Essential Articles

for the study of John Dryden

Edited by **H. T. Swedenberg, Jr.**

Professor of English
University of California
Los Angeles

ARCHON BOOKS   **Hamden, Connecticut**   **1966**

Library of Congress Catalog Card Number: 65-28670
Printed in the United States of America

CONTENTS

CONTENTS

CONTENTS

V. Literary Method

FOREWORD

Immense resources are now available for literary study in England and America. The contributions to scholarship and criticism are so numerous and often so valuable that the student preparing himself for a career in literary teaching and study may be embarrassed, not to say overwhelmed. Yet from this mass of commentary certain titles have emerged which seem to compel attention. If one offers a seminar in one of the standard areas or periods of English literature, the syllabus will show year after year some items which cannot be omitted, some pieces every serious student should know. And with each new offering of the course, one must face the task of compiling a list of these selections for the seminar's reserve shelf, of searching out and calling in the library's copies, and reserving space for the twenty or thirty or forty volumes the list may demand. As if this were not enough, one must also attempt to repair or replace the volumes whose popularity has had the unfortunate side effects of frequent circulation and the concomitant wear, abuse, and general deterioration.

We propose an alternative to this procedure. We propose to select from the many learned journals, scholarly studies, and critical books the best selections available, the selections which consistently reappear on graduate seminar shelves and on undergraduate honors program reading lists. Let us choose from those articles which time has sanctioned, those too from the best of more recent performances, and let us draw them into a single volume of convenient size. This offers a clear gain in simplicity and usefulness. The articles chosen make up a body of knowledge that cannot fail to be valuable, and they act as models of the kind of contributions to learning which we are training our students to make themselves. And if we can have ready to hand a concentration of such articles for each of the standard areas, and several individual authors, we may conduct the study of these subjects with greater confidence, knowing more fully the extent and kind of reading we can take for granted. And, while we benefit our classes and students, we can also allow the library to keep the original editions of the articles on its shelves and to fulfill its proper and usual function.

FOREWORD

We must add, finally, that each book in the series, and therefore the whole series, is the result of unselfish help from contributors and editors from all of Great Britain and the United States. We wish to acknowledge their help in rendering this useful service.

B. N. S.	Rochester, N. Y.
D. G. A.	Brunswick, Me.
H. G. R.	Atlanta, Ga.

PREFACE

Everyone concerned with the teaching and investigation of Augustan literature is aware of a renascence of interest in Dryden in the past four decades, but perhaps only those whose scholarly interests are centered on him have observed the remarkable increase in publication about him in recent years. A glance at the bibliographies points up the accelerated tempo. The Cambridge Bibliography of English Literature, published in 1941 but listing items only to 1937, has under the heading "Articles in Periodicals" eighty-one entries on Dryden, the first of which appeared in 1809. The Supplement, published in 1957 and bringing the listings to 1955, has 115 entries. The PMLA bibliography for 1962 prints eighteen titles for that one year. An extrapolation for the next twenty years based on the 1962 record, suggests that the compilers of the next supplement will require some three times as much space for Dryden as their predecessors used. Such figures may be and probably are misleading, inasmuch as the Cambridge Bibliography does not pretend to be exhaustive whereas PMLA tries to list everything; and furthermore, prophesying about the tides of scholarly and critical tastes is a risky business. Nevertheless there can be no question that Dryden is at present generating much interest and it is only reasonable to assume that there will be no diminution in his appeal in the immediate future. The direction of literary research and analysis is predictable if not mathematically measurable.

The collection of articles that make up this book may therefore be useful to the students of the future as well as those of today. The young scholar who begins a serious investigation of Dryden, or of any other major literary figure, is likely to feel depressed at the onset as he encounters the vast accumulation of learning to which the bibliographies point him. The articles reprinted here and those in the supplementary list may somewhat encourage him by providing a base on which to build his knowledge, since all of them, in the opinion of the compiler at least, have something to say that he will find useful, if only as a stimulus to disagreement. Two types of studies he will not find: the purely critical and the purely biographical. Essays in critical analysis, of which there are a number of fine examples, have

recently been collected and published in a volume edited by
Mr. Bernard N. Schilling. There seemed little point in dupli-
cating the offerings, and so only one essay appears in his and
in this volume. Biographical studies have been excluded because the substance of them can be found conveniently elsewhere.
Two books in our time have dealt learnedly and perceptively
with Dryden's life. In 1940 Mr. James M. Osborn published his
John Dryden: Some Biographical Facts and Problems in which
he surveyed the known data and raised challenging questions.
And in 1961 Mr. Charles E. Ward brought out his Life of Dryden
in which he carefully winnowed and ordered the investigations
of the past and combined them with his own research of a period
of some thirty years. For biographical data the student should
turn to these volumes.

All of the articles here reprinted originally appeared in
learned journals, and they illustrate the receptivity of editors
to a variety of approaches to scholarly problems. The first
three studies may serve as examples. Mr. Monk's survey of
Dryden studies is marked by cogent evaluations and should be
used in conjunction with his John Dryden: A List of Critical
Studies Published from 1895 to 1948. Although research done
since 1945 has brought about an adjustment in opinion on some
matters he touches upon, the student beginning his investigation
cannot do better than to start with Mr. Monk's article. The vili-
fication to which Dryden was subjected over the better part of his
career is summarized in Mr. Macdonald's essay and should be
supplemented by his invaluable bibliography John Dryden: A
Bibliography of Early Editions and of Drydeniana. Not all the
attacks described by Mr. Macdonald are to be considered of
equal importance; consequently, the student pursuing the subject
would do well to concentrate at first upon such significant documents as The Medal of John Bayes. Mr. Osborn's evaluation of
Macdonald's bibliography is a model of the scholarly review,
raising questions that are still challenging. It should be used with
his article "Macdonald's Bibliography of Dryden: An Annotated
Check-List of Selected American Libraries," Modern Philology,
XXXIX (1941), 69–98; 197–212.

Two of the articles in the prose section illustrate the fact
that Dryden as critic not infrequently reacted to ideas advanced
by others and was by no means always playing the part of the pure
theoretician. Mr. Williamson contends that the occasional nature

of the Essay of Dramatic Poesy is demonstrated by reference to
the controversy between Sobière and Sprat as well as to the well
known debate with Sir Robert Howard. Mr. Huntley argues that
the preface to All for Love is a "piece of epideictic rhetoric devoted to a censure of Rochester" and that as a whole it is more
rhetorical than critical. His other article serves as a corrective
to the over zealous attempt to make topical identifications in the
Essay of Dramatic Poesy. The unity or lack of unity in Dryden's
critical opinions has been debated many times. Mr. Trowbridge
addresses himself to this problem and concludes that consistency
in the criticism stems from Dryden's fundamental belief that
objective criteria are necessary in the judgment of art and that
without these criteria only individualistic chaos can result.
Finally, Mr. Ham's study illustrates the careful use of external
and internal evidence to establish the authorship of a tract that
casts some light on Dryden's activity as Historiographer-Royal.

The eight articles on Mac Flecknoe, Absalom and Achitophel,
and Religio Laici touch on only a few of the seemingly endless
questions that those three poems continue to raise. In one sense
Mr. Thorn-Drury's remarks on Mac Flecknoe may be considered
of interest as an historical document, a landmark in the renewed
study of the poem in the twentieth century. In another, and perhaps broader sense, it is worthy of the student's attention, for in
it he will find an example of the procedure of an accomplished
scholar in demolishing an ill-founded and carelessly constructed
thesis. Mr. Thorn-Drury was the first to suggest that Mac Flecknoe had been written as early as 1678. Mr. Brooks, as a result
of his study of Oldham, produced further evidence to support the
hypothesis. As a result, no one now doubts that the poem was
written at least four years before it found its way into print, but
the student should be aware that the precise occasion and the
exact date of its composition are as yet undetermined.* Whatever
these may be, the poem is a multi-textured work of art, and Mr.
Korn has traced out some of its strands in his essay. The two
articles on Absalom and Achitophel help us to read the poem

---

* Two recent and conflicting arguments might be noted:
Poems on Affairs of State, ed. George de F. Lord (New Haven,
1963), I, 376; George McFadden, "Elkanah Settle and the Genesis
of MacFlecknoe," Philological Quarterly, XLIII (1964), 55–72.

against the seventeenth-century background of the Absalom-Achitophel allegory and in the context of political events in the spring and early summer of 1681, particularly in regard to the publication of His Majesties Declaration to all his Loving Subjects and His Majesties Declaration Defended. The articles on Religio Laici also set it in its milieu. Details about the publication of Dickinson's translation of Father Simon's History, hypotheses about the impact upon Dryden of materialistic thinking as manifested by some of Shaftesbury's clan, and an attempt to reassess Mr. Bredvold's doctrine of Dryden's skepticism as set forth in his seminal book The Intellectual Milieu of John Dryden all suggest new perspectives on the poem.

In the fourth grouping, "Idea and Purpose," the student will find six studies which explore the impact on Dryden of contemporary thought and events. No writer was ever more responsive to the intellectual challenges of his day, but Dryden's responses are in some instances so cleverly submerged that only imaginative research can reveal the stimulus. An example is Annus Mirabilis in which the meaning and artistry are no little enhanced when the poem is set against the subversive propaganda of the 1660's. The complex of seventeenth-century philosophical systems are so subtly diffused in Dryden's works, however, that even the best efforts of scholarship have failed to give us precise answers. This is especially true of Hobbesism. Since John Aubrey remarked in passing that Dryden was strongly influenced by Hobbes, investigators have attempted to establish just how pervasive this influence was, and some have tended to see Hobbes lurking in the wings of play after play. The last of the three essays on the subject here reprinted seems to be the most cautious and reasonable estimate yet published on the subject.

A few of the elements in Dryden's astonishingly complex craftsmanship are examined in the last group. That he was steeped in Latinity has always been assumed, but his manipulation of this learning in both structure and image has remained for modern scholarship to reveal in detail. Mr. Bottkol has shown that to appreciate Dryden's renderings of Latin poetry it is necessary to go to the basic texts which he used and to examine not only them but also the commentary which he found in them as well as the Interpretatio of the "Delphin" editions. Such investigation almost invariably proves that his variations from his originals are not the result of faulty scholarship but rather of his con-

cept of translation. Dryden's indebtedness to his master Virgil
in many of his plays as well as in the great satires is documented
by Mr. Brower. A reading of his article will suggest to any
serious student that the density and allusiveness of the verse cannot possibly be fully appreciated without an awareness of Dryden's
classical memories. In like manner Miss Feder shows that the
influence of Cicero and Quintilian is strong in the structure, diction, and imagery of Dryden's criticism as well as in much of his
poetry. Miss Wallerstein analyses Dryden's dramatic method
vis-a-vis the profundity of Shakespeare's artistry, and in the
second of her articles she accounts for his poetic development
and achievement in the elegiac mode. Finally, Mr. Hemphill's
study of Dryden's heroic line demonstrates the poet's subtleties
in prosody; and Mr. Kinsley's essay illustrates how he moved in
panegyric from wit to a kind of grandeur, elevating praise to the
realm of art.

The list of "Additional Articles" is a useful supplement, it
is hoped, to the studies reprinted. These pieces exemplify additional scholarly approaches to the complex and seemingly endless
problems which the wit and judgment of John Dryden pose.

I. THREE SURVEYS

DRYDEN STUDIES: A SURVEY,* 1920–1945

Samuel Holt Monk

During the last twenty-five years, the Restoration, almost pointedly ignored in the last half of the nineteenth century, has shared with the eighteenth century the attention of critics and scholars. The cynical and amoral nineteen-twenties found the poetry and comedy of Dryden's age especially to their liking. Stuart Pratt Sherman expressed this congeniality in a remarkably self-conscious review of Mark Van Doren's Poetry of John Dryden.

> We have outlived our age of Tennyson and Wilson,
> Knight of the Grail, as Dryden outlived his Milton and
> Cromwell, his King of the Grail. Our Samuel Butler
> has ridiculed the art and science of our times as
> Dryden's Samuel Butler ridiculed the art and letters
> of his times. Long years of strife have persuaded us,
> as they persuaded Hobbes, that man has no instinct for
> decency, that his natural condition is "solitary, poor,
> nasty, brutish, and short." . . . Like Dryden we are at
> heart resolutely, or rather wantonly, materialistic.
> . . . The spiritual incapacities which follow the em-
> brace of a sensual philosophy we share with Dryden.
> We are incapable of purely imaginative creation, we
> shun sublimity and pathos, we know nothing of the love
> that has wings or the beauty that fills the heart with
> awe, and we have lost our singing voice.[1]

Fortunately such bleak romantic irony is not heard in the scholarship that a generation of literary historians has produced on the Restoration. But one hears in Sherman's farewell to romance a hint of the change in temper that has made it possible to study the age of Dryden without prejudice. And one has only to

Reprinted from English Literary History, Vol. 14 (1947), pp. 46–63, by permission of the author and The Johns Hopkins University Press.

compile and work through a bibliography of these studies to perceive how energetically that period has been explored.

Dryden has had a curious fate. Through the ebb and flow of taste since 1670 his reputation has been secure. In his own day his popularity equalled his reputation. In the nineteenth century, though his popularity was not excessive, commercial editions of his works appeared from time to time: evidence that his reputation as one of the worthies of English literature had not been eclipsed. Nevertheless, in 1920, looking back over the preceding fifty years, Van Doren could speak of Dryden as a "neglected" poet, though solid scholarly work had been done: by Christie and Noyes on the text of the poems (in the Globe and Cambridge editions respectively); by Saintsbury in his critical re-evaluation in the biography in the English Men of Letters series; by W. P. Ker in the preface and notes to the selected critical essays; by Verrall in his Lectures on Dryden. But to most critics Dryden appeared not so much a living poet as a specimen which had been classified, tagged, and assigned a permanent place in the museum of letters.

Van Doren's book announced the revival of interest in the poetry of John Dryden. Since 1920 a number of books and hundreds of articles and brief notes on every aspect of the poet and his age have gone far to re-create for us the intellectual, political, religious, and aesthetic environment in which Dryden and his contemporaries lived. With this knowledge has gone understanding, and with understanding informed critical judgments have become possible. In a unique degree Dryden and his age are one: to study the age is to arrive at some point at Dryden the poet, the critic, the playwright, the Tory, the Hobbist, and Anglican, the Catholic. The recovery of the period has been to some extent the recovery of its principal man of letters. Dryden is no longer neglected. Though not popular, as he was in his own day, or influential, as Donne has been in ours, he has been the subject of intelligent, sympathetic, and at times brilliant critical and scholarly studies.

II

The most important work has been done on bibliography, biography, the canon, and the plays. And in addition to Van Doren's fine book, there are a number of excellent critical essays. To say this is not to minimize the value of many special studies which cannot be mentioned in this paper. Dryden resembles a great block of stone from which bits have been chipped and worked into the artifacts of essays and articles. Only recently have larger works of synthesis been undertaken. Of these, Hugh Macdonald's bibliography is of fundamental importance. P. J. Dobell, T. J. Wise, and Montague Summers had made limited contributions to this complicated subject. Macdonald built on their foundations as well as on the invaluable unpublished notes of Thorn-Drury. His book is the most useful piece of Dryden scholarship since Malone's biography.[2]

Macdonald attempts to describe every edition of Dryden's works published before 1700, as well as posthumous pieces, a few quartos of the early eighteenth century, and collected editions to 1767, the date of Derrick's second edition of the Miscellaneous Works. He devotes a section also to pieces attributed to Dryden.

Not only does Macdonald give full bibliographical information, but when possible he accompanies each item with notes on biography and other topics. The section on Drydeniana lists, describes, and quotes from all or nearly all of the poems, plays, prefaces, and pamphlets in which Dryden was mentioned up to 1700, together with a few from as late as the mid-eighteenth century. There are almost two hundred of these items, supplemented by historical and interpretive material of great interest. Macdonald, therefore, not only makes available for the first time the bibliographical knowledge essential for studying and editing Dryden, but he has also compiled an allusion book so complete that it affords material for a study of Dryden's contemporary reputation and the patterns of attacks on him. In addition it gathers together material for an investigation of Dryden's life and literary career. Finally the notes contain an almost complete bibliography of modern Dryden scholarship.

A few misprints, a certain awkwardness in the arrangement of the index, and a few practices to which bibliographical purists might object mar the book, but the principal defect is Macdonald's failure to give the locations of the books that he lists. James M. Osborn was prompt to publish an annotated check list of the holdings of ten American libraries, thus making easily available to American scholars the rich resources of this country.[3]

III

In An Account of the English Dramatick Poets, 1691, Gerard Langbaine complained of the difficulty of discovering anything definite about Dryden's character. Dryden's contemporaries, he said, differ in their estimate of the poet and the man, "so that we can scarce find them agreed in any One thing, save this, That he was Poet Laureat and Historiographer to His late Majesty . . . ."[4] Macdonald, in his preface, echoes Langbaine's frustration: "I do not believe that we know or can know enough about Dryden to justify another serious biography . . ." (p. viii) Certainly Dryden's biography is a most difficult subject, but I believe that Macdonald is unduly pessimistic. It is odd that we know so little about Dryden and that what we do know is so unrevealing. Even the eighteenth-century biographers, who were close to Dryden's own time, were baffled when they looked for facts and significant details. Malone's researches, published in 1800, remain and must remain the principal source of our knowledge. As with Shakespeare, we know hundreds of facts, and from time to time new facts emerge, but they obstinately refuse to reveal the man. Dryden's enemies were numerous and vocal, but neither he nor his friends often bothered to refute scandal. Party politics, religious bias, and the venom with which the small regard the great have raised a distorting haze through which we see the essential Dryden with difficulty. In the poems and more especially in the prose, an individual voice is heard, an authentic personality is felt, but somehow Dryden does not abide our question. What was the young Dryden like? In what sort of environment did he grow up? Why was he slow in maturing as a writer? How did he pass the years between leaving Cambridge and entering on his literary career? What is the truth about his marriage? When and under what circumstances was he converted? These and other questions can be answered only by inference, if at all.

And yet a new biography can and must be written. It is not a task to be lightly undertaken, for it demands a careful search for new material in manuscripts and collections of letters in private hands or still uncatalogued in British libraries; a reevaluation of all the material now on hand; an expert knowledge of the period in all its ramifications; and tact and imaginative insight unperverted by prejudice and preconceptions. These

qualities were obviously denied to Christopher Hollis in his
Dryden, which through haste and ignorance proved so grotesque
a failure in 1933; or Montague Summers in his preposterous
article in Claude Williamson's Great Catholics, a saint's life,
in which Dryden keeps such unlikely company as that of St. Paul,
St. Catherine of Siena, and Patrick Cardinal Hayes; and in which
we are told that Anne Reeve's "prayers in her distant cloister
were by no means the least powerful factor in his conversion,"
and that the Heroic Stanzas on Cromwell are "the one sad blot
that stains Dryden's character."[5]

The new biographer of Dryden must synthesize and interpret. An impressive number of facts have been discovered in
the last quarter of a century, and Bredvold and others have done
in part for Dryden what Sherburn has done for Pope by demonstrating the falseness of much of the traditional interpretation
of his character and motives. We now know, as definitely as we
probably can, that Dryden was duly baptized; that he was employed presumably in a small post in Cromwell's government;
that he was not Collector of Customs; that the evidence that
Rochester was concerned in the Rose-Alley ambuscade is dubious; that Dryden was appointed Laureate to James II before
his conversion, a fact that removes the last ground for regarding his change of faith as mercenary.[6] Important studies have
been made in his pension and his income under William, and in
the Laureateship and his possible activities as Historiographer
Royal. The discovery that he was seriously considered for the
Wardenship of All Souls lends probability to the gossip about
his academic ambitions, especially at Magdelen, Eton, and Trinity College, Dublin, and perhaps explains the rumors that he
attempted to take orders.[7] Considerable progress has been
made in the study of Dryden's ideas: his interest in an English
Academy; his association with the Royal Society; his attitude
toward and use of the political, psychological and aesthetic ideas
of Hobbes; and finally his religion and conversion.[8] Though it
can scarcely be maintained that any of this enables us to redis-
cover Dryden as a human being, it is true that we know him
more accurately and completely than was possible twenty-five
years ago and that we can now affirm that his career was honorable, his character was not that of a gross libertine or servile
time-server, and his mind was both active and well stored.

The four major works in the field of Dryden's biography that have appeared within our period are Bredvold's Intellectual Milieu of John Dryden, Ward's edition of the letters, Osborn's John Dryden: Some Biographical Facts and Problems, and Macdonald's The Attacks on Dryden.[9]

Bredvold has removed for all time any doubts as to the sincerity of Dryden's conversion. By studying Religio Laici and The Hind and the Panther against the background of sceptical and fideistic thought in the seventeenth century, he has demonstrated that Dryden experienced no sudden change of faith, but rather a gradual clarification of his own thinking, a process that eventually led him to the authority of the Church by way of his distrust of private reason. The conversion to Rome was the ultimate fulfilment of his own nature. Dryden's naturally sceptical temper found support in the various scepticisms of Montaigne, of the Royal Society, and of Catholic apologetics. His political conservatism, which prompted his strong loyalty to the throne and his hatred of innovation, was merely a facet of his sceptical attitude. Bredvold admits but minimizes the influence of Hobbes on Dryden's mind. The largest number of echoes of Hobbes are to be found in the plays, which have been studied as evidence of Dryden's allegiance to the political doctrines of Leviathan. Bredvold wisely used the plays with caution in studying Dryden's intellectual temper, and it cannot be said that Miss Hartsock's more daring analysis of the intellectual content of the plays[10] has proved that Bredvold's caution was ill considered. Miss Hartsock treats Dryden as a mere automaton, who dipped his pen in Hobbes' ink at almost every line. She is, of course, able to point out many actual parallels, but she attributes much to Hobbes that is and has always been merely common knowledge about human nature or that is the logical outcome of plot situations. Perhaps no one but Hobbes was ever quite so Hobbesian as she makes Dryden out to be. Returning to Bredvold, the section of his book that discusses the position of Catholics under James II brings out plainly how far from prudential Dryden's conversion was and how impossible it is that he could have expected to improve his worldly position by entering the Church.

Ward's edition of the letters brings together the sixty-two known letters of the poet, eleven of which have been published casually during the last half-century. It is well to have them all together. Though they do not tell us what we should like to know, they do tell us a great deal. They are not introspective, nor do they air opinions or describe events. On the whole they are carelessly written, and they totally lack the self-conscious-ness of such a letter-writer as Pope. But they are all we have, and we should make the most of the fact that the Tonson letters reveal the relationship between the publisher and his greatest author; that the Walsh correspondence enables us to gage at first hand Dryden's kindliness to a younger poet and to glean a few remarks on the problems of writing; that the letters written late in life to his cousin Mrs. Steward show us the domestic side of his nature: his love of his sons, of Northamptonshire, of his relatives. And throughout the letters after 1688 one is aware of his uneasy position as a Catholic and of his steadfast devo-tion to his faith.

Osborn's survey of biographical facts and problems is an originally conceived and carefully executed preliminary study for a new life of the poet. In it the principal lives of Dryden from Birch's in 1734 to Saintsbury's in 1881 are analysed, and seventeen problems of varied importance and difficulty are re-examined. The survey of the lives traces our acquisition of knowledge about the poet and analyses the methods, sources, and contributions of each biographer. It is therefore in a sense a study of the rise of literary biography. Malone, of course, is the central figure, and Osborn reprints the notes that Malone had compiled for the revised second edition that was never called for.

In his examination of special problems, Osborn demon-strates the value of approaching the documents for Dryden's biography freshly and with an open mind. Time precludes a de-tailed discussion of his findings and suggestions in regard to such topics as the poet's possible work for Herringman, his ab-sences from London, or Langbaine's hostility. Most interesting is his study of the Medal of John Bayes. Arguing that Shadwell must be accepted as the author until evidence to the contrary is discovered, Osborn concludes that because of Shadwell's first-hand knowledge of Dryden the satire is an important biographi-cal document. He is able to demonstrate that behind the obvious distortions lie a number of biographical facts, many of them now supported by other evidence. The presence of these verifiable facts lends probability to other statements in the poem, which despite the malicious interpretation put on them may in them-

selves be true. The point that Osborn makes here and elsewhere
is that the future biographer of Dryden must re-evaluate every
item of gossip and may even successfully use the libels of
Dryden's enemies as a source of information. A thorough comparative study of the attacks would establish a general pattern
of charges, many of which can be traced to the Rehearsal and
to preceding libels. Variants from this pattern would be of especial interest, but care would have to be taken to distinguish
wilful invention from genuine details. The charges of moral
turpitude, veniality, base motives can be disregarded. The general line that Bredvold has taken in his studies of Dryden's pension, of the political significance of Amboyna and The Spanish
Fryar,[11] and of the poet's religious development is sound and
necessary. But Roswell G. Ham has shown that with luck and
perseverance the gossip of the day can from time to time be sub-
stantiated, and Osborn, I believe, points the way to a fruitful use
of the attacks on Dryden.

    Macdonald's essay on these attacks is useful, but more can
be done with them. His study raises one very interesting point:
why was Dryden the object of such violent dislike? Why were
the attacks so frequent, persistent, and vitriolic? Macdonald
suggests that "it is possible that there was in his character
some shade of ineffectiveness which, when it was combined with
the possession of extraordinary powers, is apt to be met by resentment." (p. 73) This is a very shrewd observation. There
is every reason to believe that Dryden's manners were not polished, that his wit in repartee was often cumbersome and crude,
that his mind was judicial and slow rather than fertile and graceful—in short, that like a writer of a later generation he wrote
like an angel but talked like poor Poll. Goldsmith came in for
a good deal of ridicule in the Johnson circle, but he had the grace
not to be remarkably successful in a worldly way, and thus did
not awaken the envy of the men who laughed at him. It is not
improbable that Dryden's greatness as a writer and his consequent worldly success aroused profound antipathies among some
who recognized the disparity between his personality and his
achievement. This matter is doubtless beyond proof, but it
seems at least likely.

IV

The Dryden canon will probably never be established with
absolute certainty, but the future editor will have to consider
a few new items. Besides printing the prologue and epilogue to
Aphra Behn's The Widow Ranter: or the History of Bacon in Vir-
ginia, Ham has published the very fine epilogue, "Spoke before
His Majesty at Oxford, March 19, 1680."[12] B. H. Newdigate has
called attention to a fragment of an ode on the marriage of two
prominent Catholics, Anastasia Stafford and George Holman,
which had been attributed to Dryden in Tixall Poetry, Edinburgh
1831, and had been included in the Aldine edition, 1832–33, but
which has been silently ignored by subsequent editors.[13] The
ascription to Dryden seems entirely probable. An occasional
song has been urged for admission to the canon, but the most
interesting discovery is Ham's publication of the dedication for
Purcell's Music of the Prophetesse, 1691, from a manuscript
almost certainly in Dryden's own hand.[14] The manuscript differs from the printed version by including some interesting
passages on the parallel of poetry, painting, and music, and on
contemporary poets as songwriters. The recovery of this un-
revised essay adds an important item to Dryden's criticism.

But if there have been additions to the works, Noyes and
Potter have laid the ghost of the Catholic tradition that Dryden,
as an act of penance on his conversion, translated all the hymns
in the Primer of 1706.[15] Their careful examination of the probabilities of the tradition, their sifting of the evidence in the case,
and their demonstration that internal evidence can prove no more
than the influence of Dryden's style and manner on the translators of the hymns leave Dryden with one hymn to his credit,
the Veni Creator Spiritus, which he himself published in Examen
Poeticum.

V

The plays have come in for a good deal of incidental discussion in the many books on Restoration drama and have been the
subject of considerable special study. Montague Summers' ex-

pensive Nonesuch Edition of the dramatic works, 1931–32, proved so faulty that the text does not bear serious examination, and his long introduction is a medley of eccentric and injudicious critical judgments and unacknowledged borrowings from other scholars. B. J. Pendlebury's <u>Dryden's Heroic Plays: A Study of the Origins</u>,[16] though superior to Chase's earlier book, is slight; but it does correctly emphasize the importance of the Renaissance heroic ideal and of Tasso. A better book is C. V. Deane's <u>Dramatic Theory and the Rhymed Heroic Play</u>,[17] which has the great merit of breadth of treatment in the survey of the forces that made for the heroic play and of relating that <u>genre</u> to critical theory. The book is weakest when the author attempts to show the influence of Descartes on heroic characters, but it is valuable in seeking to determine the degree of conflict that exists between classical formalism and the energetic spirit of heroic drama. Deane concludes by discussing the heroic play as an example of the baroque in literature.

Studies in sources are frequently tedious and not especially enlightening, but Ned B. Allen's <u>The Sources of John Dryden's Comedies</u> is more important than its title would indicate.[18] It might be called <u>The Art of Dryden's Comedy</u>. It has the great merit of actually examining the plays, a procedure sufficiently unusual to be remarked on. Although Allen is able to justify Langbaine's ill-natured charge that Dryden was a confirmed borrower, he is able also to show that he refashioned his material for his own artistic ends and always with one purpose in view: to please his audiences.

VI

The revolt against the nineteenth century, which characterized both poetry and criticism during the 1920's and 1930's, inevitably affected the reputation of Dryden. Though Johnson, Scott, and others had been fully articulate on Dryden's virtues— his power and energy, his skill in arguing in verse, his variety, his complete mastery of the couplet—nineteenth-century taste had found him wanting and had followed Hazlitt in considering him artificial or Arnold in considering him prosaic. Since 1920 it has been possible to judge Dryden's success and failure in terms of what he attempted rather than of what Keats or Tennyson achieved. No one has been so rash as to claim with Scott a place for Dryden beside Shakespeare and Milton. His warmest admirers are well aware of his defects: his almost total lack of the tragic sense of life, his inability to reach the heights and his occasional lapses into bathos; his denotative rather than connotative use of words; his tendency toward inorganic ornamentation. Dryden is not Shakespeare, Milton, Donne, or one of the Romantic poets. Having granted that obvious fact, the recent critic has gone on to insist that Dryden is none the less a poet and to explore the nature of the poetry that he wrote.

Mark Van Doren's The Poetry of John Dryden[19] was the first important critical study of the non-dramatic poems. Written as a doctoral dissertation at Columbia, it is unique in its kind for having gone through three commercial editions in the last twenty-five years. It would be futile to hope that our graduate schools could often produce such a work, but it is regrettable that they should do so so seldom. The book is a blend of judicious criticism and sound historical scholarship— so sound that its author has had to make no important revisions since it was first published.

Van Doren's interest is in Dryden's development as a poet, the forces that shaped his art, the nature of that art, and its manifestation in the poems themselves. In short, it is a study of Dryden's craftsmanship, of the objects that he made and the techniques that he used in making them. Almost every page yields such fine critical judgments as the following:

> The story of Dryden's poetry is the story of a sinewy
> mind attacking bulky materials.

> Everywhere Dryden's personal presence can be felt.
> Pope lurks behind his poetry; Dryden stands well
> forward, flush with his page and speaking with an
> honest voice if not always with an honest heart.

> The Indian Emperor must have sounded suddenly and
> loudly like a gong.

But impressionism is not Van Doren's method. He analyses the tone, the texture, the diction, the structure, the rhetoric, the versification of the poems. Van Doren's Dryden is the poet's poet, the master-builder of the guild; the craftsman who has mastered his materials and method so completely that even the confines of the heroic couplet present no obstacles to the flow of energetic thought, the changes of tempo and tone, the packed and perspicuous statements. The book is written with such engaging enthusiasm that one returns to the poems with renewed curiosity, able to see them afresh as products of an age, a temperament, and a restricted, but perfected technique.

The tercentenary of Dryden's birth in 1931 produced a spate of essays in appreciation, of which the best was Bonamy Dobrée's leading article in the Times Literary Supplement,[20] in which Dryden was praised for his single-hearted devotion to letters. But Dobrée's most interesting criticism of Dryden is in defence of the plays in his Restoration Tragedy.[21] Dryden's dramas are difficult to esteem. He had no especial aptitude for comedy, as he himself admitted, and even today when his reputation is high again, the comedies are frequently dismissed as inept or "coarse." I doubt that they are notably coarser than other Restoration comedies or than the great majority of plays that are produced annually in New York, and I suspect that the frequent recurrence of that adjective is a heritage from the last century. Dryden's best play, All for Love, suffers by contrast w'th Antony and Cleopatra,[22] but it exists in its own right as the last really fine poetic tragedy written in England. But the age, like our own, was incapable of achieving great tragedy. Dobrée, wishing to understand the heroic play, treats it as "artificial," a device that Lamb had used to justify his admiration for Restoration comedy. Admitting that Dryden did not deal in real emotions and real situations, Dobrée discusses the plays as frankly romantic fantasies that were popular because they supplied the illusion of heroism to an unheroic age. But he insists that they have a vitality of their own, that they exist on their own terms; and he draws the inevitable comparison between them and the decorative quality of baroque art.

T. S. Eliot twice essayed criticism of Dryden during our period. The three essays in the volume entitled Homage to John Dryden[23] were all published as leading articles in the Times Literary Supplement. The title essay was occasioned by Van Doren's book; the two following essays are on the metaphysical poets and Andrew Marvell. Eliot was concerned in these essays with delivering the coup de grâce to the influence of romantic poetry; with increasing the prestige of metaphysical poetry; and, one suspects, with justifying his own revolutionary method.

Near the beginning of the essay on Dryden, he declares that "to enjoy Dryden means to pass beyond the limitations of the nineteenth century into a new freedom." He argues that the then current neglect of Augustan verse was attributable to a partial and romantic perception of certain qualities in Shakespeare and Milton and to a prejudice that intellectual poetry (poetry conceived and composed in the wits, not in the soul, as Arnold had put it) cannot be poetic. And he boldly affirms that Dryden's style is natural and Milton's is artificial. "In the next revolution of taste," he concludes, "it is possible that poets may turn to the study of Dryden. He remains one of those who have set standards for English verse which it is desperate to ignore."

Having used Dryden to attack the romantic idea of poetry, Eliot proceeds to an analysis of metaphysical poetry in which his thesis is the now famous one that, in the seventeenth century, poets possessed a "mechanism of sensibility" which was unified, so that intellect, imagination, and emotion worked simultaneously and instantaneously to produce a kind of poetry that was concrete, witty, passionate, logical, and emotional. Toward the end of the century, however, a change came over the English poetic mind, a dissociation of sensibility set in, and English poetry tended to split into a poetry of statement and a poetry of sound. In Eliot's opinion the achievements of Milton and Dryden were largely responsible for this disunity. The magniloquence of the one and the wit of the other operated powerfully upon subsequent generations of poets, creating a poetry which was not whole, as metaphysical poetry had been, but incomplete, as Augustan and Romantic poetry became.

Thus Eliot used Dryden as a club with which to belabor the romantics and as a lever with which to exalt the metaphysicals. In his later three essays on Dryden,[24] he abandoned theory and wrote discriminatingly on the poetry, the plays, and the criticism; for he had won his earlier battle: Eliot's influence as poet and critic was at its height.

Eliot's theory was novel, actually, only in claiming for Donne and his school the full perfection of poetry. For the rest, it seems now to have been merely a re-phrasing of the familiar opposition between judgment and fancy, reason and imagination, the intellect and the emotions, the denotative and the connotative

in poetry. But it served one very useful purpose: it concentrated
attention on an important moment in English poetry: that moment
in which the individualistic, passionate, and introspective early
seventeenth century turned toward the more conformist, rationalistic, and objective Augustan age. Thanks to some extent to
Eliot, reasons for the change have since been sought, not in the
facile explanation of the influence of French fashion on Charles II
and his court, but in the scientific, philosophic, and psychological movements of the mid-century. English neo-classic art has
been regarded not as a fortuitous importation, but as an organic
growth out of the weltanschauung of post-Commonwealth England.
Hobbes has loomed large in these studies, of which the principal
ones are by Willey, Brooks, and Thorpe.[25]
      There have of course been protests against the new estimate
of the Augustans and against the praise of Dryden. Grierson can
see nothing in Dryden but emptiness: for him he is a poet who
knew how to say anything well, but who had nothing to say. Gran-
ville-Barker has objected to the modern taste for Restoration
drama; and C. S. Lewis, speaking frankly as a romantic, has
challenged Eliot's praise of Dryden and dispraise of Shelley.[26]
The critical war goes on, but there can be no doubt that despite
the waning of Eliot's influence and indications that the Romantics are about to be given a hearing once more, we have attained
a catholicity of taste and consequently an enlarging of pleasure
that were not possible twenty-five years ago.

VII

      And now, what remains to be done? Almost everything.
      We need first of all a definitive edition of the complete
works. The plays have never been properly edited; and the
prose, though reprinted, has been edited only in part. An edition that gives us a sound text and that assembles all of our
knowledge is essential if Dryden studies are to progress. Fortunately such an edition is in progress at the University of California at Los Angeles under the direction of Edward N. Hooker.
The new life of Dryden should not be undertaken until Hooker
and his colleagues have completed their task.
      The heroic plays will repay further study. Too much atten-
tion has been paid to peripheral matters, too little to the plays

themselves. What is the relation of the heroic play to the entire heroic tradition? What were Dryden's specific sources and how did he use them? What of his dramatic technique and its relation to the stage of his day? What of characterization? Dryden believed that he had created characters. Did he do so? What aesthetic values are implicit in the plays?

The word baroque has been used to describe the plays, and one German scholar has discussed somewhat too schematically the "baroque" elements in the Fables.[27] Is the word a useful critical term and has it value when applied to Dryden?

Almost nothing has been done on Dryden's influence in England. It has been enormous. A study of the influence of his critical opinions and his poetic technique on the writers of his own time should be made. As for the eighteenth century and after, the field is open.

Despite a large number of articles, little of real significance has been done on the criticism. Thorpe has explored the influence of Hobbes's aesthetics on Dryden; Smith has studied the long controversy with Shadwell; Walcott has shown the relationship between the "Heads of an Answer to Rymer" and the "Preface to Troilus and Cressida"; and Trowbridge has said some necessary truths about the "Essay on the Dramatic Poetry of the Last Age."[28] But there is an unfortunate tendency to treat the critical essays as elaborate devices to deceive. Too many students approach the prefaces in the spirit in which earlier biographers approached the conversion to Rome. Except in the face of evidence to the contrary (and it is not easy to find), we must believe that Dryden meant what he said. Inconsistencies abound, but they cannot be dismissed merely because they are inconsistencies. Dryden wrote his criticism experimentally and sceptically, and he was never ashamed of changing his mind. Each essay should be studied in relation to the work to which it is attached and to the critical temper of the moment. Dryden was a man of quick and eager enthusiasms, and the task in hand dominated his mind. It should also be remembered that though Dryden, in Johnson's phrase, is the father of modern criticism, he is also in his academic and literary background a man of the Renaissance. He is thus the very Janus of critics.

Many special problems need investigation. What did Dryden consider the function of criticism to be, and what seemed to him the fundamental critical problems? What is his debt to the Italian

critics and scholars? Was he in fact influenced by Spanish critics? What precisely is his debt to each of the French critics
of his own and the preceding generation? A dictionary of critical opinions, topically and chronologically arranged (two are now
being compiled), would be useful.

Finally, we need that humblest and most useful of books: a
concordance.

The work of the last twenty-five years has brought us to
the possibility of synthesis. This generation can now achieve,
not indeed the final interpretation, but an informed and sympathetic evaluation of the most representative man of letters of
the Restoration.

NOTES

* A somewhat shorter version of this paper was read before
  Group VII of the Modern Language Association at the meeting in Washington in 1946.

1 Nation 111 (1920), 620.

2 Hugh Macdonald, John Dryden: a Bibliography of Early Edi-
  tions and of Drydeniana, Oxford, 1939.
  P. J. Dobell, John Dryden: Bibliographical Memoranda,
  London, 1922.
  T. J. Wise, A Dryden Library, London, 1930.
  Montague Summers, A Bibliography of the Restoration Drama,
  London, [1934].

3 James M. Osborn, "Macdonald's Bibliography of Dryden: An
  Annotated Check List of Selected American Libraries," MP
  39 (1942), 69–98; 197–212.

4 Quoted by Macdonald, op. cit., p. 270.

5 Christopher Hollis, Dryden, London, 1933.
  Montague Summers, "John Dryden," Great Catholics (ed.
  Claude Williamson, London, 1938), p. 213 and p. 210.

6 P. D. Mundy, "The Baptism of John Dryden," N & Q 173 (1937),
  225 and N & Q 184 (1943), 286 and 352.
  Pierre Legouis, André Marvell, Paris and London (1928), p. 214
  Charles E. Ward, "Was John Dryden Collector of Customs?"
  MLN 47 (1932), 246–249.

Harold J. Wilson, "Rochester, Dryden, and the Rose-Street Affair," RES 15 (1939), 294–301.
V. de Sola Pinto, "Rochester, Dryden, and the Duchess of Portsmouth," RES 16 (1940), 177, 178.
Louis I. Bredvold, "Notes on John Dryden's Pension," MP 30 (1933), 267–274.

7   Charles E. Ward, "A Biographical Note on John Dryden," MLR 27 (1932), 206–210; "Some Notes on Dryden," RES 13 (1937), 297–306; "The Publication and Profits of Dryden's Virgil," PMLA 53 (1938), 807–812.
Edmund K. Broadus, The Laureateship, Oxford, 1921.
Roswell G. Ham, "Dryden as Historiographer-Royal: The Authorship of His Majesties Declaration Defended, 1681," RES 11 (1935), 284–298.
Louis I. Bredvold, "Dryden and the University of Oxford," MLN 46 (1931), 218–224.
Roswell G. Ham, "Dryden and the Colleges," MLN 49 (1934), 324–332.
J. A. W. Bennett, "Dryden and All Souls," MLN 52 (1937), 115–116.
Pierre Legouis, "Dryden and Eton," MLN 52 (1937), 111–115.
E. S. de Beer, "Dryden's Anti-Clericalism," N&Q 179 (1940), 254–257.

8   O. F. Emerson, "John Dryden and a British Academy," Proceedings of the British Academy 10 (1921), 45–48.
Carl Niemeyer, "The Earl of Roscommon's Academy," MLN 49 (1934), 432–437.
Louis I. Bredvold, "Dryden, Hobbes, and the Royal Society," MP 25 (1928), 417–438.
Claude Lloyd, "John Dryden and the Royal Society," PMLA 45 (1930), 967–976.
Riske, Bredvold, and Stroup, "Dryden and Waller as Members of the Royal Society," PMLA 46 (1931), 951–962.
Merritt Y. Hughes, "Dryden as a Statist," PQ 6 (1927), 335–350.
Louis Teeter, "The Dramatic Use of Hobbes's Political Ideas," ELH 3 (1936), 140–169.
Pierre Legouis, "La Religion dans l'Oeuvre de Dryden avant 1682," Revue Anglo-Americaine 9 (1932), 383–392; 525–536.

9 Louis I. Bredvold, The Intellectual Milieu of John Dryden, University of Michigan Publications, Language and Literature 12 (1934), Ann Arbor.
Charles E. Ward, The Letters of John Dryden with Letters Addressed to Him, Duke University Press, 1942.
James M. Osborn, John Dryden: Some Biographical Facts and Problems, New York, 1940.
Hugh Macdonald, "The Attacks on Dryden," Essays and Studies by Members of the English Association 21 (1936), 41–74.

10 Mildred E. Hartsock, "Dryden's Plays: A Study in Ideas," Seventeenth Century Studies, Second Series (ed. Robert Shafer), Princeton, 1937.

11 Louis I. Bredvold, "Political Aspects of Dryden's Amboyna and The Spanish Fryar," University of Michigan Studies in Language and Literature 8 (1932), 119–132.

12 Roswell G. Ham, "Some Uncollected Verse of John Dryden," London Mercury 21 (1930), 421–426. See further W. G. Hiscock, "A Dryden Epilogue," TLS March 5, 1931, p. 178 and "Oxford History," TLS October 13, 1932, p. 734. Also John Dryden: Epilogue Spoken to the King, March the Nineteenth 1681 (ed. W. G. Hiscock), Oxford, 1932.

13 B. H. Newdigate, "An Overlooked Ode by John Dryden," London Mercury 22 (1930), 438–442.

14 Roswell G. Ham, "Dryden's Dedication for the Music of the Prophetesse, 1691," PMLA 50 (1935), 1065–1075.

15 George R. Noyes and George R. Potter, Hymns Attributed to John Dryden, University of California Publications in English 6, Berkeley, 1937.

16 London, 1923.

17 London, 1930.

18 University of Michigan Publications, Language and Literature 16 (1935), Ann Arbor.

19 New York, 1920. The third edition, New York, 1945, is entitled John Dryden: A Study of His Poetry.

20 August 6, 1931, pp. 601-602. It was reprinted in A Variety of Ways, Oxford, 1932.

21 Oxford, 1929.

22 Two interesting studies of these plays are F. R. Leavis's "'Antony and Cleopatra' and 'All for Love': A Critical Exercise," Scrutiny 5 (1936), 158-69, and Ruth Wallerstein's "Dryden and the Analysis of Shakespeare's Techniques," RES 19 (1943), 165-185.

23 London, 1924.

24 T. S. Eliot, John Dryden: The Poet, The Dramatist, The Critic, New York, 1932.

25 Basil Willey, The Seventeenth Century Background, London, 1934.
    Cleanth Brooks, Modern Poetry and the Tradition, Chapel Hill, 1939.
    Clarence DeWitt Thorpe, The Aesthetic Theory of Thomas Hobbes, University of Michigan Publications, Language and Literature 18, 1940.

26 Sir Herbert Grierson, Cross-currents in English Literature of the Seventeenth Century, London, 1929. Ch. 9.
    H. Granville-Barker, On Dramatic Method, London (1931), pp. 113-155.
    C. S. Lewis, Rehabilitations and Other Essays, Oxford (1939), pp. 3-34.

27 Wolfgang Jünemann, Dryden's Fabeln und ihr Quellen, Britannica 5 Hamburg, 1932.

28 Thorpe, op. cit., pp. 189-220.
    R. Jack Smith, "Shadwell's Impact upon Dryden," RES 20 (1944), 29-44.
    Fred G. Walcott, "John Dryden's Answer to Thomas Rymer's The Tragedies of the Last Age," PQ 15 (1936), 194-214.
    Hoyt Trowbridge, "Dryden's Essay on the Dramatic Poetry of the Last Age," PQ 22 (1943), 240-250.

THE ATTACKS ON DRYDEN[1]

Hugh Macdonald

> "And as their Judgments are different, as to his
> writings; so are their Censures no less repugnant to
> the Managery of his Life, some excusing what these
> condemn, and some exploding what those commend:
> so that we can scarce find them agreed in any one thing,
> save this, that he was Poet Laureat and Historiographer
> to his late Majesty." — Langbaine on Dryden, 1691. "Dry-
> den, considering his stature, his simplicity, and the
> satisfactory nature of everything he wrote, is surpris-
> ingly elusive." — Alan Lubbock, The Character of John
> Dryden, 1925.

We probably know less about Dryden than about any man of
letters since the Restoration who has at all approached him in
importance, and what little we do know makes him almost as
puzzling to us as he evidently was to Langbaine. Much of his
life is obscure, and his contemporaries seldom mention him in
a way that allows us to form any precise conception of his personality.[2] This was not due to the obscurity of his family and
still less, of course, to any failure to obtain immediate and continuous recognition, for his social position was of service to
him from the beginning and he became poet laureate within nine
years of the publication of his first serious poem.

The Dridens were an old Cumberland family whose home
was at Staffield, near Kirkoswald.[3] They moved to Northamptonshire, where they still live in the country mansion of Canons
Ashby, and where they had by the poet's time left sufficient
mark in small ways for us to be able to gather from the county
history and such sources some notion of his ancestors and relations on both sides. It is characteristic of his own history that
the date of his birth as well as its exact place had, until recently,[4] to be accepted only on tradition. He was certainly at Cam-

Reprinted from Essays and Studies by the Members of the English Association, Vol. 21 (1936), pp. 41–74, by permission of the author and The
English Association.

bridge from the middle of 1650 until April 1655, but there follow
three mysterious years about which we are in the dark. From
a document quoted by E. Legouis in his André Marvell giving
the quantity of mourning allowed to Milton, Marvell, and Dryden
on the death of Cromwell, it is clear that he did hold some post
under Thurloe, as has been conjectured from the statements of
his enemies, though as the grant of nine yards, cut down to six
in the case of the two elder poets, was disallowed altogether in
his, it is probable that his employment had not been for very
long or of a very important nature.

From the eve of the Restoration till his death in May 1700
he wrote without cessation. A rough estimate brings the number of lines in his poems to over 20,000, excluding the enormous
Virgil, the Juvenal and Persius, and the shorter translations
contributed to Tonson's Ovid and the Miscellanies. He wrote
twenty-six plays with their prologues and epilogues, many with
dedications and long critical prefaces and all but four without a
collaborator, and he supplied at the current market rate 40 or
so prologues and epilogues to the plays of others and for special
occasions. The amount of his original prose and prose translations is in any case large, and it seems likely that there were
contributions, still unidentified, to official pamphlets, which he
would have made as Historiographer Royal. It is not easy to be
sure how far he was really the editor of the miscellanies called
indifferently by his or Tonson's name, but besides what can be
gathered from stray sentences in his correspondence with the
publisher and in the prefaces to Sylvae and Examen Poeticum it
is plain from a letter written by Stepney to Leibnitz in 1693 that
he sometimes took a direct hand in the selection of the contributors to Tonson's undertakings. An examination of the early editions of Absalom and Achitophel fully supports the testimony of
Dr. Johnson's father that its sale was very large, and the author,
anonymous but at once identified, whose sympathies had been
made clear in the dedications of two plays published during the
confusion of the Popish Plot, must have seemed to the public almost as important a person in politics as he had hitherto been
in the theatre.

The three editions of The Hind and the Panther coming
quickly on top of one another show that this controversial tract
must also have been bought up eagerly, although its arguments
could not have been congenial to many of its readers. His mar-

riage with the daughter of an earl, even if, as his enemies constantly alleged, her conduct had not always been correct, had early widened his social connexions: he had mixed with the Fellows of the Royal Society, of which he was for a time a member: he was intimate with many prominent noblemen, especially those of a literary turn, and throughout his life he found no difficulty in being on cordial terms with young writers of promise as they came along. He complains of illness in the preface to The Hind and the Panther. For this reason Southerne had to finish Cleomenes for him, and in fact during the last part of his life he had periods of ill health; but the retention of his faculties and even their increase in his old age suggests that he had generally enjoyed a corresponding bodily vigour, and he doubtless went about a good deal and was seen at other places than Wills's coffeehouse and the theatre, from which his absence at one period was observed by an irate actor. Local traditions or anecdotes associating him with places as far apart as Croxall and Ramsbury show that he was something of a traveller, apart from his periodical visits to his relations in Northamptonshire. There are many complimentary prologues to the University of Oxford besides Dryden's, and it is difficult to draw from such a master of flattery any very precise meaning when he is writing in this vein, but he possibly did have a hankering after an academic life. Obviously no evidence can be drawn from Tom Brown's burlesque account of his conversation in London about life in college, but the announcement, incorrect as it was, that he had been appointed President of Magdalen,[5] where indeed his son John was illegally foisted into a fellowship for a short time by James II, and other slight indications make one think that he may have had acquaintance with the life of the University he professed to prefer to his own. But this, like so much else about him, is conjecture.

We know almost to a day when many of his writings appeared. We know a few dates in his life, including that of his receiving the degree of M.A. from the Archbishop of Canterbury — something of an oddity in itself: we have the brief newspaper accounts of the assault on him in Rose Alley:[6] there are a good many anecdotes of uncertain authority about him and there are, of course, numerous well-known passages of self-revelation scattered throughout his prose writings. A few letters have been added to the forty-five printed by Malone, but those to Dorset which Saintsbury was not allowed to inspect now seem to have disap-

peared altogether. Evelyn baldly notes a visit Dryden paid him
at Sayes Court. Pepys, who had known him at Cambridge and
who frequently went to his early plays, mentions him only once
during the period of the diary, though he evidently knew him well
later on. A freshly elected Warden of All Souls insulted him at
a coffee-house. But there are not many records of people meeting him.[7] Of the younger men who had regard for him few except
Congreve,[8] who left it till rather late, attempted to leave any
memory of him that was not expressed in vague verse or casual
remarks. Many, no doubt, would have found it difficult to do so
had they tried, for his curious inconsistency, which made him
at times so much suspected, must have sprung from a personality difficult for even those who knew him well to grasp in a
communicable form.

There are a few other sources of information about him,
but at best our knowledge is meagre of a man who touched contemporary life at so many points and for so long, though perhaps
it would appear more substantial if it were not for a mass of hostile books and pamphlets which seem sometimes to give us a
glimpse of him and at others serve only to confuse what little
we do know on firmer foundations. Throughout his life he was
the target for attacks from every quarter, and in the attempt to
reconstruct his history these have of necessity been used by biographers. Their mere existence is probably not without significance in the estimate of his elusive character. Most of these
pamphlets were used by Malone and Scott, but as they did not
know of them all the curious collection may be worth assembling
once more. In the case of one of his most famous quarrels, that
with Blackmore, the real cause of his anger, a point not without
some importance, escaped them both. A complete survey of all
contemporary criticism of him, honest or malicious, could probably not now be made. He more than once refers to attacks of
which no trace remains, and it is not always possible to be sure
if he is speaking of verbal strictures delivered in assemblies of
critics or conveyed to him in conversation or of printed attacks
which have disappeared. That a good deal of writing of this sort
has perished altogether is probable. There are manuscripts containing libels which may be transcripts of printed sheets which
cannot now be found, and some pieces such as The Tory Poets
have so nearly been lost altogether that it is probable that others
existed which, notwithstanding the diligence of such men as

Luttrell and Wood, never got into the collections where their
survival would have been assured.

The first of Dryden's plays to be acted required the patronage of Lady Castlemaine before it was well received, and we
know from the preface to Secret Love, published in 1668, that
this play had also been severely criticized: but it is not, so far
as I know, till late in 1668, after Dryden had himself introduced
the foibles of his brother-in-law into a literary quarrel, that the
long series of attacks on his own character began. The general
discussion as to the use of rhyme on the stage had become crys-
tallized into a dispute between himself and Sir Robert Howard,
and in this famous controversy there was one pamphlet which
would be quite insignificant were it not for the fact that it may
have served as the model and source for many of those that followed. A Letter from a Gentleman to the Honourable Ed. Howard;
.·. occasioned By a Civiliz'd Epistle of Mr. Dryden's before his
second Edition of the Indian Emperour was read aloud one day in
September 1668 after church by his boy to Pepys, who found it,
as indeed it is, "mighty silly". This pamphlet is signed R. F., and
Peter Cunningham suggested that the initials stand for Richard
Flecknoe. There is no real evidence for this, and two years
later Flecknoe wrote an adulatory epigram on Dryden.[9] Dryden
did, however, pursue Flecknoe with something more than the
general contempt with which, in the fashion of the time, he always speaks of such cockshies of Restoration criticism as
Withers and Quarles; and in 1680 he had become in Dryden's
mind the poet "of scandalous memory".[10] R. F., whoever he was,
attempts to come to the victim's aid against the arguments and
sarcasm of A Defence of the Essay, perceiving, he professes,
that Sir Robert "could not so well make a Return in a Billings-
gate stile". He accuses Dryden, whom he dubs "the squire", of
plagiarism; quotes the line from Astraea Redux "An horrid still-
ness first invades the ear", always a temptation to Dryden's tormentors; talks of the loss the Church had of him when he was
diverted from entering Orders; alludes to Dryden's employment
under the Government in the "late times" and to his father having
been a "committee man". As time went on the character of his
wife, his relations with Anne Reeves, and other touches were
added, but we have here the essential framework laid for any
number of future pamphlets. The Sullen Lovers was published
in November of the same year with a preface which was the first

round in the long contest between Shadwell and Dryden. Shadwell, in his hot-headed way, interpreted Dryden's general critical attitude at this time and a specific sentence in An Essay of
Dramatick Poesy in particular as an "insolent" attack on Ben
Jonson, and under the designation "some" accused Dryden of
stealing plays and of a "bawdy and profaneness which they call
brisk writing". However, Shadwell later made amends in the
preface to The Humourists, and though the rumblings of battle
went on in their respective prefaces intermittently they seem to
have been on reasonably good terms till 1678: they were usually
writing for different theatres, and though they had friends like
Sedley and patrons like the Duke of Newcastle in common they
may not have been thrown much together. Shadwell's convivial
habits would hardly have suited Dryden, who, at least till late
in life when he was too much in Addison's company — Spence is
the authority for this — was sober and regular in his habits.
Tyrannick Love was acted in the last week of June 1669 and published later in the year with a preface defending the play from
charges of profaneness and irreligion and justifying the representation of such a character as Maximin on the stage. The
clamour seems to have gone on, and for once Dryden spared the
time to give some meaning to the words "reviewed by the Author"
on the title-page, for two years later, in the second edition, he
added a paragraph rebuking the "little critics" who had made fun
of the line:

> And he who servilely creeps after sense,

and the "fool" who had charged him "with nonsense" in The Indian
Emperor.
　　Another of Dryden's brothers-in-law, "Dull Ned", to whom
A Letter had been addressed, was inclined to take opposite views
to his on the critical problems of the drama, and he now expounded them in a preface, ineffective but showing some critical
capacity, to The Woman's Conquest (1671). In the epilogue to
another of his plays of the same year, Six Days Adventure, he
had a dig at The Conquest of Granada, which had been acted at
the end of 1670. The story of The Rehearsal, which there is no
reason to doubt was substantially the work of Buckingham, who
had a real turn for burlesque, need not be repeated. Its success
doubtless prompted a Mr. Arrowsmith, of whom nothing seems

to be known except that he is described as an M. A. of Cambridge, to put another piece of banter on Dryden's dramatic
methods. The Reformation was produced at Dorset Gardens
in September 1673, "the play being", says Downes, "the Reverse
of the Laws of Morality and Virtue it quickly made its Exit to
make way for a Moral one". It contains a scene caricaturing
Dryden at work.

> I take a subject, as suppose the Siege of Candy
> or the Conquest of Flanders, and by the way Sir let
> it always be some warlike action: you can't imagine
> what grace a Drum and Trumpet give a Play. Then
> sir I take you some three or four or half a dozen
> kings, but most commonly two or three serve my turn
> not a farthing matter whether they lived within a hun-
> dred years of one another . . . But give me leave to
> mark it for infallible, in all you write reflect upon
> religion and the clergy . . . I take some half a dozen
> youngsters of the town, people that pride themselves
> on one of my nods or a shaking by the hand at the
> Coffee-house, and let them have a copy of a song or
> two or promise of a Prologue, which does so much
> oblige, that I have all the faction of the hour that
> makes a noise on my side.

Dryden had already attained the position of almost legendary
eminence which he was to keep till the end of his life. In the
meantime "Mr. Bayes" of The Rehearsal had been dragged into
a controversy which in no way concerned the original. Marvell,
in his dispute with Parker, chose to apply this nickname to his
antagonist, as later he discomfited the Head of a Cambridge
College with whom he was having a theological argument by
labelling him "Mr. Smirke", the chaplain in The Man of Mode.
In The Rehearsal Transpros'd (1672), and in the books and pamphlets which flew about in the controversy, the authors made
very free with "Mr. Bayes" and sometimes with Dryden himself
when it suited them.

The origin of the quarrel between Dryden and Ravenscroft
is obscure. The Citizen Turned Gentleman certainly had a good
run at Dorset Gardens. This may have piqued Dryden, or he
may have considered some lines in the prologue about fighting

28

Hectors aimed specifically at his heroic plays. At any rate in
an epilogue he wrote for a special performance[11] and in the
prologue to The Assignation he is sarcastic at some gibberish
spoken by one of Ravenscroft's characters. When The Assignation failed Ravenscroft replied in The Careless Lovers (1673),
with a prologue of some force, though by the time he wrote the
address "To the Reader" he had become conciliatory. The quarrel fizzled out, but it is worth mentioning as a probable illustration of Dryden's touchiness, little as he seems ever to have
cared for dramatic writing himself, at the successful run of a
play by another and inferior hand, a trait noted by Tonson, who
recorded that he was suspicious of rivals.[12]

In the spring of 1673, about a year after the publication of
The Conquest of Granada, there appeared four anonymous pamphlets: The Censure of the Rota, The Friendly Vindication of
Mr. Dryden from the Censure of the Rota, A Description of the
Academy of the Athenian Virtuosi, and Mr. Dryden Vindicated
in a Reply to the Friendly Vindication. The Censure, which was
probably by Richard Leigh of Queen's College, Oxford, opens
with a description of the Virtuosi met at a Coffee Academy to
discuss The Conquest of Granada; they debate what they consider
to be the absurdities and defects of Dryden's plays and poems,
illustrating their censures with quotations. The Elegy on Oliver,
"one who was as great a contemnor of Kings as Almanzor", is
raked up. Dryden's supposed appreciation of himself at the expense of Ben Jonson is castigated and some of his less fortunate
lines held up to ridicule.

The Friendly Vindication, which in point of fact is another
attack, supposes Dryden at a meeting with his literary friends:
"The excellent Mr. Dryden taking into serious consideration the
Affairs of Wit and having made an Assignation to that purpose
with some flourishing Ingenuities; no less conscious than admirers of his Fame": one of the forwardest urged the immediate
discussing of the severe Censure of The Rota of Oxford: the
"admirers" proceed to discuss some of The Censure's criticisms
in a way to add to the discomfort of the poet. The failure of The
Assignation is commented on, and Dryden is accused of bringing
real persons upon the stage "with so little disguise that many beheld themselves acted for their Half-Crown".

The author of A Description, which has been incorrectly
treated as another attack, pretends that after he had lightly read

29

over The Censure, "for it deserv'd little consideration", he was
taken by a friend to see the Academy of the Virtuosi, "which was
a large room in a Coffeehouse kept for them where thrice a week
they met retir'd from Company. . . ." The friends get to the
place before the Virtuosi arrive, and by means of a tip gain admission to a room in which they find a secretary at work. They
have time to inspect the contents of the apartment and find the
Critics' owls and several of Dryden's books lying about in a
mangled condition. The Virtuosi arrive, announced under
learned names. At last Cassus, the author of The Censure,
comes in; and the secretary having supplied the Critics with
"teeth and nails"the business of the day begins. The author vin-
dicates the Heroic Poem at first by quotation from the classics,
but finding the critics unable to understand Latin he falls back
upon Cowley and continues through some pages to defend Dryden's position.

Mr. Dryden Vindicated, by Charles Blount, answers the
specific cavils of The Friendly Vindication, and charges the
author with being one of the spiteful critics"who like crabbed-
fac'd Maids, wish there were no such things as Beauty, and Hus-
bands because they have none". Dryden rarely took any notice
of attacks of the pedantic type of The Censure and The Friendly
Vindication, but in the last paragraph of the dedication of The
Assignation he refers to the dispute:"I have not wanted Friends
even amongst Strangers,[13] who have defended me more strongly,
than any Contemptible Pedant cou'd attacque me, For the other;
he is only Fungoso in the Play, who follows the Fashion at a distance, and adores the Fastidious Brisk of Oxford."

Minor controversies were rife in the years 1672–3. A curious little book, Raillerie à la Mode Considered. A Discourse
Shewing the open Impertinence and Degenerosity of Publishing
Private Pecques and Controversies to the World (1673), animad-
verts on them and the character of a detractor. "One Book
beares the Bell away one while, and then presently comes out
Reflections, Observations, Answers, Replications and Exceptions
upon it. . . . Our Laureat himself cannot escape Calumny." The
writer enumerates the Marvell versus Parker and The Rota
tracts and two books which had also been recently published,
one of them of a more serious complexion than the frivolous discussion of an imaginary circle of critics.

THE ATTACKS ON DRYDEN

Most attacks on Dryden before the time of Collier took the
form of irrelevant personal abuse or of burlesque, but in Remarques on the Humours and Conversations of the Town (1673)
a puritanical voice managed to make itself heard, not at that
period a very common occurrence. The author of this little
book for the most part gives the young country gentleman to
whom his Remarques are addressed conventional advice to avoid
the dangers of town life, but his warnings are freed from banal-
ity by a certain adroitness with which he falls on the poets. They
are called to task for making extravagant claims for their influence in the world and told that a member of any other profession
doing so would quickly find himself held up to ridicule on their
own stage. The writer evidently looked on Heroic plays with
the apprehension with which educationalists regard a gangster
film to-day or as The Beggar's Opera was regarded in its own
time. This kind of drama leads the inexperienced, he considers,
into a world of harmful unreality: its "Honour" banishes "Reason
and generosity in the contempt of Life"; its "Love" misguides
youth rather than is "capable of giving a just assistance to the
occasions of Life". Dryden is specifically aimed at; and a controversy on the subject of marriage, which the poetical discipline
was supposed to have undermined, arose and was carried on in
Remarks upon Remarques (1673), where the young gentleman is
told not to take any notice of his tutor, and in other small books
such as Conjugium Conjugium Or Some serious Considerations
on Marriage (1673) and Marriage Asserted (1674).

The next of Dryden's antagonists to spring up was Settle.
After The Empress of Morocco had been given at Court, Settle
was anxious to have it acted at the Theatre Royal, although he
was under an agreement with the Duke's Company. This, as he
explains in his Narrative, written ten years later when he had
decided to part company "with that troublesome companion Whiggism", could not be effected. It may be that Dryden made no
very strenuous effort to retain the play at Drury Lane, or possibly Settle was anxious to revenge Ravenscroft, with whom he
was on friendly terms, for Dryden's attack on Mamamouchi, or
it may simply be that Settle, who was never very level-headed,
felt in an access of vanity a desire to chastise a rival. At any
rate, The Empress was published with some caustic remarks
about "Scriblers in this Age" and their formulae for dedications

31

obviously directed at Dryden. It is hardly true to say, as has
been said, that Settle got the best of it in the squabble that
followed, for Dryden on Settle's shortcomings as a writer is
at his best in the Postscript to Notes and Observations on the
Empress of Morocco (1674).

Between 1674 and the beginning of the deluge of pamphlets
that followed Absalom and Achitophel Dryden received uncomplimentary notice from three of his greatest contemporaries,
Marvell, Otway, and Rochester. There is no doubt of Dryden's
appreciation of Paradise Lost, whatever we may think of The
State of Innocence, and we may suspect that the drubbing Marvell
gave him in his verses before the second edition (1674) was not
entirely prompted by literary considerations. Aubrey, it may
be remarked, brackets Dryden and Marvell as two of Milton's
"familiar learned acquaintance". Dryden's relations with Otway
are shadowy. They both became strong Tories, but in 1676 Dryden seems again to have shown some signs of jealousy and to
have referred to Don Carlos in a way its author naturally resented. In the preface to the printed play Otway reports a remark made by Dryden in conversation, "Igad he knew not a line
in it he would be Author of", but contented himself with crying
tu quoque as regards The Assignation. Rochester's Allusion to
Horace, critical rather than abusive, and A Trial of the Poets
for the Bays,[14] if he wrote it, were circulated in manuscript
somewhat later.

The Rehearsal had exhausted the possibilities of burlesqu-
ing Heroic plays which were themselves burlesques, but some
minor attempts in this form of criticism were made on more
promising material. The Maiden Queen seems to have early
been brought into a performance of The Knight of the Burning
Pestle; two comic versions of "Celimina of my heart" from An
Evening's Love had been printed in Mock Songs and Joking Poems
(1675), and Duffet had concocted A Mock Tempest for representation at the rival theatre.

Among the literary oddities of this time was a book by one
James Carkasse, a King's Scholar who left Westminster two
years after Dryden. This eccentric gentleman was very likely
in Bethlem, as the title-page of Lucida Intervalla (1679) intimates, at the time he wrote it. The doctor seems to have dealt
with the embarrassing question put to him by the patient as to
his fitness for release by telling him he must prove it by ab-

staining from writing verse, but is met with the answer that
many people outside write poetry,

> Bucks both and Rochester unless they mend
> Hither the King designs forthwith to send,
> Shepherd and Dreyden too, must on 'em wait.

The Kind Keeper or Mr. Limberham was produced at Dorset Gardens on the 11th of March 1679, but either because it reflected on the private habits of Shaftesbury or Lauderdale, as
has been suggested, or because it really did shock the audience,
it was allowed a run of only three days. Dryden says he took a
"becoming care" to alter it for the press. An unexpurgated manuscript was seen by Malone. The play is anything but decent and,
though a list of still more indelicate pieces has been furnished,
it was used for years afterwards as a convenient whip for the
author when nothing else was immediately available. John
Tutchin in his Poems on Several Occasions (1685) was particularly incensed with "The Bawdy Sot that late wrote Limberham".
Soon afterwards, on the 18th of December, 1679, a much more
serious business happened, the savage attack on Dryden in Rose
Alley. Malone and Scott too readily placed the responsibility
for the assault on Rochester. Contemporary rumours seem to
point at least as much to the Duchess of Portsmouth, but the
facts we have to go on are few, and here, as so often, the personal relations between Dryden and his contemporaries cannot
be satisfactorily reconstructed. There are many contemporary
allusions to the affair in prologues and elsewhere, but they show
little sympathy with the sufferer.
  Soon after Tonson's edition of Ovid's Epistles (1680) with
its long preface by Dryden came out, Matthew Stevenson produced a burlesque volume called The Wits Paraphras'd, complete with a dedication to Julian, and, one suspects, consciously
modelled on the format, &c., of Tonson's book. A little later
Captain Alexander Radcliffe, who specialized in buffoonery and
wrote a spirited "Mr. Dryden's Description of Night" for a volume
called The Ramble with a sub-title which still helps to sell the
book, produced his Ovid Travestie (1680).
  Malone and Scott have fully discussed most of the pieces
published in answer to Absalom and Achitophel and The Medal.
The furious paper war that raged at this time was made possible

by the refusal of the first Whig parliament to renew the Press
Act originally passed in 1662; and until 1685, in spite of attempts
by the Courts to invoke the Common Law to suppress seditious
publications, the Whigs were able to write what they chose with
reasonable safety. Shaftesbury was supported by an organized
press. "He had", says North, "a great Judgement and Dexterity
in managing and putting forth Libels", but he was unfortunate in
his poets, the good ones all being Tories.[15] It was a perpetual
joke among the Tories that Shaftesbury had been a candidate for
the throne of Poland in 1675, and in A Modest Vindication of the
E. of S——y (1681) Seignioro Roberto Howardensko, Jean Dry-
denuvtritz, his deputy Tom Shadworiski, and others are allotted
to the Whig leader to assist him in the formidable tasks he will
have to encounter in his new kingdom, such as the conversion
of the "Great Turk".

A Panegyrick on the Author of Absalom and Achitophel
Occasioned by his former writing of an Elegy in praise of Oliver
Cromwell lately Reprinted (1681) is short but stiff reading. The
author allows Dryden's "Laurell'd Head" to have a sweet melodious tongue, but attacks him fiercely for change and inconsistency. Hitherto Dryden had been repeatedly taunted with his
poem on Cromwell; now some one thought of reprinting it; and
the verses reappeared on a single sheet headed An Elegy on the
Usurper O.C. . . . (1681), with some lines added at the end, beginning

> The Printing of these Rhimes Afflicts me more
> Than all the Drubs I in Rose-Alley bore.

The poem was again reprinted with Waller and Sprat's poems
but, I suppose, by a less malignant enemy, as except for the substitution of "Usurper" for the "Lord Protector" of the original
title the reprint is not, on its face, obviously offensive. The
author of The Life of Boetius Recommended to the Author of the
Life of Julian (1683) is eloquent on the absurdity of raking up
this poem in the face of Dryden's long years of loyalty. "I cannot pass by Mr. Dryden's case. . . . No sooner then had he
publish'd his happy Thoughts [Absalom and The Medal] but the
Hornets were presently about him too: and, to give him (as they
thought) his mortal wound, they printed his Elegy upon Cromwel
with great clamour and joy." However, this trick seemed to be

considered suitable for every occasion, and out the poem came again in 1687, after the publication of The Hind and the Panther. Four years later it was reprinted by Tonson himself, to make up sets of the poet's collected works.

Poetical Reflections on a late Poem Entitled Absalom and Achitophel (1681) almost defies repeated attempts to read it, and one can easily agree with the remark in a contemporary news-sheet that it was of more use to the piemakers than to any one else. Malone was certainly doing Buckingham an injustice in accepting him as the author. Thorn-Drury thought it likely to have been by Ned Howard, but for this he had only the evidence of a manuscript note on the title-page of his own copy. The prose address emphasizes the point, which would have been a strong one at any other period in English history, that the author makes a principal character on his own side, i.e. the King, "a broad figure of scandalous inclination". This not unreasonable charge and that of the unfairness of producing it just before the man at whom it was aimed was on trial for his life were the most sub-stantial retorts to Absalom.

A Whip For A Fools Back who styles Honourable Marriage a Curs'd Confinement [1682], attributed to Christopher Nesse, a serious writer who managed to get himself excommunicated four times, accuses "dirty Jack" with wearisome reiteration of advo-cating polygamy. It was followed by A Key (With the Whip) (1682) which is of more interest, as it provides the first identification of the characters in Absalom, obvious as most of them were, while attempting to show the unsuitability of the biblical names chosen for them. It also accuses Dryden of softening his char-acter of Shaftesbury for a bribe. Malone dealt at length with the nature of the supposed bribe. As a matter of fact there is some bibliographical evidence to support the supposition, which seems likely enough if the entire passage on Shaftesbury is carefully read, that the celebrated twelve extra lines printed in the second edition were in the original draft of the first but omitted when the poem was in the press. The accusation of a bribe seems to have stung Dryden, for he paid particular attention to the Whip and Key in his Epistle to the Whigs. In the Litanies and other political ballads so common at this time Dryden's name pops up now and again. The Saint turn'd Courtezan [1681], a satyr on Benjamin Harris, has the expression "A Dryden's Salutation". In Azaria and Hushai (1682), probably by Pordage,[16] Lady

Elizabeth Dryden is said to have been "a teeming matron, ere she was a wife". The verse throughout is very tame and the author adopts the absurd expedient, "the utmost refuge of notorious Block heads reduc'd to the last extremity of sense", as Dryden called it, of using phraseology lifted direct from the poem he was answering:

> The Jews, a moody, murmuring, stubborn Race,

The Medal was published on the 16th of March, 1682, and was immediately answered, if the expression can be used for so unintelligible a pamphlet, by The Mushroom: or a Satyr Against Libelling Tories and Prelatical Tantivies (1682), by Edmund Hickeringill. Hickeringill, the titles of whose books were very much better than the books— The Black Nonformist was one of them— must have found his literary pursuits rather expensive, as he was mulct of £2,000 on a Scandalum Magnatum, a form of procedure open to aggrieved peers and combining the advantages of an action and a prosecution, for libelling his bishop, and eventually had to publish, at his own expense, a recantation of some of his works including The Mushroom. Among more general charges he accused Dryden of writing the preliminary verses to The Medal; but though obviously a little cracked he was quick-witted, and retorted to Dryden's sarcastic offer of the loan of feet for his enemies' verses with the first allusion to the line in The Medal:

> Thou leapst o'er all eternal truths in thy Pindaric way

which "has more than should by two". The Medal Revers'd By the Author of Azaria and Hushai (1682) is a rather feeble complaint of the Tories and of religious persecution, but it has embedded in it an unwilling tribute to Dryden's poetical powers.

In the meantime his old enemy Settle had been writing his reply to Absalom and Achitophel. In Heraclitus Ridens, where a close watch was kept on the doings of the Whig poets, it had been announced in January 1682 that "Elkanah promises to vindicate Lucifer's first Rebellion for a few guineas. Poor Absalom and Achitophel must e'en hide themselves in the Old Testament again; as I question whether they'll be safe from the Fury of this mighty cacadism."

Absalom Senior is too long, but it is not unreadable:

> Doeg, tho' without knowing how or why
> Made still a blund'ring kind of melody:

As in Azaria and Hushai a great many lines are given to a Whig historian's account of English history down to the Popish Plot. It contains a curious passage in which it is said that Dryden had aspired to become Provost of Eton.

The Loyal Medal Vindicated (1682) is dull and rambling and adds little fresh by way of abuse.

The next piece to appear is probably the best known, as it seems to be the best informed, of all the pieces attacking Dryden at this time. The Medal of John Bayes has so far as I know been hitherto attributed to Shadwell[17] on the evidence of the copy in the Dyce Collection marked by Luttrell "By Thomas Shadwell. Agts Mr. Dryden very severe 15 May". Until Thorn-Drury suggested that MacFlecknoe had been written as early as 1678—a date now I think established by Mr. H. Brooks's confirmation that the transcript of the poem in the Bodleian, dated that year, is in the handwriting of Oldham, who must have known the facts— The Medal of John Bayes was regarded as the cause of Dryden's scare-crowing of Shadwell. Although MacFlecknoe was not published till after The Medal of John Bayes (Luttrell's copy, now at Yale, being dated the 4th of October), it had been in circulation in manuscript for some time, and it was undoubtedly from some unauthorized source that the first edition was printed. So it is possible to reverse the old story and regard Shadwell's poem as an answer to Dryden's, though there is no reason for connecting them in this way. There is in the library of Trinity College, Cambridge, a copy of The Medal of John Bayes to which, I believe, attention has not been called, with the following note in manuscript on the title-page in a contemporary hand: "Shadwell is run mad."

Notwithstanding this confirmatory piece of evidence, it is not certain that Shadwell did in fact write it. Dryden, who seems to have had no difficulty in discovering who his libellers were when he wanted to, neither in The Vindication of the Duke of Guise nor anywhere else hints that Shadwell was the author, and it is difficult to reconcile his responsibility for it with the tone of his dedication to Sedley of The Tenth Satyr of Juvenal

(1687). However, if Shadwell was the culprit the attention he gets in The Second Part of Absalom and Achitophel, where his personal defects are more strongly emphasized than in Mac-Flecknoe, and the reference to him as the "dull fat fool" in one of Dryden's prologues at this time, would be accounted for. Whoever the author was he seems to have been familiar with Dryden, and in the Epistle to the Tories at the beginning and in the rough verse which follows an uncouth and grotesque "portraiture", as he calls it, of some sort is built up. The piece gives more incidents real or imaginary in Dryden's life than any other, and is tantalizing, as some of them can be neither wholly accepted nor rejected.

Satyr to his Muse was attributed to Lord Somers in Curll's edition of The Works of Rochester, . . ., 1707, from which unreliable source Jacob probably took his information. Seventeen years after the piece had been published Dryden told Mrs. Steward that the Lord Chancellor was his enemy, but to connect this with Satyr to his Muse is far-fetched; and Pope stated that the Lord Chancellor was wholly ignorant of it. One edition professes to be "Printed for D. Green", the mysterious and possibly pseudonymous publisher of MacFlecknoe. The two pieces have strong typographical resemblances and were undoubtedly the work of the same printer. Nothing else by "D. Green" is known; and the gentleman with "a curious Collection of Poetry" who announced at the end of MacFlecknoe that he intended to oblige the world with a poem every Wednesday morning seems to have abandoned the design, if the gentleman or the poems ever existed. Only the first part of the poem has anything to do with Dryden. It adds, in the most offensive language, a few more of the strange incidents of which the poet's life, according to his enemies, was composed. The Tory Poets, published before the 4th of September, is chiefly directed at Dryden and Otway. The anonymous author reflects severely on the licentiousness of the former's prologues, plays, and private morals, his ingratitude to the Duke of Monmouth, and so on. The stage was now much occupied with political plays:

'Tis now no Jest to hear young Girls talk Bawdy,

as A Lenten Prologue, published early in 1683, complains. This piece has a few uncomplimentary lines directed at the Laureate.

Directions to Fame About an Elegy on the Late Deceased Thomas Thynn Esqre, And An Elegy on other most Famous English Worthies By an Unknown Author (1682) is very rare and little known. The Bodleian has recently acquired a copy, and I know of only one other, which is now in America. Line after line of weak and rambling verse is devoted to Dryden, but it is not easy to get a clear impression of what the author is after. His mistress, Ann Reeves, is mentioned, as is usual in the pieces of this time, and a vague accusation that he will write anything for cash is made against him:

> What matter is 't how little Truth he writ,
> So that there be the Varnish of some wit?
> And yellow Boys have soundly paid for it.

L'Estrange was an almost greater source of annoyance to the Whigs than Dryden, and another very rare pamphlet published this year, A Sermon Prepared to be Preach'd at the Interment of the Renowned Observator with an Epitaph by the Rose-Ally Poet, was put out by some wag nearly a quarter of a century too early.[18] Religio Laici was published on the 20th November 1682 and, though more editions were wanted than Malone supposed, there was little in the poem to call forth abuse or praise. It was occasionally cited later on as one more example of Dryden's inconsistency, but it did not come in for much notice till it was thrown into relief by The Hind and the Panther. Dryden and Lee's play, The Duke of Guise, was produced after some trouble with the Lord Chamberlain at the end of November 1683. Shadwell soon came out with Some Reflections upon the Pretended Parallel in the Play called the Duke of Guise (1683). The "old Serpent Bays" is accused of perverting the good intentions of Lee, from whom it is said he would have filched the credit of the play, if there had been any, as he had done "in Discourse with all his own friends" when they had collaborated in Œdipus. The larger political issue was at this time somewhat narrowed to the fight over the charter of the City of London which the Court considered such a stronghold of Whiggism should only possess in a much modified form, and Thomas Hunt in A Defence of the Charter (1683) attacked the play with vigour, complaining that "they have already condemned the Charter and City and have executed the Magistrates in Effigie upon the Stage".

Another pamphlet, now very difficult to find, The True History
of the Duke of Guise Extracted out of Thuanus . . . Published for
the undeceiving such as may perhaps be imposed upon by Mr.
Dryden's late Tragedy. . . (1683) is more or less explained by
its title, and Sol in Opposition to Saturn, a single-sheet piece,
is too slight to be regarded. Dryden had no time to write for
the play a preface which he intended as a reply to Shadwell and
Hunt, as the publisher was pressing for copy, but a little later
he published The Vindication of the Duke of Guise (1683), in
which he falls on the spluttering triumvirate, Settle having also
lent a hand.

The Songs of Moses and Deborah Paraphras'd with Poems
on Several Occasions (1685), by C. Cleeve, contains a preliminary poem describing the bookstalls in St. Paul's:

> For see where Denham, Dryden, Oldham lye:
> Few read the title Page, and fewer buy,
> When to the Book Retailing Coxcomb's price,
> Perhaps the cautious Buyer will not rise,
> Come, Sir, says he, to fetch him to his Gin,
> See I'll be kind, here take The Medal in,
> Audacious Sot to use a Poet so,
> Thus Chandlers with their Penny Chapmen do,
> Into the Bargain Thread and Paper throw.

Dryden now had an encounter with Stillingfleet, possibly in
his capacity of Historiographer Royal. Soon after his accession
two papers reputed to be by Charles II, defending the Catholic
religion, were shown in manuscript by James to Pepys, who was
probing him as to what his brother's religion had really been.
These papers, together with another by Anne Hyde giving her
reasons for becoming a Catholic, were published by Royal Command. Stillingfleet wrote an answer, to which Dryden in part
replied by contributing a defence of the Duchess's paper to a
longer pamphlet printed by the King's printer. Stillingfleet then
published A Vindication of the Answer (1687), where Dryden is
roughly handled. "Romantick Heroes must be allowed to make
Armies of a field of Thistles, and to encounter Wind-mills for
Giants." Stillingfleet accuses him of attempting to divide the
clergy of the Church of England.

THE ATTACKS ON DRYDEN

Professor Bredvold has shown that there is no ground for supposing that Dryden benefited financially by becoming a Catholic, but when The Hind and the Panther was published it was naturally greeted with a series of pamphlets attacking the author or ridiculing the poem. The Hind and the Panther Transvers'd 1687 was the first and is the most readable. It seems really to have been the joint work of Montague and Prior, the latter of whom was probably also the author, though he denied it, of two pieces, A Satyr upon the Poets and A Satyr on Modern Translators, in both of which Dryden is treated wihout much respect. The Revolter, A Trage-Comedy Acted between the Hind and the Panther and Religio Laici (1687) returned to the old story that Dryden was not able to enter the Church, for which reason, it was said, he was taking his revenge on her. His "rambling conscience" was exhibited by contradictory passages from his poems, with a prose commentary to show the inconsistency between "Mr. D. the Romanist" and "Mr. D. the Protestant". The New Atlantis A Poem . . . with some Reflections upon the Hind and the Panther (1687) was published anonymously. Thomas Heyrick, the author, explains in the Advertisement prefixed to the old sheets when they reappeared with a new title, A True Character of Popery and Jesuitism (1690), that he had been, at the time, too much frightened of the Catholics, "whose usual answers are not pens", to acknowledge it. Probably his fears were quite unnecessary, as the poem is a long and tedious allegory not likely to leave in the reader sufficient energy to commit an assault. However Heyrick, a grandson of an elder brother of Robert Herrick, was something of a poet—he wrote some curious and attractive poems on the Mole and other creatures in a book of verse published at Cambridge in 1691—and The New Atlantis is more like poetry than most of the verse launched at Dryden. The Catholics, finding their faith in disrepute, decide that it can best be supported by poetry. They interview Bavius (Dryden)—

> A Proselite, whose servile Pen can write
> For fear, reward, for mischief or for spite.

They prime him on the points to be made—interrupted for a time by the appearance of a monster—a Trimmer—and eventually,

Thoughtful and dull, according to his use,

Bavius undertakes the task, which will suit him very well, for he hates the clergy, has been hit in marriage, &c. At this time an attack on Dryden, in manuscript, the work of an old enemy, was resuscitated. Martin Clifford, a forbidding-looking person if the portrait of him in Cowley's Works (1707) is a good likeness, has been credited in several contemporary pamphlets, &c., with a hand in The Rehearsal. Spratt, in dedicating his Cowley to Clifford, refers to the latter's disinclination to appearing in print, and when he died he had left four stupid unpublished letters of abuse of The Conquest of Granada. It is characteristic of the slapdash methods of many of Dryden's detractors that these letters, which had nothing to do with the present controversy, were printed as a make-weight before Some Reflections upon the Hind and the Panther (1687), by Tom Brown, who was just getting into his stride of the serio-comic employment of baiting Dryden. A folio pamphlet, The Laureat: Jack Squabbs History in a little drawn Down to his Evening from his early Dawn, by Robert Gould, was published at this time. It is very abusive, though on Dryden's death Gould wrote a poem beginning "Farewel! thou Chiefest of the Sons of Fame!"

A poem called The Laurel, still sometimes confused with The Laureat, had been published in quarto in 1685, and is one of the few pamphlets in praise of Dryden. A rare anonymous piece, The Hind in the Toil (1688), has little to do with Dryden beyond borrowing the names of some of his beasts. It contains a neat allusion to the late times:

> Plots upon plots were then found out to vail
> The grand design, and bury Oats in Meal.[19]

It was to be expected that several people should come to the rescue of the Established Church. Mrs. James, somewhat unchivalrously noticed in the preface to The Hind and the Panther, but whose fine portrait at Sion College is testimony to her capacity, had already written a prose Vindication of the Church of England, but this had not been provoked by Dryden. A Poem in Defence of the Church of England in Opposition to the Hind and the Panther (1688) keeps on the whole to a theological plane, but the accusation that Dryden was unable to take orders is repeated, and

> Friend Bayes, I fear this Fable, and these Rimes,
> Were thy dull Pennance, for some former Crimes,
> When thy free Muse her own brisk Language spoke,
> And unbabtiz'd, disdain'd the Christian Yoke.

The death of Buckingham in 1687 was not made the subject of much lamentation, but there is one poem, To the Memory of the Illustrious Prince George Duke of Buckingham (1687), which harks back to Absalom and Achitophel and "the embitter'd Song" which had accused him of "roving Change and wand'ring Fires". Another very rare pamphlet, Religio Laici, or a Laymans Faith Touching the Supream Head and Infallible Guide of the Church, not to be confused with Charles Blount's Religio Laici published five years earlier, was printed in 1688. Now that another matter altogether was in dispute Dryden's powers as a satirist, which had been preposterously derided earlier, were admitted. The author of this quarto tract says that Dryden "has a most power-ful and luxurious hand at satyr", adding that there is no one to compare with him unless it be that unknown (but supposed) worthy Author, that writ to him upon his (at last) turning Roman Catholic:

> Thou Mercenary Renegade, thou Slave,
> Thou ever changing, still to be a knave,

and thirty-two lines more in the same strain. There is at Wel-beck a manuscript copy of this poem headed "Mr. Bayes supposed by the E. of Middlesex", a disconcerting ascription, for according to more likely tradition Dorset was helping Dryden with money at this very time. Towards the end of 1686 Burnet had published his Reflections on M. Varillas History . . . and more particularly on his Ninth Book. Varillas had replied, and in A Defence of the Reflections, which appeared four or five months after The Hind and the Panther, Burnet took the opportunity to retort to the char-acter of himself as the Buzzard. If Burnet had not already given Dryden provocation he certainly received it, for the character was extremely libellous of a prospective bishop. Burnet's retort is very vague, and one can only suppose he found a difficulty in thinking of anything sufficiently caustic to say when he wrote, "it is scarce possible for him to grow worse than he was", im-proved in the History into the statement that "he was a monster of unmodesty and impiety of all sorts". It may be observed that

Thomas Burnet's explanation that his father was referring to
Dryden's plays and not to his personal character cannot be accepted in the face of both passages.[20]

Dryden had himself been at work on a translation of Varillas
at the time, as we know from an entry in the S. R. on the 29th of
April 1687, where the work is described as licensed; but the
translation was not published, and Burnet had the satisfaction
of assuming that this was because he had been able to discredit
the historian. The Reasons of Mr. Bayes Changing his Religion
(1688), by Tom Brown, and its continuation are amusing, and
Brown, working on the traditional Mr. Bayes, succeeded in leaving a comic portrait of Dryden as a pendant to the lurid John
Bayes of 1682.

Langbaine's taste for hunting plagiarisms was given ample
scope in Dryden's plays, but his hostility may have had a more
personal origin than his desire to catch poets cribbing. A New
Catalogue of English Plays with divers Remarks of the Originals
of most Plays and the Plagiaries of Several Authors by Gerard
Langbaine, Gent. . . . (1688) had appeared a little earlier as
Momus Triumphans or the Plagiaries of the English Stage Expos'd by Gerard Langbaine Esq. In an Advertisement to A New
Catalogue Langbaine says that its getting into the world under
the "Heathenish" Name of Momus Triumphans and with the title
of Esquire, to which he disclaimed all pretension, added to his
name was none of his affair. He attributed the title-page to the
machination of other people whom neither he nor his bookseller
could identify. It is difficult to know if one can believe this fantastic story. It is possible that Langbaine had been a little
ashamed of the first title-page and invented the excuse. At any
rate, after An Account of the English Dramatick Poets (1691),
the familiar "Langbaine", had been published, somebody in The
Moderator for the 23rd of June 1692 told him bluntly that being
conscious of his "porterly language" to Mr. Dryden he had pitched
on him as the person responsible for the original imposition, and
so had run full tilt at him in the present edition. An Epistle to
Mr. Dryden, some copies of which are dated Exeter Nov. 5, 1688,
and beginning "Dryden thy Wit has catter-wauld too long", need
not detain us. A more interesting piece entitled The Protestant
Satire: or Some Reason not all Rhyme In Return to Mr. Bayes's
Popish Libels must have been written about this time, though
not published apparently till 1747, when it was inserted in a very

rare volume known as Cross's Miscellany which contains a
witty reply to The Lady of the May.

Dryden lost his posts at the Revolution, and though now under the urgent necessity of earning money did not publish anything immediately. There being nothing positive to find fault
with his enemies invented a new line of attack, the foisting of
bogus pieces on him. The Address of John Dryden Laureat to
His Highness the Prince of Orange (1689) was a well-printed
folio of four leaves with the imprint of Randal Taylor. It presumably took in many people at the time, and the complete absence of anything to arouse suspicion in its appearance has led
to its being included among Dryden's own writings in the catalogue of one well-known modern library. Another piece, a bogus
Poem to King William with an apology for the poet's life, seems
only to have been circulated in manuscript until the poem was
printed in Poems on Affairs of State (1698). Annoyance was, of
course, expressed that he was now on the wrong side. In The
Murmurers (1689) he appears as Balaam:

> Thy Songs so sweet, thy Numbers so divine,
> Scarce Moses Song had won more Fame than thine:
> But now thy Glory sleeps in Shades profound,
> By Fate and gloomy Death encompass'd round.

Dryden had been accused of serious vices in some of the earlier
pamphlets. His snuff-taking and Mr. Bayes's custom of dieting,
letting blood, and taking physick before writing served now and
then as a comic relief from the days of The Rehearsal. A very
minor dramatist, Carlisle, introduced them into the prologue,
printed by Malone, to The Fortune Hunters.

His name was again dragged into a matter with which he had
nothing to do. In August 1690 William Sherlock, the nonjuror,
suddenly took the oaths under the influence, it was said, of Mrs.
Sherlock, who preferred keeping her carriage to going about on
foot. Soon a number of pamphlets, in verse and prose, were published, The Weesils, The Anti-Weesils, Advice to a Parson, and
so on, in which there is usually some echo of Absalom and Achitophel or The Hind and the Panther, the author of The Tribe of
Issachar being particularly free in his use of Dryden's lines.
One piece, Rabshahah Vapulans (1691), an answer to The Tribe
of Levi, thought by Wood to be by Dryden himself but really by

Tutchin, attacked him very savagely because priests were made
fun of on the stage:

> This <u>Art</u> was at the first found out by Bays:
> The rarest Rules in all his wise <u>Essays</u>:
> He led the <u>Dance</u>. Nor was 't in <u>him</u> so strange,
> Inspir'd by <u>Interest</u>, Madness and Revenge,
> Possess'd with Pride, and hurry'd by Despair,
> At his approach <u>whipt</u> from the <u>House of Prayer</u>.

On Dryden's exit from the political world and the settlement
of the nation's affairs some compassion for him probably became
general, and the references to him tend to become less offensive.
<u>A Search after Wit or a Visitation of the Authors In Answer to
the late Search after Claret</u> (1691), in eighty-nine stanzas, runs
over the play-writers and critics. To the lines on Shadwell
"equally admired for his Shape and his Wit" these are added:

> And was it for him, that old <u>De Jure</u> Bays
> With his Horns (<u>sic</u>) and his <u>Panthers</u> was turn'd out to graze!
> He had better have staid, and both writ at a Time,
> That one might find <u>Wit</u>, and t'other find <u>Rhyme</u>.

In <u>Poems in Burlesque with a Dedication in Burlesque</u> (1692)
there is an account of a visit to the famous coffee-house:

> To <u>Wills</u> I went, where Beau and Wit
> In mutual Contemplation sit; . . .
> To make amends there I saw <u>Dryden</u>
> Whom Pegasus takes so much Pride in,
> He suffers few beside to ride him:
> Sometimes at once he gets a Pack
> Of young raw Rhymers on his Back.

Hitherto his alleged unreadiness in conversation had been treated
as mere awkwardness, but in <u>The Humours and Conversations of
the Town exposed in two Dialogues</u> (1693) a much more friendly
view is taken: "the company of the Author of <u>Absalom and Achito-
phel</u> is more valuable, tho' not so talkative as that of the Modern
Men of Banter". Even his references to marriage, always till
now a subject for derision, are sometimes referred to without

a gibe. In A humble Remonstrance of Batchelors in and about London (1693) it is said: "we are assured from all hands, that those persons who have taken the greatest pains to expose that Holy State were all of 'em married (to prove which we could name a famous Abdicating Poet, if we were minded)."

Enemies could, however, still be fierce at times, and some verses in The Loyal and Impartial Satyrist (1694) attack the Catholic poet by the familiar method of quoting from him.

If Dryden had been constantly rebuked and attacked when he wrote he did not always escape when he was silent. In The Deliverance, A Poem to the Prince of Orange (1689) the author complained that it was left to his "Junior Pen" to caress the Prince while all the great Wits were silent. The poets had not shown much enthusiasm over the coming of William, but they indulged unlimited grief on the death of Mary. Dryden seems to have felt under an obligation to keep his political sympathies from obtruding much into his writings in return for being left in peace, but if he could do nothing to help the return of Pan and Fair Syrinx he certainly did nothing to gain the goodwill of their successors. A rumour reached Leibnitz at Dresden, rather to his surprise, that Dryden was at work on a poem on the occasion. This was not so, but there exists an interesting letter from Stepney to Tonson in which Stepney asks the publisher to submit an ode he had written to Dryden, Montague, and Congreve for correction. Stepney was puzzled as to which of three bad lines was the best, and as another was printed in its place some one must have come to the rescue, though whether or not this was Dryden there is nothing to show. Beyond expressing his opinion that an ode by the Duke of Devonshire was the best, he let the Queen's death pass unnoticed. His silence annoyed some irritable poet, who printed at the beginning of An Ode Occasion'd by the Death of the Queen (1695) a Letter to Mr. Dryden beginning with the uncompromising sentence "Though I have little Acquaintance with you, nor desire more". The author of Urania's Temple or A Satyr upon the Silent Poets (1695) is more sympathetic:

> Had that, now silent Muse been but so kind
> As to this Funeral Dirge her Numbers join'd,
> On that great Theme what Wonders had he told:
> For though the Bard, the Quill is not grown old.

Ned Howard took the opportunity, without much regard to the appropriateness of the occasion, to attach to his Elegy on the Queen's Death (1695) one of his rambling excursions into criticism, where he expressed himself as much pleased with the progress the Muses had recently made as exhibited by the poems of Dryden, Congreve, Milton, and Blackmore. It was from the last that Dryden received one of the worst insults—apparently unprovoked—which he received in the course of nearly forty years of abuse. His extreme anger with the knight-physician and the trouncing he gives him in the Preface to the Fables, the Epistle to John Driden and the Prologue to the Pilgrim have been regarded as something of a mystery, and the cause assigned either to some general remarks on the immorality of the stage in the preface to King Arthur or to some lines in A Satyr Against Wit about the stench and fumes that would arise from Dryden when he was melted down—uncomplimentary it is true, but not, I think, the cause of his annoyance. A Satyr was published just before The Fables; but this was probably not the libel of which Dryden specifically complains. This occurs in Prince Arthur. Sakil (Dorset) is distributing alms:

> The Poets Nation, did Obsequious wait
> For the kind Dole, divided at his Gate.
> Laurus amidst the meagre Crowd appear'd
> An old revolted unbelieving Bard,
> Who throng'd and shov'd, and prest, and would be heard
> Distinguish'd by his louder craving Tone
> So well to all the Muses Patrons known,
> He did the voice of modest Poets drown.
> Sakil's high Roof, the Muses Palace rung
> With endless Cries, and endless Songs he sung.
> To bless good Sakil, Laurus would be first,
> But Sakil's Prince and Sakil's God he curst.
> Sakil without distinction threw his Bread,
> Despis'd the Flatt'rer but the Poet fed.[21]

One of the last flings at Dryden came not from a political enemy or critic but from an actor on behalf of the Drury Lane Company, and was not altogether without excuse. In the verses he wrote for his friend George Granville's Heroick Love (1698) Dryden, perhaps with something of an elderly man's dislike for the changed atmosphere incident to revivals of plays, had written acrimoniously of the performances at Drury Lane, being as he admitted elsewhere especially irritated by a production of The Conquest of Granada. Dryden had begun his poem to Granville by bequeathing him his laurels in language not very dissimilar from that which he had used when giving the same legacy to Congreve. This rather typical piece of inadvertence gave Powell, one of the offended cast, an excellent opening of which he availed himself in the preface to his play The Fatal Discovery (1698): "this great wit, with his treacherous memory, forgets that he had given away his laurels upon record twice before, viz. once to Mr. Congreve and another time to Mr. Southerne. . . . Dost thou set up thy transubstantiation miracle in the donation of thy idol bays that thou hast them fresh, new, and whole, to give them three times over?"

Long as the above list of abusive and critical pamphlets is it does not exhaust the attacks on Dryden. Copies of angry verses aimed at him, especially after the publication of The Hind and the Panther, are frequently found in manuscript collections, and several are printed in the numerous volumes of Poems on Affairs of State, which were also repositories for several pieces falsely and no doubt maliciously ascribed to him. He seems to have had reason for suspecting Rymer of attempting to injure him for political reasons; and Milbourne, who had earlier professed to be his admirer, wrote an ill-natured and tiresome criticism of the Virgil. Mrs. Behn flared up in Protestant indignation and Swift pursued his name with contempt in The Tale of a Tub and The Battle of the Books.[22] Indeed it is not easy to find any parallel in English literature to so much violence and ridicule directed against one man of letters in his life-time unless Pope is a competitor. It is easy to account for the vituperation heaped upon Pope,[23] but if we know anything of Dryden it is that he was without undue vanity and that he was magnanimous to others, unless perhaps when irritated by the success of some inferior playwright. He seems to have been quite free from the infirmity, so common a cause of quarrels, when the mind doubts its own abilities and at the same time insists on their recognition. Much that he wrote, the Heroic Plays for instance, as he very well knew, was fair game and could not have escaped ridicule; many of the onslaughts were incompetent answers to his political poems and were inevitable; others, and those usually the most violent, were called forth by his acceptance of the Roman Catholic religion. His field, it is true, was wider than that of any other serious English writer, and he was therefore liable to attacks from all directions, but they were so numerous and met so many of his activities that one is tempted to wonder if there was not about him something provocative even in a negative way, some vulnerable streak of which his enemies were half conscious but which they could not locate. For some of the pieces are almost incomprehensible in their fury, as though the writers did not clearly know what it was that had angered them.[24] Saintsbury suggested his lavish flattery and his somewhat frequent indulgence in complaints as possible factors in arousing enmity, but he had the antagonism of Swift in mind, and Dryden's flattery, though more skilful than that of his contemporaries, occurs in an age when flattery, at least in dedications, was universal. Much of it was absurd, but it cannot have seemed peculiar. He sometimes seems to apologize too much. He was inconsistent, and he must have seemed more inconsistent than he was. These traits and habits were easily liable to be ridiculed, as they certainly often were. But behind them it is possible that there was in his character some shade of ineffectiveness which, when it is combined with the possession of extraordinary powers, is apt to be met by resentment. Perhaps the story of his encounter with the Warden of All Souls is suggestive. It at least stikes one as odd that this Mr. Finch, the son of a nobleman and the recently elected head of a college, should have felt himself at liberty to be quite as rude as he was. Meeting Dryden in a coffee-house he publicly wished him joy of his new religion. "Sir," said Dryden, "you are very much mistaken: my religion is the old religion." "Nay," replied the other, "whatever it be in itself I am sure it is new to you for within three days you had no religion at all."[25]

Dryden probably lacked the power of repartee for occasions of this kind.[26] Whatever it was that brought down on his head so much abuse he generally bore it with restraint, and with unmatched powers of retaliation in print he was difficult to draw.[27]

In A Discourse concerning . . . Satire prefixed to the Juvenal he says that he has been the public mark of a multitude of scribblers for many years and explains that he has left their lampoons and libels unanswered as they could do no harm.[28] One of his most persistent tormentors was passed with a remark in a letter to Mrs. Steward: "I hear Tom Brown is coming out upon me."

THE ATTACKS ON DRYDEN

When he did trouble to retaliate he probably had full justification, as he certainly had in the case of the pious but trying Blackmore.[29]

NOTES

1   This survey is based on a full bibliography of Dryden which I am preparing for the Clarendon Press. Many of the pieces are, of course, well known, and extracts from them will be found in the Scott-Saintsbury edition of Dryden's Works. I think a few have not been noticed before. I have made no reference to the Collier controversy as it has been discussed so often.

2   Saintsbury quotes a passage from Poeta de Tristitus (1682) as a description of Dryden's conversation, and Professor A. Nicoll in his Dryden and His Poetry quotes another from Rochester's Ghost as a description of his appearance. Neither has anything to do with Dryden. The first refers to Shadwell and the second to Sheffield.

3   Malone gives the family home as Staff'hill, on the authority of a genealogical tree in a Harleian MS. Dr. Allen Mawr tells me this is without doubt Staffield near Kirkoswald. Mr. Denwood of Cockermouth says that it has been traditional in his family for 200 years that the Dridens lived close to Huthwaite Hall near Isel. Of their home only an outbuilding remains. The family may have moved, or there may have been more than one branch.

4   Professor R. G. Ham called attention to the date on Dryden's Horoscope in the Ashmolean, where it is given as the 19th of August 1631: the Horoscope itself was cast for the 9th: the date was apparently the 9th of August O.S., the 19th of August N.S.

5   There were also rumours at one time that he was to be Warden of All Souls and at another President of Trinity College, Dublin.

6   An occasional fact still comes to light: for instance, that he lived for a time with Sir Robert Howard in Lincoln's Inn Fields.

7 He is mentioned under the year 1678 in Hooke's recently published <u>Diary</u>.

8 Lord Lansdowne's short account of Dryden supports the famous "character" left by Congreve.

9 In the second edition of his <u>Epigrams</u> (1671) some verses attacking Dryden were added; but this was in consequence of the epilogue to the Second Part of <u>The Conquest of Granada.</u>

10 The sentence in the dedication of <u>Mr. Limberham,</u> 1680, in which the remark occurs is, as Malone pointed out, very obscure.

11 To <u>The Maiden Queen</u> "in mans cloathes".

12 In <u>A Comparison Between the Two Stages,</u> 1702, after a reference to Dryden's public praise of Congreve, Vanbrugh, and Southern: <u>Sullen</u> adds "and yet I have seen him bite his Nails for Vexation that they came so near him".

13 The relations between Charles Blount the Deist and Dryden are of interest. Blount was a Whig and the author of a famous political Whig pamphlet, besides being so unorthodox as to commit suicide because he could not marry his deceased wife's sister. Dryden seems to have been friendly with him till his death in 1693.

14 It is difficult to accept Mr. Ham's view that this was by Settle. Possibly Buckingham had a hand in it.

15 In <u>A Character of the True Blue Protestant Poet</u> (1682) it is alleged that Settle sold his services to the party that made the higher bid.

16 Mr. Ham contends that this piece and <u>The Medal Revers'd</u> were by Settle.

17 <u>Satyr to his Muse, The Tory Poets,</u> and <u>A Lenten Prologue,</u> all dated 1682, have each been attributed to Shadwell on slight or no evidence.

18 L'Estrange died in 1704.

19 The Meal Tub Plot.

20 Percy, in his annotated Langbaine, records a story about Dryden's morals, which he seems to consider supported

Burnet's statement, but as the information was double hear-
say and its originator "an old man who in his younger years
had been a drawer at a tavern which Dryden frequented", it
is extremely unreliable evidence, to say the least of it.

21 Some of the lines are quoted by Macaulay, iii. 25, but their
significance seems to have been overlooked.

22 Both written before, though not published till after, Dryden's
death.

23 Pope, who had been made acquainted with Dryden's amiable
qualities by Wycherley, Congreve, and Sir William Trumbul,
attributed the libels on Dryden to the violence of party, but
as we have seen the attacks began too early to be accounted
for solely in this way.

24 It may be remarked that either Pope's enemies were more
competent or their objective was easier. At least they seem
on the whole more coherent. Perhaps they benefited by their
predecessors, for Savage in An Author to Let (1727) says:
"I have well perused the writings of Luke Milbourne, Shadwell, Settle, Blackmore, and many others of that stamp notable for gall writ upon Dryden. From those I have extracted
curious Hints to assist Welsted in his new satire against
Pope."

25 The Fleming MSS.

26 This can be gathered from Congreve—and from Dryden himself.

27 He perhaps sometimes wrote for a private audience: Mac-
Flecknoe was not intended for immediate publication if originally for publication at all; the lines on Tonson narrowly
escaped oblivion; and what was the Satyr which Atterbury
wanted Tonson to send him in 1687? Malone, li. 204.

28 Dr. Johnson says Dryden "is always angry at some past, or
afraid of some future censure"; but he of course refers to
literary criticism.

29 In the preface to the Lucian, published eleven years after his
death, Dryden falls on Ferrard Spence, an earlier translator,
with a severity that Spence's version does not explain. Spence
had given Dryden provocation in his preface.

MACDONALD'S BIBLIOGRAPHY OF DRYDEN

James M. Osborn

Every review of <u>John Dryden: a bibliography of early edi-tions and of Drydeniana</u>[1] should begin with a tribute to the care and industry of the compiler and an acknowledgment of the in-debtedness under which Mr. Hugh Macdonald has placed all serious students of the literature of the later seventeenth cen-tury. His book is the most important volume in Dryden scholar-ship since the publication of George R. Noyes's edition of Dry-den's poems in 1909 and the most useful volume for historians of Restoration literature that has appeared for several years. A tangible demonstration of its value is that the book has already become a fixture on the reference shelves of every university library.

The chief reason for its importance is that this book is more than a mere descriptive bibliography. Into its three hun-dred and twenty-six pages of text Mr. Macdonald has packed all the factual information he could find concerning Dryden, his writ-ings, and his literary relations with his contemporaries. The notes contain so much out-of-the-way information that no student of the period can afford to pass them by. Mr. Macdonald has here made available not only the results of his own investigations but the learning of his predecessors in Dryden bibliography, Percy J. Dobell and the late George Thorn-Drury. As every Dryden scholar knows, for more than twenty-five years Mr. Dobell has made a hobby of collecting bibliographical informa-tion about Dryden, and this book is the fruit of his labors as much as it is the work of Mr. Macdonald. After publishing his now famous catalogue, <u>The literature of the Restoration,</u> in 1918 and his stimulating volume of <u>Bibliographical memoranda</u> in 1922, Mr. Dobell placed all his information about Dryden in the hands of Mr. Thorn-Drury, then recognized as the most erudite student of the literature of the age of Dryden. Following Thorn-Drury's death, Mr. Dobell turned over Thorn-Drury's notes on Dryden to Mr. Macdonald, who also enjoyed prior use of the

Reprinted from <u>Modern Philology</u>, Vol. 39 (1942), pp. 313–319, by per-mission of the author and The University of Chicago Press. Copyright 1942 by The University of Chicago.

Thorn-Drury papers and collections in the Bodleian. Thus, Mr. Macdonald stands on their shoulders, and we can thank all three of them for the varied and valuable information that this bibliography of Dryden contains. Mr. Macdonald has shown great talent in synthesizing this mass of detail, and it is this talent which has made his bibliography such a useful reference book.

The two terms "bibliography" and "reference book" should not be used interchangeably, though both of them apply in the case of this bibliography of Dryden. Yet these words designate separate functions, and any detailed examination of Mr. Macdonald's accomplishment should, I believe, discuss his book from the two standpoints: first, as a collection of data about Dryden and other writers of his age and, second, as a detailed description of books by or about Dryden.

Considered as a reference book, this volume has the three primary virtues of abundant information, commendable accuracy, and a full index. The information is biographical as well as bibliographical, so that scarcely one of Dryden's contemporaries is mentioned by Mr. Macdonald without a note full of pertinent information. Similarly, many of the book titles are accompanied by details of publishing history, including dates from the Stationers' registers, the Term catalogues, advertisements in contemporary newspapers, and the title-page annotations of Narcissus Luttrell. A good deal of this information has already appeared in scattered publications, and much may be found in the jottings of Thorn-Drury and other antiquaries; but Mr. Macdonald has earned the gratitude of all scholars for making it conveniently accessible.

No book containing thousands of dates, page references, and other details has ever been published without its share of errors of one kind or another. In the "Annotated check list"[2] I have pointed out some of the slips observed in an attentive reading of the book. As a tribute to Mr. Macdonald's accuracy, it may be mentioned that his errors are usually errors of omission, not of commission. His dates and statements can generally be accepted as accurate, though those singled out in the "Annotated check list" may indicate the kind of information Mr. Macdonald has sometimes overlooked. Gaps are most noticeable in the Drydeniana, the sections to which Mr. Macdonald has devoted nearly half of the whole book. His preface states that he aimed to include "every contemporary book or pamphlet . . . . in which [Dryden] is praised, attacked, or alluded to"; and later he speaks of the volume as "an allusion book as well as a bibliography." The items listed in the Drydeniana are interesting enough, but so many others can be added to them that I did not attempt to insert additions in the check list.[3] Another objection to this part of Mr. Macdonald's work is that he does not appear to have settled on a clear distinction between books and pamphlets that should be described in the text and other items mentioned in the footnotes. For example, James Wright's Country conversations, mentioned in note 4 on page 56, deserves a place among the numbered Drydeniana, as do Purcell's 1695 opera based on The Indian queen (p. 90, n. 1) and several others.[4] Nor can he excuse these omissions by pleading lack of space, for the pages lavished on the tracts known as "Conversations of the town" (pp. 197–201) could well have been used to better advantage; only the last one contains anything of Dryden interest.[5] Similarly the items listed under Settle's Narrative (pp. 238–40) have, as Mr. Macdonald confesses, "little direct bearing on Dryden," and, indeed, most readers will have difficulty in finding any connection between them. Taken as a whole, the Drydeniana is the least successful section of the book.

In any reference book the apparatus is of the utmost importance. Aside from notes, the apparatus in this volume consists of a list of abbreviations and the index. The list of abbreviations is woefully weak, for it does not contain explanations of "L.P.," "S.P.," "S.R.," "L.C.," "P.," "E.," "Christie," "Malone," "Hills," and other symbols employed throughout the book. Most of these abbreviations are familiar to specialists but not to the average student who uses the book for reference purposes.

The index, on the other hand, is very full, covering more than thirty pages and even including the item: "Macdonald, Hugh, 'Attacks on Dryden,' in Essays and Studies (1936): not referred to." It is to be regretted that in the rush of publication Mr. Macdonald did not see a proof of these pages, for he would undoubtedly have corrected most of the misprints. Despite the generous length to which it runs, the index is far from complete. To take the list of Luttrell's marked copies as an example, references are lacking for the following: A Lenten prologue, page 243; The mushroom, page 228; The poet's complaint, page 235; The tryal of skill, page 222, note 3; and A ballad, page 213. Moreover, the complaint is frequently heard that the index is awkward to use. Much of the difficulty could have been avoided if the titles of Dryden's books had been listed alphabetically instead of divided into a series of categories and printed in the ten columns of the general Dryden entry. The division into categories may have been useful in organizing the bibliography proper, but a reader who is looking up The prologue to the Dutchess, for instance, will be excusably annoyed at having to look for it under "Prologues and epilogues contributed to plays of others," "Prologues and epilogues printed for the first time in miscellanies," and "Prologues and epilogues (separate)." These objections are not intended to deprecate the value of the index as a whole but merely to call attention to some of its limitations. The attempt at fulness deserves every commendation, especially such headings as those given under "Manuscripts cited," which are particularly useful for research students. The value of Mr. Macdonald's volume as a work of reference rests no less on the information he has packed into it than on the index which makes the information available.

When this bibliography of Dryden is considered solely as a bibliography, however, it should be judged by different criteria from those which apply to a reference book. Descriptive bibliography is one of the kinds of scholarship that is sometimes described as "pure" scholarship, and consequently very exacting standards are applied to it. A scholar who publishes a bibliography must expect it to stand comparison in method and workmanship with the performances of other bibliographers. In Mr. Macdonald's case, his work on Dryden should be compared with the publications of Keynes, Gibson, Fulton, Case, Murrie, Day, and other bibliographers of seventeenth-century literature. An examination of this bibliography of Dryden based on exacting standards is disappointing, for its bibliographical shortcomings are readily apparent.

Probably every student using the book has noticed Mr. Macdonald's failure to cite copies of any items except those of unusual rarity. This is directly contrary to approved procedure, and the excuse that "copies are available in the British Museum or in the Bodleian" will not satisfy the scholar who is pursuing a specific investigation. Readers wish to know which copy is the particular one described as well as the location of half-a-dozen other copies similar enough to establish the description of a

normal copy. From the methodological standpoint the citing of
copies seen is strictly required, for they are the evidence on
which the descriptions have been based. Mr. Wise side-stepped
this responsibility by confining his descriptions to books on his
own shelves, but more is expected from this Dryden bibliography
than from A Dryden library.

There are, unfortunately, other kinds of evidence omitted
in Mr. Macdonald's descriptions. With very few exceptions he
does not record pagination, though the pagination often contains
valuable clues about the printing of a book and supplies a handy
check against the collation. Another omission is the occurrence
of rules on a half-title; nine times out of ten the rules are present, but the unusual instance justifies the inclusion of full evidence. Equally reprehensible, in my opinion, is Macdonald's
practice of omitting Latin quotations from the transcriptions of
title-pages; sometimes variants in the quotation provide the only
evidence that the title-pages, which may otherwise be identical
when transcribed, are in fact different settings of type.

This matter of title-page transcription has caused a good
deal of debate, and Mr. Macdonald's bibliography is an excellent
case in point. Though he has undoubtedly lavished care on the
transcriptions, the notes in the "Annotated check list" record
enough slips of the pen to cast doubt on the trustworthiness of
the whole method of quasi-facsimile transcription. Reproduction of title-pages by photographic means has two advantages:
it eliminates errors and reveals the identity of the pages better
than any system of transcription. No man ever lived who could
transcribe a series of title-pages without error, and even if one
succeeded the result would be nothing but a translation of the
type arrangement into a series of symbols. The defenders of
transcription usually argue on the basis of cost, since plates,
even if much reduced in size, would greatly increase the expense
of publication. The answer to this objection, I believe, lies in a
calculation of all the costs in producing a bibliography. The
price of a plate is, of course, much higher than the cost of printing the transcription, even though transcriptions are one of the
most expensive forms of composition. Yet the cost of printing
is only one of the costs in the production of a bibliography; if a
proper allowance is made for the time spent by the compiler in
transcribing a title leaf, in checking and rechecking it until the
final revised proof, the computation of cost would be very differ-

ent from the mere expense of reproduction. Even more important is the principle involved: photographic facsimiles eliminate
the errors inherent in all copying and offer the reader details
that transcription cannot possibly supply. Transcription is,
after all, just a translation into symbols, a bibliographical short-
hand, a makeshift vulnerable to human weakness. In my opinion,
the use of quasi-facsimile transcription in published bibliographies will soon be generally recognized as an anachronism.

From a strictly bibliographical standpoint there are a number of other grievances that users of this book may lay at Mr.
Macdonald'd door. A surprisingly large number of items—
well over a hundred—are listed without being described exactly,
and some of the entries (e.g., 69k, 109d, 143, 147, 148, 150, 156,
157, 195c, 314) lack collations entirely. There are frequent
occasions where the system of listing has not been consistently
applied; to be specific, items such as 6aii, 15ai–iv, 16aii (and
others) should have been given separate entries instead of being
mentioned only in the notes. Love triumphant is numbered 93a,
but there is no 93b; and similarly item 21i should have been 21ai.
Under item 108 a new system of numbering is introduced [viz.
108 (1), etc.], while a series of Greek letters suddenly make
their appearance as numbers $218\alpha-\delta$. There are also frequent
occasions, many of which are discussed in the "Annotated check
list," where Mr. Macdonald's bibliographical analyses leave
much work still to be done. Indeed there are very few books
listed in the bibliography (unique items excepted) on which further investigation is not required. While Mr. Macdonald's pages
were still in proof (December, 1938) a brilliant paper by Mr. F. T.
Bowers on "Running-titles as bibliographical evidence," appeared
in the Library (XIX, 315–38), and since then Mr. Bowers has
developed the technique of using running-titles to indicate when
a whole sheet may have been canceled.[6] Equally important for
future editors of Dryden will be bibliographical investigations to
establish the genealogy of each text, to record the exemplum
from which each edition after the second was printed. Heretofore, not many bibliographies have offered this information,
though every bibliographer who wishes his work to be of importance to literary students, rather than primarily to collectors
and librarians, should report the relationship between editions.
The time is not far distant when such a statement will be considered a fundamental responsibility of the scholar-bibliographer.

A few words may properly be inserted here about the way Mr. Macdonald has treated the work of his predecessors, particularly Arthur E. Case, T. J. Wise, and Percy J. Dobell. Recognizing that Case's <u>Bibliography of English poetical miscellanies</u> is readily available to students, Mr. Macdonald does not repeat the transcriptions and collations for many of the items found in Case but sends the reader directly to Case for this information.[7] In my opinion this is a legitimate device to save space and printing expense. There are a few items (e.g., 49 and 50) in which the reader is presented with a compromise: most of Case's descriptions are given along with new information by Mr. Macdonald; but since a few details found in Case are omitted, the student should check both Macdonald and Case to make sure that no information has been overlooked. The same applies to a number of items described in Wise's <u>A Dryden library</u>. Mr. Macdonald has gone so far beyond Wise's overpositive bibliography that he has had little occasion to refer to it, yet in several instances reference should have been made. Under item 15<u>a</u>, for example, Mr. Macdonald states that he could not find a copy of <u>Absalom and Achitophel</u>, Second Part, with a misprint on page 33 and ten lines only on the last page. Wise described his copy as having these points. So too in the case of 94<u>b</u>, <u>The secular masque</u>, a copy of which Wise had described as "printed upon two quarto leaves and distributed gratis at the performance in the Theatre-Royal, Drury Lane. A specimen of this separate issue was sold for £400 in Messrs. Sotheby's rooms on March 30th, 1927" (<u>A Dryden library</u>, p. 67). Mr. Macdonald casts doubt on this separate distribution, but without mentioning Wise or the overpriced sale with which Wise may or may not have been connected. Similarly, in treating subjects discussed by Mr. Dobell in <u>Bibliographical memoranda</u>, in several places (e.g., 71<u>a</u>, 72<u>a</u>, 74<u>b</u>, 75<u>a</u>, and 105) Mr. Macdonald could well have repeated Mr. Dobell's suggestions which often contain evidence of importance for understanding the problems involved. Since copies of Mr. Dobell's book (only one hundred having been printed) are now practically unobtainable, its chief contributions could profitably have been summarized by Mr. Macdonald.

Moreover, the reader who is familiar with Dryden scholarship notices that Mr. Macdonald rarely cites his predecessors by name when repeating the results of their researches, a practice much abused by Mr. Montague Summers. Take, for instance,

the identification of the "ingenious young gentleman, my friend,"
referred to in the preface to Religio laici. Mr. Macdonald says
(p. 33), "The young gentleman was Henry Dickinson," and appends
two footnotes, the first of which points out that Halkett and Laing
erred in their identification, and the second reads as follows:
"Malone, I.i. 175, discovered that his initials were H. D. His
identity is established by the verses addressed to him by Duke,
Poems by Roscommon and others, 1717. . . . ." The casual
reader is likely to assume from the tone of this statement that
it represents a discovery, however modest, by Mr. Macdonald.
Yet the identification was made in 1808 by Sir Walter Scott in
his life of Dryden (p. 275) and, of course, was repeated by Dryden's editors, Christie and Noyes. Silence has its uses, but
such instances raise two related questions: how far a scholar
is responsible for treating problems posed by his predecessors
and how scrupulous he must be in making specific acknowledgments.

Enough evidence has now been offered, I believe, to establish
the conclusion that Mr. Macdonald's book is eminently successful
as a reference book but disappointing as a bibliography. If I have
dwelt on its deficiencies in more detail than on its merits, I have
done so because the merits of the book can best be described in
generalities. It is probably true that every book of this kind
ought to reach a second edition, since only by using the first
edition can other scholars go beyond the author in adding information from the area of their specific inquiries. But whether
or not a second edition of Mr. Macdonald's book is ever made
possible, the present one has been a boon to seventeenth-century
scholarship in general and a vigorous stimulant to the revival
of interest in John Dryden.

Notes

1 Oxford: At the Clarendon Press, 1939, pp. xiv + 358.

2 MP, XXXIX (1941), 69–98, 197–212.

3 Mr. E. N. Hooker is preparing a list of these additions to be
published at a future date.

4 Among them Gallantry a la mode, 1674 (p. 110, n. 1); A Pin-
darick poem, 1682 (p. 231, n. 1); Defoe's The pacificator,
1700 (p. 288, n. 1); Mrs. Singer's Poems on several occasions,

1696 (p. 297, n. 4); Swift's On poetry: a rapsody, 1733 (p. 303, n. 1); and Pecuniae obediunt omnia, 1698 (p. 318, n. 2). It may be observed that Mr. Macdonald, probably unconsciously, tended to omit items in which the poet is commended and to insert pamphlets, no matter how slight or derivative, in which he is attacked.

5 The most interesting allusion is not quoted by Mr. Macdonald; speaking of Dryden, the author dares to "commend him, albeit he is alive," and states "he brings the very assignations that are commonly used about the town upon the stage."

6 Papers on this subject were delivered by Mr. Bowers and Mr. Charlton Hinman at the English Institute, September 9, 1941. They will be published in the English Institute annual for 1941.

7 E.g., items 51, 52, 53, 55, 58, 59, and all the Poems on affairs of state (p. 317). After 11b, the reader is told: "For editions published between 1683 and 1748 see Case 165c–n."

II. THE PROSE

THE OCCASION OF AN ESSAY OF DRAMATIC POESY

George Williamson

Dr. Johnson introduced the invidious distinction between the general and the occasional in Dryden's criticism, declaring in the Lives that his occasional positions are sometimes interested, negligent, or capricious—inconstant to his general precepts. In a less pejorative sense An essay of dramatic poesy illustrates the occasional as well as the general, but it is unique in Dryden's criticism because it was published without any visible means of support, not as a pendant to another work. Some writers, mistaking the personal apology in the Defence of an Essay—which, as a matter of fact, is incident only to the argument about rhyme—have overplayed the occasional bias of the Essay with respect to Sir Robert Howard. But one provocation to the Essay, to which an unidentified allusion directs us, has been unaccountably neglected. This motivation helps to explain the Essay, and even its concern with dramatic principles, without challenging its conformity to its own laws.

When Dryden wrote the Essay, the French and English had already clashed in a notable exchange of opinion. The occasion actually led to diplomatic action and the banishment of the offender. The occasion especially concerned the Royal Society[1] and so provided another reason why Dryden might not be insensitive to the controversy. It is hardly necessary to remark that complimentary allusions to science are a conspicuous feature of the Essay, which was probably written before he was dropped by the Society.[2] But it does seem necessary to remark that dramatic poetry had been an issue in this clash. The famous exchange, in which the Royal Society was directly involved, had for its principals Samuel Sorbière and Thomas Sprat, and produced works which long kept a certain notoriety in England. It is, therefore, all the more strange that they have never entered the discussion of circumstances incident to the Essay of dramatic poesy.

Reprinted from Modern Philology, Vol. 44 (1946), pp. 1–9, by permission of the author and The University of Chicago Press. Copyright 1946 by The University of Chicago. This article also appeared in Seventeenth Century Contexts published by Faber and Faber, Ltd, 1960.

In the same year that Dryden published The rival ladies, with its prefatory defense of rhyme in serious plays, Samuel Sorbière published his Voyage to England[3] and raised a storm of indignation, which was embarrassing to the Royal Society because he had been "admitted a member." Thomas Sprat, the official spokesman for the Society, laid down his History long enough to write Observations on Monsieur Sorbier's Voyage into England,[4] which appeared in 1665. In the same year Sir Robert Howard published his Four new plays, with the preface now remembered chiefly for having started the controversy with Dryden. Meanwhile the Great Plague had broken out, to be followed by the Great Fire in 1666; together they closed the theaters and hindered publication for eighteen months. For these two years Dryden has nothing to show in the way of publication except his collaboration with Howard on The Indian queen, published in Four new plays. But it was in the interval, by his own account, that he wrote Annus mirabilis and the Essay of dramatic poesy, the first of which certainly appeared in 1667,[5] along with Sprat's History of the Royal Society. How Sorbière and Sprat are related to the quarrel about dramatic poetry may now be examined.

In criticizing English drama Sorbière raised issues which remained central to the controversy represented by the Essay of dramatic poesy. His chief remarks are as follows:[6]

> But the Players [Plays] here wou'd be of little Esteem in France, so far short the English come of the French this Way: The Poets laugh at the Uniformity of the Place, and the Rules of Times: Their Plays contain the Actions of Five and Twenty Years, and after that in the First Act they represent the marriage of a Prince; they bring in his Son Fighting in the Second, and having Travelled over many Countries: But above all things they set up for the Passions, Vertues and Vices of Mankind admirably well; and indeed do not fall much short in the performance. In representing a Miser, they make him guilty of all the basest Actions that have been practised in several Ages, upon divers Occasions and indifferent Professions: They do not matter tho' it be a Hodch Potch, for they say, they mind only the Parts as they come on one after another, and have no regard to the whole

Composition. I understand that all the <u>English</u> Eloquence consists in nothing but meer Pedantry, and that their Sermons from the Pulpit, and their pleadings at the Bar, are much of the same Stamp. . . . Their Comedies are a kind of Blank Verse, and suit an Ordinary Language better than our Meetre, and make some Melody: They cannot but conceive it to be a troublesome thing to have the Ear continually tickled with the same Cadence; and they say, that to hear Heroick Verses spoken for Two or Three Hours together, and to recoyl back from one to the other, is a Method of Expression that is not so natural and diverting: In short, it looks as if the <u>English</u> would by no means fall in with the Practices and manner of Representation in other Languages; and the Italian Opera's appear more extravagant, and much more disliked by them than ours. But we are not here to enter upon a Dispute about the different Tastes of Men, it's best to leave every one to abound in his own Sence.[7]

The issues raised here concern the rejection of the unities and decorum as well as the use of rhyme. Rhyme is rejected by the English because it is neither natural nor pleasing. The English (although the translated remark about opera misses the point) are open to attack because they are nonconformists to European dramatic standards—a ground of attack calculated to annoy the court of Charles II.

As one who had made a reputation out of English writers, Sorbière was especially offensive to Sprat, who would not have erred as a modern writer has erred, by praising Sorbière for ideas which he probably derived from Hobbes.[8] Hence Sprat takes advantage of any disparagement of English literature on the part of Sorbière. On the violation of the unities by the English, Sprat replies by contrasting, in too round figures, the present and the past age:

'Tis true, about an Hundred Years ago the <u>English</u> Poets were not very exact in such Decencies; but no more then were the Dramatists of any other Countries. The <u>English</u> themselves did laugh away such Absurdities

as soon as any; and for these last Fifty Years our Stage
has been as regular in those Circumstances as the best
in Europe.[9]

This contrast, properly dated, appears again in Dryden's Essay,
together with some concern for European standards.[10] But Sprat,
as we shall see, also liberalizes his terms of conformity.

The issue of decorum leads Sprat into a comparison of
French and English dramatic poetry, in which he discusses
rhymed verse:

> He next blames the Meanness of [the] Humours
> which we represent. And here, because he has thrust
> this Occasion upon me, I will venture to make a short
> Comparison between the French Dramatical Poetry
> and ours. . . . . I will therefore make no Scruple to
> maintain that the English Plays ought to be preferr'd
> before the French: And to prove this I will not insist
> on an Argument which is plain to any Observer, that
> the greatest Part of their most Excellent Pieces has
> [have] been taken from the Spaniard; whereas the Eng-
> lish have for the most part trodden in New Ways of In-
> vention. From hence I will not draw much Advantage,
> tho' it may serve to balance that which he afterwards
> says of our Books, that they are generally stoln out of
> other Authors; but I will fetch the Grounds of my Per-
> swasion from the very Nature and Use of the Stage it-
> self. It is beyond all Dispute, that the true intention
> of such Representations is to give to mankind a Picture
> of themselves, and thereby to make Virtue belov'd,
> Vice abhorr'd, and the little Irregularities of Mens
> Tempers, called Humours, expos'd to laughter. The
> Two First of these are the proper Subjects of Tragedy,
> and Trage-Comedy. And in these I will first try to
> shew why our Way ought to be preferr'd before theirs.
> The French for the most part take only One or Two
> Great Men, and chiefly insist on some one Remarkable
> Accident of their Story; to this End they admit no more
> Persons than will [barely] serve to adorn that: And
> they manage all in Rhime, with long Speeches, almost
> in the Way of Dialogues, in making high Idea's of Honour,

and in speaking Noble things. The <u>English</u> on the other
side make their chief Plot to consist of a greater variety of Actions; and besides the main Design, add many
other little Contrivances. By this Means their Scenes
are shorter, their Stage fuller, many more Persons of
different Humours are introduc'd. And in carrying on
of this they generally do only confine themselves to
Blank Verse. This is the Difference, and hence the
<u>English</u> have these Advantages. By the Liberty of
Prose they render their Speech and Pronunciation
more Natural, and are never put to make a Contention between the Rhime and the Sence. By their Un-
derplots they often change the Minds of their Spectators: Which is a mighty Benefit, seeing one of the
greatest Arts of Wit and Perswasion is the right ordering of Digressions. By their full Stage they prevent Mens being continually tir'd with the same
Objects: And so they make the Doctrine of the Scene
to be more lively and diverting than the Precepts of
Philosophers, or the grave Delight of Heroick Poetry;
which the <u>French</u> Tragedies do resemble. Nor is it
sufficient to object against this, that it is undecent
to thrust in Men of mean Condition amongst the Actions of Princes. For why should that misbecome
the Stage, which is always found to be acted on the
true Theatre of the World? There being no Court
which only consists of Kings, and Queens, and Counsellors of State. Upon these Accounts, Sir, in my
weak Judgment, the <u>French Dramma</u> ought to give
place to the <u>English</u> in the Tragical and Lofty Part of
it.[11]

Sprat concludes his comparison with an easy victory in comedy,
treating Sorbière to a lesson in humors which he might have
learned for himself:

And now having obtained this, I suppose they will
of their own Accord resign the other Excellence, and
confess that we have far exceeded them in the Representation of the different Humours. The Truth is, the
<u>French</u> have always seemed almost asham'd of the true

Comedy; making it not much more than the Subject of
their Farces: Whereas the English Stage has so much
abounded with it, that perhaps there is scarce any Sort
of Extravagance of which the Minds of Men are capable
but they have in some measure express'd. It is in
Comedies, and not in Solemn Histories, that the English use to relate the Speeches of Waggoners, of
Fencers, and of Common Soldiers. And this I dare
assure Monsieur de Sorbiere, that if he had understood our Language, he might have seen himself in all
[his] Shapes, as a vain Traveller, an empty Politician,
an insolent Pedant, and an idle Pretender to Learning.[12]

The last shape, of course, was peculiarly annoying to a defender
of the Royal Society, which felt that it had been deceived.

For our purpose it may be well to itemize the grounds of defense employed by Sprat. In the matter of unities he justifies
English drama by European standards; he argues from the nature
of drama, defines plays with respect to their ends; he argues from
the art by which a play attains its end; he finds that nature is satisfied by blank verse, that variety of plot and character are persuasive means (art) to the end of instruction, surpassing "the
grave Delight of Heroick Poetry," which characterizes French
tragedy. Decorum in characters is to be judged by nature, of
which a play is an image, and particularly by the kind of nature
appropriate to the play. In short, Sprat accepts the unities with
qualifications in the interest of delight but rejects the French
doctrine of decorum and use of rhyme in the interest of nature.
English plays are superior both in nature and in art; the English
way to the end of drama is superior because it is more lively,
and therefore more persuasive in its instruction. Such an approach, it may be observed, is not uninstructive for the Essay
of dramatic poesy.

While Sorbiere and Sprat may be said to have launched the
debate officially,[13] they by no means defined all of the issues.
If this admission seems to grant them more importance than
they deserve, it will suffice to indicate the background for the
argument which engages Dryden's "wits."[14] The Sorbiere incident was at least an event in a controversy wider but now less
substantial than Howard's Preface to Four new plays.

In that preface Howard devotes his time to a defense of English plays which is no extenuation of his own; rather, as he says with respect to rhyme, his own err by following in part the method which he condemns. Howard debates some issues that were neglected by Sprat but are discussed by Dryden, and in general broadens the argument to include the Ancients, whom the French imitate. He introduces his defense in these words:[15]

> Yet I shall presume to say something in the justification of our nation's plays, (though not of my own), since in my judgment—without being partial to my Country—I do really prefer our plays as much before any other nation's as I do the best of ours before my own.[16]

Finding the Ancients deficient in plot and wit, although their comedy has some pretenses to both, he proceeds to define the French way in terms of the Ancient pattern. Two aspects of this way, to which the English have become susceptible, are attacked: "presenting the business in relations" and writing in rhyme. The method of the Ancients was forced upon them by their subjects, but the French commit the error without the necessity. "If these premises be granted," he argues, "'tis no partiality to conclude that our English plays justly challenge the preeminence."[17] Coming when it did, Howard's Preface must have been read largely as another reply to Sorbière.

But he is ready to admit that the English differ from others less happily in one respect:

> Yet I shall as candidly acknowledge that our best poets have differed from other nations (though not so happily) in usually mingling and interweaving mirth and sadness through the whole course of their plays— Ben Jonson only excepted, who keeps himself entire to one argument. And I confess I am now convinced in my own judgment that it is most proper to keep the audience in one entire disposition both of concern and attention.[18]

Though such "pursuing accidents" may be possible, "they may

not be so proper to be presented—an entire connection being the natural beauty of all plays." To that extent Howard bows to the unities.[19] But, after the French, neither Italian nor Spanish plays offer him anything worthy of imitation. In terms of Dryden's Essay, his argument, except for rhyme, is more in accord with that of Eugenius than with that of Crites, but it agrees with Lisideius on tragicomedy. He is against both the Ancients and the French, but allows that the Ancients had reason for their method;[20] among the English he evidently rates the past age, especially Jonson, above the present.

When we come to Dryden, it must be said at once that by defending rhyme he appeared to belong to the French party;[21] in other respects he is neither more nor less ready than other members of the English party to accept elements of the French way of drama. Dryden himself placed the Essay in relation to the quarrel with Howard about rhyme, explicitly in the Defence of an Essay, and implicitly in the Essay by borrowing Howard's arguments. Others have attempted to saddle all of Crites' arguments upon Howard, but such an assimilation does not correspond to the facts; nor does it seem to have been a part of Dryden's purpose, for this allusion in his Dedication applied to no one so well as to Howard:

> Even Tully had a controversy with his dear Atticus; and in one of his Dialogues, makes him sustain the part of an enemy in philosophy, who, in his letters, is his confident of state, and made privy to the most weighty affairs of the Roman Senate.[22]

In context this remark is part of an apology for his own opinions, "which were first made public."[23] Then Dryden gives this description of the Essay:

> . . . . the relation of a dispute betwixt some of our wits upon this subject, in which they did not only speak of plays in verse, but mingled, in the freedom of discourse, some things of the ancient, many of the modern ways of writing; comparing those with these, and the wits of our nation with those of others.[24]

Needless to say, the quarrel between the ancient and modern ways of writing is also represented in the quarrel between the

French and English. Therefore, Dryden's opening remark to the reader becomes less puzzling to a modern reader: "The drift of the ensuing Discourse was chiefly to vindicate the honour of our English writers, from the censure of those who unjustly prefer the French before them."[25] Howard could have made a similar claim for his Preface. Altogether, this remark, like Howard's Preface, suggests an occasion, beyond the quarrel about rhyme, to which such a vindication of the English would be relevant. Sorbière provided such an occasion, if only by making a French party among the English all the more obnoxious.

Dryden's next sentence to the reader emphasizes the occasional aspect of the <u>Essay</u> at the expense of its general character: "This I intimate, lest any should think me so exceeding vain, as to teach others an art which they understand much better than myself." Despite this protestation, the author of the Preface to <u>The Duke of Lerma</u> took the <u>Essay</u> as a sign of such vanity in Dryden. But the <u>Essay</u> itself bears out Dryden's claim; for it has all the marks of a vindication, weighing the charges which had been made against English drama and marshaling the arguments which had been or could be used to refute them. It is not incidental to this purpose that he, like Howard, also entertains the reader "with what a good play should be"; it is, however, central to another purpose.

In the <u>Essay</u>, rhyme is the issue reserved for final and separate debate, but it was the issue which Dryden first set up, and thereby compromised his native stand. Dryden invokes European example only in support of rhyme, but even then he asserts English precedent for it — more vigorously in the <u>Essay</u>, though he is already anti-French in the Dedication of <u>The rival ladies</u>.[26] To his praise in these works of the perfecters of English rhyme he added, in his enthusiasm, the dedication of the <u>Essay</u> to one of those translators of Corneille's <u>Pompey</u> who had provided him with a dazzling argument for English rhymed plays.[27] It has long been recognized that Dryden put Howard's arguments against rhyme into the mouth of Crites, but not that Sprat anticipated Howard in arguing against rhyme, especially its unnaturalness. Therefore Neander is really answering both, as well as justifying an English use of a prominent feature of the French way of drama.

The <u>Essay</u> ought to be examined for its disposition of previous argument, apart from rhyme. It will be remembered that Crites and Lisideius are spokesmen for the Ancients and French

respectively, and that Eugenius and Neander are partners in
rebuttal. Just as Eugenius argues that Ancient plots are deficient, so Neander argues that French plots are deficient; and
as Eugenius argues that the Ancients did not follow their method
rigidly, so Neander argues that the French have departed from
theirs when they sought variety. The consequence is to render
the unities not indispensable but contingent upon variety.28 Let
us recall that the issues of plot and wit with which Crites begins
the argument had been raised against the Ancients by Howard.
Although he was probably not the "late writer" to whom Eugenius
refers, Howard had pointed out that the subjects of the Ancients
"were usually the most known stories and fables"—a fact which
Eugenius proceeds to develop into a limitation upon variety and
delight.29 On tragicomedy Lisideius definitely echoes Howard's
argument against this mixture, especially as it may frustrate
the interest and concern of the audience.30 Lisideius, moreover, answers Sprat on French plots:

> But I return again to the French writers, who,
> as I have said, do not burden themselves too much
> with plot, which has been reproached to them by an
> ingenious person of our nation as a fault. For he
> says they commonly make but one person consider-
> able in a play; they dwell upon him and his concern-
> ments, while the rest of the persons are only sub-
> servient to set him off.31

The actual words of this "ingenious person of our nation," hitherto unidentified, will be found in Sprat's remarks about the French
way in reply to Sorbière. But Lisideius also interprets Sprat's
argument in his answer:

> If he intends this by it, that there is one person
> in the play who is of greater dignity than the rest, he
> must tax not only theirs, but those of the ancients,
> and—which he would be loath to do—the best of ours.32

Sprat would not have been loath to tax an opponent with shifting
his argument. Again, Lisideius goes to considerable pains to
refute Howard's charges against the French method of relations;33
the nexus becomes obvious when he says, "But it is objected

that if one part of the play may be related, then why not all."[34]

The argument of Neander agrees in all respects save rhyme with the defense offered by Sprat, including the charge that French plays were based on Spanish plots. Neander refutes the arguments of Lisideius and Howard on tragicomedy, which he makes a special glory of the English.[35] He follows Sprat when he argues against "Lisideius and many others" who "cry up the barrenness of the French plots above the variety and copiousness of the English";[36] he agrees with Sprat on short speeches versus long harangues. It is in the interest of variety that he argues a weakness in Lisideius' answer to Sprat:

> There is another part of Lisideius his discourse,
> in which he has rather excused our neighbours than
> commended them,—that is, for aiming only to make
> one person considerable in their plays.[37]

" 'Tis evident," says Neander, "that the more the persons are, the greater will be the variety of the plot," and thus supports Sprat. He is ready to admit, however, that Lisideius has reason in what he says about relations, especially in arguing that all incredible actions be related.[38] Here, of course, he is arguing partly against Howard; but Lisideius is not allowed a victory, for the French have erred grossly in this respect, and a mean between French and English practice is best. Howard had argued that the French used relations without regard to necessity. When Neander argues "that we have many plays of ours as regular as any of theirs, and which, besides, have more variety of plot and characters,"[39] he comes pretty close to summing up Sprat's defense, including regularity as a criterion.

If Sorbière may be said to have initiated the occasion for the <u>Essay</u>, and the <u>Essay</u> itself may be allowed to reveal an appropriate orientation, the question may then be asked why Dryden delayed its publication from 1665–66, the apparent date of composition,[40] until 1668. The most obvious answer is supplied by the Plague and Fire. Actually the <u>Essay</u> was entered in the Stationers' Register, August 7, 1667, and thus was probably intended for publication in the same year as the <u>Annus mirabilis</u>.[41] The delay, which is magnified by the publication date, requires no other explanation, since The Indian emperor, though registered May 26, 1665, was not printed until late in 1667.[42] The retrospective note in the Dedication of the Essay springs from the same interval, which overlaps Dryden's retirement in the country.[43] On the other hand, because of the interruption of normal life by the Plague and Fire, the loss in timeliness was less than it would seem; Sprat's Observations reappeared in 1668. While the king's attempt to prevent any reply to Sorbière may have made Dryden's vindication more indirect, no doubt Dryden wrote the Essay chiefly to explore and define his own theories of dramatic art—not without regard to the taste of the Court, to which he owed so much—and his recent success with The Indian emperor encouraged him to undertake it.[44]

Despite the enforced delay, which made 1667 the earliest date for the publication of the Essay, there can be no doubt that it was an ambitious work or that it had a dual purpose. All this is clear from the address "To the reader." I have already quoted the first part of that address, which intimates the occasional aspect of the Essay. The latter part suggests a more general purpose:

> But if this incorrect Essay, written in the country
> without the help of books or advice of friends, shall
> find any acceptance in the world, I promise to myself
> a better success of the second part, wherein the virtues
> and faults of the English poets who have written either
> in this, the epic, or lyric way, will be more fully
> treated of, and their several styles impartially imitated.[45]

That which has been inadequately treated, or neglected in favor of a party defense, will be the main subject of a second part. This more general purpose Dryden fulfilled, at least in large part, but not as he anticipated; rather in the form of occasional essays attached to other works.[46] For the dramatic way he has many essays to show; for the epic way, several essays and parts of essays; for the lyric way, various miscellaneous passages.

This "incorrect Essay"—later honored by revision, though not of its alleged defects—still keeps a place apart in his criticism, but least for its dual motivation, which makes it, like most of his essays, both occasional and general in nature; it keeps that place, aside from merit, for its ambitious program, dialogue form, and basic principles. Yet even in "drawing the outlines of an art" Dryden had adjusted his argument both to occasion and to principle.

NOTES

1 See Vincent Guilloton, <u>Autour de la Relation du voyage de Samuel Sorbière en Angleterre, 1663–1664</u> ("Smith College studies in modern languages," Vol. XI, No. 4 [Northampton, 1930]).

2 These allusions seem less random—aside from their place in the argument—when we recall his "Apostrophe to the Royal Society" in the <u>Annus mirabilis</u> (1667).

3 <u>Relation d'un voyage en Angleterre où sont touchées plusieurs choses qui regardent l'état des sciences, et de la religion, et autres matières curieuses</u> (Paris, 1664).

4 Its apparently official character, though not official in fact, is stressed on the title-page: "Written to Dr. Wren, Professor of Astronomy in Oxford. By <u>Thomas Sprat</u>, Fellow of the Royal Society. <u>London</u>, Printed for <u>John Martyn</u> and <u>James Allestry</u>, Printers to the Royal Society." His third paragraph explains his reply: "For having now under my Hands the History of the <u>Royal Society</u>, it will be in vain for me to try to represent its Design to be Advantageous to the Glory of <u>England</u>, if my Countrymen shall know that one who calls himself a Member of that <u>Assembly</u> has escaped unanswered in the public Disgraces which he has cast on our whole Nation" (cf. Evelyn's letter to Sprat, October 31, 1664).

5 Malone believed that the <u>Essay</u> was published at the end of 1667 (cf. <u>Prose works of Dryden</u>, I, Part I, 58).

6 For convenience Sorbière and Sprat are quoted from <u>A voyage to England . . . by Mons. Sorbiere. As also Observations on the same voyage, by Dr. Thomas Sprat</u> (London, 1709); cited hereafter as <u>Voyage</u>.

7 <u>Voyage</u>, pp. 69–71. Compare Sorbière's French for the exact turn of his remarks, once seriously misrepresented by the English:

Mais les Comedies n'auroient pas en France
toute l'approbation qu'elles ont en Angleterre. Les
Poëtes se mocquent de l'uniformité du lieu, & de
la regle des vingt-quatre heures. Ils font des
comedies de vingt-cinq ans, & apres avoir repre-
senté au premier acte le mariage d'un Prince,
ils representent toute d'une suite les belles
Actions de son fils, & luy font voir bien du pays.
Il se picquent sur tout de faire d'excellens characters des passions, des vices, & des vertus; Et
en cela ils réussissent essez bien. Pour depeindre
un avare, ils en font faire à un hōme toutes les
plus basses actions qui se pratiquent en divers
âges, en diverses rencontres, & en diverses professions; Et il ne leur importe que ce soit un pot
pourry; parce qu'ils n'en regardent, disent-ils,
qu'une partie apres l'autre, sans se soucier du
total.

I'entends que toute l'Eloquence Angloise est
conduite de cette maniere; & que dans la Chaire,
& au Barreau, on ne parle pas d'autre façon. . . .

Les Comedies sone en prose mesurée, qui
a plus de rapport au langage ordinaire que nos
vers, & qui rend quelque melodie. Ils ne peuuēt
s'imaginer que ce ne soit une chose importune
d'avoir continuellement l'oreille frappée de la
mesme cadence; ils disent, que d'entendre parler
deux ou trois heures en vers Alexandrins, & voir
sauter de cesure en cesure; est une maniere de
s'exprimer moins naturelle, & moins divertissante.
En effect il semble qu'elle s'esloigne autant de ce
qui se pratique dans le monde, & par consequent
de ce que l'on veut representer; que la maniere
Italienne de reciter les Comedies en musique,
s'esgare & extravague au delà de la nostre. Mais
il ne faut pas disputer des gousts, & il vaut mieux
laisser chacun abonder en son sens (Relation
[Cologne, 1669], pp. 129–32).

If Sorbière means comedies rather than plays in general, Sprat ignores the distinction.

8 See Alan M. Boase, <u>The fortunes of Montaigne</u> (London, 1935), pp. 254–55; and compare Hobbes's <u>Answer to Davenant</u> on poetry and his <u>Human nature</u> or <u>Leviathan</u> on language. If this matter was not available to Sorbière in Latin, still the parallel is unmistakable; the ideas were no accident in Hobbes.

9 <u>Voyage</u>, p. 166.

10 In the Dedication of <u>The rival ladies</u> Dryden is worried lest the English seem eccentric by refusing rhyme in drama.

11 <u>Voyage</u>, pp. 167–69. The chief variants of the 1665 text are supplied in brackets, except for the spelling of "rhime" as "rhythm."

12 <u>Ibid.</u>, p. 169.

13 Guilloton (pp. 8–9) shows that this debate was restrained: "Dans une lettre à Louis XIV du 21 juillet 1664—quinze jours après l'arrêt qui condamnait Sorbière—l'ambassadeur Cominges dit au roi qu'il est intervenu auprès de Charles II pour empêcher certains membres de la Société Royale 'qui déjà taillaient leurs plumes' pour lui répondre, de riposter au voyageur français. Le roi d'Angleterre a dû menacer 'ces Messieurs de l'Académie' pour les obliger à lui apporter les matériaux déjà préparés pour leur réplique." Nevertheless, Sprat's "Letter to Wren" (<u>Observations</u>) was dated August 1, 1664, and some covert, though partial, replies seem to have been made.

14 The opening of the <u>Essay</u> further characterizes the wits who are introduced in the Dedication. Oddly enough, on "that memorable day" Eugenius, if he is Buckhurst, presumably shared in the victory over the Dutch rather than in that over the French. The <u>Essay</u> is described in the <u>Defence</u> as "a little discourse in dialogue, for the most part borrowed from the observations of others." Too often "others" has been restricted to foreign sources.

15 For convenience references to Howard and Dryden are made to <u>Dryden & Howard, 1664–1668</u>, ed. D. D. Arundell (Cambridge, 1929); cited hereafter as "Arundell."

16 <u>Ibid.</u>, p. 6.

17 Ibid., p. 7.

18 Ibid., p. 8.

19 Here the unity of feeling, an aspect of the unity of action or the nonmixture of the genres.

20 Of course, Thomas Rymer became the chief English advocate for the Ancients.

21 Howard had stigmatized rhyme as part of the French way, but Dryden speaks of his "adversaries" in the Dedication of the Essay.

22 Arundell, p. 20.

23 See his recapitulation of the controversy with Howard at the close of the Defence of an Essay.

24 Arundell, p. 21.

25 Ibid., p. 22.

26 Jonson provided English precedent not only for rhyme but also for dramatic regularity. He is very useful to Dryden, even doctrinally, in repudiating French influence.

27 See the allusion to Pompey in the Dedication. This translation (1664)—called the "SMEC" version by a eulogist of Orinda—was a work of the wits, including not only Buckhurst but Sedley and Waller (cf. Letters from Orinda [1705], p. 112, and Dryden's or Tonson's Miscellanies [1716], II, 94). Through these names, and because of this association, Dryden's Essay pays still more homage to rhyme. Crites alone opposes it, but Crites is given an office appropriate to his name and dismissed in the company of Neander rather than of the wits. If Crites were Roscommon, as has been suggested, he would have written the prologue to the rival Pompey translated by Katharine Philips.

28 Positively, of course, Dryden argues for both the unities and rhyme as aids to imitation.

29 Arundell, pp. 38, 7. Obviously he was not the writer if "late" means "lately deceased." Howard does not develop the consequence mentioned by Dryden; rather he argues

that these stories obliged the dramatists to resort to "relations." Cowley, now a "late" writer, characterized these stories in terms similar to those of Dryden, but with respect to epic poetry (Preface to Poems [1656]).

30 Arundell, pp. 47–48, 8.

31 Ibid., pp. 50–51.

32 Ibid., p. 51.

33 Ibid., pp. 51–55.

34 Ibid., pp. 53, 7. Howard had said that "they do by consequence maintain that a whole play might be as well related as acted." It might be remarked that Howard's show of logic eventually became a little irksome to Dryden.

35 Ibid., pp. 58, 48, 8.

36 Ibid., p. 58.

37 Ibid., p. 61.

38 Ibid., pp. 61–62. Howard argued that it was impossible to represent some parts of the stories used by the Ancients.

39 Ibid., p. 66.

40 See the Dedication of the Essay. The remark in the Dedication that he has since laid aside the writing of plays in rhyme until he has more leisure seems rather odd when we consider that although he did not defend rhyme in comedy, he laid it aside (after The maiden queen) only to write comedies.

41 The Prefatory Epistle to this poem, dated from Charlton, Wiltshire, November 10, 1666, asks Howard to see the poem through the press; it was published early in 1667, and celebrated the late fire as well as the unconcluded Dutch war. The maiden queen — apparently read by Howard between his "first perusal" and his "correction" of the Annus mirabilis (cf. Epistle) and staged early in 1667 — was entered in the Stationers' Register at the same time as the Essay, and had been published by January 18, 1668, when Pepys bought a copy "newly printed." Dryden's remark about laying rhyme aside since that time should make The maiden queen at least contemporary with the Essay.

42 The interval between registration and publication, even for Dryden's plays, usually was very much shorter. For bibliographical details concerning these works see Hugh MacDonald's Bibliography (Oxford, 1939).

43 The opening sentence of the Essay, however, seems to place the Essay later than the date assigned in the Dedication; for Dryden's phrase "in the first summer of the late war" could not have been written much before the entry in the Stationers' Register, since the "late war" was concluded in the preceding month with the Peace of Breda. This suggests, despite Dryden's protest, revision.

44 The maiden queen, however, his first attempt to embody his new formula (cf. Prologue), was saved by the king's approval (cf. Preface). In the Preface to Juvenal (1693) he speaks of the Essay as a product of the time "when I was drawing the outlines of an art, without any living master to instruct me in it; an art which had been better praised than studied here in England. . . . . I was sailing in a vast ocean, without other help than the pole-star of the ancients, and the rules of the French stage amongst the moderns, which are extremely different from ours, by reason of their opposite taste." He was speaking to the man to whom he dedicated the Essay.

45 Arundell, p. 22.

46 The groundwork for his later criticism was laid in the Essay and the "Account" of the Annus, which overlap on rhyme and the "proper wit of poetry." The Preface to Troilus and Cressida, for example, is no radical departure from the Essay. While the authorities are new—Bossu, Rapin, Longinus—the argument still owes much to Corneille's Discourses, particularly on manners and the properties of the action, even to the founding of pity and fear on the chief character—a rule not "fully enough discovered to us."

ON THE PERSONS IN DRYDEN'S ESSAY OF DRAMATIC POESY

Frank Livingstone Huntley

It will never be known exactly what historical persons lie behind the names in the dialogues of Plato and T. S. Eliot. Nor can we ever discover to what extent Dryden had actual friends in mind when he conceived his characters for the Essay of Dramatic Poesy. From the entretiens of Sarrasin and of Desmarets, he knew well the heuristic value of bringing together various speakers, each presenting a different point of view, to discuss the principles of dramatic poesy. And yet he tells us near the beginning that ". . . three of them are persons whom their wit and quality have made known to all the town; and whom I have chose to hide under these borrowed names . . ." (28:21–29:2).[1] As this appears to be a true statement, Malone wrote a long account identifying the characters with actual people.[2] Except for George Hardinge's railing Essence of Malone,[3] scarcely a word has been raised to challenge Malone's identifications of the four speakers: Crites as Sir Robert Howard; Eugenius as Charles Sackville, Lord Buckhurst, later sixth Earl of Dorset; Lisideius as Sir Charles Sedley; and Neander as Dryden himself.[4]

The purpose of this paper is to show that a mistake has been made in concentrating more on Dryden's "three persons of quality" than on his insistence that he had chosen to "hide [them] under these borrowed names"; that too great an anxiety to accept as fact the hypothesis that his persons are portraits may have prevented us from perceiving the general, dramatic functions of the speakers in the dialogue. I shall take up the four characters in the order in which Dryden introduces them. Though they may have started as portraits they soon became and remain embodiments of attitude necessitated by the argument.

Crites is the first speaker. And it so happens that his case shows most obviously the part-personal and most clearly the part-personifying function; furthermore, this is the only identification that has been seriously challenged in modern times.

Reprinted from Modern Language Notes, Vol. 63 (1948), pp. 88–95, by permission of the author and The Johns Hopkins University Press.

The background of the quarrel between Dryden and his brother-in-law is so well known that there is no need to repeat it here. On the grounds of the coincidence of some of Crites' opinions and those of Sir Robert Howard's published work, Malone settled on this identification. At one time he believed that Crites could have been Lord Roscommon[5] because of Crites' interest in Horace; but acknowledging his error, he returned to Sir Robert.[6] In 1923 G. R. Noyes[7] threw considerable doubt on Malone's identification. In Howard's prefaces Sir Robert (1) attacks the use of rime in drama, (2) argues for the preeminence of English drama over that of Greece and Rome, and (3) attacks the authority of the three unities. Of these views, however, the Crites of the Essay advances only the first, and differs radically from the second and the third. It was perhaps for this reason that the literary quarrel between Dryden and his brother-in-law had to center on the use of rime in drama. At the end of his article Noyes, though admitting that Dryden does not mention Roscommon by name earlier than 1680,[8] is inclined, like Malone, to identify Crites with Roscommon on the strength of the allusions to Horace.

Crites, characterized more at length than any of the others, is ". . . a person of sharp judgment, and somewhat too delicate a taste in wit, which the world have mistaken in him for ill-nature . . ." (29:28–29).[9] Since the purpose of the whole piece ". . . was chiefly to vindicate the honour of our English writers . . ." (27:12–15), the person to oppose the English and the modern point of view had to be a Crites. Simple though this may be, no other explanation can adequately show us why, if Dryden intended Crites to be his brother-in-law Sir Robert Howard, he made Crites so different in many of his views from Sir Robert. Crites, therefore, is not so much an individual as he is a typical ultra-conservative. The name is appropriate for a person who is a strong defender of Greek and Latin literature, but a carping criticaster of anything new.

Eugenius is the second speaker. Malone[10] identified him with Charles Lord Buckhurst (later the sixth Earl of Dorset) on the sole ground that Matthew Prior, in the dedication of his 1709 edition of Poems to Lionel, Earl of Dorset, acclaimed Lionel's late father as the Eugenius of Dryden's Essay. This single proof is taken from a preface conceived, forty years after the Essay was published, in a spirit of glowing encomium.[11]

84

DRYDEN'S ESSAY OF DRAMATIC POESY

But several pieces of evidence militate against this identification. For one thing, Dryden had dedicated his Essay to Lord
Buckhurst. If the Eugenius within the Essay is also Lord Buckhurst, he can scarcely be said to play the role of neutral arbiter
which Dryden enjoined upon his noble patron in the "Epistle Dedicatory." He opposes Crites quite roundly, and looks upon Neander "earnestly" as he "beseeches" Neander to "gratify the company, and me in particular" (79:17–21) with the characters of
Shakespeare, Beaumont and Fletcher, and Jonson. Far from
being impartial, Eugenius is definitely on Neander's side of the
argument (33:20–30). The long passage (Ker, II, 16–17) in Dryden's dedication to the same Lord Buckhurst of his essay on
Satire in 1693, which links his noble patron once more to the
Essay of Dramatic Poesy, makes no mention of Buckhurst as
the Eugenius of the Essay. Neither of the two surviving letters
written by Dryden to Buckhurst mentions the identification with
Eugenius.[12] This by itself is not extraordinary; yet the first
letter, written within ten years of the publication of the Essay,
might have offered a fine opportunity, since its subject matter
is Dryden's contemplated reply to Rymer's diatribe against the
playwrights of the Elizabethan age whom both Eugenius and Neander so revere. Finally, it appears that Charles Sackville Lord
Buckhurst had volunteered in the fleet fitted out against the
Dutch, and had taken part in the great naval battle of June 3,
1665, near Lowestoft whose effect from a distance upon the four
friends Dryden so movingly describes in his proem.[13] Would
his sense of drama, while allowing him to dedicate the Essay to
an absent friend and patron, have allowed him to include that
absent friend in a "play" whose setting and dramatic occasion
is the very day of that battle?

Eugenius, rather, signifies merely "well born." He is a
foil to Neander, for whom no claims of birth are made but whose
tastes are the same. The character within the Essay enjoys the
deference of the other persons. He puts an end to the quarrel
between Crites and Lisideius over the bad poets; and on his
general proposition that today's poets are better than any England has yet produced ". . . all of them were thus far of Eugenius
his opinion" (35:9). The other persons side with Eugenius at the
end of his argument with Crites (55:30). Throughout the Essay,
Eugenius, the "well born," stands as a symbol of the man of quality who has good taste. Can more be gained by thinking of him
as Lord Buckhurst?

Identifying the third speaker, Lisideius, gave Malone the
greatest difficulty. At last it occurred to him that Lisideius
must be Sir Charles Sedley. The grounds for this identification, which has not been questioned since, are (1) that Sedley
was a friend of Buckhurst, hence if Eugenius is Buckhurst,
then Sedley could appropriately be with him; (2) that Sedley
was a great voluptuary, and at the end of the dialogue, while
the graver Neander and Crites go home to bed, the two others
seek the pleasure of the town; (3) that Lisideius is an anagram
for Sidleyius, the Latinized form of the actual spelling of the
name "Sidley."[14]

It is difficult to determine whether the views of Lisideius
on drama coincide with those held by the author of <u>Antony and
Cleopatra</u> (1677). Nor is anything to be gained by searching
for other historical persons whose characters and views might
be made to fit Lisideius by more rigorous standards than Malone
used to identify the character with Sir Charles Sedley. But if
the mere acceptance of this identification keeps us from seeing
the allegorical function of the character, then the acceptance is
harmful.

Lisideius is prevailed upon by his friends to give the "definition" of a play, which is the starting point of the whole argument
and its primary source of unity. Lisideius knew, too, that this
was not a definition but merely his "notion" of what he thought
a play "ought to be" (36:5−8). The third speaker, Lisideius, is
the first to uphold the moderns (the French rather than the English), in the debate between the ancients and moderns. For
Eugenius before him served to tell, in arguing with Crites, not
so much what the moderns have accomplished as what the ancients had failed to do. As all the speakers do, Lisideius speaks
to certain parts of the definition of a play; but his particular
function is to counter the "just" with the "lively" portion of the
agreed-upon formula; to add to ancient "instruction" the French
"delight"; and to show that the French attain these things not so
much through the "passions and humours" in the characters as
through superiority in plotting, i.e. "the changes of fortune" of
the definition. His whole argument is based not on the well known
"justness" of the French but on the way in which the French
make plot the "lively" means to the end of the concernment in
the audience. Lisideius begins his speech with Corneille (56:
26−32), and throughout his argument, as throughout the entire

Essay, there is constant and frank allusion to Corneille's Trois Discours (1660), which has long been known to be the most important source for Dryden's Essay.

For these reasons we may well look towards France and especially towards Corneille for a clue to the origin of Lisideius. For the name does not appear on the surface to be as clearly Greek as the names Crites, Eugenius, and Neander. Is it rash to suggest, therefore, that in commemoration of the notorious controversy in France over Le Cid, the name "Lisideius" may have come to Dryden from "Le Cid" plus a Latinized-Greek masculine ending?[15] Could a young English craftsman and critic like Dryden, poring over a copy of the Trois Discours at the Howard estate in Wiltshire, fail to link his spokesman for the best in the French theatre with that reverberating victory of Corneille's over the Academicians? In this connection, one of the greatest editors of the Essay, Arnold, quotes a letter which Corneille wrote to the Abbé de Pure on August 25, 1660, on the occasion and subject matter of the famous Discourses:

> Je suis à la fin d'un travail fort pénible sur une
> matière fort délicate. J'ai traité en trois préfaces
> les principales questions de l'art poétique sur mes
> trois volumes de comédies. J'y ai fait quelques
> explications nouvelles d'Aristote, et avancé quelques
> propositions et quelques maximes inconnues à nos
> anciens. J'y réfute celles sur lesquelles l'Académie
> a fondé la condamnation du Cid, et ne suis pas d'accord
> avec M. d'Aubignac de tout le bien même qu'il a dit de
> moi.[16]

This is not to identify Lisideius with Corneille or any other historical person, but rather with an appropriate symbol for the speaker in the dialogue who upholds the new French theatre in the spirit of Corneille, one of whose antagonists in the dialogue is as carping an academician as Crites. In the words of William Strunk, who admirably epitomizes the influence of Corneille in the Essay, Corneille's ". . . own plays had been censured as departing from the ancient rules, and in the Discours he examines the ancient authorities, interprets them liberally, and, so far as he can, justifies his practice by them."[17] This practically describes the function of Lisideius, within the Essay, and describes it more profitably than does a strained identification of Lisideius with Sir Charles Sedley coupled with a dismissal of further enquiry into his meaning.

Finally, how do we know that Neander was intended to be Dryden himself? Neander's views certainly come closer to those of Dryden than do those of any of the other speakers. Malone[18] was led to the identification, also, by the anagram with Dryden's name. And "Neander" was used for Dryden in the Luctus Britannici (1700) and in Mrs. Thomas's Poems of 1727[19]—both instances of complimentary metaphor.

Although Neander uses many of Dryden's own arguments, he by no means is a constant speaker of them, any more than Crites is of Sir Robert's dicta on the drama. In the first edition of the Essay, Dryden uses direct address (89:32) in passing from his second to his third main section; and here he uses "I," meaning himself apart from Neander, and "my Lord," meaning Buckhurst quite apart from Eugenius. In the Defense, too, Dryden distinguishes between his own views and those of his imaginary character: ". . . several persons maintained their several opinions . . . ; he who answered, in behalf of our nation, was willing to give more latitude to the rule. . . . In few words my own opinion is this . . ." (130:18–26). In spite of Dryden's insistence upon the sceptical spirit of his "essai," his literal-minded brother-in-law took everything Crites said as directed towards himself and everything Neander said as coming straight from Dryden. That Neander's views come closest to Dryden's own, however, is merely to say that Dryden himself represents the "new" against the "old." In a discourse which concerns the idea of progress in letters, "Neander" is allegorically the "new man," from neo and andros, as his name so clearly implies.[20]

I cannot quite deny, in conclusion, that Dryden had actual friends in mind when he created the persons in his dialogue. I insist, however, that Malone's identifications have been too little examined, and that this readiness to accept the historical meanings of the names perhaps has blinded us to some of Dryden's dramatic intentions. Surely the latter kind of meaning is more appropriately sought in a creative work of this kind, and is more important as the Essay of Dramatic Poesy ceases to be a document published for Dryden's friends or enemies and becomes, instead, a landmark in the history of English prose criticism.

NOTES

1   I have used the first edition (1668) as edited by W. P. Ker, <u>Essays of John Dryden</u> (Oxford, 1926), 2 vols. Documentation will consist of references to the first volume of this edition by page and line numbers, and will be incorporated, as here, within my text.

2   Edmund Malone, <u>The Critical and Miscellaneous Prose Works of John Dryden</u> (London, 1800), Vol. I, part ii. Cf. the summary in Hugh Macdonald, <u>John Dryden: A Bibliography of Early Editions and of Drydeniana</u> (Oxford, 1939), p. 165, n. 1.

3   Minutius Felix [George Hardinge] <u>Essence of Malone</u> (London, 1800), pp. 83 ff; 2nd edition, enlarged, pp. 10 ff.

4   <u>The Essay of Dramatic Poesy</u> has been edited by distinguished hands, notably: Robert Urie in 1750; Malone, 1800; Scott, 1808; Arber, 1880; Saintsbury, 1882; Thomas Arnold, 1889; Strunk, 1898 and Ker, 1900. Examples of recent scholars who carry on the tradition of Malone's identifications are: Churton Collins, <u>Essays and Studies</u> (London, 1895), p. 30; J. N. Smith and E. W. Parks, <u>The Great Critics</u> (New York, 1939), p. 304; V. de Sola Pinto, <u>Sir Charles Sedley</u> (London, 1927), p. 89, n. 1 and p. 15, n. 1; L. I. Bredvold, <u>The Best of Dryden</u> (New York, 1933), p. 558; etc.

5   Malone, I, ii, 34.

6   <u>Ibid.</u>, I, ii, 117.

7   "'Crites' in Dryden's <u>Essay of Dramatic Poesy</u>," <u>MLN</u>, XXXVIII (1923), 333–37.

8   In the preface to <u>Ovid's Epistles</u>, Ker, I, 237:33.

9   That Malone had difficulty maintaining either of his first two identifications is shown by his admission (I, ii, 35) that "too delicate a taste in wit" seems to apply better to Charles Lord Buckhurst.

10   I, ii, 62.

11   Brice Harris, <u>Charles Sackville, Sixth Earl of Dorset.</u> ("Illinois Studies in Language and Literature," XXVI, Nos.

3–4, Urbana, Illinois, 1940), Preface, pp. 5–6: "Prior was either not sure of his facts or not averse to twisting them to his own ends. Grief over Dorset's recent death and too close proximity to his subject make this biography a kind of mausoleum, so that however valuable, it must yet be used with discretion."

12 Cf. Charles E. Ward, The Letters of John Dryden (Durham, N. C., 1942), No. 6 (c. 1677) and No. 22 (c. 1691).

13 The knowledge comes to us, again, from Prior's 1709 dedication, but Brice Harris (Charles Sackville, pp. 33–34) accepts the grounds as plausible. Cf. DNB, L, 87.

14 George Hardinge had greatest fun with this anagram. Cf. Essence of Malone (1800), p. 84: "The reader will not forget, that, upon the difference between SIDLEY and SEDLEY, the life and soul of the imputed anagram depend."

15 A precedent which exemplifies the linguistic principle would be Apuleius, i.e. the man who has something to do with Apulia.

16 Quoted by Arnold, Dryden: An Essay of Dramatic Poesy (Oxford, 1922), p. 146, from the Grands Écrivains edition, X, 485.

17 Dryden: Essays on the Drama (New York, 1898), Introd., xxvi.

18 I, ii, 34 f. n., 63, 118. Malone has a strong argument in quotation of the Essay (94:6–7) on Neander's writing of verse.

19 Cf. Macdonald, p. 165, n. 1. The Mrs. Thomas is, of course, "Corinna," noted for her extravagant account of Dryden's funeral.

20 This point was almost made by Arnold, Introd., p. ix, but he believed it impossible that Dryden should think of himself as a "novus homo" in the sense of a commoner desiring to rise above his station.

DRYDEN, ROCHESTER, AND THE EIGHTH SATIRE
OF JUVENAL

Frank Livingstone Huntley

The purpose of this paper is to investigate the genesis and significance of Dryden's Preface to <u>All for Love</u>. It is difficult to find its source of unity as a piece of criticism. In it Dryden compares English poetry with French; he also talks of two kinds of critics; of the kind of poet-patron represented by Dionysius and Nero; of friendship; and of "this rhyming judge of the twelve-penny gallery, this legitimate son of Sternhold."[1] At the very end, however, he mentions a topic which would perhaps have been more appropriate to the preface of a tragedy which imitates the style of Shakespeare, the justification of that imitation; but this he reserves "for a more fit occasion" (200:29), which came eighteen months later in his Preface to <u>Troilus and Cressida</u>.[2] Because Dryden seems to have been deflected, here, from his original intention, perhaps a study of the genesis of the essay will reveal the reason and the meaning. His quotation of Rochester's "An Allusion to the Tenth Satire of the First Book of Horace," in the words "he [Horace] would never have allowed him [Rochester] to have called a slow man hasty, or a hasty writer a slow drudge" (200:1–2) gives us an excuse for reexamining this essay in the light of Dryden's quarrel with Rochester, particularly as it was written when the quarrel was at its height.[3] In the light of the feud with Rochester,[4] the critical contents of this essay find a meaning; and significant too becomes the way Dryden has been fired by his purpose of censure to amalgamate sources as distant as Montaigne, Horace, and Juvenal. It will first be necessary to see what provocation Dryden had for censuring Rochester at this time; then the critical ideas of the preface itself will be analyzed as having their unity in the means toward this end, the censure being his reason for choosing his source material. Finally, special attention will be given to the main source, Juvenal's eighth satire.

The high-lights of the Rochester quarrel are well known, and may be briefly touched upon here.[5] Dryden dedicated his

Reprinted from <u>Philological Quarterly</u>, Vol. 18 (1939), pp. 269–284, by permission of the author and the publisher.

Marriage à la Mode to the Earl in 1673 when their relations
were happy. The praise of Rochester in this dedication, in
terms of the difference between French and English, may
throw some light on those passages in the Preface to All for
Love which deal with the superiority of the English over the
French:

> And not only I, who pretend not to this way, but the
> best comic writers of our age, will join with me to
> acknowledge that they have copied the gallantries of
> courts, the delicacy of expression, and the decencies
> of behavior, from your Lordship, with more success,
> then if they had taken their models from the court of
> France.[6]

In spite of the championship of Dryden, however, it is well known
that Rochester lent his support to Settle, and was largely responsible for the success of The Empress of Morocco. It addition
to the insult to Dryden contained in Settle's signing himself
"Servant to His Majesty," there were contained in the dedication
of that play to Rochester such remarks as the following: "But
my Lord, whilst I trouble you with this kind of discourse, I beg
you would not think I design to give rules to the Press, as some
of our Tribe have done to the Stage; No, that's a trick I do not
pretend to."[7] During the year 1673 Dryden, known now irrevoc-
ably as "Bayes," was attacked from other quarters as well.
A Mr. Arrowsmith took off his dramatic methods in The Reformation, which was acted at Dorset Gardens;[8] and in the spring
of that year came the Rota attacks and defenses.[9] In the midst
of the censures of the Rota and some unexpected accusations
of immorality from Puritan leaders, our poet, with the aid of
Shadwell and Crowne, undertook to answer Settle, who had risen
to fame and impudence, it must not be forgotten, under the aegis
of Dryden's one-time patron, Rochester.[10] Oil was added to
the fire by Rochester's quarrel with Dryden's new friend and
patron, the Earl of Mulgrave.[11]

After Settle, it is equally well established, Rochester raised
Crowne to a height of eminence; through his influence Crowne's
Masque of Calisto was performed at court in 1675.[12] The tradition of Rochester's quarrel with Dryden in this connection persisted into the eighteenth century. Dennis tells us in a letter:

His [Crowne's] Writings soon made him known to the
Court and Town: Yet it was neither to the Favour of
the Court, nor of Wilmot Lord Rochester, one of the
shining Ornaments of it, that he was indebted for the
Nomination which the King made of him for the writing of the Mask of Calypso [i.e. Calisto], but to the
Malice of that noble Lord, who design'd by that preference to mortify Mr. Dryden.[13]

There is an equally strong tradition that Rochester rejected
an epilogue written by Dryden for this masque.[14]
    In the same year (1675) Rochester, having thus preferred
Settle and Crowne, pushed up Otway also, the author of Alcibi-
ades. Emboldened by Rochester's protection, Otway makes
this hit at Dryden in the preface of his next play, Don Carlos
(1676):

Though a certain Writer that shall be nameless (but
you may guess at him by what follows) being ask't
his Opinion of this Play, very gravely Cock't, and
cry'd, Igad he knew not a line in it he would be Author
of; but he is a fine Facetious witty Person, as my
Friend Sir Formal has it; and to be even with him,
I know a Comedy of his, that has not so much as a
Quibble in it that I would be Author of; and so Reader
I bid him and thee Farewell.[15]

Otway dedicated his Titus and Berenice (1677) to Rochester;
and the Earl's protégée, Mrs. Barry, captured Otway's heart
as well as that of the town.
    And yet, with no accounting for the whimsies of a young
nobleman, in "A Trial of the Poets for the Bays, in Imitation
of a Satyr in Boileau," Rochester had not spared even those
whom he had set above Dryden. In that poem, first among the
poets who claim the honor and finally have to give way to Better-
ton the actor is the Poet Laureate, whose literary and moral
reputation Rochester is pleased to treat lightly:

In the head of the gang, John Dryden appear'd
That ancient grave wit so long lov'd and fear'd,
But Apollo had heard a story in town,

Of his quitting the Muses, to wear a black gown;
And so gave him leave now his poetry's done,
To let him turn priest since R[eeves] is turn'd nun.[16]

By 1676, as we can see in his dedication of Aurengzebe to Mulgrave, Dryden was rather tired of it all. Placing on the title page of this work the following quotation from Juvenal—

. . . .; sed cum fregit subsellia versu,
esurit, intactam Paridi nisi vendat Agaven,

he is stung with the poverty of his condition; with the disillusionment in a friend and former patron: he, like Statius in Juvenal, must sell his wares to a theatrical performer, when he longed to write an epic; with an allusion to Montaigne, he dilates upon the men of power at court who "make it their business to ruin wit"; and he praises the constancy of Mulgrave's friendship.[17] The use of Juvenal and Montaigne here, as well as the inclusion of much of the subject matter, forms an interesting parallel with the Preface to All for Love.

But, as we have seen, a particular work of Rochester's forms the point of departure in this Preface, namely, "An Allusion to the Tenth Satire of the First Book of Horace," which Dryden quotes.[18] Imitating his original, Rochester began this poem with a show of conciliation with his enemy:

Well, Sir, 'tis granted; I said Dryden's rhymes
Were stolen, unequal, nay dull many times;
What foolish patron is there found of his,
So blindly partial to deny me this?
But that his plays, embroider'd up and down
With learning, justly pleas'd the town,
In the same paper I as freely own.[19]

The three lines in this poem which Dryden seizes as giving him his opportunity to pay back Rochester are

Of all our Modern Wits none seems to me
Once to have toucht upon true Comedy,
But hasty Shadwell, and slow Wicherley.[20]

Dryden is aroused, in other words, not by those lines against his person, but by Rochester's calling things by their wrong names; if he can show that Rochester is wrong about others, then he can show that Rochester has been wrong about him.

So far we have seen that during the four years preceding the Preface to All for Love, Dryden had been goaded by Rochester to the point of making a volte face from his dedication of Marriage à la Mode. When we turn our attention to the Preface itself, we find that its assorted contents derive a unity in their being used as a means to the end of censuring this nobleman who was still very influential at court. Dryden implies that Rochester is a liar, by opposing throughout his essay truth to falsehood, the real to the apparent. Shadwell was not hasty, nor Wicherley slow.

He begins the Preface by saying that "the greatest wits of our nation, after Shakespeare" (191:2–3) have all been led to the subject of Antony and Cleopatra by what later we shall see is fundamental rather than incidental to the story: "I mean the excellency of the moral: . . ." (191:8). Only the variety, not the falsity, of their attempts[21] gives him "the confidence to try myself in this bow of Ulysses. . . ." (191:4–5). After describing some of the difficulties he met in forming the proper character of Antony, but without dwelling upon a discussion of that character, Dryden plunges into the virtues and faults of his play. His reason for doing this is that the virtues praised by some critics are not the true virtues and the faults condemned by some critics are not the true faults: "The fabric of the play is regular enough, as to the inferior parts of it; and the Unities of Time, Place, and Action, more exactly observed, than perhaps the English theatre requires" (192:2–5). Regularity is, however, only incidental; the real virtue of the work is that which has already been said to exist in the story, namely the excellency of the moral, and, as we shall see, the "largeness" of the model. As for the faults, he mentions the real fault of divided motivation,[22] a fault which critics have missed. On the other hand, "The faults my enemies have found are rather cavils concerning little and not essential decencies; which a master of ceremonies may decide betwixt us" (192:26–29). Stickling on matters of affectation is French; and Dryden, an English poet, cannot base his characters on punctilios (192:29–30). For him it is both "natural" and "probable" (193:2) that the rival queens

should meet and have it out; to object, on the grounds of good
manners, to such a scene is affectation—as long as the poet,
in describing scenes of passion, has kept his words from being
obscene (193:13–15). This argument of a critic's missing the
main point he illustrates by a quotation from Montaigne's essay,
De la Presumption, which is a discussion of false versus true
self-analysis.[23] It is the fault of French poets, Dryden continues,
to mistake "la ceremonie" for the thing itself, the non-essential
for the essential: "all their wit is in their ceremony" (194:1–2).
His example is Racine's changing the substance of Seneca's
character Hyppolytus into the shadow of "monsieur Hippolyte"
(195:3). The emphasis upon the excessive civility of this French
character is no digression in view of the end: to show that Rochester, educated in France, was guilty of the French habit of taking "les branches" for "le tronc" (193:21–2). As if his purpose
in introducing French poets were not clear, he makes it clear:
"I should not have troubled myself thus far with French poets,
but that I find our Chedreux critics wholly form their judgments
by them" (195:3–5).[24]

Having introduced the "poet" and the "critic," Dryden then
makes them one; and it is soon evident from the text that he is
opposing himself as the true poet-critic to Rochester as the
false poet-critic. For by a process of narrowing down, the
identification with Rochester is pointed: a poet is the best judge
(aside from a "universal genius" like Aristotle) of his own art,
unless he is "bribed by interest, or prejudiced by malice" (195:
17–18). From the category of "poet-critics" he excludes those
"who are allowed for witty men, either by the advantage of their
quality, or by common fame. . . ." (195:25–26). He also excludes
those who have no taste for tragedy (196:1–8). From this lack
of taste and knowledge come the "many satires on poets, and
censures of their writings" (196:10–11). Not only had Dryden
been attacked by a "censure" of Rochester's, as we have seen,
but the "poetaster-criticaster" whom he singles out for revenge
at this point belongs to the upper class, is esteemed a pleasant
conversationalist (196:11–12), does have a "trifling kind of
fancy" (196:12–13), which is "helped out with some smattering
of Latin" (196:13–14)—all of which characterizes Rochester.
In this context comes the first quotation from Juvenal's eighth
satire (196:16–17), the discussion of which we shall reserve for
later as supplying the epideictic framework for this essay.

DRYDEN, ROCHESTER AND THE EIGHTH SATIRE

Dryden continues his definition of the kind of critic who takes advantage of his quality (195:26) in terms of "affectation" (196:18), and the application to Wilmot is clear. For example, it is "affectation" for such men ". . . not to be contented with what fortune has done for them, and sit down quietly with their estates, but they must call their wits in question, and needlessly expose their nakedness to public view" (196:18–22). The phrase which I have italicized, it is highly probable in view of all that has gone before, contains a double entendre not to be missed by an audience aware of Rochester's notorious exhibitionism.[25] A "wit" who has an estate and does not need to write for subsistence is, to Dryden in the winter of 1677–8, without excuse for being:

> We who write, if we want the talent, yet have the excuse that we do it for a poor subsistence; but what can be urged in their defence, who, not having the vocation of poverty to scribble, out of mere wantonness take pains to make themselves ridiculous (196: 30–34)?

Once more, in the portion which I have italicized, there is evidence of Rochester's being the butt, as it is an echo from Rochester's "Satyr Against Mankind" (1675).[26] In that poem Rochester is comparing man with beast; whereas beasts kill from necessity, man

> Inhumanely, his Fellows Life betrays,
> With voluntary Pains, works his Distress;
> Not through Necessity, but Wantonness.[27]

The repetition with peculiar emphasis of "pains" and "wantonness," in a context wherein voluntary action with dire result is opposed to necessity, points the parallel; and rhetorically it becomes Dryden to hint at his enemy's self-destruction through wantonness rather than to confess that he himself is wounded by that barb.

With an allusion to Horace's observation that "no man is satisfied with his own condition,"[28] Dryden shows how this conflict between the poverty-stricken "poet" and the untalented rich man invariably turns out bad for the poet. If the poet fails, he starves; if he succeeds, "some malicious satire is prepared to level" (197:5–7) him for pleasing without leave from the tyrant:

> But while they [the rich tyrants] are so eager to destroy the fame of others, their ambition is manifest in their concernment; some poem of their own is to be produced, and the slaves are to be laid flat with their faces on the ground, that the monarch may appear in the greater majesty (197:8–12).[29]

Dryden's opposition between what we may call the poor-but-true-poet-critic and the rich-but-false-poetaster-criticaster was early recognized to have sprung from his differences with Rochester. An anonymous poem called "Rochester's Ghost addressing it self to the Secretary of the Muses" in the 1703 edition of Poems on Affairs of State quotes the line from Dryden's Preface which I have just underscored:

> 'Tis true, your Laureat well deserves the Bays,
> Witness the Genius that adorns his Plays;
> But chiefly those he writ in former days.
> Yet if in Death I may at least be free,
> As in my Lifetime he has been to me;
> To lay the Slave down flat upon his Face.
> I use his words, because the subject's base.
> So that the Monarch may in Pomp appear;
> If not an Ass, you'l read a Villain there;
> For 'tis the gen'ral Vote from King to Slave,
> Altho the Poet's good, the Man's a Knave.[30]

This kind of tyranny Dryden illustrates further by Dionysius and Nero (197:13), who were hack poets but rendered powerful by their position. Nero is mentioned in Juvenal's eighth satire, which we are coming to, and Dionysius in the essay by Montaigne already quoted.[31] Dryden's meaning is that Dionysius and Nero, tyrants of power as Rochester was a tyrant of wealth and position, also set themselves up as poets and critics, but they were false: "In the meantime the true poets were they who made the best markets, for they had wit enough to yield the prize with a good grace, and not contend with him who had thirty legions" (197: 30–33). The allusion here to Favorinus and the Emperor Hadrian may possibly come from another essay of Montaigne of much the same import as the first one quoted, "De l'incommodité de la grandeur,"[32] which in a context of talent opposed to power mentions the tyrant-poet Dionysius. Dryden has no desire to suffer Lucan's fate at the hands of such a man (198:1).[33]

As a rich powerful patron of poetry, Maecenas is the opposite to Nero and Dionysius (198:7–15), for, realizing that poetry "was not his talent" (198:10), he gave it up to patronize the true poets Horace and Virgil. There are patrons, Dryden asserts, in making his transition from the days of Dionysius to his own, who "have much of the [bad] poetry of Maecenas, but little of his liberality" (198:16–17). Here, by pretending[34] that some underling and not Rochester himself wrote "The Allusion to the Tenth Satire of the First Book of Horace," Dryden uses an épée instead of a bludgeon. With a quotation from the original of the satire in question, Dryden asserts, with no danger of being charged with libel, that the ignorant and vile imitator of Horace (198:23) and all his ilk are as ill company for Horace as was Crispinus; and that Horace

> would no more have allowed them a place amongst the critics, than he would Demetrius the mimic, and Tigellius the buffoon;
> .... Demetri, teque, Tigelli,
> Discipulorum inter jubeo plorare cathedras (198:29–32).[35]

Dryden here makes "Demetrius the mimic" and "Tigellius the buffoon" a single reference both with significant applicability to his enemy, whose escapades were well enough known. Also, Dryden knew his Horace too well not to have been aware that in Horace "Demetrius the mimic" was a trainer of actresses (mimae), and Rochester had achieved some fame as the trainer of a notorious "petticoat," the inimitable Mrs. Barry, Tom Otway's sweetheart.[36] Opposed to these petty poets, Demetrius and Tigellius, is Horace himself, who, in the words of Virgil (199:5–6, and 10–13), stands like "a landmark to set out the bounds of poetry" (199:3–4).[37] By quoting Virgil to describe Horace, Dryden makes use of the two poets previously mentioned as protected by the true patron, Maecenas.

In a final attack on "this rhyming judge of the twelvepenny gallery" (199:14–15), Dryden, by means of another singularly

99

apt quotation from Horace (199:33–34), taxes Rochester with ignorance of the difference between truth and falsehood in friendship. It is at this point that he brings in with telling force Juvenal's eighth satire.

Although there are only three direct quotations from this satire in Dryden's essay, the scheme of the whole is a very probable source of the framework of the essay—if the foregoing analysis is true. We shall first see how the satire of Juvenal is applicable to Rochester; then how the three quotations are significantly appropriate to a censure of Rochester; and finally how external evidence links the quarrel between Rochester and Dryden with the name of Juvenal.

Beginning with the question, "Stemmata quid faciunt?"—what avail your pedigrees?—Juvenal's eighth satire is an attack on those men of title who did not act in a way that befitted their high station in life. The "Argument" which heads the translation of this satire by Stepney in Dryden's The Satires of Juvenal and Persius (1693) is as convenient a summary as any:

> In this satyr, the Poet proves that Nobility does not consist in Statues and Pedigrees, but in Honourable and Good Actions: He lashes Rubellius Plancus, for being Insolent, by Reason of his High Birth; and lays down an Instance that we ought to make the like judgment of Men, as we do of Horses, who are valued rather according to their Personal Qualities, than by the race of whence they come. He advises his Noble Friend Ponticus (to whom he Dedicates the Satyr) to lead a Virtuous Life, disswading him from Debauchery, Luxury, Oppression, Cruelty, and other Vices, by his severe Censures on Lateranus, Damassippus, Gracchus, Nero, Catiline; and in opposition to these, displays the worth of Persons Meanly Born, such as Cicero, Marius, Servius, Tullius, and the Deceii.[38]

As we have seen, Dryden's purpose in the Preface to All for Love is very similar to that here expressed as Juvenal's: to censure Rochester, a nobleman, whose actions were far from being noble. Again, we have seen that the method of indirectness of Juvenal is that which Dryden has used; and the means of an opposition between "good" and "bad" is common to both. The probabilities that this satire is a source are heightened by an examination of the three quotations made from it as they apply to Rochester.

The first one (196:11–17) could be applied to several noble-men of his day:

> Rarus enim ferme sensus communis in illa
> Fortuna

became in Stepney's translation, done under Dryden's eyes:

> The Rumour's likely; for we seldom find
> Much sense with an Exalted Fortune join'd: . . . .[39]

It is in the next two quotations from the satire in a direct context of the author of "An Allusion to the Tenth Satire of the First Book of Horace" that we may look for surer applications to his foe. Since the lines beginning "Canibus pigris. . ." (200:4–7) and "ad Aethiopem cygnum" (200:12), not, in the original, with an "ad," are of a piece, it is best to quote the entire passage from Stepney's translation; the context springs from the line, "Virtue alone is true nobility":[40]

> But who will call those Noble, who deface,
> By meaner acts, the Glories of their Race;
> Whose only Title to their Father's Fame
> Is couch'd in the dead Letters of their Name?
> A Dwarf as well may for a Gyant pass;
> A Negro for a Swan; a Crook-back'd Lass
> Be call'd Europa; and a Cur may bear
> The name of Tyger, Lion, or whate'er
> Denotes the Noblest or the Fiercest Beast:
> Be therefore careful, lest the World in jeast
> Shou'd thee just so with the Mock-titles greet,
> Of Camerinus, or of Conquer'd Crete.[41]

The quotation from Lucretius which comes between these two quotations from Juvenal is, of course, of the same import— calling that which is ugly, beautiful; in Dryden's own words elsewhere:

> The sallow skin is for the swarthy put,
> And love can make a slattern of a slut. . . .
> She stammers; Oh, what grace in lisping lies!
> If she says nothing, to be sure she's wise.[42]

This subject of the wrong calling of names had come up between the two men before. In the only letter preserved from Dryden to Rochester, a letter in which Dryden takes himself to task for not answering sooner the Earl's acknowledgment of the dedication to Marriage à la Mode, Dryden quotes and comments upon a satire written by Etherege that was evidently being handed about:

> I call a spade a spade; Eaton, a bully;
> Frampton, a pimp; and brother John, a cully.
> But one of his [i.e. Etherege's] friends imagined these names
> not enough for the dignity of a satyr, and chang'd them thus:
> I call a spade, a spade; Dunbar, a bully;
> Brounckard, a pimp; and Aubry Vere, a cully.[43]

But why "ad Aethiopem cygnum"? The surface meaning can only be: "But I'll not drive this argument to (or to the point of) calling an Ethiopian a swan." But there may very well be a double entendre on "Black Swan," for if Dryden is censuring Rochester as a nobleman who is not noble (in Juvenal's sense), it is becoming for him to hint at a famous escapade of Rochester: his setting himself up in 1676, as Alexander Bendo in Tower Street next door to the tavern which was known from its sign as "The Black Swan." It was well remembered by Dryden's audience that the notorious broadside which advertised the noble quack ended as follows:

> They that will do me the favour to come to me, shall
> be sure from three of the Clock in the Afternoon, till
> Eight at Night, at my Lodgings in Tower-Street, next
> door to the sign of the Black Swan, at a Goldsmith's
> House to find
>
> > Their Humble Servant,
> > Alexander Bendo[44]

The play upon Juvenal's phrase becomes triple when it is remembered that "black swan" is proverbial for rara avis, from
Juvenal's sixth satire (line 164),[45] which Dryden himself was
to translate by the couplet:

> Suppose all these, and take a Poet's word,
> A Black Swan is not half so Rare a Bird.[46]

The quotations from Juvenal's eighth satire in Dryden's essay
support the contention that the essay is a censure of Rochester.

Finally, there are several pieces of evidence that link the
quarrel between these one-time friends with the name of Juvenal. The first of these is doubtful but is given here for what
it may be worth. It is a "Satire on the Times," ascribed to
Rochester but not generally accepted as part of the Rochester
canon.[47] Beginning

> Not Rome in all her Splendour, could compare
> With those great Blessings happy Britons share,

the poem, as far as I am aware, was first printed in the 1697
edition of State-Poems.[48] On page 32 of this volume appears
the only evidence of its authorship, an attribution which in itself, of course, is untrustworthy. In the 1705 edition of Poems
on Affairs of State, it appears in the order and ascription just
given, on page 184; but here its heading is "Nobilitas sola atque
unica virtus est," the twentieth line of Juvenal's eighth satire.
The poem was printed again in the 1739 edition of the works of
Rochester, Roscommon, and Dorset, where it is introduced with
the double quotation:

> Satire on the Times
> Nobilitas sola atque unica Virtus est. Juv. Sat. viii
> Virtue alone is true Nobility. Dryd.[49]

In the poem the author, taking his cue from Juvenal's eighth
satire, satirizes members of the court of Charles II who are
other than they appear to be: first, Charles himself; second,
ambassadors from the court, like Sunderland; third, "com-
manders both by sea and land"; finally, the "wits" of the court.[50]

After the Rose Alley Ambuscade, the only two pieces of evidence that link the names of Dryden and Rochester also link them with the name of Juvenal. Rochester's poem entitled "An Imitation of the First Satyr of Juvenal" unmistakably refers to the episode:

> Who'd be a <u>Wit</u>, in Dryden's cudgell'd Skin?
> Or who'd be <u>safe</u>, and <u>senseless</u>, like Tom Thynne?[51]

Of not such certain ascription is the poem in <u>Poems on Affairs of State</u> called "Satire on the poets, being a Translation out of the 7th Satyr of Juvenal."[52] In this poem Dryden is called a "drudge" and the unfortunate affair of Rose Alley is certainly hinted at in this couplet:

> More I could say, but care not much to meet,
> A Crabtree Cudgell in a narrow Street.

Two poems, one certainly Rochester's and the other probably his, in which Dryden and the Rose Alley Ambuscade are mentioned, are imitations from Juvenal. On Dryden's side of the quarrel, we know that after the night of July 18, 1679, he does not mention Rochester except in the Preface to his translation of Juvenal, where he quotes "An Allusion to the Tenth Satire of the First Book of Horace."[53]

But to return to the essay. Free of his enemy, Dryden closes with an assertion of his own intentions in writing the play, namely, to make a "regular" play on a "larger" model than that of the Greek (200:25-30). For a very good critical reason, appropriateness, he calmly announces his farewell to rime, which he had upheld for so many years. The question of Shakespeare's style as the object of limitation intrigues him, but he postpones discussion of it. He tells us instead that his favorite scene in the play to follow is that between Antony and Ventidius in the first act. It is a scene of <u>true</u> friendship.

The Preface to <u>All for Love</u> is a piece of epideictic rhetoric devoted to a censure of Rochester; taking his cue from Juvenal's eighth satire on the subject of true and false members of the peerage, Dryden has used it as a framework to reprove the Earl for his habit of calling things by their wrong names. External evidence supports the interpretation of this Preface as having its genesis in Dryden's conviction that Rochester had been false as a poet, critic, and friend. From that conviction the essay takes its form, by it the sources are brilliantly amalgamated, and because of it the essay is more significant as rhetoric than as criticism.

NOTES

1 Essays of John Dryden, ed. W. P. Ker (Oxford, 1926), I, 100:14–16. Hereafter, to avoid excessive footnoting, the references to this Preface will be embodied in the text; the first number will refer to the page of the first volume, the second numbers indicating the lines on that page.

2 Fred G. Walcott, "John Dryden's Answer to Thomas Rymer's The Tragedies of the Last Age," PQ, XV (1936), 197.

3 All for Love was published, with its preface, early in 1678. Cf. Eyre and Rivington, A Transcript of the Stationers' Registers, 1640–1708 A.D., III, 56; it is registered under the name of Herringman, "January 31, 1677" (i.e. 1677/8).

4 Although, as will become clear in subsequent footnotes, others have commented on the connection of this essay with Rochester, no one so far as I am aware has traced that connection throughout the entire essay, or attempted, by it, to unify its disparate elements. Cf. Dryden's Works, ed. Scott-Saintsbury, V, 335–37; cf. Prinz, John Wilmot Earl of Rochester (Leipzig, 1927), p. 117: ". . . . Dryden, in his Preface to All for Love, wrote a sort of reply to the censure exercised upon him by the Allusion."

5 One of the clearest and most authoritative accounts is that in Alexandre Beljame, Le Public et les hommes de lettres en Angleterre au dix-huitième siècle (Paris, 1897), pp. 92–113.

6 "Dedication" of Marriage à la Mode, Selected Dramas, ed. G. R. Noyes (Chicago, 1910), p. 149.

7 Quoted by Beljame, p. 101, n. 2. "Servant to His Majesty" appeared on the title-page of the 1673 edition "with sculptures"; again on that of The Conquest of China (1676); of

Ibrahim (1676); of The Female Prelate (1680), although Dryden was poet laureate.

8 Hugh Macdonald, "The Attacks on Dryden," Essays and Studies by Members of the English Association, XXI (1935), 50–51

9 Loc. cit.

10 Cf. the chronological table of Dryden's works in Ker, I, lxxv. The reply to Settle is, of course, the Notes and Observations on the Empress of Morocco (1674).

11 Beljame, pp. 100–2.

12 Ibid., p. 102; cf. Collected Works of John Wilmot Earl of Rochester, ed. John Hayward (London, 1926), Introd., p. xxx. Hereafter, wherever possible, all references to Rochester's works will be to this edition.

13 Quoted by Beljame, p. 102, n. 2, from Dennis, Original Letters, Familiar, Moral and Critical, 1721, I, 49.

14 The epilogue is printed in Scott-Saintsbury, X, 332; cf. evidence for the tradition there. Hayward, p. xxxi, accepts the tradition as fact.

15 Quoted by Beljame, p. 105; for text cf. The Works of Thomas Otway, ed. Ghosh (Oxford, 1932), I, 174:57–66.

16 Works, p. 131. Hayward (ibid., p. xxxviii) dates this poem "some years before Etherege's Man of Mode (1676)." Prinz (p. 70) is vague on the date; hopes to show this poem is unreasonably ascribed to Rochester; but (p. 102) admits that there is not much positive evidence against Rochester's authorship.

17 Scott-Saintsbury, V, 179, title page, from Juvenal, Sat. vii, 86–7; the preface which parallels the one under investigation occupies pp. 186–200.

18 Cf. supra, p. 1; Ker, I, 200:1–2. Chronology is difficult in Rochester's works, and it is difficult to state exactly when this poem was written or when Dryden first came upon it. It was first published in the 1680 edition of Rochester's works (on p. 40, according to Prinz, p. 341). As far as internal evidence is concerned, the latest allusion is that to Nat. Lee's Sophonisba or Hannibal's Overthrow in

> When Lee makes temp'rate Scipio fret and rave,
> And Hannibal a whining, Amorous Slave.

This play was published in 1675 (cf. Allardyce Nicoll, Restoration Drama, etc., pp. 119, 307). Rochester's poem antedates Dryden's essay: that is all that is necessary as for their dates. Cf. Spingarn, Critical Essays of the Seventeenth Century (Oxford, 1908), II, 353.

19 Works, p. 55. It would be interesting to discover whether Rochester actually wrote a poem to which he refers in "In the same paper," but in view of the calumny of this apparently frank statement, I am inclined to think that he is only following his original. There is no commentary on this line in Hayward; nor in Vivian de S. Pinto, Rochester (London, 1935).

20 Ibid., p. 56.

21 By "their" he probably alludes to the Countess of Pembroke's Antonie (1590, pub. 1592, a translation of Garnier's Marc Antoine); Daniel's Cleopatra (1594); Samuel Brandon's The Tragi-Comoedi of the Virtuous Octavia (1598); Fletcher and Massinger's The False One (c. 1620, pub. 1647); Thomas May's Cleopatra Queene of Aegypt (1654); Mrs. Phillips' (1663) and Waller's (1664) translation of Corneille's La Mort de Pompée (1642); the travesty on the story in the fifth act of D'Avenant's Playhouse to be let (1663); Sir Charles Sedley's Antony and Cleopatra (acted Feb., 1676/7), etc.

22 The meaning of the term "machine" in 192:20 (Ker, I, 316).

23 Book II, essai xvii.

24 A "Chedreux critic" is evidently an English critic who "affects" the non-essential (to Dryden) criteria of the French. The term, coming from "Chedreux wig," might very well include Rochester insofar as Rochester took it upon himself to criticize Dryden. There was a Chedreux wig in Etherege's The Man of Mode (1676), in which the character Dorimant was taken to be a portrait of Rochester (Allardyce Nicoll, Restoration Drama, p. 224). In view of the evidence that a "Chedreux wig" was associated with a man of fashion,

it is unlikely, in spite of A. A. Tilley (CHEL, VIII, 429) that by the term "Chedreux critics" Dryden has in mind Thomas Rymer.

25   Cf. in an earlier context of this essay Dryden's emphasis upon modesty: ". . . . expressions . . . are a modest clothing of our thoughts, as breeches and petticoats are of our bodies" (193:11–13). The scandal of Rochester's running around naked, which he later repudiated, is witnessed by a letter of Robert Harley (Portland Abbey MSS., Welbeck Abbey, September 11, 1677). The event alluded to took place three or four months before Dryden's penning the lines italicized above. Again, concerning the episode, Savile wrote to Rochester: ". . . . there has been such a story made concerning your last adventure as would persuade us grave men that you had stripped yourself of all your prudence as well as your breeches. . . ." Both pieces of evidence are cited by Hayward, pp. xl–xli.

26   This poem was issued as a broadside in 1675 (Hayward, p. 329).

27   Works, p. 39.

28   197:1–2, from Satires, I, i, 1–3, Qui fit . . . . illa contentus vivat, etc.

29   My italics. Scott notes on this passage (Scott-Saintsbury, V, 333): "This passage, though applicable to many of the men of rank at the court of Charles II., was particularly levelled at Lord Rochester, with whom our author was now on bad terms." And he comments on the "prophesy" contained in what Dryden had said, in the dedication to Rochester of 1673, about the man of wit becoming its tyrant.

30   My italics. Poems on Affairs of State, 1703, II, 130–31. I am indebted for this reference to Professor George Williamson.

31   Juv., Sat., VIII, 71–2: "Haec satis ad iuvenem quem nobis fama superbum / tradit et inflatum plenumque Nerone propinquo; . . . ." As for Dionysius, cf. Montaigne, Essais, Bk. II, xvii (ed. Villey, Paris, 1922, II, 414): "Dionysius le pere n'estimait rien tant de Soy que sa poësie."

32 Coming originally from Spartianus' Life of Hadrian, ch.
xv, Montaigne's account of this story in "De l'incommodité
de la grandeur," Book III, essai vii, is as follows (Essais,
ed. Villey, III, 180–81): "Mais, pour achever par ou j'ay
commencé, Adrian l'Empereur debatant avec le philosophe
Favorinus de l'interpretation de quelque mot, Favorinus
luy en quicta bien tost la victoire. Ses amys se plaignans
à luy: Vous vous moquez, fit-il; voudriez vous qu'il ne fut
pas plus sçavant que moy, luy qui commande à trente
legions?" Dryden had used this anecdote a decade previously in Defence of the Essay, Ker. I, 111; cf. Ker's note,
I, 305–6.

33 For the story of Lucan's death cf. Harper's Dictionary, ed.
Peck. The association of Lucan the poet, who was killed
by Nero out of sheer jealousy for his poetic talent, is natural here; but the association might have come to Dryden
through reading Montaigne, Book II, essai viii, who tells
how just before death Lucan recited from his Pharsalia:
"Le bon Lucanus estant jugé par ce coquin de Nero, sur
les derniers traits de sa vie, comme la plupart du sang
fut desjà escoulé par les veines," etc. (Essais, ed. Villey,
II, 96–7).

34 In the words "Some of their little zanies yet go further"
(198:21). In a long note at this point, Malone, The Critical
and Miscellaneous Prose Works of John Dryden (London,
1800), II, 24–25, suggests that perhaps Dryden in this
phrase is alluding to Crowne. Prinz recognizes the rhetorical artifice (pp. 117–18): "Although he probably knew
the real author of the satire, he chose to impute it to one
of the 'Zanies' of the great, a fiction that allowed him
greater freedom. . . ."

35 Horace, Sat., I, 10, 90; this is the satire which Rochester
"imitated."

36 Cf. Loeb Horace, ed. Fairclough (1926), Index, p. 496, and
references at Sat. I, 10, line 18; Tigellius is generally
identified with Hermogenes, and Demetrius with the "simius"
of Sat., I, 10, 18. For Rochester's training of Mrs. Barry,
the famous actress, cf. DNB (III, 317), and Hayward, pp.
xxxiii–iv.

37 Ker notes (i, 317) Aen. xii, 891, lines which Dryden translated:

> An antique stone he saw; the common bound
> Of neighboring fields, and barrier of the ground: . . .
> (Scott-Saintsbury, XV, 184).

38 The Satires of Decimus Junius Juvenalis. Translated into
English Verse. By Mr. Dryden, and Several other Eminent
Hands, ed. 1693, p. 146.

39 Ibid., p. 151. The original is Juv., Sat., VIII, 73.

40 Juv., Sat., VIII, 20: Nobilitas sola atque unica virtus est.
Dryden's quotations are, respectively, lines 34 ff. and line 33.

41 Dryden's Juvenal, ed. 1693, p. 149.

42 Lucretius, IV, 1152–6; Dryden's Works, ed. Scott-Saintsbury,
XII, 350–51.

43 Ibid., XVIII, 94. Malone (Vol. I, part ii, p. 6), dates this
letter from internal evidence July, 1673.

44 Works, p. 160. The date of this escapade is well established
as 1676, prior to the writing of Dryden's Preface. Rochester
was forbidden the court for his satire on the king and "labouring Nelly" (printed by Hayward, p. 154; cf. title of poem).
Also, within this advertisement, Rochester wrote: "The
knowledge of these Secrets, I gathered in my Travels abroad
(where I have spent my time ever since I was Fifteen Years
Old, to this my Nine and Twentieth Year) . . . ." [ibid., p.
159]. The travels were actually not that lengthy, but the age
Rochester gives is his true age: he was born in 1647, and
the age of twenty-nine would make the date of writing 1676,
which tallies with the external evidence of the aforementioned
satire. For information on the lodgings of Tower Street
and the well known section called, from the sign of the tavern there, "Black Swan Court," cf. Harben, A Dictionary of
London, 1918, pp. 273, 118; also Cunningham, London, 1931,
p. 293, article "Great Tower Street."

45 OED.

46 Dryden's Juvenal, ed. 1693, p. 98.

47 The poem is not included by Hayward in his edition, although
    that editor serves notice that his collection of Rochester's
    poems is in no sense the canon (Works, "Prefatory Note,"
    p. ix). The poem does not appear in Rochester's first
    collected edition, Poems on Several Occasions, Printed at
    Antwerpen; and it is also missing from the 1691 edition,
    "considered to be the best collection of Rochester's authen-
    tic lyrics" (Prinz, p. 351).

48 "A Satyr, by the Lord R---r" ["Must I with patience ever
    silent sit," etc.] appears on p. 32, and on page 33 "A Satyr,
    By the same Hand" is the satire in question. Cf. the bib-
    liographical description in Prinz, pp. 323–4.

49 The Works Of the Earls of Rochester, Roscommon, and
    Dorset: The Dukes of Devonshire, Buckinghamshire, &c
    with Memoirs of their Lives. M.DCC.XXXIX., p. 74.

50 The earliest version I have seen, that in State-Poems,
    1705, has initials and asterisks for the names which are
    spelled out in the 1739 edition. It would be interesting to
    discover an earlier version to see whether the names are
    the same, or whether Dryden himself was ever mentioned
    among the "wits." But such speculation is useless and be-
    side our purpose, which is merely to mention all the links,
    actual and ascribed, between Dryden, Rochester, and the
    satire of Juvenal which plays so important a part in the
    Preface to All for Love.

51 Works, p. 86.

52 Poems on Affairs of State, 1703, II, 142. The poem is re-
    ferred to by Hayward (p. 395) in connection with the Rose
    Alley Ambuscade.

53 Essays, ed. Ker, II, 18:27–31; cf. Ker's note, p. 277.

THE PLACE OF RULES IN DRYDEN'S CRITICISM

Hoyt Trowbridge

I

A fundamental task in the interpretation of any literary critic is to determine the nature and status of the general criteria which lie behind his judgments of specific works and writers. Discussion of Dryden's criticism has largely turned upon this question. The critics of the neoclassical period—the writers, let us say, from Ben Jonson to Samuel Johnson—are agreed in general to have been characterized by their use of "rules": that is to say, of objective norms or canons, established by reason, which they applied in the judgment of particular works of art. Did Dryden share this faith in rules, or did he appeal to other criteria, perhaps subjective and antirational? If he did make use of rules, we should inquire also as to their derivation and status—the sort of reasoning by which they were supported and the kind and degree of validity which he supposed them to possess.

To the first of these questions, three answers have been suggested. The clearest example of the first answer is to be found in George Saintsbury's History of criticism. According to Saintsbury, Dryden was the Shakespeare of criticism. He judged poems as Shakespeare wrote them, by "aiming at delight, at truth, at justice, at nature, at poetry, and letting the rules take care of themselves." If at times he seems to have appealed to critical rule and system, he did so only in deference to fashion and fools. In the last analysis, Dryden judged poems simply by his own impressions, by his own intuition of poetic quality.[1]

In his Life of Dryden, Dr. Johnson tells a very different story. Writing some eighty years after Dryden's death, Johnson knew that many changes had taken place during the intervening period. He seems to have feared that Dryden's doctrines and judgments might seem commonplace to the sophisticated reader of 1780. We ought to remember, Johnson says, that in

Reprinted from Modern Philology, Vol. 44 (1946), pp. 84–96, by permission of the author and The University of Chicago Press. Copyright 1946 by The University of Chicago.

Dryden's time these ideas were new. In that age, sound principles of criticism were known to few: "Audiences applauded by instinct, and poets perhaps often pleased by chance." It was Dryden who first taught the English to criticize by rule: "Dryden may be properly considered as the father of English criticism, as the writer who first taught us to determine upon principle the merit of composition." Dryden's great achievement, Johnson believed, had been to establish a groundwork of critical standards and principles, upon which other men had continued to build; for a criticism by instinct or intuition he substituted a criticism by law.[2] This is the exact opposite of Saintsbury's view.

The third solution combines the two above. A representative instance is Margaret Sherwood's discussion in her essay on Dryden's theory of drama. In her opinion, Dryden had no consistent position. He wavered continually between French rules and English freedom, judging at one time by the canons of rationalism, at another by subjective impression or intuitive response.[3] This is the answer given by most students of Dryden's thought; few have been able to find any single criterion underlying the variety of his critical opinions and judgments.

The second question, though almost as important as the first, is much less frequently considered. The most relevant discussion is that of Professor L. I. Bredvold, who represents Dryden as a Pyrrhonist, a skeptical antirationalist. In religion the natural expression of this philosophy is "fideism," an attack upon natural reason in the interests of revelation and ecclesiastical authority. In politics the same distrust of reason leads to a defense of tradition and authority — in Dryden's case, to a moderate constitutional Toryism. His thought, in these two fields, is consistent both in its distrust of reason and in the conservative conclusions to which this assumption leads.[4] In criticism, according to Bredvold, Dryden's thought is unsystematic and tentative; as a Pyrrhonist, he distrusted reason and was always ready to change his mind. Appealing at one time to the rules, at others to nonrational criteria, his criticism is essentially unstable and inconsistent. In so far as he did make use of rules, their status was that of hypotheses or provisional generalizations, tentatively held and easily dropped in favor of other criteria.[5] In criticism, as in religion and politics, Pyrrhonic skepticism or antirationalism is the continuing substratum, beneath the surface contradictions, which gives unity and integrity to Dryden's thought.

These, then, are the questions with which we are concerned, together with some of the solutions which have been offered by scholars and critics. The evidence to be presented here is drawn primarily from a single work, Dryden's Defence of An essay of dramatic poesy; it will be supplemented, however, by material from other critical essays by Dryden and, in connection with Bredvold's thesis, by evidence drawn from some of Dryden's sources and from the writings of his contemporaries. I will not attempt here to analyze Dryden's practice as a critic; my purpose is to recover his theory of criticism and to define its nature, as he himself conceived it.

The Defence was written in 1668 as a reply to the preface to Sir Robert Howard's play, The Duke of Lerma, which, in turn, was an attack upon Dryden's Essay of dramatic poesy. Considered as a whole, the Defence is not of first-class importance. The main point at issue was the propriety of rhyme in serious plays—a question of considerable practical importance at the time but of comparatively minor theoretical interest. Howard was an amateur, a fourth-rate poet whose views were too superficial to have much intrinsic value,[6] and Dryden's rebuttal is largely devoted to ad hoc satire on Howard's frequent obscurities, mistranslations, grammatical faults, and errors of reasoning. The Defence nevertheless contains, in two or three passages, a serious and reasoned treatment of certain crucial theoretical questions. For all his superficiality, Howard had raised some fundamental problems, which Dryden considered more fully in his reply than he had occasion to do in any of his later works. These passages give the essay a unique value and interest for the student of his critical thought.

Howard speaks in his preface as a friend of reason but an enemy of dogmatism; he accuses Dryden of attempting to establish laws by dictatorial fiat. In poetry he defends liberty of taste and opinion against the rules:

> . . . . Nor do I condemn in the least any thing of what
> Nature soever that pleases, since nothing cou'd appear
> to me a ruder folly than to censure the satisfaction of
> others; I rather blame the unnecessary understanding
> of some that have labour'd to give strict rules to things

> that are not Mathematical, and with such eagerness
> persuing their own seeming reasons that at last we
> are to apprehend such Argumentative Poets will grow
> as strict as <u>Sancho Pancos</u> Doctor was to our very
> Appetites; for in the difference of <u>Tragedy</u> and <u>Comedy</u>,
> and of <u>Fars</u> it self, there can be no determination but
> by the <u>Taste</u>; nor in the manner of their Composure;
> and who ever wou'd endeavour to like or dislike by
> the Rules of others, he will be as unsuccessful as if
> he should try to be perswaded into a power of be-
> lieving, not what he must, but what others direct him
> to believe.[7]

For Howard, evidently, there was no middle ground between
mathematical demonstration and the anarchy of uncontrolled
individual preferences; if, therefore, the rules were not susceptible to demonstration, it followed that taste alone could
be the guide. The poet must be free to dress his play "in
such a fashion as his fancy best approves" and the audience,
by the same token, to judge the result by its own satisfaction.
The poet might preserve the unities if he liked, might rhyme
or not as pleased him best; and the audience was to respond
according to its taste. Howard's argument, denying the possibility of a criticism by rule, left all questions of better and
worse in poetry to be determined by personal preference.
It was for this reason that his preface needed a serious refutation.

In opposing this antinomian view, Dryden makes three important claims: first, the negative contention that taste—the
mere liking or disliking—cannot be taken as the criterion of
poetic value; second, as the positive counterpart of this contention, that it is possible to ground the rules on objective principles and to support them by reasoned arguments; and, finally,
that such principles are not dogmatic, since they are not
claimed to be demonstrative. In short, there is a middle ground
between individual taste and arbitrary law, and it is in this
area that sound criticism ought to operate. Taken together,
these three propositions constitute Dryden's general position
as to the function and status of rules in criticism.

II

Dryden's first argument, against the validity of taste as a criterion, is made in reply to Howard's statement that "in the difference of <u>Tragedy</u> and <u>Comedy,</u> and of <u>Fars</u> it self, there can be no determination but by the Taste." After noting the ambiguities of this proposition, Dryden replies to what he takes to be its sense—"that betwixt one comedy or tragedy and another, there is no other difference but what is made by the liking of the audience." This statement, which seems to reject all objective standards, Dryden flatly denies:

> The liking or disliking of the people gives the
> play the denomination of good or bad, but does not
> really make or constitute it such. To please the
> people ought to be the poet's aim, because plays are
> made for their delight; but it does not follow that
> they are always pleased with good plays, or that
> the plays which please them are always good. The
> humour of the people is now for Comedy; therefore,
> in hope to please them, I write comedies rather than
> serious plays: and so far their taste prescribes to
> me: but it does not follow from that reason, that
> Comedy is to be preferred before Tragedy in its
> own nature; for that which is so in its own nature
> cannot be otherwise, as a man cannot but be a ration-
> al creature: but the opinion of the people may alter,
> and in another age, or perhaps in this, serious plays
> may be set up above comedies.[8]

This argument rests upon the assumption that the value of a work of art is entirely independent of opinion. Each work and each kind has an unchanging intrinsic value, which would be the same "were there neither judge, taste, nor opinion in the world," and the function of criticism is to judge each in accordance with its real worth. But, since this real value is not determined by opinion, the liking or disliking of the people cannot be the criterion by which it is judged. Taste can have no authority, for real value "cannot be otherwise" than it is, while taste is constantly changing; to depend upon taste is to be at the mercy of whim and caprice. In order to be valid, therefore, criticism requires an external rule, some standard or measure which is independent of opinion.

Those who believe (with the majority) that Dryden's thought was radically inconsistent, varying without pattern from year to year, may find this passage unconvincing as evidence of Dryden's permanent views. If, as the Defence certainly shows, Dryden believed in 1668 that uncontrolled taste had no authority in criticism, this fact would not necessarily prevent an appeal to taste in his other writings. On this point, however, Dryden's position did not change; he returns again and again to the assertion that taste in itself has no validity or authority but must always be checked and guided by some objective criterion of poetic worth.

His attack upon the taste of the people, as we see it in the Defence, is repeated in many other works. In the Essay of dramatic poesy itself, he had already said emphatically: "If by the people you understand the multitude, the hoi polloi, 'tis no matter what they think; they are sometimes in the right, sometimes in the wrong: their judgment is a mere lottery."[9] In the prefaces to An evening's love (1671) and to All for love (1678) he again expresses his contempt for the popular audience; their applause is valueless, he says, because "the crowd cannot be presumed to have more than a gross instinct, of what pleases or displeases them."[10] The same attitude is shown in the dedication of The Spanish friar, during the eighties, and again in the Discourse on satire in the nineties, the last decade of Dryden's life.[11] The reason for this contempt, though clear in all these passages, is most explicitly stated in the preface to Troilus and Cressida (1679), when he attacks "that audience which loves Poetry, but understands it not."[12] Having no ground but instinct, the people's opinion proves nothing as to the real merit of a poem or play.

Although the theoretical basis of these remarks seems clear, they might perhaps be discounted as an expression of mere class prejudice. But the same idea appears elsewhere in a more general form, without application to any particular social class. Dryden distinguishes in several places between a "blind admirer" and a true critic.[13] The blind admirer, whether in the stalls or in the upper gallery, is distinguished from a true critic by his lack of understanding. Such men, though often enthusiastic lovers of poetry, judge it without discrimination, by a mere "gross instinct" of what pleases. They know what they like, as we say, but cannot explain why. Such men are to be found in all parts of society; a lack of principle, though characteristic of the mob, is to be found in every class. The true critic, by contrast, not only loves poetry but understands it, too; he is able to defend his inclination by his reason, because he admires not "blindly" but "knowingly."[14] As a result, his views are likely to be both sound and convincing; in the long run, since they are grounded on principle, they will win out. Such views, Dryden says, are "of God."[15]

This idea is most fully developed in the dedication of Dryden's Aeneis (1697), where he adapts from the French critic, De Segrais, an analysis of the reading public into three groups. The classification is based upon capacity for true judgment, which is assumed to depend not on sensitivity or enthusiasm but on understanding and a grasp of principle. The first two groups, having either no principles or very inadequate ones, have but little capacity for right judgment. The third and highest group, which is also the smallest, includes the "best judges," the judices natos. This is the part of the audience which Vergil, in common with all true poets, had particularly wished to please:

> . . . . the most judicious: souls of the highest rank, and truest understanding. These are few in number; but whoever is so happy as to gain their approbation can never lose it, because they never give it blindly. Then they have a certain magnetism in their judgment, which attracts others to their sense. Every day they gain some new proselyte, and in time become the Church.[16]

Their judgments are sound and enduring because they are never given blindly, out of mere taste, instinct, or subjective impression. The essence of true criticism, as distinguished from a blind enthusiasm for poetry, is an appeal beyond taste to the enduring criteria of reasoned principle.

The second of Dryden's arguments against Howard is a proof that objective criteria can actually be established. Howard had claimed that "the general rules laid down for Playes" were wholly undemonstrable and groundless, because "the great foundation that is laid to build upon is nothing, as it is generally

stated."[17] If Dryden's attack on taste was to stand, it was necessary to defend the ground or foundation on which the rules were
to rest. He had shown that they were necessary, if critical judgment was to conform to real literary value; he must now show
that they are possible.

Dryden's proof is based upon the nature of an art, as he
conceived it:

> .... let us consider what this great foundation is,
> which he says is nothing, as it is generally stated.
> I have never heard of any other foundation of Dra-
> matic Poesy than the imitation of Nature; neither
> was there ever pretended any other by the Ancients
> or Moderns, or me, who endeavour to follow them
> in that rule. This I have plainly said in my defini-
> tion of a play; that it is a just and lively image of
> human nature, &c. Thus the foundation, as it is
> generally stated, will stand sure, if this definition
> of a play be true; if it be not, he ought to have made
> his exception against it, by proving that a play is
> not an imitation of Nature, but somewhat else, which
> he is pleased to think it.
>
> But 'tis very plain, that he has mistaken the
> foundation for that which is built upon it, though
> not immediately: for the direct and immediate
> consequence is this; if Nature be to be imitated,
> then there is a rule for imitating Nature rightly;
> otherwise there may be an end, and no means con-
> ducing to it.[18]

This argument assumes that an art is a skill directed to some
end and that the existence of an end implies some means of
attaining it. Rules of poetic production, formulating the means
appropriate to attain the poet's end, are therefore inherent in
the nature of poetry as an art; and these same rules provide
the standards by which the products of his art are to be judged.
If the end is to imitate nature, this aim constitutes the foundation upon which the rules, as means to that end, may be erected.

This argument, like that against the validity of uncontrolled
taste, appears in Dryden's later works as well as in his reply
to Howard. The conception of an art, which provides the major

premise of this argument, is to be found almost everywhere in his critical writings. It is implied, for example, in his use of the term "artificial" in praise of a poet's work, or "inartificial" in condemnation.[19] It appears also in the familiar distinctions between nature and art, genius and skill, or fancy and judgment. With other critics of the neoclassical period, Dryden assumes that good poetry cannot be composed without genius, a creative power implanted in the poet by nature; but he always contends that true poetry requires, in addition, the judgment to "manage" this power, to apply it with skill to the task at hand.[20]

The same idea of art is expressed metaphorically in several places. Dryden compares the poet to a gunsmith or watchmaker, a wrestler, a physician, and an architect or builder.[21] The inference drawn from all these analogies is the necessity of skill; and in the last two, more specifically, of skill based on theoretical insight or knowledge. As Dryden says in the preface to An evening's love, the writer of farce—a type of the bad poet—is like a mountebank doctor, a mere "empiric"; for, even if he succeeds, it is by inferior means and without understanding what he does. The good poet, on the other hand, is like the true physician: he understands the principles of his art, the reasons for what he does and the causes of his success. "What the one performs by hazard, the other does by skill."[22] Or, again, in condemning plays written without a plan, Dryden says that poets who succeed in such undertakings "ought to have sacrificed to Fortune, not to the Muses."[23] To succeed by chance is no credit to an artist, for discrimination in the choice of means is inherent in the very definition of an art. For Dryden, if not for some critics of later times, a poet without art is a contradiction in terms.

In its complete form, as a proof of the existence of standards, Dryden's argument against Howard reappears in his Parallel of poetry and painting (1695). In this essay, which was prefixed to Dryden's translation of Du Fresnoy's poem, De arte graphica, Dryden commends his author as "one who perfectly understood the rules of painting; who gave the best and most concise instructions for performance, and the surest to inform the judgment of all who loved this noble art."[24] Taking Du Fresnoy's rules as authoritative for painting, Dryden presents an extended parallel between the sister-arts: first, in their ends and their kinds, which are the same or very similar, and then

in their means, which are analogous. The comparison is fruitful because both are arts and because, as such, they proceed by
parallel paths toward a common goal: "I must now consider
them, as they are great and noble arts; and as they are arts,
they must have rules, which may direct them to their common
end."[25] The end in both arts is to please, and the general rule
for attaining it is the imitation of nature, which is "justly constituted as the general, and indeed the only, rule of pleasing,
both in Poetry and Painting."[26] Upon this general rule, as a
foundation, the more specific rules are grounded; they formu-
late the various subordinate or particular causes by which the
artist's purpose may be effected:

> Having thus shewn that imitation pleases, and
> why it pleases in both these arts, it follows, that
> some rules of imitation are necessary to obtain that
> end; for without rules there can be no art, any more
> than there can be a house without a door to conduct
> you into it.[27]

In the Parallel, as in the Defence, Dryden argues that both
poetry and criticism—both performance and judgment—are
founded on rational principles. Considered by one as rules of
production, by the other as standards of evaluation, these principles were essential to the perfection of both. Poetry deserved
to be called an "art" when it achieved its purpose by rationally
determined means, and criticism was sound when it judged the
poet's performance by the appropriateness of these means to
the chosen end. If poetry were not an art, there could be no
such standards in criticism; but, since it is an art, its rules
provide the canons of a rational artistic judgment.

It was Dryden, according to Dr. Johnson, who first established this view in England. Before his time, "audiences applauded by instinct, and poets perhaps often pleased by chance,"
but Dryden "taught us to determine upon principle the merit
of composition." This conception of his historic mission is
confirmed by Dryden himself in the Discourse on satire, published in 1693. Looking back some twenty-five years to his
apprentice days in criticism, Dryden says that in the Essay of
dramatic poesy he had tried to draw "the outlines of an art,
without any living master to instruct me in it." In England

121

at that time, the art of poetry had been praised but not studied:

> Shakespeare, who created the stage among us, had rather written happily, than knowingly and justly, and Johnson, who, by studying Horace, had been acquainted with the rules yet seemed to envy to posterity that knowledge, and, like an inventor in some useful art, to make a monopoly of his learning.[28]

It was a primitive time—"before the use of the loadstone, or knowledge of the compass." Dryden's achievement, as he himself conceived it, had been to teach those arts to his countrymen: to show, both by example and by argument, that rules were essential to poetry and that in these same rules might be found the objective criteria of a sound and reasonable criticism. Dr. Johnson's discussion is, in fact, hardly more than a paraphrase of Dryden's own statement in the Discourse on satire.

If this conclusion has been denied by many students of Dryden, the reason probably lies in a gratuitous assumption that rules are inherently opposed to the true spirit of poetry. When Saintsbury wrote that Dryden aimed at delight, truth, justice, nature, and poetry and let the rules take care of themselves, he obviously assumed that rules were incompatible with these positive qualities. But Dryden's view was very different. To him delight was the end of poetry, the imitation of nature its most general and basic means; the more specific rules were simply less general means to the same end. They were not incompatible with delight, nature, or poetry; they were, in fact, an important source of these effects. Without them, in his view, poetry was not an art, and criticism had no criteria.

More generally, Saintsbury's misunderstanding of Dryden may be ascribed to his failure to transcend the limitations of his own critical position. As Dorothy Richardson has recently shown, Saintsbury was a part of the "art for art's sake" movement; his views were formed under the influence of Pater and Swinburne, Gautier, Baudelaire, and Flaubert.[29] He often seems to have valued the older critics in so far as they anticipated his own ideas, and he sometimes found these ideas where they did not actually exist. This was the case, I think, in his treatment

122

of Dryden. Saintsbury himself believed that the best, if not the
only, criterion of poetry was "that immediate and magical effect
on the senses of the mind—that direct touch of the poetic nerve"[30]
—and he read this impressionism into Dryden. The wish, it
seems, was father to the thought.

III

The third and last part of Dryden's reply to Howard brings
us to our second main question. Assuming that rules are necessary in criticism, what is the intellectual status of these criteria?
On what sort of evidence do they rest? Can they be established
demonstratively, or do they admit some degree of uncertainty?
On this problem we part company with Saintsbury and Johnson,
since they did not discuss it, and turn to Professor Bredvold,
whose conception of Dryden as a skeptic has a direct bearing on
the question.

According to Howard, Dryden wanted to govern poetry by
dictatorial prescription. "Things that are not Mathematical,"
in his opinion, ought to be governed wholly by fancy or individual
preference; Dryden's attempt to judge poetry by rule constituted
a dogmatic infringement of the poet's liberty. But Dryden denies
any dictatorial intention. He had made no claim of certainty for
the rules laid down in the Essay of dramatic poesy. It was a
"sceptical dialogue," presenting several different views, with
the reasons which could be offered in support of each, but making no attempt either to reconcile these views or to judge among
them:

> He is here pleased to charge me with being
> magisterial, as he has done in many other places
> of his preface; therefore, in vindication of myself,
> I must crave leave to say, that my whole discourse
> was sceptical, according to that way of reasoning
> which was used by Socrates, Plato, and all the
> Academics of old, which Tully and the best of the
> Ancients followed, and which is imitated by the
> modest inquisitions of the Royal Society. That it
> is so, not only the name will show, which is an Es-
> say, but the frame and composition of the work.

> You see it is a dialogue sustained by persons of
> several opinions, all of them left doubtful, to be
> determined by the readers in general; and more
> particularly deferred to the accurate judgment of
> my Lord Buckhurst, to whom I made a dedication
> of my book. [31]

Of course Dryden had his own convictions, which were voiced
in the Essay by his spokesman Neander, but these convictions
were not forced upon the reader. His own views, like those of
the other speakers, were presented as "problematical," and
the reader was expected, with Lord Buckhurst, to determine
the issue "in favour of which part you shall judge most reasonable." [32] Dryden considered his position reasonable, but he did
not claim that its validity had been conclusively established.

The distinction which Dryden had in mind here is illustrated
concretely in connection with his argument, already quoted above,
in support of the existence of rules: "If Nature be to be imitated,
then there is a rule for imitating Nature rightly; otherwise there
may be an end, and no means conducing to it." He then goes on:

> Hitherto I have proceeded by demonstration;
> but as our divines, when they have proved a Deity,
> because there is order, and have inferred that
> this Deity ought to be worshipped, differ after-
> wards in the manner of the worship; so having
> laid down, that Nature is to be imitated, and that
> proposition proving the next, that then there are
> means which conduce to the imitating of Nature,
> I dare proceed no further positively; but have
> only laid down some opinions of the Ancients and
> Moderns, and of my own, as means which they
> used, and which I thought probable for the attain-
> ing of that end. [33]

Dryden distinguishes in this passage between two degrees of
certainty, the demonstrative and the probable. Although the
existence of rules of some sort seemed to him demonstrable,
the arguments in support of particular rules were all of a
merely probable order. They were to be received, therefore—
as he says elsewhere in another connection— "with a doubtful

academical assent, or rather an inclination to assent to probability."[34] Thus he agrees with Howard that mathematical
certainty is unattainable in criticism, but he contends that individual fancy is not the only alternative. Rejecting both taste
and demonstration, he finds a mean between these extremes in
the realm of probable arguments. Since the rules are confessed
to be merely probable, his position could not fairly be called
dogmatic; on the other hand, since they had sufficient plausibility
to justify assent, he also avoided the opposite extreme of an-
archic individualism.

The source of this view, according to Bredvold, is the
skeptical tradition which descended from Pyrrho of Elis through
Sextus Empiricus and Cicero to Montaigne, Charron, Sir Thomas
Browne, and others, and so to Dryden and his contemporaries.
Bredvold shows that Dryden was acquainted with this tradition
and that he makes use of skeptical arguments against reason in
several of his works, especially in the religious and political
writings. I believe, however, that Dryden's position should be
dissociated in some degree from that of historic Pyrrhonism;
while he agreed with the skeptics at some points, he differed
from them at others. The true source of his "problematical"
way of thinking, in my opinion, lies in a quite different quarter.

It is important, first of all, to distinguish between two types
of skeptical philosophy: the "probabilism" illustrated in ancient
times by Carneades, and the more thoroughgoing skepticism of
Pyrrho and Sextus Empiricus.[35] This distinction is much emphasized by Sextus, our chief source of information about Greek
skeptical thought. In the opening chapter of the Hypotyposes, he
differentiates three main types of philosophic system: the Dogmatic, including Aristotle, Epicurus, and the Stoics; the Academic, illustrated by Cleitomachus and Carneades; and the Pyrrhonic
or truly skeptical. As he explains in a later chapter, the Academic philosophers were skeptical as far as they denied that
things can be "apprehended" or known with certainty. But they
differed from the Pyrrhonists in recognizing several degrees
of uncertainty, ranging from the improbable (or seemingly false)
to the probable, the probable and tested, and, finally, the probable, tested, and "irreversible." On this basis, using probability
as the guide of life, a man might reasonably assent, in practice,
to many things that were not "apprehensible." From the point of
view of Sextus and the extreme Pyrrhonians, the Academic writers were dogmatists in disguise.[36]

This distinction is collapsed by Cicero, who identifies not only the later Academics but even Socrates and Plato with the skeptical sect. As against the dogmatic stoicism of his opponents, Cicero represents himself (in the Academica) as a skeptic; his guiding principle, however, is not a Pyrrhonic suspension of all belief but an Academic probabilism. As he says:

> Nor between us and those who suppose themselves
> to know [i.e., the Stoics and other dogmatists] is there
> any difference, except that they do not doubt that those
> things which they defend are true, while we accept
> many probabilities which are easily followed but which
> we can scarcely claim to affirm.[37]

Near the close of the dialogue, in a passage which throws much light on Dryden's views, Cicero refutes the claim of Lucullus that without certainty there can be no basis for the arts. Although their principles cannot be "apprehended"—and must therefore be considered to be uncertain—Cicero contends that probable knowledge is quite sufficient for the arts. "We abolished," he says, "what never existed, leaving, however, what was enough for them."[38]

It is obvious, from his reply to Howard, that Dryden understood skepticism in Cicero's sense. Whether or not he knew Sextus, he did not distinguish, as Sextus did, between Academicism and true skepticism. His Essay of dramatic poesy was skeptical, he says, because it was constructed "according to that way of reasoning which was used by Socrates, Plato, and all the Academics of old, which Tully and the best of the Ancients followed, and which is imitated by the modest inquisitions of the Royal Society."[39] He concedes, as Cicero does, that certainty is unattainable in criticism, but he contends, in opposition to Howard, that probabilities are sufficient for the establishment of rules. To Dryden, skepticism meant, at most, the probabilism of Cicero and the Academy; though skeptical in one sense, since he denied that demonstrative certainty could be attained in literary criticism, he was clearly not a Pyrrhonist in the sense defined by Sextus.

But Dryden must be dissociated in some degree even from Cicero and the probabilists. His critical method was formulated in terms of a distinction between demonstrative and probable reasoning. As with the parallel Ciceronian distinction between "apprehension" and probability, the immediate consequence of this disjunction is to establish probable arguments as a legitimate mode of reasoning; in this respect Dryden agrees with Cicero and the Academics against the Pyrrhonists. But Dryden's distinction did not eliminate all intellectual certainty; on some questions, even outside mathematics, demonstration seemed to him possible. In theology, as we have seen, he counted the argument from design as a demonstration; and in criticism, while particular rules were always merely probable, the existence of rules in general seemed to him certain.[40] For Cicero, on the other hand, certainty existed nowhere; no proposition could be "apprehended," and all arguments were merely probable. At this point Dryden differs radically from skeptics of all varieties.

The source of Dryden's way of reasoning should be sought, therefore, in some other tradition. The most plausible origin, in my opinion, is to be found in the logical treatises of Aristotle. Aristotle distinguishes in many places between "science" and "dialectic." The method of science, as elaborated in the Analytics, is demonstration, which provides, with intuitive reason, the only grounds of certain knowledge; the method of dialectic, a process of reasoning from probable premises, yields only tentative or approximative results.[41] The appropriate method, in each department of inquiry, is determined by the nature of its subject matter; dialectic, though an inferior method, is necessarily and properly employed in the sciences which deal with variable things. Thus ethics, for example, must be content with probabilities:

> We must be content, then, in speaking of such subjects and with such premises to indicate the truth roughly and in outline, and in speaking about things which are only for the most part true and with premises of the same kind to reach conclusions that are no better. In the same spirit, therefore, should each type of statement be received; for it is the mark of an educated man to look for precision in each class of things just so far as the nature of the subject admits; it is evidently equally foolish to accept probable reasoning from a mathematician

and to demand from a rhetorician scientific
proof.[42]

In a loose sense, as denying the possibility of an ethical
"science," this statement might be called skeptical. Its effect,
however, is the opposite of skeptical; for it saves demonstrative certainty in some fields, while at the same time justifying
probable arguments and tentative or approximative results in
others.

This distinction is preserved, through various transmuta-
tions, in the main tradition of modern logic. In the handbooks
of the early seventeenth century, it is sometimes phrased as a
distinction between Science and Opinion; the former employs
demonstration, which "consisteth of necessary, certaine, and
infallible Propositions, and of such things as cannot be otherwise," but the method of proof in matters of opinion is the
"Dialecticall Syllogisme," which is "made of probable and
credible Propositions." Opinion does not give rise to certainty
but is "knowledge of things casuall, which may be sometime false,
sometime true."[43] In a somewhat different form, the distinction is preserved even in the antischolastic "new" logics of Dryden's maturity. It appears in the Port-Royal logic, a classic of
the Cartesian reformation in philosophy, as a weapon against
both Pyrrhonism and Academicism. True reason, the authors
say,

> places all things in the rank which belongs to them;
> it questions those which are doubtful, rejects those
> which are false, and acknowledges, in good faith,
> those which are evident, without being embarrassed
> by the vain reasons of the Pyrrhonists, which never
> could, even in the minds of those who proposed them,
> destroy the reasonable assurance we have of many
> things.[44]

Another formulation, obviously influenced by Locke, is given to
the distinction by Isaac Watts, a generation later:

> Where the Evidence of the Agreement or Dis-
> agreement of the Ideas is so strong and plain, that
> we cannot forbid nor delay our Assent; the Proposi-

tion is call'd certain, as every Circle hath a Centre;
the World did not create it self. An Assent to such
Propositions is honour'd with the name of Knowledge.
But when there is any Obscurity upon the Agreement or Disagreement of the Ideas, so that the Mind
does not clearly perceive it, and is not compell'd to
assent or dissent, then the Proposition, in a proper
and philosophical Sense, is call'd doubtful or uncertain; as the Planets are inhabited; the Souls of Brutes
are mere Matter; the World will not stand a thousand
Years longer; Dido built the City of Carthage, &c.
Such uncertain Propositions are call'd Opinions.[45]

It is notable that Watts illustrates demonstration by geometry
and, in theology, by a version of the argument from design:
"the World did not create it self."

The philosophers and scientists of Dryden's period make
active use of the distinction between demonstrative and probable proofs; they, too, employ it for an explicitly antiskeptical
purpose. Meric Casaubon, for example, describes rational belief as a mean between the "vicious extremities" of credulity
and incredulity—between superstition and skepticism. Sound
reasoners distinguish between probability, the "ordinary grounds
of reason," and "certain knowledge, or science," which is
grounded on the knowledge of causes; employing each type of
evidence as it is appropriate, human reason is able to discover
truth in all things natural, civil, and divine.[46] Closer to Dryden
are Glanvill and Boyle, the apologists for the Royal Society.
Like Dryden, these men called themselves skeptics; however,
they preserve certainty—in some fields and under proper safe-
guards—by a distinction between demonstrative and probable
arguments. A probabilist in natural science and in many other
fields of thought, Glanvill specifically admits demonstration in
mathematics and in divinity: "Our religious foundations are
fastened at the pillars of the intellectual world, and the grand
Articles of our Belief as demonstrable as Geometry."[47] A
similar conclusion is defended by Locke in Book IV of the Essay.
True "knowledge," which is certain, may be attained either by
direct intuition or by demonstration; where these are impossible,
the mind must depend upon probability as the ground of "judgment" or "assent." Like Dryden, Glanvill, Boyle, and Watts,

Locke does not limit demonstration to mathematics: though knowledge is admittedly "very short and scanty," demonstration is possible wherever the agreement of two ideas with some third, intermediate idea can be intuitively perceived.[48] According to Locke, this definition permits a demonstrable foundation for the rules of morality, as well as certain knowledge of the existence of God.[49] Here he claims rather more for demonstration than many of his contemporaries were willing to do.

In general, these statements differ markedly both from Aristotle's formulation and from each other; they disagree as to the nature of demonstration and also as to the spheres of its legitimate application. On the essential point, however, they are closer to each other and to Aristotle than they are to any version of the skeptical or academic philosophies; though un-Aristotelian in several respects, all these writers distinguish between probable and demonstrative proofs and use the distinction to guarantee certainty in some fields of thought. Their debt to Aristotle is explicitly acknowleged by Boyle and Tillotson,[50] and it seems equally clear in Glanvill, Locke, and Dryden.

Whatever the source of Dryden's method of reasoning, it is not skeptical in spirit or intent. His criticism, as Johnson recognized, is a criticism by rule. In this field, as in religion and politics, his fundamental aim was to establish some kind of objective standards as a check against the anarchy of individual preference and opinion. In opposition to the antinomianism of Howard, he argued that sound criticism requires the use of objective rules or canons, grasped by the understanding and supported by reasoned arguments; he found these rules in the means which reason and experience had shown to be conducive to the ends of poetry. He agreed with Cicero that certainty can never be attained in criticism but that probability is a sufficient basis for the arts; the rules, therefore, are tentative or hypothetical and are to be accepted with a "doubtful academical assent." Here we may agree with Bredvold. But this conception of critical method is formulated by Dryden in terms of a distinction between demonstration and probability. For him, as for many others in his time, this distinction was antiskeptical in intention and effect; by recognizing degrees of knowledge, proportional to the nature of evidence, they were able to save reason from the attacks both of the Pyrrhonists and the Academics. In criticism, we must conclude, Dryden believed that rational principles were both necessary and possible: literary evaluation, as he understood it, was a process of rational judgment, which determined the merit of works and writers by the application of probable rules.

NOTES

1 George Saintsbury, A history of criticism and literary taste in Europe, II (2d ed.; New York and Edinburgh, 1905), 388–89.

2 Lives of the English poets, ed. Hill (Oxford, 1905), I, 410–11; cf. also p. 366.

3 Dryden's dramatic theory and practice (New Haven, 1914), pp. 27–29, and passim.

4 The intellectual milieu of John Dryden (Ann Arbor, 1934), esp. pp. 11–15, 70–72, 108–10, 115–20, 132–34.

5 L. I. Bredvold, The best of Dryden (New York, 1933), pp. xxxiv–xxxviii.

6 For a similar judgment of Howard compare Paul Spencer Wood, "The opposition to neo-classicism in England between 1660 and 1700," PMLA, XLIII (1928), 190–91. For other and generally more favorable opinions see D. D. Arundell, Dryden and Howard (Cambridge, 1929), pp. ix–xi; Paul Hamelius, Die Kritik in der englischen Literatur des 17. und 18. Jahrhunderts (Leipzig, 1897), p. 48; and James E. Routh, The rise of English classical criticism (New Orleans, 1915), p. 22.

7 J. E. Spingarn (ed.), Critical essays of the seventeenth century, II (Oxford, 1908), 106–7. Hereafter cited as "Spingarn."

8 W. P. Ker (ed.), Essays of John Dryden (Oxford, 1926), I, 120–21. Hereafter cited as "Ker."

9 Ibid., p. 100.

10 Ibid., pp. 195 and 135–36.

11 Ibid., I, 246, and II, 50–51.

12 Ibid., I, 221, 226.

13 Ibid., pp. 138, 196.

14 Ibid., II, 115.

15 Ibid., pp. 225, 258.

16 Ibid., pp. 223–26.

17 Spingarn, II, 108.

18 Ker, I, 123.

19 Ibid., p. 49.

20 Ibid., p. 220; cf. also pp. 8, 106–7, 228–29; II, 45, 92–93, 138, and passim.

21 Ibid., I, 147, 220, 136, 46.

22 Ibid., p. 136.

23 Ibid., p. 46.

24 Ibid., II, 115.

25 Ibid., p. 133.

26 Ibid., p. 137.

27 Ibid., p. 138.

28 Ibid., pp. 16–17.

29 Dorothy Richardson, "Saintsbury and art for art's sake in England," PMLA, LIX (1944), 243–60.

30 Quoted by Richardson (ibid., p. 259, n. 74).

31 Ker, I, 124.

32 "Epistle dedicatory" (ibid., pp. 23–27).

33 Ibid., I, 123.

34 "Life of Plutarch," in Works, ed. Scott and Saintsbury (London, 1882–93), XVII, 35.

35 Bredvold recognizes this distinction (Intellectual milieu, p. 18) but does not apply it in his analysis of Dryden. "Pyrrhonic" and "skeptical" are used throughout his study as synonymous terms.

36 Hyp. i.33.220–35; cf. also Montaigne, "Apologie de Raimond Sebond," Essais, ed. Villey (Paris, 1930), II, 337–39, 455–57; Arnauld and Nicole, Port-Royal logic, Part IV, chap. i; and Hume, Enquiry concerning human understanding, chap. xii.

37 "Nec inter nos et eos, qui se scire arbitrantur, quicquam interest, nisi quod illi non dubitant quin ea vera sint, quae defendunt, nos probabilia multa habemus, quae sequi facile, adfirmare vix possumus" (Acad. pr. ii. 3. 8).

38 "Sed quo modo tu, si nihil comprehendi posset, artificia concidere dicebas neque mihi dabas id, quod probabile esset, satis magnam vim habere ad artis, sic ego nunc tibi refero artem sine scientia esse non posse. An pateretur hoc Zeuxis aut Phidias aut Polyclitus, nihil se scire, cum in eis esset tanta sollertia? Quod si eos docuisset aliquis quam vim habere diceretur scientia, desinerent irasci: ne nobis quidem suscenserent, cum didicissent id tollere nos, quod nusquam esset, quod autem satis esset ipsis relinquere" (ibid. ii. 47. 146).

39 Ker, I, 124. Dr. Johnson, with characteristic precision, describes the Essay as "artfully variegated with successive representations of opposite probabilities" (Lives, I, 412). Even when only one line of argument is presented, Dryden often makes clear that the evidence is not conclusive; his opinions are "set not up for a standard to better judgments," and those who think differently are free to present their reasons (Ker, II, 81–82; cf. I, 190, and II, 53, 248).

40 Ker, I, 123; cf. also Conquest of Granada, Part II, Act IV, scene iii (Works, IV, 190): "By reason, man, a godhead may discern/ But how he would be worshipped cannot learn" (cited by Bredvold, Intellectual milieu, p. 117). Elsewhere, however, he states that we have "the highest probabilities" for religion, but can demonstrate nothing ("Life of Lucian," Works, XVIII, 66; cf. preface to Religio laici).

41 Anal. pr. i. 1. 24ᵃ 22–ᵇ16; Anal. post. i. 1. 71ᵃ 5–11, 71ᵇ 9–23; Topics 100ᵃ29, 104ᵃ 8; Eth. Nich. vi. 3. 1139ᵇ18–36; and passim.

42 Eth. Nich. i. 3. 1094ᵇ18–28 (Oxford trans.).

43 M. Blundevile, The arte of logick (London, 1617), Book V,
    chaps. xvii, xx, xxi. Cf. also Thomas Spencer, The art of
    logick (London, 1628), Part II, chaps. liv, lv; Robert Sander-
    son, Logicae artis compendium (4th ed.; Oxford, 1640),
    chap. xvii; Gerard Vossius, De logices et rhetoricae (1668),
    chap. xiii.

44 The Port-Royal logic, trans. Baynes (8th ed.; Edinburgh,
    n. d.), pp. 4–5; cf. pp. 299–308.

45 Logick (4th ed.; London, 1731), p. 175; see also pp. 253–
    59, and passim.

46 Meric Casaubon, Of credulity and incredulity (London, 1668),
    pp. 6–7.

47 Joseph Glanvill, Scepsis scientifica, ed. Owen (London,
    1885), pp. 179–80. See also "Of scepticism, and certainty,"
    pp. 44–51, and "The agreement of reason and religion,"
    pp. 5–6, 20, and passim, in Essays on several important
    subjects in philosophy and religion (London, 1676). Cf.
    Robert Boyle, "The reconcileableness of reason and reli-
    gion," Theological works, ed. Boulton (London, 1715), I,
    417–29; and John Tillotson, "Preface," Works (8th ed.;
    London, 1720), fol. B1^v–B2^r; cf. also p. 585.

48 Essay concerning human understanding, ed. Fraser (Ox-
    ford, 1894), Book IV, chaps. i–iii and xiv–xvi.

49 Ibid., chap. iii, pp. 208, 212; cf. also chap. x.

50 See the passages cited above, n. 47.

DRYDEN AS HISTORIOGRAPHER-ROYAL: THE AUTHORSHIP OF HIS MAJESTIES DECLARATION DEFENDED, 1681

Roswell G. Ham

The dignified but unremunerative position of Poet Laureate came to Dryden six days after the death of D'Avenant in 1668.[1] It was not, however, until August 18, 1670, that Charles in a joint patent designated him Historiographer-Royal as well, and "for his great Witt and elegant Style in Verse & prose" granted him

> the rights priviledges benefitts and advantages, therevnto belonging as fully and amply as Sir Geoffery Chaucer knight Sir john Gower knight john Leland Esquire William Camden Esquire Beniamin johnson Esquire james Howell Esquire Sir William Davenant knight or any other person or persons haveing or exerciseing the place or employment of Poet Laureat or historiographer or either of them in the time of our Royall progenitors.[2]

The list is a singular medley, out of which those names appertaining to the laureateship and its functions have been sufficiently discussed. But to the post of Historiographer-Royal, or General, as it was occasionally termed, has been directed little attention, and virtually none at all to its bearing upon John Dryden. He was appointed, we read, for his excellency as much in prose as in verse, was paid the comfortable stipend of £200 a year—though with no designated part of the salary depending upon the post of historiographer[3]—and presumably was active in the exercise of his duties. But exactly what were they? Could we but answer that question, it might be possible to subdivide in a more satisfactory fashion his various political and literary activities, and in addition, begin to identify, perhaps, a considerable body of anonymous prose tracts as issuing from his hand.

Reprinted from Review of English Studies, Vol. 11 (1935), pp. 284–298, by permission of the author and the publisher.

First, as to the antiquity of the post, we may note that, among the historians mentioned in the patent, Leland appears to have been appointed King's antiquary, without, however, either predecessor or follower. Camden was royally esteemed, given great encouragement, and made Clarenceux king-of-arms; but so far as discovered he was never officially designated the Royal historiographer.[4] On the other hand, a certain Bernard Andreas, to whom the patent makes no allusion, under Henry VIII combined the title as did Dryden with that of Poet Laureate.[5] One explanation of the reappearance of the Historiographer, after the lapse of so many years, is very likely to be found somewhere in the travels of Charles II, particularly in France. "C'est à la fin du XVIᵉ siècle qu'apparaît le titre officiel d'historiographe."[6] The list of French historiographers had been distinguished by the names of Pierre Pascal and the earlier Balzac; it was to have in its line Boileau, Racine, and Voltaire. From this Gallic precedent very likely it was that James Howell argued for his designation to the post in 1661. "Among the prudentest and best policed nations," said he, "there is a Minister of State appointed and qualified with the title of Historiographer Generall."[7] Whether this was his original suggestion or that of Charles himself, Howell received the appointment, and apparently so much esteemed it as a climax to his career that upon his tombstone in the Temple Church he was noted Regius Historiographus, with the pertinent addition, in Anglia primus.[8]

What we may know, then, concerning the requirements of the office, as held by John Dryden, is to be deduced from its character under Howell; and happily with him there enter no complexities of the laureateship. In one place, he writes of himself as "a free historian"; and, indeed, his published works, especially those issued immediately upon his appointment, were of such a character. Tractarian and in general the political apologetics for royalty, they utilized history as a justification of theory. Thus among the Twelve Treatises, published in 1661 over his new title of "His Majesties Historiographer Royal" are to be found the following suggestive captions: His Majesties Royal Declaration, Sway of the Sword, and Vindication of his Majesty. Later, 1664, he published A Discours of Dunkirk with some Reflexes upon the late surrender thereof and A Discourse Concerning the Precedency of Kings.[9] No single title in the lot is history in our accepted sense of the word.

DRYDEN AS HISTORIOGRAPHER-ROYAL

With this background in mind we may turn our attention to Dryden. In the period of Dryden's incumbency, 1670–88, there is an apparent lacuna of no tractarian or historical activity for a full decade after appointment, unless we may consider his tragedy of Amboyna, 1673, as a royally inspired attack upon the Dutch. But in the same area no title seems any more definitely to partake of the laureate's function. It is not until 1680 that we have a clear indication that his post of historiographer was anything more than a sinecure. In that year a correspondent of November 27 startles us by his allusion to the purchase of "that History of Dryden's".[10] To what work this unnoted and chance remark may refer remains unsettled, for in the accepted canon of the poet-historian there is no clear title in print. Somewhat questionably it may have been the Annus Mirabilis or Amboyna, though each seems a bit too far removed in time and character to be acceptable. Probabilities point either to a lost or to an unidentified work.

Looking over the bibliography of Dryden, we may note certain titles as of the same general character as those of Howell. The active years naturally fall during the stormy 'eighties, a period of immense tractarian ferment. Quite definitely both the play of The Duke of Guise, 1683, and its elaborate Vindication, of the same year, were in the correct mode. Likewise Maimbourg's History of the League, "translated into English by His Majesty's Command by Mr. Dryden," 1684, carries on the tradition. Most important to us are the long political disquisitions that preface and conclude the work. A Defence of the Papers Written by the late King of Blessed Memory, and Duchess of York, 1686, "by authority," and a translation of The Life of St. Francis Xavier, 1688, drew this particular activity to a conclusion. But what of Absalom and Achitophel, The Medal, and The Hind and the Panther? What of certain of his political prologues and epilogues? From contemporary gossip we know that several of these were inspired by royal command. They are argumentative or apologetic in character. The fact that they are also great poetry need not conceal their essential kinship to the work of both Dryden and Howell in a more prosaic field. Finally, it is probable that Dryden in these years either supervised or composed a number of the tracts published "by Royal Command." Their identification, while tantalizing, is not impossible.

In this connection new evidence has recently been published corroborative of Dryden's activity as historiographer, with some considerable illumination as to his duties. Until the appearance in 1933 of the second volume of Winston Churchill's study of Marlborough it had remained unobserved that Dryden was closely identified with an unpublished narrative of the early years of James II. Some allusion to this work had appeared in the writings of Charles James Fox, but the latter had curiously failed to identify its editor. Thus he remarked that:

> There were in the Scotch College [Paris] two distinct manuscripts, one in James's own hand, consisting of papers of different sizes bound up together, the other a sort of historical narrative, compiled from the former. The narrative was <u>said</u> to have been revised and corrected, as to style, by Dryden the poet, (meaning probably Charles Dryden, the great poet's son) and it was not known in the College whether it was drawn up in James's life, or by the direction of his son, the Pretender.[11]

That it was not Charles but John Dryden, his father, who edited this narrative would appear conclusive from a letter dated 1740, from Mr. Thomas Inesse (or Inese), one-time principal of the Scots College. Inesse remarked that to the adaptation of James's Memoires there was appended a note, in the hand of his predecessor, to this effect:

> [Transcribed in 3 volumes in 4^0 from the Kings original Memoires by M. Dryden the famous Poet, in the year 1686, and afterwards revised by his Majesty, and in Severall places corrected in his own hand.]

He thus comments:

> There are besides some other Markes upon this Copy of Mr. Dryden by which it would appear that A. D. 1686 when it was made it was making ready for the Press and probably it had been published, if the unhappy Revolution had not soon after fallen out.

> This Copy is indeed very valuable in itself being
> made under his late Majesty's eye, and no doubt all
> the differences in it from the Original have been made
> by H. Ms. directions or by himself. . . .[12]

Whether the text in Dryden's hand was subsequently lost is left
in some obscurity. In any event we have here a dim sketch of
Dryden pursuing his appointed task, at times under the closest
supervision of the King, at others acting in the capacity of what
we should now term "His Majesty's Ghost-writer."

We approach at this point the specific problem of a tractarian work variously assigned and denied the authorship of the
historiographer. The twenty-page pamphlet entitled His Majesties Declaration Defended, 1681,[13] was, with two other works
assigned to him, easily dismissed by Mr. Henry B. Wheatley
in his bibliography of the poet. He remarked that "There does
not seem to be any evidence for the attribution of these treatises
to Dryden." But it was not so simple. For Mr. Percy J. Dobell,
in his John Dryden, Bibliographical Memoranda,[14] observed
that he had in his possession a copy with the contemporary
manuscript notation, "Written by Mr. John Dryden." These
early attributions, however, have been found notoriously unreliable, if for nothing else than the fact that anonymous works
by force of gravity tend to be attracted to the greatest contemporary names. And so it might rest.

But we must note the date of its appearance— some five
or six months before the publication of Absalom and Achitophel,
Pt. I. The latter may have been undertaken at the hint of Charles
some time in February or March, 1680–1.[15] It was shortly
afterwards, May 26, 1681, that The Observator discussed the
whiggish Letter from a Person of Quality— the immediate provocation of our pamphlet— "as one of the most daring papers
yet come to light"; and again, on June 22, mentions His Majesties Declaration Defended as an "Answer to that Cursed Letter
you and I were talking of tother day; and an Excellent Piece."
Thus, apparently falling between the two dates, its publication
would easily adjust itself to the time scheme of Dryden's activity, actually during the composition of his poetic masterpiece.
Its title is interesting, as a kind of reminiscence of Howell's
similar activity with His Majesties Declaration. All this, how-

ever, is inconclusive evidence, except to show that the piece might by time and character have issued from the King's Historiographer.

More immediately to the point is a new bit of external evidence recently discovered in Echard's History of England. The quotation is so much to the point of our discussion that I venture to reprint it almost in full. The King's Declaration itself came after the dissolution of the Oxford Parliament:[16]

> On the same Day [remarks Echard] it was Order'd by his Majesty in Council, That the said Declaration be forthwith Printed and Publish'd, and Read in all Churches and Chappels throughout this Kingdom; which for the most part was Chearfully obey'd, and with remarkable Success. To weaken the natural Effects of a Thing so Popular, there came out two celebrated pieces, the First Entituled, A Just and Modest Vindication of the Proceedings of the two last Parliaments, ascrib'd to the ingenious Pen of Sir William Jones. . . . The second Piece was call'd A Letter from a Person of Quality to his Friend,[17] concerning his Majesty's late Declaration, &c. the Author of which very freely tells us, "That there never was more Occasion for a Parliament, than at the Opening of the last, held at Westminster; never had People juster Fears, nor of weightier Consideration, to be secured against; never were our Liberties and Properties more in Danger; nor the Protestant Religion more expos'd to an utter Extirpation both at Home and Abroad." Speaking of the Person of the King, he informs us, "In his Private Capacity as a Man, he can only Eat and Drink, and perform some other Acts of Nature; but that all his Actings without Himself, are only as a King, and in his Politick Capacity he ought not to Marry, Love, Hate, make War, Friendship or Peace, but as King, and agreeable to the People, and their Interest he governs." And as to the Lords rejecting Fitz-Harris's Impeachment, he says Their Votes wou'd not have born a Conference. This Author was soon after lash'd by the Satyrical Pen of Mr. John Dryden, who undertook to expose the Exorbitancies of Him and his Friends, and to vindicate the Honour and Dignity

of the House of Lords, as to the Case of Fitz-Harris, and to shew that they ought in such Matters to be sole Judges. Without which, he says, The Number of Impeachments wou'd be so increased, that the Peers wou'd have no time for any other Business of the Publick. Again, The Commons may make Spaniels of the Lords, throw them a Man, and bid them go Judge, as we command a Dog to Fetch and Carry.[18]

The sentences quoted as by Dryden may be readily identified upon p. 18 of His Majesties Declaration Defended.

Still we may enquire with what authority Echard spoke when he assigned the pamphlet to Dryden. Something of an answer is discoverable in the historian's bibliography. Born c. 1670, Echard had received his B. A. by 1691, and immediately thereafter launched into a literary career that should have brought him into contact with Dryden. His preface to a translation of Plautus, 1694, is noteworthy for an extended panegyric to the poet, amply repeated the same year in the Terence, which has commonly been attributed to him. Dryden was then so much the arbiter of all matters concerning translation and so susceptible to praise that it seems most likely that they corresponded. But probabilities unhappily do not always carry conviction, and so we are forced to fall back upon gossip. An allusion of 1718 is called to the attention of Dryden's bibliographers for whatever it is worth. Its coincidence at this point is striking.

For a number of years during the second decade of the eighteenth century, the Rev. John Thomlinson of Rothbury, Cumberland, kept a diary rich in antiquarian and literary interest. His principal source of information seems to have been an uncle, born 1651 and graduated from Emmanuel College, Cambridge. The latter gives, perhaps, whatever authenticity may be allowed the following entry:

> 1718. Aug. 3rd. Eachard's history commended by Dr. Ellison. Uncle says he never heard it commended before—he flags in his Roman History, the two first volumes only good—Dryden corrected his first volume which made it excellent.[19]

According to a statement in his Preface to Vol. III, Echard wrote only the first two volumes of his Roman History; and elsewhere (adv. to 2d Edit.) he remarked that aid was lent him in respect to style "by persons of the greatest judgment in these matters, whose names I ought not to mention without their particular leave." This much we do know certainly, that Dryden was ever unsparing of his advice and active assistance to the minor writers of his time, and that a certain plausibility would be added to the chance remark by his definite interest in historical composition. For our purposes, of course, there remains this conclusion: if Echard was so assisted by Dryden, the truth of his attribution to the latter of the Declaration Defended becomes much less open to challenge. He would have been sufficiently close to the final source of information to make it first hand and authentic.

It is, however, upon internal evidence that we must finally rest our case for Dryden's authorship; and here the task of tracing parallels of thought and phrase holds a singular interest. The Declaration Defended anticipated Absalom and Achitophel by only a few months, not to mention The Medal and The Duke of Guise, with a considerable body of brilliantly argued tory doctrine. Could it be proved Dryden's it might illuminate various fine points of the latter creations in addition to rendering valuable testimony upon his activity as historiographer. It is too long and too elaborate in argument for any but the briefest survey in this place. But by the quotation of a sufficient number of passages, apposite to Dryden's in thought or style, we may produce something of an outline that should serve the twofold purpose of clinching the argument for his authorship, and of revealing some added subtleties of his political theory.

After certain preliminary remarks the author sets himself the task of answering, head by head, the various arguments of "The Person of Quality," reproducing them verbatim and italicizing them in the text in the same manner as that subsequently employed by Dryden in his Vindication of The Duke of Guise. The second printed page immediately produces a notable parallel of which the context is immaterial, beyond the fact that the quotation is very much more to the point in the doubtful than in the canonized work. In this and in nearly all other cases, The Declaration Defended has priority in time—a fact to be remembered, since Dryden frequently imitated himself but rarely his contemporaries. The writer is discussing the subject of addresses:

> My Lord Mayor [he remarks] might have only been
> troubled to have carried the Addresses of <u>Southwark</u>,
> &c. of another nature: without his offering them with
> one hand, and the City Petition with the other; like the
> Childrens play of, this Mill grinds Pepper and Spice;
> that Mill grinds Ratts and Mice. (<u>Decl. Def.</u>, p. 4.)

In the <u>Vindication of The Duke of Guise</u> we have:

> Hitherto there is nothing but boys' play in our
> authors: <u>My mill grinds pepper and spice, your mill
> grinds rats and mice</u>. (<u>Vind.</u>, II, 127.)[20]

The next paragraph defends the King against the charge of a
subtle design to break the power of Commons:

> if it succeeded, not capable of making him so truly
> Great as he is by Law already. If we add to this,
> his Majesties natural love to Peace and Quiet, which
> increases in every man with his years, this ridicu-
> lous supposition will vanish of itself. (<u>Decl. Def.</u>, p. 5.)

The analogous quotation—earlier in this case—is of interest
not so much from phrase as from its parallel thought:

> A King who is just and moderate in his nature,
> who rules according to the laws, whom God made
> happy by forming the temper of his soul to the con-
> stitution of his government. . . . (<u>All for Love</u>, Ded.,
> II, 5.)

The charge that the King had exceeded his powers in having his
<u>Declaration</u> "read publicly in Churches" brings this response:

> And if the Clergy obey him in so just a Design,
> is this to be nam'd a blind Obedience! . . . 'Tis
> enough that this Declaration is evidently the Kings,
> and the only true exception which our Answerer has
> to it, is that he would deny his Majesty the power of
> clearing his intentions to the people. (<u>Decl. Def.</u>, p. 5.)

It is noteworthy that Dryden alluded at least twice subsequently to this reading of the King's Declaration, "publicly in churches." His interest in it may thus have had an earlier expression:

> Men cite his Majesty's last Declaration against those
> who dare trifle with parliaments; a Declaration by the
> way, which you endeavoured not to have read publicly
> in churches. . . . (Vind. II, 113. Cf. Hist. of the
> League, Ded., II, 433.)

The sixth page contains an interesting allusion to Sancho Panza as governor of the Isle of Barataria being, like Charles, deprived of his food because, forsooth, he was a public person; and so throughout the tract its author reveals himself as a man of letters. The same page has a curious usage, "quatenus a King," that may be compared to the "Quatenus subjects" of the Vindication, II, 120. Immediately thereafter follows some treatment of the Commons' desire to curtail the King's prerogatives:

> Oh, but there is a wicked thing call'd the Militia in
> their way, and they shew'd they had a moneths mind
> to it, at the first breaking out of the Popish Plot. If
> they could once persuade his Majesty, to part gra-
> ciously with that trifle . . . their argument would be
> an hundred times more clear. (Decl. Def., p. 6.)

When the representatives of the Commons were either mortally afraid, or pretended to be so, of this airy invasion, a request was actually made to the King, that he would put the militia into their hands. (The History of the League, Postscript, II, 465.)

> Kings, who disband such needless aids as these,
> Are safe—as long as e'er their subjects please:
> (Prologue to The Loyal Brother, p. 123.)

The argument continues in the same vein:

> he shall be Kept so bare of Money, that Twelve Holland
> ships shall block up the River, or he shall be forc'd to
> cast himself upon a House of Commons, and to take
> Money upon their Terms, which will sure be as easie,
> as those of an Usurer to an Heir in want. (Decl. Def., p. 6.)

> Alph. Is there any seeming kindness between the King
>   and the Duke of Guise?
> Cril. Yes, most wonderful: they are as dear to one an-
>   other as an old usurer and a rich young heir
>   upon a mortgage.
>   (Duke of Guise, V, i, ll. 32 ff.)

> The thrifty Sanhedrin shall keep him poor;
> And every shekel which he can receive,
> Shall cost a limb of his prerogative.
>   (Abs. and Achit., p. 114, ll. 390 ff.)

The Declaration Defended, p. 6, remarks upon a design to push
the King into a French war, the same end in view. With this
compare the Prologue to The Duke of Guise:

> Push him to wars, but still no pence advance,
> Let him lose England, to recover France.

I am able to find no parallels for the matter upon pp. 7–8, which
is largely given over to an airy consideration of the Duchesses
of Mazarine and Portsmouth and of their influence. It is handled
in a style akin to Dryden's best manner. Page 9 has a reference
to "the most ingenious of your Authors, I mean Plato Redivivus,"
who reappears on p. 13. That Dryden had attentively read this
whiggish pamphleteer of 1680 is evident from the Postscript to
The History of the League (II, 463. Cf. Malone's note.) The
same page of the Declaration Defended contains a long section
demonstrating the parallel to English conditions of the Guisard
League in France, a theme to which Dryden subsequently devoted his tragedy The Duke of Guise, a Vindication, and a History.
    The next quoted passage contains a remarkable argument
that the author apparently derived from Hobbes. Dryden's debt
to the philosopher of Malmesbury has been recognized and was
acknowledged. Thus Noyes in a note upon a kindred passage in
Absalom and Achitophel makes the following remarks:

> Unlike most Tories, [Dryden] grounds the royal power
> not on divine right, but on a covenant made by the
> governed, to avoid the anarchy of a state of nature

where all have a right to all. He thus shows his
sceptical turn of mind by accepting a fundamental
tenet of Hobbes. He will not, however, agree with
Hobbes that this covenant once made is irrevocable,
since such a conclusion leaves the people defence-
less. Yet he sees, as well as Hobbes himself, that
to admit that the governed can revoke their covenant, opens the door to anarchy.[21]

The Defender's argument is much to the same effect:

But what can we think of his next Axiome,
that it was never known that Laws signified anything to a People, who had not the sole guard of
their own Prince, Government and Laws?
Here all our Fore-fathers are Arraign'd at
once for trusting the Executive power of the Laws
in their Princes hands. And yet you see the Government has made a shift to shuffle on for so many
hundred years together, under this miserable oppression; and no man so wise in so many ages to
find out, that Magna Charta was to no purpose,
while there was a King. I confess in Countreys,
where the Monarch governs absolutely, and the Law
is either his Will, or depending on it, this noble
Maxim might take place; But since we are neither
Turks, Russians, nor Frenchmen, to affirm that in our
Countrey, in a Monarchy of so temperate and whole-
some a Constitution, Laws are of no validity, because they are not in the disposition of the People,
plainly infers that no Government but that of a Commonwealth can preserve our Liberties and Priviledges:
for though the Title of a Prince be allow'd to continue,
yet if the People must have the sole guard and Government of him and of the Laws, 'tis but facing an whole
hand of Trumps, with an insignificant King of another
sute. And which is worst of all, if this be true, there
can be no Rebellion, for then the people is the supream
power. And if the Representatives of the Common
shall jarr with the other two estates, and with the King
it would be no Rebellion to adhere to them in that War:

146

to which I know that every Republican who reads this,
must of necessity Answer, <u>No more it would not</u>. Then
farewell the Good Act of Parliament, which makes it
Treason to Levy Arms, against the present King, upon
any pretences whatsoever. For if this be a Right of
Nature, and consequently never to be Resign'd, there
never has been, nor ever can be any pact betwixt King
and People, and Mr. <u>Hobbs</u> would tell us, <u>That we are
still in a state of War</u>. (Decl. Def., pp. 9–10.)

The argument has many parallels in Dryden, both of phrase and
thought, of which the following perhaps may serve:

> <u>What shall we think</u>! Can people give away,
> Both for themselves and sons, their native sway?
> Then they are left defenseless to the sword
> Of each unbounded, arbitrary lord:
> And laws are vain, by which we right enjoy,
> If kings unquestion'd can those laws destroy.
> Yet if the crowd by judge of fit and just,
> And kings are only officers in trust,
> Then this resuming cov'nant was declar'd
> When Kings were made, or is forever barr'd.
> > (Abs. and Achit., p. 119, ll. 759 ff.)

> Our temp'rate isle will no extremes sustain
> Of pop'lar sway or arbitrary reign,
> But slides between them both into the best;
> Secure in freedom, in a monarch blest.
> > (The Medal, p. 131, ll. 248 ff.)

> He should have leave to exercise the name,
> And hold the cards, while commons play'd the game.
> > (The Medal, p. 131, ll. 233–34.)

> If Kings may be excluded, or depos'd,
> When e'er you cry Religion to the Crowd,
> That Doctrine makes Rebellion Orthodox,
> And subjects must be Traytors to be sav'd.
> > (The Duke of Guise, Act. 1, scene i.)

> Not only crowds, but Sanhedrins may be
> Infected with this public lunacy, . . .
> If they may give and take when e'er they please,
> Not kings alone, (the Godhead's images,)
> But government itself at length must fall
> To nature's state, where all have right to all.
>> (Abs. and Achit., p. 119, ll. 787 ff.)

The eleventh page has some material upon the duplicity of the Irish witnesses, which remind one of the couplet in Absalom and Achitophel:

> Against themselves their witnesses will swear,
> Till viper-like their mother Plot they tear.
>> (Abs. and Achit., p. 122, ll. 1012–13.)

The twelfth deals with the succession and Divine Right:

> We read of a divine Command to obey Superior Powers; and the Duke will lawfully be such, no Bill of Exclusion having passed against him in his Brother's life. (Decl. Def., p. 12.)

> Yes, I can tell them one other way to express their loyalty, which is, to obey the King, and to respect his brother as the next lawful successor: their religion commands them both, and the government is secured in so doing. (Vindication, II, 112.)

In an identical juxtaposition in both places follows the praise of the Duke's rival, Monmouth:

> I am not ashamed to say, that I particularly honour the Duke of Monmouth. (Decl. Def., p. 12.)

> And I am of their number who truly honour him [Monmouth]. (Vindication, II, 112. Cf. also Preface to Abs. and Achit., II, 296–97.)

But Monmouth would shortly discover the rapacity of his adherents:

Conquerors are not easily to be curbed. And it is yet
harder to conceive, that his [Monmouth's] pretended
Friends, even design him so much as that. At present,
'tis true, their mutual necessities keep them fast together, . . . but suppose the business compassed, as
they design'd it, how many, and how contradicting interests are to be satisfied! Every Sect of High Shooes
would then be uppermost; and not one of them endure
the toleration of another. (Decl. Def., p. 12.)

> And frogs and toads, and all the tadpole train,
> Will croak to Heav'n for help from this devouring crane.
> The cutthroat sword and clamorous gown shall jar,
> In sharing their ill-gotten spoils of war. . . .
> (The Medal, p. 132, ll. 304 ff.)

And the Protestant successor himself, if he be not
wholly governed by the prevailing party, will first be
declared no Protestant; and next no successor . . . .
none but a pack of Sectaries and Commonwealthmen
[will be] left in England. (Decl. Def., p. 13.)

our associators and sectaries are men of commonwealth principles, and though their first stroke was
only aimed at the immediate succession, it was most
manifest that it would not there have ended, for at the
same time they were hewing at your royal prerogatives;
so that the next successor, if there had been any, must
have been a precarious prince, and depended on them
for the necessities of life. (History of the League,
Ded. II, 432.)

Now comes an attack upon the Person of Quality into which more
of the rhetorician entered than of the Historiographer:

> I will forgive him two false Grammars and
> three Barbarisms, in every Period of his Pam-
> phlet. (Decl. Def., p. 13.)

Correctness was ever a shibboleth to the laureate—witness his
earlier attack upon Elkanah Settle:

149

> what is here is only selected fustian, impertinence,
> and false grammar . . . for I am sure there are no
> four lines together, which are free from some
> errour, and commonly a gross one. (Notes and Ob-
> servations on The Empress of Morocco, II, 279.)

Page 15 of the Declaration Defended has much to do with the
various petitions of Commons for the removal of Charles's
friends:

> without Process, order of Law, hearing any De-
> fence, or offering any proof against them. (Decl.
> Def., p. 15.)

The argument appears elsewhere, and frequently. He asks:

> whether frequent votes did not pass in the House
> of Commons at several times for removing and
> turning out of office those who on all occasions
> behaved themselves most loyally to the King, with-
> out so much as giving any other reason of their
> misdemeanours than publick fame,—that is to say,
> reports forged and spread by their own faction; or
> without allowing them the common justice of vindi-
> cating themselves from those calumnies and asper-
> sions. (History of the League, Postscript, II, 420.)

> > No groundless clamors shall my friends remove,
> > Nor crowds have pow'r to punish ere they prove,
> > For gods and godlike kings their care express,
> > Still to defend their servants in distress.
> > > (Abs. and Achit., p. 122, ll. 995 ff.)

As to the King being a public servant with the right in his private
capacity only to eat and drink, there is sketched on the next page
a sorry picture of Charles's misadventures under the Scottish
kirk, a matter less capably handled but to the same effect in his
Postscript to The History of the League (II, 442).

Page 18 is concerned with the Fitz-Harris matter, which nowhere in Dryden's accepted works is given such consideration.
Nor has p. 19 or p. 20 much more to the immediate point, though

the final page provides an allusion to Æsop's ass, for which he
showed some fondness in the Vindication (II, 113), also the statement that his opponent admits himself an angry man, which was
a line of attack later employed upon Hunt, and, finally, some
triumphing over his whiggish enemies as their dissolution com-
menced to set in:

> his party is mouldring away, and as it falls out, in
> all dishonest Combinations, are suspecting each
> other so very fast, that everyman is shifting for him-
> self, by a separate Treaty: and looking out for a
> Plank in the common Shipwreck. (Decl. Def., p. 20.)

Identical to this in substance is the following:

> the scene is changed, and they are more in danger of
> being betrayed every man by his companion, than they
> were formerly by the joint forces of their enemies.
> (Hist. of the League, Postscript, II, 456.)

Thus, 1681–1684 witnessed the growing estate of the Historiographer Royal—years in which he wielded an influence
comparable to that of the great pamphleteers of the next century. And that His Majesties Declaration Defended was possibly the first important exercise of his powers in the political
field does not seem an unsafe deduction from the evidence at
hand. It has with some show of authority been attributed to his
pen; it is completely in accord with his tory doctrine, containing as it does hardly an idea that he does not advert to somewhere in his accepted writings; and it has, finally, notable
similarities both to his phrasing and rhetorical usage. Parallels between diverse authors might easily occur, but not so ex-
tensively nor so systematically as here; nor, as remarked,
would Dryden scarcely have echoed in his admitted works the
phrase and thoughts of an anonymous pamphleteer—other than
himself. He was both proud and vulnerable. If, then, I have
seemed to quote from it at too great length, it has been from
the desire not merely to fix its authorship, but to provide some
taste of its style, otherwise denied because of excessive rarity.
The Declaration Defended seems to have been Dryden's. Its
importance to his other poems and pamphlets in the same vein

is that the ideas in this tract were developed with an illuminating clarity not always touched elsewhere. It displays him in the full possession of his official manner. 'Tis pity that no other such historiographer was present to carry forward the tradition.

NOTES

1 E. K. Broadus, The Laureateship, Oxford, 1921, p. 60.

2 "Chaucer, Dryden and the Laureateship," a note by Eleanore Boswell, R.E.S., vii, 27, 338.

3 L. I. Bredvold, "Notes on John Dryden's Pension," Modern Philology, xxx, 268–9.

4 D.N.B. Articles: Camden, Leland.

5 Broadus, op.cit., p. 25.

6 Nouveau Larousse Illustré. Article: historiographe.

7 Broadus, p. 62.

8 Notes and Queries, clv, 445.

9 W. A. Vann, Notes on the Writings of James Howell, passim.

10 Hist. MSS. Comm., 12 Rpt., App., pt. vii, p. 175.

11 C. J. Fox, A History of the Early Part of the Reign of James the Second, London, 1808, p. xx. Quoted by Churchill.

12 Winston S. Churchill, Marlborough, His Life and Times, New York, 1933, II, 61. Without offering a final conclusion, I may suggest that Clarke's edition of The Life of James the Second, London, 1816, gives us substantially the work of Dryden in Part I of the biography, detailing the events before 1660. The problem is, however, highly involved and will require additional study.

13 His Majesties /DECLARATION /DEFENDED: /In a LETTER to a Friend. / BEING AN /ANSWER /TO A /Seditious Pamphlet, /CALLED /A LETTER from a Person of Quality / to his Friend: /CONCERNING /The King's late Declaration touching the Reasons /which moved him to Dissolve /THE TWO LAST /PARLIAMENTS /AT /WESTMINSTER and OXFORD. /LONDON: /Printed for T. Davies, 1681. / Colla-

tion: Folio, 20 pp. consisting of 1–2 t–p, verso blank; 3–20 text. Signatures, beginning with p. 3 are A2, 2 leaves; B–D in 2's; E, 1 leaf; preceded by one leaf bearing title-page. (Yale Library.)

14 Pp. 17–18.

15 Cf. Malone, Prose Works of John Dryden, I, i, 141–142.

16 Publ. April 8, 1681.

17 A Letter from a Person of Quality to his Friend concerning His Majesties late Declaration touching the Reasons which moved him to dissolve the Two last Parliaments at Westminster and Oxford. n.d. (Yale Library.)

18 L. Echard, The History of England, London, 1718, iii, 626–27.

19 Six North Country Diaries, ed. J. C. Hodgson (Surtees Soc.), London, 1910, p. 130.

20 All quotations from Dryden's prose are from Malone, The Prose Works of John Dryden, London, 1800. The verse is quoted from The Poetical Works of John Dryden, ed. Noyes, Cambridge, 1908.

21 The Poetical Works of John Dryden, p. 954.

III. <u>MAC FLECKNOE</u>, <u>ABSALOM AND ACHITOPHEL</u>, <u>RELIGIO LAICI</u>

DRYDEN'S MAC FLECKNOE. A VINDICATION[1]

G. Thorn-Drury

In the course of what he describes as stating the case for
Dryden's authorship of Mac Flecknoe "clearly and impartially,"
Mr. Babington cites Scott's opinion that "there existed no contemporary poet to whom so masterly a production could have
been ascribed." From this sentence he has omitted the words
"even with remote probability," and with them, he seems to
have given up all idea of dealing with such considerations as
they suggest. He is free, therefore, to abstain from making any
appeal to the "ear" of those who are familiar with Dryden and
Oldham, and need not attempt to explain how the latter, who in
his published satires presses all sorts of words into the service
as rhymes, and is very often content to get on without any, was
able upon one occasion to achieve the almost uniform correctness of this poem.

Upon the broad question of its poetical qualities, Scott's
view, in agreement with that of every competent critic who
has ever written upon Dryden, will satisfy most people, but
in the aspect of the case presented by Mr. Babington, in which
personal character is so seriously involved, something more
may, and, in the writer's judgment, ought to be said.

The morality of Dryden appears to vary in Mr. Babington's
estimate with the exigencies of his argument; for he, who we
are invited on p. 31 of his paper to think "would have been too
magnanimous to chastise in 1682 a man who had died four years
before," is presented on p. 34 as one who, in circumstances of
peculiar meanness, stole the best work of a dead friend, of
whom he had written with affectionate regret.

It is not in these terms that Mr. Babington states his conclusion, but he goes so far as to admit that it is "a rather ugly
one"; it is indeed, and he does not make it less hideous by de-

Reprinted from Modern Language Review XIII (1918), pp. 276-81 by permission of Modern Humanities Research Association and of the Editors.

scribing the thievish conduct of which he accuses Dryden by
any form of words such as "adopted as his own." This is the
euphemism which he employs, and whether it was intended
to do so or not, it cannot but suggest, even to those who know
little more of Dryden and Oldham than their names, a ribald
travesty of the second of the beautiful lines:

> Farewell too little and too lately known,
> Whom I began to think, and call my own;

This is not the occasion for any review of the attacks that were
made upon Dryden's life and work by some of his contemporaries: it is sufficient to say that his name remains, after all,
one of the greatest in English literature, and when an odious
charge such as this is brought against him, we have a right to
require of his accuser some adequate measure of care, accuracy and knowledge.

Mr. Babington tells us that in a MS.[2] in the Bodleian Library, among other pieces copied out fair, in Oldham's writing,
for the printer or to hand to friends, he found "Mac Fleckno,
A Satyr," bearing the date "A⁰ 1678." This discovery of what
he takes to be the author's autograph MS. is the foundation of
the indictment he has preferred against Dryden. He goes on to
say that he is apparently the first person who has had occasion
to make "a thorough examination" of this MS.

It is submitted that something considerably short of a thorough examination of that portion of it upon which he relies for
his conclusion will demonstrate that, so far from being the
author's MS., it is only a partial transcript and a bad one at
that.

To begin with, Mr. Babington is mistaken in stating that he
found in the MS. "Mac Fleckno, A Satyr," if he intended to suggest, as every one would understand him to do, that it contains
the complete poem. Mac Flecknoe as printed consists of 217
lines, of which 115 only, written on three pieces of paper, one
of them separated by a number of leaves from the other two,
are all that are there.

It is, comparatively speaking, a small point, but it should
be noted that the other pieces in this MS., which Oldham published as his, and which bear dates, are dated, not as this particular piece is, with the year only, but with the month as well,

with, in some cases, the addition (as Mr. Babington noticed, without attaching any importance to the fact) of the places where they were composed.

People who are interested in Dryden are aware that the <u>Mac Flecknoe</u> of 1682 has a number of obvious errors of the press, corrected in 1684[3], of which the following are perhaps the most striking.

(a)   Sir Formals oratory Wit be thine: 1. 168.
          (For <u>Wit</u> read <u>will</u>)
(b)   This is thy Promise, this thy wondrous way, 1. 187.
          (For <u>Promise</u>, read <u>province</u>,)
(c)   He said: but his last words were scarcely heard;
          For Bruce and Longvil had a trap prepared,
          And down they sent the yet declining bard. ll. 211–3.
          (For <u>declining</u> read <u>declaiming</u>)

All these errors occur in the Bodleian MS. which also introduces in l. 41 the reading—truly surprising, if it were in the author's hand—"And big with <u>him</u>" instead of <u>hymn</u>. Oldham may have been as unattractive a character as Mr. Babington, his prospective editor, thinks him; he was not a born fool.

The year to which this piece is assigned in the MS. may or may not be correct. Oldham may have put upon it what he understood, but mistakenly, to be the date of its composition; on the other hand, there is no apparent difficulty in supposing that Dryden did in fact write it in 1678, that it was circulated in MS. and in 1682 was printed from a transcript containing errors, some of which appeared also in that copied by Oldham.

The description of him in the heading as "The True Blew-Protestant Poet" was not, as far as is known, justified at the earlier date by anything Shadwell had then written.

If it be objected that the second of these suggestions with reference to the date of composition is not feasible, because he and Dryden were upon friendly terms at a later period, as is evidenced by Mr. Babington's statement that the prologue to <u>The True Widow</u> was written in 1679, it should be remembered that the writing of prologues and epilogues was with Dryden a matter of business, and that though the precise date of it cannot now be ascertained, this particular prologue was, in all probability, produced before March 21st, 1678.

Mr. Babington finds, so he says, much significance in the subject-matter of the poem; apparently, because 1678 is also the accepted date of Flecknoe's death.

If, which is open to doubt, the passage in the dedication of The Kind Keeper about the poet of "scandalous memory" has any reference to him at all, it affords no ground whatever for supposing that he died in 1678, nor need anyone wonder, as Mr. Babington does, whether words of Dryden in the same place suggested the form of anything alleged to have been written in that year, for the simple reason that The Kind Keeper appeared, not as he supposes in 1678, but in 1680.[4]

One is not much impressed with the parallels: the pregnant brain, the "vile uses" to which the writings of others may or ought to be put, Nature and Art, and even Hannibal as the implacable foe, strike one as being mere common-places, and if it be urged that stress is to be laid rather on the names of particular persons that are introduced, one can only say that most, if not all of them, are almost equally common-places of the period in like connexions: but whatever view may be taken of them, it is obvious that if Mac Flecknoe was available in 1678, the occurrence in it of words and phrases which it is sought to claim for Oldham by reference to his published writings, may point to a conclusion quite different from that at which Mr. Babington wishes to arrive.

Something must be said—a great deal less than might be—about the way in which, apart from any consideration of the Bodleian MS., this charge has been presented.

Scott, one feels sure, would have disclaimed, upon all grounds, the distressing title of "proto-editor," which is conferred on him by Mr. Babington, but the latter appears never to have heard of, or, at least, never to have consulted Malone's laborious work. If he will look at Malone's Dryden, he will find set out in full (I, 169) the statement from the last page of Mac Flecknoe, which he says has been overlooked or ignored by all editors, and (I, 170–3) a collation of the first edition, which, according to him, it does not appear that any of them has examined.

The statement that Scott thanks Malone for a transcript of the title-page of it, is simply Mr. Babington's invention, and there is, beyond the fact that he says it was published not by Tonson but by D. Green, no more ground for suggesting that

DRYDEN'S MAC FLECKNOE. A VINDICATION

Scott "seems interested in Dryden's sudden change of publisher."
There was, of course, no change of publisher: the state of the
text of the Mac Flecknoe of 1682 is sufficient to show that the
publication was unauthorized, and there is no more mystery about
it than there is about the appearance of other things, e.g. Oldham's A Satyr against Virtue, transcripts of which found their
way into bookseller's hands.

It is entirely misleading to suggest, as Mr. Babington allows himself to do, that what he describes as two difficulties
in connexion with the authorship of Mac Flecknoe have never
been recognised or dealt with as such by any editor of Dryden.

With regard to the first of these, it is true that we read in
Scott (Dryden I, 223), "we cannot believe Shadwell's assertion,"
but an impartial statement should have included the qualification
of his disbelief which he expressed as follows (op.cit. X, 433–4),
"From this (Shadwell's) averment, which is probably made far
too broadly, we can only infer that Dryden like Swift in the same
predicament left his adversary to prove what he had no title to
call upon him to confess; for that he seriously meant to disavow
a performance of which he had from the beginning sufficiently
avouched himself the author can hardly be supposed for a moment." Mr. Babington says "All later editors have substantially
endorsed Scott's views," and, "most other editors treat Shadwell as a liar"; statements which, by the light of the passage
just quoted, seem to require modification.

The second supposed difficulty hinges on the date, Oct. 4,
1682, which it is said is "universally accepted" as the day on
which Mac Flecknoe appeared.

The date in question was almost certainly obtained by Malone
from the title-page of the copy which was once Narcissus Luttrell's. That business-like collector was in the habit of inscrib-
ing upon his tracts the prices he paid for those he bought — he
generally succeeded in getting discount — and the date upon which
each came into his possession: sometimes, but most certainly
not always, this was also the date of publication. It was most
probably not so in the case of this poem, for in The Loyal Protestant of Thursday, February 9, 1681/2, in the course of an attack
upon Shadwell, the following passage occurs — "he would send
him (Shadwell) his Recantation next morning, with a Mac Flecknoe, and a brace of Lobsters for his Breakfast; All which he
knew he had a singular aversion for." It is, of course, conceiv-

able, though one is inclined to think that the expression "a Mac Flecknoe" makes it unlikely, that the reference is only to a written copy of the poem, but the fact that it was in existence and apparently well-known early in 1682 disposes of the suggested difficulty of two attacks by Dryden upon Shadwell, with a very brief interval between them.

Mr. Babington appears to be entirely unaware of

(a) the evidence contained in Mulgrave's Essay upon Poetry, 1682, which Dryden says he publicly valued before he knew who the author was[5]:

> The Laureat here may justly claim our praise,
> Crown'd by Mac-Fleckno with immortal Bays;
> Op.cit., p. 10.

(b) the repetition of this couplet in the second edition, of 1691, with two notes to explain that the Laureat is "Mr D——n" and Mac-Fleckno "A famous Poem of his."

(c) the passage in The Laurel, A Poem On The Poet-Laureat, 1685, pp. 21–2:

> Your too keen Satyr, does oblige your Foe,
> As harmless Tom's kind dulness still does you.
> Your Fleckno's kind (tho' still severe enough)
> It arms him Cap-a-pe with Nonsense Proof.

(d) the thrice-repeated statement of Langbaine:

> Now that Mr. Dryden may not think himself slighted in not having some Verses inserted in his Commendation; I will present the Reader with a Copy written by Mr. Flecknoe, and leave him to Judge of his Wit, and Mr. Dryden's Gratitude by comparing the Epistle Dedicatory to his Kind Keeper, and his Satyr call'd Mack Flecknoe, with the following Epigram.— An Account of the English Dramatick Poets. 1691, p. 176.

> For whatever becomes of his own Pieces, his Name will continue whilst Mr. Dryden's Satyr call'd Mack Flecknoe, shall remain in Vogue.—Ibid., p. 199.

DRYDEN'S MAC FLECKNOE. A VINDICATION

> Mr. Dryden, I dare presume, little imagined,
> when he writ that Saytr of Mack-Flecknoe, that the
> subject he there so much exposes and ridicules,
> should have ever lived to have succeeded him in
> wearing the Bays.—Ibid., p. 443.

His ignorance of contemporary publications leaves him in
a ridiculous position with regard to one part of his attack, which
he has casually introduced in a foot-note (p. 26): he is aware of
Sir A. Ward's statement that Dryden does not appear to have
acknowledged Mac Flecknoe before 1692, but rashly assuming
that the knowledge of Sir Adolphus upon the subject is rather
less than his own, he has brought against this great master of
plain English the absolutely preposterous charge of having in
1693, when he wrote "and (if it be not too vain to mention anything of my own) the poems of Absalom and Achitophel and Mac
Flecknoe," "expressed himself so artfully" that he could always
disclaim the second poem, when the fact is he had himself published it under his own name in the previous year.[6]

Mr. Babington has never, it would seem, heard of the suggested identification of Flecknoe as the "R. F.," the writer of
A Letter to the Honourable Ed. Howard, Esq. occasioned by a
Civiliz'd Epistle of Mr. Dryden's before his Second Edition of
his Indian Emperour[7] which it is thought may have provoked
Dryden's ill will, and he is content to ascribe to Oldham attacks
for which he makes no attempt to hint at a motive, beyond offering the amiable suggestion that one of them was due to the fact
that the victim of it was at the time either seriously ill or recently dead!

The statements to which Mr. Babington commits himself
upon the subjects of Rochester's Works, their editors (save the
mark!), and their contents, his idea that Giles Jacob was a contemporary of Oldham and a literary authority to be quoted with
Dryden, and many other points in his paper, invite comment,
but, as these are matters not directly concerned with his main
purpose, it is withheld.

NOTES

1 See Dryden not the Author of "Mac Flecknoe," by Percy L.
Babington, pp. 25 ff. ante.

2 Rawlinson, poet. 123; 14616 in the Summary Catalogue.

3 Miscellany Poems. . . . By the most Eminent Hands . . . London, Printed for Jacob Tonson, 1684, where Mac Flecknoe, Absalom and Achitophel and The Medal, without in any case the author's name, occupy pp. 1-104.

4 The dedication was probably written in the autumn of 1679, but here, as in the case of Dryden's Juvenal, the date on the title-page is adopted as that of publication.

5 Sylvae: Or, The Second Part of Poetical Miscellanies . . . 1685, a3 verso: see also A Discourse on Epick Poetry, Malone, III, 438.

6 Miscellany Poems: In Two Parts. . . . Published by Mr. Dryden. . . . The Second Edition . . . 1692.

7 Gentleman's Magazine, Dec. 1850. Pepys' Diary, ed. Wheatley, VIII, 108. Essays of Dryden, ed. Ker, I, 306.

WHEN DID DRYDEN WRITE MACFLECKNOE?—
SOME ADDITIONAL NOTES

Harold Brooks

Since the late G. Thorn-Drury published the results of his research,[1] 1678 has been generally accepted among Dryden scholars as the year when MacFlecknoe was written. Yet a few
doubts have been raised,[2] and in additional support of his conclusion, one or two fresh points seem worth enumerating.

(1) A couplet in Rochesters Farewell:

> Lewd Messaline was but a Tipe of thee
> Though highest, last degree of Letchery

is a clear debasement of MacFlecknoe, ll. 29, 30:

> Heywood and Shirley were but Types of thee[3]
> Thou last great Prophet of Tautology.

Rochesters Farewell was probably not by Rochester: but its
contents show that it was written before the end of 1680; in
particular, it suggests that Mulgrave may be killed by the
Moors at Tangier; this was no longer a possibility after the
peace of which Luttrell had news December 25, 1680.

(2) Besides those cited by Thorn-Drury and P. L. Babington,[4] there are other parallels between MacFlecknoe and
John Oldham's writings; some of them bear upon the date of
composition. I note an echo of MacFlecknoe, ll. 5, 6:

> In Prose and Verse was own'd without dispute
> Through all the realms of Non-sense, absolute.

Reprinted from Review of English Studies, Vol. 11 (1935), pp. 74–78,
by permission of the author and the publisher.

in Oldham's A Satyr, in Imitation of the Third of Juvenal, where
he describes French intruders who

> . . . love to reign without dispute
> Without a Rival, full, and absolute.

The piece was "Written, May, 1682," so that though the borrowing might come from a printed copy of MacFlecknoe if that was
published in January, it is fresh evidence that Dryden's poem
was not provoked by The Medal of John Bayes, which did not
itself appear till May. Moreover, Oldham's third Satyr upon the
Jesuits, written between June 3, 1679, and the end of 1680, and
most probably in summer 1679, has three reminiscences of
MacFlecknoe. Babington remarked the resemblance between
Oldham's comparison beginning

> As the great Carthaginian . . .

and the similar one in MacFlecknoe, ll. 112 ff.; but not that a
couplet in the same passage

> Now through all Age, when Time or Place soe're
> Shall give you pow'r, wage an immortal War:

contains a verbal echo of MacFlecknoe, l. 12,

> To Reign, and wage immortal War with Wit.

I had marked as inspired by MacFlecknoe another passage from
this satire

> Pray that kind Heav'n would on their hearts dispense
> A Bounteous and abundant Ignorance,
> That they may never swerve, nor turn awry
> From sound and orthodox Stupidity.

when I discovered that Professor J. L. Hill, in an article in St.
Edmund Hall Magazine, 1931, had already drawn attention to it.
Here it is rather a matter of thought and style than of verbal
resemblances: one may, however, compare MacFlecknoe, l. 18,

WHEN DID DRYDEN WRITE MACFLECKNOE?

> Who stands confirm'd in full Stupidity.

and the passages where Flecknoe sheds oblivion on his successor, and urges him to

> advance
> Still in new Impudence, new Ignorance.

(3) These parallels are not likely to be coincidences. Oldham was perhaps the most wholesale borrower who ever made new poetry of what he took, and he was keenly interested in Dryden in 1678 and 1679. His autograph drafts of the Satyrs upon the Jesuits,[5] written for the most part in 1679, contain reminiscences of the Epilogue to The Man of Mode and the Prologue to The Kind Keeper; Oldham specifically refers in the margins to pages of The Indian Emperor and Aureng-Zebe from which he is borrowing, and twice scribbles down lines from All for Love, to which these Satyrs owe several phrases.

(4) The transcript of MacFlecknoe preserved in the same MS., and with the date "A⁰. 1678" at its head, is undoubtedly in Oldham's autograph. Van Doren[6] describes the MS. as "containing most of John Oldham's works transcribed by a single hand as if for the printer, under the title Poems on Several Occasions," and further on is inclined to think that "the safest deduction" is "that the whole of the volume at Oxford was transcribed after Oldham's death by an admirer, perhaps a literary executor." This is an unfortunate lapse. The fair copies of Poems written on Several Occasions do not extend beyond p. 64ᵇ. They are followed by a mass of MS. in the same hand, which includes drafts of many of Oldham's poems with erasures and tentative revisions such as can have been the work of no pen but the author's. Letters from Oldham's friends and exercises by his pupils, each in its original writing, have been covered with verses in the principal hand. In addition, an independent Bodleian MS. (Ballard XX. 23) contains a signed letter by Oldham, endorsed "Oldham the poet an original": the handwriting is the same as that of the bulk of the Rawlinson MS. and of the MacFlecknoe transcript.

(5) Oldham was careful and accurate in recording the times when he wrote his own pieces. Thirteen of them are dated in the Rawlinson MS. Four of these, together with nine others, are

dated in the first published editions. These four poems bear the same date both in the MS. and printed versions. From the evidence of a Latin letter in the MS. one can prove that the heading of the piece "Upon ye Marriage of ye Prince of Orange . . . 9^{ber} 5, at Bedington," gives the precise day of composition. The internal and other evidence never conflicts with the stated dates. This care and accuracy makes it the more unlikely that Oldham dated MacFlecknoe at random. All the printed dates and three of the MS. ones are definitely stated as those of composition. Besides MacFlecknoe, and undated transcripts of two of Rochester's poems, the MS. includes a copy made by Oldham of a piece which on stylistic grounds can hardly be his own, entitled The Epicure, subscribed "Philomusus," and headed "Wrote ye last day of ye year 1675." One concludes that when Oldham dated a poem, his own or another's, he meant to indicate when it was composed; Belden's suggestion, that he perhaps affixed the date to MacFlecknoe as that of the action,[7] now seems unlikely to be correct.

(6) The year 1678 was the most natural time for Oldham to have concerned himself with MacFlecknoe. As I hope to show in a future publication, he was then consciously dedicating himself to the work of a serious satirist. He had adopted heroic rhyme as the proper medium for heroical satires from Whitsuntide 1678. The particular deficiency of satire, regarded as a species of the heroic poem, was its lack of action and epic machinery. In 1678 and 1679 Oldham was seeking models which would help him in overcoming this defect: he studied Davideis and Paradise Lost, Jonson's prologue to Catiline, and Buchanan's Franciscanus et Fratres. In mock-heroic poetry he found satire already combined with pseudo-epic action and machinery. As we should expect, he was interested in mock-heroic at this time: he was translating Boileau's Le Lutrin; his fair copy of the first canto is dated October, 1678. What more natural than that he should also turn his attention to MacFlecknoe?

(7) If MacFlecknoe was written in 1678, Oldham's Satyrs upon the Jesuits take their place chronologically as well as logically as the step which led from it to Absalom and Achitophel MacFlecknoe is incomparably finer and more enjoyable than the Satyrs upon the Jesuits. Nevertheless, in MacFlecknoe the onslaught is personal, the action only mock-heroic. Oldham made the public cause his own, and attempted the heroic vein in earnest. But he confined himself to monologue, and accepted as

WHEN DID DRYDEN WRITE MACFLECKNOE?

true heroic style the false one of contemporary drama: it was unfortunate, too, that the public feeling he expressed sprang so largely from a popular paroxysm of ignorant cruel fear. In Absalom and Achitophel, Dryden introduced more action and multiplied the characters; his style was at its loftiest and most vigorous; the political passion that moved him was deep-seated and worthy. And so Absalom, as Verrall said, is more than a satire, it is a heroic poem. Of the rival dates, 1682 conflicts and 1678 agrees with the natural place of MacFlecknoe in the evolution of Restoration satire and of Dryden's art.

NOTES

1   See his "Dryden's MacFlecknoe; a Vindication," Modern Language Review, July, 1918; and "Some Notes on Dryden," Review of English Studies, 1925, vol. i, pp. 187 ff.
See also Dryden Poetry and Prose, ed. Nichol Smith, 1925, vol. i, pp. 188–89.

2   Thorn-Drury's latest critic, Christopher Hollis (in his Dryden, 1933, p. 100, note), thinks the letter in The Loyal Protestant was written in February, 1682/3, pleading that confusion has arisen between the New Style dating and the Old; but Thorn-Drury quoted the date of the number of The Loyal Protestant as Thursday, February 9, 1681/2, and February 9, 1682/3 was not a Thursday. The Loyal Protestant in question, No. 114, is in the Bodleian (Nichols Newspapers, vol. 4.a. n⁰ 300), with full date, and exactly as Thorn-Drury described it.

3   Mr. C. H. Wilkinson reminds me that the phrase was certainly in Dryden's mind about 1678: see The Kind Keeper (acted March, 1677/8), 1680, p. 41. "Dioclesian, and Julian the Apostate, were but Types of thee."

4   "Dryden not the Author of MacFlecknoe," Modern Language Review, January, 1918.

5   Preserved in the Bodleian, MS. Rawlinson Poet, 123.

6   The Poetry of John Dryden (first published 1920; revised edition 1931); appendix on "The Authorship of MacFlecknoe."

7   "The Authorship of MacFlecknoe," Modern Language Notes, December, 1918.

MAC FLECKNOE AND COWLEY'S DAVIDEIS

A. L. Korn

The close relationship of Cowley's Davideis to Dryden's
Mac Flecknoe reveals very well the peculiar affiliation of Dryden's burlesque with its serious epic forerunners. The style
of Mac Flecknoe, if we include within the term especially Dryden's archetypal linguistic patterns, finds its most immediate
and living counterpart not so much in ancient epic—in Virgil,
for example—as in the "heroick poesy" of Dryden's own age.
In fact, of the three most celebrated epics of Dryden's period
—Davenant's Gondibert, Cowley's Davideis, and Paradise Lost
—we may suspect that Cowley's was the one most likely to suggest itself to Dryden (in the 1670's, at least) as a source of
materials for a burlesque poem. Not that Dryden lacked regard
for Cowley, for there was never a time when he did not acknowledge in his predecessor a very distinguished poet. Nevertheless,
scattered through preface and essay and beginning in the 1670's,
Dryden's casual praise of Cowley seems to have grown increas-
ingly discriminative.[1] A similar note of critical reservation
echoes in the very talk of the coffee-house. "Not being of God,
he could not stand," Rochester once remarked of Cowley, re-
moving him by a phrase from the rank of writers of the first
order.[2] The remark is exactly right. Its levity of manner
deepens its "serious wit"; and Dryden, recollecting the judgment long afterward in "The Preface to the Fables" (1700),
recognized its truth and agreed.

A few years earlier, in the rambling "Discourse Concerning the Original and Progress of Satire" (written in 1692), Dryden recalled likewise that "about twenty years ago" he had looked
into Cowley—"the darling of my youth"—and had found his
works marred by "points of wit, and quirks of epigram, even in
the Davideis, an heroic poem, which is of an opposite nature to

Reprinted from Huntington Library Quarterly, Vol. 14 (1951), pp. 99–
127, by permission of the author and the publisher.

those puerilities."[3] If we can trust Dryden's memory of an approximate date, we may believe that several years before the composition of Mac Flecknoe[4] he had already sketched the groundwork for his last word on the author of the Davideis: Cowley would always be remembered as a "great poet" although he could no longer be called a "good writer."[5]

This final judgment should be given a measure of attention in any study of the epic antecedents of Mac Flecknoe. When Dryden wrote his burlesque in his late forties, his thoughts were turning from the drama to speculation on a possible fable for a serious heroic poem.[6] Mac Flecknoe reflects experience crowding the poet (Shadwell was certainly crowding him) at a moment when Dryden's career was entering a new and transitional phase. Above all, Mac Flecknoe reveals a division in Dryden between his love for Cowley's themes, the expressive aims of the older poet, and a growing disenchantment with the Cowlean style. It was as if Dryden's affection for "my better master Cowley"[7] were suffering a delicate but inevitable readjustment. Although his passion for the "great" Cowley was still glowing and responsive, his faith in his former idol as a writer of "judgment" was by now well on the wane.

Dryden's disaffection with Cowley as implied in Mac Flecknoe was nevertheless an unusual case of critical alienation: it vented itself neither in mere ridicule nor simply in an overt act of the critic's judicial bent of mind. The release his disenchantment found in Mac Flecknoe was nothing if not resourceful, an expression of what was most free and happy and baffling in Dryden's own temperament. We may well believe that the genial, rosy-cheeked John Dryden impressed certain of his contemporaries, those not attuned to the hidden movement of his thought, as somehow remote.[8]

It is possible that Paradise Lost may have aroused in Dryden a profound interest in the idea of a modern epic.[9] It is possible, too, that the notion of the renovated epic — with Paradise Lost as its avatar — may have turned Dryden's mind in the direction of the mock-poem. Yet it was Cowley's epic and not Milton's, I think, which exerted a direct and altogether creative influence upon what Dryden would have called the "invention" of Mac Flecknoe. Likewise, a similar distinction may be applied to the relationship of Mac Flecknoe to the earlier seventeenth-century character writings, both in prose and verse.[10] However

much Dryden's poem owes as satire and as a portrait of Shadwell as Dunce to the character writers, as mock-heroic it owes
an equal debt to Abraham Cowley—at least, for what Mac Flecknoe eventually became.

The first major critic to detect a resemblance between Mac
Flecknoe and the Davideis was Dr. Johnson. Unfortunately, he
did not go into details. His life of Cowley is a critique on taste,
not a treatise on Cowley's place in literary history. Hence,
Johnson's few "facts" concerning the influence of the Davideis
barely emerge from behind their enveloping purpose, which was
to disparage Cowley's "metaphysical" style: "By the Spectator
[the Davideis] has once been quoted, by Rymer it has once been
praised, and by Dryden, in Mac Flecknoe, it has once been imitated."[11] Probably what Johnson was thinking of was that a
familiar couplet or two in Mac Flecknoe is an evident parody
of one of Cowley's most showy poetic flights.[12] Yet Johnson's
allusion to a basic article of the neo-classical faith—the notion
of poetic imitation—has its bearing on the design of Dryden's
poem as a whole. When fully construed the remark should lead
to a train of fresh insights into the underlying principle of Dryden's burlesque method. This was indeed a method of parody.
But I should prefer to take Johnson's hint and in a broader sense
call it a mode of burlesque imitation.

The theory of poetic imitation was an extremely elastic body
of ideas in neo-classical literary doctrine.[13] Apart from referring to a technique of loose translation,[14] the ubiquitous term
also covered an important feature of general poetic practice.
Thus, by employing special devices of style, an author might
establish an affinity, a blood relationship, between his own work
and another's creation. Showing considerable freedom of invention, he could "pursue the course of a composition, so as to
use parallel images and examples."[15] He might occasionally
borrow from an earlier poet an entire line. More obliquely, an
author could rely on methods of allusion and "transfuse" (a
favorite word of the period) something of the spirit of an earlier
work by means of verbal or phonetic or metrical echoes. In the
special case of satire and the poetry of ridicule, he could adopt
one of the more minute methods of achieving comic incongruity
and indulge himself in explicit parody of another writer's subject matter and style.

MAC FLECKNOE AND COWLEY'S DAVIDEIS

Now, it is unlikely that Johnson when he pointed to an un-
specified connection between Mac Flecknoe and the Davideis
had in mind anything so elaborate as imitation in the sense just
described, so wide in potential choice of means and range of
appeal. Yet his casual observation assumes, I feel, the rest
of the doctrine.[16] Are the Davideis and Mac Flecknoe linked
together, although not consecutively, by an extended and witty
parallelism? Likewise, when viewed from our own historic
vantage, is the one poem—although comic in aim and mock-
heroic in method—a wayward but deliberate "imitation" of the
other in its loftier kind? A minute analysis suggests that Mac
Flecknoe was contrived to remind us (just as we suspect it must
have reminded the coffee-house wits) of the Davideis not only
in one passage but in a succession of organically related passages throughout Dryden's poem as a whole. If this is true it
is too simple to assume that Mac Flecknoe was intended simply
as a burlesque of ancient epic conventions as found, say, in the
Aeneid. Although the work was unquestionably that, it was also
something more. Ultimately, it was a genial criticism—very
genial—of the neo-classical epic of Dryden's own period, and
in particular of Cowley's attempt to Christianize the epic, "to
Baptize it in Jordan," and so force a marriage between sacred
history and the Virgilian manner and style.[17]

Overt parody of the Davideis in Mac Flecknoe sometimes
takes the form of ludicrous garbling of certain of Cowley's images and metaphors. The most memorable instance of such
fooling is undoubtedly Dryden's allusion to the old district of
Barbican, the unsavory location of one of the nursery playhouses,
and the setting for Shadwell's coronation:

Where their vast Courts the Mother-Strumpets keep,
And, undisturb'd by Watch, in silence sleep. (ll. 72–73)[18]

As has long been known, the couplet is an indecorous lowering of
the language of Cowley's awesome vision of Hell:

Where their vast Court, the Mother-waters keep,
And undisturb'd by Moons in silence sleep. (Bk. I, p. 244)[19]

Likewise, the following couplet from Cowley's description of
Hell—"Beneath the dens where unfletcht Tempests lye, / And

173

infant <u>Winds</u> their tender <u>Voyces</u> try"—is echoed in Dryden's
contemptuous reference to the Nursery school for young players:

> Where unfledged Actors learn to laugh and cry,
> Where infant Punks their tender voices try. (ll. 76–77)

The Hell-passage (Dryden must have known it by heart) seems
also to have provided the root metaphor and basic imagery in
the couplets celebrating the degree of Shadwell's dullness:[20]

> Some Beams of Wit on other souls may fall,
> Strike through and make a lucid intervall;
> But Sh---'s genuine night admits no ray,
> His rising Fogs prevail upon the Day. (<u>Mac Flecknoe</u>, ll.
> 21–24)

> There is a place deep, wondrous deep below,
> Which genuine <u>Night</u> and <u>Horrour</u> does o'reflow;
> No bound controls th' unwearied space, but <u>Hell</u>
> <u>Endless</u> as those dire <u>pains</u> that in it dwell.
> Here no dear glimpse of the <u>Suns</u> lovely face,
> Strikes through the <u>Solid</u> darkness of the place;
> No dawning <u>Morn</u> does her kind reds display;
> One slight weak beam would here be thought the <u>Day</u>.
> (<u>Davideis</u>, Bk. I, p. 244)

Such are the inescapable examples of the influence of the
<u>Davideis</u> upon Dryden's burlesque technique. We may distin-
guish, however, between the level of explicit parody of the <u>Dav-
ideis</u> in <u>Mac Flecknoe</u> and the level of implicit parody or, simply, burlesque imitation. In the first type, as in the passages
noted, we may feel that Dryden as parodist is calling attention
to certain absurdities in Cowley's style: to what a zealously
correct critic of the day might have considered ludicrous in
Cowley's "poetical fictions."[21] Implicit parody, on the other
hand, need not necessarily suggest disparagement or conceal
a frown. Its effects are sometimes more subtle than those of
explicit parody; and they may frequently prove more amusing.
Above all, they may depend on the good qualities of what is being parodied rather than merely on the dubious. The main distinction is that the good features have been lifted out of their

proper native context and made to serve different and incongruous ends. The humor of explicit parody approaches rather the humor of ridicule. Implicit parody—the humor of high-spirited and witty imitation—may resemble more closely the humor of sheer play. In implicit parody the poetic fancy or imagination seems to embark on a kind of holiday. Perhaps that is why sportive literary humor, as David Daiches has remarked, often reveals "the highbrow masquerading as the philistine."[22]

No doubt it would be impossible to fit neatly all of Dryden's parody of the Davideis into the one or the other of the two categories. Yet the basic distinction is sometimes helpful in differentiating between distinctive modes of Dryden's burlesque humor. Thus, aside from the familiar specimens of explicit parody in Mac Flecknoe, the poem abounds in mimicry or imitation of a more ambiguous and sportive kind. One notices, for example, an implicit but nevertheless striking parallel between the substance itself of Dryden's poem and that of the Davideis, a relationship extending to Cowley's general subject matter and linking it with its thematic counterpart in Mac Flecknoe. I refer to the biblical or pseudo-biblical allusions running through Mac Flecknoe and to the integral part a biblical background plays in the design and organization of the poem as a whole.

It is sometimes said that the temper of the age made it almost inevitable that Milton and Cowley in their attempts at a "modern" epic should have settled upon a biblical theme or subject. The same truth may be applied to Mac Flecknoe. The mock splendor of the poem is partly the result of its elegant motley, its outrageous blending together of various shades of Christian and pagan coloring. In Cowley's "Sacred Poem of the Troubles of David" the union of scriptural and classical source materials is far less felicitous. The critical paradox of these two poems, the serious failure and the witty success, is that while in the one the poetic fusion of inharmonious elements is achieved with utmost brilliance, in the other it is hardly realized at all. Only by great strain and the sacrifice of art for erudition does Cowley manage to bring together in one uncongenial and never-completed design[23] his double set of norms—the "Christian" and the "Classical"—comprising his twofold knowledge of heroic story.

Apart from digressions into other chapters of Old Testament history, Cowley's poem treats mainly of the events of his hero's youth. We hear principally of David's winning favor at court, his love for Michal, friendship with Jonathan, persecution by his royal patron, and early years of exile among the tribes. In the foreground of Cowley's rather cluttered baroque stage are two tremendous personages: Saul, the Hero as King, and Samuel, the Hero as Prophet. Towering in the center of the picture is the shepherd-boy, musician, lover, and warrior, David himself. Being a poet, he too is gifted with prophecy. One day he will be king. Above all, he will live to become the founder of a royal messianic line.

The parallel element in Mac Flecknoe emerges most clearly in Dryden's ambiguous management of his succession-theme, showing Flecknoe and Shadwell each in the role of the Hero as Prophet. Although Dryden presents his heroic pair primarily as an old king and his successor to the throne of Nonsense, the two royal personages are more than merely secular rulers: they are priests as well as potentates— "prophets," in an ironical sense of the word—dedicated to spreading the gospel of Unreason throughout the land. The burlesque perspective of the poem is such that the reader must always read with a divided mind. He must try to maintain in the precarious focus of his double lens Dryden's portrayal of his two heroes in their simultaneous roles as prophets and princes. As the poem rises to its climax, Dryden even emphasizes the secondary motif in his comic characterization. In an abruptly terminated tableau, Flecknoe is represented as a pseudo-biblical prophet passing on to his anointed disciple, as Elijah did to Elisha, the mantle of "divine" prophecy.

Dryden's opening lines, comprising a brief introduction and a part of Flecknoe's initial harangue, establish the primary pattern of the narrative. Flecknoe is described as a "monarch," an "aged Prince," the governor of an "Empire," and the head of a "State." The secondary motif appears for the first time in lines 29–30, but will return throughout the course of the poem:

> Heywood and Shirley were but Types of thee,
> Thou last great Prophet of Tautology.

The next few lines, in which the identification of dunces with
prophets is underscored, deserve more attention than they have
received from Dryden's annotators:

> Even I, a dunce of more renown than they,
> Was sent before but to prepare thy way:
> And coarsely clad in Norwich Drugget came
> To teach the Nations in thy greater name. (ll. 31–34)

These are by no means the only lines in Mac Flecknoe to carry
with them biblical overtones.[24] They are but the first of the two
most significant passages, one occurring early in the poem and
the other at its close, in which Dryden echoes for burlesque purposes a well-known biblical text:

> For this is he [John the Baptist] that was spoken
> of by the prophet Esaias, saying, The voice of one cry-
> ing in the wilderness, Prepare ye the way of the Lord,
> make his paths straight.
> And the same John had his raiment of camel's
> hair, and a leathern girdle about his loins; and his
> meat was locusts and wild honey.[25]

The Globe Edition points out in the preceding couplets a
possible thrust (although presumably the Irish priest Flecknoe
is referring to himself) at Shadwell's Norfolk birthplace.[26]
Within the larger context of the poem the lines have additional
ramifications requiring the reader to follow out the biblical
parallel. Having emerged out of his native hinterland, Flecknoe
appears as a dingy St. John come to "prepare the way" for the
"greater name" of Shadwell. Just as St. John himself was but
the last of a line of prophets who foretold the coming of the
Messiah, so Flecknoe and Shadwell are but the last in a hieratic
procession reaching back to Heywood and Shirley. The later
reference to "ancient Decker" is a variation on the basic theme.
During Restoration times Dekker was remembered not only as
a dramatist but also as an author of city pageants and as a
writer of popular prognostications. His place in the chain of
succession, if it is not that of a biblical prophet, suggests the
role of the prophet and prognosticator Merlin, who foretold the
return of King Arthur to the throne of Britain—a legend fre-

quently applied to the Stuart rulers and well-known to Dryden's
contemporaries:[27]

> For ancient <u>Decker</u> prophesi'd long since,
> That in this <u>Pile</u> should Reign a mighty Prince. (ll. 87–88)

Throughout the remainder of <u>Mac Flecknoe</u> Dryden's skill
in weaving together his three strands of ironic allusion—to kings,
to prophets, and to poets—is sustained and reinforced. In accord not only with biblical precedent but also with contemporary
conceptions of kingship, Flecknoe acts as <u>rex et sacerdos</u>. Like
Samuel, who had anointed both David and <u>King Saul</u>, he himself
administers the sacred chrism before turning over his scepter
to his royal offspring.[28]

> The King himself the sacred Unction made,
> As King by Office, and as Priest by Trade. (ll. 118–19)

In combining the three strands of allusion Dryden by no
means ignores the tradition of pagan prophecy. What is perhaps
surprising—less so, however, when we remember <u>Absalom and
Achitophel</u>—is that the strictly classical allusions in the poem
should carry no more than their just share of the total burlesque
implication. The Goddess Fame, of course, is a stock Virgilian
figure long familiar in the native poetic tradition, where she had
appeared prominently during the sixteenth and seventeenth century in the courtly masque. The same is true of the designation
of London as Augusta, an epithet frequent in the civic pageantry
and coronation poetry of the period. The brief comparison of
Shadwell to the young Ascanius and to Hannibal, the reference
to Romulus and the Tiber, the apt appearance of the prophetic
owls or vultures presaging Shadwell's rule, and the close parody
of Virgil in the lines describing Shadwell's "lambent dullness"
are among the most apparent instances in the poem of specifically classical matter turned to purposes of burlesque.[29] Under the same heading there is perhaps one other noteworthy
passage. Here Dryden's allusion seems to point not so much
to biblical prophecy as to the "raging god," the <u>furor poeticus</u>,
of Platonic-Renaissance convention.[30]

> The Syre then shook the honours of his head,
> And from his brows damps of oblivion shed

178

> Full on the filial dullness: long he stood,
> Repelling from his Breast the raging God;
> At length burst out in this prophetick mood. (ll. 134–38)

The closing lines, following with ludicrous abruptness Flecknoe's peroration, serve as a climax to the biblical strain running
through the poem. The passage also contains a jest at the expense of Shadwell's own writings—the trap door employed in
his comedy The Virtuoso.

> He said, but his last words were scarcely heard,
> For Bruce and Longvil had a Trap prepar'd,
> And down they sent the yet declaiming Bard.
> Sinking he left his Drugget robe behind,
> Borne upwards by a subterranean wind.
> The Mantle fell to the young Prophet's part
> With double portion of his Father's Art. (ll. 211–17)

The "drugget robe" links the close of the episode with the earlier
allusion to "Norwich drugget," a material commonly worn by
hard-up authors. In the final couplet, in which the royal garment
is transformed into the mantle of inspiration, it is possible that
Dryden has one eye on Shadwell's notorious girth and the other
on the Hebrew word for the shepherd's mantle [addereth] derived from a root meaning "to be wide."[31] In any event, the
couplet echoes (with certain unseemly explosives added) the
biblical account of Elijah's leave-taking of Elisha, when "they
two stood by Jordan":

> And it came to pass, when they were gone over, that
> Elijah said unto Elisha, Ask what I shall do for thee,
> before I be taken away from thee. And Elisha said, I
> pray thee let a double portion of thy spirit be upon
> me . . .
> He took up also the mantle of Elijah that fell from
> him and went back, and stood by the bank of Jordan.[32]

In terms of the burlesque machinery of the poem, the trap
door and the subterranean wind thus take on an added humor
when set in the fuller perspective of the biblical parallel. Just
as Elijah "went up by a whirlwind to heaven," so presumably

the ruler of the realms of Nonsense must have vanished with
equal velocity in the opposite direction.

The mock-heroic function of such passages of biblical
allusion in <u>Mac Flecknoe</u> is everywhere clear. They are not,
however, to be classed along with verses in which Dryden's
borrowing from Cowley takes the form of explicit verbal parody of Cowley's text. In the passages summoning up the incongruous shades of St. John and Elijah the burlesque imitation of the sacred poem is generic rather than particular, but
it is also in polite accord with Cowley's theory of heroic verse
as a fusion of Christian substance with classical art, or artifice.

As for the narrower satiric function of the passages, this
too is deliberate and shrewdly achieved. When Dryden wrote
<u>Mac Flecknoe</u> the traditional Renaissance conception of the poet
as <u>vates</u>, as inspired prophet and seer, had lost much of its
former prestige. If it suited the purpose of the satirist, the
notion served as a general target of ridicule along with "enthusiasm," whether religious or poetic, and other evidences of that
"Inspiration, called commonly, private spirit." The phrase
happens to be Hobbes's, but Hobbes's assault was only an opening skirmish in the general Restoration attack upon enthusiasm.[33]
In accord with the temper of the times, Dryden drew his most
telling weapons of satire from the prevalent psychology. The
first was the ridicule of inspiration as exemplified in the "En-
thusiastical Impostors of our Age"—far-gone religious or political dissidents, particularly members of conventicles, or
Latitudinarians of various degrees, "True-Blood Protestants,"
and emergent Whigs. Likewise, in the literary polemics of the
period and by a natural transference of terms of abuse, the victim of "enthusiasm" might be identified with a pretentious rival
author, a Settle or a Shadwell. In Dryden's dispute with his
former friend and fellow-playwright his charge, however, was
not merely that Shadwell's mind was a breeding place of irrational vapors.[34] Worse still, Shadwell was a walking symbol
of that False or Unsteady Wit personified in the Dullard and the
Dunce:

> Sh--- alone my perfect image bears,
> Mature in dullness from his tender years;
> Sh--- alone of all my Sons is he

> Who stands confirm'd in full stupidity.
> The rest to some faint meaning make pretence,
> But Sh--- never deviates into sense. (ll. 15–20)

With this well-known passage may be compared the Hobbesian notion of the sluggish and "deviating" intellect: the antithesis of that "Celerity of Imagining, (that is, swift succession of one thought to another;) and steddy direction to some approved end," which distinguishes "Naturall Wit."

> On the Contrary a slow imagination, maketh that
> Defect, or fault of the mind, which is commonly
> called DULNESSE, Stupidity, and sometimes by
> other names that signifie slownesse of motion, or
> difficulty to be moved.[35]

Not a little of the irony and paradoxical force of Dryden's comic characterization in Mac Flecknoe consists, in short, in the way Flecknoe and Shadwell embody at one and the same time a sub-human stupidity and supernatural powers of "inspiration." In terms of the direct satire, they are stuffed owls betokening an idiotic senselessness. In terms of their burlesque implication, they are also emblems of a "mystique" glory whose effulgence distinguishes them as Prophet and Prince. Ultimately, it was in the achievement of his burlesque goal that Dryden placed himself most in debt to Cowley's venture in the heroic kind.

Supplementing the passages of minute parody noted earlier, there are numerous examples in Mac Flecknoe of Dryden's use of various phrases and formulas characteristic of the style of the Davideis. For instance, Saul had thus observed the anointing of the boy David by the Prophet Samuel:

> He saw the reverend Prophet boldly shed
> The Royal Drops round his Enlarged Head. (Bk. I, p. 245)

In a later passage, foreshadowing the "Kingly Day" when Saul is elected by lot to reign over Israel, Samuel performs the same sacred office for Saul:

> Then takes the sacred Viol, and does shed
> A Crown of mystique drops around his head. (Bk. IV, p. 375)

181

In his echoing of the passages, Dryden's adaptation suits his triple purpose of retaining phonetic coloring (including the exact rhyme), injecting psychological overtones into his satire of Shadwell as Dunce, and at the same time imitating Cowley's subject matter.

> The Syre then shook the honours of his head,
> And from his brows damps of oblivion shed
> Full on the filial dullness . . . (ll. 134–36)

"Honours," incidentally, is both Virgilian and Cowlean.[36] In the Davideis Cowley briefly refers to the drops of oil used by Samuel in the act of consecration. In Dryden's lines, by a kind of prestidigitation, the mechanistic theory of the humors— "damps of oblivion"—usurps the place of that divine elixir or "grace" symbolized in the chrism and traditionally supposed to shine forth from the face of majesty.

A more perplexing specimen of Dryden's variations on the theme of "anointed dulness" in Mac Flecknoe is the following reference to Shadwell's alleged habit of plagiarizing his betters. The surface meaning of the passage, the ironic comparison of an act of plagiarism to literary borrowing, or "transfusion," is in no way obscure.

> When did his [Jonson's] Muse from Fletcher scenes purloin,
> As thou whole Eth'ridg dost transfuse to thine?
> But so transfused as Oyls on waters flow,
> His always floats above, thine sinks below. (ll. 183–86)

Now the fuller context of Cowley's couplet on Saul's "Crown of mystique drops," the sacred oil used in the rite of coronation, reads as follows:

> Drops of that Royal Moisture which does know
> No Mixture, and disdains the place below.

Cowley's learned gloss on these lines points out that "Oyl mixt with any other liquor, still gets uppermost, is perhaps one of the chiefest Significancies in the Ceremony of Anointing Kings and Priests."[37] The phonetic resemblance of the two sets of rhymes (flow:below; know:below) and the similar references

in both Dryden and Cowley to the physical action of oil when
mixed with denser liquids are perhaps only accidental similarities in the two passages. Yet the presumption is irresistible,
when we consider all the other less oblique references to the
Davideis recurring throughout Mac Flecknoe, that here too a
passage from Cowley's poem possibly served Dryden as a spark
to kindle his own invention. If so, Dryden's purpose as elsewhere was to violate normal standards of appropriateness and
so reduce highbrow poetic materials to a sublime nonsense.

Thus, in a deeply buried and quite cryptic allusion rudely
dislodged from its original context, Dryden here seems to have
adapted (consciously or unconsciously) a symbolic interpretation of the rite of royal consecration—the notion of the sacred
oil as a symbol of the infusion of immanent grace—to the process of poetic or literary borrowing. Whereas in true "transfusion" the precious borrowed matter becomes one in substance
with an author's own creation, in a piece of plagiarism the combination and mixture of elements is imperfect: the inferior matter of the plagiarist "sinks below." In terms of the hidden
analogy, Etherege's comedy compared with that of Shadwell is
as sacred matter compared with profane: lacking the true poet's
"grace" Shadwell as borrower works no miracles.

By deliberate design or through less conscious intention,
Dryden's echoing of the Davideis sometimes shows his mind—
or, better, his "fancy"—working in its most playful or even
perverse capacity. The modern reader may well feel that in a
passage so apparently plain and yet so private as the one just
examined we are close to the threshold in Dryden of a creative
principle—that remote stage in its formative process when his
poem was "only a confused mass of thoughts, tumbling over one
another in the dark; when the fancy was yet in its first work,
moving the sleeping images of things toward the light, there to
be distinguished, and there either chosen or rejected by the
judgment."[38]

Distinct from Dryden's echoings of particular lines or couplets in the Davideis,[39] there are certain stock epithets in Cowley's poem which Dryden appears to have borrowed for the sake
of heightening his mock-heroic effect. As a device for producing
what he called "pathos," Cowley from time to time designates
his characters by means of stock formulas, as in the following
passage describing the High Priest of Nob, who sheltered David

during his flight from Saul: "The good old <u>Priest</u> welcomes his
fatal <u>Guest,</u> /. . . Much more the Reverend <u>Sire</u> prepar'd to say,
/Rapt with his joy . . ." (Bk. III, p. 324). A similar formula is
used later to designate Samuel: "The good old <u>Seer</u> 'gainst <u>Kings</u>
was too severe" (Bk. IV, p. 371). Reminiscent of Spenserian
usage (more than one "good old <u>Aged</u> man" wanders through
<u>The Faerie Queene</u>) such flourishes cannot of course be called
peculiar to Cowley. They are rather to be considered as locu-
tions generally deemed suitable for poetry either in the "legislative" or "high" style; in fact, they appear as a permanent part
of Dryden's mature manner.[40] Yet when taken together with
Dryden's other echoings of the <u>Davideis</u>, such stock formulas
increase the resemblance between the diction and general texture of <u>Mac Flecknoe</u> and Cowley's poem:

> Here stopt the good old Syre; and wept for joy,
> In silent raptures of the hopefull boy. (<u>Mac Flecknoe</u>, ll. 60–61)

The absurdity of heralding Shadwell as "boy" is not lessened
when the reader remembers his Falstaffian size: "A Tun of Man
in thy large Bulk is writ." In 1678 Shadwell was between thirty-
five and forty. For a choice contemporary audience the incongruity of the term may well have added piquancy to the poem's
mock-heroic flavor. In a lengthy gloss on the phrase "The
Inn'ocent <u>Boy</u>," as applied to Isaac awaiting his sacrifice, Cowley had thus expatiated on exegetical tradition:

> Our English Translation, <u>Lad</u>, which is not a word
> for verse, the Latin, <u>Puer</u>, <u>Boy</u>. <u>Aben Ezra</u> is cited
> to make him [Isaac] at that time but ten or twelve
> years old. . . . Others 33, because at that age our
> <u>Saviour</u> (whose <u>Type</u> he was) was sacrificed. Some
> of the Jews 36. none of which are contrary to the
> <u>Hebrew</u> use of the word <u>Boy</u>; for so all young men
> are termed, as <u>Benjamin</u>, . . . and <u>Josephus</u>, <u>Joshua</u>,
> and <u>David</u> when he fought with <u>Goliah</u>. The <u>Painters</u>
> commonly make him very young, and my description
> agrees most with that opinion, for it is more poetical
> and pathetical than the others.[41]

In the same class of Hebraic formulas may also be placed
the poetical designation of Flecknoe as "Father Flecknoe":

> Let Father Flecknoe fire thy mind with praise
> And Uncle Ogleby thy envy raise. (ll. 173-74)

The allusion to patriarchal "envy" is curious. It is possible that Dryden here is recalling a particular portion of the super-natural machinery of the Davideis in which Saul is seduced into jealousy through the agency of the Hell-hag Envy, who has assumed the shape of "Father Benjamin"—"the first and chief of Saul's progenitors."[42]

It is evident from such recurrent correspondences that the Davideis, although by no means a model Dryden followed slav-ishly, has left a pervading impression on the diction, the tex-ture of allusion, and general style of Mac Flecknoe. In several instances, Dryden's overt parody of Cowley takes its humor from his indecorous wrenching of the foundations of Cowlean metaphor, as in the reference to the "Mother-waters." In other deft borrowings from Cowley's stock of heroic epithets Dryden injected into Mac Flecknoe a suggestion of ancient Hebrew folk-ways, suitable for supplying "sacred" atmosphere and describ-ing in mocking vein an aged prophet and his younger disciple.

This classification does not exhaust the means by which Dryden was able to evoke in his reader's mind the cadence of Cowley's heroic tread. In the following passage the resem-blance between the two works is one of general similarity in the metrical handling of the couplet, together with an immoderate use of parallel repetition. In its echoing of Cowley's parade-ground measure the passage achieves a martial beat and cere-monial self-consciousness equaled only in the Davideis.[43] As explicit parody displaying in exaggerated form Cowley's man-nered use of parallel repetition, this is the most prominent ex-ample of its kind in the whole of Mac Flecknoe. Cowley is de-scribing Abdon, Jonathan's "loyal esquire":

> Abdon alone his gen'erous purpose knew;
> Abdon a bold, a brave, and comely Youth,
> Well-born, well-bred, with Honour fill'd and Truth,
> Abdon his faithful Squire, whom much he lov'd,
> And oft with grief his worth in dangers prov'd.
> Abdon, whose love to'his Master did exceed
> What Natures Law, or Passions Power could breed,

> Abdon alone did on him now attend;
> His humblest Servant, and his dearest Friend.
>> (Bk. IV, p. 385)

> Sh--- alone my perfect image bears,
> Mature in dullness from his tender years;
> Sh--- alone of all my Sons is he
> Who stands confirm'd in full stupidity.
> The rest to some faint meaning make pretence,
> But Sh--- never deviates into sense.
> Some Beams of Wit on other souls may fall,
> Strike through and make a lucid intervall;
> But Sh---'s genuine night admits no ray,
> His rising Fogs prevail upon the Day.
>> (Mac Flecknoe, ll. 15-24)

In this celebrated passage the burlesque imitation of Cowley is exceedingly dense. Although in substantial image and metaphor the couplets are related to Cowley's Hell-passage in Book I of the Davideis, in their verse pattern and their excessive use of parallelism they promiscuously echo other typical couplets scattered through Cowley's entire work.[44]

Like the general correspondence in the prophet-king motif, the minute stylistic resemblances between Mac Flecknoe so far noted have been with but one or two exceptions easily apparent. More tenuous but not improbable is the implicit parallelism between Dryden's description of the old Nursery playhouse in Barbican[45]—the setting for Shadwell's coronation—and Cowley's elaborate account in the Davideis of the "Prophets Colledge," where David finds refuge from Saul. If the passages may be regarded as in some sense related, it is not simply because of any line-for-line resemblance by way of verbal parody (although such lines exist). Nor is it because of any passing similarity in metrical pattern and phrase. The connection between the two sections consists rather in the way each of them shows its author appealing to the reader's familiarity with the same seventeenth-century literary convention. Broadly, it is the convention of describing a great national edifice, a St. Paul's or Windsor Castle, a subject of both topical and "topological" interest in the panegyric verses of the period. In the Davideis the description of the "prophets Colledge,"[46] its location

186

MAC FLECKNOE AND COWLEY'S DAVIDEIS

Midst a large Wood that joyns fair Ramahs Town
(The neighborhood fair Rama's chief renown),

its "Well-furnisht-Chambers," its "Halls and Schools," the
Synagogue where "Musick and Verse seem'd born and bred up
here," comprises over two hundred lines. The corresponding
section of Mac Flecknoe establishing the location of the Nursery

Close to the Walls which fair Augusta bind,
(The fair Augusta much to fears inclin'd) (ll. 64–65)

and describing the school for "unfledged Actors" takes up but
twenty-five lines.

Although very different in length and in specific content,
the two passages may nevertheless be linked together in function
and theme. They may be regarded as set pieces describing a
national or royal monument: in the Davideis, a tribal college
for indoctrinating the "Sons of the Prophets"; in Mac Flecknoe,
a kind of Royal Academy dedicated to the cultivation of the arts
of nonsense. As such, the passages are suitably included in
poems celebrating a princely practitioner of the arts, a David
or a Shadwell. In the same manner the two selections are akin
to other seventeenth-century panegyric verse treating comparable subject matter: for example, Waller's St. James's Park,
Otway's Windsor Castle, and the section in Davenant's Gondibert
—more notable still—devoted to the House of Astragon, with
its nest of Baconian savants, its museums, and libraries.

Cowley himself in his notes to the Davideis confesses that
his description of the "Prophets Colledge" perhaps savors too
much of topicality: "The Description of the Prophets Colledge
at Naioth, looks at first sight, as if I had taken the pattern of it
from ours at the Universities."[47] Is there any reason to suspect that the seventeenth-century reader of Dryden's verse-
caricature of the Nursery, with its picture of fledgling heroes
and minuscule tragedy-queens, might have found in Mac Flecknoe an oblique reference to the contemporary vogue for speculation on the subject of the ideal college? The answer depends
partly on the weight to be given to a single clue provided by Dryden himself: the allusion to the Nursery as a "Monument of
vanisht minds." In this instance, however, Davenant's heroic
romance is the source from which Dryden borrowed a memorable line for sharp ironic effect.[48]

Canto V in Book II of Davenant's poem is a lavish account
of the palace of Astragon, where Davenant's hero recovers from
the exertions of battle. There Gondibert observes the Baconian
wonders of Astragon's great academy of the arts and sciences
—a kind of research foundation modeled upon The New Atlantis
and its House of Solomon, or after Bacon's prescriptions in The
Advancement of Learning. Davenant's hero is permitted to inspect the instruments of the scholars devoted to the new astronomy. He visits "Great Nature's Office," a museum of natural
history containing records of "ev'ry fish, and foule, and beest";
passes on to "Nature's Nursery,"[49] with its living specimens
of all varieties of plants; and progresses finally to the inspiring
spectacle of the stuffed whale, the "dry'd" elephant, and the
" skeletons of every kind":

> This to a structure led, long known to fame
> And call'd, THE MONUMENT OF VANISH'D MINDES.[50]

In Gondibert this last of the marvels of the House of Astragon is devoted to monuments of unaging intellect: Egyptian papyri,
Chaldean hieroglyphs, the lore of Persian magi, the wisdom of
the "talking Greeks," and the Holy Scriptures:

> Such heaps of written thoughts (gold of the dead
> Which Time does still disperse, but not devour) . . .

In Dryden's journey to the Byzantium of Golden Lane he brings
his reader's gaze to rest—whether justly or not—upon the
Nursery's hardened, sterile vulgarity:

> Near these a Nursery erects its head,
> Where Queens are formed, and future Hero's bred;
> Where unfledged Actors learn to laugh and cry,
> Where infant Punks their tender voices try,
> And little Maximins the Gods defy.
> Great Fletcher never treads in Buskins here,
> Nor greater Johnson dares in socks appear.
> But gentle Simkin just reception finds
> Amidst this Monument of vanisht minds. (ll. 74–82)

Instead of referring to man's long-reaching intellectual heritage,
Davenant's phrase comes to denote—by a turn on the word

"vanisht"—an abyss of mindlessness. It is clear that Dryden's
purpose in inserting the line bodily into a passage describing
a school for puny players, the site of the Dunces' accession to
their thrones, is consistent with his general method in the same
verses of twisting to his own cause tempting bits from the Davideis. Again he has chiseled off a noble fragment of a contemporary heroic poem to serve as a touchstone certifying Folly's
latest priesthood.

It is no part of my present purpose to raise the large question of Dryden's formal theories of the epic and the relation of
these theories to his mock-heroic method and goal. Instead, I
have tried chiefly to show that among the epics of Dryden's time
the Davideis was a much more important and pervasive influence upon the style and design of Mac Flecknoe, and on what
might be called its burlesque iconography, than has commonly
been recognized. It would be going too far to claim that the
miniature action of Mac Flecknoe has any extended similarity
to Cowley's copious and digressive history of David and his
wanderings. It would likewise be a mistake to look for detailed
correspondences between Cowley's fuller development of the
characters of David, Samuel, or Saul, and Dryden's representation of Flecknoe and Shadwell as "anointed" prophets garbed in
the huge masque of comedy.

The resemblance between Cowley's work and Dryden's is
often an elusive one. Apart from significant instances of explicit parody the parallelism is sometimes implicit, sometimes
generic rather than particular. Indeed, it is difficult to settle
upon a consistent terminology by which to designate the range,
complexity, and creative distinction of Dryden's mimicry of the
poet he still loved and once called his master. For that reason
I have adopted, perhaps loosely, the term "imitation": an art
in which Dryden was always a virtuoso, whether as translator
of Virgil, adapter of Antony and Cleopatra, or re-fashioner of
Boccaccio and Chaucer, as in the Fables.

A further word should be said perhaps about Dryden's
choice of the Davideis as the object of his humor. Why did he
select this particular poem and its author—"the darling of my
youth"—for his facetious and sportive ends? And why did he
not borrow more freely from Davenant's Gondibert or, for that
matter, Paradise Lost?

Like Cowley's, the influence of Davenant's poetry on the
verse of the younger Dryden was a strong one.[51] By the late

189

1670's, however, Gondibert itself must have been somewhat
passé and therefore not inviting as a target for topical parody.[52]
The poem had already, in fact, been ridiculed by others. Such
are the implications of the passage Dryden wrote or approved
in 1680 in his revision of Sir William Soame's translation (an
authentic "imitation") of Boileau's L'Art Poétique. The passage
follows a laudatory account of Spenser's handling of his stanza.

> Then D'Avenant came, who, with a new-found art,
> Chang'd all, spoiled all, and had his way apart;
> His haughty muse all others did despise,
> And thought in triumph to bear off the prize,
> 'Til the sharp-sighted critics of the times,
> In their Mock-Gondibert, exposed his rhymes;
> The laurels he pretended did refuse,
> And dashed the hopes of his aspiring muse.[53]

Apart from the question of the stanza, to have burlesqued Gondibert would probably have required making merry with its romantic trappings and whole air of martial and amorous enterprise.
It is not easy to see how Gondibert would have suited so well as
did the Davideis Dryden's primary purpose of attacking the
dunces.

Other than Dryden's predilection for the heroic couplet,
his reasons for avoiding Miltonic features in Mac Flecknoe were
of a very different order.[54] It is true that in the unacted State
of Innocence (1677) he turned the blank verse of Paradise Lost
into his own favorite measure. But there is little if any evidence
that he could have been tempted for humorous purposes to tamper with the Miltonic substance and style. Dryden recognized
in Paradise Lost a transcendent achievement: "One of the greatest, most noble, and most sublime poems which either this nation
or age has produced."[55] A successful "sacred poem" nobly conceived and nobly accomplished, Paradise Lost simply did not
lend itself, in the 1670's at least, to the light approach.

I have suggested several of the more apparent considerations which might have prompted Dryden in Mac Flecknoe to
focus his burlesque humor on the Davideis rather than on Gondibert or on Paradise Lost. But the word "considerations," I feel,
places the problem in too conventional a frame. As a young man
Dryden had been deeply stirred by Cowley. He had long loved

Cowley's verses and many of them he very likely knew by heart.
Now, in Mac Flecknoe, and from the vantage of his middle years,
he could look upon the older poet with critical detachment. Com-
pounded also of sympathy, this was a detachment nourished on a
mysterious and rich appreciation: Dryden was alive to every
quality of Cowley's art. In English parody it might be hard to
find another example in which the peculiar distance maintained
by the parodist toward the poet parodied is at times so shadowy,
so difficult to label or assess. Perhaps the reason is that in
parodying Cowley John Dryden was also parodying something
in his earlier self.

Undoubtedly there were other less intangible attractions of
the Davideis as a model for Dryden's mock-heroic poem. For
one thing, Cowley's work was written in the heroic couplet, a
verse form in which Dryden in his plays had already demonstrated his own virtuosity. To clinch the matter, Cowley's handling
of "poetical fictions," his manner of "describing things which
really exist not," as in his description of Hell's "vast Court"
and silent waters, had already by 1678 disturbed Dryden enough
to cause him, smiling, to step forward in Cowley's defense.

In "The Author's Apology for Heroic Poetry and Poetic
License" (1677), written apparently not many months before
Mac Flecknoe, Dryden had chivalrously shielded Cowley from
the type of witticisms to which his style was frequently vulnerable:

> For if the mass of waters be the mothers [see Mac
> Flecknoe, "Mother-Strumpets"], then their daughters,
> the little streams ["infant Punks"], are bound, in all
> good manners, to make courtesy to them, and ask
> them blessing. How easy 'tis to turn into ridicule
> the best descriptions, when once a man is in the hu-
> mour of laughing, till he wheezes at his own dull
> jest! But an image, which is strongly and beautifully
> set before the eyes of the reader, will still be poetry
> when the merry fit is over, and last when the other
> is forgotten.[56]

Dryden's insight is one which perhaps helps to explain the temper, essentially sunny, of his burlesque imitation of the Davideis in Mac Flecknoe. Cowley's poem was, after all, good and

bad at the same time. If it had been overwhelmingly fine, its very sublimity (as in <u>Paradise Lost</u>) might have made the fun risky. On the other hand, if the work had been consistently worthless or dull, the humor would have been too cheap and the occasion no test of Dryden's skill. The distinction is one which perhaps can best be explained by an appeal to a familiar theory of comedy. For just as "high" comedy requires characters of a certain polish and wit, so "high" burlesque or parody demands likewise that the matter or manner imitated be of a definite weight, dignity, and brilliance. However, it helps if the work in question has its points of possible weakness: places where the gilding is a trifle thin, the framework somewhat shaky. The <u>Davideis</u> seems to have fulfilled these qualifications.

It is worth noticing, too, that in echoing the tone of the <u>Davideis</u> or in borrowing certain Cowlean formulas, Dryden throughout <u>Mac Flecknoe</u> shows a high sense of artistic discretion. As a poem sophisticated and in the current, <u>Mac Flecknoe</u> did not escape, as we have seen, the predilection of the period for extracting the substance of an heroic poem from biblical sources. A clumsy touch in harmonizing his ironic allusions to sacred history and his purpose of ridiculing Shadwell as dunce would have been disastrous for Dryden's ultimate aims. How superbly he reconciled these antithetical elements has already been suggested and may here be reviewed.

First, he saw to it that the primary pattern of his poem should impress upon the reader's mind the picture of Flecknoe and Shadwell as the King and the Prince, a convention wholly in accord with epic precedent in all ages. But in addition he introduced into his narrative a secondary pattern, never overstressed but evoked largely by means of incidental reference and ironic allusion. Finding its ultimate sanction perhaps in the growing spirit of skepticism—in a "libertine" approach to matters commonly considered sacrosanct—the pattern was one in which Flecknoe and Shadwell emerge fleetingly as pseudo-messianic figures. Besides oblique allusion to prophecy and to scriptural story in the poem, there is above all the counterpoint of Cowlean phrase and cadence to keep the manner and tone of the <u>Davideis</u>—the serious portrayal of the prophet as hero—marching through the reader's mind.

To stress the Cowlean element in <u>Mac Flecknoe</u> is by no means to rule out its other literary affiliations, both ancient

and modern.[57] In the larger comic tradition, Mac Flecknoe
echoes the engaging and intellectualistic irony of Lucian and
certain of Lucian's Renaissance successors. Although difficult
to measure, an indebtedness of Mac Flecknoe to Erasmus and
The Praise of Folly is perhaps perceptible even in the design
of Dryden's poem.[58] A fuller study would surely reveal that
the strategy of Dryden's satire is determined not so much by
the conventions of epic as by the rules of classical oratory:
rules parodied, to our delight, in the manner of Erasmus' mock-
encomium. So, on the miniature stage of Mac Flecknoe, Shadwell's sacred ancestry, his mental equipment, his achievements
poetical and otherwise (including the gustatory) are displayed
with somewhat the same bewildering aplomb exemplified by
Dame Folly in her version of the art of public praise.

Mac Flecknoe as a whole may therefore be called a mock-
panegyric enclosed in a neat mock-epic frame. One cannot
doubt that in the second of its two aspects the poem owes a good
deal to the conventions of ancient epic. Considered as narrative
and as a burlesque handling of an epic episode, Mac Flecknoe
has been described by one of its critics as a consistent attempt
to adapt classical conventions to comic purposes: "Dryden employed skilfully the epic conventions best suited to his action.
He made use of the Goddess Fame, of the debate and the harangue, of the prophecy, omen, and vow, and the supernatural
disappearance of mortals."[59] All this is helpful and true. Yet
it is well to remember that the poem is ambiguous and ironical
and that certain of these devices had ample precedent in the
Bible, to say nothing of the Christianized neo-classical epic of
Dryden's own age. In one important instance, of course, the
supernatural disappearance of mortals, Dryden's specific handling of the device points to a verse in Scripture.

Because of the way in which the Davideis places numerous
portions of the text of Mac Flecknoe in a novel perspective,
opening up revealing vistas into Dryden's mind and his age, it
is an oversimplification to suppose that the poem's narrative
scheme or mock-epic characterization is chiefly a burlesque
of ancient practice. In fact, all attempts to over-regularize
Mac Flecknoe for the sake of finding a single model or analogue
must necessarily collapse if for no other reason than that the
nonsense-theme of the poem has been incorporated in its total
structure. In Mac Flecknoe, through the integrative fusion of

types and conventions normally kept distinct, disorder itself
has been civilized and brought within the rule of a unified
artistic effect, even though it is but the powerful mirth of
the grotesque. Because of his "celerity of imagining" and swift-
paced "direction to some approved end," Dryden succeeded
where Cowley had failed.

NOTES

1 See, for example, Dryden's remarks on Cowley's "poetical
fictions" in "The Author's Apology for Heroic Poetry and
Poetic Licence" (1677), Essays of John Dryden, ed. W. P.
Ker (Oxford, 1926), I, 188, and A. H. Nethercot, "The Repu-
tation of Abraham Cowley; 1660–1800," PMLA, XXXVIII
(Sept., 1923), 595–96, 600.

2 Ker, II, 258.

3 Ibid., II, 108–109.

4 The date now generally accepted is 1678; see Hugh Macdonald, John Dryden: A Bibliography (Oxford, 1939), pp. 28–
29.

5 Ker, II, 258.

6 See the Dedication to Aureng-Zebe (1675), in Dryden: The
Dramatic Works, ed. M. Summers (London, 1932), IV, 84;
also Ker, II, 37–38, 272.

7 Dedication to Aureng-Zebe, in Summers, IV, 83. Dryden
is referring to Cowley not as a poet but as his moral guide
—a "better master" than Epicurus.

8 See Hugh Macdonald, "The Attacks on Dryden," Essays and
Studies of the English Association, XXI (1936), 45, 73–74.

9 See Gilbert Highet, The Classical Tradition (New York,
1949), p. 314.

10 The relationship is emphasized by Mark Van Doren, in The
Poetry of John Dryden (Cambridge, 1931), p. 171.

11 Lives of the Poets, ed. G. Birbeck Hill (London, 1905), I,
49. For comprehensive studies of Cowley's reputation see
A. H. Nethercot, op.cit., pp. 588–641; A. H. Nethercot,

Abraham Cowley: The Muses' Hannibal (London, 1931), pp. 280 ff.; Jean Loiseau, Abraham Cowley's Reputation in England (Paris, 1931).

12 See below, pp. 173–4.

13 The bibliography of the subject is discussed at length in Harold F. Brooks, "The 'Imitation' in English Poetry, especially in Formal Satire, before the Age of Pope," Review of English Studies, XXV (April, 1949), 124–40. For brief but informative comment on the neo-classical practice of borrowing, see Francis Gallaway, Reason, Rule, and Revolt in English Classicism (New York, 1940), pp. 210 ff., and James Sutherland, Preface to Eighteenth Century Poetry (Oxford, 1948), pp. 56–57, 133–36. The best detailed study of Dryden's method of borrowing materials supplied by his immediate forerunners is found in Helene Maxwell Hooker, "Dryden's Georgics and English Predecessors," The Huntington Library Quarterly, IX (May, 1946), 273–310.

14 See Brooks, pp. 127–28. Dryden discusses imitation as a mode of translation in his "Preface to the Translation of Ovid's Epistles" (1680), Ker, I, 237 ff.

15 Johnson's Dictionary, vb. imitate 3.

16 Oliver Elton, in The Augustan Ages (Edinburgh and London, 1899), p. 231, long ago noted the overlapping of genres and mingling of modes in the poetry of the period: "These three kinds, satire, imitation, translation, become indistinctly divided when they are practised, in a common metre, by a syndicate of wits, the 'mob of gentlemen' reinforced by some professional poets, for purposes ranging from personal aggression to literary criticism."

17 For Cowley's theory of the heroic poem based on Scripture see his "Preface to the Reader" in The English Writings of Abraham Cowley: Poems, ed. A. R. Waller (Cambridge, 1905), pp. 11–14; also Basil Willey, The Seventeenth Century Background (London, 1934), pp. 224–32, and Leah Jonas, The Divine Science (New York, 1940), pp. 160–65.

18 All quotations from Dryden's poetry, unless otherwise noted, are from John Sargeaunt's text in The Poems of John Dryden (Oxford, 1929).

195

19 All quotations from the Davideis are from Waller's edition, referred to hereafter as Poems. Scott noted the parody of Cowley in his edition of Dryden: The Works of John Dryden, ed. Sir Walter Scott and revised by George Saintsbury (Edinburgh, 1885), X, 448. G. Birbeck Hill quoted the same passage from the Davideis in his edition of The Lives of the Poets, I, 49.

20 First pointed out by Van Doren, op.cit., p. 22.

21 See below, p. 191.

22 A Study of Literature for Readers and Critics (Ithaca, 1948), pp. 197–98.

23 He completed only four out of twelve projected books; see "The Preface to the Reader," Poems, pp. 11–12.

24 Compare, for example, "And blest with issue of a large increase," Mac Flecknoe, l. 8; Deut. 16:15: "Because the Lord thy God shall bless thee in all thine increase"; "He paused, and all the people cry'd Amen," Mac Flecknoe, l. 144; Neh. 8:6, where Ezra reads the Law to the tribe: "And all the people answered, Amen, Amen, with lifting up their hands: and they bowed their heads, and worshipped the Lord with their faces to the ground."

25 Matt. 3:3, 4.

26 The Poetical Works of John Dryden, ed. W. D. Christie (London, 1907), p. 144.

27 See R. Florence Brinkley, Arthurian Legend in the Seventeenth Century (Baltimore, 1932), pp. 11–12, 200.

28 The conception of the anointed king as a ruler modeled upon David was not merely a seventeenth-century notion but part of a widespread tradition reaching back to the kingworship of the ninth century; see Ernest H. Kantorowicz, Laudes Regiae: A Study in Liturgical Acclamations and Medieval Ruler Worship (University of California Publications in History, Vol. XXX [Berkeley and Los Angeles, 1946]), 57: "This is the meaning of the idea of the Frankish 'Regnum Davidicum' . . . He was the novus Moyses, the novus David. He was the priestly king, the rex et sacerdos."

For the David-formula in the seventeenth century, see
Richard F. Jones, "The Originality of Absalom and Achitophel," Modern Language Notes, XLVI (April, 1931), 211–
18.

29   Lines 108, 112, 129–30. For annotations of Dryden's classical allusions in Mac Flecknoe see especially The Poetical
Works of John Dryden, ed. G. R. Noyes (revised ed.; Cambridge, 1950). For "lambent," Noyes cites Aeneis, ii, 931,
Dryden's translation. Cowley, however, had already used
the word in the Virgilian sense in the Davideis, where he
comments as follows (Poems, p. 359): "Lambent fire is,
A thin unctuous exhalation made out of the Spirits of Animals, kindled by Motion, and burning without consuming
anything but it self. Called Lambent, from Licking over,
as it were, the place it touches. It was counted a Good
Omen. Virg. describes the whole nature of it excellently
in three verses, Aen. 2." It is not impossible that the connotations of "lambent" as emphasized by Cowley ("unctuous
exhalation," "Spirits of Animals," "Licking over") may have
been in Dryden's mind in applying the word to Shadwell.
An additional Virgilian allusion seems to be the reference
to Shadwell's voyage on the Thames (Mac Flecknoe, ll. 38
ff). Tillotson, in the Twickenham Pope, II, 158 n., groups
the passage with Aeneas's voyage up the Tiber (Aeneid,
vii) and the opening of Canto II in The Rape of the Lock.

30   The passage has been cited as an example of Dryden's
genius for suggesting the style of Virgil; see R. A. Brower,
"Dryden's Epic Manner and Virgil," PMLA, LV (March,
1940), 135. Brower comments that "here Dryden combined
the Homeric (and Virgilian) picture of Zeus with Virgil's
description of the inspired Sibyl" (Aeneid, VI, 77–79). The
allusion is more than probable; but this does not rule out
the practically simultaneous phonetic echo of the Davideis
in the immediately preceding couplet (Mac Flecknoe, ll.
134–135); see below, pp. 181–2.

31   See Cowley's note (Davideis, Bk. III, p. 361, note 56) on the
"outward Robe or Mantle" given to David by Jonathan: "a
loose garment not exactly fitted to their bodies (for the profession of Taylors was not so ancient, but clothes were

made by the wives, mothers & servants even of the greatest persons) & so might serve for any size or stature." In On the Death of Mr. Crashaw (Poems, p. 50) Cowley had compared himself to Elisha and Crashaw to Elijah:

> Lo here I beg (I whom thou once didst prove
> So humble to Esteem, so Good to Love)
> Not that thy Spirit might on me Doubled be,
> I ask but Half thy mighty Spirit for Me.

32 II Kings 2:9, 13. The allusion was noted by J. Churton Collins in his edition of The Satires of Dryden (London, 1897)

33 Leviathan, Everyman edition, p. 37. See also George Williamson, "The Restoration Revolt Against Enthusiasm," Studies in Philology, XXX (Oct., 1933), 581 ff.

34 See Ruth Wallerstein, "To Madness Near Allied: Shaftesbury and His Place in the Design and Thought of Absalom and Achitophel," The Huntington Library Quarterly, XV (Aug., 1943), 446–47.

35 Leviathan, p. 33.

36 See Davideis, Bk. II, p. 306, note 1, and Aeneis, x, l. 172, Dryden's translation: "And shook the sacred honours of his head" (Et laetos oculis afflarat Honores). Tillotson, in the Twickenham Pope, II, 191–92, notes that Pope borrowed the word in Canto IV, l. 140, of The Rape of the Lock: "The long contended Honours of her Head."

37 Davideis, Bk. IV, p. 399, note 28.

38 "Epistle Dedicatory to the Rival Ladies" (1664), Ker, I, 1. See also C. D. Thorpe, The Aesthetic Theory of Thomas Hobbes (Ann Arbor, 1940), pp. 189 ff.

39 There are doubtless other echoes or correspondences which I have missed or have omitted for reasons of space: for example, "The King himself the sacred Unction made," Mac Flecknoe, l. 118; "Himself the Sacrifice and Offring's made," Davideis, Bk. IV, p. 384; "At once his Sceptre and his rule of Sway," Mac Flecknoe, l. 123; "At once his Murder and his Monument," Davideis, Bk. I, p. 247; "To far Barbadoes on the Western main," Mac Flecknoe, l. 140; "From sacred Jordan to the Western main," Davideis, Bk. IV, p. 366.

40   See Religio Laici, l. 221, and Aeneis, ii, ll. 789, 948.

41   Davideis, Bk. II, pp. 291, 311, note 28.

42   Ibid., Bk. I, p. 248.

43   R. L. Sharp, From Donne to Dryden (Chapel Hill, 1940),
      p. 189, points out that in certain of Dryden's early poems
      "the tone of Cowley, rather heavy and martial, was re-
      peated by Dryden in almost its unique quality; what we can
      identify as Cowley's tone—and it is necessary to forget
      conceits for the time being—seems also identifiable as
      Dryden's." For the general influence of Cowley on the
      younger Dryden, see also Sharp, pp. 119–20, 186–89.

44   Dryden gains his burlesque effect partly through imposing
      an antithetical logical structure ("But Sh---," etc.) upon a
      pattern which in Cowley was merely one of monotonous
      aggregation of detail plus parallel repetition.

45   For an account of the Nursery's location and troubled his-
      tory (it ended in the eighteenth century as an Anabaptist
      meeting house), see Leslie J. Hotson, The Commonwealth
      and Restoration Stage (Cambridge, 1928), pp. 176–96.

46   Poems, pp. 258 ff. Tillotson, in the Twickenham Pope, II,
      167, comments that Pope's description in The Rape of the
      Lock of Hampton Court ("Close by those Meads for ever
      crown'd with Flow'rs,/Where Thames with Pride surveys
      his rising Tow'rs," etc.) "refines on the vulgar structures
      described in similar terms in Mac Flecknoe, ll. 64 ff., the
      Dispensary, pp. 1 f., 38 f." If the present interpretation is
      correct, Cowley's "Prophets Colledge" would seem to ante-
      date Mac Flecknoe as an ancestor of the convention.

47   Poems, pp. 278–79, note 47.

48   The borrowing was first noted by J. Churton Collins in his
      edition of The Satires of Dryden (London, 1897).

49   It is possible that in his description of the dramatic Nur-
      sery Dryden's memory made an associative leap to the
      botanical nursery described in Gondibert; spaniel-like,
      Dryden's fancy then pursued the scent to the point of seiz-
      ing from Davenant the borrowed line. The nursery-formula

appears also in <u>Absalom and Achitophel</u>, II, 324–25, and in <u>The Hind and the Panther</u>, III, 997–98.

50 <u>Gondibert</u>, in <u>The Works of the English Poets</u>, ed. Alexander Chalmers (London, 1810), VI, 403.

51 See Van Doren, pp. 34–35; also Sharp, p. 189.

52 But see the opening lines of <u>Mac Flecknoe</u> and compare Davenant's description of King Aribert in <u>Gondibert</u> (Chalmers, VI, 375):

> Of all the Lombards, by their trophies known
>   Who sought Fame soon, and had her favour long,
> King Aribert best seem'd to fill the throne;
>   And bred most bus'ness for heroick song.

53 Scott-Saintsbury, XV, 228.

54 A single echo of Milton appears in <u>Mac Flecknoe</u>, ll. 106–107: "The hoary Prince in Majesty appear'd,/High on a Throne of his own Labours rear'd"; see <u>Paradise Lost</u>, II, 1–5: "High on a throne of royal state," etc. Sutherland, in the Twickenham <u>Pope</u>, V, 96–97, notes that Pope echoes <u>Mac Flecknoe</u> in the <u>Dunciad</u>, II, 1 f.: "High on a gorgeous seat, that far outshone/Henley's gilt Tub, or Fleckno's Irish Throne," etc.

55 Ker, I, 178–79.

56 Ker, I, 188.

57 Critics have occasionally acknowledged a vague resemblance to Boileau's <u>Le Lutrin</u>; see Richmond P. Bond, <u>English Burlesque Poetry: 1700:1750</u> (Cambridge, 1932), p. 156: "He [Dryden] knew Boileau's mock-epic, but the indebtedness is not detailed; it is rather one of spirit."

58 Dryden was well aware of the relationship of <u>Mac Flecknoe</u> to <u>The Praise of Folly</u>; see his remarks on "Varronian" satire, in "A Discourse Concerning the Original and Progress of Satire," Ker, II, 67.

59 G. L. Diffenbaugh, <u>The Rise and Development of the Mock-Poem in England from 1660 to 1714</u> (Urbana, 1926), p. 23.

THE ORIGINALITY OF ABSALOM AND ACHITOPHEL

Richard F. Jones

Ever since Scott published his edition of Dryden's works,
here has been little disposition to attribute any great degree
of originality to Absalom and Achitophel in respect to the Bib-
ical story selected to carry the satire. For Scott shows that
not only had a Bible story been previously used in a poem,
closely resembling Dryden's, for political purposes but that
he very story of Absalom had been employed in 1680 to represent Monmouth's revolt against Charles.[1] Yet the extent to
which the life of King David had been applied to political situations in the seventeenth century, and especially the degree to
which "Achitophel" had become, prior to Dryden's poem, a conventional term for disloyal politicians have hardly been sufficiently recognized.

The work largely responsible for the popularity of this
Biblical episode in political writings was Nathanael Carpenter's
Achitophel, or the Picture of a Wicked Politician, the contents
of which were first contained in three sermons preached before
he University of Oxford. These, Wood says, were very much
applauded by all the scholars that heard them, and were eagerly
desired to be printed.[2] The first edition was published in Dublin
in 1627, but was immediately withdrawn in order that certain
passages suspected of attacking Arminianism might be deleted.
The popularity of the work is evidenced by its enjoying five
more editions, three published at London, 1629, 1633, 1638, and
two at Oxford, 1640, 1641. In the dedication Carpenter defines
his composition as "a sacred Tragedy, consisting of four chief
Actors, viz. David an anointed King: Absolon an ambitious
prince: Achitophel a wicked politician, and Hushai a loyal sub-
ect: a passage of history for variety pleasant, for instruction
useful, for event admirable." The author's purpose, however,

Reprinted from Modern Language Notes, Vol. 46 (1931), pp. 211–218,
by permission of the author and The Johns Hopkins University Press.

is much the same as that of the "character" writers of the period, though his method is different. By thoroughly analyzing the story of Absalom and Achitophel as it is revealed in the Scriptures, he draws a "character" of a crafty politician, and applies it to local conditions, especially to the machinations of the Catholics.

It seems that Achitophel first became a popular term with the Puritans on the eve of the civil war to designate what they considered to be the evil influences surrounding the king. One speaker in supporting certain puritan policies characterized his time as an "Age (Mr. Speaker) that hath produced and brought forth Achitophells, Hammans, Woolsies, Empsons, and Dudlies. . . . And I doubt not, but when his Majesty shall be truly informe of such matters, as we are able to charge them withall, we shall have the same justice against them, which heretofore hath been against their Predecessours, in whose wicked steps they have trodden."[3] About the same time another puritan orator in speak ing of the enemies of parliament proclaimed that all members of the latter had banded together "To defeat the Counsels of these Achitophels, which would involve us, Our Religion, our being, our Lawes, our liberties . . . in one universall and general desolation, to defeat I say, the Counsels of evil Achitophels."[4] Achitophel, as the representative of the whole tribe of wicked politicians, became so popular that he passed into ballad literature. After portraying with great gusto the imminent destruction of the bishops, the puritan poet concludes,

> Thus did the counsell of Achitophell
> Unto these Doctors prove a dismal Cell.[5]

Naturally the story proved popular in the pulpit, and due application was made of it to contemporary conditions, both from the puritan and the royalist points of view. In a sermon preached before the House of Commons, Sept. 24, 1645, and ordered printed by that body, Samuel Gibson first discussed the narrative and then applied it to the political crisis of his own day, with the fervent prayer that "all the enemies of the King and Parliament be as that young man Absolom, and that old Fox Ahitophel."[6] But the story could serve both parties equally well. The same year a Royalist thoroughly analyzed it, with a running application to the sad state to which the

Puritans had reduced England, and concluded in this manner: "This is the true Story of this Rebellion, faithfully extracted out of the Holy Writ, where it is Recorded; Scarce to be parallel'd untill these unhappy Times, whence it seemes they have taken their President. <u>It needs no other Application.</u>"[7]

Thus we see that in the unsettled conditions preceding and attending the civil war both Royalist and Puritan utilized the Bible story, or at least made use of the name of Achitophel to express their political condemnations. The restoration of Charles provided an even closer parallel with certain episodes in David's life, especially his exile and restoration,[8] which was seized upon with avidity by preachers and poets eager to stand in the good graces of their sovereign. One ecclesiastical congratulator says, with the air of a man making a new discovery, "If we compare the example of that king who is the present subject of our admiration with King David, as to those things we have spoken of him, we shall find them extreamly like one unto another," and the whole purpose of his sermon "is only to shew you the admirable conformity that is between those two Kings."[9] In some sermons of the day the parallel was developed to the farthest possible limits, one preacher listing and discussing fifteen particulars in which the lives of the two kings were similar. He even compares the cave in En-gedi in which David took up his abode, with the hollow oak where Charles is said to have hidden.[10]

The sermons which have just been cited are sufficiently numerous to compel the conclusion that the association of the English sovereign with David must have accompanied the former until his death, though his life as king hardly conformed to scriptural teachings. Indeed, Charles himself seems to have courted the comparison. While his fate was still in the balance, the monarch addressed a letter to the peers of England in which he sought to make political capital of the parallel: "Again we call upon our Peers, who cannot be insensible that the Streams of your own Honour must necessarily fail, when the Fountain which should feed them is diverted; We advise you to learn of the Hebrews, who after that absence of their <u>King David</u> (more than seven times doubled by our sufferings) grew to contention for bringing home their persecuted Prince."[11] While it is quite possible that Charles gave the cue to his clerical adulators, the inference is unnecessary in view of the well established tradition regarding the use of the comparison. This letter, however, assumes some importance in the light of a widely accepted account, which has its origin in the 1716 edition of Tonson's Miscellany Poems (II. 1), that Dryden undertook his poem at the instigation of Charles, for it strengthens this account, and indicates that the king may have been responsible for the form of the satire as well as its purpose.

Although the story of David's exile and restoration comprises the greater part of the parallels cited, Achitophel is by no means slighted, but is used generally to designate the enemies of the king.[12] As the poems mentioned in a previous note show, he still represented the false politician; in fact, he became so widely and frequently used as the prototype of traitors that a verb was coined from his name, the surest evidence of the identification of a type with a name. In a poem of the period, the failure of the Puritans is ascribed to their plotting against each other:

> So all their Projects broke, not any held
> One by another out-Achitophel'd.[13]

And for a number of years Achitophel served a useful purpose in affording a term of reproach to be leveled at the discomfited Puritans. In speaking of the way in which the puritan leaders had misled the ignorant people, Samuel Parker remarks, "So easie a thing is it for your crafty Achitophels to arm Faction with Zeal, and to draw the Multitudes into Tumults and Seditions under Colour of Religion."[14] George Vernon applies the name more specifically in his attack on John Owen, when he says the latter "crept into his [Cromwell's] favour, was nourished in his bosome, and continued his Achitophel to his dying day."[15]

One might say that any political disturbance of any importance during this period was sure to inspire reference to the Biblical traitor. In a sermon preached on the anniversary of the gunpowder plot and largely inspired by the recent popish plot, Henry Dove introduces the deadly parallel, concluding with the words, "I shall leave it to your memories to run the parallel between David's Conspirators and these Traytors, in the secresie of their Counsels, designs laid deep as Hell, and black as utter darkness, in the maliciousness of their calumnies and imbitter'd slanders, in the insolence of their insurrection and bold-fac'd Rebellion."[16] But no political situation could possibly furnish so close a parallel as Monmouth's disaffection. Here was the story of a king's son egged on by politicians to revolt against his father and adopting practices suggestive of the Scriptures. The application of the Biblical story to the affair was inevitable. We are not surprised, then, to find one who signs himself C. F. addressing a Letter[17] to Monmouth, which urges him to desist from his treasonable course, and makes the most out of the example of Absalom and his wicked politicians. In a very short tract published the same year an ever closer parallel is traced between the scriptural characters and Monmouth and Shaftesbury.[18] Certainly by the time Dryden's satire appeared, the comparison had been considerably overworked. It is not strange, then, to hear one of Shaftesbury's adherents say, evidently in scorn of Dryden's originality,

> Let them with their Poetick Malice swell.
> Falsely apply the Story, known so well,
> Of Absolom, and of Achitophel.[19]

It is not hard to understand why the vicissitudinous life of King David, and especially the episode of Absalom and Achitophel, should have figured prominently in the treatises, sermons, speeches, and poems of a period so troublesome for English kings as the seventeenth century. Even though it was not until the last years of the reign of Charles II that a clear parallel for Absalom was furnished, he could very well be used to represent rebellion in general. As for Achitophel, political strife was so intense and feeling ran so high that every faction needed some term into which could be packed all the hatred and contempt inspired by the supposedly wicked and deceitful practices of the other factions. Such a term as Achitophel was all the more useful when it was expedient to attack the counsellors of a ruler rather than the ruler himself, as in the case of Charles I, to castigate living Puritans for the deeds of Cromwell who was beyond punishment, and to show some tenderness to the son of a king. Yet when everything is taken into consideration, the wide use of the story is still remarkable. Dryden, or possibly Charles, could not have shown less originality in the selection of the vehicle for the satire. This fact, of course, does in no way detract from Dryden's originality in his treatment of the parallel, nor from his vigorous satire and energetic verse.

NOTES

1 Works of John Dryden, 1808, IX, 197–207.

2 Athenae Oxoniensis, ed. P. Bliss, 1815, II, col. 421.

3 Mr. Grimston's Speech, In the High Court of Parliament, 1641, p. 15.

4 Densell Hollis, Speech at the delivery of the Protestation to the Lords of the upper House of Parliament, 4 May, 1641, p. 7.

5 The Prentises Prophicie, 1642, p. 3.

6 The Ruine of the Authors and Fomentors of Civill Warres, p. 27. This is one of the very few instances where the spelling of the name follows the authorized version. Richard Garnett (Age of Dryden, p. 21n.) thinks it "worth remarking that although not yet a Roman Catholic, Dryden in this name employs the orthography, not of the authorized version, but of the Vulgate." Needless to say, Dryden was merely following the usual spelling of the name in the seventeenth century.

7 The italics are the author's; see Absolom's Rebellion. As it is Recorded in the 2 Sam. Chap. 15, 16, 17, 18 & 19. With some Observations upon the Severall Passages thereof. Too fit a Patterne for the present Times, whereinto we are Fallen. Oxford, 1645. Other examples of the conventional use of Achitophel are found in certain royalist effusions such as Francis Wortley's Characters and Elegies, 1646, p. 27, in which the author compares the treason of Britanicus [Marchmont Needham?] to that of Achitophel, and expresses the wish that all traitors may meet Achitophel's fate; and Mercurius Britanicus His Welcome to Hell: With the Divills Blessing to Britanicus, 1647, in which occur the lines

> Nay thou shalt set thy house in order too,
> And in thy death Achitophell out-do,
> *   *   *   *   *   *   *   *   *
> And therefore, in thy death thou shall excell
> That great grave Councellor Achitophell.

And another Royalist advises the puritan "Masters of Wit
and Statecraft to have before their eyes the unsuccessful
ends of Achitophel, the Oracle of the times he lived in."
Peter Heylyn, Cosmographie, 1652, "To the Reader."

8 Verrall says the "parallel was obvious enough, and it was
indeed a common habit in political sermons to compare
Charles with David." He also refers to such a comparison in Dryden's Astraea Redux and in Lee's verses prefixed to The State of Innocence, in which the latter urges
Dryden to develop the parallel (Lectures on Dryden, pp.
56-58). A. W. Ward states that the parallel "was a commonplace of restoration poetry" (Cam. Hist. Eng. Lit.,
VIII, 41). Scott refers (op.cit., IX, 200n.) to John Rich's
Verses on the blessed and happy Coronation of Charles
the II, 1661, in which occur the lines,

    Preserve thy David, and he that rebells,
    Confound his Councells, like Achitophels.

Other poems that may be cited are John Quarles' Rebellion's Downfall, 1662, and an undated ballad, probably of
this period, entitled His Majesties miraculous Preservation By the Oak, Maid, and Ship.

9 Anthony Hulsius, The Royal Joy. Or, A Sermon of Congratulation, p. 11. This was preached at Breda, May 23,
1660, the day before Charles' departure for England. In
a sermon preached June 28, 1660, William Creed claims
that "The Author of this book of Samuel, or the Kings,
seemes to have been a Register of our times, and to have
foretold of these same changes, we in our days have lived
to see," and he elaborates upon the comparison of the modern with the ancient king. Judah's Return to their Allegiance,
and David's Return to his Crown and Kingdom, 1660, p. 1.

10 R. Feltman in a sermon preached May 29, 1660, and entitled
Davids Recognition, with a Parallel betwixt his and our
present Soveraigns Sufferings and Deliverances. For another elaborate comparison consult Clement Barksdale's
sermon delivered May 24, 1660, The Kings Return. See
also James Buck's St. Paul's Thanksgiving, May 10, 1660;
R. Mosson's England's Gratulation For the King and his

Subjects Happy Union, May 10, 1660; George Willington's The Thrise Welcome and happy Inauguration of our most Gracious Sovereign, King Charles, 1660. The sermons and other references cited in this article, for the majority of which I am indebted to my wife, are only representative, and their number could easily be augmented by further investigation.

11 A Letter from His Ma^ty. King Charles II^d. To his Peers the Lords in England, 1660. Since Thomason gives March 20 as the date of publication, this letter preceded all the sermons that have been noticed.

12 See especially W. Creed's Judah's Return.

13 H. Beeston Winton, A Poem to His most Excellent Majesty Charles the Second, 1660, p. 6. Two years later Wither, in Verses intended to the King's Majesty, expresses a desire for

> So much worth, at least, as did commend
> His loyalty, whom David call'd his friend;
> And wit enough to make a parallel
> Of evry traytor with Achitophel.

14 A Letter to a Friend Concerning some of Dr. Owen's Principles and Practices, 1670, p. 27.

15 A Defence and Continuation of the Ecclesiastical Politie, 1671, p. 684.

16 A Sermon Preached before the Honourable House of Commons . . . November 5, 1680.

17 A Letter to his Grace the Duke of Monmouth, this 15th of July, 1680. By a true Lover of his Person and the Peace of this Kingdom. This is to be found in the Somers Tracts, ed. Walter Scott, VIII, 216. See also Scott's edition of Dryden's Works, IX, 199–200.

18 Absolom's Conspiracy; or The Tragedy of Treason, London, 1680. See the Harleian Miscellany, 1811, VII, 530. Malone pointed out that several months before the appearance of Dryden's poem, a satire entitled The Badger in the Fox-Trap, applied the name Achitophel to Shaftesbury:

> Some call me Tory, some Achitophel,
> Some Jack-a-Dandy, some old Machiavel.

See <u>Critical and Miscellaneous Prose Works of John Dryden</u>, ed. E. Malone, 1800, I, 141n. Malone, although he was familiar with Carpenter's book, thought Dryden was entirely original in his choice of the Biblical story.

19 <u>A Loyal Congratulation To the Right Honorable, Anthony, Earl of Shaftesbury</u>, London, 1681.

THE CONCLUSION OF DRYDEN'S
ABSALOM AND ACHITOPHEL

Godfrey Davies

Edmond Malone[1] stated in the "advertisement" to his edition of The Critical and Miscellaneous Prose Works of John Dryden that he found in the received accounts of his author's life and writings, "so much inaccuracy and uncertainty, that I soon resolved to take nothing upon trust, but to consider the subject as wholly new."[2] Here the attempt is made to apply this excellent rule to the conclusion of Dryden's most famous poem.

Lines 939 to 1025 of Absalom and Achitophel, which comprise David's speech at the end, raise several problems. The first is the extent of Charles II's responsibility for them. The second is the probable time when the King desired Dryden to write the poem, and when Dryden wrote it, for the dates are likely to help explain the substance of the conclusion. The third concerns the reason why he, assuming his responsibility, prescribed this particular ending.

The belief that Charles II suggested to Dryden a scriptural basis for a poem on contemporary politics and prescribed its conclusion rests upon two statements of later date. In the fourth edition of Dryden's Miscellaneous Poems (1716) appeared an unsigned note (on B_2): "To the Reader. In the year 1680 Mr. Dryden undertook the Poem of Absalom and Achitophel, upon the Desire of King Charles the Second."[3] Joseph Spence, in his Anecdotes,[4] after noting that the King gave Dryden the hint for The Medal, continued: "This was said by a priest that I often met at Mr. Pope's: and he[5] seemed to confirm it; adding, that King Charles obliged Dryden to put his Oxford speech into verse and to insert it toward the close of his Absalom and Achitophel.

Reprinted from Huntington Library Quarterly, Vol. 10 (1946), pp. 69–82, by permission of Mrs. Godfrey Davies and the publisher.

DRYDEN'S ABSALOM AND ACHITOPHEL

This evidence by itself can scarcely be regarded as conclusive, since the first part of it was committed to print thirty-
five years after the satire was written, and the second was
spoken nearly twenty years later still. However, the fact on
which both pieces of evidence agree—that the King suggested
the subject—can probably be accepted, particularly as the poet
laureate would, perhaps, hardly have ventured otherwise on the
frank description of the royal amours with which the satire
opens. The King had early in his reign likened himself to David,
and the aptness of the comparison may well have struck both
him and others afresh in 1681. Indeed, the analogy[6] between the
indulgent David and his rebellious son and Charles and Monmouth was so apparent as to suggest that not the idea but permission or encouragement to use it was what Dryden needed.

The probability is that Charles suggested to Dryden the
object as well as the framework of his satire, the kind of propaganda he needed as well as the vehicle. These two subjects can
be treated fully only by an examination of the whole poem. Attention is here directed merely to the conclusion in order to
determine, in the first place, the date when it is likely that the
royal "desire" was expressed to the poet. Two sets of circumstances may supply the answer to that question.

Ever since the dissolution of the Oxford Parliament on
March 28, 1681, there had been a roaring torrent of Tory addresses and pamphlets which had stressed such points as the
danger of a civil war as lamentable as the Great Rebellion, the
sedition inherent in dissent, and the benign rule of the King.
Undoubtedly the tide had turned and was now running as strongly
with the Tories as it had run with the Whigs for about thirty
months since the discovery of the Popish Plot. The royal cause
was triumphant, and the Whigs had failed either to carry through
Parliament their bill to exclude the Roman Catholic James, Duke
of York, from the throne, or to maintain their hold on public
opinion. The immediate threat of civil war had proved more
powerful than the remoter threat of a Popish successor to Charles,
then fifty-one years old and apparently in good health. But hatred
of Roman Catholicism was a lasting passion with Tories as well
as Whigs. Churchmen might soon recover from their fright at
the alleged prospect of a rebellion unless concrete evidence
was afforded of a real danger. Proof could be supplied only if
prominent Exclusionists could be convicted of treason.

Some time in June Charles made up his mind to have Whig leaders prosecuted. His decision did not rest on any popular demand. Addresses and Tory pamphlets had not called for individual victims. Therefore, the King required that his new policy be supported by new propaganda. Having determined to put Shaftesbury on trial for his life, he needed a writer who would make conviction easier by covering the Earl with obloquy. No Tory writer, including Dryden, had up to this time singled out Shaftesbury as the great conspirator and, excepting Dryden, no one apparently so stigmatized him in the interval between his arrest and trial. Therefore, the suggestion is at least plausible that the King turned to Dryden in June or July, perhaps more probably in the latter month, after the ignoramus on College's bill (see below) had revealed an unexpected difficulty in securing a conviction. Thereupon Dryden wrote "a pamphlet designed to achieve a particular end, pointed to the occasion, topical and allusive in every line." [7]

The concluding passage of <u>Absalom and Achitophel</u> fits the inference that Charles spoke to Dryden after a decision to put Shaftesbury and College upon trial for treason. The Whig leader's arrest was urged in the committee for foreign affairs on June 21, 1681,[8] and took place on July 2, when, after examination before the Privy Council, he was sent to the Tower.[9] There he was promptly visited by the Duke of Monmouth. If Dryden set to work soon after this date, he would have had ample time to have written his poem and had it printed by November 17, when it was published.

An indication that the latter part of the poem, at least, was written in September or October is furnished by the circumstances of the trial and execution of Stephen College, the notorious "protestant joiner." Lines 1000–1001

> Why am I forc'd, like Heav'n, against my mind,
> To make Examples of another Kind?

may well refer to this affair. College had been arrested on June 29 and arraigned at the Old Bailey on July 8, when a Whig jury threw out the bill with "ignoramus." He was then successfully indicted at Oxford, where his offense had taken place, tried and found guilty on August 17, and executed two weeks later. The witnesses against him were those who had formerly

testified to an Irish plot,[10] and in his line: "Against themselves
their Witnesses will Swear," Dryden may have been recording
what had actually happened. Many ballads testify to the exultation loyal writers felt at the verdict,[11] and Dryden may have
shared this sentiment. Certainly his final lines, that God-like
David was restored, may well have been inspired by the dejec-
tion in Whig circles at College's indictment and conviction at
Oxford. As Roger North wrote, "It is not to be conceived what
a Thunderclap it was for the Faction, to hear that a prime Instrument of their's should be brought to answer, much more to
attaint of Treason. They thought their whole Party safe en-
sconced behind the Sherriffs of <u>London</u> and <u>Middlesex</u>, with their
Partisans of <u>Ignoramus</u>; and that the Law was enervous as to
them."[12]

However, granting that Dryden wrote his satire while Shaftesbury was awaiting trial, and some of it after College's execution,
the question still remains whether there is any reason for believing that the King prescribed how the poem should end. Spence's
anecdote that the King obliged the poet to versify his Oxford
speech is improbable in itself. Charles addressed the two
Houses only in his opening speech on March 21, 1681, except
for a few words when ordering the Lord Chancellor to dissolve
Parliament a week later. By its very nature, an opening speech
would normally have few or none of the elements of a manifesto
designed to appeal to public opinion against the House of Commons.[13] Indeed, much of the speech was inapplicable to the
situation that developed during the spring and summer.

The King began by explaining that he had been forced to
part with his last Parliament by the Commons' unwarrantable
proceedings, which were such as to occasion wonder that his
patience lasted so long and not that he at length grew weary.
He declared that he would neither use arbitrary government
nor suffer others to use it, and that he always would be as careful to preserve the liberties of the subject as any Parliament
could be. He called attention to the need for a further prosecution of the Popish Plot and the more speedy conviction of re-
cusants so that, if possible, the country might be rid of that
party altogether. He warned members against trying to conceal a design to alter the foundation of the government behind
imaginary fears for Protestantism, and urged them to remember that without the safety and dignity of the monarchy neither

religion nor property could be safe. He professed his willingness, if means could be found, to provide for a Protestant ad-
ministration if a Papist (i.e., James) ascended the throne, but
refused to permit any alteration in the succession. He concluded with the advice "that the rules and measures of all your
votes may be the known and established laws of the land; which
neither can, nor ought to be departed from, nor changed, but
by act of parliament. And I may the more reasonably require,
That you make the laws of the land your rule, because I am resolved they shall be mine."[14]

For convenience of comparison, this precis of the speech
the King actually delivered is here followed by a summary of
the concluding lines of Dryden's poem: Lines 939–954—The
royal clemency has been attributed to fear, not to innate mercy,
and so has caused the opposition leaders to believe that they
can encroach more and more on the prerogative. They contend
that a king exists for the convenience of his subjects, whereas
he is the hereditary pillar of the state. Lines 959–972—If Monmouth shakes that pillar, he will fall with it. But his father will
even now grant forgiveness if he will but ask it.[15] He has been
deluded by specious appeals to be a patriot, a word which means
one who "would by law supplant his prince." He cannot pretend
to be a keener champion of religion and law than the King. Even
Shaftesbury, when chancellor,[16] was never so regarded. Lines
973–990—The saints have long been rebels, and now they wish
to change the succession to the throne. But the royal assent is
essential to make a parliamentary bill the law of the land. To
exclude the rightful heir and to impose one of their own choice
would give the Exclusionists, by implication, the right to depose
the King, although they feign concern for his safety. Lines 990–
1025—Henceforth the King will take his stand in the known laws
of the realm and no longer permit a rebellious faction to usurp
the royal power and remove ministers from office. For the
future the King will protect his servants, but he may be forced
to make examples of his opponents. Since they demand law and
are not content with the royal mercy, they shall suffer the utmost rigor of law.[17] The very witnesses they have encouraged
shall now testify against them. The issue is not doubtful, for
the fury of the factious mobs is exhausted, and they cannot stand
against lawful power, which will retreat no further.

Almost the only point common to both speeches is the King's
intention to rule according to the laws of the realm.[18] But the

emphasis is different. In the speech at Oxford it is upon the royal will to rule as a constitutional monarch but in the poem it is also upon the enforcement of the laws against rebels. Furthermore, if Spence correctly reported the anecdote, Dryden clearly disobeyed the royal command in many particulars, omitting most of what the King said and including much he did not say. The question, therefore, naturally arises, Must the anecdote be entirely ignored? The correct answer seems to be that Pope, Spence's informant, knew that Dryden had a source but named the wrong one. Although no direct evidence can be adduced as proof, the thesis here advanced is that Charles advised Dryden to incorporate in his satire the substance of the official defense of the dissolutions of Parliament. It is entitled <u>His Majesties Declaration to all His Loving Subjects Touching the Causes & Reasons that moved Him to Dissolve the Two last Parliaments. Published by His Majesties Command.</u>19 At the end of this tract is printed: "At the Court at Whitehall, April the Eighth, 1681. It is this day Ordered by His Majesty in Council, That this Declaration be forthwith Printed and Published, and Read in all Churches and Chapels throughout this Kingdom. Francis Gwyn."

This manifesto, from its very nature, is a more likely source for Dryden than the Oxford speech, because, like his satire, it was designed to win adherents and overthrow opponents. The <u>Declaration</u> had such a remarkable influence on public opinion and was so closely related to Dryden's political writings that it requires a brief analysis. Commencing with a brief restatement of the royal speech which opened Parliament on October 21, 1680, it proceeded to denounce the arbitrary orders and illegal votes of the Commons, with special stress on the resolutions against loans to the King and the enforcement of penal laws against dissenters. Passing to the Oxford Parliament, it recalled the offer to accept any expedient to preserve the Protestant religion in the case of a Popish successor. Unsatisfied, the Commons had insisted on a total exclusion from the throne of the lawful heir, although the King had frequently declared he could never, in "honour, justice, and conscience," consent to it. "We cannot, after the sad experience we have had of the late Civil Wars, that murder'd our father of blessed memory, and ruin'd the monarchy, consent to a law, that shall establish another most unnatural war, or at least make it necessary to maintain a standing force for the preserving the government and the peace of the kingdom." After a mention of the dispute between the two Houses over Fitzharris, whether he should be impeached or tried by the courts, the promise was made to call frequent parliaments and in all things to govern according to the laws of the kingdom. Appealing to the loyalty of all who remembered the rise and progress of the late troubles, the Declaration closed with a warning that "religion, liberty, and property were all lost and gone, when the monarchy was shaken off, and could never be reviv'd till that was restored."

The effect of this manifesto was immediate and far-reaching. It evoked the utmost enthusiasm in all Churchmen and Tories. It brought down a veritable flood of addresses from quarter sessions and corporations, counties and boroughs. As an opponent stated, the addresses "construe the King's Declaration as the erection of the royal standard and . . . intend these papers for the muster-rolls of those that are to fight under his Majesties ensigns."[20]

Many of these addresses were regularly printed in the London Gazette, sometimes in double issues, though their number necessitated their postponement or even the omission, except for a mention, of some of them. The first, April 18, was from the quarter sessions of Middlesex. "Ex uno disce omnes." It not only concurred in the Declaration but either adopted its language or expressed the same ideas in superlatives. Clearly the strongest appeals the Declaration made were to memories of the Civil Wars. Nearly all the addresses refer to the Great Rebellion as a time when, in the words of the Middlesex justices of the peace, "most illegal and arbitrary powers . . . most tyrannically disposed of the lives and fortunes of your good subjects at their pleasures, and left them neither religion, liberty, or property." The King replied in person that he would endeavor as much as in him lay to maintain the legal rights and properties of his subjects. Other addresses promised support alike against Papists and fanatical, ambitious, and antimonarchial parties that might "precipitate us again into the dismal miseries of a Civil War, and enslave us to the insupportable tyranny of an armed multitude."[21] The constant association of Papists and dissenters as equally dangerous[22] inevitably led addressers to demand that the laws against dissenters be put in force[23] after the insertion in the London Gazette[24] of a paragraph to prove that the statute 35 Elizabeth[25] against nonconformists was still valid.

The Whigs strove against this torrent of Tory propaganda by counter-petitions, already forbidden,[26] newspapers, whose publishers were, like Francis Smith of the <u>Protestant Intelligence</u>, liable to be committed to Newgate for high treason,[27] and pamphlets. For present purposes specific reference need be made only to the tract entitled <u>A Letter from a Person of Quality to his friend, concerning His Majesty's late Declaration.</u>[28] This Whig statement elicited replies from two famous men. George Savile, Earl (later Marquis) of Halifax, wrote <u>Observations Upon a late Libel, called A Letter.</u>[29] John Dryden compiled <u>His Majesties Declaration Defended . . . Being an Answer to . . . A Letter from a Person of Quality,</u>[30] which was published before June 22 when it was mentioned by the <u>Observator.</u>[31] This tract should be compared in detail with <u>Absalom and Achitophel</u> to detect both similarities and differences. Here all that can be attempted is to indicate some of the points Dryden made or omitted in what was primarily a reply. The very form he adopted—citing a passage from <u>A Letter</u> and then commenting on it—may have restricted his scope and account for some at least of the differences between his pamphlet and his poem.

Among the points Dryden made were: The King has a natural love for peace and quiet (p. 5): the faction will not be satisfied until they have the King as fast as they had his father (p. 7); the Whigs, since the discovery of the Popish Plot, have been lopping off the royal prerogatives and seizing sovereignty and arbitrary power while professing to fear the King's encroachments on the constitution (p. 11); the Whigs hope to attach Monmouth to their side "by some remote hopes" of the Crown, although they did not name him as heir to the throne in the Exclusion Bill at Oxford (p. 12); sectaries and commonwealths men were active (p. 13); the House of Commons voted that Protestant dissenters should not be persecuted, "but if it be true what has been commonly reported since the Plot, that Priests, Jesuits, and friars mingle amongst anabaptists, quakers, and other sectaries, and are their teachers, must not they be prosecuted neither?" (p. 17); His Majesty is well known to be an indulgent Prince to the consciences of his dissenting subjects (p. 17).

There are many notable features in this defense of the Dec
laration. Perhaps the most remarkable is the moderation shov
throughout as compared with the virulence of the addresses.
They contained inflammatory sentences such as one emanating
from Ludlow[32] and referring to the "most barbarous and horri
murder of that glorious martyr your royal father of ever bless
memory." But Dryden gave the merest hint, if that, of the exe
tion of Charles I (see the second item in the above summary).[3]
He mentioned commonwealths men but otherwise did not recall
the days

> Where Sanhedrin and Priest enslav'd the Nation
> And justifi'd their Spoils by Inspiration.

He raised the question of enforcing the laws against dissenters
only to dodge it by implying that if Papists should be persecute
their pupils, the dissenters, should also suffer. In general Dry
den does not go beyond the Declaration and in one important
respect—the execution of Charles I—falls short of it. It is
very curious that he persistently avoided, both in prose and
verse, this most telling point in the Tory propaganda. Did he
fear lest his own past should be raked up against him if he delv
into the history of the Civil Wars?[34]

Absalom and Achitophel was obviously written later than
His Majesties Declaration Defended and dealt with a different
situation. During the earlier period Charles II was on the defensive. His defenders, like Dryden, Halifax, and L'Estrange,
had to justify his dismissal of two parliaments within three
months—which recalled, as the Whigs pointed out, the abrupt
dissolutions of parliaments at the beginning of Charles I's reig
and the eleven years of unparliamentary government that followed. For several months they are content with an offensive-
defensive attitude, although from the beginning the addressers
took the offensive with all the reckless abandon of a Rupert on
the field of battle. So old a hand at Tory propaganda as L'Estrange viewed the first addresses with a jaundiced eye. In the
fourth Observator occurred this short dialogue:

Q. You do not take address-making to be a trade, I
   hope; do ye?
A. Yes, that I do; and so is Petition-making.

DRYDEN'S <u>ABSALOM AND ACHITOPHEL</u>

For a while L'Estrange is apparently more concerned, by reference to, or quotation from, the <u>Declaration,</u> to reveal the
benevolent and constitutional rule of the King than to brand his
opponents as seditious. Dryden's attitude in his pamphlet is
much the same. But by June the volume and exuberant loyalty
of addresses had convinced Charles that he could now safely
pass to the attack. Dryden's poem reflects the new attitude of
the court. Shaftesbury and his satellites, hitherto ignored in-
dividually, are now the target. They are traitors and their followers seditious by nature and principle. They must be crushed,
and Dryden wrote his matchless lines to accomplish their downfall. But when he came to the end of his satire, he reverted to
his earlier defensive position—a more vigorous defense than
formerly but still a defense for two-thirds of his lines. It is
still modeled fairly closely though not exclusively on the <u>Dec-
laration.</u>
    Naturally enough, the poet could not incorporate the com-
plete contents of a tract with ten folio pages, but not a few of
his most telling points are to be found there. The lines

> Without my leave a future King to choose,
> Infers a Right the present to Depose

are a reasonable paraphrase of "We have reason to believe . . .
that if We could have been brought to give Our Consent to a Bill
of Exclusion, the Intent was not to rest there, but to pass further,
and to attempt some other Great and Important Changes even in
Present."
    The couplet,

> Votes shall no more Established Pow'r controul,
> Such Votes as make a Part exceed the Whole,

may well have been inspired by the complaint in the <u>Declaration:</u>
"By which Vote, without any regard to the Laws establish'd,
they [Commons] assumed to themselves a Power of Suspending
Acts of Parliament; . . ."
    The lines,

> No groundless Clamours shall my Friends remove
> No Crouds have pow'r to Punish e'r they Prove,

may have been suggested by "Strange illegal Votes, declaring divers eminent Persons to be enemies to the King and Kingdom, without any Order or Process of Law, . . . or any Proof so much as offer'd against them."

In addition to these specific resemblances there are other lines which seem to have been, or may have been, derived from the general tenor of the Declaration rather than any particular sentence or phrase in it.

The couplet,

> Unsatiate as the barren Womb or Grave;
> God cannot grant so much as they can Crave,

is a picturesque way of saying what the Declaration had complained of more prosaically—that the gracious concessions offered by the King had all been rejected as insufficient. "That one was made for many" may have been suggested by the passage about "Old beloved Commonwealth-principles." But even if the ingenious student can detect more parallels than the above, the fact remains that Dryden not only in the conclusion but throughout the poem made no mention of one point on which the Declaration was so emphatic—that the King was resolved to have frequent Parliaments. Can it be that the King, whose French pension depended on his not listening to parliament,[35] was responsible for the striking omission? There was surely no point in reminding people of the promise which had served its turn by quieting the apprehensions of men who feared that the King was going to imitate his father and rule without parliament. Actually, Charles II ignored his pledges and the Triennial Act for the last four years of his reign.

The conclusion to Absalom and Achitophel has been criticized from Dr. Johnson's day. He pointed out that there is "an unpleasant disproportion between the beginning and the end." "Who can forbear to think of an enchanted castle," he asked, "which vanishes at once into air, when the destined knight blows his horn before it?"[36] Translating this simile into the politics of 1681, the castle would be the Whig party, the knight the King, and the horn the Declaration. Another criticism is that Dryden does not adhere closely to his main theme. From a dramatic and artistic point of view, to ignore the chief villain, Achitophel—apart from a casual reference—is a serious blemish.[37] From

a historical point of view too, the substitution of the party for
the leader is unexpected, for the time of publication demanded
a final fling at Shaftesbury on the eve of his trial for treason.
The main body of the poem has relevance to events that took
place from the beginning of July onward, though with some backward glances. No Tory propaganda in the spring refers to
Shaftesbury and Bethel, and Dryden in his pamphlet equally ignores them. The prominent parts assigned to them in the poem
can be explained by the arrest of the one and the share the other
had in securing <u>ignoramus</u> juries in London. Assuming that
Dryden wrote his poem not long before its publication, he was
dealing with subjects of topical interest, and trying to influence
public opinion on current issues.

But the conclusion drops Shaftesbury and his individual sup-
porters, and reverts to the Whig party as revolutionary and to
the King as obliged to restrain sedition. The defensive attitude
is a return to that of the <u>Declaration</u> and to Dryden's defense of
it. The shift in emphasis was very astute. The <u>Declaration</u> had
been most successful. Moreover, Charles knew that the vocifer-
ous loyalty of the addresses was not shared by all. He knew
that between the Whigs and Tories was a middle group—Trim-
mers, like Halifax—adverse to absolutism and any bloody revenge upon the Whigs. These moderates had been won over by
the promises of constitutional government and gentle rule in
the <u>Declaration</u>. What more natural than to revive those parts
of it which claimed that the Whigs were trying to wreck the constitution and that the King was its true guardian?

Accordingly, the conclusion is keyed to an older tune. With
the exception of the few lines on Monmouth, and the longer passage at the end, there is little here that could not have been set
down in the spring of 1681. Although Tory writers like L'Estrange were no longer citing the King's <u>Declaration</u> in the summer, Dryden deliberately devoted much of his conclusion to the
very arguments the King had set forth early in April. Is there
any other likely explanation than that Spence's anecdote is true
in substance if erroneous in detail and that Dryden did receive
a royal order or hint to close his poem with an adaptation in
verse of the King's <u>Declaration</u>?

NOTES

1 For an appreciation of one who is "still our greatest authority on the life of Dryden" see David Nichol Smith, ante, III (Oct. 1939), 23–36.

2 Vol. I, Part I (London, 1800), vi.

3 This seems to be the authority for Edmond Malone's (Critical and Miscellaneous Prose Works of John Dryden, 1800, I, pt. I, pp. 141–42) remark that "Tate, who was likely to be well informed, relates, that this poem was undertaken. . . ." Of course the year, 1680, is a slip for 1681.

4 Ed. S. W. Singer (1820), pp. 171–72.

5 I have assumed that "he" refers to Pope and not to the priest, but the point makes no difference to my argument.

6 For a list of early sermons on texts from 2 Samuel on the Absalom-Achitophel theme see William Crowe, The Catalogue of our English Writers on the Old and New Testament (Second Impression, London, 1668). The moral the Church of England drew is summed up by Joseph Hall, "Let no man look to prosper by rebellion," and "How easily may the fickle multitude be transported to the wrong side." Works (Oxford, 1837), I, 443. At the beginning of November, 1645, Lichfield published at Oxford Absalom's Rebellion. As it is recorded in the 2 Sam. Chap. 15, 16, 17, 18, & 19. With some observations upon the severall passages thereof. Too fit a patterne for the present times. Falconer Madan, Oxford Books, II, 408. For important notes on contemporary applications of the story of David and his ambitious son, see Hugh Macdonald, John Dryden, A Bibliography (Oxford, 1939) p. 18; and R. F. Jones, "The Originality of Absalom and Achitophel" in Modern Language Notes (April, 1931).

7 Walter Raleigh, Some Authors (Oxford, 1923), p. 162.

8 W. D. Christie, Life of Shaftesbury (London, 1871), II, app. VII.

9 Ibid., II, 412–13.

10 At least as early as June the Whigs were saying, presumably with reference to the arrest of Lord Howard of Escrick and

the trial of Fitzharris, that "every true Protestant is in daily hazard through their sham-plots, and vile and execrable villains hired to swear away his life." An Impartial Account of the Nature and Tendency of the late Addresses, dated June 28. Reprinted in State Tracts . . . Privately Printed in the Reign of Charles II (London, 1693), p. 437.

11 Dict. Nat. Biog., sub College. Edward Fitzharris, author of The True Englishman Speaking plain English, advocating the King's deposition and the Duke of York's exclusion, was executed on July 1, 1681. He may have been one of the "examples" to which Dryden refers.

12 Examen (London: Fletcher Gil Gyles, 1740), p. 588; cf. Observator, August 31; September 24.

13 The Oxford speech hardly figured in the controversy that followed the dissolution. One of the very few references to it was in the address from Haslemere, presented to Charles II on or about May 23. See London Gazette, May 23–25, 1681.

14 Cobbett's Parliamentary History (London: T. C. Hansard, 1808), IV, 1303–5.

15 Lines 957–60, appealing to Monmouth to repent, were added in the second edition.

16 When he would be keeper of the King's conscience.

17 The Observator of July 16, 1681, explains the reasons for enforcing the penal laws against dissenters. The King is obliged to act in his own defense. The dissenters, instead of being the quieter, are the more troublesome for being indulged. "Let the King give them what he will, they look upon it either as their due, or that he durst not do otherwise."

18 See Malone, pp. 154–55.

19 London: John Bill, Thomas Newcomb, and Henry Hills, 1681. According to Roger North, Lord Keeper Guilford prepared and "composed mostly" the Declaration. Lives of the Norths, ed. Augustus Jessop (London, 1890), I, 206.

20 An Impartial Account. Reprinted in State Tracts, p. 437.

223

21 Address from Southampton, London Gazette, May 12–16.

22 As the summer wore on, Tories tended to identify Papists and dissenters. See Observator, August 18: "The Spirit of Popery, speaking out of the mouthes of Phanatical Protestants."

23 Address from York, in London Gazette, May 26–30; cf. Sir Roger L'Estrange, Observator, April 26.

24 April 18–21.

25 G. W. Prothero, Select Statutes and other Constitutional Documents (Oxford, 1906), pp. 89–92.

26 A proclamation against tumultuous petitions had been issued December 12, 1679. See An Impartial Account in State Tracts, p. 426.

27 London Gazette, under date April 15. A proclamation of May 12, 1680, had prohibited unlicensed newsbooks and pamphlets.

28 Reprinted in State Tracts, pp. 187–92.

29 Edited by Hugh Macdonald (Cambridge, 1940).

30 London: T. Davies, 1681. The Letter is mentioned in the Observator of May 26.

31 Commended as "an excellent piece."

32 In London Gazette, May 30–June 2.

33 He also said that the King has learned from the unhappy example of his father not to perpetuate a parliament.

34 Cf. A. W. Verrall, Lectures on Dryden (Cambridge, 1914), pp. 19–20.

35 David Ogg, England in the Reign of Charles II (Oxford, 1934), II, 614.

36 Lives of the English Poets (The World's Classics: Oxford, 1933), I, 320–21.

37 As a student of history I leave to my literary colleagues the question how far Dryden's reputation as an artist gains by this explanation of what has generally been deemed a flaw in his satire.

RELIGIO LAICI AND FATHER SIMON'S HISTORY

Charles E. Ward

The English translator of Father Simon's Histoire critique du Vieux Testament has long been identified as one Henry Dickinson, about whom nothing more than his name has been known. Since his work provided the occasion for Dryden's Religio Laici, and thus becomes a book of passing importance, I should like to present a few new facts about him and his translation—hitherto unnoticed—which may serve to supplement Professor Bredvold's treatment of him and of his influence on Dryden's thinking in 1682.[1]

Professor Bredvold has pointed out that Father Simon's Histoire critique was first published in Paris in 1678, and again in Amsterdam, by Elzevir, in 1680. The English translation appeared in late 1681.[2] When Dryden, almost a year later, brought out Religio Laici, he included, as the penultimate paragraph in his preface, the following:

> It remains that I acquaint the reader that the verses were written for an ingenious young gentleman, my friend, upon his translation of the Critical History of the Old Testament, compos'd by the learned Father Simon: the verses therefore are address'd to the translator of that work, and the style of them is, what it ought to be, epistolary.

This passage suggests an intimacy with Henry Dickinson, which the facts that I have assembled do not entirely confirm; perhaps it should be read only as an indication of his habitual kindliness to his younger contemporaries.

Nearly all of the facts that I can discover about Dickinson are to be found in a very interesting and informative Chancery

Reprinted from Modern Language Notes, Vol. 61 (1946), pp. 407–412, by permission of the author and The Johns Hopkins University Press.

suit which Jacob Tonson instituted against Dickinson concerning the business arrangements for the publication of the Critical History.[3] Tonson begins his Bill by saying that he was acquainted with Henry Dickinson of London and that the latter "about May 1681 proposed printing a book he was translating out of French and which was entitled infer [sic] histoire critique de vieax Testament affirming it was a learned discourse & contained nothing but what was agreeable to sound doctrine and good manners." Dickinson, it appears, proposed that if Tonson would arrange to have it printed and pay half the costs, he would pay the other half. They would then share equally in the profits. To this proposal Tonson readily agreed. "Soon after," according to Tonson, the translator delivered the copy or "the greater part thereof"; and Tonson, carrying out his part of the bargain, dispatched it "to Miles Fletcher for printing with directions to apply to Dickinson for the remaining part thereof." All seems to have gone well until the book was nearly printed. At that time Tonson learned—from whom, he does not reveal—that the book "had been publicly burnt in Paris and did contain several things which might bring the publisher into some danger." Apparently frightened by the prospect of a possible action against him, Tonson informed Dickinson that he would not proceed with the printing. Dickinson thereupon sought to allay his fears by asserting that there was nothing harmful in the book; and to reinforce Tonson's belief in his honesty in the matter, he promised to send the stationer a note to that effect under his hand and seal. Sufficiently reassured, Tonson completed the printing of the History; but before he published it, he demanded the note, which, he now alleges, Dickinson refused to give him. At this point Tonson washed his hands of the whole affair.

Dickinson, however, seems to have been reluctant to see his book remain unpublished. "Shortly after," in Tonson's words, "Dickinson sent for your orator to y[e] Fleece Tavern in Fleetestreete and proposed your orator should publish the book and put his name thereto as the Publisher and undertake to pay all charges of paper and printing and Dickinson would relinquish all his share in the impression. Your orator refused being apprehensive of danger and offered to quit all his interest in the book and to deliver the same to Dickinson if he would pay the charges of paper and printing which offer Dickinson accepted. . . ." Later Dickinson asked Tonson to help him with the sale of the book, offering him 6d for every copy he sold. Tonson agreed to this solution. Subsequently he "caused all the books to be sent to Dickinson's Lodgings in Doctors Comõns and Dickinson employed Walter Davies to sell and publish the books for him, who did so, and the name of Walter Davies was printed in the title page of the said books as the publisher thereof, and Dickinson procured advertisements of the printing of the books to be put into the Gazette and other news books that the same was to be sold by Walter Davies."

But the books sold very slowly. About January, 1681/2, Dickinson, informed that the book was unlikely ever "to goe off for ready money," and plagued by the printer and the suppliers of the paper for their money—about £150—sent for Tonson and laid before him a new plan. He pointed out to the stationer that the book had now been "exposed to sale" and that no exception had been made to it; and he proposed that if Tonson "would pay all the money due the printers and for the paper your orator should have the book to his own use and make what advantage he could telling your orator he had obtained the principal end he aimed at in the translation which was the pleasing of his father and that your orator might make a profit by bartering the same for other books in the way of his trade." So Tonson, as he deposes, "not having heard of the offence that the said book had given and being sensible that he stood engaged for the paper and printing" agreed to this offer. He paid off remaining debts of more than £100, and Dickinson, acting in good faith, ordered Walter Davies to give an account to Tonson of the books he had sold and he himself sent a number of copies to Tonson's shop "pretending that these were all that remained unsold."

Some months later, about May, 1682, Dickinson gave Tonson "a supplement of the said criticall Historie which he said he had translated telling your orator he gave it freely to him and hoped it might give him profit."[4] Looking upon himself as the sole owner, Tonson proceeded to sell some and to barter away for other books the greater part of them "in the usual way of booksellers dealing with one another." And though he was frequently in the company of Dickinson thereafter and often offered to give him copies of books which he had received in barter for the History, Dickinson had shown no interest. But as soon as the greater part of the impression had been disposed of in one way or another, the translator suddenly demanded an accounting, asserting that Tonson had been acting merely as an agent for him, with an allowance for the printing and selling costs. Since he had understood that the books were now his, Tonson reveals that he has not kept accounts; and he counter-charges that Dickinson had originally retained a large number of copies which he has sold for his own benefit. At the end of his complaint Tonson admits that "your orator cannot have dis-covery of the third and last agreement otherwise than by the corporal oath of Dickinson your orator's witnesses being now in places unknown and therefore he is remediless."

These then are the important sections in Tonson's com-plaint. Were it possible to have access to Dickinson's answer, if he made one, we might be given further details regarding the Critical History. But we have enough here to enable us to see a bit more clearly the background of Dryden's poem. First, with respect to Henry Dickinson. He was, it is clear, a young man interested in the law, with his residence in Doctor's Com-mons. It seems reasonably certain that he was not himself greatly interested in Father Simon's Histoire critique or in the religious issues involved; for if Tonson is telling the truth, Dickinson undertook the translation only to please his father.

It is somewhat ironic that such a filial gesture should have introduced into England a book of great scholarship which was to provide the ablest poet of the time the occasion for a poem of considerable significance in his intellectual development. Dickinson, it seems certain, was only three years up from Cam-bridge, where he had been a member of Dryden's old college.[5] This common interest may have provided a basis for an acquaint-anceship of sorts, especially since Dryden was generally helpful to young literary men. I can hardly believe, however, that there was friendship between them. Dickinson was so inconspicuous a figure that it is impossible to follow his career. He wrote, however, at least one more piece, which brought him into trouble with the authorities. Luttrell records on September 28, 1683: "about this time came out a scandalous libell against Dr. Tillot-son, entitl'd Queries about the Dean of Canterbury, writt by one Mr. Dickinson, of Doctors Commons, who was taken by a mes-senger for the same, and carried before the Councill, where he was severely checked; and the attorney generall was commanded

to exhibit an information against him."[6] This testimony is
corroborated by the Calendar of State Papers, Domestic (1683,
pp. 428, 433), where it is recorded that Robert Moon, bookseller,
was taken with Dickinson. Though Dickinson gave bail for his
appearance, the action against him seems to have been dropped,
for no further mention is made of him. Whatever further work
Dickinson may have done—and none has ever been identified—
he was hardly a serious aspirant for a literary reputation.

Another important piece of information that comes from
Tonson's Bill of Complaint is that Dickinson's translation was
almost a drug on the market. Not only did it not "goe off for
ready money": it was difficult—if we can believe Tonson—to
barter it away. It is now possible to explain the apparent two
issues of the Critical History. Tonson's fear, as we have seen,
dictated the transfer of the original sheets to Walter Davis,
who attached his title page and imprint. This is the "Walter
Davis issue," as described by Professor Bredvold. But when
Tonson's fears had been sufficiently allayed, Dickinson in-
structed Walter Davis to return to Tonson those same original
sheets. Then, with the addition of the supplement and the com-
mendatory verses, Tonson put his own title and imprint to the
same sheets, retaining, however, the Davis title page. This
is the "Tonson issue." They are, of course, the same. Dickinson's translation, then, was not a popular book; indeed, it
made hardly a stir in the book-buying market of 1682.[7] Father
Simon's History could not have been known by very many people
in England before the appearance of Dryden's Religio Laici in
November, 1682.

Dryden's own acquaintance with the History begins apparently with the Dickinson translation. There is no indication
that he was aware of the Paris edition of 1678 or of the Amsterdam edition of 1680. How early he knew of the existence of the
English translation is uncertain. But since we can now push
forward by some months the date of Dickinson's work, we may
be able to assume that Dryden was familiar with it earlier than
we have believed. Tonson's assertions make it clear that the
book was nearly completely translated in May, 1681, and that
the printing was completed before the end of the year; for the
Davis issue was selling very badly before January, 1681/2.
Since Dryden's Absalom and Achitophel, also with Davis' name
on the imprint, came out about November 17, 1681, it seems

clear that both Dryden's poem and Dickinson's translation were
going through the same stationers' hands and perhaps the same
printing shops at the same time. Under these circumstances,
there is every likelihood that Dryden was well aware of the
Critical History before the end of 1681. Since the Religio Laici
did not appear for at least a full year, we may conjecture that
he spent considerably more time studying Father Simon and
the literature of religious thought than we have believed. Instead of providing Dryden with a summer of thinking and writing, as Professor Bredvold has suggested, Dickinson's translation may well have provided him a full year of thinking and
writing.

NOTES

1   See L. I. Bredvold, The Intellectual Milieu of John Dryden,
    University of Michigan Publications, XII (1934), pp. 98–
    107. Professor Bredvold here examines at some length
    Father Simon's Critical History and the English transla-
    tion. He points out that "Dryden's acquaintance with it
    was perhaps the most critical event in his intellectual life."
    (p. 106.)

2   It was advertised in the Loyal Protestant and True Domes-
    tic Intelligence for January 14, 1681/2.

3   Tonson's Bill of Complaint is dated June 13, 1683. PRO C
    8/284/205.

4   The supplement referred to here was undoubtedly the answer
    to Spanheim's letter which is described thus on the title
    page which Tonson provided for himself soon after he re-
    ceived it: "With a Supplement, being a Defence of the Criti-
    cal History, in Answer to Mr. Spanheim's Treatise against
    it. Both Translated into English by H. D." (See Bredvold,
    op.cit., p. 162.)

5   He had been admitted Pensioner at Trinity on March 3,
    1672/3. He took his LL. B. in 1678. See W. W. Rouse Ball
    and J. A. Venn, Admissions to Trinity College, Cambridge,
    London, 1913, II, 506.

6 Narcissus Luttrell, A Brief Historical Relation of State Affairs, London, 1857, I, 282.

7 It is curious that Tonson should have retained the Walter Davis title page when he re-issued the book under his own imprint in the summer of 1682. He perhaps had some kind of trade agreement with Davis to share profits (and responsibility?) in certain books. For example, Walter Davis' name appears on the Tonson imprint of all the London editions of Absalom and Achitophel until the fifth (Macdonald, 12h).

DRYDEN AND THE ATOMS OF EPICURUS[*]

Edward N. Hooker

My starting point is a single poem, John Dryden's <u>Religio Laici</u>. The Latin title of this English poem might be rendered as The Faith, or Beliefs, of a Layman. <u>Religio Laici</u> is a fine poem; one critic, in fact, described it as the finest didactic poem in the English language. Of its art and beauty, however, I shall refrain from speaking. What I propose to do is to show, first, that the poem was a political act, a bold stroke delivered at a time of political crisis; and, second, that it manages to raise the curtain for us, revealing a dramatic upsurge of intellectual forces—philosophic systems, beliefs, assumptions, dogmas,—that gave a special meaning and flavor to the moment of history.

That moment of history was the period from 1678 to 1682, in which occurred the events described by a recent historian as "The Attempted Whig Revolution"—the period near the end of which, in November, 1682, <u>Religio Laici</u> appeared. Trouble had been brewing before 1678, but in September of that year two perjured rascals uncovered a sham plot against the King and the Protestant religion; and when, shortly afterwards, the justice of the peace before whom they had sworn out their "informations" was found in a ditch, murdered (or slain by his own hands), the tide of fear, hatred, and hysteria was let loose. At that fearful instant the architects of the revolution began actively to direct the course of popular passions, some in the hope of overthrowing the monarchy, some with the intention of excluding James, the King's successor, from the throne, some out of a simple craving for personal power. Whatever the mixture of motives, the grand designers appear to have had as their object an abrupt and rather drastic change in the mode of government.

Reprinted from <u>English Literary History</u>, Vol. 24 (1957), pp. 177–190, by permission of Mrs. E. N. Hooker and The Johns Hopkins University Press.

DRYDEN AND THE ATOMS OF EPICURUS

Among the chiefs of the conspiracy were the Duke of Buckingham and the Earl of Shaftesbury, two extraordinarily brilliant, ambitious and frustrated men.

Dryden had thrown himself into the controversy from the start, in 1678, taking the side of the King because in his eyes that was the side of stable, constitutional government. He wrote two plays with a strong political undercurrent. In addition, he composed a series of brilliant political poems, including MacFlecknoe and the astonishing, rollicking Absalom and Achitophel, and the razor-sharp satire, The Medall. It was in The Medall that Dryden recalled a memorable piece of Shaftesbury's past, when he had engaged his talents in the service of Cromwell and the Puritan "saints":

> Next this (how wildly will ambition steer!)
> A vermin wriggling in th' usurper's ear.
> Bart'ring his venal wit for sums of gold,
> He cast himself into the saintlike mold:
> Groan'd, sigh'd, and pray'd, while godliness was gain,
> The loudest bagpipe of the squeaking train.

All of Dryden's work published at this time shows a dominating political motive, and reflects the urgency of the political crisis. All, that is, until we come to Religio Laici. Dryden's critics and editors have been bothered by the fact that in the midst of wild political controversy, Dryden seems to pause cheerfully to give us a leisurely account of his religious beliefs. The oddity of the thing has been neatly expressed by George Saintsbury:

> That a man who had never previously displayed
> any particular interest in theological questions,
> and who had reached the age of 51, with a reputa-
> tion derived, until quite recently, in the main from
> the composition of loose plays, should appear be-
> fore his public of pleasure-seekers with a serious
> argument in verse on the credibility of the Christian
> religion, and the merits of the Anglican form of doc-
> trine and church-government, would nowadays be
> something more than a nine days' wonder.

To a modern reader with even a small acquaintance with Dryden there is another oddity about the poem which smites one as soon as he commences reading it. The beginning which is a rather stately and magnificent overture, suggests in a crowd of images that human reason, while it is sufficient for our ordinary, practical needs, is grotesquely inadequate to solve the ultimate problems of man's destiny, his relationship to the world in which he lives, and the sources and means of happiness or frustration. This is the way the poem opens:

> Dim as the borrw'd beams of moon and star
> To lonely, weary, wand'ring travelers,
> Is Reason to the soul; and, as on high
> Those rolling fires discover but the sky,
> Not light us here, so Reason's glimmering ray
> Was lent, not to assure our doubtful way,
> But guide us upward to a better day.
> And as those nightly tapers disappear,
> When day's bright lord ascends our hemisphere;
> So pale grows Reason at Religion's sight;
> So dies, and so dissolves in supernatural light.

That reason should be described as a pale, glimmering light is a bit of a shock, coming from a chronic rationalist, a poet who had argued, debated, reasoned, and butted his way through verse and drama for twenty years. It is doubly shocking, coming from an early member of the Royal Society and a man who prided himself on being modern. Only a few years before Religio Laici Dryden had committed an act of—well, I will let you name the crime. He had not only rewritten John Milton's Paradise Lost; he had converted the old Puritan's epic into a rhymed opera entitled The State of Innocence. A comparison of the two is instructive. In Paradise Lost the angel Raphael, questioned eagerly by our forefather Adam, intimates gently that there are some questions into which man was not supposed to probe:

> Solicit not thy thoughts with matters hid;
> Leave them to God above; Him serve, and fear!

Shortly thereafter, Adam began to question Raphael about the sex-life of angels. The questioning drew from the angel a blush "celestial rosy red," but remarkably little scientific information. In Dryden's opera things are different. Questions are raised and debated, and one is left with the impression that Dryden would gladly have answered them <u>all</u> if the end of the last act had not rolled around too soon.

Of course a man so habitually ratiocinative as Dryden would not write a poem to repudiate reason. It becomes apparent upon reading it that <u>Religio Laici</u>, instead of rejecting reason, has something to say about the scope and limits of reason, about its abuse, and about the social consequences of an irresponsible exploitation of it.

Some years ago I had the notion that <u>Religio Laici</u> was part of a political and philosophical controversy and that in writing the poem Dryden was supporting one side of a fierce debate which was agitating men of that time. One afternoon in 1951, as I was reading in the British Museum, I discovered two books that formed part of the controversy. Both were composed as replies to another work which had previously been published, a work which they both regarded as crammed with errors of a particularly sinister breed. With a little more hunting I succeeded in finding the book they referred to, the irritating substance which set off a series of angry reactions by way of reply and counter-reply for about eight years.

The book which precipitated the trouble bore on its front the imposing title of <u>A Treatise of Humane Reason</u>. It was published somewhere around August 1674. There was no author's name attached to it, either then or when it was reprinted the following year. But the excitement stirred up curiosity, and it was not long before the identity of the author was discovered. He turned out to be one Martin Clifford, who at that time served as Master of the Charterhouse in London. The sober article about him in the <u>Dictionary of National Biography</u> notes simply that he was distinguished in those days for his licentious tastes and his powers of buffoonery. Nothing in the records of Martin Clifford suggests a philosophical bent or an interest in religion. Rather the contrary. But we <u>do</u> know that he was a protégé of the feckless Duke of Buckingham, a worthy whom Dryden was to describe, in 1681, in these lines:

> A man so various, that he seem'd to be
> Not one, but all mankind's epitome:

> Stiff in opinions, always in the wrong;
> Was everything by starts, and nothing long;
> But in the course of one revolving moon
> Was chymist, fiddler, statesman, and buffoon. . . .

Clifford's treatise is a rather remarkable performance, so deft and shrewd as to arouse the suspicion that a greater talent than Clifford's had a share in the writing. On the surface a plea for toleration, it managed to assure non-conformists of all types that they were the real champions of truth. The underlying attitude of the writer (or writers) emerges in the assumption that apart from the knowledge of physical nature, truth is so uncertain that every man's reason is valid; where all may possibly be mistaken, each is equally right. Learning inherited from the past is likely to be error or deceit; each man is qualified to decide for himself, with or without knowledge. Perhaps the most revealing feature of the treatise is the notion that dissent and divergence are in themselves ultimate values, regardless of what they stand for or what they diverge from.

By 1675 the replies to Clifford had begun to appear in print. There were probably a number of answers which directly or indirectly tried to counteract the effects of Clifford, but at least two still survive from 1675 which on their very title-pages proclaim their intention. Both of these are anonymous, as if they feared to reveal themselves to foes who were powerful and dangerous. The more interesting of the two answers was a book called Plain-Dealing, published by a Cambridge book-seller, Henry Dickinson, whose shop was located on Trinity Street (on a site now occupied by Bowes and Bowes), and only a stone's throw from the gatehouse of Trinity College, which was Dryden's college. Whether it was the product of a Cambridge scholar or a group of Cambridge men, Plain-Dealing in several respects anticipates the position which Dryden took a few years later in Religio Laici. What Plain-Dealing objected to most vigorously in Clifford's treatise was its complete Pyrrhonism (or full-blown scepticism), its tendency to Socinian subtlety, and its subservience to the philosophy of Thomas Hobbes, who, it asserted, was Clifford's "old master."

The only defense of Clifford's Treatise of Humane Reason which I have been able to find is a book called An Apology for the Discourse of Humane Reason, published anonymously but

236

written by a friend of Clifford's named Albertus Warren, a devout admirer—and one of the few admirers—of Thomas Hobbes. Warren had written the Apology in 1677–1678. Two years later, in 1680, he added a supplement and published the whole work, with a dedication to the Earl of Shaftesbury, who, he tells us, had been a most valued friend and patron to Clifford. Why Albertus Warren failed to publish in 1678 what he had written in behalf of Clifford, is any man's guess; but there was a cogent reason for its publication in 1680, for by that time Shaftesbury was exerting all of his astonishing energies to bring dissention to a climax.

In the replies to Clifford which were written from 1675 to 1682, one of the main concerns of the writers was that the principles advocated in the Treatise of Humane Reason tended to the fragmentation of human society rather than its unity. In 1681, a young man entered the lists with arguments against dissention and factionalism. ". . . . in our poor Island," he wrote, "there are as many different Passions and Affections, Plots. and Agitations, Factions and Fashions, Opinions and Religions, almost as (there are) men." This particular plea for moderation and unity was written from the standpoint of a clergyman, and it was entitled Religio Clerici. One can see a kind of inevitability in the fact that Dryden's poem, coming one year later and supplementing the arguments from a secular point of view, was given the title of Religio Laici.

Dryden's Religio Laici, then, is primarily neither a religious poem nor a poem about religion. There are various bits of evidence besides what I have suggested, to support the conclusion that it was composed as part of a specific controversy, and intended to counter a set of ideas that had been cherished and fostered by the Duke of Buckingham and the Earl of Shaftesbury. Shaftesbury and Buckingham had used the ideas as a convenient instrument in the political battle which culminated during the years 1678–1682 in what we have called the Attempted Whig Revolution.

Thus far I have attempted to outline the immediate occasion of Dryden's poem. But the poem deals with the scope and limits of human reason, and therefore has implications beyond the immediate occasion. To explore these implications, to sketch in Dryden's position, and to cast at least a little light upon the complex of ideas and attitudes against which he was reacting, is the task to which I shall set myself.

In Religio Laici we find four modes of thinking specified in which, Dryden is convinced, human reason has failed. First of all, the great philosophic systems, constructed with the utmost of human ingenuity, fall short of religion in accounting for the origin of the world and of the life in it; the best of the philosophers merely guessed, and his guess was no better than that of Epicurus, whose world consisted of an infinity of atoms whirling, bumping in infinite space until some of them, by merest chance, leap into a common rhythm and an intelligible form. Philosophic systems, again, have failed in defining the way to happiness, for they have all attempted to comprehend the summum bonum in a formula for adjustment, instead of recognizing that, except on a purely bovine level, men are incapable of happiness unless their imagination and faith are touched and informed.

The second abuse of human reason is represented by the Deists, to whose position Dryden devotes much of the first half of the poem. The summary of the Deists' tenets is given in terms which make it clear that the poet is thinking of Lord Herbert of Cherbury's five common notions. He has no objections to the beliefs of Deism; he merely intimates that unaided reason is given rather too much credit. The error of the Deist is the belief that nothing of unique value is embedded in tradition or history, that it is possible to wipe the slate clean (as Descartes did) and start all over again, and by the pure exercise of reason to discover "all ye know, and all ye need to know."

The third abuse of reason involves an excessive reliance on tradition, combined with the assumption that under certain circumstances reason may determine infallibly which elements in tradition are valid. The error consists in dogmatic certainty in an area in which certainty is inadmissible.

The fourth abuse of reason occurs in what Dryden describes as the operations of "the private spirit." The error grows, first, out of the assumption that the conclusions of individual reason, even when it is exercised without training and without knowledge, are precious discoveries; and, secondly, out of the belief that in areas where mathematical certainty is not to be expected, there is no real knowledge and that, therefore, one man's conviction is bound to be as valid as anyone else's.

If it seems strange that these thoughts can be elicited from a poem on the Faith of a Layman, I must point out that Dryden

.himself, in the prose-preface to the poem, carefully informs
us that he is following a particular philosophic tradition. "Being naturally inclin'd to scepticism in philosophy," he wrote,
"I have no reason to impose my opinions in a subject which is
above it. . . ."

Dryden's scepticism, the frame of reference within which
Religio Laici was composed, has been widely misunderstood—
and quite needlessly. By the time Religio Laici was published
at the end of November, 1682, he was already at work on another literary project, and within four months of the poem's
appearance the first volume of Plutarch's Lives was in the hands
of the printer. Plutarch was a prime favorite of Dryden's, a
sage with whom he was likely to identify himself. He described
Plutarch's scepticism in much the same way as he described his
own: each was content "only to propound and weigh opinions,
leaving the judgment of his readers free, without presuming to
decide dogmatically." In this position of moderation, Plutarch
found himself opposed to two philosophical extremes. First,
that of the dogmatic system-makers, the Stoics and Epicureans,
who "pretend" too much to certainty in their dogmas, and to
impose them with too great arrogance." And, second, the other
extreme, the wholesale sceptics, or the Pyrrhonists, who "bring
all certainty in question," and, with a peculiar kind of dogmatism, insist that nothing is more likely than anything else.
Plutarch, as a sceptic of the later academy, though he recognized little certainty in human knowledge, yet had the wisdom
to see that knowledge and experience will incline "the balance
to that hand where the most weighty reasons, and probability
of truth, were visible." There are areas in our lives, such as
moral philosophy, which admit of so few doubts that the dogmatic scepticism of "the private spirit" is an untenable position.
Such, in brief, was Plutarch's—and Dryden's—philosophic
scepticism.

After the opening of the poem, as we have seen, Dryden
proceeds to examine the inadequacies of the rational systems,
with specific allusion to the Stoic and Epicurean philosophies.
Apart from his reference to Epicurus, and to the dance of the
atoms, which miraculously leap into form, there are abundant
clues as to which system Dryden had primarily in mind; for
the early part of the poem is sprinkled with phrases and images
taken from the great Latin poem by Lucretius, expounding the

atomistic philosophy of Epicurus. The fact is scarcely surprising in view of Dryden's intense interest in—and even obsession with—the atomistic theory. Twenty-two years before <u>Religio Laici</u> he had written a poem to Sir Robert Howard, in which he referred to a work by Sir Robert in the following words:

> . . . this is a piece too fair
> To be the child of chance, and not of care.
> No atoms casually together hurl'd
> Could e'er produce so beautiful a world.

And in the intervening twenty-two years the jarring atoms of Epicurus appear in a variety of Dryden's works, and in a variety of forms: through analogy, in the field of politics by reference to the jarring factions, and in the field of religion by reference to the jarring sects.

The deep concern over the effects of the atomistic theory was not confined to John Dryden. Scientists found it a highly useful working hypothesis in their investigations in physical nature. But by 1660 the working hypothesis had been blown up into a very different shape, and in its altered shape was being peddled as the final truth concerning nature, man, and human society. The new monster had a wide appeal. In 1662 Edward Stillingfleet wrote in <u>Origines Sacrae</u> that of all theories the Epicurean at that time was making the greatest noise in the world. A few years later John Wilkins, the remarkable Bishop of Chester who had been for years the leading spirit in that amazing group of scientists laboring at Oxford (a group which became the nucleus of the Royal Society), commented on the extravagant and irrational opinions then afloat, inspired by Epicurus and his atoms. A little later Ralph Cudworth, probably the most learned member of the Cambridge Platonists, remarked that of late there had been an extraordinary enthusiasm for Epicurus. From all sides came testimony to the effect that Epicurus had indeed risen from the dead, and that the atomistic theory had burst its seams.

Of course no ancient philosopher is revived on whim or impulses; he is revived only if his ideas serve to give coherence and meaning to drifts, attitudes, tendencies already existing in another age. And the reason why Epicurus became "guide, philosopher, and friend" to so many in the two decades before

Religio Laici is apparent in a remark made by Samuel Parker in 1681. Parker, a rather hard-headed individual who had an overriding contempt for Platonic mysteries and airy notions said plaintively that the very craftsmen and mechanics of his time had philosophized themselves into an atomistic atheism. "And," he complained, "They are able to demonstrate out of [Hobbes'] Leviathan . . . that all things come to pass by an eternal Chain of natural Causes" and that human nature is a mere machine! Parker had a feud with Descartes as well, but his chief bête noir was Thomas Hobbes, the champion of what Parker called the "folly and nonsense of meer mechanism."

Hobbes, as we know, chiefly by the publication in 1651 of his Leviathan had become the foremost English champion of atomism and mechanism, reducing all things to matter in motion. Opponents, who rose by the score to refute him, had little success, partly because they met him on his own grounds and fought with weapons of Hobbes' choice; while Hobbes, sitting within the security of his tight little system, from which all strictly human experience was excluded, could out-chop logic with any competitor. But Hobbes was formidable partly because the intellectual climate favored the dogmatists and systemmakers who had already made the brilliant discovery that you can hope to find a simple, inclusive formula to describe nature and man—if you assume that man is a machine. Strip man of his history, strip him of civilization, strip him of his critical and creative powers, of his imagination and his aspiration, and your formula may apply even to him.

Hobbes was formidable, as I intimated, because he was in the swim. He was soon reinforced by an abler, more subtle mind—that of Spinoza, whose Tractatus Theologico-Politicus was published in 1670. That Spinoza's work threatened religion seemed apparent at once to theologians; among others, to Richard Simon, whose Critical History Dryden was reading just before or during the days when he was composing Religio Laici. But religion was not the circumference of Spinoza's intention or influence. James Tyrrell, who was a lawyer, historian, and personal friend of John Locke, placed Spinoza and Hobbes in the same tub: both sages maintaining that man's actions and thoughts are bound up in an inexorable chain of determinism, which obliterates the power of choice and, therefore, the human distinction between good and evil.

241

It is extremely difficult to determine precisely how much
effect Spinoza's Tractatus had in England between 1670 and
1682. It is difficult because there are many twanging the same
string of the harp. One of these, strangely enough, was La
Rochefoucauld, whose Maxims were published in France in 166❙
and first translated into English in 1670. Though there are
vaguenesses and ambiguities in La Rochefoucauld's intentions,
the reader will find a clear inclination on the part of the author
to view man's action and choices as the result of the condition
of his body. One of the maxims puts the matter baldly: "Force
of character and weakness of character are misnomers; they
are in fact nothing but good or bad physique." The import of
his doctrine was recognized by the 18th-century philosopher
Francis Hutcheson, who complained that the old Epicurean notions had been revived in the 17th century by Hobbes, La Roche
foucauld, and others.

La Rochefoucauld's position and prestige insured him a
hearing in England. One of his followers (who probably drew
upon the ideas of Hobbes as well) was the famous wit, courtier,
rake, and poet John Wilmot, Earl of Rochester, who admitted
to Gilbert Burnet that at one period of his life he had been drun
for five years uninterruptedly. Somewhere between 1674 and
1679 Rochester gave vent to a poem entitled A Satyr against
Mankind, in which human beings appear as "reas'ning engines,"
reason as a pretentious futility, and the criterion of good and
evil as the power of a thing to titillate our senses. The glitter-
ing example of such men as Rochester was fresh in Dryden's
memory when he remarked of the political wildmen among
Shaftesbury's followers: They "are generally men of atheistic
principles, nominal Christians, who are beholding to the front
only, that they are so called; otherwise Hobbists in their politics and morals."

By 1680 the spread of Epicurean atomistic doctrine had
washed up so many monsters that one of the great men of the
age, Robert Boyle, known to us as the father of modern chem-
istry, felt impelled to take up the cudgels against it. This he
did, in a book called A Discourse of Things above Reason . . .
By a Fellow of the Royal Society. Boyle's discourse is tactful,
deft, and ingratiating—quite worthy of a brilliant and a humble
mind. His general position is a philosophical scepticism rough
similar to that of Plutarch and Dryden; a position Baconian

242

rather than Cartesian. From this vantage-point he delivers his blows at the dogmatic systems of rationalism and atomism. To the philosophers who deny the existence of everything which cannot be weighed or measured, or of which they have no clear and adequate idea, Boyle observes quietly that it is no easy matter to perceive, or to have clear and adequate ideas of the world of infinite space inhabited by infinite multitudes of whirling atoms—the world which Epicurus, Gassendi, and their atomistic followers have offered us.

I cannot examine all of the abuses of reason which Dryden analyses in <u>Religio Laici</u>; but in what has been said, I hope I have come close to the core of his meaning. He was not a philosopher. He was a playwright and a poet with an acute and comprehensive mind, who joined battle against dogmatist and atomist because their ideas appeared to threaten the values of human society and to menace the stability of the state—especially as Shaftesbury and Buckingham had coralled and harnessed them for their own purposes.

In writing a poem about the scope and limits of human reason Dryden was no anti-rationalist or anti-intellectualist. Part of what he had to say was expressed in our time by Austin Warren in an essay on the novelist E. M. Forster. Said Warren: "Complete rationalism, like glaring sunlights dries up the vegetation." The comment which this statement demands is that when rationalism narrows and hardens to the point of denying the special powers of the human mind and the special qualities of civilized experience, it is no longer rationalism; it is the off-spring of dogma out of fantasy.

I am tempted to illustrate; and the illustration that comes to hand is from a popular work on biology published within the past few years, and written by a rather distinguished mathematician and theoretical physicist, who is arguing for the mechanistic school of thought. I quote:

> According to this point of view, basic manifestations of life like growth, motion, reproduction, and even thinking depend entirely on the complexity of the molecular structures forming living organisms, and can be accounted for, at least in principle, by the same basic laws of physics which determine ordinary inorganic processes.

HOOKER

It would undoubtedly be highly convenient to have the processes of thinking reduced to a simple formula of physics—but I am afraid that we shall have to face the problems of human nature and human society with tools and insights other than those supplied by cybernetics.

One trouble with such expressions of rambunctious rationalism as that which I have quoted is that they drive men of a different temperament to another extreme, an extreme of antirationalism like that adopted by Mark Rampion, a character in one of the most brilliant novels of our century. Rampion remarks in a diatribe against the rationalists:

> By torturing their brains they can get a faint notion
> of the universe as it would seem if looked at through
> non-human eyes. . . . The results of . . . all these
> famous theories about the cosmos and their practical
> applications—they've got nothing whatever to do with
> the only truth that matters. And the non-human truth
> isn't merely irrelevant; it's dangerous. It distracts
> people's attention from the important human truth.
> It makes them falsify their experience in order that
> lived reality may fit in with abstract theory.

Both extremes of view flourished in Dryden's age, and he held no brief for either. He was aware that man is a strange and complex creature,—as Alexander Pope felicitously put it, a being darkly wise and rudely great—a child of nature who refuses to thrive on a formula—a creature whose mind is fit to inhabit two worlds and is dwarfed and distorted if it is confined to one. To shrink in distaste, as Dryden did, from the overreaching usurpations of constricting dogma and corroding scepticism, is another way of affirming one's conviction that our good depends on the realization of all man's powers and capacities in mutual aid and support. Our age has reason to understand the ancient secret: that there is no quick and easy road to the New Jerusalem.

NOTE

* This paper, read to his colleagues at the University of California at Los Angeles, is the last work to come from the pen of Professor Edward Hooker (1902–1956), one of the founding editors of <u>ELH</u> and a distinguished student of the late seventeenth century.

DRYDEN'S APPARENT SCEPTICISM IN RELIGIO LAICI

Elias J. Chiasson

Professor Bredvold's view of Dryden as a philosophic sceptic in the general tradition of Pyrrho, Sextus Empiricus, and
Montaigne, or as a "fideist" after the fashion of certain Roman
Catholic apologists,[1] continues to be the generally accepted one.
Samuel Monk, in summing up the direction that Dryden studies
have taken, says: "Dryden's naturally sceptical temper found
support in the various scepticisms of Montaigne, of the Royal
Society, and of Catholic apologetics."[2] It is this scepticism,
so the story goes, which drove Dryden to the shelter of the
Roman Catholic Church.

Mindful of Dryden's later conversion, Bredvold is certain
that Dryden's position, even when he wrote Religio Laici, had
no real affinities with Anglicanism. He says: "If the question
of his sincerity is to be raised, it would therefore seem more
discerning to raise it in connection with his Anglicanism in
the . . . [Religio Laici], rather than with his conversion a few
years later." That this is his point is clear, for he says that
in 1682 Dryden was "far along on the road to the Roman communion. . . ."[3]

The purpose of this article is to show that there is no need
to posit anything so special as pyrrhonistic scepticism or Catholic fideism to explain Dryden's position,[4] and that Dryden belongs to that tradition of Christian humanism which had, in varying degrees and with varying speculative or practical emphases,
been common to patristic, medieval, and Renaissance Christen-
dom. In its broadest extension, such a humanism denotes a
world view which distinguishes between the order of grace and
the order of nature, which subordinates the second to the first,
and which recognizes not the destruction but the perfection of

nature by grace. Such a view does not permit exalting the super-natural at the expense of the natural, on the one hand, or exalting the natural at the expense of the supernatural on the other, or even, while accepting both orders, insisting on their divergence. Tertullian during the patristic period, the Averroists and William of Occam during the medieval period, Luther and Calvin at the Reformation, various sceptics of the sixteenth century, and the "Baconians" and Deists of the seventeenth and eighteenth centuries illustrate that at no time was such a unified view of life universally embraced.[5]

But from the time of Hooker to the Restoration and beyond, Anglicans continued to assert the central imperatives of this Christian humanism. After the Restoration, certain changes occur which presage but do not yet officially announce the disappearance of that "massive but flexible tradition. . . ."[6]

The Cambridge Platonists, for example, continued to insist on the closest and most intimate relation between religion and philosophy. Truth, whatever its source, from reason or revelation, has its origin in God. Recognizing the limitations of man's cognitive faculties as a result of the Fall,[7] they affirmed the necessity of supplementing "the truth of natural inscription" with the "truth of divine revelation. . . ."[8] Viewing reason as the distinctive quality of man, they affirmed, much like Hooker and the medieval tradition, that reason is the very voice of God.[9] Encouraged by the conviction, central to any Christian humanism, that "all Truth is Catholic," they turned to the pagan philosophers for much of their inspiration. The contemporary need, as Cudworth saw, in view of the antagonisms which surrounded him,[10] was a "philosophy of religion confirmed and established by philosophical reasons. . . ."[11] Here faith anticipates and completes the findings of reason, and philosophy is the handmaid of religion.[12] Since Truth, whatever its source, is ultimately grasped by reason, there can be no conflict between faith and reason, or between revealed and natural truth. As Whichcote observes, "Our reason is not confounded by our religion, but awakened, excited, employed, directed, and improved. . . ."[13] With a Dryden-like metaphor, Culverwel points to the relationship which properly exists between reason and revelation: "The light of Reason doth no more prejudice the light of faith, then the light of a Candle doth extinguish the light of a Star."[14] Whichcote suggests a similar relationship by his choice of verbs: "Reason discovers what is natural, and reason receives what is supernatural."[15]

The Latitudinarians preserved a similar distinction between nature and grace. For while it is true that most Latitudinarians tended to "frame a reasonable system of belief and then demonstrate that it was actually the same as the traditional faith,"[16] they constantly emphasized that natural religion must be supplemented by the disclosures of revelation. Stillingfleet is typical in defending revelation by an appeal to reason and arguing that there are cogent "grounds for divine revelation from natural light," but at the same time insisting that "the immediate dictates of natural light are not to be the measure of divine revelation. . . ."[17] The sermon tradition from Isaac Barrow through Robert South to Tillotson illustrates the habit of mind we have been describing. Barrow, in a sermon delivered in 1661, exhorts us to obtain Wisdom "by the faithfull exercise of our Reason, carefull observation of things, diligent study of the Divine Law, watchfull reflexion upon our selves, vertuous and religious practice; but especially by imploring the Divine influence, the original spring of light, and the fountain of all true knowledge. . . ."[18] A similar spirit may be found in South's sermon preached in 1691. "Let a Man," he says, with imagery which suggests the manner of Dryden, "carefully attend to the Voice of his Reason, and all the Dictates of Natural Morality. . . . For though Reason . . . is, indeed, but a weak, and diminutive Light, compared to Revelation . . . it ought to be no disparagement to a Star, that it is not a Sun."[19] Tillotson is equally convinced that there is "a natural and immutable and eternal reason for that which we call goodness and virtue," to which man may arrive "under the influence of God's grace and assistance which is never wanting to our sincere indeavours. . . ."[20]

The conclusion therefore would seem to be that the Anglican tradition (to which Dryden properly belongs) preserved, with varying emphases, the traditional balance between reason and faith. If because of the absence of a principle of infallibility, which could settle certain controversial questions by means of dogmatic pronouncements, Anglicanism was to make its appeal finally to reason, the nature of this reason must not be disregarded.[21]

At this point it is essential, if we hope to understand Dryden, to make distinctions not always made in present Dryden criticism. For example, it must not be too readily assumed that controversialists, both Anglican and Catholic, are the most reliable judges of the precise drift of each others' opinions. One must furthermore also avoid labelling as "fideistic" positions which seem quite consistent with positions which, when held by another, one calls rationalistic.[22] To exaggerate the rationalism of the seventeenth-century Anglican, for example, would be as unsatisfactory as to exaggerate the fideism of seventeenth-century Catholicism.[23] To say that Anglicans unhesitatingly made their appeal to reason demands, as we have seen, a clear understanding of the nature of that reason. Similarly, the mere exploitation by a Catholic of the importance of the principle of infallibility is not _necessarily_ fideistic. Nor is it a mere seventeenth-century apologetic device, but perhaps the central difficulty which complicates the reunion of Catholicism with what it views as the separated brethren.

The difficulty of Anglicans with Catholic infallibility was not, generally speaking, a reflection of greater Anglican confidence in the power of human reason, but a resistance to the _exclusive_ character of Catholic claims. Certainly in the seventeenth century, Anglicanism, Sectarianism, and Catholicism were agreed on the necessity for some principle which would protect the faith against the obvious fallibility of human reason. Hooker is typical of the Anglican anchoring of the truth in reason — not reason _sans phrase_, but reason protected by tradition and Scripture and illuminated by the Grace of God.[24] The Sectarians, less dependent on tradition and relying primarily on revelation, found their stay in the _inner light_. Catholics, convinced that both Protestant positions were either gross or more subtle varieties of reliance on the individual reason, insisted on the competence of the Church to examine the findings of reason, revelation, and tradition, and to enforce dogmatically the results of this examination. Methodologically these three concepts of infallibility do not differ greatly. Much of the difficulty was caused not by the concept itself, but by the precise location of this infallible power. To a thoroughgoing rationalist, any one of the three would be an illegitimate restriction of the power of reason.

DRYDEN'S APPARENT SCEPTICISM IN RELIGIO LAICI

Before proceeding to an examination of Religio Laici, one might cite a passage from Dryden's life of Plutarch in which Dryden sets forth what he conceives to be the highest achievement and yet the serious limitations of the unregenerate, pagan mind (ancient or modern). "I have ever thought," he says, "that the wise men in all ages have not much differed in their opinions of religion; <u>I mean as it is grounded on human reason</u>: for reason, <u>as far as it is right</u>, must be the same in all men; and <u>truth being but one</u>, they must consequently think in the same train." The wise pagans "doubtless believed the identity of one Supreme Intellectual Being, which we call God." Of Plutarch he says that Plutarch "could not know" the way to salvation "without revelation, and the revelation was not known to him." Plutarch therefore suffered the general pagan disability of being able to believe "no more than" could be deduced "from the principles of nature. . . ."[25] The references to the oneness of Truth, and the hierarchical balance of reason and revelation required for its attainment suggest Hooker and the Cambridge Platonists and the general tradition which we have described, not the variety of scepticism generally alleged.

Dryden does not substantially change his position in Religio Laici. For while in the extended image which opens the poem Dryden does deprecate the complete sufficiency of reason, his apparently melancholy conclusion that "reason's glimmering ray" can but "guide us upwards to a better day" is but the orthodox Christian-humanistic position, already described, that reason without faith cannot come to the fullness of Christian truth. There is, as yet, no real reason to suppose that Dryden is rejecting reason as operative on its own object. Since reason does have the power to "guide us upward to a better day," it can scarcely be said to be inoperative, unless one wishes to say that it is inoperative in Hooker, the Cambridge Platonists, and such men as Barrow and South.

As he does in his life of Plutarch, Dryden in the Religio Laici makes the traditional concession that reason can arrive at God's existence ("one first principle must be") while insisting on the impossibility of reason arriving at His Nature ("But what or who, that UNIVERSAL He . . . Not even the Stagirite himself could see."). Dryden would undoubtedly have agreed with Laud: "The <u>quod sit</u>, that there is a God, blear-eyed reason can see; but the <u>quid sit</u>, what it is, is infinitely beyond all the fathoms of reason. . . ."[26] Laud is typically Anglican on this point: "Though reason without grace cannot see the way to heaven nor believe this Book in which God hath written the way, yet grace is never placed but in a reasonable creature. . . ."[27] Like Laud, Dryden makes a distinction between reason and faith. Reason can establish the preambles of faith; it requires a grace to believe the Truth presented.

Dryden's reference to Hooker in the Preface to Religio Laici[28] would suggest that he conceived himself to be in a tradition which by no means repudiated the place of reason in the discovery of religious truth. His reference to the "light of nature as the next in dignity" is scarcely a repudiation of the power of reason. What he is specifically opposed to is the Deists' professed ability "to be able to find out that there is one supreme agent or intellectual agent which we call God; that praise and prayer are his due worship; and the rest of those deducements. . . ." Such religious sophistication (and here Dryden includes the pagans) Dryden, after the manner of some of the Fathers, attributes to "the faint remnants or dying flames of revealed religion in the posterity of Noah. . . ." Here Dryden is certainly more restrictive than Hooker who would have allowed a greater competence to the human mind. Nevertheless the Pauline reference prevents us from concluding that Dryden sees the unregenerate pagan mind as completely powerless with respect to religious and moral duties. If Dryden's belief in the oneness of Truth, referred to earlier, can be appealed to, his restrictiveness here will seem less severe. It is furthermore to be remembered that Dryden's restrictions on what is attainable "by our discourse" is immediately followed by the caveat: "I mean as simply considered, and without the benefit of divine illumination." Like Hooker,[29] Dryden defines faith as "the seal of heaven impressed upon our human understanding."

The brunt of Dryden's attack is directed not against reason but against the rationalism of the Deists, that is to say, against the absence in their system of a concept of grace—flowing from the fact of the Incarnation. Against the deistic confidence in the rationally conceived common notions, Dryden asserts the primacy of the faith. His claim that "Reason saw not, till Faith sprung the light" and that therefore "'Tis Revelation what thou think'st Discourse" does not fracture the synthesis of reason and faith, for in Dryden reason does see, though admittedly only after the act of faith. He merely asks that the Deists recognize the unconscious debt that they owe to a long tradition of religious experience. In pursuit of his argument, Dryden asks why, if the common notions of prayer "to one sole God" and an afterlife of happiness or reprobation are available to the unregenerate reason, why the pagans, Plato, Aristotle, Plutarch, Seneca, or Cicero ("those giant wits") were so contradictory and confused about such matters.

That Dryden's intention is not to reject the order of nature is clear from his admission that man is capable of a natural movement towards remorse, a movement which, however, is inadequate because of the disproportion between God offended and man offending: "See then, the Deist lost: remorse for vice/ Not paid, or paid, inadequate in price." In other words, Dryden is insisting on the traditionally accepted meaning of the Incarnation as a dramatic instance of the mercy of God with which man can coöperate but which he must not attempt to supplant with his own private ethic, no matter how noble. This is the traditional view, tirelessly reiterated,[30] that "no natural man can do anything towards a supernatural work."[31]

Dryden then proceeds to assert the necessity of Scripture if man is to know this particular economy of grace. He does so in the context of the formidable argument of the Deists, based on the fact that since Revelation was of a certain time and place, pagans—past and present—remain out of this so-called economy of grace which the orthodox insist upon. Dryden feels the cogency of this argument, but rejects the implications the Deists would draw, insisting, as the overwhelming majority of Christian theologians would insist, that salvation outside the economy of the Incarnation is impossible. Buttressing himself with a natural movement of charity and with an assertion of St. Paul (Rom. II. 14) that the pagans, not knowing the law, are a law unto themselves, Dryden says: "tho' no name be for salvation known,/ But that of his eternal Son's alone;/Who knows how far transcending goodness can/Extend the merits of that Son to man?" Dryden's Pauline emphasis, which Rand refers to as the very foundation of Christian humanism,[32] strongly suggests that Dryden's "scepticism" is of a very special kind indeed. Dryden's assertion that "those who followed Reason's dictates right" "may [also] see their Maker's face" corrects the impression that he perhaps made earlier about the exclusive character of Christian ethics, while preserving (by means of the subjunctive may) the view of salvation as a gift. This is, of course, far from submission to the Deists. Their precise point was that the common notions (rationally derivable) can perform a function which Dryden, like most Anglicans, restricts to a very special economy—the economy of grace, the only known centre of which lies in the mystery of the Incarnation.

Dryden then moves to a discussion which Bredvold sees as most explicitly pointing to Dryden's scepticism. This is the digression in praise of the translator of Father Simon's Critical History of the New Testament, and is devoted, in large measure, to the problem of finding "a generally accepted method for interpreting, for purposes of church discipline and morality, the truth which God reveals in His Scripture."[33] This, as we have seen, was a problem perennial to any system of Christianity which lays no claim to being infallible. But there is no evidence, in spite of Bredvold, that Dryden was unduly affected by the attempt of Father Simon to undermine the Protestant confidence in Scripture. He falls back, as other Anglicans had done, on the assurance that on all needful points Scripture is plain. The poem at this point, as a matter of fact, reflects the serenity of Dryden in the face of the potent Catholic argument that admitted difficulties of interpretation point to the necessity of an infallible Church. To suppose, with Bredvold, that the couplet, "Such an omniscient Church we wish indeed, / 'T were worth both testaments; and cast in the creed" is a reflection of Dryden's disturbance at the fundamental lack of authority within Protestantism is to read Religio Laici in the light of the later Hind and the Panther. To suggest that a poem which is consistently critical of the Deists, the Puritans and the Catholics, is suddenly startled into a tone of yearning for the bosom of the Catholic Church is to suggest a Romantic not a Neo-Classic poem. As a matter of fact, this precise attitude, which reflects not yearning for but dismissal of the reality behind the principle of Catholic infallibility, can be found in Anglicans whose intellectualism is not at all suspect. Chillingworth, for example, says: ". . . if I knew any one Church to be infallible, I would quickly be of that Church."[34] William Sherlock, whom Bredvold does not place on the road to Rome, says in A Discourse Concerning a Judge of Controversies in Matters of Religion (1686):

"Now could they prove that the Church of Rome is infallible, this indeed would be an irresistible Reason to return to her Communion. . . ."35

Like any other Anglican, Dryden cites Father Simon's argument for the necessity of an infallible judge of tradition only to reject it. But typical of Anglicanism, he falls back to a position which methodologically is much like that of Rome. For, says he, "In doubtful questions 't is the safest way/To learn what unsuspected ancients say;/For 't is not likely we should higher soar/In search of heav'n than all the church before." Bredvold's comment on this conservatism in Dryden is that Dryden here yielded "an obedience to the Church of England by law established, more strict than it theoretically could claim and more blind than that Church, in its fear of being identified with Popery, would want to claim."36 While Bredvold may be correct on the theoretical right of Anglicanism to demand the allegiance of the faithful, because of the individualistic principle which informs it, many Anglicans, among them Hooker, Donne, Laud, and countless others,37 did not hesitate to make this demand, especially against the excessive individualism of the Sectarians. To think of Dryden's attitude as a hankering for authority which removed him from the central tendency of Anglicanism is to mistake the nature of Anglicanism. This is as misleading as Bredvold's view that the Catholic position "that reason appeals to evidence but faith accepts authority" was but a distinction "which the Protestants refused to recognize as valid."38 For while Hooker (to quote but one instance) defines ecclesiastical law as that "which out of the law either of reason or of God men probably gathering to be expedient, they make it a law,"39 Hooker means by reason not the private reason of the individual but rather the corporate reason of the Church. He insists that that "which the Church by her ecclesiastical authority shall probably think and define to be true or good, must in congruity of reason overrule all other inferior judgments whatsoever."40

Like Hooker Dryden does not fall back on the authority of the Church prematurely. For in Dryden the place of reason in the elucidation of the divine text is by no means ignored. Dryden's assertion is clear that if the simple soul "Plods on to heaven, and ne'er is at a loss," nevertheless there are some born to instruct as others to be taught who "must study well the sacred page." The function of such elucidators is to discover "Which doctrine, this, or that, does best agree/With the whole tenor of the Work divine, /And plainliest points to Heaven's reveal'd design." His specific charge against the Puritans is that in them reason has been replaced by the inner light: "Each was ambitious of th'obscurest place, / No measure ta'en from knowledge, all from GRACE. /Study and pains were now no more their care; /Texts were explain'd by fasting and by prayer:/This was the fruit the private spirit brought, /Occasion'd by great zeal and little thought." The distinction that Dryden makes between knowledge and grace by no means suggests any thorough-going repudiation of the activity of reason in religion. Indeed Dryden is anxious to "stem" both the "tides of ignorance" (Puritans) and "pride" (Roman Catholics). It is true that temperamentally Dryden is satisfied with religion in its more simple expression. In the Preface to the Religio, he tells us that the Apostles' Creed is the one best fitted to his weak understanding. But this is an attitude by no means foreign to Anglicanism.[41]

Dryden's opposition to Puritan "ignorance" suggests very strongly that he would be at one with Hooker in insisting that "the benefit of nature's light" must not be "thought excluded as unnecessary, because the necessity of a diviner light is magnified."[42] It would seem clear that to Dryden, as to Hooker, reason is not merely a supplement but a "necessary instrument, without which we could not reap by the Scripture's perfection that fruit and benefit which it yieldeth."[43] Furthermore the nature of Dryden's criticism hardly suggests a lack of confidence in reason. He speaks of pre-Reformation times as times "o'er grown with rust and ignorance" when "want of learning" was exploited by priestcraft. Such ignorance gave way to "a knowing age" which refused to accept Roman claims of infallibility. This is quite in the spirit of Hooker who refuses "to be tied and led by authority," and who rejects the notion "that authority of men should prevail with men either against or above Reason, is no part of our belief."[44]

But again like Hooker, when this anti-authoritarianism was pushed within Protestantism by the Puritans, Dryden demurs. Hooker has insisted that "ten thousand general councils" cannot overweigh "one demonstrative reason alleged, or one manifest testimony cited from the mouth of God himself to the contrary. . . ."[45] But faced with the Protestant "genius for schism,"[46] he also insists that even in matters of doctrine where no clear proof is presented, if it can be shown that "a number of the learnedest divines" are unified on a particular point, a "somewhat reasonable man" would submit. For although it would not be clear "what reason or what Scripture" had led to such unanimity, the reasonable man would be deterred from opposition by a recognition of "the common imbecilities which are incident into our nature."[47] Dryden, aware that this "good" of the Reformation has had "full bad a consequence" whereby "he was gifted most that loudest bawl'd," falls back on the proposition that in "doubtful questions 't is the safest way/To learn what unsuspected ancients say." Moreover, "if after hearing what our Church can say," reason still demurs, Dryden like Hooker, both of them persuaded of "the common imbecilities . . . incident into our nature," recommends that the "private Reason 't is more just to curb/Than by disputes the public peach disturb." Hooker, in his conflict with the Puritans, had already cited the desirability of "some definitive sentence, which being given may stand, and a necessity of silence on both sides afterwards imposed."[48]

The conclusion to be drawn is that while Dryden sharply criticizes the Deists' substitution of the common notions for the central fact of Christianity—the Incarnation—this cannot with any justification be called scepticism, unless Christianity by definition is a scepticism. For Dryden, reason is of course powerless to achieve our salvation despite the fact that as "the Light of Nature" it is "the next in dignity" to the light of Revelation. But if, as Saint Paul and Anglicans generally say, the pagans are saved by the merciful application of the Incarnation to them, and not by virtue of their natural light, Dryden's criticism of the Deists' claims should not be thought of as unusual. Further, if Dryden prefers his religion simple, he is at one with a number of Anglicans whose central intellectualism is not generally suspect.[49] His opposition to Roman Catholicism is on what he sees as rational grounds; his criticism of the Puritans is on the grounds of their lack of intellectual credit. His traditionalism can be matched at many points within Anglicanism, and constitutes no evidence of scepticism in him. Indeed it would seem that scepticism in the Religio Laici can be found only at the cost of exaggerating the rationalism of seventeenth-century Anglicanism, and of too readily assuming that seven-

teenth-century Roman Catholic "fideism" has no recognizable
methodological affinities with this Anglicanism. One is led to
the further conclusion that if Dryden had not become a Catholic,
and had not written the Hind and the Panther, the evidence of
his turning to Rome and of his leanings to scepticism would,
with respect to the Religio, have remained quite unsuspected.[50]

Dryden's opposition to Deism, Sectarianism, and Catholicism represents, therefore, not a lack of confidence in human
reason but an attempt to reassert a basic Christian humanism
which he found to be endangered by the secularism of the Deists,
the anti-intellectualism of the Sectarians, and the excessive
claims of the Catholics. That he will eventually recognize Catholicism to be a Christian humanism which most adequately re-
solves the traditional tensions between nature and grace has no
bearing on his position at the time of the Religio Laici. At this
point, he is securely within the tradition of Anglican Christian
humanism.

NOTES

1   L. I. Bredvold, The Intellectual Milieu of John Dryden (Ann
    Arbor, 1934).

2   Samuel Holt Monk,"Dryden Studies: A Survey," ELH, XIV
    (1947).

3   Bredvold, Intellectual Milieu, 121.

4   A. W. Secord, JEGP, XXIV (1935), 463, reviewing Bredvold's
    book is convinced of Dryden's fideism, but is less careful
    than Bredvold in defining it as "the medieval distinction be-
    tween reason and faith." Such a definition would make
    Catholicism generally and a whole array of Anglicans fi-
    deistic.

5   Among the pertinent studies of this question are: D. Bush,
    The Renaissance and English Humanism (Toronto, 1939);
    G. G. Walsh, Medieval Humanism (New York, 1942); H. Haydn,
    The Counter-Renaissance (New York, 1950); H. Baker, The
    Wars of Truth: Studies in the Decay of Christian Humanism
    in the Earlier Seventeenth Century (Cambridge, Mass. 1952).

6   Baker, Wars of Truth, 98.

7   John Smith, Selected Discourses (Cambridge, 1859), 61.

8   Ibid.

9   Benjamin Whichcote, Moral and Religious Aphorisms (London, 1753), 76.

10 The contemporary need was to counter the twin dangers of Puritan bibliolatry and Hobbistic materialism.

11 Ralph Cudworth, The True Intellectual System of the Universe (London, 1845), Preface.

12 Smith, Selected Discourses, 442.

13 Whichcote, Select Sermons (London, 1698), 298.

14 Quoted in M. L. Wiley, The Subtle Knot (Cambridge, Mass., 1952), 93.

15 Whichcote, Aphorisms, 99.

16 G. R. Cragg, From Puritanism to the Age of Reason (Cambridge, Eng., 1950), 68. However, S. L. Bethell, The Cultural Revolution of the Seventeenth Century (London, 1951), 15, takes issue with G. N. Clark's assertion that post-Restoration writers "tried to justify Christianity itself not on the ground that it was divinely revealed but on the ground that it was reasonable." On the contrary, says Bethell, "Seventeenth-century thought, both earlier and later, has a subtlety and precision that eludes such broad-meshed categories."

17 Edward Stillingfleet, Origines Sacrae (London, 1666), Bk. II, Ch. V, passim.

18 This sermon and one by South and Tillotson respectively are conveniently reproduced in Seventeenth-Century Verse and Prose, eds, White, Wallerstein, Quintana (New York, 1952). For the present quotation see ibid., II, 186.

19 Ibid., II, 185.

20 Ibid., II, 204.

21 Throughout the Anglican tradition there was general agreement that, in the words of Donne (Works, ed. H. Alford, II, 7), "no natural man can do anything towards a supernatural work. . . ."

22   Bredvold is especially confusing on this point. At page 81, Bredvold says that Hooker and Chillingworth "appealed unhesitatingly to reason." And yet Hooker (Polity, III, viii, 18) insists that men's reason in divine matters must not be thought of as working independently of "the aid and assistance of God's most blessed Spirit." Furthermore, it is difficult to see why Chillingworth's professed willingness to adopt Roman Catholicism if infallibility were indeed a fact (Anglicanism, eds. P. E. More and F. L. Cross, 113), as well as Sherlock's (cited in Bredvold, 94), is consistent with the sturdy rationalism of Chillingworth and Sherlock, and yet that a similar suggestion in Dryden is conclusive evidence of his hankering for authority.

23   Bredvold's treatment of Edward Worsley (Intellectual Milieu, 94) illustrates the unsatisfactoriness of such exaggerations. Worsley, a Catholic apologete, defends himself against the allegation of impugning reason by conceding that "Reason euer precedes Faith, and is grounded vpon those rational motiues which Induce to Belieue" but that "Faith, precisely considered as Faith, relies vpon a quite Different Obiect, God's pure Reuelation. . . ." Bredvold regards this as a "tangle of logic" and as a typical example of fideistic apologetic, in spite of the fact that, as this paper shows, this position is common to Hooker and Laud and the majority of Anglicans.

24   Hooker, Polity, III, viii, 18.

25   John Dryden, Works, ed. Scott-Saintsbury, XVII, 33. This passage is quoted in Bredvold, Intellectual Milieu, 114, as evidence of Dryden's "rationalism" in spite of Dryden's clear distinction between revelation and reason.

26   Anglicanism, eds. P. E. More and F. L. Cross (Milwaukee, 1935), 100.

27   Ibid., 102.

28   I find it impossible to conclude, with Bredvold (Intellectual Milieu, 119), that the Preface to Religio Laici makes it clear that Dryden had "Hooker and other Anglican 'philosophizing divines' in mind. . . ." As a matter of fact, Dryden there associates himself with "venerable Hooker" in resisting the extreme individualism of the sectarians.

29 Even Hooker, who cannot be suspect of disregarding or understressing the rights of reason, insists (Polity, III, viii, 15) that "other motives and inducements, be they never so strong and consonant unto reason, are notwithstanding uneffectual of themselves to work faith concerning this principle [i.e. the reliability of Scripture], if the special grace of the Holy Ghost concur not to the enlightening of our minds."

30 This is not to deny, of course, the subtle changes which were occurring in the way in which the relationship between nature and grace was being viewed. Cf. Bethell, The Cultural Revolution, 58, for a description of the narrowing of the concept of reason that is responsible for the grave differences in tone which complicate the apparent agreement between Hooker and Tillotson.

31 John Donne, Works, ed. H. Alford (London, 1839), II, 7.

32 E. K. Rand, Founders of the Middle Ages (Cambridge, Mass., 1929), 35.

33 Baker, Wars of Truth, 191.

34 Anglicanism, 113.

35 Quoted in Bredvold, Intellectual Milieu, 94.

36 Bredvold, Intellectual Milieu, 126.

37 Donne's view of the self-elected saints as the white spots of leprosy in the Church, and Browne's recognition that every "man is not a proper Champion for Truth" as well as Burton's fear of the "fopperies" of private judgment, can be matched by Taylor's comment on the sectarian insistence that conscience is above law: "And so Suspicion; and Jealousie, and Disobedience, and Rebellion are become Conscience; in which there is neither knowledge, nor revelation, nor truth, nor charity, nor reason, nor religion." For these references see Donne, The Works, IV, 511; Browne, Religio Medici (Everyman, ed.), 8; Burton, Anatomy of Melancholy (Bohn Library), III, 372; Taylor, Ductor Dubitantium, in L. P. Smith, The Golden Grove (Oxford, 1930), 145.

38   Bredvold, Intellectual Milieu, 94.

39   Hooker, Polity, I, iii, 1.

40   Ibid., V, viii, 5.

41   Cf. Anglicanism, 121–131, for representatives of those
     who prefer the Apostles' Creed rather than the more theo-
     logically explicit Creeds without, however, intending to
     undermine the content of those Creeds.

42   Hooker, Polity, I, xiv, 4.

43   Ibid., III, viii, 10.

44   Ibid., II, vii, 6.

45   Ibid., II, vii, 5.

46   Herschel Baker's phrase, Wars of Truth, 193.

47   Hooker, Polity, II, vii, 5.

48   Ibid., Pref., vi, 4.

49   Bredvold, Intellectual Milieu, 87, quotes the Independent
     John Owen's answer to the Franciscan John Vincent Canes,
     the first of whom Bredvold considers rationalistic, the sec-
     ond fideistic: "This Protestants think sufficient for them,
     who as they need not to be wise above what is written; nor
     to know more of God, than he hath so revealed of himself,
     that they may know it. . . ." This seems to be essentially
     the position of Dryden, and so it is difficult to see how a
     sturdy rationalism in Owen can become metamorphosed in-
     to conclusive evidence of Dryden's hankering for authority.

50   I am now preparing an article which discusses the general
     question of Dryden's Catholicism.

NOTE: Titles of books have not been underscored in this
       article since they were not italicized in the original

IV. IDEA AND PURPOSE

JOHN DRYDEN AND A BRITISH ACADEMY

Oliver Farrar Emerson

The chartering of a British Academy in 1902 lends added interest to preceding suggestions of founding such an institution. One of these has already been presented in the excellent account by Miss Edith M. Portal of the Academ Roial of King James I, as detailed in the Proceedings of 1915–16.[1] This attempt of Edmund Bolton to found a British Academy in 1614 was under the influence of the continental Academies, especially those of Italy, although he might have followed, had he known of it, the example of a great Englishman in a long past age. The first French Academy was established by the English Alcuin (Alcwine), whom Charlemagne had called to France in 782 in order to supervise reforms in Education.

After the establishment of the French Academy in 1635 it was natural, especially considering the strong French influence upon England during the reigns of the Charles Stuarts, that an Academy for England should have been proposed. It is even said that, in the very year of the French Academy's founding, a somewhat similar institution was suggested, a Minerva's Museum under the patronage of Charles I, but the suggestion came to nothing. By far the most important of these proposals for a British Academy in the seventeenth century is connected with a far greater name in English literary annals than that of Edmund Bolton, although the connexion has never been made as clear as might have been done. Thus, the first proposal in the second half of the seventeenth century has always been associated with the appointment of a committee by the Royal Society in 1664, while another, sometimes placed in the same decade, has been attributed exclusively to the Earl of Roscommon. Unquestionably the first, and probably the second as I shall hope to show, is to be more directly attributed to one of the greatest men in the English lit-

Reprinted from Proceedings of the British Academy, Vol. 10 (1921), pp. 45–58, by permission of the publisher.

erature of the period, the poet, dramatist, miscellaneous essayist John Dryden.

To deal with the first proposal, a lack of regard for chronological sequence has obscured the importance of Dryden's suggestion of a British Academy in the Dedication of the Rival Ladies. Writing of the language of the play, in which he questions with becoming modesty whether he has been as careful as he ought, he says:

> I am sorry that, speaking so noble a language as we do, we have not a more certain Measure of it, as they have in France: where they have an "Academy" erected for that purpose, and endowed with large privileges by the present King.

Now the Rival Ladies, probably produced in the latter part of 1663, was "entered on the Stationers' Books June 5, 1664" (Malone in Prose Works of Dryden, i, 57), and doubtless published shortly thereafter. As Malone points out, it was not usual to publish plays until they "had run their course on the stage." The entry on the Stationers' Books, with the accompanying proposal of Dryden in the Dedication, antedated the appointment of the Royal Society's committee on the improvement of English by almost exactly six months, and the actual issue of the play and Dedication by several months at least. The Royal Society's move in the matter did not occur until December 7, 1664.

Dryden had been made a member of the Royal Society as early as November 26, 1662, the year of receiving its royal charter. It may be, therefore, that he was the first to mention, in conversation with his fellow members, the idea of a British Academy. At least the language of the Society's vote, considering Dryden's advocacy already published, may indicate that Dryden was partly in mind in appointing the committee. The vote of the Society reads:

> It being suggested that there were persons of the Society whose genius was very proper and inclined to improve the English tongue, and particularly for philosophical purposes, it was voted that there should be a committee for improving the English language; and that they meet at Sir Peter Wyche's lodgings in Grays-Inn

once or twice a month, and give an account of their proceedings when called upon. The persons following, or any three or more of them, were nominated to constitute the committee: Mr. Aershire, Sir Robert Atkins, Mr. Austen, Sir John Birkenhead, Dr. Clarke, Dr. Crowne, Mr. Dryden, Mr. Ellise, Mr. Evelyn, Sir John Finch, Mr. Godolphin, Mr. Henshaw, Mr. Hoskins, Mr. Neile, Sir Thomas Notte, Mr. Sprat, Mr. Southwell, Sir Samuel Tuke, Mr. Waller, Mr. Williamson, Mr. Matthew Wren. It was ordered that this committee at their first meeting choose a chairman out of their number. — Birch's History of the Royal Society, i, 499.

Although not specifically made a member of the committee by this record, Sir Peter Wyche was made chairman, the committee thus consisting of twenty-two members, not twenty-one as sometimes stated.

As will be seen the committee included, besides Dryden, only the poet Waller of those who would now be considered as having the "genius" "very proper and inclined" to the subject of the vote. But Waller, as we know from his own statement some years later, was not active in the Royal Society at any time. In 1682 he was in arrears for his annual dues, and when called upon pleaded that "he, being perpetually in parliament, had never been able to attend the Society, either to serve them or receive any advantage thereby." The record is in Birch, vol. iv, p. 130, and in confirmation we have the testimony of Clarendon that Waller was "nursed in parliaments", his membership having begun as early as 1621, when he was only sixteen years of age.

On the other hand Dryden, who had already publicly suggested a British Academy after the French model, was through life an avowed believer in improving English by some such means. Besides, Dryden was in other respects strongly under French influence. He had written the Rival Ladies in rimed verse, and vigorously defended rime in the dedication. He had already collaborated with Sir Robert Howard in producing the Indian Queen in the same form, and he was almost immediately to enter the controversy which produced his famous Essay of Dramatick Poesie (written in part in 1665), and his Defence of the Essay (1668). In any case, to Dryden alone belongs the first public advocacy of

an Academy for England, after that of France had taken up its
labours. Indeed, the first public advocacy in the seventeenth century one may say, since Richard Carew's suggestion of 1605 was
in a private letter, and Bolton's elaborate proposal was not actual
ly published until long after Dryden's day, that is in <u>Archaeologia</u>,
xxxii, 124, December 17, 1846.

How far at this time Dryden had thought out the work of a
British Academy is not clear. Later he twice mentioned a dictionary and a grammar as essential, and twice a <u>prosodia</u>, on
which he is known to have made some progress as a favourite
study, although nothing was ever published. From another member of the Royal Society's committee we have a more extended
record of what he thought a British Academy should undertake.
John Evelyn, in a letter to the chairman Sir Peter Wyche (June 20
1665), makes an even dozen suggestions for such an institution.
From the letter we learn that the meetings of the committee had
been appointed for Tuesday afternoons, and that, on account of
his duties as government Commissioner for Kent in charge of the
sick and prisoners in the Dutch War, Evelyn could not meet with
his fellow members. On this account, "to save the imputation of
being unwilling to labour", he sends what he calls "these indigeste
thoughts" the importance of which deserves statement in his own
words:

> I conceive the reason both of additions to, and the
> corruption of the English Language, as of most other
> tongues, has proceeded from the same causes; namely,
> from Victories, Plantations, Frontieres, Stapes of
> Com'erce, pedantry of Schooles, Affectation of Travel-
> lers, Translations, Fancy and style of Court, Vernility
> & mincing of Citizens, Pulpits, Political Remonstrances,
> Theaters, Shopps, &c.
> The parts affected with it we find to be the Accent,
> Analogy, direct Interpretation, Tropes, Phrases, and
> the like.
> 1. I would therefore humbly propose that there
> might first be compil'd a Gram'ar for the Præcepts;
> which (as did the Romans, when Crates transferr'd the
> art to that city, follow'd by Diomedes, Priscianus and
> others who undertooke it) might onely insist on the Rules,
> the sole meanes to render it a learned, & learnable tongue.

2. That with this a more certaine Orthography were introduc'd, as by leaving out superfluous lettres, &c.: such as o in Woomen, People; u in Honour; a in Reproach; ugh in Though, &c.

3. That there might be invented some new Periods and Accents, besides such as our Gram'arians & Critics use, to assist, inspirit, and modifie the Pronunciation of Sentences, & to stand as markes beforehand how the voice & tone is to be govern'd; as in reciting of Playes, reading of Verses, &c. for the varying the tone of the voyce, and affections, &c.

4. To this might follow a Lexicon or Collection of all the pure English-Words by themselves; then those which are derivative from others, with their prime, certaine and natural signification; then, the symbolical: so as no innovation might be us'd or favour'd; at least 'till there should arise some necessity of providing a new Edition, & of amplifying the old upon mature advice.

5. That in order to this, some were appointed to collect all the technical Words; especially those of the more generous employments: as the Author of the "Essaies des Merveilles de la Nature, et des plus nobles Artifices" has done for the French; Francis Junius and others have endeavour'd for the Latine: but this must be gleaned from Shops, not Bookes; and has ben of late attempted by Mr. Moxon.

6. That thinges difficult to be translated or express'd, and such as are as it were incom'mensurable one to another; as determinations of Weights and Measures; Coines, Honors, National Habits, Armes, Dishes, Drinkes, Municipal Constitutions of Courts; old and abrogated Costomes, &c. were better interpreted than as yet we find them in Dictionaries, Glossaries, & noted in the Lexicon.

7. That a full Catalogue of exotic Words, such as are daily minted by our Logodœdali, were exhibited, and that it were resolved on what should be sufficient to render them currant, ut Civitate domentur; since without restraining that same indomitam novandi verba licentiam, it will in time quite disguise the Language.

There are some elegant words introduc'd by Physitians
chiefely and Philosophers, worthy to be retained; others,
it may be fitter to be abrogated; since there ought to be
a law, as well as a liberty in this particular. And in
this choyce, there would be some reguard had to the
well sounding, and more harmonious words, and such
as are numerous, and apt to fall gracefully into their
cadences and periods, and so reccom'end themselves
at the very first sight as it were; others, which (like
false stones) will never shine, in whatever light they are
placed; but embase the rest. And here I note, that such
as have lived long in Universities doe greatly affect
words and expressions no where in use besides, as may
be observed in Cleaveland's Poems for Cambridg: and
there are also some Oxford words us'd by others, as
I might instance in severall.

8. Previous to this it would be inquir'd what particular Dialects, Idiomes and Proverbs were in use in
every several Country [County] of England; for the Words
of the present age being properly the Vernacula, or Classic rather, special reguard is to be had of them, and this
consideration admits of infinite improvements.

9. And happly it were not amisse, that we had a Collection of the most quaint and Courtly expressions, by
way of Florilegium, or Phrases distinct from the Proverbs: for we are infinitely defective as to civil addresses, excuses & formes upon suddaine and unpre-
meditated (though ordinary) encounters: in which the
French, Italian & Spanyards have a kind of natural grace
& talent, which furnishes the conversation, and renders
it very agreeable: here may come in Synonimes, Hom-
oinymes, &c.

10. And since there is likewise a manifest rotation
and circling of Words, which goe in & out like the mode
& fashion; Bookes would be consulted for the reduction
of some of the old layd-aside words and expressions had
formerly in delicijs; for our Language is in some places
sterile and barren, by reason of this depopulation, as I
may call it; and therefore such places should be new cultivated, and enrich'd either with the former (if significant)
or some other: For example, we have hardly any words

that do so fully expresse the French clinquant, naïveté,
ennuy, bizarre, concert, façoniere, chicaneries, con-
summé, emotion, defer, effort, chocq, entours, débouche;
or the Italian vaghezza, garbato, svelto, &c. Let us
therefore (as the Romans did the Greeke), make as
many of these do homage as are like to prove good
citizens.

11. Something might likewise be well translated
out of the best Orators & Poets, Greek and Latin, and
even out of the Moderne Languages; that so some judgement might be made concerning the Elegancy of the
style, and so a laudable & unaffected imitation of the
best be reco'mended to Writers.

12. Finaly, There must be a stock of reputation
gain'd by some publiq Writings and Compositions of the
Members of this Assembly, that so others may not
thinke it dishonor to come under the test, or accept
them for judges and approbators: And if the designe
were arriv'd so far, I conceive a very small matter
would dispatch the art of Rhetoric, which the French
propos'd as one of the first things they reco'mended
to their late Academitians.

These suggestions of the far-seeing Evelyn are wonderfully
like a foretaste of the New English Dictionary, the English Di-
alect Dictionary, and other modern works of reference.

As is well known, the project of the Royal Society fell through.
Various things, some quite extraordinary in themselves, account
for this, and are indicated in part by another passage from Evelyn. In a letter to Pepys (August 12, 1689), Evelyn says of the
committee's undertaking:

But by the death of the incomparable Mr. Cowley,
distance and inconvenience of the place [that is, of the
committee's meetings], the contagion and other circumstances intervening, it crumbled away and came to nothing.

Evelyn was writing, it will be seen, almost a quarter century
after the Royal Society's committee had been appointed, and he
puts together without chronological sequence several reasons for

269

the project's failure. The "distance and inconvenience of the place" of meeting, Gray's Inn the lodging of Sir Peter Wyche the chairman, may have been a minor reason for the committee's inactivity in the winter of 1664-5. Yet more important must be counted "the contagion", or Great Plague, which broke out in the very month of the committee's appointment, December 1664, and caused a general derangement of London life in the early part of 1665. The theatres were closed in May and remained closed for more than a year and a half. The Court, and all who could get away, retired to the country. Milton spent the summer at Chalfont St. Giles, and Dryden went to his father-in-law's home at Charlton, Wiltshire, where, as he tells us in the Dedication, writing his Essay of Dramatick Poesie "served as an amusement". The Royal Society itself suspended its weekly meetings on June 28 and did not resume them until March 14, 1666, according to Weld' History of the Royal Society, i, pp. 182, 190.

The "other circumstances intervening" may well have included the opening of the Dutch War in 1665, and its active prosecution into the summer of 1666. The Plague also continued in the latter year, and hardly had it begun to spend its force when, on September 2, the Great Fire laid waste London homes and public buildings. So great was the need that Gresham College, the meeting-place of the Royal Society, was "restored to its original use and made an Exchange", as Sprat tells us in his History of the Society (p. 253). He adds that Henry Howard of Norfolk offered for its use his own home, Arundel House, but meetings of the Society were again given up for a time. The rebuilding of London occupied men's assiduous attention, and the establishment of a British Academy gave way before this far more pressing matter.

The one other event mentioned by Evelyn as contributing to the crumbling away of the Royal Society's venture—"the death of the incomparable Mr. Cowley" July 28, 1667—deserves a word, in order to avoid a wrong impression. For here alone, in writing so many years after the fact, Evelyn was clearly in error. Although it is sometimes so stated, Cowley was not a member of the Society's committee, as shown by the record of Birch, and indeed on other accounts could not have taken an active part in the Society's deliberations at this time. Although made a member March 6, 1661, Cowley was not long actively engaged with it. He was not in the list of Fellows drawn up May 20, 1663, and probably for a very good reason. Neglected by the king, for whom he had

written his Song of Triumph and whose father he had served so
faithfully, the melancholy Cowley, as he styles himself in his
Complaint, had already retired in disappointment to Barn Elms,
Surrey, where Evelyn visited him as early as May 14 of that
year, and where he remained in retirement until his death. Indeed, except for the implication of Evelyn's remark, we have no
knowledge of Cowley's interest in a British Academy, although
his relation to the founding of the Royal Society is well known.
In the notice of his death (Birch, Hist. of Roy. Soc., ii, 220), there
is no reference to his concern in the project for which the committee had been appointed.

II

The probable relation of Dryden to the next plea for a British
Academy has been wholly overlooked in discussions of the subject.
That plea was made by Thomas Sprat in his History of the Royal
Society, published in 1667. Yet here develops a curious fact not
hitherto noted. Part of Sprat's History, as he tells us in the Ad-
vertisement to the Reader, had been "written and printed above
two years before the rest". Again, at Section XXI (p. 120) of the
Second Part, Sprat says:

> Thus far was I come in my intended work when my
> hand was stop'd and my mind disturb'd from writing by
> the two greatest disasters that ever befel our Nation,
> the fatal infection, which overspread the City of London
> in Sixty five; and the dreadful firing of the City itself in
> the year insuing.

Now Sprat's digression, as he calls it, to urge the founding
of an Academy for England, is in the first part of the History, and
thus in the part first printed. "Above two years" before the writing of the last part, and the publication of the whole in 1667, puts
the printing of the first and most of the second part as early as
the first months of 1665, when the "fatal infection" was well advanced. Probably it was in the preceding year, as indicated by
other evidence.

For one thing, Sprat makes no mention of the Royal Society's
appointment of a committee with something like the purpose of a

British Academy. This is almost conclusive proof that this part
of the book must have been written and probably printed before
December, 1664. Other evidence for this view is also at hand.
In the first months of 1664 Sprat had been engaged on another undertaking. Early in that year Sorbière had printed his Relation
d'un Voyage en Angleterre, in which he had criticized the English
in no uncertain terms. Sprat immediately prepared a biting answer, called Observations on M. de Sorbier's Voyage into England,
the Dedication of which is dated August 1, 1664. We may reasonably assume, therefore, that Sprat began his History only after
completing his answer to Sorbière. He would thus have had ample
time to write the first part before the Royal Society had appointed
its committee in December. It as naturally follows that Dryden's
Dedication to the Rival Ladies must have been printed before
Sprat had proceeded far with his History. In all probability, also,
he was encouraged to make his recommendation of a British Academy by the public advocacy of Dryden.

The suggestion of Sprat seems to have had but little influence.
Perhaps this was partly because the Royal Society at this time
had itself fallen under severe criticism. Sprat devoted a large
portion of his History to the "Detractors of so noble an institution"
The Third Part is given up to asserting at length "the Advantage
and Innocence of the work, in respect to all the Professions, and
especially of Religion". Sprat tried to show that experimental
science did not injure education, the Christian religion, or the
Church of England. Notwithstanding this defence, however, the
eminent Restoration preacher Robert South, at the dedication of
the Sheldonian Theatre Oxford in 1669, ridiculed the work of the
Royal Society, and Sprat's History was attacked by Henry Stubbe
in three pamphlets of 1670. It was the seventeenth-century phase
of the warfare between science and religion.

III

For the third suggestion of a British Academy in the second
half of the seventeenth century, entire credit has always been
given to Wentworth Dillon, Earl of Roscommon. In fact he founded
a Society with some such end in view, although its establishment
has been variously placed in time. Johnson's Roscommon, in his
Lives of the Poets, is responsible for bringing it into closer re-

lation to Dryden's first advocacy than is warranted. Following him, Malone in his Prose Works of Dryden (vol. i, Pt. II, p. 9) says:

> Some years after this Dedication was written [that is Dryden's Dedication to the Rival Ladies] Lord Roscommon, as Fenton informs us, . . . formed the plan of a Society for refining our language and fixing its standards.

Johnson's Life also led Monroe (Mod. Phil., viii, 107) to place the founding of the Roscommon Academy with great definiteness "about 1662", thus antedating Dryden's first proposal. But Johnson, as we can now see, was merely using with great freedom Fenton's note on Waller's poem Upon the Earl of Roscommon's Translation of Horace, De Arte Poetica (Works of Edmund Waller, p. lxxvi). He had made no independent investigation.

The reference to Roscommon's Society as of "about 1662" rests on Johnson's apparent connexion of it with the Earl's first marriage in April of that year. Fenton, to whom it is best to go at once, is by no means so definite. Instead of making a biography, as Johnson was doing, he was merely writing a note to one of Waller's poems, and incidentally including some allusions to events in Roscommon's life. Though Fenton also places the following paragraph immediately after Roscommon's first marriage, neglecting entirely his second marriage a decade later (1673), he clearly connects the Society for "refining" English with the last years of Roscommon's life. He says:

> And about this time, in imitation of those learned and polite assemblies with which he had been acquainted abroad, particularly one at Caen (in which his Tutor Bochartus dy'd suddenly whilst he was delivering an Oration), he began to form a Society for the refining and fixing the standard of our language, in which design his great friend Mr. Dryden was a principal assistant. A design of which it is much easier to conceive an agreeable idea, than any rational hope ever to see it brought to perfection among us. This project, at least, was entirely defeated by the religious commotions that ensu'd on King James's accession to the

throne: at which time the Earl took a resolution to pass the remainder of his life at Rome; telling his friends it would be best to sit next the chimney when the chamber smok'd. Amid these reflections he was seized by the gout, and being too impatient of pain he permitted a bold French pretender to physic to apply a repelling medicine, in order to give him permanent relief; which drove the distemper into his bowels, and in a short time put a period to his life in the year 1684 [that is 1684/5, Roscommon's death occurring in January, 1685].

Fenton does not connect the founding of Roscommon's Society with "his literary projects" as does Johnson, but the latter was doubtless right in this particular. All that we know of Roscommon's life in London up to 1680 indicates that the Court and gambling engrossed his attention. Only in the last four years of his life did he make a new and surprising reputation for himself as poet and critic, publishing his translation of Horace's Ars Poetica in 1680, and his poetical Essay on Translated Verse in 1684. The latter date is approximately the time with which Fenton connects the project which "was entirely defeated by the religious commotions that ensu'd on King James's accession to the throne". The only error is in relation to the latter fact. Charles II did not die until February 6, 1685, while on January 21 Roscommon had been buried with great pomp in Westminster Abbey.

Fenton's error with regard to the accession of James I cannot overthrow his general accuracy in attributing the failure of the Roscommon venture to the religious troubles attendant upon the possible accession of James, and to the gout which carried Roscommon off so near the death of Charles II. The "religious commotions" continued from the passage of the Exclusion Bill by the Commons in October 1680, through the discovery of the Rye House Plot in 1683, to the end of Charles II's reign. During the later years especially, the thought of Englishmen was far removed from any such unessential to the country's safety as a British Academy of learned men. A second time important national events affected the latter project. But the connexion of the failure of Roscommon's Society with the religious troubles, King James's accession, and the gout which hastened Roscommon's death, is a clear indication that the Society which he founded on the model of that at Caen must have been close to the end of the Earl's life.

JOHN DRYDEN AND A BRITISH ACADEMY

Meanwhile Dryden, who was the only man of his time to take a lifelong interest in the idea, had again brought forward the project of a British Academy in his Dedication of Troilus and Cressida, when that play was published in the early part of 1679. The occasion seemed especially opportune. In February the Earl of Sunderland had been recalled from his ambassadorship in France to become Secretary of State, and his sister was the wife of Thomas Howard, the brother of Dryden's Lady Elizabeth. Sunderland was a man of such keenness of intellect that Dryden withheld the usual fulsome flattery of his dedications, while the new Secretary's former employment in France had already acquainted him with the work of the French Academy. He was ambitious in his new position. It seemed reasonable that Dryden might, with some chance of success, offer him the opportunity of rivalling the great French minister Richelieu, and become the patron of an English "which foreigners may not disdain to learn".

Malone, under the influence of Johnson as we have seen, ventures that in this proposal to Sunderland Dryden alluded to Roscommon's scheme, but I find no evidence to that effect. Fenton accords to Dryden the position of "principal assistant" to Roscommon, but all the circumstances more naturally suggest that Dryden was again first to bring forward his earlier proposal, and that it was taken up by Roscommon and Dryden together. Their relations were especially cordial at this time. In the Preface to Ovid's Epistles (1680), Dryden quotes Roscommon's translation of Horace as "excellently rendered". Roscommon wrote complimentary verses for Dryden's Religio Laici of 1682. Dryden returned the compliment in verses To the Earl of Roscommon upon his Essay on Translated Verse in 1684, and he twice refers flatteringly to that work in the Preface to the Second Miscellany of 1685. It can scarcely be believed that, if Roscommon's Society had been in existence, Dryden would not have made some allusion to it in his Dedication to the Earl of Sunderland.

Dryden's Dedication of the Troilus and Cressida makes clearer than his former brief suggestion what he thought the necessary labour of a British Academy. He would have the great minister he was addressing

> Make our language as much indebted to his care,
> as the French is to the memory of their famous Richelieu.
> You know, my Lord, how low he laid the foundations of
> so great a work; that he began it with a Grammar and a

Dictionary, without which all those remarks and observations which have since been made had been performed
to as little purpose, as it would be to consider the furni-
ture of the rooms before the contrivance of the house.
Propriety must first be stated, ere any measures of
elegance can be taken. Neither is one Vaugelas sufficient
for such a work; it was the employment of the whole
Academy for many years; for the perfect knowledge
of a tongue was never attained by any single person.
The court, the college, and the town must be joined in
it. And as our English is a composition of the dead and
the living tongues, there is required a perfect knowledge
not only of Greek and Latin, but of the old German, the
French, and the Italian; and to help all these, a conversation with those authors of our own who have written
with the fewest faults in prose and verse. . . . I am
desirous, if it were possible, that we might all write
with the same certainty of words and purity of phrase
to which the Italians first arrived, and after them the
French; at least that we might advance so far as our
tongue is capable of such a standard. . . . We are full
of monosyllables, and those clogged with consonants;
and our pronunciation is effeminate: all which are enemies to a sounding language. It is true that, to supply
our poverty, we have trafficked with our neighbour nations, by which means we abound as much in words as
Amsterdam does in religions; but to order them, and
make them useful after their admission is the difficulty.
A greater progress has been made in this since his
majesty's return than perhaps since the conquest to his
time. But the better part of the work remains unfinished;
and that which has been done already, since it has only
been in the practice of some few writers, must be di-
gested into rules and method, before it can be profitable
to the general.

Then comes the strong personal appeal, in a tone of such
confidence as almost to imply some private understanding and encouragement:

Will your Lordship give me leave to speak out at
last? and to acquaint the world, that from your encourage-

ment and patronage we may one day expect to speak and write a language worthy of the English wit, and which foreigners may not disdain to learn. Your birth, your education, your natural endowments, the former employments which you have had abroad, and that which to the joy of good men you now exercise at home, seem all to conspire to this design: the genius of the nation seems to call you out, as it were by name, to polish and adorn your native language, and to take from it the reproach of its barbarity.

Dryden's eloquent appeal, as we know, was of no avail. Earlier in the Dedication he had pointed out that, before his peaceful project could be undertaken, "the quiet of the nation must be secured, and a mutual trust betwixt prince and people renewed". That task, however, was to be too great for any man or group of men. Had Sunderland planned the founding of a British Academy, the "religious commotions", as Fenton called them, and the generally unsettled state of the country would have hampered him, quite as it has been said to have defeated Roscommon's project. Besides, Sunderland lost his secretaryship in 1681, and although he regained it two years later he was clearly in no position to take up any unnecessary venture. Yet our interest is with the project, rather than with the failure. And it is but a tardy act of justice to the memory of the great poet, that we to-day recognize the renewed advocacy of a British Academy at this time as initiated by Dryden himself, rather than by any other, and that we accord to him the praise of an exalted conception, even though it was to be unfulfilled for many years.

IV

Nor is this all that may be placed to Dryden's credit in this connexion. To the end of his life something like a British Academy was in his mind. Twice again he was to refer to it publicly, though with less hope than when he wrote the Dedication of Troilus and Cressida. In his Discourse on the Origin and Progress of Satire, addressed to the Earl of Dorset in 1693, he says:

We have as yet no English Prosodia, not so much as a tolerable dictionary, or a grammar; so that our

> language is in a manner barbarous; and what govern-
> ment will encourage any one or more who are capable
> of refining it, I know not: but nothing under a public
> expense can go through with it. And I rather fear a
> declination of the language, than hope an advancement
> of it in the present age.

In the Dedication of the Third Miscellany during the same
year, he again mentions the project of a public effort, although
again with some note of pessimism:

> For after all our language is both copious, sig-
> nificant, and majestical, and might be reduced into a
> more harmonious sound. But for want of public en-
> couragement in this iron age we are so far from mak-
> ing any progress in the improvement of our tongue,
> that in a few years we shall speak and write as bar-
> barously as our neighbours.

Again, however imperfect may have been Dryden's idea of a
British Academy, and the possibility of "refining" English, one
must be impressed with his frequently repeated interest in the
English language, and in efforts to make it a better medium of
expression. His proposals of an Academy for England are repeated during quite thirty years—in 1664, in 1679, and in 1693.
He made important references to English, sometimes of praise
and sometimes of blame it is true, in his Essay of Dramatick
Poesie (written 1665); in the Account of Annus Mirabilis (1667);
in the Defence of the Epilogue (1672); in the Preface to Albion
and Albanius, and in that to the Second Miscellany (1685); in the
Preface to Don Sebastian (1690); in the Dedication to the Pas-
torals, and the Discourse on Epick Poetry (1697); in the Preface to Fables Ancient and Modern (1700), the year of his death.
In addition, he has severe criticism of Sir Robert Howard's
English in the Defence of the Essay of Dramatick Poesie (1668),
and that of Settle in Remarks on the Emperor of Morocco (1674).
Nor did Dryden offer precepts only. Conscious effort as a
stylist was expressed as early as the Dedicatory Epistle to the
Rival Ladies:

JOHN DRYDEN AND A BRITISH ACADEMY

> I have endeavoured to write English, as near as I
> could distinguish it from the tongue of pedants and that
> of affected travellers.

He more than once mentions correcting his own works, when new
editions made that possible, for example the Indian Emperor, as
noted in the Defence of the Essay of Dramatick Poesie. The considerable changes made in the Essay of Dramatick Poesie, when
it was reprinted in 1684, give notable testimony to the pains he
took to improve his own style in prose. His best acknowledgement of care in regard to poetic technique is in the Discourse of
Epick Poetry, where he says:

> I have long had by me the materials of an English
> Prosodia, containing all the mechanical rules of Versi-
> fication, wherein I have treated with some exactness of
> the feet, the quantities and the pauses.

It is a distinct misfortune that this first treatment of English
Metrics by an Englishman, and a poet as well, was never printed,
and is not now known to be in existence.

Finally, looking back on all his labours towards the end of
his life, Dryden could reasonably assume of his influence what
has since been freely acknowledged. Writing of our language and
poetry in the Postscript to a Discourse on Epick Poetry, he says:

> Somewhat (give me leave to say) I have added to
> both of them in the choice of words and harmony of
> numbers, which were wanting, especially the last, in
> all our poets, even in those who being endowed with
> genius yet have not cultivated their mother-tongue
> with sufficient care; or, relying on the beauty of their
> thoughts, have judged the ornament of words and sweet-
> ness of sound unnecessary.

Again, writing to his cousin Mrs. Steward on June 9, 1699, less
than a year before his death, Dryden hopes that the King and
Court "will consider me as a man who has done my best to improve the language, and especially the poetry". It is not too much
to believe, that the British Academy of the twentieth century will

honour in no uncertain way this early and lifelong exponent of its high aims and purposes.

NOTE

1 Compare <u>Archaeologia</u>, xxxii, 148, for an earlier discussion of that attempt. For a general treatment of the whole subject, see "An English Academy" by B. S. Monroe in <u>Modern Philology</u>, viii, 107, and for a still earlier brief consideration the writer's <u>History of the English Language</u>, pp. 90–93. See also Spingarn, <u>Critical Essays of the Seventeenth Century</u>, ii, 337; Flügel, <u>Anglia</u>, xxxii, 261.

THE PURPOSE OF DRYDEN'S <u>ANNUS MIRABILIS</u>

Edward N. Hooker

I

Dryden's first long narrative poem appears so simple and lucid that nobody has seen fit to be puzzled concerning its intention. Yet its purpose has been generally misinterpreted, and our failure to catch its main intent has led to a false emphasis upon certain features of it and a mistaken evaluation of its proper intellectual and therefore esthetic effect.

Perhaps Dryden himself is partly responsible for the errors of critics concerning his poem, because he calls it "historical, not epic," in that it exhibits "but broken action, tied too severely to the laws of history"[1]—that is, it relates, without poetic fiction, things which actually happened, and in the order in which they happened. Furthermore, he says in his dedication to the city of London and its official representatives, "To you, therefore, this Year of Wonders is justly dedicated, because you have made it so; you, who are to stand a wonder to all years and ages; and who have built yourselves an immortal monument on your own ruins." <u>Annus Mirabilis</u>, then, is not merely an historical poem, but also a panegyric inspired by the vigor, courage, and resourcefulness of the metropolis.

So critics have understood it—where they have taken the trouble to discuss what seems almost too plain to invite discussion. Dr. Johnson took the work to be a simple historical poem, in which Dryden "had subjects equal to his abilities, a great naval war and the Fire of London." What can be expected of such an undertaking, thought Dr. Johnson, is a series of vivid pictures of scenes and events; and the great fault which he found with the poem as a whole is that the author "affords more sentiments than description, and does not so much impress scenes upon the fancy,

Reprinted from <u>Huntington Library Quarterly</u>, Vol. 10 (1946), pp. 49–67, by permission of Mrs. E. N. Hooker and the publisher.

as deduce consequences and make comparisons."[2] To Mark Van Doren Annus Mirabilis "was almost the last echo of Lucan in English," a narrative poem that was "not a tale but a chronicle."[3] He also recognizes that it is a panegyrical poem, continuing the strain sounded previously in "To His Sacred Majesty" and "To My Lord Chancellor"; and that the panegyrical strain gives it a kind of unity, culminating nicely in the prophecy concerning London's future greatness. The poem is, says Van Doren in summary, "Dryden's most ambitious official compliment."[4] That, and nothing more? It is difficult to become excited over a poem with so simple a design, even if it is the work of a major poet.

But one may be sure that Dryden had something else in his mind when he wrote. In fact, he himself tells us as much, in words that meant far more to his contemporaries than they do to men of today. He dedicates his poem to the City, whose fame and glory have been dearly won in three terrible "trials"; an expensive war, "a consuming pestilence," and "a more consuming fire." Now "trials" are the afflictions which God sends down upon the virtuous to test and strengthen them. Having introduced his explanation for the calamities of London, Dryden continues:

> To submit yourselves with that humility to the
> judgments of heaven, and, at the same time, to raise
> yourselves with that vigour above all human enemies;
> to be combated at once from above, and from below;
> to be struck down, and to triumph, —I know not whether
> such trials have been ever paralleled in any nation: the
> resolution and successes of them never can be.

Here he repeats his theme with a slight variation; it is the City's rise through "trials" to strength and success.

But in the variation there is a significant word, which appear once and is quickly brushed away. The citizens had submitted themselves "to the judgments of heaven." Judgments suggest something quite different from trials, for a judgment, in the parlance of popular theology, is a punishment for grievous sins, as well as a warning of God's wrath to come if the sufferers continue in evil-doing. Having barely suggested that idea, Dryden seems immediately to reject it, returning a few phrases later to interpreting London's calamities as trials. Later the City's troubles are referred to as "sufferings" and "afflictions." Lest anyone miss his intention Dryden puts it bluntly: the plague and the fire "are not more the effects of God's displeasure (frequent examples of them having been in the reign of the most excellent princes) than occasions for the manifesting of your christian and civil virtues."

By this time the careful reader has begun to suspect that there were men engaged in representing London's calamities as judgments inflicted upon a sinful people, and that Dryden was anxious to interpret the events in a different way. The latter part of the dedication presents three reasons why the disasters could not have been judgments. First, "heaven never made so much piety and virtue to leave it miserable." Second, virtuous individuals may end unhappily, but there is no example of virtuous nations coming to that fate. And third, the Providence which granted spectacular success to the country's naval forces could not intend utterly to ruin that nation at home. From these considerations Dryden arrives at the conclusion that the City's afflictions have been merely trials, which are now ended; and that it will speedily arise, like the phoenix, from its own ashes.

At this point we may state the problem. Why was Dryden anxious to show that what some men had construed as judgments consisted only of a series of trials? Who were the men thus bent upon seeing in London's woes the signs of God's wrath foretokening utter ruin? Why did these men insist upon this interpretation of the plague and fire? And finally, in view of the fact that Dryden intimates a clear connection, why were the misfortunes of the City taken to be an omen of the nation's doom?

The answers to these questions are to be found in history. After we have set them forth, we shall inquire how they affect our reading of Dryden's poem.

II

How did Dryden and his party view the course of events from the Restoration up to the Year of Wonders? Some light will be thrown upon their attitude by Bishop Parker, whose De rebus sui temporis commentariorum libri quatuor was published in 1726, and in the following year translated into English by Thomas Newlin. One would not go to Parker for an impartial summary of historical events in the Restoration, for he was a fierce royalist and a somewhat heated Churchman, who hated all Cromwellians, resented all dissenters, and opposed Comprehension and Toleration to the top of his bent. But he represents, in however inflated the form, many of the attitudes and beliefs which prevailed among the court party, with which Dryden had identified himself.

We learn at once from Parker that despite the apparently universal rejoicing that accompanied the return of Charles II, all was not peace and harmony. Various dissident groups still remained, and still cherished their hopes for a happy commonwealth, for a kingdom of God on earth, or at least for a place where one might worship without oppression or restraint. It is understandable that the harmony of the realm did not improve when it became evident that the spirit of the Declaration of Breda was not to be carried into effect, and the conduct of hundreds of ejected ministers, who braved poverty and ruin rather than to conform, shows that the courage to resist was not dead.

More specifically, however, Bishop Parker informs us that in the early years of the Restoration a good deal of agitation was stirring against the government. During these years, he says, innumerable libels of a seditious kind were published by republicans and dissenters, and of these the most flagrantly seditious were fantastic accounts of prodigies, omens, and portents from sky and sea, monstrous births and marvellous occurrences by land, all of them construed as dire warnings of the impending wrath of God, of divine judgments to be visited upon an erring nation.[5] And the title prefixed to these rebellious pamphlets recounting the aberrations of nature, was <u>Annus Mirabilis</u>![6]

Was it a strange coincidence that Dryden in 1667 made use of a title which opponents of the Church and government had employed in their propaganda only a few years previously? Let us look at the "seditious libels" which aroused such contempt, hatred, and fear in the doughty Bishop of Oxford.

Parker intimates that there were several, but only three such pamphlets seem to be extant, and only two of them are listed in Wing's Short-Title Catalogue.[7] The first was called <u>Mirabilis Annus, the Year of Prodigies</u>, and was published in 1661. The second, appearing in 1662, was entitled <u>Mirabilis Annus Secundus; or, The Second Year of Prodigies</u>. The third, printed late in 1662 and not long after the second, was called <u>Mirabilis Annus Secundus or, the Second Part of the Second Years Prodigies</u>. All three of them omit the names of printer and publisher on the title pages— a caution undoubtedly well taken.

The first of these tracts included over a hundred accounts
of strange apparitions and prodigious events, with frequent mention of the names of the persons concerned as well as of the
places and dates of occurrences. There is no doubt whatever of
the strong seditious tendency of the work; it was carefully calculated to arouse discontent against the Church and against the
King and his ministers who supported the Church. To make it
perfectly obvious that the omens should be regarded as a warning to the nation of judgments to come for their enduring an iniquitous monarch and an oppressive establishment, the tract included a collection of historical parallels pointing to national
calamity, to the downfall of a monarch, and to civil war.

A general hue and cry followed the distribution of this pamphlet, and the cries of sedition were so loud that apparently some
of the dissenters themselves were offended or alarmed by the
work of their party. So much is indicated by the Preface to the
second tract, the author or authors of which attempt (probably
disingenuously) to disclaim any connection with or responsibility
for the previous publication. After asserting that the stories related in the first <u>Mirabilis Annus</u> were largely true, the Preface
goes on to discuss the charge of sedition which had been brought
against the authors of that tract:

> . . . we shall only say, That if any such thing were in-
> tended or designed by them, we cannot but openly tes-
> tifie our Abhorrency of such Practices. The publishing
> of the Works of God ought not by any means to be made
> use of as a project to further and promote that which
> is so plainly repugnant to the Word of God. And we do
> ingenuously confess (though the Authors design might
> be never so innocent) yet that Collection of Parallels
> might well have been spared, in regard there was at
> least <u>an appearance</u> of ground for those Imputations
> which were cast upon the <u>Book</u> and the <u>Author</u> also for
> their sakes.

As to the innocence of his own intentions the writer of the Preface
wants nobody to be confused:

> And truly, we can appeal to the <u>all-knowing God</u>, that
> our design is not to stir up any to <u>Sedition</u>, but season-

able <u>Repentance</u>; not to <u>Treason</u> against <u>man</u>, but
<u>Loyalty</u> and <u>Subjection</u> to JESUS CHRIST. . . .

These are fair words, but the contents of the tract do not
bear them out. The amazing tales are so slanted as to make
it apparent that God's wrath is directed at the King and his
Church. We are told, for example, of a special church-service
in which an uncanny magpie by its inspired chattering confounded
the prelatical parson in his attempts to deliver a sermon, and
threw the bishop into confusion when he proposed to dismiss the
congregation; the point of the story is made unmistakable by the
information that the congregation and clergy had been summoned
to the service to express their affections to the King.[8] Equally
pointed is the account of the great storm that occurred on Tuesday, February 18, 1661. During the storm the Great Fane at
Whitehall was blown down, the triumphal arches erected throughout London in honor of the King were shattered and torn, and
from the arch in Leadenhall-street the King's Arms were wrenche
loose and demolished.[9] Who could mistake such warnings?

The import of the third pamphlet is not less obvious. It was
brought out under the same authorship, and it consisted of a batch
of prodigies that had been left over from the previous publication.
Three examples will illustrate the meaning which contemporaries
found lurking in the work.

On April 13, 1662, we are told, the famous preacher Robert
South of Christ Church, Oxford, delivered a sermon before the
King at Whitehall. Just as he reached that moment when he would
assert that the era of the late Rebellion was not a happier period
than the present, he was stricken with a Qualm and forced to
leave the pulpit.[10]

An even clearer manifestation of the anti-monarchical sentiments of the tract is found in the story of the two wastrels who
made their way to Tyburn to witness the execution of three regicides, Berkstead, Okey, and Cobbet. After the execution, finding
a portion of Colonel Berkstead's liver near the fire where his
bowels were to be incinerated, one of the rascals seized the liver,
wrapped it in a cloth, and along with his companion betook himself speedily to a tavern. Here the precious pair managed to get
roaringly drunk, and in their riotous mirth they placed the Colonel's liver on the coals and, after it was sufficiently toasted, soon
fell to consuming their unconventional feast. Then the bolt fell.

Both were stricken at once; one died a few hours later, and the other seemed not like to continue long in this world. Thus God avenged a regicide![11]

Our third example is a direct, grim warning, though it has an overtone of humor for the modern reader. In October, 1662, great stores of mackerel were caught by the fishermen. So plentiful was the catch "that they have been sold in <u>Cheapside-</u>Market at reasonable rates; a thing which hath rarely happened heretofore, but upon some signal Changes and Revolutions."[12]

Such were the prodigies related of the years immediately following the return of Charles II. With Charles had come May-poles and the spirit of Merry England, but the authors of the tracts were not primarily concerned with the frailties of the Old Adam in us; they were intent on bigger game. The prodigies were set forth as prophecies, giving fair warning of approaching judgments upon a nation for tolerating an iniquitous monarch and oppressive clergy, or heralding "some signal Changes and Revolutions." In short, they led the people to expect disaster and civil war if they continued to submit to the Stuart regime.

These pamphlets, then, were alarming enough in themselves. But there was a special reason why they must have been feared: for years the minds of the people had been conditioned to expect disasters of extraordinary reach, which were to occur in the 1660's. The number of the year 1666 seemed to be fraught with supernatural significance, partly because 666 had the properties of a mystic symbol, and partly because 666 is mentioned in the very obscure "prophecy" of Revelations 13:18. A judicious and learned man like Selden could write upon this Scriptural passage without pretending to lay bare the future, but the temptation was too much for lesser minds. William Lilly, the famous astrologer, basing his foresight squarely upon both astrology and the Bible, predicted a series of broils and tumults to follow upon 1660 and to end, in 1666, in the pulverization of all false religions.[13] He could be even more specific. After examining a number of old prophecies, he arrived at the conviction that "in 1666. there will be no King here, or pretending to the Crowne of England."[14] Such predictions prepared the minds of Dryden's contemporaries to detect the republican odor in warnings concerning the horrible turmoil that lay in wait for England in the 1660's.

The ground, then, was made ready. But how effective were the <u>Mirabilis Annus</u> tracts themselves? Quite apart from Bishop

Parker's rage, which indicates that they were considered dangerous, there is good reason for believing that friends of King and
Church were perturbed.[15] In 1663, a year after the publication
of the Mirabilis Annus Secundus, John Spencer, fellow of Corpus
Christi in Cambridge, published A Discourse concerning Prodigie
a work of notable wit and learning, the success of which warrante
a corrected and enlarged edition two years later. The author was
no ordinary man. An eminent and erudite Hebraist, he was
largely responsible for constructing the foundation on which the
science of comparative religion was erected. Not only was he a
follower of Bacon, and strongly sympathetic with the new movement in natural philosophy, but he was also a writer skilled in
that style of urbane raillery which suited so well the cultivated
Restoration taste. Two years after the second edition of his
Discourse he was elected Master of Corpus Christi College by
unanimous vote. Such a man would probably not have undertaken
the book if the subject had not appeared important and the occasion serious.

That Spencer when he assumed his task had in mind the serie
of pamphlets called Mirabilis Annus is made manifest by his pref
atory remark:

> That which further engaged my thoughts upon the Argu-
> ment, was a consideration of the Seasonableness there-
> of. We have been of late perswaded by three or four
> several impressions of Books (more then were ever
> vented in any Ethnick or Christian Common-wealth in a
> much larger period of time) that England is grown
> Africa, and presents us every year since the Return
> of His Majesty, with a new Scene of Monstrous and
> strange sights; and all held forth to the people, like
> black clouds before a storm, the harbingers of some
> strange and unusual plagues approaching in the State.[16]

Furthermore, he was convinced of the rebellious designs of the
individuals who were circulating the tracts and eagerly devour-
ing their contents. All such sullen murmuring, false reports,
rumors, and libels hovering about the tales of prodigies and omer
he described briefly as "feminine sedition." They were the products of malcontents, lusting for revolution. Only when men are
sick of the present times, he said, do they long for variety and

look to prophecies and signs which seem to give them hopes and promises of a change.

> As <u>Nature</u> hath seated in some bodies a kind of restless desire of change, and motion from their present state; so <u>humor</u>, or interest, hath placed in some minds a kind of perpetual motion, an eternal desire of change and alteration: And therefore <u>Prophecies</u>, <u>Omens</u>, <u>Stories of Prodigies</u>, shall be readily attended to and contended <u>for</u>, for these things feed that humor; because encouraging in losers the hopes of a better game by some new shuffling and cutting, and in all persons not pleased with what pleaseth God, of a great change of Affairs in State.[17]

Reports of omens and prodigies are "symptomes of that common itch in men to tell strange stories," but these "camel-stories" are also dangerous. Therefore, by undermining their authority, Spencer proposed to secure the peace and tranquility of common life, to maintain the honor of religion (as against superstition, which he defines as religion scared out of its wits), and "to serve the just interest of State." In attacking superstitious prophecy he assumes the stand of scientist and philosopher. As scientist he affirmed his belief in the faithfulness of nature to its original laws of motion. What appears to be a "signal," or warning, prodigy is merely an event about the causes of which we are ignorant a result of some unusual impediment in the course of nature, which yet does not destroy nature's general constancy and harmony. Why, he asks, would God interrupt nature in her regular motions in order to provide warning to those stiff-necked creatures who refuse to heed either the great examples of divine justice in the Bible, or the sermons of His clergy, or the lash of private afflictions? As a philosopher he adhered to the chain-of-being theory, which, interestingly enough, he employed to support his scientific assumptions; for the chain-of-being idea denies that any one event or phenomenon can be interpreted out of its context in the universal system. The diversity of men's minds, the "elegant variety of Beings in the world," and the "grateful disparity of occurrences which the history of every age of the world entertains us with," all warn us against the danger of drawing dogmatic conclusions from isolated or few or unrelated instances. Thus Spencer empties the "signal" prodigy of all significance.

There remained the "penal" prodigy, or judgment, and this
was a subject far more gnarled and knotty, for the tradition of
centuries had accustomed men to look upon certain dreadful and
unusual events such as the defeat of armies, the devastations of
the plague, and the coming of lean or unseasonable years, as
punishments inflicted upon a nation for its iniquities. Moreover,
Dryden and his contemporaries were all familiar with tales of
God's judgments falling upon the sinful, upon the profane swearer
and the Sabbath-breaker—illustrations of divine wrath such as
one may find in The Life and Death of Mr. Badman. Against the
overcredulous faith in judgments Spencer points out simply,
"God often blasts the cause of truth and goodness by adverse
Providences."[18] Because we know not His purposes, it is a
dangerous kind of effrontery to set up our private interpretation
of God's judgments as a criterion of right and wrong superior
to His precepts and to the commands of His representatives on
earth—especially as our interpretation will be based on self-
interest or party bias. So Spencer pleads:

> It were therefore heartily to be wish'd, that men
> had that largeness of heart, as not to think Heaven
> and Earth concerned in the standing or falling of
> their little Interests, Forms, and Opinions; that they
> would leave off (that worst kind of inclosure) the in-
> tailing Salvation soly upon their own party, and not go
> about to hedg in the Holy Dove, by appropriating the
> graces and influences thereof to themselves.[19]

In short, "The Ends of the Divine Judgments being thus various
and unsearchable, they cannot be preferred Rules of trial in any
sacred or civil differences. . . ."[20]

The restlessness and perturbation which Spencer had sensed
when he published his Discourse concerning Prodigies in 1663
did not subside. In 1665 he wrote:

> 'Tis a time wherein (as 'tis usual) Folly is as busy
> as Wisdom. Never greater talk of terrible Signs,
> Revelations, Prophecies and Visions in our own and
> other Kingdoms then now.[21]

Up until the time of the great plague in 1665, we see, the air was
full of rumors concerning strange prodigies and omens, which al

pointed toward terrible judgments to be heaped upon the nation. Under the burden of this expectation it was obvious that if national disasters occurred many people would interpret them as God's punishment administered to a people who had turned from Him toward pleasures and evil kings and an oppressive episcopacy. It seemed possible that in a crisis the King and Church might fall. What could be done to dissuade the people from resting their faith on judgments?

This problem was complicated by the fact that even the clergy of the Established Church were divided in their opinions of judgments. The distinguished Dr. Isaac Barrow in his "Sermon on the King's Happy Return" warned of the heinous provocations that lay in the dissoluteness of the times, and he urged that we have reason to be fearful of God's just displeasure.[22] Yet, like John Spencer, he condemned the assurance of bold men who professed to read God's intentions with certainty; and in his sermon called "The Unsearchableness of God's Judgments" he remarked that God may act upon rules too profound or subtle for our weak intellects. Such rules

> we may not be able to perceive from the Meanness of our Nature, or our low Rank among Creatures; for beneath Omniscience there being innumerable Forms of Intelligence, in the lowest of these we sit, one Remove from Beasts. . . .[23]

We must therefore conclude nothing from judgments. (It is interesting to note that, again like Spencer, Barrow employs the chain-of-being theory to combat the popular inclination to prophesy from judgments.)

But on the other hand, that mighty preacher, ex-Presbyterian, and future Archbishop of Canterbury, John Tillotson, saw in the judgment an unmistakable sign of God's will and intention. In a sermon called "Of the End of Judgments, and the Reason of their Continuance," preached in 1667, he proclaimed that the plague of 1665 and the fire of 1666 had unquestionably been judgments of God upon England because the nation had turned away from Him; and because after those calamities the nation returned to its evil ways, a third judgment, the sally of the Dutch fleet up the Thames, had descended upon the people.[24]

It is hardly necessary to prove that the puritans of the day were quick to recognize the calamities of 1665–1667 as visitations of God. Their own historian, Daniel Neal, proclaimed that the oppressions of the magistrates and the vices of the nation brought down the judgments of heaven upon England, and he listed the judgments: the Dutch war, the plague, and the fire.[25] The political excitement was intense, and the danger acute (or so it seemed We know that, during the Dutch war, government circles were fearful lest the dissenters should rise in support of their co-religionists in Holland.[26] And we know that during this time there was a resurgence of strength and courage among the Presbyterians (partly because of their successful ministry during the plague) and that parliament viewed the trend with concern.[27] In this general state of tension and horrified anticipation Samuel Pepys entered in his Diary, on February 25, 1665/66, a record of a conversation which he had had with Lord Sandwich: "He dreads the issue of this year, and fears there will be some very great revolutions before his coming back again."

We are now better able to answer certain questions concerning Dryden's aims in the writing of Annus Mirabilis. As early as 1661 a group of sober citizens, clearly opposed to the Church, some of them anti-monarchical, thinking wistfully of the good old days and the good old cause, some of them restive and sullen under the oppressions of government and magistrates, some of them pious souls genuinely horrified at the wanton conduct of King and clergy and the effect of this upon the common people, published a series of anonymous pamphlets, issued without imprint, describing many "signal" prodigies that warned of approaching judgments or heralded "some signal Changes and Revolutions." They were understood by the court party to be seditious, and their effect upon the people was feared. One effect which they had was to lead the English people to expect some sort of national calamity which would appear as heaven's condemnation of the government and Church; and with such an appearance of divine encouragement a rebellious people might rise again, as they had twenty-five years previously. The pamphlets were loaded with dynamite, because they strongly recalled and reinforced old prophecies, superstitions, and astrological predictions. Measures were taken, therefore, to counter their influence. Some friends of the court undertook to explain that the judgments of God were unsearchable and that He visited His wrath alike upon the wicked and the righteous; which is to say, that a calamity might be no judgment at all but only an accident of nature, or that it might be a trial to afflict

292

the virtuous. Yet even some of the clergy of the Established
Church feared judgments and expected them. The air was tense,
and nerves were quivering. Then fell the first blow: the plague,
in 1665. Out of it the Presbyterians emerged with heightened
prestige and courage. In 1666 came the great fire of London.
Besides, there was the costly and indecisive war with the Dutch.
London, of course, was the seat of government and the source
of England's power as well. If these calamities of the City be-
tokened God's displeasure, then indeed the regime was doomed.

It was at this juncture that Dryden stepped forward and,
taking over <u>the very title</u> of the seditious tracts, composed a
poem to show that the disasters were merely trials (or, if they
were allowed to be judgments, then they were judgments upon a
people for persisting in their old spirit of rebellion against their
rightful sovereign); to show that the disasters were but momen-
tary interruptions in the path to wealth and glory, and that they
had served to draw the King and his people together in the bonds
of mutual suffering and affection. Such was Dryden's answer to
the disaffected and seditious. Such was <u>Annus Mirabilis</u>. It
stands as a political document as well as a poem, and it is remarkably adroit. Only a short while after it was published Dryden was nominated to the dignity of poet laureate.

III

How does this explanation of Dryden's intention affect our
reading of the poem? Without attempting a detailed and exhaustive analysis, it may be profitable to note something of the poet's
plan and maneuvering.

In the first place, it is obvious that Dryden is not writing
an historical poem about a <u>Year</u> of Wonders, for the action begins
with York's naval victory of June 3, 1665, and continues through
the time of the great fire, which started on the night of September 1 and burned on until September 6, 1666. Nor is he writing
of the <u>Wonders</u> of that period, for he religiously avoids the great
plague, which reared up in June, 1665, and raged until January
of the following year — a visitation more terrible and wonderful
than the events described in the poem. Nor is the poet composing a panegyric to the city of London, because the praise of the
City for its courage, enterprise, and loyalty occupies a relatively
insignificant place in the poem.

Why he omitted an account of the plague is easy to understand. It was an unmitigated disaster, and he was much concerned to prevent emphasis upon this aspect of history. Moreover, he could not have welded it into his plan without ridiculously distorting the truth, for the King and his officials had been unheroic and many of the divines of the Church had shamefully deserted their posts. The plague was better left untreated.

Dryden's plan will be clearer if we outline the divisions of the poem.

I. (stanzas 1–12) An account of the importance of trade to England, together with an explanation of the necessity for the war against the Dutch.

II. (st. 13–18) A sketch of the preparations for the war, emphasizing the King's genius in naval affairs and the auspicious signs.

III. (st. 19–23) A relation of the first naval battle and York's great victory, a sign that heaven favors the cause of Charles II.

IV. (st. 24–31) The story of the attempt at Bergen, together with an illustration of the riches to be got by trade.

V. (st. 32–38) A digression on the vanity of human wishes — and the vanity of foreign alliances; leading up to

VI. (st. 39–45) A view of the sinister designs of France; and the harshness of the French king contrasted with the mercy and virtue of Charles II.

VII. (st. 46–53) An account of the preparations for battle, with praise of the English leaders, both favorites of fortune.

VIII. (st. 54–137) Story of the four-day naval battle, with praise for the generosity, courage, and virtue of the English leaders.

IX. (st. 138–154) An account of the return and repair of the ships, the skill of shipwrights and the genius of the King, and the inscrutable designs of heaven and kings, who must be obeyed without question.

X. (st. 155–166) A digression on the history of shipping, with praise for English enterprise and the practical contributions of the Royal Society to navigation.

The seditious tracts which Dryden was answering agreed that the approaching disasters which would fall upon the nation were provoked by the iniquities of state and Church, of the King and his leaders. In reading <u>Annus Mirabilis</u> one cannot help noticing that the King and his chosen leaders are carefully represented as great and noble, and all splendid achievements are credited to them. The King himself is portrayed as a natural leader with a special genius in naval undertakings; he has extraordinary discrimination in selecting his admirals, he is generous and bountiful, vigilant in watching over his people, and wise in his provision for them; and, above all, his wisdom and virtue establish him (as if his divine right were not enough!) as the favorite of heaven.

Dryden's insistence that heaven and fortune are on the side of Charles could not be overlooked. The King's very birth was auspicious (st. 18); the fact that the Duke of York won the first notable victory of the war shows that heaven intended conquest to stem from the royal line (st. 19); the Dutch themselves in this battle had to acknowledge that heaven was present to favor the English fleet (st. 22); Charles's chosen leaders, Rupert and Albemarle, are favorites of nature and fortune (st. 49); the Duke reminds the sailors that heaven has chosen them to uphold the glory of Great Britain (st. 75); fate has pledged the victory to the King (st. 81); the fates of Charles and his two admirals led the fleet irresistibly to victory (st. 191); the great fire is halted by a miracle, following upon the King's prayer (st. 271, 283); and the King supplies God's own place in his mercy and bounty to the distressed (st. 286). Thus Dryden opposes the superstitious acceptance of the vulgar prophecies.

So exalted a notion of the King and his chosen leaders stands in sharp contrast with Dryden's picture of the English people, who appear admirable only when they exhibit their loyalty and obedience to the King, and when they exert those talents for trade and shipping which can be given scope only by the fulfillment of the King's great design. By a dexterous twist the two comets which at the start give promise (apparently) of glorious success to Charles's arms (st. 18), later become dire influences accompanying God's wrath against the town (st. 291). In so far as the fire might be thought of as a manifestation of God's wrath, it was directed, not against the King or state, but against the people. It began, Dryden explains carefully, in the "mean buildings" of the town, and it was never allowed to touch the King's palace or his naval magazines, and only by the King's prayer was it finally checked. True, the flames were allowed to destroy St. Paul's, but Dryden intimates that the destruction came about only because the great church had been debased by rebellion and profaned by civil war. He does not tell us who started the fire, but in the exquisite stanza describing the ghosts of the regicides descending from the Bridge he lets us know what sort of people would rejoice in the fire. While the King in the midst of the conflagration was weeping with pity and exercising his fatherly care, what were the London crowds doing? Why, the wealthy were bribing the poor to assist them in saving their possessions, and the poor were haggling and bargaining for a higher price: "So void of pity is th' ignoble crowd. . . ." It was clearly on account of the sins of the people that punishment had fallen upon London.

But Dryden was not interested greatly in scolding the Londoners; it was rather his aim to enlist them in support of their King. He intimates quietly that the ignoble crowd had sinned grievously (that crowd which had driven the young Charles into exile, and which perhaps had circulated the very pamphlets from which the poet derived the title of his work). But the wrath which their errors had drawn upon them was not a wrath aimed to destroy. It was to purge them of their vices and tie them in tighter bonds of love and loyalty to their sovereign; it was a trial and not a judgment. It was to teach them that heaven's will and kings' designs are best effected when they "passive aptness in all subject find."

If the poem is not a panegyric to the city of London, what motif can be found to unify the two main parts, the account of the naval battles and the account of the fire? For one may assume that there is some unity beyond mere chronological sequence. That unity, let us suggest, is to be sought in the passage following upon the description of the four-day naval battle. The battle had ended inconclusively, to the intense disappointment of Rupert and, presumably, the English nation. Rupert blamed his stars, but, says Dryden, he was wrong. Heaven's will is unsearchable, and kings' designs inscrutable. Great works come slowly to maturity, and what appears to be a check or a defeat may be the "rudiments of great success." Ours not to question why; our plain duty is loyalty and obedience to the King. In spite of disappointment the English, under the careful direction of Charles, undertake to fit out a new fleet. This finished, battle is joined with the Dutch navy, and a glorious English victory ensues. Thus the loyalty and obedience of the people are rewarded.

Then, in the moment of victory, as the English are swelled with pride and joy in their success, the great fire springs up to lay them low. Yet, however calamitous the fire, heaven stops it short of the royal palace and the naval magazines. It is not a judgment upon the state or Church, and the effect of it is to heighten the people's loyalty to their King. With this great end achieved, what at first seemed to be pure disaster has come to appear as preparation for the final effort; and now Charles's mighty designs can proceed. "Already we have conquer'd half the war, / And the less dang'rous part is left behind. . . ." And so the way is open to London's future greatness, and it is certain that Britannia shall rule the waves.

With high good judgment Dryden does not attempt to give a direct answer to all of the threats in the <u>Mirabilis Annus</u> tracts. Instead, he appeals ingeniously to the self-interest of the citizens. The glory of their city and nation rests upon trade and the enormous riches that it can bring them. By great good fortune the genius of Charles II is perfectly suited to the command of ships and navies; his wisdom has revealed the aptitude of his people; and his care will develop their capacities for greatness. Since the plague and fire were visited upon the people, not their leaders, the people must purge themselves of sin and fractiousness, and support the designs of heaven and their sovereign in "passive aptness."

Dryden's poem was a piece of inspired journalism. It was published separately, and in the same size as most of the tracts which Restoration readers were familiar with. It seems to have been printed in fair numbers; there are, to my knowledge, at least four states represented in copies of the first edition still extant. The very title page shows a journalistic flair, displaying topics most likely to catch the eye of readers who were excited by current events and controversies. Altogether, the poem must be taken as part of a pamphlet-war. Dryden gave the official point of view dignity and prestige by setting it forth in skilful verse.

Conceived as a means to counter certain vague and superstitious terrors that filled the air, and in particular to oppose certain seditious tracts the effects of which, it was feared, would call the people forth to rebellion in times of disaster, Annus Mirabilis was developed as a plea that citizens should leave off their waywardness, pay their loyalty and obedience to their anointed leader, and vote him all the supplies which his purposes required. And the whole of it became an eloquent panegyric to trade, and a noble proclamation of Britain's manifest destiny.

NOTES

1 "An Account of the Ensuing Poem," prefixed to Annus Mirabilis.

2 Life of Dryden, in Works of Johnson, ed. Murphy (1824), VI, 376–77.

3 The Poetry of John Dryden (Cambridge, Eng., 1931), p. 218.

4 Ibid., p. 118.

5 Bishop Parker's History of His Own Time, trans. Thomas Newlin (1727), pp. 23–25.

6 Ibid., p. 26.

7 Edmond Malone first called attention to the fact that Dryden's title was not new and that a "prose tract thus entitled was published in 1662" (Critical and Miscellaneous Prose Works of Dryden, II, 249), but neither he nor any succeeding editor has commented on the tract or related it to Dryden's purpose in composing the poem.

8 Mirabilis Annus Secundus; or, the Second Year of Prodigies (1662), p. 45.

9 <u>Ibid.</u>, p. 59.

10 <u>Mirabilis Annus Secundus: or, the Second Part of the Second Years Prodigies</u> (1662), pp. 32–33.

11 <u>Ibid.</u>, pp. 35–36.

12 <u>Ibid.</u>, pp. 25–26.

13 <u>The Worlds Catastrophe</u> (1647), pp. 32–34.

14 <u>Monarchy or No Monarchy</u> (1651), p. 57.

15 The political unrest brought about by purposeful or irresponsible "vulgar prophecies" had been recognized in the sixteenth century, and laws were passed making them serious offenses. Cf. Thomas Tomkis, <u>Albumazar</u>, ed. Hugh Dick (Berkeley, 1944), Introduction, pp. 25–29.

16 <u>Discourse concerning Prodigies</u> (2d ed., 1665), sig. a5^{r-v}.

17 <u>Ibid.</u>, p. 407.

18 <u>Ibid.</u>, p. 357.

19 <u>Ibid.</u>, p. 370.

20 <u>Ibid.</u>, p. 367.

21 <u>A Discourse concerning Vulgar Prophecies</u> (1665), p. 6. This work was issued with and bound up with the second edition of the <u>Discourse concerning Prodigies.</u>

22 <u>Works</u>, ed. Tillotson (3 vols., 1700), I, 126.

23 <u>Ibid.</u>, III, 229.

24 Tillotson, <u>Works</u> (3 vols. 1752), I, 84–85.

25 <u>History of the Puritans</u> (2 vols., N. Y., 1871), II, 252–58.

26 Von Ranke, <u>History of England, principally in the Seventeenth Century,</u> (6 vols., Oxford, 1875), III, 433.

27 <u>Ibid.</u>, pp. 447–48.

POLITICAL ASPECTS OF DRYDEN'S <u>AMBOYNA</u>
AND <u>THE SPANISH FRYAR</u>

Louis I. Bredvold

To contend that Dryden was a man without faults would be futile; he confessed his sins too freely for that. However, there are good reasons for questioning the appropriateness of the tone of apology so common in discussions of the poet as a man. There is too great a discrepancy, for instance, between the customary estimate of him and the portrait sketched in admiration and affection by Congreve.[1] Dryden's many friendships, which survived even the most violent and prolonged differences of political opinion, are further testimony of his excellent personal qualities. It is especially difficult to reconcile evidence of the esteem in which his contemporaries held him with those biographical incidents which reflect so little credit on him—which would make it appear that throughout his life he was guided by political considerations of a low order, and that he changed his affiliations freely, according to the dictates of prudence. One begins to suspect that his reputation has been too much in the hands of his enemies. Quite evidently, a revaluation of his personality involves a critical examination of the facts of his life, particularly of his supposed political activities and changes. This paper will deal with two such episodes in connection with his plays <u>Amboyna</u> and <u>The Spanish Fryar</u>, its purpose being to reopen the case in behalf of Dryden's character, and to indicate the need for a critical review of his biography.

No one cares to urge that <u>Amboyna</u> has literary merit. Dryden himself admitted in the Epistle Dedicatory that, though it succeeded on the stage, it "will scarcely bear a serious Perusal, it being contriv'd and written in a Month, the Subject barren, the Persons low, and the Writing not heighten'd with many labour'd

Reprinted from <u>University of Michigan Publications, Language and Literature</u>, Vol. 8 (1932), pp. 119–132, by permission of the author and the publisher.

scenes." After that statement by the author himself, who ranks as one of the greatest English critics, who would champion the piece as great literature?

But it seems that Dryden's own disparaging remark about the play never discouraged anyone from regarding it as political pamphleteering. There is a very old tradition that it was written at the request of Lord Clifford for the purpose of agitating public opinion into support of the Dutch War, declared March 18, 1672. Thomas Bruce, Earl of Ailesbury, so recollected it as he wrote his memoirs at Brussels in 1728. The king's counsellors, he says, employed "One Dr. Stubbs of Warwick to write a treatise to support what they had advised the king to. They took the poor man from a good practice in physick and then slighted him, and which turned his brain. I am not certain, but I do believe that it was at that time that Mr. Dryden was employed to compose the tragedy of Amboyna, where the Dutch exercised unheard of cruelties towards our factors there (more like barbarians than Christians), and chased us from thence."[2] Chesterfield, in 1737, repeated the same story: "When the Court had a mind to fall out with the Dutch, Dryden wrote his Amboyna, in which he represents the Dutch as a pack of avaricious, cruel, ungrateful rascals."[3] Scott, also, said that in writing Amboyna Dryden's muse was "lent to the court, who were at this time anxious to awake the popular indignation against the Dutch."[4] Chesterfield and Ailesbury, followed by Scott, clearly believed that the play had been staged early in the war, and that it had really done something, at a critical moment, to rally popular support for the government. Thus arose, it seems, the habit of referring to Amboyna as a glaring illustration of the author's mercenary nature.

That such summary disposal of the episode does Dryden less than justice the following brief résumé of events will show. The declaration of war against the Dutch on March 18, 1672, was undoubtedly a shock to the English people, and the events leading up to the declaration brought severe criticism on the ministry. Moreover, a large part of the English public regarded France as the more dangerous enemy, and felt that in the Dutch War England was fighting against her natural ally. Consequently, throughout the year 1672, the government was in need of good pamphleteering. If Amboyna had appeared in that year, as Chesterfield and Ailesbury erroneously assumed, it would have been a clear case of ministerial propaganda. But the generally accepted date for the presentation of the play is April or May, 1673. By that time the political situation had greatly changed. In February, 1673, Parliament had assembled, and had shown no serious opposition when the king asked for supplies. "That the war must be carried on under circumstances which were still very favorable was the universal conviction," says von Ranke. "The proposal to grant £70,000 monthly for eighteen months, that is to say £1,260,000, was supported by the former opponents of the crown, and passed without challenge."[5] Inasmuch as the session of Parliament was over before the end of March, Dryden's play appeared only after the support of the Dutch War had ceased to be a real political issue. Consequently, unless we have reason to change the generally accepted date of the play, we shall have to reject the tradition which attributes to it either a serious political purpose or an important political result.

Also, if we are to assume that Amboyna was written at the request of Lord Clifford, the leader of the war party, for the purpose of arousing war sentiment, a further difficulty is encountered in the tone of Dryden's dedication. Let us suppose that the play was started as early as January, before Parliament met, and staged as early as April, although this supposition does not agree with Dryden's own statement that he wrote the play in four weeks. Then why should Dryden, in June, when the war was still going on, print the play with a dedication to Clifford, in which he said of it that it "will scarcely bear a serious Perusal," and that "the Subject was barren, the Persons low"? What bungling pamphleteer is this? Is the mercenary writer publicly ridiculing the service for which his lord pays him wages? The natural inference seems rather to be that neither Dryden nor Clifford connected the play with that statesman and his politics, and that in the publication of June, 1673, it was the dedication only, and not the play, that concerned Clifford.

A plausible deduction from Dryden's own statements, as well as from the situation as it has been described, is that Amboyna was a "pot-boiler," and for a "pot-boiler" that depends on playing up war sentiment there is no good word to be said; certainly, Dryden said none. But there is something to be said for Dryden's dedication to Lord Clifford. The Parliament which, in February and March, voted supplies for the Dutch War, had also constrained the king to withdraw his Act of Indulgence, and had passed the Test Act, which forced the Duke of York, and all other Catholics, from office. Clifford opposed the Test Act. On June 18, two days after the Act went into effect, he resigned the treasurership, "to the amazement of all the world," says his friend John Evelyn. Politically, he was a broken man, and he evidently took his fall with bitterness. On August 18, Evelyn, we learn from his diary, took farewell of him, "not without almost mutual tears." In October he died, rumor having it that he committed suicide.

On June 26, eight days after the resignation of Clifford, <u>Amboyna</u> was entered in the Stationers' Register, and published with a dedication to the fallen statesman; Dryden admitted, in the words already quoted, that the play was a poor thing; "but" — he addresses Clifford with fine grace and loyalty — "I had not satisfied myself in staying longer, and could never have paid the Debt with a much better Play." It is generally believed, on very good grounds, that Clifford, more than any other man, was responsible for Dryden's appointment as Poet Laureate; and we may infer from this dedication that it was also due to Clifford's influence that Dryden had so far received regularly his annual pension, even from a constantly depleted and embarrassed Treasury. The moment this patron ceased to have any political power, and suffered the mortification of failure, Dryden hastened to render him homage with a public profession of his own obligations and gratitude. Whether he apprehended any untoward consequences for himself when he made this gesture it would now be impossible to guess; perhaps not, and no one is disposed to contend that Dryden was a heroic character. But even to claim highmindedness for him is so novel and temerarious that this incident of the dedication deserves to be pondered.

One of the earliest and most damaging libels on Dryden alleges that he wrote <u>The Spanish Fryar</u>, in 1680, during temporary estrangement from the Court, in anger because his pension had not been paid; and that the following year, upon resumption of payments, he returned to the service of the Court or Tory faction. This story is told circumstantially in <u>The Laureat</u>, a four-page pamphlet in verse, which appeared without imprint in 1687.

> Thy pension lost, and justly without doubt,
> When servants snarl, we ought to kick 'em out;
> They that disdain their Benefactors Bread,
> No longer ought by Bounty to be fed.
> That lost, the Visor chang'd, you turn about,

> And strait a True Blue Protestant crept out;
> The Fryar now was writ: and some will say
> They smell a Male-content through all the Play.
> The Papist too was damn'd, unfit for Trust,
> Call'd Treacherous, Shameless, Profligate, Unjust,
> And Kingly Power thought Arbitrary Lust.
> This lasted till thou didst thy Pension gain,
> And that chang'd both thy morals and thy strain.

Dryden never deigned to reply to the charge, which stained his name in the esteem of his contemporaries and posterity; and even those biographers who have been reluctant to accept the disagreeable inferences regarding Dryden's character have not refuted the statements of fact which compel such inferences.

Malone, for instance, records the story with the warning that however Dryden "might complain of the tardiness of payment it is highly improbable that he should thus express his resentment at a delay which he must have known arose solely from the poverty of the Exchequer."[6] Scott believed that Dryden, when he wrote the play, was "not encouraged, if not actually discountenanced at court," adding as partial explanation that Dryden was then "sharing in some degree the discontent of his patron Mulgrave."[7] Dryden's later return to the royal side, Scott goes on to say, was facilitated because "if he had shared in the discontent which for a time severed Mulgrave from the royal party, that cause ceased to operate when his patron was reconciled to the court, and received a share of the spoils of the disgraced Monmouth."[8] It may be said at once that Scott's theory about Mulgrave's connection with the episode is contrary to the facts. The Spanish Fryar was produced in 1680; but it was in 1682 that Mulgrave incurred the displeasure of Charles and was banished from the court. And as for Mulgrave's receiving "a share of the spoils of the disgraced Monmouth"—this happened in 1679.[9] Scott's attempt to explain Dryden's defection, therefore, only added error and confusion.

Refutation of this rumor has seemed all the more difficult because of the apparent confirmation of it in a Royalist satire on Shaftesbury in 1680, in which Dryden is assigned to the "King of Poland," that is, Shaftesbury, as laureate, with Shadwell as his deputy.[10] Certainly, the Tory author of this pamphlet was no friend of Dryden's; but one may question whether he was well

informed. His reasons for assigning Dryden to the party of the
Whig leader he states thus: "for writing panegyrics upon Oliver
Cromwell, and libels against his present master, King Charles II
of England."[11] Only the second accusation could have been of
any consequence in 1680, and it can only mean that Dryden was
seriously believed to be the author of Mulgrave's Essay on Satire,
in which Charles and his mistresses had been disrespectfully
described. The same assumption was made in The Laureat:

> Thy pension lost, and justly without doubt,
> When servants snarl, we ought to kick 'em out;
> They that disdain their Benefactors Bread,
> No longer ought by Bounty to be fed.

As both pamphleteers assign the same reason for Dryden's supposed alienation from the Court, the value of their testimony depends on whether or not they had reliable information on this
point or were merely retailing malicious and irresponsible gossip.

As early as November, 1679, London rumor attributed the
authorship of the Essay on Satire to Dryden; this he promptly
denied,[12] though his denial was by many people not taken at its
face value. Strangely enough, even in quarters close to the Court,
the responsibility was laid at his door, for the Earl of Rochester
and the Duchess of Portsmouth, the king's French mistress, had
the poet cudgelled in Rose-Alley, Covent Garden, on the night of
December 18, 1679. There would, therefore, seem to be some
excuse for the pamphleteer who, in 1680, accused Dryden of writing "libels against his present master, King Charles II of England."

The authorship of the Essay, however, was not in itself the
main point of the charges we are examining; the interest of Dryden's enemies attached to the sequel—the loss of pension and
place, the disaffection of the poet, and his unprincipled change
of sides. Did his critics know the truth about these matters?
Was Charles as angry at Dryden as they were? Finally, and
above all, was the pension stopped?

If we look in the only place where we can expect to find an
answer to the last question, namely, in the Calendar of Treasury
Books, we discover that on December 22, 1679, only four days
after the notorious Rose-Alley ambuscade had become the talk
of the town, the Treasury issued a money warrant for the pay-

305

ment to John Dryden of £75 on his annuity, and the payment was actually made early in January. A similar payment of £75 was made on June 28, 1680, and on December 16, 1680, he received £50. During this year of his supposed alienation from the court he received a total of £200. But in 1681, when, according to our informants, Dryden was brought back into the fold by a renewal of payments, he received in fact only one payment, of £100, on July 12.[13] So far as there was any irregularity in these payments it was exactly the reverse of that assumed by the libels we have been examining. They were, it is true, not the full amount of his pension, which had been paid with regularity up to the summer of 1677, when an additional annuity of £100 was given him. The Exchequer, however, was so embarrassed that the salaries of ambassadors as well as of the king's household were in arrears. The Poet Laureate was paid £150 in 1678, 1679, 1682, and 1683; the payments in 1680 and 1681, therefore, need no far-fetched explanation.

Since the records show that Dryden's pension was never "lost" and that he was never "kicked out" for "snarling" it may reasonably be concluded that his status at Court remained unaltered from 1679 to 1681, and that the whole legend about his temporary defection was a fabrication. Dryden's supposed connection with the Essay on Satire was denied in print by Mulgrave in 1682; after that the truth was available to anyone, even to the author of The Laureat, had he wanted it. Whether Charles learned the truth in 1679, or whether he concerned himself about the matter at all, we may never know. But we do know that the Essay on Satire did not interfere with the drawing of warrants for the payment of the Laureate's pension.[14]

The Spanish Fryar, however, is also a document in the case. Does one, as The Laureat put it, "smell a Male-content through all the play"? Is it merely anti-Catholic, or is it also permeated with Whig sentiment?

As one might expect, a number of passages touch on such political problems as were hotly debated at that time. Thus, the "fierce Raymond," "tribune of the people," asserts the right of the subject to take up arms against the king's person "in defence of the crown":

Raymond. — What treason is it to redeem my king,
And to reform the state?

DRYDEN'S <u>AMBOYNA</u> AND <u>THE SPANISH FRYAR</u>

<u>Torrismond.</u> — That's a stale cheat;
The primitive rebel, Lucifer, first used it,
And was the first reformer of the skies.

<u>Raymond.</u> — What, if I see my prince mistake a poison,
Call it a cordial,—am I then a traitor,
Because I hold his hand, or break the glass?

<u>Torrismond.</u> — How dar'st thou serve thy king against his will?

<u>Raymond.</u> — Because 't is then the only time to serve him. [15]

Such an argument is likely to be misunderstood when quoted apart
from its context. The sentiments of Raymond are appropriate to
his character, but the sympathy of the audience is not with him,
but with his enemy, Torrismond. Likewise, the following discussion of royal authority, raised by the question of loyalty to Queen
Leonora, must be understood in relation to the dramatic movement:

<u>Torrismond.</u> — Kings' titles commonly begin by force,
Which time wears off, and mellows into right;
So power, which, in one age, is tyranny,
Is ripened, in the next, to true succession:
She's in possession.

<u>Raymond.</u> — So diseases are:
Should not a lingering fever be removed,
Because it long has raged within my blood?
Do I rebel, when I would thrust it out?
What, shall I think the world was made for one,
And men are born for kings, as beasts for men,
Not for protection, but to be devoured?
Mark those who dote on arbitrary power,
And you shall find them either hot-brained
    youth,
Or needy bankrupts, servile in their greatness,
And slaves to some, to lord it o'er the rest.
O baseness, to support a tyrant throne,
And crush your freeborn brethren of the world!
Nay, to become a part of usurpation;
To espouse the tyrant's person and her crimes,
And, on a tyrant, get a race of tyrants,
To be your country's curse in after ages. [16]

Dryden did not intend his audience to receive this speech with Whig enthusiasm; the violence of Raymond, indeed, serves rather to caution us against his cause. When the plot is all unraveled, Torrismond denounces Raymond as the "tribune of the people! Thou zealous, public blood-hound!" Only unnatural straining of the letter could turn Raymond's speeches into evidence against Dryden's loyalty.

Another burning political question debated in The Spanish Fryar was whether ministers owed any responsibility to Parliament. The House of Commons had bitterly pursued the fallen Danby, whom the opposition wanted to try for high treason. On March 22, 1679, Charles II went before both houses and spoke as follows:

> I met you here to put an end of that which may
> hinder our business, for I perceive the prosecution
> of my Lord Treasurer has put a stop to all business.
> I declare I have given him his pardon under the Great
> Seal of England before this Parliament met and if
> there be anything wanting in form of circumstance
> I will give it him ten times over, for I will secure
> him in his person and his fortune, which is no more
> than I commonly do to my servants when they quit
> my service, as the Duke of Buckingham and my Lord
> Shaftesbury well know.[17]

Charles was determined to protect Danby from political persecution as well as from trial for criminal correspondence with France; and the Whigs, contending that the royal pardon was abused, made the matter a leading political issue. Those who wish to find Whig sentiments in The Spanish Fryar should not overlook the following dialogue between the unfortunate schemer, Bertran, and Leonora, Queen of Aragon:

> Bertran. — This 't is to serve a prince too faithfully;
> Who, free from laws himself, will have that done,
> Which, not performed, brings us to sure disgrace;
> And if performed, to ruin.
>
> Leonora. — This 't is, to counsel things that are unjust;
> First to debauch a king to break his laws,

308

> Which are his safety, and then seek protection
> From him you have endangered; but, just heaven,
> When sins are judged, will damn the tempting devil
> More deep than those he tempted.

Bertran. — If princes not protect their ministers,
What man will dare to serve them?

Leonora. —None will dare
> To serve them ill when they are left to laws;
> But, when a counsellor, to save himself,
> Would lay miscarriages upon his prince,
> Exposing him to public rage and hate;
> Oh, 't is an act as infamously base,
> As, should a common soldier skulk behind,
> And thrust his general in the front of war:
> It shows, he only served himself before,
> And had no sense of honour, country, king,
> But centred on himself, and used his master
> As guardians do their wards, with shows of care,
> But with intent to sell the public safety,
> And pocket up his prince.[18]

The applicability of this passage, however, depends entirely upon whether or not one regards Danby as a scoundrel—as it is highly improbable Dryden did. The general principle that he expresses through the queen was, in fact, not peculiarly Whig. It was not a mark of opposition to the Court; it was voiced by Charles II himself on November 26, 1680, when he answered the Address from the House of Commons to remove from his councils and presence the Earl of Halifax. The king said:

> That he doth not find the Grounds in the Address
> of this House to be sufficient to induce him to remove
> the Earl of <u>Halifax</u>: But he answers them, at the same
> time, "That, whenever this House shall, in due and
> regular course, prove any Crime either against the
> said Earl of <u>Halifax</u> or any other Person, who either
> now is, or shall hereafter be, in his Council, he will
> leave him or them to their own legal defence, without
> interposing to protect them."[19]

After that speech, at any rate, it would hardly be justifiable to label as "disaffected" the utterance of Dryden's royal heroine.[20]

In her references to "the people" Leonora reveals herself a most hardened Tory:

> I fear my people's faith;
> That hot-mouthed beast, that bears against the curb,
> Hard to be broken even by lawful kings,
> But harder by usurpers.[21]

Even Raymond refers to the city militia with a tone of contempt, as if his function for the moment were merely to reveal the cheap tricks of Whig demagogy:

> Raymond. — Yet you may give commission
> To some bold man, whose loyalty you trust,
> And let him raise the train-bands of the city.
>
> Leonora. — Gross feeders, lion talkers, lamb-like fighters.
>
> Raymond. — You do not know the virtues of your city,
> What pushing force they have; some popular chief,
> More noisy than the rest, but cries Halloo,
> And, in a trice, the bellowing herd come out;
> The gates are barred; the ways are barricadoed,
> And One and all's the word; true cocks o' the game,
> That never ask for what or whom they fight;
> But turn them out, and show them but a foe,
> Cry— Liberty! and that's the cause of quarrel.[22]

This is hardly the strain Shaftesbury would expect from his laureate!

Finally, there is the closing couplet of the play, summing up its moral:

> But let the bold conspirators beware,
> For heaven makes princes its peculiar care.

It is a fitting conclusion to a play which in its serious plot exploits particularly the Tory attitude toward legitimacy and regularity of succession. Apart from the satire on the Catholics, it would be absurd to "smell the Male-content" in The Spanish Fryar.[23]

Nor need we attach any great significance to this satire. In the first place, it is not directed at all Catholics, but only against the clergy, or even more particularly, against the orders. Dryden's lifelong distrust of priests has always been noted, and this distrust was probably shared by many, even among Catholic laymen, at that time. In the second place, the play is not ornamented, as one would expect, with topical allusions to the Popish Plot and its ramifications.[24] Nor are there in the plot of the play any pointed parallels that would suggest Whig prejudices on the part of the author. As for the dedication of "a Protestant Play to a Protestant patron," to which so much importance has been attached, it was probably written in 1681, too late to be evidence of Whiggism in 1680. And he would have been a strangely stupid Tory who, either in 1680 or 1681, would have admitted that Protestantism was the exclusive property of the Whigs.

We may defer, in conclusion, to an intelligent contemporary judge, Charles II, who would have known if the poet laureate had written a "disaffected" play. <u>The Spanish Fryar</u>, it has recently been discovered,[25] had the honor of performance at court in March, 1680, and again in November, 1684.

Thus the whole structure of the calumny falls to the ground; every part of it proves to be contrary to fact. It is asserted that Dryden's pension was stopped because he wrote the <u>Essay on Satire</u>; but Dryden did not write the <u>Essay</u>, and his pension was not stopped. It is asserted that <u>The Spanish Fryar</u> was written while he was in opposition to the Court, but that play was loyalist and legitimist in sentiment, even though "Protestant"; and it must have been written before the date assigned for his disaffection. And just as there is no evidence of any departure from the Royal party, so there is none of any "return." Instead of the vacillating pamphleteer that has been painted, changing from party to party for mercenary reasons, Dryden appears to have been in these years a firm, consistent and loyal Tory.

NOTES

1   In his Dedication of Dryden's <u>Dramatic Works</u>, 1717.

2   <u>Memoirs of the Earl of Ailesbury</u> (Roxburghe Club, 1890), pp. 11–12. In 1672 Ailesbury was only a youth, and his information could have been only the current rumor. It should

be added, also, that he was very bitter against Clifford and the other "evil Counsellors" of the Cabal. See his Memoirs, pp. 12 f.

3 Quoted in Johnson, Lives of the Poets, ed. Birkbeck Hill (Oxford, 1905), I, 356, n. 3.

4 Sir Walter Scott, Life of Dryden in Works, ed. Scott-Saintsbury (Edinburgh, 1882), I, 138.

5 Leopold von Ranke, History of England (Oxford, 1875), III, 531–532.

6 Edmund Malone, The Life of Dryden (London, 1800), p. 119.

7 Scott, Life of Dryden, ed. cited, I, 197.

8 Ibid., I, 202. Cf. the context, pp. 195–203, and IX, 303.

9 Cf. Narcissus Luttrell, Brief Relation (Oxford, 1857), I, 27.

10 Cf. Dryden's Works, ed. Scott-Saintsbury, I, 198, and IX, 438–439.

11 Somers Tracts, ed. Walter Scott (London, 1812), VIII, 317.

12 Historical Manuscripts Commission, 7th Rep., App., p. 477b, and 12th Rep., App., Part VII, p. 164.

13 Calendar Treasury Books, ed. W. A. Shaw, VI (1913), 318, 390, 576, 593, 767, 768; and VII (1916), 197, 222.

14 With the account in the text the reader is asked to compare Christie's hesitating discussion in his Memoir, Political Works of Dryden, Globe edition, pp. xlvi–xlvii. But, of course only fragmentary information about the payments of the pension was available when Christie wrote.

15 The Spanish Fryar, V, ii, ed. Scott-Saintsbury, VI, 505–506.

16 The Spanish Fryar, IV, ii, ed. cited, VI, 493–494.

17 Historical Manuscripts Commission, Lindsey MSS., 1895, p. 404.

18 The Spanish Fryar, IV, ii, ed. cited, VI, 486–487.

19 H. C. Foxcroft, The Life of Halifax (London, 1898), I, 260.

20   It is hardly necessary to refer to another speech by Leonora, denouncing, in passing, "arbitrary power in Kings."— The <u>Spanish Fryar</u>, IV, sc. ii, ed. cited, VI, 485. It is either Whig or Tory, as you please. Tories did not, of course, believe in "arbitrary power"; they were <u>accused</u> by the Whigs of advocating it.

21   The <u>Spanish Fryar</u>, III, iii, ed. cited, VI, 465–466.

22   <u>Ibid.</u>, IV, ii, ed. cited, VI, 488–489.

23   G. W. Whiting arrives at much the same conclusion in "Political Satire in London Stage Plays; 1680–83," <u>Modern Philology</u>, XXVIII (1930), 32.

24   In the Dedication of <u>Limberham</u>, Dryden referred to the depression in the theatrical business: "the great plot of the nation, like one of Pharaoh's lean kine, has devoured its younger brethren of the stage." The temptation to make capital of the Popish Plot was, therefore, great. <u>Limberham</u> was advertised in the Term Catalogues in November, 1679, and <u>The Spanish Fryar</u> must have been performed as early as February, 1680.

25   Cf. Allardyce Nicoll, <u>Restoration Drama</u> (Cambridge, 1923), p. 311.

DRYDEN, HOBBES, AND THE ROYAL SOCIETY

Louis I. Bredvold

When students of Dryden have encountered the problem of his relation to the Royal Society and the new science, they have generally passed by on the other side. They have, of course, included in their biographical narratives the fact that he was chosen a member of the newly organized Society on November 19, 1662, and admitted at the next meeting, November 26; but with no significance attached except that Dryden must at this time have enjoyed the social status of a gentleman.[1] As to any intellectual sympathy with the new movement, comment has been meager and conflicting; Christie declares that Dryden "had no accurate knowledge" of science, whereas Scott, more generously but equally without documentation, says that "Dryden, who through life was attached to experimental philosophy, speedily associated himself with those who took interest in its progress." In an elaborate study of the new science in relation to literature,[2] Mr. Carson S. Duncan has been cursory, but severe, in his treatment of Dryden. Although he found that the poet had introduced here and there some imagery derived from science—thus obeying, says Mr. Duncan, "the injunction of Bishop Sprat"[3]—yet he found also imagery drawn from such sources as astrology or the Ptolemaic astronomy. "From all which," concluded Mr. Duncan, "it follows that Dryden was not deeply impressed with the new philosophy. It seems never to have occurred to him that it was a serious matter to know the truth about nature, or at least to be consistent about its representation." "Dryden was practically unaffected by the new intellectual impulse."[4] As to the sources of his poetic imagery, Dryden went all his life both to the new and the old science. But he would probably have defended the latter

Reprinted from Modern Philology, Vol. 25 (1928), pp. 417–438, by permission of the author and The University of Chicago Press. Copyright 1928 by The University of Chicago. The material of this essay appeared in revised form in The Intellectual Milieu of John Dryden published by the University of Michigan Press, 1934.

as he does the supernatural in poetry, by an appeal to folk-lore. "It is enough that, in all ages and religions, the greatest part of mankind has believed the power of magic, and that there are spirits or spectres which have appeared. This, I say, is foundation enough for poetry."[5] Without raising further, therefore, the question of Dryden's knowledge of science as shown in his metaphors and similes, this paper will approach more directly the larger question whether or not "Dryden was practically unaffected by the new intellectual impulse," or whether he at least possessed any characteristic attitudes or ideas which might indicate sympathetic interest in the Royal Society and the new science.

I

First of all, there are two common errors to be avoided in defining the intellectual impulse of the new science. One is to describe the new science as mainly Baconian in nature, as merely collection and classification of specimens. Bacon's prestige with the Royal Society and his great influence in fostering the inductive method must of course be admitted. The scientists of the seventeenth century were his disciples in their respect for facts and their suspicion of hasty generalization; the gentlemen virtuosi collected rarities with truly Baconian zeal. But the most significant element of the new science was not to be found in these collectors' cabinets, so frequently ridiculed in the literature of the time; neither is it to be found in the works of Bacon. The new philosophy of science, or, as it was then called, the "new philosophy of motion," was the result of the application of mathematics to physics and astronomy; and Bacon had completely ignored mathematics. "In this respect," says Whitehead, "Bacon completely missed the tonality which lay behind the success of seventeenth century science. Science was becoming, and had remained, primarily quantitative."[6]

It is also a mistake to suppose that the profoundest effect of the Copernican system upon general ideas was the shift of the center of the universe from the earth to the sun. The shock of this revelation, great as it had been at first, was not greatly felt in England, at least, after 1660. And during the process of popularizing the heliocentric theory, other problems of deeper and more permanent import emerged and became the real storm center. These deeper problems, again, were the result of the application of mathematics to astronomy and physics.

The development of mathematics and its triumphant application to the phenomena of motion constitutes undoubtedly one of the greatest revolutions in the history of thought. It has so completely permeated even the "common sense" view of the world of the average modern man that only by effort can we understand the conception of motion which preceded it. The medieval interpretation was animistic. The Middle Ages asked the question, "Why do bodies move?" And their answer was that they move because they have a desire to. Gravitation is due to each thing seeking its appropriate place; nature abhors a vacuum; Kepler, in his Mysterium cosmographicum (1597), explained that planets move because they have "moving souls" (animae motrices);[7] Gilbert described the magnetic force he had discovered as "of the nature of soul, surpassing the soul of man"; Harvey believed that the motion of the heart and blood is due to "innate heat," which is not fire nor derived from fire; and the blood, he said, is not occupied by a spirit, but is a spirit, "celestial in nature, the soul, that which answers to the essence of the stars . . . . is something analogous to heaven, the instrument of heaven."[8] Medieval thought sought for the essence of motion as an answer to the question why bodies move. As a matter of fact, the new science of the seventeenth century did not answer this question, but only deprived it of its interest. The new science demonstrated that all motion is regular and mathematically measurable, and thenceforth the real question became, "How do bodies move?" Thus Kepler, after many years of astronomical calculations, ultimately rejected his "moving souls" as unnecessary. The seventeenth century, as a period in the development of thought, is particularly notable for its many geniuses in the related fields of mathematics, physics, and astronomy, who by a vast cooperative effort added stone to stone in this new philosophic structure, until Newton completed it, a new universe of cause and effect, a vast machine, whose every mystery must be amenable to the laws of mathematics.[9]

Thus arose in a new and much more perplexing and dangerous form the ancient problem of materialism. Even Descartes felt constrained to regard living organisms as machines, although he of course admitted that man has also a "rational soul," and thus established the famous and influential Cartesian dualism. But there were many who accepted the mechanical theory without adding to it this idealistic superstructure which contradicted it. Hence the great popularity in the seventeenth century of the atomistic philosophy of Democritus, Epicurus, and Lucretius, who not only affected the general tone of sophisticated society by stimulating "libertine" thought, but influenced as well the new science.[10] The French philosopher Gassendi combined ancient atomism with the new science of his own day, thereby preparing for Newton's rejection of the vortex theory of Descartes and the foundation of modern atomism. Voltaire, in his Elements of the Philosophy of Newton, pointed out, probably not without some malicious satisfaction, the great prestige and importance, in the eyes of the pious Newton, of the materialistic ancient atheists and their modern disciple:

> Newton suivait les anciennes opinions de Démocrite, d'Epicure et d'une soule de philosophes rectifiées par notre célèbre Gassendi. Newton a dit plusieurs fois à quelques françois qui vivent encore, qu'il regardait Gassendi comme un esprit très juste et très sage, et qu'il ferait gloire d'être entièrement de son avis dans toutes les choses dont on vient de parler.[11]

As for the materialistic implications of the new science, however, they were much more hospitably received among lay gentlemen, such as cultivated the gay cynicism of "libertine" thought, than among professional men of science. On the other hand, those members of the Royal Society who were doing significant scientific work were also pious men who held dear that religious and idealistic tradition which their scientific work was putting on the defensive. From this dilemma sprang much of the characteristic thought not only of the seventeenth century, but of the modern era. As Whitehead says, "The history of thought in the eighteenth and nineteenth centuries is governed by the fact that the world had got hold of a general idea which it could neither live with nor live without."[12] But the apologetics of the Royal Society will be understood better if we first consider Hobbes, the most distinguished and the most uncompromising of the contemporary adherents of the dreaded materialism.

317

II

The mental history of Hobbes is typical of the mathematical and physical preoccupations of the seventeenth century. His philosophical awakening came at the age of forty, when he accidentally opened a book of Euclid and became enchanted by the certainty of mathematical demonstration. Along with Euclid he studied Galileo, from whom, it appears, he derived his fundamental mechanical theory, which he proceeded to apply both to the world and to man.[13] Science is the study of causes, but all causes are ultimately reducible to motion. A complete science should begin with a study of simple motions, then proceed to more complex motions in geometry, thence to physics, until we reach the most complex motions in "moral philosophy, in which we are to consider the motions of the mind . . . . what causes they have, and of what they be causes."[14] To complete his scheme Hobbes also insisted that the soul is material, a sort of thin, filmy substance, which could thus be assumed to be a part of the mechanical world. The customary theological definition of soul as "incorporeal substance" he ridiculed as meaningless. The soul, he said, has dimension as the body has, though he admitted it has no color. In response to his theological critics, Hobbes declared himself willing to accept on faith such incomprehensible beings as God and the angels, though he suggested with fine irony that "the Scripture favoureth them more, that hold angels and spirits corporeal, than them that hold the contrary."[15]

In spite of this thoroughgoing mechanistic view of the world, Hobbes always professed himself a Christian and a submissive adherent of the Church of England as by law established. Obedience to authority, he said, is the cardinal virtue in political and ecclesiastical matters. But it was well understood already by his contemporaries that under this outward acceptance of Christianity he attempted to conceal a nature in which the religious instincts remained undeveloped. His reaction was significant when early in his philosophical career he was asked for comment on Descartes' Discours. His own mechanical and materialistic philosophy was already definitely formulated, and he opposed it to the idealism of Descartes. His manner was as tart as his reasoning keen; he reduced the whole spiritualistic philosophy to corporeal motion, "et ainsi l'esprit ne sera rien autre chose qu'un mouvement en certaines parties du corps organique."[16]

As both men were irritated by their mutual lack of sympathy, their relations never passed beyond an acquaintance. And the philosophy of Descartes, which had so much in common with Plato, Augustine, and Anselm, became for half a century in England one of the most trusted modes of escape from Hobbism and materialism, especially among the Cambridge Platonists and the members of the Royal Society.

For Hobbism spread rapidly, and after 1650 the philosopher of Malmesbury, already past sixty, became for nearly thirty years more the center of a storm of controversy which reverberated throughout Europe. That he had many friends and disciples is certain, although some of the names in the long list given by his friend John Aubrey are open to suspicion.[17] His popularity with Charles II and the court was a thorn in the side of his enemies, though it does not appear to have rested entirely on a philosophical basis:

> Order was given that he should have free accesse to his majesty, who was always much delighted in his witt and smart repartees. The witts at Court were wont to bayte him. But he feared none of them, and would make his part good. The king would call him the beare: "Here comes the beare to be bayted!"[18]

But he enjoyed also the friendship and esteem of such men of letters as Davenant and Waller, and even of Cowley, a member of the Royal Society.[19] On the whole, however, his disciples seem to have been more ready to talk than to write, and his great vogue is best apparent from the number, the seriousness, and the persistence of his opponents.

Hobbes fought indeed alone against all the leading thinkers of his time. Already in 1645 he had entered upon a long controversy with Bishop Bramhall on free-will and necessitarianism.[20] The Cambridge Platonists attacked from various points of view the "mechanic" philosophy of Hobbes. Of these the most important were Ralph Cudworth and Henry More, both of them members of the Royal Society and both declared adherents of the new science. More had said already in 1647 that "it is plain to any man that is not prejudic'd" that Galileo's "System of the world is more naturall & genuine than that of Tycho's."[21] Cudworth objected only to a materialistic interpretation of the new science. Imbued with the notion that truth is purest at its source in antiquity, he sought there for a truer philosophy. In his erudite work, The True Intellectual System of the Universe (1678), he distinguished between the ancient theistic and atheistic atomisms, the former of which he believed to be derived from Moses. From such heights of learning he felt himself able to weigh and estimate the atomistic science of his contemporaries, who were only reviving ancient doctrine, "and that with no small pomp and ostentation of wisdom and philosophy."

Though directing their polemics especially against Hobbes, both More and Cudworth, significantly, approved of Descartes, even though with some reservations. In the Preface to his treatise on The Immortality of the Soul, a treatise refuting Hobbes's doctrine that the soul is material,[22] More declares that he thinks

> it is the most sober and faithful advice that can be offered to the Christian World, that they would encourage the reading of Des-Cartes in all publick Schools and Universities. That the Students of Philosophy may be thoroughly exercised in the just extent of the Mechanical powers of Matter, how farre they will reach, and where they fall short. Which will be the best assistance to Religion that Reason and the Knowledge of Nature can afford. For by this means such as are intended to serve the Church will be armed betimes with sufficient strength to grapple with their proudest Deriders or Opposers. Whenas for want of this, we see how liable they are to be contemned and born down by every bold, though weak, pretender to the Mechanick Philosophy.[23]

Cudworth gives Descartes the high praise of having revived the right kind, the theistic atomism of Moschus, whom Cudworth identified with Moses.

> For Renatus Cartesius first revived and restored the atomick philosophy, agreeably, for the most part, to that ancient Moschical and Pythagorick form; acknowledging besides extended substance and corporeal atoms, another cogitative incorporeal substance,

320

and joyning metaphysicks or theology, together with
physiology, to make up one entire system of philosophy.

But he unreservedly condemns Hobbes, though not naming him:

> But shortly after this Cartesian restitution of
> the primitive atomology, that acknowledgeth incor-
> poreal substance, we have had our <u>Leucippus</u> and
> <u>Democritus</u> too, who also revived and brought upon
> the stage that other atheistick atomology, that makes
> <u>senseless and lifeless atoms to be the only principles</u>
> <u>of all things in the universe</u>; thereby necessarily ex-
> cluding, besides incorporeal substance and immortal-
> ity of souls, a Deity and natural morality; as also
> making all actions and events materially and mechan-
> ically necessary.[24]

These attempts to read Hobbes out of the new scientific movement did not, however, draw him into controversy, any more than
did the sermons and pamphlets of "every young Churchman mili-
tant," who, as Warburton says, "would needs try his arms in
thundering upon Hobbes' steel-cap." But the members of the
Royal Society penetrated his armor, stirred him to counterattack,
and in mathematics and physics won a whole series of easy victories, each of which seems to have left Hobbes more sore and
obstinate than enlightened. He was indeed constantly on the wrong
side of scientific questions; he was incompetent enough as a mathematician to try to demonstrate the quadrature of the circle; he
rashly contradicted Boyle on the nature of the vacuum. Both as
scientist and mathematician he had been discredited in discerning circles even before 1660.[25] It was his reputation and influence with the larger public that made a continued polemic against
him necessary. The situation was especially delicate because the
royal patron of the new science also showed a marked partiality
for this charlatanical but dreaded enemy of the scientists.[26] And
though dangerous as an enemy, Hobbes would have been far more
insidiously dangerous as a friend and member of the Royal Society.
The leaders of the new scientific movement could never have admitted the modern Democritus to their ranks without endangering
their cause. Their most subtle and persistent difficulty was to
explain to the public the difference between the Hobbists and the

members of the Royal Society; to explain how these Christian scientists could accept the new philosophy of motion and yet escape an atheistic materialism.

III

The Royal Society had of course enemies of all kinds. They alienated many churchmen and scholars by attacking the Aristotelian scholasticism which still dominated the universities. Here the Royal Society had to contend with a powerful vested interest, and they fought it vigorously and openly. But they suffered even more from the suspicion that they were undermining religion. Sprat, in his History of the Royal Society (1667), approaches this subject with the statement that it is "the weightiest and most solemn part of my whole undertaking; to make a defense of the Royal Society, and this new Experimental Learning, in respect to the Christian Faith. I am not ignorant, in what a slippery place I now stand; and what a tender matter I am enter'd upon."[27]

Sprat's discussion of the matter is eminently tactful, and also somewhat evasive. There is none of the direct attack on Hobbes found in More and Cudworth. The facts about the situation are more easily gathered from Boyle. This recognized great champion of both religion and science[28] was also one of the chief antagonists, along with Wallis and Ward, of Hobbes, to whom his references are frequent and explicit. In the Preface to An Examen of Mr. T. Hobbes his Dialogus Physicus de Natura Aeris (1662) he says he is writing to defend the experimental method which Hobbes scorned. He adds:

> It was also suggested to me that the dangerous
> opinions about some important, if not fundamental,
> articles of religion, I had met with in his Leviathan,
> and some other of his writings, having made too great
> impressions upon divers persons, (who, though said
> to be for the most part either of greater quality, or
> of greater wit than learning, do yet divers of them de-
> serve better principles,) these errors being chiefly
> recommended by the opinion they had of Mr. Hobbes's
> demonstrative way of philosophy; it might possibly
> prove some service to higher truths than those in

controversy between him and me, to shew, that in
the Physics themselves, his opinions, and even his
ratiocinations, have no such great advantage over
those, of some orthodox Christian Naturalists.[29]

In his Usefulness of Natural Philosophy (1663) he objects that

it has long been the custom of such men [i.e., atheists],
to talk, as if themselves, and those of their mind, were
not alone the best, but almost the only naturalists; and
to perplex others with pretending, that, whereas it is
not conceivable, how there can be a God; all things are
by the principles of the atomical philosophy, made
clear and facil.[30]

In the second part of this work (1671) he says:

I forget not that there are several divines (and
some of the eminent ones) that out of a holy jealousy
(as they think) for religion, labour to deter men from
addicting themselves to serious and thorough inquiries
into nature, as from a study unsafe for a Christian,
and likely to end in atheism, by making it possible
for men (that I may propose to you their objection as
much to its advantage as I can) to give themselves
such an account of all the wonders of nature, by the
single knowledge of second causes, as may bring
them to disbelieve the necessity of a first.[31]

In 1675 Boyle writes that whereas atheists had formerly been in
the habit of attacking the historical and doctrinal parts of Christian
theology, they in this age attacked the very notion of God and religion. "For these libertines own themselves to be so upon the account of the Epicurean, and other mechanical principles of philosophy"; and, he adds, they recognize no authorities except such as
"Leucippus, Democritus, Epicurus, &c.," who "explicate things
by matter and local motion."[32] "The modern Atheists," wrote
Rev. Joseph Glanvill, another member of the Royal Society, "are
pretenders to the mechanick principles . . . . the modern Sadduce
pretends that all things we do, are performed by meer matter,
and motion, and consequently that there is no such thing as an

immaterial being."[33] Obviously, the scientists of the Royal
Society, even though they themselves may have been secure from
the charge of atheism, could hardly escape the charge of cultivating a philosophy which led to atheism in others. How did they
defend themselves against this charge?

Officially they did nothing. Officially the Royal Society, as
Sprat says, "is abundantly cautious, not to intermeddle in Spiritu
things," and such subjects as God and the soul were not discusse
at their meetings.[34] Nevertheless, there was considerable unanimity of opinion among the members. It is well known that Des
cartes was respected by them as a philosophical as well as a
scientific genius. Through the Royal Society as well as through
the Cambridge Platonists, Cartesianism became a very importan
element in English idealistic thought in that century. But the me
bers of the Royal Society adopted also another mode of defense
against materialism, namely, a critique of the very science they
were promoting, a critique which varied all the way from timidit
in generalization to philosophical skepticism.

Sprat testifies to the extreme caution of the Society from its
very inception. Their motto Nullius in Verba was a hit at the
tyranny of scholasticism, but it soon became apparent that the
tyranny of Epicurus or Democritus, or of any "modern dogmatists," would be equally unwelcome.[35] In fact, no philosopher
was accorded the seat of authority, not even Descartes. Com-
panies, Sprat says repeatedly, are to be preferred before single
endeavors in philosophical matters, as "exhibiting more warines
and coldness in thinking, and rigorous examination." Altogether
Sprat fears that "to this fault of Sceptical doubting, the Royal
Society may perhaps be suspected, to be a little too much inclin'
because they always professed, to be so backward from setling o
Principles, or fixing upon Doctrines." To which Sprat replies
that generalizing is for the future, and in the mean time dogmati
is more dangerous than skepticism.[36]

Among the workers in the Royal Society, no one was more
wary and cold in scientific thinking, more reluctant to dogmatize
from the new science, than Robert Boyle. It is therefore particu
larly important to note that he cultivated this critical, not to say
skeptical, attitude toward science with a conscious intent to serv
religion. In his Excellence of Theology (1673), Part II, section 3
he criticizes the belief that physics has one prerogative over divinity, namely, "the certainty, and clearness, and thence resultin

satisfactoriness of our knowledge of physical, in comparison of any we can have of theological matters, whose being dark and uncertain, the nature of the things themselves, and the numerous controversies of differing sects about them, sufficiently manifest." In reply Boyle does not urge the certainty of divinity, but the real uncertainty of science.

> That physical certainty, [he says] which is pretended for the truths demonstrated by naturalists, is, even where it is rightfully claimed, but an inferior kind or degree of certainty, as moral certainty also is. For even physical demonstrations can beget but a physical certainty, (that is, a certainty upon supposition, that the principles of physic be true,) not a metaphysical certainty, (wherein it is absolutely impossible, that the thing believed should be other than true) . . . . And there are I know not how many things in physicks, that men presume they believe upon physical and cogent arguments, wherein they really have but a moral assurance; which is a truth held by so few, that I have been invited to take the more particular notice of them in other papers, written purposely to show the doubtfulness and incompleteness of natural philosophy; . . . . the most even of the modern virtuosi are wont to fancy more of clearness and certainty in their physical theories, than a critical examiner will find. 37

Boyle, then, sought a reconciliation of the new science with religion by limiting the sphere of reason; he weakened the materialistic interpretation of the new science by emphasizing the uncertainty of science itself.

This criticism of scientific knowledge was carried still further by Joseph Glanvill, whose volume, The Vanity of Dogmatizing (1661), was reprinted in 1664 as Scepsis scientifica, with a Dedication to the Royal Society which resulted in his election to membership. 38 A passage from this Dedication will explain his purpose and its relation to Hobbes as well as to the new science. The work of the Royal Society, he says, is

> the improving the minds of Men in solid and useful notices of things, helping them to such theories as

may be serviceable to common life, and the searching
out of the true laws of Matter and Motion, in order to
the securing of the Foundations of Religion against all
attempts of Mechanical Atheism.

For the ingenious World being grown quite weary
of Qualities and Formes, and declaring in favour of the
Mechanical Hypothesis, (to which a person that is not
very fond of Religion is a great pretender) divers of
the brisker Geniuses, who desire rather to be accounted
Witts, then endeavour to be so, have been willing to accept Mechanism upon Hobbian conditions, and many
others were in danger of following them into the preci-
pice. So that 'tis not conceivable how a more suitable
remedy could have been provided against the deadly influence of that Contagion, then your Honourable Society,
by which the meanest intellects may perceive, that
Mechanick Philosophy yields no security to irreligion,
and that those that would be gentilely learned and ingenious, need not purchase it, at the dear rate of being
atheists.

It is impossible and unnecessary here to examine in detail
the skepticism of Glanvill. We are concerned more with the
occasion of his thought than with an evaluation of it. It must suffice to say that Glanvill has a place in the history of philosophy
as an acute and ingenious thinker, whose critique of causation
anticipates in some respects that of Hume himself. These scientific skeptics were, indeed, not naïve theorizers; they were
versed in the tradition of philosophical skepticism. Boyle knew
the work of Sextus Empiricus,[39] and Glanvill shows an acquaintance not only with Sextus, but with such modern disciples as
Montaigne and Charron.[40] Perhaps they were also indebted to
Sir Thomas Browne, although his imaginative flights and complete humiliation of the reason must have appeared to them rather
too uncritical. And yet Glanvill conveyed, in rhythms that recall
Browne, a sense of the mystery of the world both in its vastness
and in its infinite minuteness, and of the miracle of man among a
these unexplainable wonders:

Whatever I look upon within the amplitude of
heaven and earth, is evidence of humane ignorance;

> For all things are a great darkness to us, and we are
> so unto our selves: The plainest things are as obscure,
> as the most confessedly mysterious; and the Plants we
> tread on, are as much above us, as the Stars and
> Heavens. The things that touch us are as distant
> from us, as the Pole; and we are as much strangers
> to our selves, as to the inhabitants of America.[41]

Both Glanvill and Boyle, however, refused to be identified with
the extreme skeptical position that truth is unknowable.[42] They
were far from intending to discourage scientific and philosophic
activity. But they believed that he is least likely to go astray who
is most keenly aware of the weakness and deception of human faculties. And in "Hobbism" they saw the grand modern illustration
of stiff confidence in opinion, of the vanity of dogmatizing.[43]

IV

It is now possible to return to Dryden and ask whether he
was aware of the developments we have sketched. We should the
more expect their influence to be noticeable because they came
so largely in the period from 1660 to 1680, the very years when
Dryden was equipping himself with those ideas which make his
political and religious poems, as a group, a remarkable expression of the conservative temperament. Religio Laici and The
Hind and the Panther constitute the terminus ad quem in a study
of Dryden's intellectual history.[44] But for material on his development up to 1680 we have to depend quite largely on his
dramas.

A valuable clue is given us in the notes collected in 1679–80
by John Aubrey toward a life of Hobbes: "Mr. John Dreyden, Poet
Laureat, is his great admirer, and oftentimes makes use of his
doctrine in his plays—from Mr. Dreyden himselfe."[45] And although Aubrey was too enthusiastic a friend of Hobbes to be
trusted in all matters, yet this note can hardly be without foundation. Its authoritative source is confirmed by the many parallels
to the doctrines of Hobbes to be found in Dryden's plays. In political thought, for instance, the monarchical absolutism of Hobbes
is also the doctrine of Dryden's stage creatures,[46] and must have
been particularly grateful to the ears of the court audience for

which Dryden wrote. And yet this resemblance alone would not be decisive proof of indebtedness; a narrow political outlook was almost inevitable in heroic drama, and is common enough in the plays of Orrery, for instance, who has hardly been suspected of an admiration for Hobbes. More conclusive, I believe, and for the purpose of this study, more important, is the frequent reference in Dryden to the dilemma of free-will and necessity—the great ethical problem raised in a new form by Hobbism. In 1664, in his Dedication of The Rival Ladies to Lord Orrery, he implies that free-will is a delusion:

> Here [in Orrery's plays] is no chance, which you have not foreseen; all your heroes are more than your subjects, they are your creatures; and though they seem to move freely in all the sallies of their passions, yet you make destinies for them, which they cannot shun. They are moved (if I may dare to say so) like the rational creatures of the Almighty Poet, who walk at liberty, in their own opinion, because their fetters are invisible; when, indeed, the prison of their will is the more sure for being large; and, instead of an absolute power over their actions, they have only a wretched desire of doing that, which they cannot choose but do.[47]

Almanzor, the hero of The Conquest of Granada (1670), is troubled by the same problem:

> O Heaven, how dark a riddle's thy decree,
> Which bounds our wills, yet seems to leave them free!
> Since thy fore-knowledge cannot be in vain,
> Our choice must be what thou didst first ordain.
> Thus, like a captive in an isle confined,
> Man walks at large, a prisoner of the mind:
> Wills all his crimes, while Heaven the indictment draws,
> And, pleading guilty, justifies the laws.[48]

A sufficient number of such allusions can be found before 1680 to indicate that Dryden was interested in the subject.[49] Perhaps the most surprising expression of determinism is in The State of Innocence (1674), his operatic version of Paradise Lost, a philosophical perversion of the epic to which it is hard to believ

328

Milton would have given his consent. In the opera the newly created Adam seems to have an innate understanding of seventeenth-century philosophy. When he first becomes conscious, he rises and speaks as a Cartesian:

> What am I? or from whence? For that I am
> I know, because I think, etc.[50]

But when Gabriel and Raphael are sent down jointly to instruct Adam in the doctrine of the freedom of the will, they find him a most reluctant and obstinate scholar.

> Gabriel: The Eternal, when he did the world create,
> All other agents did necessitate:
> So what he ordered, they by nature do:
> Thus light things mount, and heavy downward go.
> Man only boasts an arbitrary state.

> Adam: Yet causes their effects necessitate
> In willing agents; where is freedom then?
> Or who can break the chain which limits men
> To act what is unchangeably forecast,
> Since the first cause gives motion to the last?

The lengthy discussion appears to have been unsuccessful, for after his instructors have departed Adam is still lamenting his "hard state of life" in the divine disposition which has been explained to him.[51] These pages of argument read like a brief summary of the famous Bramhall-Hobbes controversy, with Adam, despite his innocence, taking the part of Hobbes.

But it would be a mistake to rush, from such passages and from Aubrey's note, to the conclusion that Dryden was at this time a disciple of Hobbes, any more than of Descartes. He must have been interested in necessitarianism, speculated on its implications, and enjoyed testing out its argumentative strength in verse. Sympathetic intellectual curiosity is one of Dryden's marked characteristics. But this very suppleness of his mind served also to liberate him from the dogmatism and egotism of Hobbes. In his old age he spoke of Hobbes's translation of Homer as "bald," adding that he studied "poetry as he did mathematics, when it was too late."[52] It was a curt dismissal. In 1685, in a discussion of himself as translator of Lucretius, he incidentally

329

clearly draws the distinction between himself and Hobbes, both in temperament and ideas:

> If I am not mistaken, the distinguishing character of Lucretius (I mean of his soul and genius) is a certain kind of noble pride, and positive assertion of his opinions. He is everywhere confident of his own reason, and assuming an absolute command, not only over his vulgar reader, but even his patron Memmius. For he is always bidding him attend, as if he had the rod over him, as our poet and philosopher of Malmesbury. This is that perpetual dictatorship, which is exercised by Lucretius; who, though often in the wrong, yet seems to deal bona fide with his reader, and tells him nothing but what he thinks; in which plain sincerity, I believe, he differs from our Hobbes, who could not but be convinced, or at least doubt, of some eternal truths, which he had opposed. . . . . For there is no doubt to be made, but that he [Lucretius] could have been everywhere as poetical, as he is in his descriptions, and in the moral part of his philosophy, if he had not aimed more to instruct, in his System of Nature, than to delight. But he was bent upon making Memmius a materialist, and teaching him to defy an invisible power: in short, he was so much an atheist, that he forgot sometimes to be a poet. These are the considerations, which I had of that author, before I attempted to translate some parts of him. And accordingly I laid by my natural diffidence and scepticism for a while, to take up that dogmatical way of his, which, as I said, is so much his character, as to make him that individual poet.[53]

These passages, it is true, come too late in Dryden's life to constitute alone any sure indication of his attitude toward Hobbes before 1680. But when they are considered along with his earlier comments on the new science, the Royal Society, and his own distrust of dogmatism, they lose their casual appearance; and the impression grows that Dryden's attitude toward Hobbes must from the beginning have involved reservations and that he found himself more naturally on the side of the Royal Society, with its eminent spokesmen Boyle and Glanvill.[54]

V

There can be no doubt of Dryden's real appreciation of the new science. In an Epistle to Dr. Charlton, written in 1662, he praises English science, especially Bacon, Gilbert, Boyle, and Harvey. There is the famous apostrophe to the Royal Society in Annus Mirabilis, in which, after prophesying remarkable progress in navigation, he adds:

> This I foretell, from your auspicious care
>   Who great in search of God and nature grow;
>   Who best your wise Creator's praise declare,
>   Since best to praise His works is best to know.

Even more direct and forceful are two passages, heretofore strangely neglected, in the Essay of Dramatic Poesy (1668). One is a recognition of the remarkable scientific advance after Copernicus:

> Is it not evident [asks Crites, who is otherwise
> on the side of the Ancients] in these last hundred years
> (when the study of philosophy has been the business of
> all the Virtuosi in Christendom), that almost a new Nature
> has been revealed to us?—that more errors of the school
> have been detected, more useful experiments in philosophy
> have been made, more noble secrets in optics, medicine,
> anatomy, astronomy, discovered, than in all those credu-
> lous and doting ages from Aristotle to us?—so true it is,
> that nothing spreads more fast than science, when rightly
> and generally cultivated.[55]

Later in the same essay he makes Lisideius allude to "what the philosophers say of motion that, when it is once begun, it continues of itself, and will do so to eternity, without some stop put to it"[56] —which is a simple statement of what was later to become Newton's first law of motion.

But we can go even further. That "natural diffidence and skepticism" which Dryden in 1685 declared part of his character, he already in 1668 identified with the skeptical attitude of the Royal Society. When his brother-in-law, Sir Robert Howard, charged him with being "magisterial" in the Essay of Dramatic Poesy, his reply was that

331

> in vindication of myself, I must crave leave to say,
> that my whole discourse was sceptical, according to
> that way of reasoning which was used by Socrates,
> Plato, and all the Academies of old, which Tully and
> the best of the Ancients followed, and which is imitated
> by the modest inquisitions of the Royal Society. That
> it is so, not only the name will show, which is an Essay,
> but the frame and composition of the work. You see it
> is a dialogue sustained by persons of several opinions,
> all of them left doubtful, to be determined by the
> readers in general.[57]

In the true spirit of the Royal Society he asks, in the Preface to
An Evening's Love (1671), "why should there by any Ipse dixit
in our poetry, any more than there is in our philosophy?"[58]
That skepticism which separated Dryden from Hobbes and
Lucretius was therefore no passing whim; it was both an early
and a permanent intellectual characteristic. In the Preface to
Religio Laici (1682) he confesses that he was "naturally inclined
to scepticism in philosophy." He criticizes the Deists, and even
some leaders in the Anglican church, for their confidence in religious rationalism. He says:

> Our modern philosophers, nay, and some of our
> philosophizing divines have too much exalted the
> faculties of our souls, when they have maintained
> that by their force mankind has been able to find that
> there is one supreme agent or intellectual Being
> which we call God . . . . They who would prove
> religion by reason, do but weaken the cause which
> they endeavour to support: 'tis to take away the pil-
> lars from our faith, and to prop it only with a twig.

It was this distrust of reason, this philosophical skepticism, that
drove Dryden toward conservatism and authority in religion, and
ultimately to the Catholic church, just as his distrust of the popu-
lace was one reason for his increasing conservatism and Toryism
in politics.

VI

On such evidence the case must rest. Fragmentary and meager as it is, it would at least seem sufficient to indicate that Dryden was not unresponsive to the intellectual impulses aroused by the new scientific movement. All that we know of Dryden's intellectual character, his sensitiveness to all winds of doctrine, his curiosity, his wide and sympathetic interests, should in fact have led us to expect just such a conclusion. Few poets have consciously cultivated so many contacts with the world as Dryden. He wrote in 1674:

> Mere poets and mere musicians are as sottish
> as mere drunkards are, who live in a continual mist,
> without seeing or judging anything clearly. A man
> should be learned in several sciences, and should have
> a reasonable, philosophical, and in some measure a
> mathematical head, to be a complete and excellent
> poet; and besides this, should have experience in all
> sorts of humours and manners of men.[59]

Again, in 1679, in his Preface to Troilus and Cressida, he says that the "manners" are to "be gathered from the several virtues, vices, or passions, and many other commonplaces, which a poet must be supposed to have learned from natural Philosophy, Ethics, and History; of all which, whosoever is ignorant, does not deserve the name of poet."[60] Dryden proves so baffling because, with a multiplicity of ideas, he appears to have no system; he incorporates ideas, often contradictory ones, into his writings with an eye more to their rhetorical than their philosophical value. Carneades, one of the most famous of Greek skeptics, appeared before the Roman Senate on two successive days, and shocked the moral sense of that venerable assembly by brilliantly attacking the second day all that he had brilliantly defended on the first; skepticism offers peculiar advantages to the artist in expression. Dryden loved reasoning in verse so well that he could not resist an opportunity for a debate, whether in a play or a poem; and he lent of his fire and strength to both sides. But in spite of this inclusiveness of Dryden's intellectual interests, there is a consistency of temperament in his work which allies him with certain tendencies and groups of his time more than with others. It is the problem

333

of criticism to find the perspective from which this larger consistency becomes apparent.

Since the material is so meager for even a descriptive study of Dryden's mind, it would be rash, at least in the present state of Dryden scholarship, to make any large assertions regarding the genesis of his ideas. It is not contended here that Dryden was a skeptic because he was a member of the Royal Society and knew Boyle and Glanvill; skepticism could in that age be acquired in many ways. The purpose of this study is to emphasize the significance and representative nature of Dryden's mind. His ideas are closely related to the important movements of his age. He was interested in the Royal Society, understood its spirit, and recognized that he was like minded with it; he understood the new philosophy of motion, vaguely perhaps in its scientific aspects, but with an acute interest in its deterministic implications regarding human nature; and he rejected the dogmatic materialism of Hobbes and Lucretius. And when we look for the meaning and importance of his distrust of the reason in Religio laici and The Hind and the Panther, or for the interpretation of his ingenuous changeableness in literary opinions, we must go, among other places, to his intellectual experiences with the new science, with Hobbes, and with the Royal Society.

NOTES

1 Malone, Critical and Miscellaneous Prose Works of John Dryden, I (1800), 49–50; Scott, Life of Dryden, in Works of Dryden (ed. Scott and Saintsbury), I, 46–47; W. D. Christie, "Memoir" in Globe edition of Poetical Works, p. xxv; J. Churton Collins, Essays and Studies (1895), p. 18. Saintsbury, in his volume in the "English Men of Letters Series," does not even mention Dryden's membership in the Royal Society.

2 The New Science and English Literature in the Classical Period (Menasha, Wis., 1913).

3 See Sprat, History of the Royal Society, Part III, sec. xxxv (2d ed., 1702), pp. 413–19.

4 Op. cit., pp. 43–45 and 179.

5 Essay on Heroic Plays, in Works (ed. Scott and Saintsbury), IV, 22.

6   A. N. Whitehead, Science and the Modern World (New York, 1925), p. 66.

7   Höffding, History of Modern Philosophy (London, 1900), I, 168–69.

8   T. C. Albutt, Science and Medieval Thought (London, 1901), pp. 41 ff.

9   See W. Whewell, History of the Inductive Sciences (London, 1837), and Philosophy of the Inductive Sciences (London, 1840); E. A. Burtt, The Metaphysical Foundations of Modern Physical Science (1925), with Bibliography; A. J. Snow, Matter and Gravity in Newton's Physical Philosophy (1926), with Bibliography; also the volumes by Albutt and Whitehead referred to above.

10   See Lange, History of Materialism (Eng. trans.; Boston, 1877); Kurd Lasswitz, Geschichte der Atomistik (Hamburg, 1890); L. Mabilleau, Histoire de la philosophic atomistique (Paris, 1895).

11   Quoted by Lange, op. cit., I, 267, n. 12. Gassendi was not in fact an atheist, but outside of scientific circles he was regarded with suspicion, and the "libertines" appealed to his authority.

12   Whitehead, op. cit., p. 74.

13   W. R. Sorley, History of English Philosophy (Cambridge, 1920), pp. 49–50. But this early indebtedness to Galileo has been questioned by Frithiof Brandt, Den Mekaniske Naturopfattelse hos Thomas Hobbes (Copenhagen, 1921), pp. 72–81.

14   Elements of Philosophy, Part I, chap. vi, especially secs. 5 and 6, in English Works (ed. Molesworth), I, 131–32.

15   Human Nature, chap. xi, secs. 2–5; ed. cit., IV, 59–62.

16   Descartes, Troisièmes objections contre les Méditations, in Œuvres (ed. Simon), pp. 198–99.

17   Brief Lives (ed. A. Clark; Oxford, 1898), I, 365–72.

18   Ibid., p. 340. This story is told in a quite different manner by Sorbière: "Il a fait peur je ne sçay comment au Clergé de son pays, aux Mathematiciens d'Oxfordt, & à leurs ad-

herants; c'est pourquoy S[a] M[ajesté] me le compara tres-
bien à l'ours, contre lequel il fait battre les dogues pour les
exercer" (Relation d'un Voyage en Angleterre [Cologne, 1666],
p. 76).

19 Cowley's ode to Hobbes was published before the Royal Society was founded, but there is nothing to indicate that he did
not to the end continue to admire both the opposing parties.

20 A controversy discussed and deservedly emphasized as "of
great importance in the history of seventeenth-century
thought" by Marjorie H. Nicolson, "Milton and Hobbes,"
Studies in Philology, XXIII (1926), 409.

21 Philosophical Poems (Cambridge, 1647), p. 390.

22 Op.cit. (London, 1662), chaps. viii–xii, pp. 34–49.

23 Ibid., Preface.

24 True Intellectual System (London, 1743), Book I, chap. iii,
sec. 38, pp. 174–75.

25 See the correspondence of Christian Huygens, in Œuvres
Complètes (La Haye, 1888 ff.); especially the letters from
Huygens to J. Wallis, March 15, 1656 (Vol. I, No. 272); and
from Huygens to R. Moray, November 4, 1661 (Vol. III, No.
916): "Dans le Dialogue de Monsieur Hobbes je ne trouve
rien de solide, mais seulement de pures visions. C'est par
faute d'esprit ou par ce qu'il se plait à contredire qu'il ne
recoit pas les veritables raisons des effets du vide, qui sont
dans le liure de Monsieur Boile. Quand a ce qu'il adjouste
de la duplication du cube, je ne l'ay pas voulu regarder par
ce que je scay demonstratiuement que la chose est impossible
Et d'ailleurs il y a long temps qu'en matiere de Geometrie
Monsieur Hobbes a perdu tout credit aupres du moy."

26 Ibid., letters from Moray to Huygens, September 13 and October 19, 1661 (Vol. III, Nos. 893 and 909). According to
Sorbière, Charles II would have liked to have Hobbes elected
to the Royal Society (Relation [ed. cit.], p. 75).

27 History (ed. cit.), Part III, sec. xiv, p. 345.

28 Stillingfleet, in a letter of October 6, 1662, urged Boyle to
publish his papers on behalf of Christianity against Hobbes.

See Boyle, Works, V (1744), 516. See also letters from
Peter du Moulin, December 28, 1669 (V, 594); from J. Beale,
June 26, 1682 (V, 505); from Cudworth, October 16, 1684
(V, 549)—all indicative of the way Boyle was relied on to
save the day.

29 Works, I, 119.

30 Usefulness of Natural Philosophy, Part I, Essay 5, in Works,
I, 459.

31 Ibid., pp. 429-30. Meric Casaubon, no friend to the new
science, had expressed this objection in A Letter . . . . to
Peter du Moulin . . . . Concerning Natural experimental
Philosophie, and some books lately set out about it (Cambridge, 1669). After a lengthy attack on the presumption of
the new science, he continues (p. 30): "Now I crave leave to
tell you, that it is (as all good things, more or less) very apt
to be abused and to degenerate into Atheism. Men that are
much fixed upon matter and secondary causes and sensual
objects, if great care be not taken, may in time, (there be
many examples) and by degrees forget that there be such
things in the world as Spirits, substances really existing and
of great power, though not visible, or palpable by their nature;
forget I say, that there is a God, and that their souls are immortal." In this same year Dr. du Moulin, who was like
Casaubon a prebendary of Canterbury, saw his Latin poem
in praise of the Royal Society suppressed by the licenser,
Dr. Gunning, later Bishop of Ely. See Boyle's Works, I, 60,
and V, 594.

32 Preface to Some Considerations about the Reconcileableness
of Reason and Religion (ed. cit.), III, 510.

33 Philosophia Pia (1671), pp. 23, 32.

34 History (ed. cit.), Part III, sec. xiv, and Part II, sec. xi, pp.
83 and 347.

35 History (ed. cit.), Part I, secs. xiii–xv, pp. 28–35.

36 Ibid., pp. 100–109.

37 Works (ed. cit.), III, 432. Cf. Burtt, op.cit., pp. 178–82, and
Whitehead's discussion of modern science as "predominantly
an anti-rationalistic movement" (p. 23). Although passages

from Boyle could be patched together to make a criticism of human knowledge almost as complete as that of Glanvill, yet Nourrisson has undoubtedly exaggerated his skepticism in his essay in Philosophies de la Nature (Paris, 1887), pp. 43–84.

38 On December 7, 1664, "Lord Brereton presented a book written by J. Glanvill, dedicated to the Society, the dedication of which was read. Mr. Glanvill was proposed candidate by Lord Brereton" (Birch, History of the Royal Society, p. 500). Glanvill was elected and admitted December 14, 1664. Scepsis scientifica was licensed for publication on October 18, 1664.

39 See reference in A Free Inquiry into the received Notion of Nature, printed in 1686, but written about 1666 (Works [ed. cit.], IV, 376 and 359).

40 Ferris Greenslet, Joseph Glanvill (New York, 1900), pp. 95 ff. For references to Montaigne and Charron, see Scepsis scientifica, pp. 114 and 172.

41 From "Address to the Royal Society," Scepsis scientifica.

42 Boyle, ed. cit., I, 374; and Glanvill, Scire, or Reply to Albius (1665), p. 3.

43 The skeptical attitude toward science was not without influence. In 1688 Matthew Prior, then at St. John's College, Cambridge, wrote a grandiose ode On Exod. III. 14. — I Am That I Am, the theme of which is the inadequacy of reason to understand the world and the necessity of exercising faith and reverence to reach the high abode of the mysterious God who revealed himself to Moses. A few lines will show how definitely Prior applied his critique to materialistic science:

> Man does with dangerous curiosity
> These unfathom'd wonders try:
> With fancied rules and arbitrary laws
> Matter and motion he restrains;
> And studied lines and fictious circles draws:
> Then with imagin'd sovereignty
> Lord of his new hypothesis he reigns.

(Prior, Poetical Works [ed. R. B. Johnson; London, 1907], I, 23–27.) The scepsis scientifica has again become a familiar and important conception in the discussions of the present century, as, for instance, in Émile Boutroux, "La Religion et les limites de la science," Science et religion (Paris, 1908).

44 To supplement and complete the present study, the writer is preparing parallel discussions of Dryden's relation to the political and religious controversies of his time.

45 Brief Lives, I, 372. For the date of the notes see Introduction, p. 16.

46 Mr. Merritt Y. Hughes has pointed out parallels in his article, "Dryden as Statist," Philological Quarterly, VI (1927), 334–50; but Mr. Hughes relied only on internal evidence, without noting either the remark of Aubrey or the contemporary accusation that Dryden got his political ideas from Hobbes, in Censure of the Rota (see Mark Van Doren, The Poetry of John Dryden [New York, 1920], p. 21).

47 Works (ed. cit.), II, 132–33.

48 Conquest of Granada, Part II, Act IV, sc. iii (Works, IV, 190–91).

49 I have collected the following, with references to the Scott and Saintsbury edition:

> Indian Queen (1664), Act II, sc. iii (II, 246)
> Indian Queen (1664), Act III, sc. ii (II, 257)
> The Tempest (1667), Act III, sc. v (III, 175)
> Tyrannic Love (1669), Act I, sc. i (III, 389)
> Tyrannic Love (1669), Act III, sc. i (III, 410)
> Tyrannic Love (1669), Act IV, sc. i (III, 430)
> Conquest of Granada, Part I (1670), Act II, sc. i (IV, 56–57)
> Conquest of Granada, Part II (1670), Act III, sc. i (IV, 162)

In the Dedication to Aureng-Zebe (1676) there is an interesting passage: "Our minds are perpetually wrought on by the temperament of our bodies; which makes me suspect, they are nearer allied, than our philosophers or school-divines will allow them to be."

50 State of Innocence, Act II, sc. i (V, 133–34).

51 Ibid., Act IV, sc. i (Works, V, 152–56).

52 Preface to the Fables (1700), in Essays (ed. W. P. Ker), II, 252.

53 Preface to Sylvae (1685) (Essays, I, 259–60).

54 A very interesting passage in the Essay on Heroic Plays (1672) by no means implies discipleship: "I dare further affirm, that the whole doctrine of separated beings, whether those spirits are incorporeal substances (which Mr. Hobbes, with some reason, thinks to imply a contradiction), or that they are a thinner or more aerial sort of bodies (as some of the Fathers have conjectured), may better be explicated by poets than by philosophers or divines. For their speculations on this subject are wholly poetical; they have only their fancy for their guide; and that, being sharper in an excellent poet, than it is likely it should in a phlegmatic, heavy gownman, will see farther in its own empire, and produce more satisfactory notions on those dark and doubtful problems" (Essays [ed. Ker], I, 153). A man who held such theories of knowledge and psychology would certainly never have been recognized by Hobbes as a hopeful disciple. Dryden had a very unHobbesian interest in the realms of mystery, and he repeatedly defended the use of the supernatural in epic poetry.

55 Essays (ed. Ker), I, 36–37.

56 Ibid., p. 63.

57 Ibid., p. 124.

58 Ibid., p. 138. Cf. also Defence of the Epilogue (1672), I, 163.

59 Postscript to Notes and Observations on the Empress of Morocco, in Works (ed. Scott and Saintsbury), XV, 406.

60 Essays (ed. Ker), I, 214.

THE DRAMATIC USE OF HOBBES'S POLITICAL IDEAS

Louis Teeter

The influence of the writing of Thomas Hobbes on the philosophical "climate" of the Restoration courtier and wit has been frequently analysed and emphasized. Taine wrote of them that Hobbes

> érigeait leurs moeurs en théorie, donnait le manuel
> de leur conduite, et rédigeait d'avance les axiomes
> qu'ils allaient traduire en actions.[1]

The literary historians of the period have agreed in this appraisal and indicated the indebtedness of contemporary poets and playwrights.[2]

That this influence included his political ideas as well as his psychology has been generally assumed as axiomatic. Was not Hobbes the greatest theorist of monarchial absolutism of his time? and were not the poets and dramatists dominated by a Stuart court? Courthope, for example, speaking of Hobbes's political thought, writes that

> A theory so favorable to the principles of the Restoration was, of course, promoted by all the social powers of the age.[3]

An assumption of such an influence has been frequently made by students of Dryden. Professor Bredvold in a discussion of that poet's use of Hobbesian doctrines remarks parenthetically:

> In political thought, for instance, the monarchical
> absolutism of Hobbes is also the doctrine of Dryden's stage creatures, and must have been particu-

Reprinted from English Literary History, Vol. 3 (1936), pp. 140–169, by permission of the author and The Johns Hopkins University Press.

larly grateful to the ears of the court audience for
which Dryden wrote.[4]

Another student of Dryden's political thought finds many of
Hobbes's ideas in his plays, and agrees with Mark Van Doren
that his distrust of the crowd was due to the teaching of the
Leviathan.[5]

Yet a careful examination of Hobbes's characteristic contributions to political theory and the attitude of his contemporaries towards them gives little support to the belief that an expression of them in the drama would have been "welcome to the
court." His absolutism was derived from premises that were
acceptable to no one and dependent upon conditions which were
shocking to all believers in divine right. The orthodox royalists
of his time were quite aware of this incompatibility and never
tired of denouncing the danger of his theories. The first part
of this article will be devoted to justifying these statements and
discussing certain passages in the plays which seem to represent the actual opinions of the dramatists. In no case, I believe,
will typical Hobbesian doctrines be found in the mouths of such
characters as can be considered as speaking for the dramatist
himself.

That is not to say, however, that Hobbes had no influence in
this field. The drama is a narrative art in which many opinions
not sanctioned by the author must be expounded. A drama concerned as was Restoration tragedy with state affairs must give
to its tyrants, usurpers, and rebels political principles of a
plausible and characteristic nature. If these principles can have
the added piquancy of novelty so much the better, and if Hobbes
were anathema to the royalists he might very well be a political
guide to stage villains. It is to an investigation of this possible
relationship that the concluding section of this article will be
devoted.

What Hobbes actually said is perhaps most clearly interpreted
against the background of his life.[6] He was prematurely born in
1588, his mother having been frightened by tales of the Spanish
Armada. As he later wrote, Fear and he were twins, and, one
may add, his brother visited him frequently throughout his life.
In his first attempt at philosophy he formulated a defense of absolutism for which he feared the Long Parliament would never
forgive him, and he decided to shift for himself.[7] He fled to Paris

where he was soon at home in scientific circles. When the Prince of Wales arrived from England Hobbes was appointed his tutor in mathematics, and only mathematics, for he had already acquired his reputation for atheism.

It was during this period that he wrote the Leviathan, the most finished statement of his political theory, and had it printed in London in 1651. After the Restoration he was accused of having written it in order to facilitate his return to England, and Clarendon said that Hobbes had told him apropos of the book that "the truth is I have a mind to go home."[8] Whether this accusation was true or not, Hobbes did boast in 1656 that his doctrine had "framed the minds of a thousand gentlemen to a conscientious obedience to present government, which otherwise would have wavered in that point."[9] This was certainly not a claim calculated to endear his doctrines to the cavalier emigrés.

As was natural, Hobbes, that aged twin of Fear, viewed the Restoration with a certain anxiety. He was, however, received kindly by Charles and taken under the protection of a monarch who was as willing to sacrifice his family's political dogmas to a "bear-baiting" as his own dignity to a jest. From the shelter of the court, Hobbes became the patron saint of the Restoration rakes, whose commonplace books were full of extracts from his writings. His political ideas were, however, anathema to all parties. This will hardly seem astonishing if they are examined with care.

It is important to realize that the dominant emotion behind Hobbes's political thought was fear; the goal to which he was willing to sacrifice everything was security. And by the time he came to formulating his theory the Stuart doctrine of divine right was obviously unsuited for the comfort of a "diffident" man. It was a theory that demanded the sacrifice of property and even life itself from the loyal; not in such divinity could Hobbes find the protection he sought. Hardly a religious man, he attempted rather to build his commonwealth solidly on the self-interest of the individual. If it could be shown that enlightened self-interest demanded absolute obedience, he would be striking at the root of most sedition and social unrest. The origin of government he found then in the selfish desire of man to escape from the insupportable war of the state of nature. Before, or without government,[10] man lived in "continual feare, and danger of violent death," for men, complete egotists and with a right to all that they could obtain, were driven by the passions of competition, diffidence, and glory to a condition of constant warfare against each other. Even the strongest could find himself caught at a fatal disadvantage by the weakest. It was thus to the advantage of everyone to escape from this condition and secure some common power capable of enforcing obedience and securing protection.

Such power could be secured only by uniting the separate strengths of the individuals, the natural right of each

> to use his own power, as he will himself, for the preservation of his own nature; that is to say, of his own life.[11]

This donation of power was secured by contract.

> The only way to erect such a common power, as may be able to defend them from the invasion of foreigners, and the injuries of one another . . . is to confere all their power and strength upon one man, or upon one assembly of men, that may reduce all their wills, by plurality of voices, unto one will: which is as much as to say, to appoint one man, or assembly of men, to bear their person: and every one to own, and acknowledge himself to be author of whatsoever he that so beareth their person, shall act, or cause to be acted, in those things which concern the common peace and safetie; and will therein to submit their wills, every one to his will, and their judgements, to his judgement. This is more than consent, or concord; it is a real unity of them all, in one and the same person, made by covenant of every man with every man, in such manner, as if every man should say to every man, I authorize and give up my right of governing myselfe, to this man, or to this assembly of men, on this condition, that thou give up thy right to him, and authorise all his actions in like manner. This done, the multitude so united in one person, is called a Commonwealth, in Latin <u>Civitas</u>. This is the generation of that great Leviathan, or rather (to speak more reverently) of that mortal god, to which we owe under the immortal God, our peace and defence.[12]

344

Now the contract theory had been historically the doctrine of those who desired to limit the sovereign, and Hobbes, in making it the basis of complete absolutism, was attempting to turn the rebels' own weapons against them. The particular novelty of his approach was not so much the assumption that the power given was irrevocable (this was the "donation" conception of contract) as that the contract was not between the people and the sovereign, but between the people themselves. The sovereign was thus not a party to the agreement at all and so could not be held under any circumstances to have broken it.

Hobbes at different times gave two accounts of the sovereign's source of power, both of which had reverberations in contemporary drama. He held at one time that rights could not really be given and that the sovereign's power was simply his "natural right" to everything which he possessed as a human being, but which his subjects had given up by contract.[13] The king was, in relation to his subjects, in a state of nature. Hobbes's final conclusion on the subject, however, was that given in the quotation above. The king possessed by contract the sum total of individual powers, which he exercised for his subjects. There could logically, then, be no complaint against him, as the malcontent would be really protesting against his own actions.[14]

The nature of sovereignty so evolved is absolute. The sovereign, being no party to the contract, can under no circumstances be considered as having broken it; there is no appeal for a would-be rebel. Even the most tyrannous and depraved of actions must be accepted, for it is the sovereign who establishes by fiat the standard of justice and injustice. For, "where there is no common power, there is no law: where no law, no injustice. Justice and injustice . . . are qualities, that relate to men in society, not in solitude."[15] The Sovereign possesses all those powers necessary for effective dominion: the judicial power, control of religious opinion, the right to carry on war and to reward and punish. Sovereignty is indivisible: there can be in a state but one sovereign power. If the king does not possess it, some other part of the government must. Hobbes admitted that a commonwealth could possess a Sovereignty identical in kind with that of a monarchy. The latter had certain advantages over other forms of government, but a democracy also possessed the essential sovereignty.

Now this doctrine of absolutism, complete as it was, was entirely unacceptable to that very party whose loyalty to the English monarchy was the most thorough-going. In part, of course, it was because the royalists suspected any contract theory, but their opposition went still farther. Hobbes, in evolving a system that would make for the security of men, had succeeded in sacrificing most of the things held sacred by the upholders of divine right. It may help to throw light on the incompatibility of these two systems of political thought if we consider Hobbes's as being also in a way a divine right theory, a Scotist divine right. The opposition between the relative importance of reason and justice on the one side and will on the other had long been a problem of theological importance. The followers of Aquinas laid emphasis on the justice of God's acts, the followers of Dun Scotus on His power. Thomistic theology said God acted in the way He did because that was the just and reasonable way; the Scotists insisted that this subordinated God to justice, and that the position must be reversed: what God did was just and reasonable because He so willed it. It was in terms of the orthodox Thomistic theology that the divine right of kings had been formulated. Obedience was owed to kings, not because by God's support they could compel it, but because their power was from God, and hence just.

Hobbes was a Scotist in theology. To him

> The right of nature, whereby God reigneth over men
> and punisheth those that break his laws, is to be de-
> rived, not from his creating them, as if he required
> obedience as of gratitude for his benefits; but from
> his irresistible power.[16]

It followed that the Leviathan, or "Mortall God" created by the needs of men, was divine in the essential attributes of God himself—His power.

> For . . . he hath the use of so much power and
> strength conferred on him, that by terror thereof,
> he is enabled to perform the wills of them all, to
> peace at home and mutual aid against their enemies
> abroad.[17]

The implications that prevent this Scotist divine right from being an aid and comfort to the descendants of Charles I and the loyalists driven from England by the armed force of the rebels

are obvious. When applied to God the question as to whether
power or justice be the more important is, in a way, merely
academic, since it could be assumed He would always possess
both. Not so, however, with Leviathan. That Mortal God, Charles
the First, had lost his power most definitely at Naseby, and by
losing it had lost his divinity. Without power he was no longer
a god, for:

> Though sovereignty, in the intention of them that
> make it, be immortal; yet is it in its own nature,
> not only subject to violent death, by foreign war; but
> also through the ignorance, and passions of men, it
> hath in it, from the very institution, many seeds of
> natural mortality, by intestine discord.[18]

The obvious corollary of such a position was that obedience was
owed to whatever party could seize power; a conclusion that could
never be admitted by a Stuart or a Tory. More than any other of
Hobbes's ideas, at least in politics, this aroused the ire of the
faithful. John Whitehall accuses him of providing the commonwealth with philosophical justification;[19] Clarendon says the
Leviathan was a sly address to Cromwell;[20] and Wallis writes
that

> his great Leviathan . . . which, upon deserting his
> royal master in distress . . . was written in defence
> of Oliver's title, or whoever, by whatsoever means,
> can get to be upmost; placing the whole right of gov-
> ernment merely in strength, and absolving all his
> Majesty's subjects from their allegiance, whenever
> he is not in a present capacity to force obedience.[21]

In 1669 a certain David Scargill made a public recantation at Cambridge in which he admitted that he had

> lately vented and publicly asserted in the said univer-
> sity, diverse wicked, blasphemous and atheistical
> positions, (particularly, that all right of dominion
> is founded only in power: that if the devil be omnip-
> otent he ought to be obeyed; that all moral righteous-
> ness is founded in the positive law of the civil magis-

trate only: . . .) professing, that I gloried to be an
Hobbist and an atheist.

    I do disclaim, renounce, detest and abhor . . . :

1. That all right of dominion is founded only
   in power.
2. That all moral righteousness is founded
   only in the law of the civil magistrates.[22]

Anyone holding such beliefs, Scargill admits, would comply in
his own interest with the order of any invader or usurper.

    Perhaps the best detailed record of the contemporary loyal-
ist's attitude to Hobbes is found in the decree published by the
University of Oxford on that day in 1683 when Russell was executed for treason. Coming from the great center of loyalism
at a time when Charles was completely triumphant, it gives us
an unusually detailed statement of what the royalists considered
bad political theory. It is entitled:

> The Judgement and Decree of the University of Oxford,
> passed in their Convocation, July 21, 1683, against cer-
> tain pernicious books and damnable doctrines destructive
> to the sacred persons of princes, their state and govern-
> ment, and of all human society.[23]

There are twenty-seven propositions then presented, of which
three are definitely referred to Hobbes and four, though given
without reference, are undoubtedly his. Those of Hobbes are:

1. All civil authority is derived originally from
   the people.
7. Self-preservation is the fundamental law of
   nature, and supersedes the obligation of all
   others, whensoever, they stand in competition
   with it. (Hobbes, de Civ. Leviathan.)
10. Possession and strength give a right to govern,
    and success in a cause or enterprise proclaims
    it to be lawful and just: to peruse it is to comply
    with the will of God, because it is to follow the
    conduct of his providence. (Hobbes. Owen's
    Sermon before the Regecides. Jan. 31, 1648.
    Baxter. Jenkin's Petition. October 1651.)

12. The foundation of civil authority, is this natural
    right; which is not given, but left to the supreme
    magistrate upon men's entering into societies,
    and not only a foreign invader, but a domestic
    rebel, puts himself again into a state of nature,
    to be proceeded against not as a subject but an
    enemy; and consequently acquires by his rebellion
    the same right over the life of his prince, as the
    prince for the most heinous crimes has over the
    life of his subjects.
13. Every man after his entering into a society re-
    tains a right of defending himself against force;
    and cannot transfer that right to the common-
    wealth, when he consents to that union whereby
    a commonwealth is made. And in case a great
    many men together have already resisted the com-
    monwealth, for which every one of them expected
    death, they have liberty then to join together to
    assist and defend one another; their bearing of
    arms, subsequent to the first breach of their duty,
    though it be to maintain what they have done, is
    no new unjust act; and if it be only to defend their
    persons it is not unjust at all.
14. An oath superadds no obligation to a pact and a
    pact obliges no further than it is credited: and
    consequently if a prince gives any indication that
    he does not believe the promises of fealty and
    allegiance made by any of his subjects, they are
    thereby freed from their subjection, and notwith-
    standing their pacts and oaths, may lawfully rebel
    against, and destroy their sovereign. (Hobbes,
    de Cive Leviathan.)

Having presented their manifesto to the king, the university
burned the works of Hobbes along with those of the notorious
Bellarmine and Buchanan.

I have given these Hobbesian extracts, partly because they
contain those doctrines which most enraged his loyal contemporaries and which we shall find reflected in the drama and partly
because it seems necessary to make it quite clear that typically
Hobbesian political doctrines could not have been used sympa-

thetically by a Restoration dramatist in the hope of pleasing the court. If the "absolutism of Hobbes is also the doctrine of Dryden's stage creatures," then according to contemporary opinion they were a seditious crew indeed. As a matter of fact, no king who is not a tyrant ever claims the sovereignty of Hobbes or demands obedience in the terms of the Leviathan. Hobbes had his contemporary triumphs, but they were not through serving as a political guide to loyal dramatists.

It might be here objected that we have contemporary evicence of Dryden at least having made use of Hobbes. John Aubrey in the notes he collected for a life of Hobbes jots down: "Mr. John Dryden, Poet Laureat, is his great admirer, and oftentimes makes use of his doctrine in his plays — from Mr. Dryden himself."[24] It will be noticed, however, that Aubrey does not specify that the doctrine was political; it seems likely, therefore, that Dryden was referring to ethical and psychological ideas, for example, the dilemma of free-will and necessity, the frequent use of which in his plays has been pointed out by Professor Bredvold.[2] The other reference to the poet's intellectual debt, however, is more precise. Professor Bredvold has called attention to Richard Leigh's accusation in The Censure of the Rota (1676) that Dryden in The Conquest of Granada had secured "the Reason and Political Ornaments from Mr. Hobs."[26] Leigh's poem, however, was a satirical attack on Dryden, and if Hobbes was made the dramatist's political god-father it was because Hobbes was politically anathema to all right-thinking people. Dryden could hardly have welcomed the charge and could with justice have denied it if it meant that he agreed with the principles of the Leviathan.

Like all generalizations this one must be controlled by its exceptions. Thus there is a passage in Dryden's Indian Emperor which I am inclined to believe is indebted to Hobbes. Alibech has pointed out to the loyal Guyomar that the besieged people are starving to death and suggested that the country would actually be much better off if the Spaniards were admitted to the town. It is really the duty of anyone with his country's good at heart to betray Montezuma to the Spaniards. Guyomar is outraged.

> Take heed, fair maid, how monarchs you accuse:
> Those reasons none but impious rebels use:
> Those who to empire by dark paths aspire,
> Still plead a call to what they most desire;

> But kings by free consent their kingdoms take,
> Strict as those sacred ties which nuptials make;
> And whate'er faults in princes time reveal,
> None can be judge where can be no appeal.[27]

The line italicized represents, I believe, the sole favorable reference in the drama to the contract theory. It is by no means characteristically Hobbesian and one may doubt if that philosopher would have appreciated the marital analogy, even for the sake of a rhyme. The insistence that there can be no appeal from the contract is, of course, as old as the "translation" theory. The only reason for considering that Hobbes may have been in Dryden's mind is the neat way in which the loyalist adopts the social theory and urges it against the utilitarian position taken by Alibech. The actual form in which he expresses it is not Hobbesian, but the inspiration to use what was traditionally a revolutionary argument as an attack on revolution was perhaps derived from Hobbes.

An amusing example of a distorted use of Hobbes occurs in Lord Orrery's Tryphon. Tryphon has killed his king and usurped his throne. He justifies himself to the loyal subject Nicanor by explaining that the king had first determined to kill him, and that self-preservation, nature's dictate, not ambition, had driven him to the crime of regicide. Nicanor, however, returns the argument against him.

> Ah, Sir, though this had been the state of things,
> Yet subjects, Sir, should die to save their Kings . . .
> Nature, whose Dictates in defense you bring,
> Ties subjects by their Deaths to save their King:
> Nature is Reason, Sir, and that does show
> More to our Kings then to ourselves we owe,
> For in a subjects Death but one does fall,
> But a King's life contains the Life of all.[28]

Tryphon's defense might well have been taken direct from the Leviathan where Hobbes had pointed out that

> A covenant not to defend myself from force, by force,
> is always void. For, as I have showed before, no man
> can transfer, or lay down his right to save himself from

351

> death, wounds, and imprisonment, the avoiding whereof
> is the only end of laying down any right: and therefore
> the promise of not resisting force, in no covenant trans-
> ferreth any right; nor is obliging. For though a man
> may covenant thus, unless I do so, or so, kill me; he
> cannot covenant thus, unless I do so, or so, I will not
> resist you when you come to kill me.[29]

Even those in the audience who had not read Hobbes were probably aware of his teaching in this matter since the royalists consistently pointed out its heterodoxy.[30]

More unusual is Orrery's attempt to defend passive resistance in Hobbesian terms; yet that he was so doing seems clear.
The justification of complete obedience to a sovereign by an
appeal to the laws of nature was foreign to the drama and more
typical of Hobbes than of any other writer. The scene itself indicates the genesis of Orrery's innovation. The dramatist has
had Tryphon, a conventional usurper, justify himself by an appeal
to the law of self-preservation, a doctrine particularly associated
with the teaching of Hobbes. Thus with Hobbes's heterodoxy in
his mind it probably occurred to Orrery that it would be ingenious
to have his loyal subject damn the usurper out of his own mouth.
His perversion of the Leviathan is indeed clever. The laws of
nature, that is reason, teach us to do everything to preserve our
lives (so far, Hobbes), but the king's life is ours (Hobbes had
said that the multitude was united in the person of the king),[31]
so we must, reason shows, preserve his at the expense of our
own. It is quite possible that the famous frontispiece to the Leviathan picturing that mortal god as a giant made up of innumerable
little men may have contributed to this distortion of the book's
thesis. In any case, Orrery's dramatic exposition may well have
impressed by its specious sophistry a contemporary audience
which knew enough of Hobbes to recognize his first law of nature.

With the exception of such garbled passages as those I have
indicated, the use of Hobbes by politically orthodox characters
in the drama was confined to a few ideas which were the common
possession of innumerable political philosophers. The frequent
references in Dryden to the danger of any temporal claims by
the priesthood, for example, can hardly be referred to any specific
source; any monarchist was committed to a belief in the subordination of the clergy to the secular power. Sometimes, it is true,

the phrasing seems an echo of Hobbes. The outburst of Cortez in <u>The Indian Emperor</u> against the priests:

> And you
> Who saucily, teach monarchs to obey,
> And the wide world in narrow cloisters sway;
> <u>Set up by Kings as humble aids of power</u>,
> <u>You that which bred you</u>, viper-like, devour.
> <u>You enemies of crowns.</u>[32]

may have been influenced in the lines I have italicized by the twelfth chapter of the <u>Leviathan</u>, wherein Hobbes says that religion has been cultivated by those who wished to teach subjects obedience to the state.[33] The idea was not original with Hobbes, of course. To go no further, Machiavelli had praised Numa Pompilius for inventing the Roman religion and using it for the advantage of the state.[34] But in the drama the idea had been characteristically expressed by Machiavellian "atheists." That Dryden should have given it to a loyal character is perhaps indicative of a less traditional source.

There is a long, obviously polemical passage in <u>The Conquest of Granada</u> which has been frequently cited as an example of Hobbes's influence. Yet an analysis of the ideas expressed will show, I believe, that it is almost completely royalist commonplace, and no more indebted to Hobbes than to a dozen other writers. The passage, which is but distantly related to the actual events in the play, is as follows:

Boabdelin
> See what the many-headed beast demands.—
> Cursed is that king, whose honour's in their hands.
> In senates, either they too slowly grant,
> Or saucily refuse to aid my want;
> And, when their thrift has ruined me in war,
> They call their insolence my want of care.

Abenamar
> Cursed be their leaders, who that rage foment,
> And veil, with public good, their discontent:
> They keep the people's purses in their hands,
> And hector kings to grant their wild demands;
> But to each lure, a court throws out, descend,
> And prey on those they promised to defend.

Zulema

>Those kings, who to their wild demands consent,
>Teach others the same way to discontent.
>Freedom in subjects is not, nor can be;
>But still, to please them, we must call them free.
>Propriety, which they their idol make,
>Or law, or law's interpreters, can shake.

Abenamar

>The name of commonwealth is popular;
>But there the people their own tyrants are.

Boabdelin

>But kings who rule with limited command,
>Have players' scepters put into their hand.
>Power has no balance, one side still weighs down,
>And either hoists the commonwealth or crown;
>And those, who think to set the scales more right,
>By various turnings but disturb the weight.

Abenamar

>While people tug for freedom, kings for power,
>Both sink beneath some foreign conqueror:
>Then subjects find too late they were unjust,
>And want that power of kings, they durst not trust. [35]

The passage may be analysed as follows:

>The first speech of Boabdelin is not characteristically Hobbesian. It is scarcely emphatic enough as to the absolute necessity of the king controlling the finances,[36] and seems scarcely more than a petulant complaint that he is compelled to depend upon a niggardly senate.
>Abenamar's speech is more an expression of Stuart cynicism than of serious theory.
>Zulema's insistence that subjects have no liberty is perhaps from Hobbes,[37] but his suggestion that they should be called so is certainly not. This piece of policy might have stemmed from Clarendon, who had suggested that a clever king would permit the people to think themselves free.[38]
>That property is really at the mercy of the sovereign was taught by Hobbes[39] and was a conception not

usually emphasized by orthodox absolutists. It was a
power denied the king by Bodin, whose Republic had
been a university text-book since 1606, and its expression here may be due to the Leviathan.
That the people were tyrants in a commonwealth
was a commonplace.[40]
Mr. Hughes finds in the last lines of the passage
a reference to Hobbes's second law of nature, but
just why is not clear.[41] The lines seem conventional
enough in sense and phrasing.

Abandoning then the barren pursuit of any serious formulation of Hobbes's ideas, let us turn to that wider field in which
rebels, usurpers, tyrants, and Machiavellians bedeck themselves
with finery stolen from the Leviathan and rant Florentine à la
Malmesbury. For, as I hope to show, Hobbes played in the drama
much the same role as that played by Machiavelli before him.[42]
Many of his most characteristic ideas were indeed closely related to opinions that had been expressed by stage villains from
the time of Marlowe.
Hobbes's doctrine that dominion was founded on power,
which the obscure Scargill penitently recanted, bears a specious
resemblance to the Elizabethan usurper's conviction that nothing
succeeds like success. When Photinus in Beaumont and Fletcher's
The False One urges rebellion on the grounds that

> If we prosper,
> 'Twill be styl'd lawful, and we shall give laws
> To those that now command us.[43]

he was but anticipating the doctrine attributed to Hobbes in the
tenth proposition of the Oxford decree: "success in a cause or
enterprise proclaims it to be lawful and just." But to the Elizabethan mind, which did not carefully discriminate between de
facto and de jure power,[44] the latent antithesis in this idea was
not developed. It was not until the Restoration that it was un-
equivocally expounded as a political principle by the villainous,
and the ingenuity with which it is used for dramatic effect is one
of the clearest examples of the use of Hobbes's ideas.
The distinction between de jure and de facto sovereignty,
between "Thomistic" and "Scotist" divine right, which was latent

in the principle of Hobbes was theatrically used by Dryden in The Indian Queen. The Inca and his daughter have been captured and Zempoalla has vowed to sacrifice them to her gods. Traxalla, however, who has fallen in love with the princess, invokes the principle of divine right in an attempt to save her life. "Princes are sacred," he points out. Zempoalla counters with an expression of Hobbes's conception of regal divinity.

> True, whilst they are free;
> But power once lost, farewell their sanctity:
> 'Tis power to which the gods their worship owe,
> Which, uncontrouled makes all things just below.[45]

She goes even further: "Thou do'est the pleas of saucy rebels use. . . ." Now to find the divinity of kings to be an argument of "saucy rebels" is indeed an innovation in the drama and is attributable to the royalists' shocked interpretation of Hobbes's doctrine of dominion founded on power.

In Dryden and Lee's The Duke of Guise this principle was given a twist that would have pained the old enemy of faction, though he would have been forced to admit that the conclusion was a legitimate corollary of his position. I am referring to the passage in which the conspirators of the league decide that not they, but the king is a rebel. Says Bussy:

> 'Tis a plain case; the king's included in the punish-
> ment, in case he rebel against the people.[46]

Polin is unable to understand how the king can rebel, but the paradox is explained by the Curate of St. Eustace:

> I'll make it out: Rebellion is an insurrection against
> the government; but they that have the power are
> actually the government; therefore, if the people have
> the power, the rebellion is in the king.

Bussy remarks that this is "a most convincing argument for faction" but the priest retorts:

> For arming, if you please, but not for faction;
> For still the faction is the fewest number:

> So what they call the lawful government,
> Is now the faction; for the most are ours.

Now if we were confining our investigations to strictly logical influences we would have to free Hobbes from the charge of
serving the leaguers, for in the last speech the curate implies
that they have not yet the power (since they are yet to arm), and
bases their right on numerical superiority. Such a majority right
is not Hobbesian, but is taken from the sixteenth-century mo-
narchomachs, with which Dryden was familiar. We are, however,
dealing with one of those mosaics of contradictory ideas so typical of Dryden's dramatic arguments. The Hobbesian influence
is found in the curate's earlier point that the particular body of
the state which has the actual power, i.e., the sovereignty of the
Leviathan, is the real government. Hobbes had written:

> that King whose power is limited, is not superior to
> him, or them that have the power to limit it; and he
> that is not superior, is not supreme: that is to say
> not sovereign. The sovereignty therefore was always
> in that assembly which had the right to limit him.[47]

It might be urged that Hobbes does not explicitly justify the rebellion of the powerful. But the implications of an idea originally
controlled by the dominating purpose of the man who formulated
it may, upon falling into different hands, be differently developed.
Hobbes was, of all men who ever wrote, the farthest from a desire to encourage rebellion on any grounds whatsoever. Yet, as
we have seen, he was commonly accused of justifying successful
rebellion. Similarly distorted, the implications concerning a
rebellious king-without-power undoubtedly latent in the passage
I have quoted could be used, as Dryden used them, to put his
villains au courant with the latest developments in casuistical
disloyalty.[48]
It is this doctrine, obscured by poetic and dramatic trim-
mings, which lies behind an exchange between Arcos, the Spanish Ambassador and Boabdelin in The Conquest of Granada. The
ambassador has closed his attack on Boabdelin's title to the
Moorish throne by pointing out:

> You have no right, except you force allow;
> And if yours then was just, so ours is now.

To which Boabdelin replied:

> 'Tis true, from force the noblest title springs;
> I therefore hold from that, which first made kings.[49]

Professor Bredvold, who has not taken into consideration the ambassador's lines, suggests that the king's speech is from Hobbes.[50] But Hobbes most notoriously had <u>not</u> made kingship the product of force but of contract. He had, it <u>is</u> true, recognized sovereignty by conquest,[51] but merely as one of the historical origins of the state. The idea had been more forcefully expressed by orthodox theorists, among others by Bodin[52] and King James himself.[53] The conception had not, however, found favorable expression in the drama, but had been taken over by the Machiavellian villain who identified conquest with usurpation. Machiavel in the prologue to <u>The Jew of Malta</u> first formulated the traditional handling of this theme when he said

> Many will talk of title to a crown:
> What right had Caesar to the empery?
> Might first made kings,

and in the subsequent drama only the politically wicked so expressed themselves.

In the light of this dramatic tradition we can correctly interpret Dryden's handling of the theme. Arcos (and it must be remembered that he does represent the legitimate claim, while Boabdelin is actually a usurper as he is accused) has denied to the Moorish king any ethical right to the throne and added ironically that even if he claims by power his title is weak. But Boabdelin pounces upon the word "force" and, giving it the conventionally orthodox implications as to the "origin" of his power, urges it as proof of the right of his claim. Arcos, however, has read Hobbes, and points out the inconsistency of his argument.

> Since then by force you prove your title true,
> Our's must be just, because we claim from you.

The Spaniard has ironically applied Hobbes to Machiavelli with devastating effectiveness.

Hobbes's doctrine of the purely civil origin of justice was one of the "atheistical positions" recanted by Scargill and damned

358

by the Oxford decree. Not only was it ethically shocking, it was politically dangerous. The strength of the theory of divine right lay in its identification of obedience with moral standards that transcended the transitory, the expedient or the merely civil. The sovereign's right to be obeyed was unassailable precisely because it did rest upon the immutable foundation of divine justice. If there were no right beyond the will of the king, then he could claim no sanction beyond what he was actually in a position to impose. The doctrine of non-resistance, of course, insisted that no matter what crimes a monarch committed, rebellion was not justified; but this was not the same as saying that he could do no wrong.[54] The most exaggerated claims that are made for kingly power both in the Elizabethan and Restoration drama were made in terms that everyone would have known to be "destructive to the sacred persons of princes." This truth, so consistently ignored by literary critics of the drama, has been succinctly phrased by one of the most trenchant historians of political theory.

> A theory of sovereignty in which law and right become
> one and in which no right exists except that of the
> Sovereign's creation, was held by no one in the six-
> teenth century. Such a view was impossible to any-
> one who held that right was divine. It was wholly
> incompatible with the theory of the divine right of
> Kings. Just so far as men came to believe in sov-
> ereignty to this extent, the right of the Sovereign lost
> its divinity. Historically it is those who lost faith in
> the divinity of right, and of Kings, who believed in
> the absolute right of the political sovereign.[55]

However politically unorthodox it might be, the conception had certain dramatic possibilities that the poets were quick to hit upon for their own uses. It was, of course, eminently suited for a tyrant's rants. Dryden, ever ready to make such innovations, used the idea as early as Tyrannic Love, where Maximin boasts:

> Our Gods are Gods, 'cause they have power and will;
> Who can do all things, can do nothing ill.
> Ill is rebellion 'gainst some higher power:
> The world may sin, but not its emperor.[56]

Probably the most extended exposition of this doctrine occurs in Crown's Calisto. Jupiter, who expresses the idea, is speaking both as God and king, which slightly confuses the matter, but his latter position is sufficiently emphasized.

> I cannot err, what e'er my actions be;
> There's no such thing as good or ill to me.
> No action is by nature good or ill;
> All things derive their natures from my will.
> If virtue from my will distinct could be,
> Virtue would be a power supreme to me.
> What no dependency on me will own,
> Makes me a Vassal and usurps my throne.
> If so I can revenge me in a thrice
> Turn all the balance, and make Virtue Vice.[57]

If this passage be compared with a typically "Machiavellian" one from the anonymous Nero of 1624 it can be seen just how the Hobbesian doctrine gave a new turn to an old dramatic theme. Nero, who has just had Proculus killed, says

> This 'tis to be commander of the world.
> Let them extol weak pity that do need it,
> Let men cry to have law and justice done
> And tell their griefs to heaven that hears them not:
> Kings must upon the people's headless corses
> Walk to security and ease of mind.
> Why, what have we to do with th'airy names
> That old age and philosophers found out,
> Of justice and ne'er certain equity?
> The gods revenge themselves and so will we:
> Where right is scand, authority's o'erthrown;
> We have a high prerogative above it.
> Slaves may do what is right, we what we please:
> The people will repine and think it ill,
> But they must bear, and praise too, what we will.[58]

The two passages are similar in their emphasis on the danger to a king of a system of justice independent of his will. Nero, however, shifts inconsistently between two conceptions of justice. On the one hand he explicitly asserts his belief that justice is merely a fiction made up by wise men; on the other he seems to admit the existence of a moral standard, which is hostile to powerful rule and which kings must ignore. This wavering between the two conceptions was characteristic of pre-Restoration tyrants. But the tyrants of Dryden and Crowne have gone an important step further. They no longer either oppose themselves to morality, or deny it; instead, they create it. And this conception, entirely new to the stage,[59] would seem plausibly enough to stem from Hobbes.

The idea, frequently used as a sheer rhetorical heightening of ruthless power, is sometimes employed for more subtle and paradoxical effects. Thus, Crowne uses it in a passage that will repay comparison with a scene in Valentinian. In Fletcher's play the tyrant, having violated Lucina, explains to her:

> Know I am above the faults I do.
> And those I do I am able to forgive too.[60]

In Caligula Crowne gives his tyrant the advantage of a knowledge of Hobbes's supposed identification of morality with the will of the sovereign. The result is a novel variation of an old theme that must have pleased his audience. Caligula tells the recalcitrant heroine:

> Madam, my time, nay more, my life you waste:
> Yes, Madam, now 'tis treason to be chaste.

The virtuous Julia is not moved by this frontal attack. "Sir, for the world I'd not my honour lose." But feminine virtue could have no sanctuary from a dramatist's conception of a "mortall God." Caligula overwhelms her.

> Oh! I'm the fountain whence all honour flows.
> Yes, Madam; sure you are not to be told . . .
> I can make virtue scorn'd and vice esteem'd,
> I can make hell ador'd, and Heav'n blasphemed,
> Success, dominion, and the longest sword,
> Make any creeds believ'd, or gods ador'd.[61]

Dryden has heightened the impression of Maximin's power in Tyrannic Love by an amusingly absurd combination of two of

Hobbes's ideas. The emperor's daughter in a display of independence has insisted that her free-will at least is beyond her father's control. But Maximin tells her:

> I'll find that power o'er wills, which heaven ne'er found.
> Free will's a cheat in any'one but me;
> In all but kings 'tis willing slavery;
> An unseen fate which forces the desire;
> The will of puppets danced upon a wire.
> A monarch is
> The spirit of the world in every mind;
> He may match wolves to lambs, and make it kind.
> Mine is the business of your little fates;
> And though you war, like petty wrangling states,
> You're in my hand; and, when I bid you cease,
> You shall be crushed together into peace.[62]

The passage illustrates to perfection the clever way in which Dryden made use of any handy theory for dramatic effect. It is a weird mosaic of contradictory conceptions and unwarranted applications of ideas. To start with, Dryden is applying the Hobbesian denial of free-will, an idea of which he made frequent use in other ways, to an entirely irrelevant situation. Hobbes had given an explanation which seemed to make of free-will nothing but a cheat, for he had said that while a man was indeed free to do that which he wanted to do, his desires themselves were rigorously bound in a chain of causation. A man must desire to do that which he feels free to do. This compulsion applied to kings as much as to any one, of course, but Hobbes had expounded the traditional conception of the sovereign as the vital force in the state in such a form that Dryden was here enabled to make a telescoped application of two unrelated ideas. In the Philosophical Rudiments Hobbes had written that

> They who compare a city and its citizens with a man
> and his members almost all say, that he who hath the
> supreme power in the city is in relation to the whole
> city, such as the head is to the whole man. But it ap-
> pears by what hath been already said, that he who is
> endued with such a power, whether it be a man or a
> court, hath a relation to the city, not as that of the

head, but of the soul to the body. For it is the soul
by which a man hath a will, that is, can either will or
nill; so by him who hath the supreme power, and no
otherwise, the city hath a will, and can either will
or nill.[63]

and

the chief ruler . . . whose will contains the will of each
man.[64]

Now if the word "will" be twisted out of its purely political
meaning and taken in a psychological sense the passage can be
made to imply that it is only through the king that a subject has
any will at all. Such a transition in thought would be facilitated
by Hobbes's insistence that the actions of the king are really the
actions of the subject (by the terms of the social contract) even
when the subject thinks he is willing otherwise. It was such a
play upon ideas that Dryden probably had in mind when he penned
Maximin's lines.

It may be that the doctrine attacked in the fourteenth proposition of the Oxford decree had some connection with the claims
of characters like Almanzor and Montezuma, who admitted allegiance no longer than the king respected their interests. The
idea is, however, an essentially commonplace one, though there
is a passage in Settle's Cambyses which is more explicit than
usual. The villain Prexaspes, whose word has been doubted by
Cambyses, says

Since he does distrust
My faith and Loyalty, it were but just,
That he should find me false who thinks me so.[65]

Whether Hobbes could be held responsible or not, it is probably
true that the pit would have considered Prexaspes a "Hobbist."

The famous huffing scene between Almanzor and Boabdelin
is heightened in dramatic interest, and certain obscurities in the
king's position are cleared up when it is realized that Dryden is
playing off two rival political theories against each other in the
characters of the two men. Almanzor, who dwells—for the purposes of this scene, at least—in the Stoic's state of nature, is

faced by a king who has read Hobbes, and their disagreement as to the source and validity of political coercion makes good theatre.

The exchange takes place after Almanzor, having given his aid to the weaker of the warring factions simply because it was the weaker, is condemned to death by Boabdelin. After paying his respects to his own heroic indifference to death, Almanzor at once propounds a fundamental problem in political science: On what grounds could the king claim a right to condemn a man who refused to accept the state's authority? Almanzor recognizes the existence of a state whose members are bound by its law: "Obeyed as Sovereign by thy subjects be," but explicitly denies that he himself is a member of it, or subject to its coercion. He himself is in the state of nature.

> But whence hast thou the right to give me death?
> Obey'd as sovereign by thy subjects be,
> But know that I alone am king of me,
> I am as free as nature first made man,
> Ere the base laws of servitude began,
> When wild in wood the noble savage ran.

Boabdelin retorts ironically

> Since, then, no power above your own you know,
> Mankind should use you like a common foe;
> You should be hunted like a beast of prey:
> By your own law, I take your life away.

But Almanzor, as hero, has the last word.

> My laws are made but only for my sake;
> No king against himself a law can make.
> If thou pretend'st to be a prince like me,
> Blame not an act, that should your pattern be.
> I saw the opprest, and thought it did belong
> To a king's office to redress the wrong:
> I brought that succour which thou ought'st to bring,
> And so, in nature, am thy subjects' king.[66]

Almanzor's first speech is an expression of the traditional juristic state of nature. The original condition of mankind according to this conception was an idyllic state in which laws and government were unknown and each man was his own ruler. Government was an "unnatural" creation made necessary by man's fall from his original virtue. The Stoic ethics, with its fusion of the conception of self-sufficiency and the doctrine of following nature, implied that the thoroughly rational, that is to say, thoroughly "natural" man had no need of an "artificial" government; he was outside of the legal and political relationships binding on his fallen brethren. This whole complex of ideas had been adopted by the Elizabethan dramatists and used for manifold dramatic purposes. Chapman in particular had used it in Bussy D'Ambois to heighten and justify the independence of his hero.[67] Bussy, in a speech much like Almanzor's, appeals to nature against the laws of the state.

> Since I am free,
> (Offending no just law), let no law make
> By any wrong it does, my life her slave:
> When I am wrong'd, and that law fails to right me,
> Let me be king myself (as man was made),
> And do a justice that exceeds the law. . . .
> Who to himself is law, no law doth need,
> Offends no law, and is a king indeed.[68]

The kings in the two plays both accept the state of nature as a norm, but arrive at sharply divergent conclusions as to its application. Henry says of Bussy that

> kings had never borne
> Such boundless empire over other men,
> Had all maintain'd the spirit and state of D'Ambois.[69]

Yet Boabdelin, taking Almanzor at his own valuation, insists: "By your own law, I take your life away."

What is the explanation of Boabdelin's retort? From what point of view could it be argued that the law of nature justified the civil authority in punishing criminals? The answer becomes clear when it is recognized that Boabdelin (a usurping Hobbist, let it be remembered) is translating Almanzor's Stoic state of nature into the Hobbesian form in which everyone had the right to kill when it was to his advantage. At one stage of his thought, as I have pointed out, Hobbes had said that the power of the king was simply his natural right as a man which he had not given up as had his subjects by contract. Judging by the twelfth proposition of the Oxford decree, this explanation impressed his contemporaries and may have been what Dryden had in mind when penning Boabdelin's lines.

The line

Mankind should use you like a common foe,

however, indicates that the king is not merely referring to his own right, but to the right of the whole organized state against a recalcitrant individual. Hobbes had recognized the possibility that some independent individuals might refuse to enter into the general contract and insist upon going their own lonely way like Almanzor. Hobbes had explained in the Leviathan just what position they occupied in respect to the state into whose formation they had not entered.

> Because the major part hath by consenting voices
> declared a sovereigne; he that dissented must now
> consent with the rest; that is, be contented to avow
> all the actions he shall do, or else justly be de-
> stroyed by the rest. . . . And whether he be of the
> congregation or not, and whether his consent be
> asked, or not, he must either submit to their de-
> crees, or be left in the condition of war he was in
> before; wherein he might without injustice be de-
> stroyed by any man whatsoever.[70]

It was this strain of thought that lay behind the speech of Boab-delin and is so heroically and irrelevantly answered by Almanzor.

Hobbes's original contributions to the Polybian state of nature and his analysis of the fundamental passions that drive men probably never found expression in the drama at all as a political theme.[71] To the modern student of Hobbes the most character-istic element in his description of the state of nature is its insecurity. Even the strongest must fear the weakest who may at any time be able to overcome him by treachery. It was not this phase, however, that impressed his contemporaries, who turned rather to the passage in De Cive in which Hobbes had said that

"Man is to Man an arrant Wolf." His cynical evaluation of human nature and his antiprimitivistic picture of man unprotected by organized government seems to have shocked everyone's most cherished illusions.[72] The popular conception was that Hobbes had held up for admiration the "natural" man as gratuitously cruel and treacherous. It is only by dipping into some of the contemporary attacks that one can come to appreciate what the audiences of Dryden and Lee would have recognized on the stage as a "Hobbist."

The most illuminating, and certainly the wittiest of these attacks was published by John Eachard in 1672. Mr. Hobbe's State of Nature considered in a Dialogue between Philautus & Timothy presents Hobbes in the character of Philautus voicing those ideas generally accredited to him. When first accosted by Timothy, Philautus refuses to walk with him on the grounds that Timothy will undoubtedly take advantage of him in some unguarded moment and kick him. Such conduct is only what the intelligent man would expect from a member of the human race, for

> I must tell thee, that men naturally are all ravenous
> and currish, of a very snarling and biting nature; to
> be short, they are in themselves meer Wolves, Tygers
> and Centaurs.[73]

Later in their conversation Timothy explains ironically that after reading Hobbes's description of the state of nature he had looked about him expecting to find the whole world shouting "hang him with his own guts, give him a pound of melted lead for a julip to cool his pluck," and generally revelling in torture and cruelty.[74] It is difficult to appraise just what the connection between such a common interpretation of Hobbes and the effect of such plays as Tyrannic Love and Nero might have been. These plays with their cruel tyrants and their scenes of torture and mutilation represented in part a return to Elizabethan models; yet to the audiences that beheld them they must have appeared as dramatic illustrations of Hobbes's doctrines. It may not be too far-fetched to see in the reappearance of this dramatic type a recognition on the part of the dramatists that the horror aroused by Hobbes offered them a fertile field in which to work and an opportunity to give the old an air of novelty. The possibility of such

a connection is strengthened when we discover Settle, one of the
most assiduous dramatists of the horror school, having one of
his villains appeal to a state of nature much like that of Timothy.
The career of Crimalhaz in The Empress of Morocco has been
made up of regicide, murder and usurpation. He insists, however,

> This work, which we so roughly do begin,
> Zeal and Religion may perhaps call Sin.
> No; the more Barb'rous garb our Deeds assume,
> We nearer to our First perfection come,
> Since Nature first made Man wild, savage, strong,
> And his Blood hot, then when the world was young:
> If Infant-times such Rising valours bore,
> Why should not Riper Ages now do more.
> But whilst our Souls wax Tame, and Spirits Cold,
> We Only show th'unactive World grows Old.[75]

A primitivistic appeal against the artificial demands of religion
and morality had, of course, characterized the Machiavellian
villain since the time of Marlowe, but such villains had not explicitly appealed to a primitive state of ruthless savagery.
Paradoxically enough, it had been the Stoic conception on which
they had built.[76] Crimalhaz, who is unquestionably in the Machia
vellian tradition, avoids this confusion and quite frankly justifies
his treachery and cruelty by citing man's natural wildness and
barbarism. It seems probable that Settle was making use of the
popular misinterpretations of Hobbes's state of nature.

In conclusion then, we can insist that the influence of Hobbes'
political ideas on the Restoration drama was, like Machiavelli's
on the Elizabethan, almost completely theatrical. His principles
were logically incompatible with the form of absolutism accepted
by the court party and were recognized by them as being incompatible. But the very notoriety of his ideas made them valuable
to the dramatists who wished to have their political villains up
to date and echoes of the Leviathan are to be found in the speeche
of many tyrants and usurpers. The situations and characters to
whom his ideas were applied, however, were inherited from the
Elizabethan drama and were not seriously modified by the Hobbes
ian influence; indeed many of the ideas accredited to Hobbes
had been adumbrated by the conventional Machiavellian. The

THE DRAMATIC USE OF HOBBES'S POLITICAL IDEAS

Elizabethan drama would certainly have been different had not
Machiavelli been thoroughly misunderstood. So much can not
be said for Hobbes in the Restoration period. The dramatic
appetite had been already trained, and the fare to satisfy it was
in all essentials already cooked. Yet certainly we can claim
for Hobbes a piquant seasoning of the dishes. The analogy is
not unhappy. In the plays his influence is pervasive, sharp and
only too often intangible.

NOTES

1 Histoire de la Litterature Anglaise, 10th ed., Paris, 1899,
3.34.

2 See in particular: Leslie Stephens, Hobbes, pp. 67–69; R. G.
Ham, Otway and Lee, New Haven, 1931, pp. 46–49; J. Prinz,
John Wilmot, Earl of Rochester, Leipzig, 1927, pp. 16–18;
W. J. Courthope, History of English Poetry, London, 1903,
3.459.

3 Courthope 3.459.

4 The Intellectual Milieu of John Dryden, Ann Arbor, 1934,
p. 66. This statement is reprinted from an article in MP 25
(May, 1928). It is significant that when Professor Bredvold
came to an analysis of Dryden's political thought he decided
that "it is less easy to find characteristic Hobbesian political
theory in his drama." Milieu, p. 135.

5 Merritt Y. Hughes, "Dryden as Statist," PQ 6 (1927), 339–
40. The reference to Van Doren is to The Poetry of John
Dryden, Cambridge, 1931, p. 17.

6 I am not, of course attempting a complete analysis of
Hobbes's philosophy. For a full discussion John Laird's
Hobbes, London, 1934, is excellent.

7 J. Aubrey, Brief Lives, ed. Clark, 1.334. The Elements of
Law circulated in manuscript in 1640 although not published
until 1651.

8 A brief view and survey of the dangerous and pernicious
errors to church and state in Mr. Hobbes's Leviathan, 2nd
imp., Oxford, 1676, p. 317.

9 Hobbes, The English Works of Thomas Hobbes, ed. Molesworth, 7.336. All subsequent references will be to this edition.

10 Whether Hobbes conceived of the state of nature analytically or historically need not here concern us.

11 Works 3.116.

12 Ibid. 3.157–158.

13 Ibid. 4.88, 129; 2.68 ff.

14 Ibid. 3.163.

15 Ibid. 3.115.

16 Ibid. 3.345.

17 Ibid. 3.158.

18 Ibid. 3.208.

19 Leviathan found out (1679). Quoted by J. A. Thomas, "Some contemporary critics of Thomas Hobbes," Economica, 9 (1929), 188.

20 Brief View, p. 317.

21 Quoted by Hobbes in "Considerations upon the Reputation, Loyalty, Manners and Religion of Thomas Hobbes," 1662, Works 4.413.

22 Somers Collection of Tracts, London, 1812, 7.370–71.

23 I quote from G. W. Cooke, The History of Party, London, 1836, 1.346–355.

24 Brief Lives 1.372.

25 Bredvold, p. 66.

26 Bredvold, p. 118.

27 The Indian Emperor 4.2 (Works, ed. Scott and Saintsbury, 2.377). All further reference to Dryden's plays will be to this edition.

28 Tryphon 1.1 (Two New Tragedies, London, 1672), pp. 4–5.

29 Works 3.127.

30 Cf. propositions 7, 12, 13, and 14 of the Oxford decree.

31 Works 3.158.

32 The Indian Emperor 5.2 (Works 2.400).

33 Works 3.98–99.

34 Discourses, Bk. 1, Ch. 11 (Works, ed. Detmold, 2.127–28).

35 The Conquest of Granada, Part II, 1.2 (Works 4.130).

36 Works 3.234–37.

37 But see Works 3.199, "Liberty of the subject consistent with the unlimited power of the sovereign."

38 A Brief View, p. 71.

39 Works 3.232–37.

40 See Dunning, History of Political Theories from Luther to Montesquieu, New York, 1905, p. 258.

41 "Dryden as Statist," p. 348. I presume he means the third law.

42 John Eachard has his mouthpiece Timothy remark that the young men who have not read Machiavelli consider Hobbes new. Mr. Hobbes's State of Nature considered in a Dialogue between Philautus & Timothy in Dr. Eachard's Works, 11th ed., London, 1705, p. 11.

43 The False One 5.2 (Works of Beaumont and Fletcher, ed. Waller and Glover, 3.359).

44 When Convocation in 1606 compiled a series of canons on the nature of political authority they specifically insisted upon the legitimate authority of a successful usurpation— much to the disgust of James.

45 The Indian Queen 3.1 (Works 2.253).

46 The Duke of Guise 1.1 (Works 7.25).

47 Works 3.179.

48 This treatment occurs in several plays. Cf. The Spanish Friar 5.2 (Works 6.507) where Lorenzo says "the beaten party are rebels to the conquerors."

49 The Conquest of Granada, Part I, 1.1 (Works 4.47).

50 Bredvold, p. 135. Professor Bredvold recognizes that the idea is not sympathetically presented.

51 Works 3.159.

52 Republic 2.2.

53 The Trew Law of Free Monarchies in Political Works, ed. McIlwain, p. 55.

54 It is not, perhaps, too irrelevant to point out that this phrase is the product of Whig theory, and kings became incapable of sin, only when they became incapable of sovereign power. Cf. D. Ogg, England in the Reign of Charles II, Oxford, 1934, 2.453.

55 J. W. Allen, History of Political Thought in the Sixteenth Century, London, 1928, p. 393. Italics mine.

56 Tyrannic Love 5.1 (Works 3.456).

57 Calisto 2.1 (Works, ed. Maidment and Logan, 1.264). Genest, who could scent "divine right" in astonishing places, considers this passage incredibly servile on the part of Crowne. Some Account of the English Stage 1.181.

58 Tragedy of Nero 2.2, Mermaid ed. Italics mine. In the italicized line I have followed the 1624 quarto reading of "scand" instead of the Mermaid's "scant."

59 There are passages in the earlier drama which come very close to this position. Thus in Fletcher's The Bloody Brother the tyrannous Rollo says

> I sit above in power, where power is given,
> Is all the right suppos'd by Earth and Heaven.
> (Works 4.273)

But a closer examination of the whole passage shows it to be a conventional piece of "Machiavellianism."

60 Valentinian 3.1 (Works 4.38).

61 Caligula 3.1 (Works 4.402).

62 Tyrannic Love 4.1 (Works 3.430).

63 Works 2.89.

64 Ibid., p. 84.

65 Cambyses, London, 1672, 1.1.

66 The Conquest of Granada, Part 1, 1.1 (Works 4.43).

67 I hope to consider elsewhere the strangely ignored question of Chapman's influence on the genesis of Almanzor.

68 Bussy D'Ambois 2.1. 194 ff.

69 Bussy D'Ambois 3.2. 95 ff.

70 Works 3.162. Cf. proposition 12 of the Oxford decree: ". . . a domestic rebel, puts himself again into a state of nature, to be proceeded against . . . as an enemy."

71 In his Bellamira, Sir Charles Sedley has Merryman, who is about to sleep with his friend's mistress, justify himself by saying:

> Besides, in matter of Women, we are all in the State of Nature, every man's hand against every man, whatever we pretend.
>
> (Bellamira 3.4. 112 ff.)

This libertine interpretation of the motive of competition is "Hobbesian" but hardly political.

72 J. A. Thomas, "Some Contemporary Critics of Thomas Hobbes," Economia 9 (1929), 185–91, finds all parties united in indignation at Hobbes's conception of human nature.

73 Dr. Eachard's Works, p. 5.

74 Ibid., p. 48.

75 The Empress of Morocco, London, 1673, 3.2.

76 The fundamental confusion of this strain of dramatic thought is particularly well illustrated in the anonymous Selimus, 1594, 1, lines 305 ff.

THE PLACE OF HOBBESIAN IDEAS IN DRYDEN'S TRAGEDIES

John A. Winterbottom

There are a number of considerations which might lead one to make a systematic survey of Dryden's tragedies with the expectation of finding in them evidence of Hobbes' influence. In the first place, even a casual reading of the tragedies will reveal many characters whose behavior and attitudes can readily be explained on the basis of some of the assumptions Hobbes makes about human nature and human society. Elsewhere in Dryden's works, one finds at least three direct references to Hobbes. One of them, it is true, is adversely critical of Hobbes' translation of the Iliad, and another is acidulous at the expense of his dogmatism; but a third refers with some approval to Hobbes' rejection of such metaphysical paradoxes as "incorporeal substances."[1] At least these references suggest that Dryden was rather closely acquainted with Hobbes' works. Confirmation of this supposition together with evidence that Dryden not only knew but used Hobbes, occurs in Aubrey's Brief Lives: "Mr. John Dryden, Poet Laureat, is his [Hobbes'] great admirer, and oftentimes makes use of his doctrine in his plays."[2] It is very probable, too, that we are predisposed to assume some affinity between major figures in the intellectual life of an age, particularly when, as with Dryden, one of them is generally regarded not as an independent thinker but as a mirror of his time.

A number of literary historians, impelled perhaps by some such considerations as these, have examined Dryden's plays, including the tragedies, and have concluded that Hobbesian ideas have played a significant part in making them what they are. Wolfgang Mann suggests that Hobbes' philosophy is mirrored "in ziemlich starkem Masse" in Dryden, and he goes on to analyze speeches from The Indian Emperor and Tyrannic Love to support his point.[3] Bredvold, much less tentative than Mann, flatly attri-

Reprinted from Journal of English and Germanic Philology, Vol. 57 (1958), pp. 665–683, by permission of the author and the publisher.

butes Hobbesian beliefs to the characters in Dryden's plays: "In political thought . . . the monarchical absolutism of Hobbes is also the doctrine of Dryden's stage creatures, and must have been particularly grateful to the ears of the court audience for which Dryden wrote."[4] But by far the most vigorous and thoroughgoing treatment of the thesis is to be found in Mildred Hartsock's essay, "Dryden's Plays: A Study in Ideas,"[5] in which she attempts to show by exhaustive analysis of speeches and behavior that Hobbesian ideas constitute a major shaping force in the conception of Dryden's dramatic characters and of the political milieu within which they exist. "All of the pertinent evidence," she says, "irresistibly suggests that the psychology of Hobbes, basing man's activity upon the passions—recognizing reason to be sure, but emphasizing the priority of emotions—had so permeated Dryden's thought as to condition, whether consciously or not, his creation of dramatic character."[6] And later, having discussed the political relationships in the plays, she concludes: "Dryden was familiar with the writings of one of the foremost political theorists of his time, and he at least found nothing basically incompatible between the opinions of Hobbes and his own ideas."[7]

Insofar as the position taken by these writers is based upon what we find in the tragedies, it is, I think, untenable. The evidence presented in its support consists, in the main, of isolated speeches taken from context and analyzed to show the presence in them of Hobbesian ideas. This is a method well calculated to demonstrate an acquaintance on Dryden's part with the ideas of Hobbes, but it seems to me totally inadequate for examining the intellectual foundations on which the tragedies are raised. The latter purpose would demand the answers to questions scarcely touched on by these writers—such questions as, What kind of people espoused Hobbesian ideas and how do they fare in the plays? What philosophical notions are represented in the speeches and behavior of their antagonists? In a given play as a whole, which set of beliefs prevails? Taking the corpus of the tragedies in its entirety, are there ideas or attitudes which seem to persist from play to play? By examining these questions in this paper I have attempted to show that, although Hobbesian ideas are very likely present in the tragedies, they are by no means espoused by Dryden himself; and, further, that certain other lines of thought which were popular during the latter half of the seventeenth century provide a much more plausible philosophical basis for the tragedies.

II

Of central importance in Hobbes' analysis of human nature is his attack on the traditional concept of Reason and the virtues believed to flow from it. For Hobbes' Reason is not to be thought of as the reflection in man of a divine order embracing the cosmos, a principle of moral control whereby man is redeemed from bestiality; for him it is merely a flunkey to the passions, a "power of reckoning" engaged in the discovery of means to accomplish ends determined solely by the passions. Manifestations of orderly behavior are not evidence of anything like a higher nature in man; they result merely from the denial of the lesser passions in the hope of satisfying the greater. Thus, for example, man's capacity for living in peaceable communities results from the motion of the most powerful of all his passions, fear of violent death, which leads him to restrain his appetite for power and possessions and to accept the restraints of community life in return for a guarantee of security.[8]

As Miss Hartsock assumes,[9] dramatic characters created in accordance with the Hobbesian conception of human nature might be expected to exhibit certain predictable qualities. First, they would be extremely egotistic, their energies being devoted primarily to self-preservation and self-aggrandizement. Second, since passion would have primacy over reason in determining behavior, they would show little emotional stability. Third, as creatures of passion and appetite, they would be characterized by blunted moral sensibilities.

It is quite possible, as Miss Hartsock demonstrates, to discover characters in the tragedies who seem to have been conceived quite deliberately for the purpose of displaying this pattern of qualities; and even among characters obviously intended for our admiration there are occasional lapses into behavior which lends itself readily to analysis on the basis of Hobbesian assumptions about human nature. But a careful look at a few of the heroic tragedies as wholes rather than as assemblages of unrelated speeches and actions any one of which can be excised and analyzed for its ideological content will, I think, bring us to a conclusion different from Miss Hartsock's.

The Indian Emperor (1665), the first of the heroic tragedies wholly by Dryden, is dominated by the spectacular figure of Montezuma. He is a person of great natural nobility, fearless, possessed of an illustrious military record, respected by his followers as a powerful and provident monarch. Yet he is the helpless victim of an ignoble love for the daughter of a woman he has wronged, and in the heat of passion he is capable of the grossest neglect of his responsibilities as emperor. Surely, one would say, a fine example of the Hobbesian man sunk in appetite. And the case for the dominance of Hobbesian ideas in the play is further strengthened if one examines such characters as Odmar, the emperor's son, or Cortez, the conquistador, for each is ensnared in a love which leads him at one time or another to violate his honor.

These are persuasive examples, yet we cannot accurately assess the impact of the play without considering Guyomar, who conforms not in the least to the Hobbesian conception of man. In the body of the play one can see a carefully developed contrast between Guyomar as the vessel of honor and virtue on the one hand, and Montezuma, Odmar, and Cortez as the toys of passion on the other. Each of the four is confronted at some point in the play with a choice between love and honor. Montezuma's test comes when he finds himself faced with the problem of what to do with Cortez after he has captured him. His own life has already been spared by Cortez and honor bids him return the favor. But he is infatuated with Almeria who, for reasons of her own, relentlessly insists that Cortez must die. During the ensuing struggle within himself, Montezuma is perfectly aware of the moral issue involved, yet he ultimately follows the urging of his passion and condemns Cortez to death.

> How gratitude and love divide my breast!
> Both ways alike my soul is robbed of rest,
> But—let him die.   (Vol. 2, III.iv, p. 368)[10]

Cortez is placed in a somewhat similar dilemma when he is asked by Cydaria, the Indian princess whom he loves, to refrain from engaging her people in battle. Cortez knows that his side is almost certain of victory and that his duty to his sovereign demands that he proceed to battle. But, like Montezuma, he follows the dictate of his passion; he accedes to Alibech's prayer.

> Honour, be gone! What art thou but a breath?
> I'll live, proud of my infamy and shame,
> Graced with no triumph but a lover's name.
> (Vol. 2, II.ii, p. 348)

It is undeniable that we have in these instances the sort of behavior one would expect from the stage creatures of a dramatist imbued with Hobbesian psychology. But that Dryden's sizing up of human nature does not stop with Montezuma and Cortez is evident from the fact that Guyomar is placed in a situation very similar to the two just described and yet he behaves quite differently. He is urged by his beloved, Alibech, to save his nation by usurping power from Montezuma, who has been rendered fatuous and incapable of command by his ill-conceived passion. It is Alibech's contention that, under Guyomar's leadership, the Indians might yet have a chance against the Spaniards. But Guyomar is shocked at the suggestion that he rebel against his father and, though he feels that his choice may cost him his love, decides to follow the course of honor.

> Tis hard with me whatever choice I make;
> I must not merit you, or must forsake:
> But in this strait, to honour I'll be true,
> And leave my fortune to the gods and you.
> (Vol. 2, IV.ii, p. 377)

Guyomar's rectitude is pointed up once more in one of the battle scenes, this time in contrast with the moral flabbiness of his brother Odmar. The pair are ranging the field in company when they see Alibech, loved of both, and Montezuma, their father, simultaneously in danger of capture. The question for each is which of the two he will attempt to rescue. Alibech who engages his passion, or Montezuma whose rescue is demanded by the dictates of filial honor. With the cry "I'll follow love!", Odmar goes to the rescue of Alibech, while Guyomar, shouting "I'll follow piety!", goes to save his father (Vol. 2, II.iv, p. 351).

Very significant, too, is the fact that Guyomar is made the center of attention in the closing lines of the play. Again, he behaves like anything but a Hobbesian creature of passion and appetite. Offered a high post among his conquered compatriots by the victorious Cortez, Guyomar chooses instead to go off to the north where life will be hard but where it can be lived with honor.

THE PLACE OF HOBBESIAN IDEAS IN DRYDEN'S TRAGEDIES

It would, I think, be quite proper to see in Montezuma, Odmar, and Cortez certain aspects of the Hobbesian view of human nature, though it would have been quite possible to conceive such characters long before Hobbes ever wrote. However, one would have an ill-balanced view of the play if he concluded, therefore, that the play is intended in any way to support the correctness of the Hobbesian view. Surely the traditional view that, though human passions are powerful, moral control is yet possible is vigorously represented in the character of Guyomar. Indeed, considering the deliberateness with which Dryden plays him off to his own advantage against other characters and the emphasis he places upon him in the final scene, it may be argued that Guyomar determines the moral tone of the play.

In the <u>Conquest of Granada</u> Parts I and II (1670) there is a very large group of characters, perhaps a majority of those in the plays, whose behavior could be adequately explained on the basis of Hobbesian assumptions about human nature. Boabdelin, the Moorish emperor, is capable of any degree of treachery to maintain his power. Abdalla and Abdelmelech are typical Drydenesque infatuates. They are both in love with the heartless Lyndaraxa; they can see how contemptible she is and they realize that the only sensible course is to have nothing more to do with her. Yet they ignore the dictates of reason and having degraded themselves in life, they die wretchedly as a direct consequence of their unholy passion. Lyndaraxa herself, with her egotism, her swelling ambition, her lust for power, and her total lack of moral restraint, fits precisely with many aspects of Hobbes' view of human nature. Yet, having recognized this parallelism between the thinking of Hobbes and Dryden, one has still to consider Almanzor, the dominant figure of the play, and to ask how far he reflects the ideas of Hobbes.

It is true that, at the beginning of the <u>Conquest</u> plays, Almanzor is in many ways like a Hobbesian man who, never having emerged from the state of nature, has never acquired the sense of his own limitations on which, according to Hobbes, morality is grounded. He thinks of himself as the center and the sum of things. He sees the world either as a field of action created for his sole delectation or as a lump of insensate matter to be kneaded at his will. He has boundless self-confidence and, like the typical hero of the Tamburlaine strain, he minimizes the importance of any steps between the act of willing and accomplishment. For

him to have willed is tantamount to have done. And yet Almanzor's career cannot be understood unless we see that he is not
the same man at the end of the play as he was at the beginning.
Despite Miss Hartsock's implication that we do not find growth
in Dryden's characters,[11] it is precisely the concept of growth
that is the key to an understanding of Almanzor.

Even at the beginning of the play Almanzor differs from
Lyndaraxa in that there is one principle of restraint in his nature—a sense of honor. True, it is honor in the military sense,
and it is limited pretty rigidly to a certain magnanimity in battle
and loyalty to his friends. But in the course of the play he learns
to accept certain other limitations on his behavior. First, there
is the discipline of Platonic love to which he is introduced by
Almahide. Through her he learns that the animal impulses must
be kept under the severest control in any love worthy of high-
minded people. Second, he accepts the restraints implied by
the parent-child relationship when he kneels reverently before
his new-found father on the field of battle. Third, he accepts the
restraints of the Christian religion at the behest of his mother
who appears to him as a ghost; later it is in obedience to a divine
voice speaking from heaven that he avoids killing the man who,
as it turns out, is his father. Finally, through an act of obeisance
to Ferdinand and Isabella of Spain he accepts the political restraints implied by full membership in a hierarchical society.
It is true that he is but a novice in the arts of restraint by the
time the plays are ended, but the transformation is not one that
could have taken place at all had Dryden been committed in significant degree to the Hobbesian view of human nature.[12]

To find Dryden's hero in full maturity we must examine
the play Aureng-Zebe (1675). In this play, too, there are numerous characters who square with the Hobbesian interpretation of
human nature. There is the familiar figure of the infatuated emperor, so at the mercy of his passions that the duties of his office
are forgotten. Arimant corresponds closely with Abdalla and
Abdelmelech of the Conquest plays, for he, too, is so abandoned
in his love for an unresponsive lady that he loses all human dignity, all claim to rationality, and becomes a mere pawn. Morat
is the bombastic hero in the line of Tamburlaine and Lyndaraxa.
But, again, the play cannot be understood through a study of these
characters alone, for the center of the play is Aureng-Zebe,
whose personality is very different from those just alluded to.

Like the conventional hero, he is a person of great energy and great accomplishments. Those about him recognize him as a being apart, one to whom the usual limitations on human capabilities do not apply. But there the resemblance stops, for he displays none of the crude egotism, ruthless ambition, or the disregard of the claims of society which characterize his brother Morat. No hero of the conventional sort would be capable of Aureng-Zebe's scrupulous respect for a father who he knows is attempting to seduce the woman he loves. Nor could such a hero summon up the self-abnegation displayed by Aureng-Zebe when he offers to combine with Morat to crush the emperor's enemies and then to retire into private life to avoid any suspicion of rivalry with Morat.

It is true that on one occasion Aureng-Zebe, frustrated in his effort to help his father, convinced that Indamora has been unfaithful to him and that Morat's schemes have succeeded, gives way to cynicism in a speech declaring that the "world is made for the bold impious man" (Vol. 5, II.i, p. 236). Virtue, he implies, since it brings with it no material reward, is not worth the candle, and in suggesting this he seems to confirm the Hobbesian opinion that the satisfaction of appetite is the only valid motive in human conduct. But the significance of this speech, of which Miss Hartsock makes much, can be understood only in the light of what comes immediately after it. Dianet, Aureng-Zebe's lieutenant, enters, and there ensues a scene in which Dianet tempts Aureng-Zebe to rebel against his father. Yet, despite his disillusionment and the excellent reasons he has for despising his father, Aureng-Zebe refuses to yield.

> Ill treated, and forsaken, as I am,
> I'll not betray the glory of my name:
> 'Tis not for me, who have preserved a state,
> To buy an empire at so base a rate. (Vol. 5, II.i, p. 237)

A major point in this play and, indeed, in all the plays so far discussed seems to be that, although man's passions are potent forces which can sometimes usurp reason's position of control and so upset the balance of his soul, man has the power to fight off such incursions, if he will but use it. Man is not as one of the gods whose souls are never ruffled by the winds of passion, nor is he a mere vane to those blasts. As Aureng-Zebe says on an-

other occasion when his passions almost betray him into wrong-
doing,

> Strong virtue, like strong nature, struggles still;
> Exerts itself, and then throws off the ill.
>
> (Vol. 5, I.i, p. 219)

If my analysis of these plays has any validity, then, Dryden's
conception of what human nature can and should be is very different from what we find in Hobbes. Dryden grants that the passions
are powerful, but he believes they can be controlled by a force
within the individual which seems to be akin to Reason as it was
traditionally conceived. Hobbes is unwilling to grant the existence,
much less the efficacy, of Reason in the sense of a principle of
order. One must look beyond Hobbes for parallels to Dryden's
way of thinking about human nature in the tragedies.

Dryden's preoccupation in the tragedies with characters who
are trying either to satisfy or to control their passions reflects
one of the absorbing interests of his time. During the latter half
of the seventeenth century innumerable popular treatises appeared
on the passions—their nature, their uses, and methods of controlling them. Many of these works, probably a majority, took the
Aristotelian position that, under the watchful eye and wise guid-
ance of Reason, the passions could be the source of much good—
this in opposition to the Stoic view which held that the passions
were so dangerous as to require complete extirpation.[13] But
even among the writers of this period who affirm the potential
usefulness of the passions and the possibility of controlling them,
one senses an underlying uneasiness. Influenced by the Christian
conception of the Fall and fundamental depravity of human nature,
they are much impressed with the difficulty of achieving a harmonious relation between the passions and Reason. The power
of Reason is limited; the passions, if not inherently evil, are
easily corruptible; consequently the human soul is often the scene
of a bitter conflict between the recalcitrant passions and their
rightful governor, Reason. The ancient analogy of the wise and
virtuous prince beset by rebellious subjects is almost universally
alluded to among these writers.

One of the contributors to the literature of the passions was
Walter Charleton, a physician of some distinction who flourished
during the middle third of the century and held posts in the royal

household under Charles I and Charles II. A person of numerous interests, he was one of the earliest members of the Royal Society and it was he who, in 1662, sponsored Dryden for membership. In the course of a long life he published voluminously on scientific and philosophical subjects. For one of his scientific works, Chorea Gigantum (1663), Dryden composed a verse epistle in praise of the author. The chances seem rather good, then, that the two men knew each other and exchanged ideas.

In 1674, Charleton brought out an adaptation of J. F. Senault's popular treatise De l'Usage des Passions, under the title The Natural History of the Passions. In it occur two ideas which, it seems to me, contribute infinitely more than anything Hobbes has to say to an understanding of the psychology underlying Dryden's tragedies. First, in the Epistle Prefatory, Charleton introduces the commonplace analogy between the soul and a battleground.

> It seem'd to me no less inconceivable, whence that dismal ψυχομαχια or intestin war which every man too frequently feels within himself, and whereof even St. Paul himself so sadly complained, when (in Epist. ad Roman, cap. 3) he cries out, video aliam legem in membris meis repugnantem legi mentis meae; should arise, if not from a Duumvirate as it were of Rulers contending for superiority within us, and inclining us two contrary ways at once.[14]

Second, while he admits that the passions can be formidable troublemakers and that the struggle for supremacy between them and Reason is a real one, he insists that Reason has the power to win out. "By virtue of his Understanding," he says, "Man is capable of Wisedom, which alone is able to teach him how to subdue and govern all his affections . . . I commit Errors in Passion . . . only because I make not a right use of that finite indeed, yet sufficient Understanding God hath given me, in the conduct of that cupidity my passions excite in me."[15]

The "intestin war" of which Charleton speaks is being waged in the souls of nearly every major character Dryden presents in his tragedies. Maximin and Lyndaraxa are the only ones in whom the passions hold such absolute sway that no opposing force is ever in evidence. It is true that in Montezuma Reason has been reduced to a feeble sense of guilt, and in Abdalla and Abdelmelech

Reason is merely an abstraction to be argued over. Nevertheless there are a number of characters, such as Guyomar, Aureng-
Zebe, and Almanzor, in whom virtue and Reason do triumph,
though frequently not without a real struggle. Moreover, it is
around these figures that the moral and dramatic significance of
the tragedies I have analyzed tends to gather, so that to attribute
to these plays anything like a Hobbesian bias or tone is to distort
their meaning.[16]

III

Hobbes' political theory is a natural outgrowth of his assumptions about human nature. Since Reason, for him, is so feeble a
force in the moral economy of the individual, it can hardly be expected to provide a sound foundation for the state, as it did for
more traditional thinkers such as Hooker. In the hypothetical
"state of nature" man finds himself engaged in ceaseless warfare and life is "nasty, brutish, and short," for no individual has
sufficient power to impose on his fellows the restraints essential
to a civilized society. Only under the spur of fear of violent death
is man capable of visualizing the means to extricate himself from
this impasse. The solution is a contractual arrangement whereby
each individual agrees to delegate his power to a single person,
the monarch, who will use that power to create an orderly society
in which the individual can live in safety if he will accept certain
restrictions on his appetite for power and possessions. Thus the
Hobbesian monarch is essentially a receptacle of power which,
when dispersed among warring individuals, can lead only to continual destruction and death but which, when gathered in the monarch, becomes a fountainhead of order and security. The monarch's will becomes the will of the state; his word becomes absolutely binding upon his subjects.

Miss Hartsock has pointed out that there are numerous examples in Dryden's tragedies of monarchs of the Hobbesian type.
Such monarchs, in theorizing about their office, invariably think
of it in terms of power. Montezuma, for example, remarks that
"Kings and their crowns have but one destiny: / Power is their
life: when that expires they die" (Vol. 2, V.ii, p. 404). And Boabdelin in the Conquest plays, pontificating about his position, says
" 'Tis true from force the noblest title springs; / I therefore hold

from that, which first made kings" (Vol. 4, I.i, p. 47). The image
of the monarch as a figure whose essence is power and who sums
up in his person all the power inherent in his subjects is most
forcefully presented in a speech by the emperor Maximin in Tyrannic Love (1669).

> I'll find that power o'er wills, which heaven ne'er found.
> Free-will's a cheat in anyone but me;
> In all but kings, 'tis willing slavery;
> An unseen fate which forces the desire;
> The will of puppets danced upon a wire.
> A monarch is
> The spirit of the world in every mind:
> He may match lambs and wolves and make it kind.
> Mine is the business of your little fates:
> And though you war, like petty wrangling states,
> You're in my hand; and, when I bid you cease,
> You shall be crushed together into peace.[17]
>   (Vol. 3, IV.i, p. 430)

It is true, then, that a conception of monarchy similar to, if
not necessarily derived from, the Hobbesian conception is present
in Dryden's plays. Nevertheless, the fact that Dryden could conceive such characters when the need arose scarcely justifies the
contention that the plays imply espousal of the Hobbesian position.
To discover the true status of the Hobbesian monarch in Dryden's
tragedies we must inquire how he fares in the plays in which he
appears and how he fits into the pattern of the tragedies as a
whole.

In general it can be said that those monarchs who theorize
so freely about their power are notably unsuccessful as rulers.
Thus Montezuma, incapacitated by his love for Almeria, contrib-
utes at least by default to the subjection of his people to the
Spaniards. Boabdelin in the Conquest plays, despite his mouth-
ings about monarchic power, is a pitiable caricature who must
rely on his rival in love to preserve his throne. In Tyrannic Love,
Maximin meets his death as a direct consequence of the notion,
expressed in the speech quoted above, that the lives of others
are at the disposal of his slightest whim.

It is in this latter play, however, that one sees in germ another attitude toward the ruler-subject relationship which in suc-

ceeding plays is to become predominant. It reveals itself in the
speeches of Berenice, the emperor's sorely tried spouse. She
is systematically humiliated by Maximin, who crowns a long
series of insults to her when he makes it clear to everyone that
he prefers the Egyptian princess, Catherine. Berenice has one
admirer, Porphyry, who is eager to rid her of Maximin, but she
steadfastly refuses his help on the ground that violence to Maximin cannot be countenanced by a subject and a wife. On the question of the ruler-subject relationship she thus would seem to be
in perfect agreement with Maximin; but the theoretical ground
on which she takes her stand is quite remote from his. There
is no suggestion on her part that fear, awe, or prudence should
motivate a subject's obedience. Rather it is the compelling necessity of being faithful to a trust. The ruler-subject relationship,
like that between husband and wife, is based on mutual confidence,
and it would be dishonorable for a subject to betray such a trust
no matter what the provocation. Thus, when Porphyry urges her
to let him kill Maximin, she refuses with the following lofty sentiments:

> We both are bound by trust, and must be true;
> I to his bed, and to his empire you.
> For he who to the bad betrays his trust,
> Though he does good, becomes himself unjust.
> (Vol. 3, II.i, p. 399)

Like Maximin, Leonora, queen of Aragon in The Spanish Friar
(1681), believes that it is the place of the monarch to will and of
the subject to obey. Any resistance on the part of subjects must
be ruthlessly crushed. Thus she confides to Bertran, who fills
the dual role of her lover and her advisor:

> I fear my people's faith;
> That hot-mouthed beast, that bears against the curb,
> Hard to be broken even by lawful kings,
> But harder by usurpers.   (Vol. 6, III.iii, pp. 465-6

In contrast with her attitude is that of Sancho, the rightful king of
Aragon who was deposed by Leonora's father. Torrismond, who
has had notable success in defending Leonora and her kingdom
from the Moors, has been to visit Sancho in his dungeon. He describes the visit in part as follows:

> He was so true a father of his country,
> To thank me, for defending even his foes,
> Because they were his subjects.   (Vol. 6, III.iii, p. 469)

The contrasting metaphors of the masterful rider on the rebellious horse and the solicitous father throw into sharp relief the differences between the two conceptions of the ruler-subject relationship. It is significant that Sancho is restored to his throne at the end of the play.

The non-Hobbesian conception of the relationship between ruler and subject adumbrated in Tyrannic Love and made more explicit in The Spanish Friar is accorded much fuller definition in Don Sebastian (1690). Again, in this play as in those that preceded it, the monarch with Hobbesian views is represented, this time in the person of Muley-Moluch, emperor of Barbary. His conception of his function in the state and of his relationship to his subjects is suggested in the following speech to a religious leader who has refused to legalize a divorce the emperor wants:

> Slave, have I raised thee to this pomp and power,
> To preach against my will? Know, I am law;
> And thou, not Mahomet's messenger, but mine!
> Make it, I charge thee, make my pleasure lawful.
>   (Vol. 7, III.i, p. 375)

But, whereas in Tyrannic Love the mouthpiece of Hobbesian philosophy is the most colorful figure in the play, in Don Sebastian he is relatively insignificant. The truly imposing figure is Don Sebastian himself, and his view of kingship is quite the opposite of that of his Moorish counterpart.

Dryden says of Sebastian in the preface to the play, "In the drawing of his character, I forgot not piety, which any one may observe to be one principal ingredient of it, even so far as to be a habit in him" (Vol. 7, p. 311). It is this quality that shines pre-eminent when, at the climax of the play, having discovered that he has unwittingly committed incest, Don Sebastian voluntarily gives up the Portuguese throne lest it be polluted by his continued possession. In doing so he demonstrates his belief that a ruler must qualify for his office through moral purity rather than through the mere acquisition of power and that the throne should function as a spring of moral inspiration rather than as a mere disciplinary force intended to guarantee order.

On the question of the proper relationship between ruler and subject, Dryden develops an interesting contrast between the Moors and their Portuguese captives. Among the Moors, self-interest is the governing motive. "What's royalty, but power to please myself," says Muley-Moluch (Vol. 7, II.i, p. 348). The same attitude is reflected in the cynicism of Mustapha, leader of the rabble:

> Both rich and poor for their own interest pray,
> 'Tis ours to make our fortune while we may.
> (Vol. 7, I.i, p. 346)

Between Don Sebastian and his subjects, on the other hand, there exists a kind of generous rivalry to see who can outsacrifice the other. The subjects, having given their blood to defend their vanquished monarch on the battlefield, give up their freedom in order to remain with him in his captivity;[18] while Don Sebastian, having drawn the lot which marks him as one of three victims whose lives are to redeem those of the other captives, refuses to accept leniency from the Moors until the safety of his subjects is guaranteed:

> You could not, give me leave to tell you sir,
> Have given me life but in my subjects' safety:
> Kings, who are fathers, live but in their people.
> (Vol. 7, I.i, p. 338)

The most searching analysis of this relationship between ruler and subject is provided, oddly enough, by a renegade, a Portuguese named Alonzo who, because of a fancied insult, has left the service of Don Sebastian and attached himself to Muley-Moluch. Despite his defection from his rightful sovereign, he continues to conceive of the ruler-subject relationship in the most idealistic terms, and when a treacherous courtier invites him to conspire against the life of Muley-Moluch, he replies in language that recalls Berenice's notion that the ruler-subject relationship is based on trust:

> He trusts us both; mark that! Shall we betray him;
> A master, who reposes life and empire
> On our fidelity? I grant he is a tyrant,
> That hated name my nature most abhors: . . .

THE PLACE OF HOBBESIAN IDEAS IN DRYDEN'S TRAGEDIES

> But, while he trusts me, 'twere so base a part
> To fawn, and yet betray . . .   (Vol. 7, II.i, p. 356)

The discrepancy between these professions and his behavior toward Don Sebastian arouses in him such remorse that Alonzo
eventually returns to his old allegiance, proving its genuineness
by saving Don Sebastian from the suicidal impulse attendant on
his discovery that he has committed incest.

Clearly, the ruler-subject relationship as it is conceived in
these plays is not based on the ideas of Hobbes. For him, the
state is a product of human ingenuity spurred by fear; it is not,
as it was for Aristotle and his intellectual descendants, the inevitable embodiment of an inborn quality of the human soul. Indeed, there is a sense in which, for Hobbes, the state runs directly counter to human nature, for he believed that man is
dominated by his acquisitive appetites, which in themselves can
lead only to perpetual conflict, deprivation, and death. Man in-
vents the state in order to avoid these consequences and the
state is worthy of preservation, at least in any given form, only
so long as its usefulness for this purpose is evident.

In Dryden, on the other hand, the ruler-subject relationship
is not thought of as a purely ad hoc arrangement, a set of rules
devised by human wit in an effort to prevent the game of getting
and keeping from becoming a destructive free-for-all. It seems
rather to be the spontaneous expression of some elemental need
in human nature, and it is sanctioned not through the quid pro quo
of a contractual understanding, but through some instinct for
order, some deep sense of responsibility which makes the be-
trayal of a trust abhorrent. As such, it has about it an absolute
quality. It is not terminable merely because one of the parties
to it defaults in his obligations, and it brings with it something
of the same satisfaction and demands something of the same
reverence as the marriage bond or the father-child relationships.[19]

Indeed, the father-child analogy, which Dryden uses more
than once for the ruler-subject relation, was the core of a way
of thinking about human society with which Dryden was much
more in sympathy than he was with the ideas of Hobbes. Figgis
traces the appearance of the comparison back to St. Thomas and
cites off-hand some half-dozen instances of its use by succeeding writers.[20] In fact, by the seventeenth century it had become
the merest cliché insinuating itself into innumerable political

389

tracts, unbidden by the writers and, no doubt, virtually unnoticed by the readers. It was rescued from this state by the efforts of Sir Robert Filmer, an apologist for the Royalist cause, who in 1680 published a volume entitled <u>Patriarcha</u>. In it he derives from the stale metaphor a systematic theory of the origin and sanction of monarchic power. "I see not then," he says, "how the children of Adam, or of any man else, can be free of subjection to their parents. And this subordination of children is the fountain of all regal authority by the ordination of God himself. . . . Nor leaves it any place for such imaginary pactions between Kings and their people as many dream of."[21]

Filmer's attitude toward Hobbes was mixed. He agreed with him in his assertion of the monarch's right to the exercise of absolute power; he could not agree with him about the means by which this power was conferred. Hence, the disparaging reference to "pactions" between kings and subjects in the remarks of Filmer quoted above. Edward Gee, writing in 1658, describes the patriarchal school in such a way as to summarize neatly the distinction between its way of thinking and that of Hobbes: "The drift of their opinions is to make the rise and right of government natural and native, not voluntary and conventional."[22]

In brief, therefore, it seems to me that Filmer and Dryden are at one with Hobbes in approving the authoritarian state, but they diverge from Hobbes in their conception of the theoretical basis of the state. For Hobbes the state is an invention of the human intellect and it is to be judged by its utility. For Filmer and Dryden it is a spontaneous expression of human nature, and as such it is beyond the need or possibility of rational justification.

IV

It is, after all, scarcely surprising that Dryden should find little in Hobbes that he could present with approval in his heroic tragedies. These plays were written for the court, which, at least in its public and ceremonial aspects, professed to live by the Aristotelian ideal of heroic virtue and honor. Indeed, heroic tragedy may have enjoyed its great popularity partly because it helped to sustain the illusion that the aristocratic ideal of honor was a vital force when in reality it had entered its decline. In the realm of political theory the court took its stand during much of this period on the Divine Right of Kings, a doctrine which in essence maintained that monarchy was the natural form of government for human society and that to tamper with it was to interfere with the natural expression of the divine order. Hobbes, on the other hand, very soon ceased to believe in the sense of honor as an adequate basis for social behavior, and eventually concluded that fear was the only safe foundation upon which the restraints necessary to social living could be based. Hobbes was, in fact, the radical thinker of the age in urging that man could make and remake his government according to his will, and it was to the rising middle class that his theories gave aid and comfort rather than to the class which owed the existence of its privileges to ancient custom and tradition.

In view of what prudence demanded, it is hard to see how Dryden could have championed in his plays the ideas of a person like Hobbes, or how, had he done so, his plays would have been popular. But there is reason to believe that personal predilection alone would have made it difficult for Dryden to accept the view of Hobbes. As Professor Bredvold has pointed out, the drift throughout Dryden's life was toward increasing conservatism in matters of politics and religion. It is entirely probable that such a movement in his personal life would carry him away from the position of Hobbes and in the direction of belief in the traditional theories about human conduct and human government. It is true that Professor Bredvold sees as one source of Dryden's conservatism the general revival of interest in Pyrrhonism which tends to cling to the old ways of doing things because it can see no reliable way of acquiring the truth about human society upon which reforms might be based. This, it must be admitted, is scarcely a position which would lead to a passionate and exclusive devotion to traditional ways of thought. Nor do we find such devotion in the tragedies. Fidelity to his basic convictions does not exclude, for Dryden, a sympathetic understanding of other points of view; and, when it suits his dramatic purposes, he can write poignantly about the feeling most of us occasionally have —that the power of passion is irresistible and that the demands of duty are grossly at variance with common sense. Nevertheless, the assumptions about human nature and society which have a determining effect on the tragedies seem to me to be, first, that human behavior emerges from an internal struggle in which there is a genuine possibility that virtue may win out and, second, that man is bound to society through natural obligation, not through a political structure devised by wit and preserved at the discretion of its human architects.

NOTES

1 The Works of John Dryden, ed. Scott and Saintsbury (Edinburgh, 1883), XI, 216; XII, 291; IV, 24.

2 John Aubrey, Brief Lives and Other Selected Writings, ed. Anthony Powell (London, 1949), p. 261.

3 Wolfgang Mann, Drydens heroische Tragödien als Ausdruck höfischer Barockkultur in England (Tübingen, 1932), p. 15.

4 L. I. Bredvold, The Intellectual Milieu of John Dryden (Ann Arbor, 1932), p. 66.

5 In Seventeenth Century Studies, second series, ed. Robert Shafer (Princeton, 1937).

6 Ibid., p. 127.

7 Ibid., p. 143.

8 In interpreting Hobbes I have made extensive use of a study by Leo Strauss entitled The Political Philosophy of Thomas Hobbes (Oxford, 1936).

9 Op.cit., pp. 88–127.

10 Quotations from the plays of Dryden are cited by reference to volume, act, scene, and page in the Scott-Saintsbury Works (Edinburgh, 1883).

11 Op.cit., p. 96.

12 For a fuller treatment of this development in Almanzor see the writer's article "The Development of the Hero in Dryden's Tragedies," JEGP, LII (April, 1953), 161–73.

13 See, for example, Thomas Wright, The Passions of the Minde in Generall (London, 1630), p. 18; Timothy Nourse, A Discourse Upon the Nature and Faculties of Man (1686), pp. 106–107; Jacques Abbadie, The Art of Knowing One-self (tr. T. W. Oxford, 1695), p. 24. R. S. Crane discusses this antistoical strain in the thought of the seventeenth century in his article "Suggestions toward a Genealogy of the 'Man of Feeling,'" ELH, I (December, 1934), 214–20.

14 Walter Charleton, The Natural History of the Passions (London, 1674), Epistle Prefatory.

15 Ibid., pp. 172–73. The date 1674 for Charleton's translation of Senault makes it too early to have influenced directly any of Dryden's tragedies before The Conquest of Granada. However, Dryden must have known Charleton at least as early as 1662 when Charleton sponsored him for membership in the Royal Society, and it is perfectly possible that the two may have discussed Senault's ideas. Senault's book appeared in French in 1641 and was available in English as early as 1649 in the translation of Henry Carey, second earl of Monmouth.

16 I have omitted consideration of Tyrannic Love and All for Love because they do not readily lend themselves to the argument at this stage in my paper. Maximin in Tyrannic Love is clearly the helpless thrall of passion, the Hobbesian man if you will, but his chief antagonist, St. Catherine, is characterized by a blend of stoicism and Christianity rather than by the Aristotelian attitude toward the passions with which I am here concerned. However, the upshot of this play is similar to that of the plays I have analyzed in that the Hobbesian man goes down in defeat.

In All for Love, it is true, a considerable amount of sympathy is generated for a pair of lovers who are entirely given over to passion. It is worth noting, however, that according to his preface, Dryden felt limited in the amount of pity he could work up for Antony and Cleopatra precisely because they were so incapable of exercising any control over their passions. The last clause of the relevant passage in particular runs quite counter to the Hobbesian position. "That which is wanting to work up the pity to a greater height, was not afforded me by the story: for the crimes of love, which they both committed, were not occasioned by any necessity, or fatal ignorance, but were wholly voluntary; since our passions are, or ought to be, within our power" (V, 326–27).

17 The extent to which the Hobbesian concept of monarchy is distilled in this speech can be gauged by setting it beside the following quotation from Leo Strauss' The Political Philosophy of Thomas Hobbes: "[Hobbes] conceives the sovereign power not as reason but as will . . . . [He] expressly turns against the view still predominant in his age that the holder of the

sovereign power is in the same relation to the State as the head to the whole man. The holder of the sovereign power is not the 'head', that is, the capacity to deliberate and plan, but the 'soul', that is, the capacity to command, in the State" (p. 160).

18 The following quotation from Leviathan suggests how foreign to Hobbes is the notion of a subject-ruler relationship based on other than prudential considerations: "The obligation of the subjects to the sovereign, is understood to last as long, and no longer, than the power lasteth, by which he is able to protect them" (ed. Oakeshott, Part 2, Chap. 21, p. 144).

19 A cogent statement of this conception of the ruler-subject relationship occurs in the epilogue to Albion and Albanius, an opera eulogizing the career and character of Charles II. It is interesting to note how, by a play on words in the last two lines, this relationship is linked to an ordering, creating principle in the cosmos—the fiats of Jahweh in Genesis or perhaps the orthos logos of the Stoic philosophers.

> He plights his faith and we believe him just;
> His honour is to promise, ours to trust.
> Thus Britain's basis on a word is laid,
> As by a word the world itself was made.   (VII, 284)

20 J. N. Figgis, The Divine Right of Kings (Cambridge, 1922), pp. 150-51.

21 Sir Robert Filmer, Patriarcha and Other Political Works, ed. Peter Laslett (Oxford, 1949), p. 57. It should be emphasized that Patriarcha was simply a crystallization of ideas which were already deeply imbedded in the thought of the seventeenth century (see Laslett's introduction, pp. 20-33). Patriarcha itself had been written in manuscript and circulated within Filmer's circle forty years before its publication. Moreover, earlier treatises by Filmer, notably The Anarchy of a Limited or Mixed Monarchy (1643) and Observations upon Aristotle's Politiques (1652), had embodied the essential ideas of Patriarcha though in a less developed form. In short, the political theory of Patriarcha was readily available to Dryden throughout his literary career.

22 Ibid., p. 38.

V. LITERARY METHOD

DRYDEN'S LATIN SCHOLARSHIP

J. McG. Bottkol

From the days of Luke Milbourne[1] it has been a commonplace that Dryden was not only a free translator but also a scholar
of very feeble attainments in classical learning. It has custom-
arily (and carelessly) been assumed that Dryden was loose in
translating <u>because</u> of his weakness as a Latinist. It is not my
purpose here to make an apology for Dryden as an exact translator; rather, I wish to confute the long-accepted opinion that
Dryden was not vividly aware of the scholarly problems confront-
ing him as a translator. The evidence for this argument will be
drawn from sources scarcely examined since Dryden's death—
the actual contemporary texts and editions of the Latin classics
used by him in the process of translation.

George Saintsbury, still the best known, if the least accurate,
of Dryden's recent editors, dismisses the question of the poet's
scholarship with a blanket condemnation:

> This system [i.e., paraphrase] of Dryden's
> makes it at once unnecessary and impossible to an-
> notate his Translations as if they were written from
> the point of view of the scholar. An equal proportion
> of notes and text would hardly suffice to point out his
> verbal variations, omissions, and additions, while an
> attempt to account for any of the three classes would,
> save in very rare instances, be labour wholly lost.[2]

To account for Dryden's every divagation from the original would
indeed be an Augean labor, but to give no account of the "three
classes" of "verbal variations, omissions, and additions" beyond
attributing them summarily to lack of scholarship is, I hope to
show, evidence of editorial slothfulness.

Reprinted from <u>Modern Philology</u>, Vol. 40 (1943), pp. 241–255, by permission of the author and The University of Chicago Press. Copyright
1943 by The University of Chicago.

A similar judgment—perhaps an echo of Saintsbury's—is found in A. W. Ward's chapter on Dryden in the Cambridge history of English literature:

> From the point of view of exact scholarship, nothing can be said in favour of a method [of translation] which does not show any reverence for the text, and very little for the style, of the original author.[3]

With Mr. Ward's stricture on Dryden's stylistic failings I have no present quarrel, but I wish emphatically to disagree with the confident assertion that he showed no "reverence for the text." One must ask at once, what text? A modern text like Sabbadini's Virgil or Postgate's Corpus poetarum Latinorum? This question, ignored by Saintsbury and Ward, is the crucial point. Did they, in comparing Dryden's translations with the original, use a modern Latin text, or did they turn up the seventeenth-century editions actually used by Dryden? It is plain from their statements that they did not do the latter, and their failure to do so vitiates any conclusions they may offer on this head.

The lapse of even a single generation of scholars brings about appreciable changes in the text and scholarly interpretation of the classics. The emendations and conjectures of our grandfathers' day give way before new surmises or new discoveries, and the scholars of today may expect the same of their successors. The lapse of two hundred and fifty years and the renovation of classical scholarship on scientific principles during the nineteenth century have removed us a vast distance from the scholarship of Dryden's time. Therefore, the student who compares Dryden's translation with a modern text is working in the dark and is quite unable to account for variations, omissions, or additions except by an easy accusation of the poet's scholarly incompetence. Yet, if the contemporary authorities on which Dryden himself relied are compared with the translations, it at once becomes plain that, in all but a small number of examples, his departures from the original are due to aesthetic or stylistic reasons—not to ignorance or imperfect knowledge of Latin. In the time of Busby, to translate word for word was a license scarcely allowed even to schoolboys; Dryden, the most eminent poet of his day, was as much concerned to produce an acceptable

English poem as he was to reproduce the matter of the original.
This convention of translation is unpopular today, and its premises
are indeed debatable; but we are not concerned here with a question of artistic convention or taste, but only with that of scholarship, a much more palpable issue. Dryden is often wilful and prolix in exercising his prerogatives as a poetic translator; he is
almost never ignorant.

In comparing all of Dryden's translations from Latin with
their seventeenth-century editions of the originals, the investigator
will come to the inescapable conclusion that the poet was a much
more conscientious scholar than has been admitted by even his
friendliest critics. Omissions, seeming mistranslations, and
apparently unwarranted intrusions will, in a large number of instances, be found attributable to peculiarities in the texts used
by Dryden. These peculiarities form three main classes:

1. The Latin text itself, which abounds in variant
readings differing widely from those current in modern texts. Also, portions of the text included in seventeenth-century canons of the text have since been excised as spurious.

2. The commentary, or "explanatory notes" which
accompanied the text. In following these aids, appended
by the most learned authorities of his time, Dryden
often gives interpretations of the original unfamiliar
to modern editors or includes editorial matter given
by way of fuller explanation. The influence of the
commentators is apparent on every page of Dryden's
work, and it is by far the most copious source of his
expansions of the original.

3. The Interpretatio, or running translation into
Latin prose which accompanies the original in all the
"Delphin" editions of the classics. Occasionally, in
following this authority, Dryden is led into renderings
which would seem mistranslations today.

It is necessary now to pass to the names and characteristics of
the editors upon whom Dryden relied.

It is an easy matter to discover from his prefaces and notes
the editions used by Dryden for most of his translation. For
Juvenal he went to Prateus,[4] one of the editors of the great series

published in usum serenissimi Delphini. For Virgil he used almost exclusively another volume of the Dauphin's library, the
very popular edition of Ruaeus.[5] For Persius he abandoned
Prateus for the epochal work of Casaubon,[6] whose name is not
yet forgotten in connection with that difficult poet. For Ovid,
Dryden gives us no sufficient indication of his editor. In his
Preface to Ovid's Epistles (1680) we read:

> The title of them in our late editions is Epistolae
> Heroidum, the Letters of the Heroines. But Heinsius
> has judg'd more truly, that the inscription of our
> author was barely, Epistles. . . . .[7]

This proves Dryden's familiarity with the great edition of Niklaas
Heinsius (1652).[8] Most probably one of the "late editions" referred to by Dryden was the Variorum of Borchard Cnipping,[9]
which was based on the monumental labors of Heinsius. While
it is plain that Dryden knew Heinsius, it is much more likely,
as will appear, that he habitually used an edition with full explanatory notes, as those of Heinsius are purely textual. A comparison of the various annotated editions which fall between 1652
(the date of the Heinsius edition) and 1680 (the date of the Preface
to Ovid's Epistles) points to that of Cnipping as the one used by
Dryden, although the influence of other editors is apparent here
and there. Since Cnipping's text is almost exactly that of Heinsius,
and since Dryden relied on Cnipping's commentary, it can be inferred that his edition was the one used by Dryden. Dryden translated also some hundreds of lines from Lucretius, four idyls of
Theocritus, three odes and an epode of Horace, the first book of
the Iliad, and one other selection from Homer. For these last
four poets Dryden gives us no indication of his editors. Largely
because of the scantiness of the selections and the huge number
of possible editions, I have been unable to find conclusive evidence
as to Dryden's editors for Lucretius, Horace, and Homer. However, the translations of the Eclogues, Georgics, and Aeneid of
Virgil, five satires of Juvenal, all of Persius, and large sections
of Ovid make up the overwhelming bulk of Dryden's work in translation. Indeed, it makes up over half of all Dryden's nondramatic
verse. A weighing of the evidence drawn from these alone is ampl
proof of Dryden's careful methods of work.

After reading thousands of lines of Dryden's translations together with the contemporary Latin texts, one can reconstitute

his actual working method: he sat with a favorite edition open before him (Prateus, Ruaeus, Casaubon, or Cnipping), read the original carefully, often the Latin prose Interpretatio, and invariably studied the accompanying annotations. When he came to a difficult or disputed passage, he repeatedly turned to other editors, studied and compared their varying opinions, and then chose to follow one authority or another or even to make a new interpretation for himself. Also he had open before him on the table one or more earlier English translations, particularly those which were written in heroic couplets. From these he often took rhymes, stray phrases, even whole lines and passages.[10] That this is not a fanciful picture must now be proved by concrete evidence of Dryden's close attention to the scholarly authorities of his day.

We may begin with Ruaeus' text of Virgil. Here I wish to demonstrate the method of internal proof, by which we could be certain that Dryden had made use of this edition rather than another, even if he had not told us himself.[11] In many places Ruaeus' readings agree with those of modern editors[12] but differed from those of his contemporaries. In the first book of the Aeneid Ruaeus rejects a reading of the Codex Romanus:

> Pars optare locum tecto . . . . [i. 429].[13]

> Optare.) Non aptare, ut quidam legunt. Optare enim est eligere. . . . [Ruaeus, ad. loc. cit.].

> Some for their dwellings choose a spot of ground . . . .
> [Dryden, I, 590].

It is plain that Dryden has followed the reading and interpretation of Ruaeus. In the twelfth book of the Aeneid, where the reading of Servius and of most manuscripts is preferred by Ruaeus, and hence by Dryden, to the limina of the Medicean, we have a similar example:

> . . . . . nec nota potentum
> Munera . . . . [xii. 519–20].

> Munera.) Munia, dignitates. Pauci quidam legunt, limina [Ruaeus, ad loc. cit.].

> Nor pompous cares, nor palaces, he knew . . . .
> [Dryden, XII, 756].

Of the five modern editors, only Fairclough follows the Medicean in reading limina. These might be called "negative" examples, as there is no difficulty here for a student reading a modern text parallel to Dryden. They merely show that Dryden was using Ruaeus rather than "pauci quidam." The converse and positive examples are the readings in Ruaeus which vary from those of modern editors. To a student using a modern Latin text, these passages seem to confirm Dryden's reputation for incorrigible carelessness. For example, the five modern editors agree on their reading of this line:

> . . . . ita digerit omina Calchas . . . . [ii, 182; Conington et al.]

> . . . . as Calchas did ordain [Dryden, II, 242].

This certainly seems to show no reverence for the text, unless we look into Dryden's editor:

> . . . . ita digerit omnia Calchas . . . . [Ruaeus ii. 182].

In the Interpretatio which corresponds to this passage, Ruaeus paraphrases for the Dauphin's benefit thus:

> . . . . sic Calchas disponit omnia . . . . [Ruaeus, ad loc. cit.].

Dryden has followed his authority exactly. Similarly, in a later passage, where we find exitium in the modern editors (except Sabbadini), we read in Ruaeus:

> Heu! nunc misero mihi demum Exilium infelix
> . . . . [x. 849–50].

A person using any of the modern texts but that of Sabbadini would be unable to understand Dryden's rendering of the line:

> 'T is now my bitter banishment I feel . . . . [Dryden, X, 1212].

Again, when Dryden seems incapable of accuracy even with simplest numbers:

> . . . . caedit <u>binas</u> de more bidentes . . . . [v. 96; Conington <u>et al.</u>]

> <u>Five</u> sheep, according to the rites, he slew . . . . [V, 129].

he is guilty of no textual or arithmetical slovenliness, for the number is <u>quinas</u> in Ruaeus.

With Juvenal, we might suspect Dryden of bowdlerizing a passage concerning the lechery of the <u>Graeculus esuriens</u>. Housman gives the lines thus:[14]

> † praeterea sanctum nihil aut ab inguine tutum,
> non matrona laris, non filia uirgo, neque ipse
> sponsus leuis adhuc, non filius ante pudicus.
> horum si nihil est, <u>auiam</u> resupinat amici. [iii. 109–12]

The translation is faithful enough until we come to <u>aviam</u>:

> Besides, there's nothing sacred, nothing free
> From bold attempts of their rank lechery.
> Thro' the whole family their labors run;
> The daughter is debauch'd, the wife is won: ⎫
> Nor scapes the bridegroom, or the blooming ⎬
> son. ⎭
> If none they find for their lewd purpose fit,
> <u>They with the walls and very floors commit</u> [III, 187–93].

Seemingly, Dryden has substituted "walls and very floors" for "grandmother." Actually, Dryden was faced with a very difficult line because of the inferior reading (<u>aulam</u>) given him by his editor, Prateus. Dryden's rendering of this textual crux is brilliantly ingenious. Although only one word is concerned, I repeat the whole passage from Prateus' text in order to give the reader an idea of the continual variation in detail of a seventeenth-century text from any modern one:

> Praeterea sanctum nihil est, & [ab inguine][15]
>   tutum
> Non matrona laris, non filia virgo, neque ipse
> Sponsus laevis adhuc, non filius ante pudicus.
> Horum si nihil est, aulam resupinat amici
>   [Prateus iii. 109–12].

A strong indication of Dryden's scholarly conscience is his use of Casaubon's edition of Persius. It would have been easier to continue with Prateus' edition, which Dryden had already used for Juvenal. Prateus was more "recent" and his volume was much more conveniently arranged, but Dryden recognized the superior authority of the great Frenchman and used his edition almost exclusively. Casaubon is historically perhaps the most important editor of Persius, but most of his emendations have been removed from modern texts; thus Dryden's rendering of this line from the first satire is puzzling if we follow the reading of Prateus, Conington, or Summers:[16]

> Auriculas asini quis non habet? [i. 121; Prateus
>   et al.]

> King Midas has a snout, and ass's ears. [Dryden,
>   I, 240].

Dryden, however, was following Casaubon, not Prateus; Casaubon, on the authority of the Vita Persi substituted Mida for quis, thus referring the line to Nero: ". . . . reddidimus autem Persio suam scripturam: quam a Cornuto interpellatam Neronis metu . . . ." (Casaubon, p. 153). In the third satire of Persius, where in Prateus, Conington, and Summers the text stands:

> non pudet ad morem discincti vivere Nattae [iii. 31]?

we find Dryden ignoring the proper name:

> Dost thou not blush to live so like a beast,
> So trim, so dissolute, so loosely dress'd [III, 57–58]?

Casaubon, on manuscript authority, took Nattae not as a proper name out of Horace but as nattae, a common noun—"fuller"; his further comment accounts for Dryden's rendering:

.... nattae semper in membranis .... proprie sic
vocabant qui sordidas artes exercebant, vt fullones
.... posteà ad animum transtulêre && [sic] vitae
dissolutae homines atque inhonestae ita dixerunt, qualis
fere est vita pullatae turbae, & eorum quos discinctos
Latini, Graeci ἀκλύτοις vocant .... Zonae usus apud
veteres indicium faciebat emendatae vitae & sobriae
.... [Casaubon, p. 248].

A careful student might have noted from a modern apparatus
criticus that Casaubon had read Mida for quis, but neither Summers nor Conington mentions his modification of Nattae. Nor
would the student be any the wiser in examining the translation
of this line:

Mire opifex numeris veterum primordia vocum
.... [vi. 3; Prateus et al.]

Great master of the Muse, inspir'd to sing
The beauties of the first created spring;
The pedigree of nature to rehearse,
And sound the Maker's work, in equal verse
.... [VI, 5–8].

For the phrase primordia vocum, which Persius borrowed from
Lucretius, Casaubon substitutes another, more familiar, phrase
from Lucretius—primordia rerum. Dryden is following Casaubon,
adding on his own account the vaguely Lucretian second line. Without Casaubon before us, we should be certain to condemn Dryden
for pure invention. As it is, we see that he has justification even
for the line which he does invent, for the "beauties of the first
created spring" and the over-Christian "Maker's work" are implicit, for Dryden at least, in the Lucretian reminiscence—
primordia rerum.

Dryden's numerous translations from Ovid furnish similar
evidence of the need for attention to the translator's contemporary
Latin texts. In the selection from the fifteenth book of the Metamorphoses, which Dryden calls "Of the Pythagorean Philosophy,"
the use of a modern text would indicate a stupid mistranslation.
The text given in Postgate's Corpus reads:

> unguibus et <u>puro</u> . . . . ore [xv. 397].

> . . . . with his <u>broad</u> bill and crooked claws
> [<u>Pyth. Phil.</u>, l. 589].

Dryden is quite correct, for Cnipping, his editor, follows Heinsius
in reading <u>pando</u> for <u>puro</u>. In Dryden's version of the first book
of Ovid's <u>Ars amatoria</u> we find an inexplicable translation of a
line which reads in Postgate:

> at cum pompa frequens <u>certantibus ibit ephe-</u>
> <u>bis</u> . . . . [<u>Ars amat.</u> i. 147].

> But when the <u>statues of the deities,</u>
> In chariots roll'd . . . . [<u>Art of love</u>, ll. 172–73].

In Heinsius and Cnipping, however, the reading confirms Dryden:

> At cum pompa frequens <u>coelestibus ibit ebur-</u>
> <u>nis</u>. . . .

Occasionally, as he tells us himself,[17] Dryden refuses to
follow the reading of his editor; often he shows a good sense of
<u>Textkritik</u> in rejecting a variant unsuited to the sense. Thus,
in the twelfth book of the <u>Aeneid</u>, Ruaeus retains a reading which
pictures the despondent Turnus with "downy" cheeks, but Dryden
refuses to see the hero in this unsuitable adolescence:

> <u>Pubentesque</u> genae, & juvenili in corpore pallor
> [xii. 221; Ruaeus].

> <u>A livid deadness</u> in his cheeks appears [XII, 335].

Of the five modern editors of Virgil, only the conservative Sabbadini reads <u>pubentes</u> instead of the more fitting <u>tabentes</u>. Dryden forsook Ruaeus here and edited the text in a manner since
confirmed by the majority of modern editors. Again, Dryden
may make an independent interpretation of his own, even where
there is no question of changing a reading. In this circumstance
he is likely to inform the reader that he is doing so:

> . . . . nunc & de cespite vivo
> Frange aliquid . . . . [Persius vi. 31–32; Casaubon].

> From thy new hope,* and from thy growing store,
> Now lend assistance, and relieve the poor [VI, 72–73].

> * From thy new hope, &c. The Latin is, Nunc et de
> cespite vivo frange aliquid. Casaubon only opposes the
> cespes vivus, which, word for word, is the living turf,
> to the harvest, or annual income; I suppose the poet
> rather means, sell a piece of land already sown, and
> give the money of it to my friend, who has lost all by
> shipwreck; that is, do not stay till thou hast reap'd,
> but help him immediately, as his wants require.[18]

I have been arguing that Dryden was a much more scrupulous
textual scholar than has hitherto been understood or acknowledged,
and I have offered in evidence concrete examples of his meticulous
attention to textual matters. If there is any one trait which characterizes the careful textual student, it is the skeptical frame of
mind which refuses to accept a single editor's opinion as final.
I can think of no better statement of this attitude than Dryden's
own strictures on textual critics:

> As authors generally think themselves the best
> poets, because they cannot go out of themselves to
> judge sincerely of their betters; so it is with critics,
> who, having first taken a liking to one of these poets,
> proceed to comment on him, and to illustrate him; after
> which, they fall in love with their own labors, to that
> degree of blind fondness, that at length they defend and
> exalt their author, not so much for his sake as for their
> own.[19]

That Dryden was anything but homo unius libri is everywhere apparent in his translations.

Another factor which is likely to lead to confusion in comparing Dryden's translations with a modern Latin text is that of
passages excised by recent editors. In many places lines which
were even in Dryden's time under suspicion had not then been
excluded from the accepted text. The incautious student is likely

to be amazed when he reads Dryden's "expansion" of a line and
a half in the Metamorphoses:

> Interea medias fallunt sermonibus horas
> concutiuntque torum . . . . [viii. 651 f.; Postgate].

> . . . . And shorten'd the delay by pleasing chat.
>   "A beam there was, on which a beechen pail
> Hung by the handle, on a driven nail:
> This fill'd with water, gently warm'd, they set   ⎫
> Before their guests; in this they bath'd their feet, ⎬
> And after with clean towels dried their sweat.   ⎭
> This done, the host produced the genial bed . . . ."
>   [Baucis and Philemon, ll. 71–77].

But Heinsius and Cnipping did not suspect lines which were to be
expunged by many later editors even from the apparatus criticus:

> Interea medias fallunt sermonibus horas:
> Sentirique moram prohibent erat alveus illic
> Fagineus, curva clavo suspensus ab ansa:
> Is tepidis impletur aquis; artusque fovendos
> Accipit. in medio torus . . . . [viii. 651–55].

In the translation of Virgil's first Eclogue it would be easy to
charge that Dryden was supplying extra details from his imagination:

> de caelo tactas memini praedicere quercus
>   [Ecl. i. 17; Sabbadini].

> Yon riven oak, the fairest of the green;
> And the hoarse raven, on the blasted bough,
> By croaking from the left, presag'd the coming
>   blow [Pastoral I, 24–26].

But in Ruaeus the line is followed by another, since excised:

> Saepe sinistra cava praedixit ab ilice cornix
>   [Ecl. i. 18].

So far we have been examining Dryden's Latin texts exclusively, ignoring for the moment the accompanying commentaries. These commentaries not only take the place of a modern apparatus criticus but also include explanatory material, parallel passages, conjectures as to the interpretation of difficult passages—all much in the format, to take a contemporary example, of Jebb's edition of Sophocles. It was the helpful practice of the "Delphin" editors to give about half of each page to annotations, and these scholarly aids were not wasted on Dryden, for we have the fullest evidence that he read all the notes carefully and that they exert a constant influence on his translations. They, much more than peculiarities of the text itself, account for many oddities in the translations which must remain inexplicable to anyone not making use of the seventeenth-century editions of the classics. Literally every page of Dryden supplies numerous evidences of the omnipresent influence of the commentators.

Without Ruaeus, for example, we should be unable to explain the singular rendering of this passage from the Aeneid:

> . . . . dirae ferro & compagibus arctis
> Claudentur belli portae . . . . [i. 297–98].

> Janus himself before his fane shall wait,
> And keep the dreadful issues of his gate,
> With bolts and iron bars . . . . [I, 402–4].

Ruaeus' comment on these lines is a bare cross-reference to a later passage in the seventh book of the Aeneid. Dryden was careful to consult the commentary at that point, and his translation incorporates the substance of the later note: "Custos limine Janus.) Vel quia statua ejus erat in limine bifrons: vel quia praeerat omnibus januis . . . ." (Ruaeus, ad vii, 610). In the second book of the Aeneid we find that Dryden's modification of a proper name is also due to Ruaeus:

> . . . . primusque Machaon . . . . [ii. 263].

> Nor was the Podalirian hero last . . . . [II, 343].

> Primusque Machaon.) Aesculapii filius, Podalirii frater . . . . [Ruaeus, ad loc. cit.].

409

The editor's gloss on a strange word or custom often causes a similar explanation in the translation—a kind of concealed footnote. Again from the Aeneid:

> . . . . saevosque gerunt in bella dolones . . . .
> [vii. 664].

> And poles with pointed steel their foes in battle
> gore [VII, 923].

> . . . . Dolonibus: contis ingentibus ligneis; quibus
> . . . . praefixum erat ferrum . . . . [Ruaeus, ad loc.
> cit.].

Dryden often chooses to embody material we should put into footnotes in the translation itself. The prejudice of the age was against a pedantic display of learning,[20] and Dryden wrote only a few scattered notes with great reluctance, as we know from the "Postscript" to his Aeneis.[21] This dislike for pedantic ostentation often accounts for the intrusion of information only implied in the original. A reference in Virgil to the ceremony by which the Romans closed their treaties is explained in Ruaeus by a quotation of the ancient sacrificial formula; Dryden compresses this information (rather cryptically) into an extra line corresponding to nothing in the original:

> . . . . & caesa jungebat foedera porca [viii, 641].

> A fatted sow for sacrifice is led,
> With imprecations on the perjur'd head [VIII,
> 851–52].

> Caesa porca.) . . . . Fecialis, minister san-
> ciendi foederis, sic aiebat: Si prior defecerit publico
> consilio, dolo malo: tu illo die, Jupiter populum
> Romanum sic ferito; ut ego hunc porcum hodie feriam.
> Id ubi dixit, porcum silice percussit . . . . [Ruaeus,
> ad loc. cit.].

In the sixth Eclogue Virgil transforms the sisters of Phaethon into trees. Dryden, following Ruaeus, makes them weep tears of amber for good measure:

Tum Phaetontiadas musco circumdat amarae Corticis,
atque solo proceras erigit alnos [Ecl. vi. 62–63].

> The sisters mourning for their brother's loss;
> Their bodies hid in barks, and furr'd with moss;
> How each a rising alder now appears,
> And o'er the Po distils her gummy tears . . . .
>   [Pastoral VI, 89–92].

Ovidius . . . . ait ex earum ramis electrum, sive
succinum in Eridanum lacrymarum instar stillare
[Ruaeus, ad loc. cit.].

Without Ruaeus how bewildering is the mention of the river Po!
Again in connection with mythology, we discover Dryden com-
pressing the matter of a long note into the neatest of antitheses
within a single line. Not having seen Ruaeus, we should hardly
be able to catch the import:

> Quid loquar? aut Scyllam Nisi . . . . [Ecl. vi. 74].

> Why should I sing the double Scylla's fate?
> (The first by love transform'd, the last by hate
>   . . . .) [Pastoral VI, 105–6].

> . . . . Duplex vulgo Scylla distinguitur: altera
> Nisi Megarensium regis filia, quae patrem, execto
> fatali ejus capillo, prodidit hosti Minoi, cujus amore
> flagrabat . . . . Altera Phorci filia, quae cum amaretur
> a Glauco, per Circes invidiam mutata est inferiori
> parte corporis . . . . [Ruaeus, ad loc. cit.].

The curious translation of a line in the second Georgic rests upon
Ruaeus' interpretation of the passage:

> . . . . nec miseros fallunt aconita legentes . . . .
>   [Georg. ii, 152].

> Nor pois'nous aconite is here produc'd,
> Or grows unknown, or is, when known, refus'd
> . . . . [II, 209–10].

Nascuntur [aconita] & in Italia teste Servio: sed
poeta mira arte utitur ut rem excuset: nam ea dicit
non obesse, quia sunt omnibus nota, nec fallunt legentes
[Ruaeus, ad loc. cit.].

An amusing instance of the rationalistic temper of the age is
Ruaeus' warning to the Grand Dauphin that stars do not really
fall; Dryden likewise does not wish to be caught in a popular
superstition:

Saepe etiam stellas vento impendente videbis
Praecipites coelo labi . . . . [Georg. i. 365–66].

The seeming stars fall headlong from the skies
. . . . [I, 502].

Consentiunt omnes nullam coelo stellam labi,
sed hoc e vulgi mente dictum esse, cui labi videtur
[Ruaeus, ad loc. cit.].

In the first satire of Juvenal an obscure reference to the
birds which nested in the temple of Concord is the occasion for
a long note by Prateus. Dryden read this note carefully and
made it the substance of the translation:

Quaeque salutato crepitat Concordia nido [i.
116].

. . . . Concord, where the stork on high   ⎞
Seems to salute her infant progeny,   ⎬
Presaging pious love with her auspicious cry   ⎠
[I, 173–75].

Concordia, in cujus aedis fastigio aves nidi-
ficantes sonitum edunt & crepitant, quoties ad nidos
redeunt, & pullos quasi salutant, pabulum afferentes.
Cornices intelligit Politian. . . . Alii tamen . . . .
Ciconias significari volunt, quia pietas illis inest,
admirabilis . . . . & quoniam Concordia Ciconiae
forma colebatur . . . . [Prateus, ad loc. cit.].

The editors used by Dryden were more inclined to find hidden
personal references in Juvenal and Persius than is now the
fashion. Without the commentary, the reader is likely to be
startled by the sensational turn Dryden gives to a line in Juvenal:

> Qui bona donavit praesepibus, & caret omni
> Majorum censu, dum pervolat axe citato
> Flaminiam: puer Automedon, nam lora tene-
>   bat
> Ipse lacernatae cum se jactaret amicae [i. 59–62].

> Whose coursers kept, ran out his father's land;
> Who, yet a stripling, Nero's chariot drove,
> Whirl'd o'er the streets, while his vain Master
>   strove
> With boasted art to please his eunuch-love [I,
>   92–95].22

> Ipse lacernatae cum se jactaret amicae.)
> Satirice habitu virili foeminam describit, inquit Vetus
> Schol. At vulgo indigitari putatur juvenis Sporus qui
> Neroni pro uxore fuit . . . . [Prateus, ad loc. cit.]

Exactly similar is a line in Persius, to which Dryden wrote a
footnote as well as expanding the translation. It will be seen that
he is following Casaubon scrupulously, although without acknowledgment:

> Si Puteal multa cautus vibice flagellas . . . .
>   [iv. 48].

> If thy lewd lust provokes an empty storm,
> And prompts to more than nature can per-
>   form;
> If with thy guards23 thou scour'st the streets
>   by night,
> And dost in murthers, rapes, and spoils de-
>   light . . . . [IV, 120–23].

> Si Puteal flagellas, id est, si tanta est tua
> petulantia & lasciuia, vt nocturnus praemiator grasseris,

413

cum obuiis rixam contrahēs, & pudori matronarum
illudens, nullum denique insolentiae genus praeter-
mittens. Hoc genere insignem primum se fecit Nero,
cum foras erumperet illius probra, quem ad modū
disertè scribit Dio. Existimo circa illa tempora,
aut non longe pòst scripsisse Persium istud carmen:
vt valde mirer e tot interpretibus huius poetae
nemini istius interpretationis hactenus, quod sciam,
venisse in mentem [Casaubon, p. 354].

This is an extreme example of the necessity for a knowledge of
texts actually used by Dryden.

Persius combines constant allusiveness with compressed
brevity of expression. Because he is such a difficult writer,
Dryden is more than usually indebted to his editor for explanatory
paraphrases. In many places his translation is more of Casaubon
than of Persius. The following example is typical; note how
Dryden expands the "synecdoche" on Casaubon's authority:

> His mane edictum, post prandia Calliroen do
> [i. 134].

> Such, all the morning, to the pleadings run; ⎫
> But, when the bus'ness of the day is done, ⎪
> On dice, and drink, and drabs, they spend ⎬
>   their afternoon [I, 273–75]. ⎭

> Studia eorum exponit, quibus satirarum suarum
> lectione interdicebat: ait istos duo solum curasse:
> forum, propter auaritiam: & lupanaria, amore
> voluptatis . . . . Callirhoes voce heic, (nomen id
> scorti quondam celeberrimi) vniuersa voluptuariorum
> studia, atq. occupationes συνεκδοχικῶς intelliguntur
> (Casaubon, pp. 167 f.].

In Persius' fifth satire Dryden again translates Casaubon's paraphrase of a difficult line rather than the original itself:

> Haereat in stultis breuis vt semuncia recti.
> Haec miscere nefas . . . . [v. 121–22].

414

> Virtue and Vice are never in one soul:
> A man is wholly wise, or wholly is a fool [V,
> 175–76].

> Haereat . . . .) vt sapiens vlla ex parte sit, qui
> non totus sapit Ratio Stoicorum: quia virtutes se
> mutuò consequantur: ut qui unam habeat omnes habere
> sit necesse. & contrà: qui vna careat omnibus nudatum
> esse necessariò . . . . [Casaubon, p. 432].

But, even with Casaubon, Dryden was not a man of one book,
for he was conscientious enough to consult Prateus occasionally.
This can be seen from the translation of a single word in the first
satire of Persius:

> . . . . Nolo . . . . [i. 11].

> FRIEND. Once more forbear [I, 27].

> Nolo.) concludens satiram omnino se scrip-
> turum, veniam facti petit, quod alter verbo negat
> [Casaubon, p. 52].

> Nolo) Non sinam, inquit monitor: ab his abstineas
> jubeo [Prateus, ad loc. cit.].

A little further on it is plain that Prateus' note was again preferred to that of Casaubon:

> Ten' cirratorum centum dictata fuisse
> Pro nihilo pendas [i. 29–30]?

> That's he whose wondrous poem is become
> A lecture for the noble youth of Rome [I, 62–
> 63]!

> . . . . cirratos dici pueros qui ludum frequentant,
> item capillatos & crinitos, etiam pueri sciunt [Casaubon,
> p. 80].

> Cirratorum.) Id est, nobilium juvenum, quorum
> cirrati solent esse capilli . . . . [Prateus, ad loc. cit.]

The same is true with Ovid; Dryden did not commit himself
wholly to the interpretations of a single authority. In the story
of Meleager and Atalanta he drew a picturesque mythological
detail from the "Delphin" editor, Crispinus.[24] This information
is not given in Heinsius or Cnipping:

> .... natis in corpore pennis
> Allevat; & longas per brachia porrigit alas:
> Corneaque ora facit; versasque per aëra mittit
> [Metam. viii. 543–45].

> .... but with wings endued,
> And horny beaks, and sent to flit in air;
> Who yearly round the tomb in feather'd flocks
> repair [Mel. and Atal., ll. 400–402].

> Porrigit) .... Ideo vero Meleagri nomine in-
> signitae illae aves, quod certis quibusdam temporibus
> in Boeotiam ex Africa circa Meleagri tumulum con-
> volarent [Crispinus, ad loc. cit.].

Likewise peculiar to Crispinus is the note which results in the
unappetizing menu that Dryden sets upon the table of Baucis and
Philemon:

> .... epulasque foci misere calentes .... [Me-
> tam. viii. 671].

> By this the boiling kettle had prepar'd
> And to the table sent the smoking lard ....
> [Bauc. and Phil., ll. 106–7].

> Epulas) Lardum nempe cum oleribus ....
> [Crispinus, ad loc. cit.].

However, Cnipping was still at Dryden's elbow. In his notes to
the tenth book of the Metamorphoses, Crispinus does not give the
other name for the constellation Boötes, which Dryden evidently
found metrically convenient:

> Tempus erat quo cuncta silent; interque
> Triones

Flexerat obliquo plaustrum temone Boŏtes
[Metam. x. 446–47].

'T was depth of night: Arctophylax had driv'n
His lazy wain half round the northern heav'n
. . . . [Cinyras and Myrrha, ll. 264–65].

Bootes.) Sydus est Bootes, qui & Arctophylax
appelatur [Cnipping, ad loc. cit.].

It has now been sufficiently demonstrated that a critic of
Dryden's translations must exercise extreme caution in pointing
out "errors." It is impossible to do so without a careful examination of all the editors which Dryden may have used, as was shown
in connection with Cnipping and Crispinus. Genuine errors do
occur, but they are much more infrequent than has usually been
assumed. On rare occasions Dryden is careless in reading his
editor and may make a slip in geography, as in these words from
Virgil:

. . . . Grynaeus Apollo . . . . [Aen. iv. 345].

. . . . Aeneas Phoebi monita de quaerenda Italia,
neque Grynii, neque Patarae accepisset; sed in insula
Delo . . . . nomina Grynaei & Lycii, unus idemque
Apollo, ejusque oraculum, non locus significatur . . . .
[Ruaeus, ad loc. cit.].

. . . . the Delphian oracle . . . . [IV, 496].

Or the translator may be guilty of a genuine misunderstanding of
the Latin:

Tum Salii ad cantus, incensa altaria circum
. . . . [Aen. viii. 285].

The Salii sing, and cense his altar round
With Saban smoke . . . . [VIII, 377–78].

Dryden once refers an action to the wrong character:

> At juveni oranti subitus tremor occupat artus,
> Diriguere oculi . . . . [Aen. vii. 446–47].

> And frighted Turnus trembled as she spoke.
> Her eyes grow stiffen'd . . . . [VII, 623–24].

In another place Dryden seems wilfully to pervert the plain sense of the original:

> . . . . bijugique ad fraena leones . . . . [Aen. x. 253].

> Fierce tigers, rein'd and curb'd, obey thy will
> [X, 356].

All these may be called downright mistakes, for Dryden with a little more attention to his editors might have avoided them; they are all careless and seemingly involuntary.

Yet the reader may well ask: Why are Dryden's translations so much longer than their originals? The answer has two parts: (1) he was writing in heroic couplets, which encourage a tendency to give two lines for one, and (2) he inserted extraneous details of his own volition. This last point militates in no way against an apology for Dryden's scholarship, because such additions are always perfectly voluntary and conscious. This tendency toward expansiveness belongs in criticism to the province of style, not to that of classical learning, and cannot be treated here. I give two random examples to make plain that Dryden's scholarship is in no way concerned. Dryden refurbishes a shrine in Ovid with the utensils of Roman Catholic worship:

> Primus Ophionides Amycus penetralia donis
> Haud timuit spoliare suis; & primus ab aede
> Lampadibus densum rapuit funale coruscis
> . . . . [Metam. xii. 245–47].

> Bold Amycus from the robb'd vestry brings
> The chalices of heav'n, and holy things
> Of precious weight: a sconce, that hung on
>   high,
> With tapers fill'd, to light the sacristy . . . .
>   [XII, 342–45].

Dryden is fond of inserting sly digs at his political enemies. In Ovid's seventh Epistle, which Dryden translated in 1680, there is a plain allusion to the Exclusion Bill of Shaftesbury:

> Quis sua non notis arva tenenda dabit [Epist. vii. 16]?

> What people is so void of common sense,
> To vote succession from a native prince [Dido to Aeneas, ll. 17–18]?

These modifications are typical of hundreds inserted by Dryden with the intent of giving a "modern" flavor and vivacity to his work; it would be a pedant who could object to his translation of Ovid's Palatia coeli:

> Hic locus est; quem, si verbis audacia detur,
> Haud timeam magni dixisse Palatia coeli [Metam. i. 175–76].

> This place, as far as earth with heav'n may vie,
> I dare to call the Louvre of the sky [I, 226–27]. 25

These examples of genuine errors and conscious modifications will serve to qualify our estimate of Dryden's scholarly ability. His errors are almost negligibly few, his intentional modifications many. The charge of scholarly incompetence and textual carelessness has been shown to be unfounded. Dryden cannot be called a professional expert in classical studies,26 but there are few great translators who can claim that title. Dryden was engaged in reinterpreting the classics for his own generation, a recurring necessity in any living tradition of literature, and he wrote within a convention which demanded (not allowed) greater license in translation than is now permissible. Dryden's critics have confused this license with ignorance, mistaking for scholarly ineptitude his vigorously asserted prerogatives as a poetic translator. The critics may therefore be charged on two counts: ignorance of seventeenth-century classical learning and failure to allow for the convention of translation within which Dryden was working.

It is the purpose of this paper not only to establish the fact that Dryden was a competent and conscientious classical scholar

but also to caution prospective editors of Dryden that the text of
the translations has yet to be properly edited. The edition of
Professor Noyes is invaluable in its fidelity to the earliest editions
of the translations, but it does not claim to take into account the
evidence of Dryden's classical authorities. Not only would a full
edition throw light on Dryden's careful methods of work but it
would in places eliminate from the text typographical errors
which have stood unquestioned from the first edition to the present.
Thus the ridiculous line in the first Georgic would be restored to
the form in which Dryden wrote it:

> . . . . hinc ille avium concentus in agris,
> Et laetae pecudes, & ovantes gutture corvi
> [Georg. i. 422–23].

> From hence proceeds the birds' harmonious
> voice:
> From hence the cows exult, and frisking lambs
> rejoice [I, 569–70].

Although corvi is properly "ravens," there can be no real doubt
that Dryden wrote "crows" not "cows" — Dryden could never have
been guilty of an exulting cow. There is in addition a mass of new
material — political allusions, borrowings from earlier translators
and from other poets,[27] stylistic and metrical matters — which
have not yet been noticed because so little close attention has been
directed to the translations. If Dryden is ever to be accorded the
honor of a new and comprehensive edition of his works like those
recent and monumental editions of Spenser, Milton, and Pope, let
us pray that the editor of the translations does not call their
author a poor scholar.

NOTES

1 Notes on Dryden's Virgil, in a letter to a friend, with an
  essay on the same poet (London, 1698).

2 The works of John Dryden, ed. Sir Walter Scott and George
  Saintsbury (Edinburgh, 1882–93), XII, 1.

3 (New York and Cambridge, 1933), VIII, 56.

4   Ludovicus Prateus (Louis Desprès) (ed.), D. Junii Juvenalis et A. Persii Flacci satirae (Paris, 1684).

5   Carolus Ruaeus (Charles de la Rue) (ed.), P. Virgilii Maronis opera (Paris, 1675).

6   Isaac Casaubon (ed.), Auli Persi Flacci satirarum liber (Paris, 1605).

7   The poetical works of John Dryden, ed. G. R. Noyes ("Student's Cambridge edition" [Cambridge, Mass. (1909)]), p. 90. All quotations of Dryden are taken from this source.

8   I have been obliged to use the Elzevir reprint of Heinsius: Operum P. Ovidii Nasonis editio nova (3 vols.; Amsterdam, 1658–61). The opinion cited by Dryden is in the Notae, I, 3: "Epistolas tamen Ovidius ipse libro III. Artis Amatoriae videtur nuncupare. . . . ."

9   Borchard Cnipping (ed.), P. Ovidii Nasonis opera (4 vols.; Leyden, 1670). The heading of the Epistles reads: "P. Ovidii Nasonis Epistolarum Heroidum Liber."

10 A separate article rather than a single footnote would be necessary for a discussion of Dryden's debt to earlier English translations. His borrowings are of three types: rhymes, phrases, and entire lines or even passages. Dryden is indebted in varying degrees to at least fifteen of his predecessors: to Creech and Evelyn for Lucretius; to Sandys for Ovid; to Holyday and Stapylton for Juvenal; to Holyday for Persius; to Ogilby, Lauderdale, Roscommon, Stafford, Cowley, Denham, Waller, Godolphin, Normanby, and Addison for Virgil. For example, in translating the second book of the Aeneid, Dryden borrowed without acknowledgment five lines from Denham's fragment The destruction of Troy: an essay upon the second book of Virgils Aeneis (London, 1656). The lines in Dryden's Aeneis, with the corresponding pages in Denham's translation are: Dryden, ii, 274/Denham, p. 11; Dryden, ii, 318/Denham, p. 13; Dryden, ii, 351/Denham, p. 14; Dryden, ii, 442/Denham, p. 17; Dryden, ii, 514/Denham, p. 19.

11 ". . . . Gilbert Dolben . . . . who, when I began this work, enrich'd me with all the several editions of Virgil, and all

the commentaries of those editions in Latine; amongst which I could not but prefer the Dolphin's, as the last, the shortest, and the most judicious" (Dryden's "Postscript to the reader," ed. Noyes, p. 708).

12 I have taken the editions of these five modern editors of Virgil as typical: John Conington (4th ed.; revised by Henry Nettleship [London, 1881]); T. L. Papillon and A. E. Haigh (New York, n.d.); H. Rushton Fairclough ("Loeb Classical Library" [London, 1930]); Remigio Sabbadini (Rome, 1930).

13 Ruaeus includes the prooemium in his numbering of the lines of the first book of the Aeneid. Hence, four lines must be deducted to make this correspond to the numbering of a modern text.

14 In Postgate's Corpus poetarum Latinorum (London, 1905–20).

15 All obscene words are deleted in the "Delphin" text but, incredibly, are brought together again in an appendix: "Resecti Versus . . . . Nemini Probo Legendi. Ex Edicto Jul. Scaligeri. . . . ." I have restored the text from this source.

16 John Conington (ed.), The satires of A. Persius Flaccus (Oxford, 1893); and W. C. Summers in Postgate's Corpus poetarum Latinorum.

17 ". . . . I have forsaken Ruaeus (whom generally I follow) in many places, and made expositions of my own in some, quite contrary to him" ("Dedication of the Aeneis," ed. Noyes, pp. 513–14). The whole passage, too long to quote, is worth examining.

18 This is Dryden's note 5 (ed. Noyes, p. 381).

19 Discourse concerning satire, ed. Noyes, p. 303.

20 An illuminating example of this prejudice in a work admired by Dryden may be found in Roscommon's An essay on translated verse (London, 1684), p. 5:

"The Soil intended for Pierian seeds,
Must be well purg'd from rank Pedantick Weeds.

> Apollo starts, and All Parnassus shakes,
> At the rude Rumbling Baralipton makes.
> For None have been, with Admiration, read,
> But who (beside their Learning) were Well-Bred."

21 ". . . . the few Notes which follow are par manière d'àcquit, because I had oblig'd myself by articles to do somewhat of that kind. These scattering observations are rather guesses at my author's meaning in some passages than proofs that so he meant. The unlearn'd may have recourse to any poetical dictionary in English, for the names of persons, places, or fables, which the learned need not; but that little which I say is either new or necessary" ("Postscript to the reader," ed. Noyes, p. 709).

22 Dryden's own note 16 to this line gives another interpretation as well: "His eunuch-love. Nero married Sporus, an eunuch; tho' it may be, the poet meant Nero's mistress in man's apparel" (ed. Noyes, p. 326).

23 Dryden's note 10: "If with thy guards, &c. Persius durst not have been so bold with Nero as I dare now; and therefore there is only an intimation of that in him which I publicly speak: I mean, of Nero's walking the streets by night in disguise, and committing all sorts of outrages, for which he was sometimes well beaten" (ed. Noyes, p. 372).

24 Daniel Crispinus (ed.), Publii Ovidii Nasonis opera (4 vols.; Lyons, 1689).

25 This is an interesting symptom of the growth of French cultural influence during the seventeenth century. Sandys in 1626 translated the same words—Palatia coeli—as "White-Hall."

26 Dryden evidently knew much less Greek than Latin. Mark Van Doren (The poetry of John Dryden [New York, 1920], p. 271) asserts (without proof) that Dryden did not use the original at all in translating the first book of the Iliad. I have never been able to verify this statement, and Professor Van Doren, after a lapse of twenty years, could not find his notes on the subject, although he was kind enough to make a search at my request. I very much doubt whether any American library contains a sufficient number of seventeenth-

century editions of Homer to settle the point—those of Harvard, Yale, and Congress do not. Dryden's editor for Theocritus has been identified and well examined by F. H. Pughe in John Dryden's Uebersetzungen aus Theokrit (Breslau, 1894), pp. 5–10.

27 A typical unnoted example is l. 110 of Dryden's translation of Ovid's Ars amatoria, Book I: "Some to undo, and some to be undone." This is word for word the thirty-second line of Denham's Cooper's hill.

DRYDEN'S ODES AND DRAGHI'S MUSIC

Ernest Brennecke, Jr.

The study of any choral lyric, properly so called, and designed to be sung and otherwise performed by a group of executants on a specific public occasion, must be considerably hampered when its original musical setting is not at hand. Indeed the appreciation of such a poem as <u>Alexander's Feast</u> can be only partial at best if the text is read with the comparatively simple apparatus that one usually brings to bear upon a sonnet by Sidney. When the music to a choral ode was no afterthought but rather an integral part of the whole performance, the divorcement of the words from their setting results in an inevitable loss of understanding and of proper response. The ideal way to absorb any choral lyric, whether it be by Pindar, the author of the Book of Judges, or Dryden, would be to hear, if not to participate in, the complex display of sound through which its author intended it to be proclaimed. And since one cannot be present at the original performance of any save contemporary compositions of the kind, it becomes imperative to reconstruct, through the vigorous use of both study and imagination, the original circumstances and the original music which accompained the poem.

We cannot hope to accomplish much of this reconstruction with many choral lyrics of the past, having too meagre a supply of the necessary data. But with Dryden's "occasional" odes, in particular with his two Cecilian productions, we are unusually fortunate. We may occasionally even hear them sung by chorus, soloists, and orchestra in a public concert which approaches the conditions attending their first performances. The music to which they are now usually sung, however, was composed by Handel a generation after Dryden's death, and gives us less insight than we require into the quality of the poet's actual achievement. A

Reprinted by permission of the Modern Language Association from <u>Publications of the Modern Language Association</u>, Vol. 49 (1934), pp. 1–34, and by permission of the author.

detailed view of Dryden's accomplishment can now be obtained
only through a study of the musical settings which he himself
heard and which were composed by his own musical collaborators.
Unfortunately, the original score of Alexander's Feast has been
lost. But the very competent setting of his Song for St. Cecilia's
Day of 1687, by Giovanni Baptista Draghi, is preserved in at least
two manuscripts, and has been examined by the writer.

Three functions will be served by the following discussion
of the original extant music for the Cecilian poems. First, it
will provide the sentimental satisfaction of "hearing" what was
actually heard when the poems were first delivered to the world.
Second, it will demonstrate that the poet consciously designed
his ode as a part of a larger production, in which the poetry, far
from being an independent entity, shared significance and importance with the music. Third, it will demonstrate that many
of the striking features of Alexander's Feast can be properly
understood only as the direct results of Dryden's experiences
in writing the 1687 ode and in observing its treatment at the hands
of the Cecilian musicians. The final result of the discussion will,
it is hoped, be an intensified appreciation of Dryden's composition,
properly recognized as extraordinary poetic solutions to extraordinary poetic problems.

I

The celebrations of St. Cecilia's Day in London from 1683
to 1710 have been described in W. H. Husk's valuable monograph[1]
and the circumstances need only to be very briefly summarized
here. An organization of professionals and amateurs called The
Musical Society arranged annual concerts on the Saint's day,
November 22, delegating the details to the management of six
"stewards of the feast." The stewards commissioned an ode
from a poet and delivered his text to a composer. When the
musical score was completed it was rehearsed by a chorus of
sixty voices, soloists, and an orchestra of about twenty instruments. The performance usually took place in Stationers Hall,
preceded by divine service at St. Bride's and followed by a feast.

The ode[2] for the first festival in 1683 was written by Christopher Fishburn, about whom little is known. His poem for this
occasion, a rather inept piece, had the good fortune to be set by

A
𝕸𝖚𝖘𝖎𝖈𝖆𝖑 𝕰𝖓𝖙𝖊𝖗𝖙𝖆𝖎𝖓𝖒𝖊𝖓𝖙

PERFORM'D

On NOVEMBER XXII. 1683.

IT BEING THE

Feſtival of St. CECILIA, *a great* Patroneſs *of* Muſic;

WHOSE

MEMORY is ANNUALLY honour'd by a public *Feaſt* made on that Day by the MASTERS and LOVERS of 𝕸𝖚𝖘𝖎𝖈, as well in *England* as in Foreign Parts.

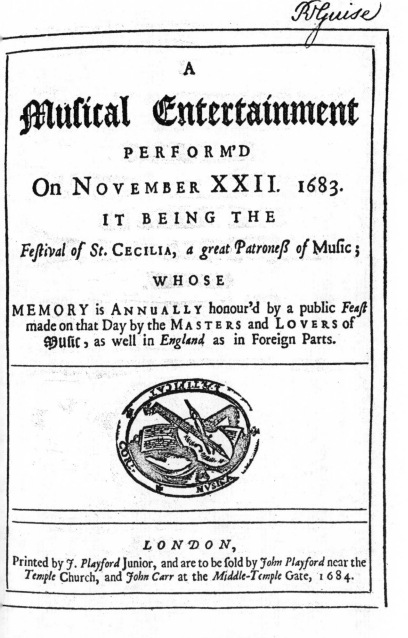

LONDON,

Printed by *J. Playford* Junior, and are to be ſold by *John Playford* near the *Temple* Church, and *John Carr* at the *Middle-Temple* Gate, 1 6 8 4.

6

Verse.

Welcom, welcom, to all the Pleasures that de-

Welcom, welcom, to all the Pleasures that de-

Welcom, to all the Pleasures that de-

Welcom,

light, of ev'ry Sense, the grate—ful Ap—pe—tite.

light, of ev'ry Sense, of ev'ry Sense, the grateful Ap-pe-tite.

light, of ev'ry Sense, the grate-ful, grate—ful Ap-pe-tite.

Chorus.

Hail, hail great Assembly of A-pol-lo's Race,

Hail, hail great Assembly of A-pol-lo's Race,

Hail, hail great Assembly of A-pol-lo's Race,

Hail, hail great Assembly of A-pol-lo's Race,

Hail great Assembly.

Hail great Assembly.

Hail, hail great Assembly of A-pol-lo's Race,

hail to this hap——py place, hap—py place, this

hail to this hap

hail to this hap——py place, to this

hail to this hap——py place, this Musical - As-sem-bly;

hail to this hap

hail to this hap——py place;

hail to this place;

Purcell, for the usual four-part chorus, treble, alto, tenor, and bass soloists, and an orchestra of strings only. No percussion or wind instruments were used.

The completed composition[3] opens with a symphony[4] for the orchestra, consisting of two short sections: first a grave and massive movement using free contrapuntal imitation, then a lively dance in triple time. The poem itself is treated as follows.

> 1. Welcome to all the Pleasures that delight
>   Of ev'ry Sense, the grateful Appetite!
>   Hail, great Assembly of Apollo's Race!

In a slow movement in minor, the word "welcome" is sung first by the bass soloist, then by the tenor, then by the alto. All three together sing lines 1 and 2. In line 3, the alto sings "hail" on a sudden change of harmony, and is then joined by the tenor and bass for the words "great Assembly." The full chorus then enters with the word "hail," and after a silent beat sings "Hail, great Assembly of Apollo's Race," in simple triad harmony, probably forte.

> 4. Hail to this happy place,
>   This Musical Assembly, that seems to be
>   The Ark of Universal Harmony!

Lines 4–6 are sung to a solid marching rhythm by the whole chorus, with little repetition of the words. The rhythm is then carried out and the movement completed in a ritornello for the orchestra.

> 7. Here the deities approve
>   (The God of Music and of Love,)
>   All the talents they have lent you,
>   All the blessings they have sent you;
>   Pleas'd to see what they bestow
>   Live and thrive so well below;

For lines 7–12, Purcell invented a "ground-bass" theme, three measures in length, which is repeated without alteration nineteen times.[5] The alto soloist enters with a suave melody at the first repetition,

continuing through the eighth, after which the violins
and violas play further variations over the bass to the
end. This movement has proved to be one of Purcell's
most successful compositions, and is also found adapted
to the harpsichord, in the second part of his Musick's
Handmaid under the name of A new ground.

>   13. While joys celestial their bright souls invade,
>   To find what great improvement you have made.

To the singularly amateurish lines 13–14, there is a
brisk trio for two solo trebles and tenor, followed by a
ritornello for the strings in the same manner.

>   15. Then lift up your voices, those Organs of Nature,
>   Those Charms to the troubled and amorous
>   Creature;
>   17. The Pow'r shall divert us a pleasanter way;
>   For Sorrow and Grief
>   Find from Music relief,
>   And Love its soft charms must obey.

At line 15 the bass soloist sings a strong and vigorous
air in triple time, and is joined by the chorus for the
repetition. The chorus continues in the same rhythm
through line 20, then repeats lines 15 and 16.

>   21. Beauty, thou Scene of Love,
>   And Virtue, thou innocent Fire,
>   Made by the Powers above
>   24. To temper the heat of desire;
>   Music, that Fancy employs
>   In Rapture of innocent Flame,
>   We offer with Lute and with Voice
>   To Cecilia, Cecilia's bright Name.

After a beautiful independent slow passage of only four
measures of alla breve, the tenor soloist sings lines
21–28 as an expressive air, with repetition of both words
and music of lines 21–24. The orchestra repeats the
number.

> 29. In a Consort of Voices, while Instruments play,
>   With Music we celebrate this Holy Day;
>   Iô Cecilia.

With line 29, the music shifts brilliantly from minor
to major. The tenor sings lines 29–31; then the chorus,
entering successively with soprano, alto, tenor, and bass,
presently joined by the violins in independent parts,
brings the composition to a spirited conclusion.

Several things are worth noting in the above performance: its
brevity (the delivery could not have consumed more than twenty-
five minutes),[6] the feebleness and puerility of the words, in both
idea and expression, and the unfailing competence of the music.
Purcell was given only the slenderest of opportunities to display
his phenomenal dramatic skill, yet his music was undoubtedly
responsible for the initial success of the Cecilian idea.

For the "second entertainment" in 1684, John Oldham was
commissioned to write the ode. It was a remarkable improvement over Fishburn's effort, at least in style and construction.
But it shows no great advance in idea. The opening faintly fore-
shadows Dryden in its allusions to instruments:

> Begin the song! Your instruments advance!
>   Tune the voice and tune the flute,
>   Touch the silent, sleeping lute,
> And make the strings to their own measures dance, . . .

The second stanza is likewise interesting:

> Hark! how the waken'd strings resound,
> And sweetly break the yielding air!
> The ravish'd sense how pleasingly they wound,
> And call the list'ning soul into the ear!
> Each pulse beats time, and ev'ry heart
> With tongue and fingers bears a part.
>   By harmony's entrancing pow'r
> When we are thus wound up to extacy,
>   Methinks we mount, methinks we tow'r,
> And seem to antedate our future bliss on high.

The rest of it is thoroughly conventional.

The musical setting, "in two, three, four, and five Parts," was entrusted to John Blow, Purcell's renowned teacher, whose confidence in his powers was so great that he committed his score to the press before the performance. Copies are now preserved in a number of libraries.

The composition opens with an overture in G minor for the strings (which comprise the entire orchestra), a <u>maestoso</u> movement in <u>alla breve</u> time. The first four lines of the poem are set to an expressive recitative for alto with a figured bass, and after a <u>ritornello</u> are repeated by a five-part chorus singing vigorously in free imitation. The air, "Bring gentlest Thoughts," is again given to the alto, and is followed by a four-part chorus in stricter fugal style, ending with "For this is Music's Sacred Jubilee." There is some drama in the staccato repetition of the word "this" by the full chorus against florid counterpoint in the violins. The tenor soloist joins the alto in a duet, "Hark, how the wakened strings resound," with effective repetition of "hark" and some elegant voice-leading. Set off by <u>ritornelli</u>, the alto and then the chorus deliver the lines, "By Harmonies entrancing Pow'r" in the solid tonality of C major. "How dull were life" is treated in a bass and treble duet in G, with the accompaniment of one violin and bass. The tenor soloist delivers "Without the sweets of melody," and after a <u>ritornello</u> there follows the most successful piece in the score, the bass solo, "Music's the cordial of a troubled Breast," with accompaniment of two violins and bass. This number, which offers the singer some excellent opportunities for tone and declamation, was reprinted in Blow's later collection of airs, <u>Amphion Anglicus</u>. The final chorus, "Come then with tuneful Breath," is treated conventionally in a four-part chorus.

The setting is throughout melodious and competent. And in spite of the fact that Burney made a famous to-do over Blow's supposed "crudities" and his "licentiousness as a contrapuntist" (having been outraged by a few un-Handelian progressions), this setting contains nothing that shows greater technique and little that shows

a stronger imagination than Purcell's music of the preceding
year. And its general plan is considerably more stilted.

Nahum Tate wrote the poem for 1685. It is an amusing effort,
opening:

> Tune the viol, touch the lute,
> Wake the harp, inspire the flute,
> Call the jolly swains away;
> Love and Music reign today.

Pastoral effects are attempted in the following lines: kids and
lambkins, then nymphs and jolly swains, are joined finally by
Angels "in consort from above." There is some imitation of
Oldham, and some anticipation of future Cecilian poetry, in the
fourth stanza:

> What charms can Music not impart,
> That through the ear finds passage to the heart!
> In vain the Muse indites a lover's tale,
> In vain his doleful words declare
> His passion to the cruel fair,
> 'Tis Music only makes his song prevail, etc.

The final stanza again calls upon the jolly swains, and victorious
heroes, to celebrate the occasion.

Tate's doggerel was set by William Turner, a composer of
modest attainments, chiefly renowned for his extraordinarily pure
and flexible alto voice. He sang as a chorister in Lincoln Cathedral as well as in the Chapel Royal, was appointed a vicar choral
in St. Paul's and a lay vicar at Westminster. He was to play a
considerable part in the production of Dryden's ode in 1687. His
own music for the ode of 1685 was not printed, and no manuscript
has survived.

The celebration for this year was apparently a disastrous
failure, the novelty of the idea having worn out and neither the
poet nor the musician being able to maintain public interest.
The Musical Society, in discouragement, promoted no festival
for the following year. Thus ended the first phase of the Cecilian
tradition, having produced only one musical composition, and no
poetry, of any significance. The right form and the right quality
of expression for these occasions was still to be invented.

II

It was decided to revive the Feast in 1687. Determined to avoid all chances of another and perhaps fatal fiasco, the stewards came to Dryden for the ode. And they could not have chosen more wisely. Dryden had already exhibited his extraordinary powers as an "occasional" poet. He possessed to a unique degree that sensitivity to public events which made him an incomparable laureate. His responses were, broadly speaking, those of the masses, and his command over vocabulary and metrical diction was imperial. Depending equally on study, intuition, and conscious design, he very naturally handled the Cecilian situation with unprecedented competence—though not with complete mastery, as will be shown.

He had at hand the fumbling efforts of his predecessors, and at least some familiarity with the music of the period. He had certainly heard the anthems of Blow and Purcell. He knew the music of the theatre,[7] which was not strikingly different from that of the church at the time, and he had very possibly been present at one or more of the Cecilian festivals. There is one other significant poem which he may have read. Although there was no London celebration in 1686, there may have been one at Oxford, and at Oxford a young Fellow of New College, Thomas Fletcher, wrote an Ode on the Feast of St. Cecilia, 1686. It was not published until seven years later, in Fletcher's Poems on several occasions, but it contains a passage similar to a portion of Dryden's poem. It opens conventionally, with some poor rhymes—noise and verse, sacred day and Cecilia.[8] But in its second stanza we find:

> Methinks I now behold sweet Orpheus sit
> On Strymon's bank, and tune his lyre
> To sounds which life and vig'rous joys inspire:
> Round him the list'ning beasts their food forget,
> Forget to play,
> And without motion round the charmer stay.
> But nimbler trees when they the music hear,
> (Music which gives them ear,)
> Leap forth, and wanton round the place;
> Trees skip, like beasts; beasts stand unmov'd, like trees
> Pines, elms, and cedars in long rows advance,
> An aged oak leads up the dance:

> Two hundred years it stood the wood's chief pride,
> So long Jove's bolts and struggling winds defied;
> Now from its bed of earth away it tears,
> And round its spreading roots a weighty mountain bears.

— which whole idea Dryden compressed into three short lines:

> Orpheus could lead the savage race;
> And trees unrooted left their place,
> Sequacious of the lyre.

It is interesting to speculate on the hints that Dryden may have picked up here and there. Van Doren has, for instance, suggested the partial derivation of his scheme from Oldham,[9] and his Angel may even have come from Tate. Verrall states with more confidence that the idea of chaos and cosmos derived from Milton's At a Solemn Musick and On the Morning of Christ's Nativity.[10] The evidence of the words nature, jarring, diapason, used by both poets, is persuasive. But it is both more fascinating and more useful to note the virtuosity with which Dryden created almost the precise form and style for which the occasion was waiting. His first stanza tells every reader that here is genuine poetry; his whole ode immediately tells every musician that here is a genuine libretto, displaying virtues that well over-balance its defects as such. The cosmic conception of the first stanza provides something of the desired opportunity for massive chorus work and eloquent declamation. There follows the series of contrasted strophes, treating successively the lyre, the trumpet, the flute, the violin, the organ. And having begun with harmony and cosmos, he ends with dissolution and chaos. Van Doren declares that in this ode each verse became "for practical purposes an orchestra, the poet drawing upon his vowels and cadences as a conductor draws upon his players."[11] This is a fair statement of the achievement if one disregards the occasion, but it would probably be nearer to the facts to observe that the poet knew his audience, which demanded something imposing and sensational, and that he knew his musicians, who wanted variety, "singability," and plenty of opportunities for the display of their own proper technique and art — and a form that would result in little or no distortion in the process of being set.

It would be going much too far to assume that Dryden at the start knew precisely how the musician would treat every phrase in his ode. There is indeed no doubt that he had only very broad notions of the effects that could be produced. He was certainly aware of the function of these verses as complementary to the music. But it is one thing to be merely aware of such a relationship, and quite another thing to have direct and intense personal experience of it. Such direct experience, which was to have a telling effect in the sequel of 1697, was provided by the handling that his poem was now accorded. We shall see how certain defects in this first ode, when considered purely as a composer's vehicle, significantly failed to reappear in Alexander's Feast.

The composer chosen was Giovanni Baptista Draghi, generally known to his English contemporaries as Signor Baptist. He was a musician of no mean talents. He was possibly born in Ferrara, and it has been conjectured that he was a relative of Antonio Draghi, composer of operas and maestro di capella at Vienna.[12] He is supposed to have been one of those musicians who came to England with Mary d'Este, Princess of Modena, consort of James II. He rapidly made his way as an expert player of the harpsichord and became a favorite court musician, quickly adapting his style to that of the English masters. He wrote anthems, ballad airs, dance tunes, and madrigals. He appears in an interesting passage in Pepys's diary (February 12, 1666–67).

Draghi joined with Locke in composing music to the opera Psyche, and when Locke died, in 1677, succeeded as organist to the Queen's chapel, a position he was still holding in 1684. Draghi later published Six select suites of lessons for the harpsichord, was music master to Queen Anne in her youth, and probably contributed part of the music to D'Urfey's opera, The Wonders in the Sun, or The Kingdom of the Birds, which was performed at the Queen's Theatre, Haymarket, in July, 1706.

III

The complete manuscript score of Draghi's setting of the ode, From Harmony, possibly in the composer's handwriting, was preserved in the library of the Sacred Harmonic Society.[13] Upon the dissolution of the Society in 1882 the library, including this item, was acquired by the Royal College of Music. There is another copy in the British Museum, contained in a large manuscript folio (add. MS 33287). This folio contains, among others,

Sign.r Baptists Song

On St. Cecilias Day

1687

Performd att Stationers

Hall

Blow's Cecilian ode of 1684 and, in different and rather later hands, both Purcell's Sound the trumpet of 1687 and Draghi's ode. It is imperfect in the middle and end, however, and names only one of the singers, Mr. Abell, whereas the R. C. M. MS. names twelve. The only fact which would indicate that the latter copy is not one of the earliest is that on page 7 we find the re-mark, "Just here begins Dr. Turner," and all authorities[14] agree that Turner received his doctorate no earlier than 1696. But on page 6, which repeats some of page 7, the remark reads, "Just here begins Mr. Turner," and he is called "Mr. Turner" in six additional places in the manuscript. The "Dr." may have been only a respectful slip. The care and profuseness with which the singers' names are assigned to the various passages in the MS., and its wealth of directions as to orchestration and performance, make it highly probable that this was either a composer's or a conductor's copy. Through the courtesy of Prof. Sir Hugh P. Allen, Director of the R.C.M., I have been enabled to study a photographic reproduction of this MS. It consists of ninety folio pages of music paper, each ruled with twelve staves. The title page reads: "Signr. Baptists Song / On St. Cecilias Day / 1687 / Performd att Stationers / Hall." At the end is found the signa-ture, "Sigr. Baptist / Draghi / Finis &c: / Sigr. Baptist Draghi / Composed by Mr. Baptis/." Dryden's name is nowhere mentioned. The numbering of some of the pages has been revised, the sequence in which they now appear being, after the title page, pp. 1, 2, 1, 2, 3, . . . 87.

The scoring is for five-part chorus (two trebles, alto, tenor, and bass), and for string orchestra, likewise in five parts, with the addition of trumpets and flutes in certain passages. This was the first time that wind instruments were used in a Cecilian ode. Obvious as the device seems to us at this day, it was a startling novelty in 1687. Dryden must be credited with demand-ing it by his text, and Draghi must be credited with fulfilling that demand. Hawkins, discussing the trumpet, remarks that "Purcell was the first who composed songs with symphonies for that instru-ment."[15] In the same year Purcell wrote his ninth royal ode, the "welcome song," Sound the trumpet, beat the drum, in which he first introduced parts for those instruments. It thus appears that he and Draghi were about abreast in their use of an expanded accompanying orchestra.

Turner was assigned to the principal counter-tenor rôle. The other counter-tenor parts were given to Messrs. Abell,

Boucher, and Robart. Of these the most colorful personality was John Abell, a celebrated alto singer and performer on the lute.[16] Boucher, or Bouchier, was a theatre singer and gentleman of the Chapel Royal. Robart is frequently mentioned as a singer in other choral odes of the period.

The tenor parts were undertaken by Messrs. Marsh, John Church, and Freeman. Marsh and Church were also composers of inferior note. The bass parts were given to James Hart, Daniel Williams, John Bowman (an actor and theatre singer), Leonard Woodson (gentleman of the Chapel Royal), and the Rev. John Gostling.

Gostling (c. 1650–1733) had a voice of immense compass and volume. He was M.A. at St. John's College, Cambridge, was sworn in as gentleman of the Chapel Royal on February 25, 1678–79, and was subsequently minor canon of Canterbury, vicar of Littlebourn, chaplain to the King, and prebendary of Lincoln. He was a lover of the viol da gamba and a great favorite of Charles II. One of Purcell's most famous anthems, They that go down to the sea in ships,[17] was written especially for the very low range of Gostling's voice, "which was a deep bass, that hardly any person but himself was then, or has since been able to sing it," as Hawkins remarked.

IV

In setting most of Dryden's words, Draghi did not have to work out an independently proportioned musical plan, as so many composers must when they treat poetic passages. The poem itself provided him with a fairly explicit structure. The first and last stanzas obviously called for choral movements of great scope, and the five interior stanzas demanded contrasted solos, duets, trios, and short choruses with varied instrumental accompaniments and interludes. Draghi's principal departures from Dryden's structure are found in his significant breaking up of the opening and closing stanzas.

His general treatment of the text followed the English tradition, which had always[18] demanded an "underlaying" of the text, except when a few words had to be repeated again and again for the sake of carrying out a purely musical idea. This "underlaying" tended, at its best, to translate the verbal idea into legitimate

436

musical devices; at its worst it resulted in rather cheap onomato-
poeia. Draghi's sure feeling for good vocal line, however, saved
him from many of the natural pitfalls of this custom. Furthermore, the English tradition which he was consciously adopting
was refreshingly free from the stilted conventional Italian opera
"tags," ornaments and clichés, which were to disfigure so many
of Handel's recitative passages. English composers, from Mar-
beck through Dowland, Gibbons, and Lawes, had developed a
recitative which, when sung in strict time, did as little violence
as possible to the words and generally preserved their proper
accent. Its greatest defect was an occasional superabundance of
colorature. Draghi's problems were: first, to reproduce the
spectacular fire and drama of the poem; second, to "underlay"
each word with musical meaning, so far as possible, without violat-
ing good taste; and third, to produce music which would have independent value. Although he was by no means a composer of out-
standing genius, he did attack these problems in a thoroughly
competent manner. The experienced hand is apparent on every
page of his score.

The composition opens with a pompous introduction
in full chords for the string orchestra, in C minor,[19]
leading to a simple homophonic passage containing some
interesting harmonic clashes (Example A). At the twelfth
measure the first violins announce a lively fugue subject,
which is properly answered by the four other string
parts and is ingeniously worked out (Example B). On
page 5 the fugue reaches its climax, giving way to alternate passages for single strings and full orchestra.
On page 7, where we find the cue, "Just here begins Dr.
Turner," the solo counter-tenor sings "From harmony,
from heavenly harmony" to the expressive motif which
has already been announced by the solo first violin. He
touches his high C on the first syllable of "heavenly."
After a rest of a beat, the full chorus and orchestra
enter (Example C): "From harmony, from harmony,"
followed by Mr. Abell and Mr. Turner, "From harmony,
from heavenly harmony," and then the full chorus again
—the whole vocal passage repeating precisely what the
orchestra had announced before Mr. Turner's entrance.
"Here the violins rest," and with a thorough-bass accompaniment the five-part semichorus (two voices to a

part) announces and develops a strongly rhythmical theme
fitted to the words, "this universal frame began." (Example D). The entire chorus joins in the contrapuntal
development, ending in a grandiose <u>Adagio</u> (Example E).
A <u>symphony</u> for strings in four parts repeats the theme
as a fughetta. There follows a florid recitative for "Mr.
Gozling" (Example F) to the words "When Nature underneath"—here the voice sinks to the C below the bass
clef—"a heap of jarring"—an elaborate descending
passage in semi-quavers—"atoms lay, and could not
heave her head, the tuneful voice was heard from high"
—ascending in arpeggio to the D above the staff. Then
"one of ye Boys, Solus," in a colored ascending treble
passage: "Arise, ye more then dead" (Example G).
Whereupon Mr. Turner, Mr. Marsh and Mr. Woodson
engage in a very interesting vocal trio (Example H),
carrying out the idea of the following words. Mr.
Woodson (bass): "Then cold;" Mr. Turner: "and hot;"

A Opening
STRINGS

Mr. Marsh (tenor): "and moist;" all: "and dry;" then
alternately: "in order to their stations leap;" together:
"and Musick's pow'rs obey." The theme set to the
words "in order to their stations leap" is then rede-
veloped as a fughetta for strings. The chorus breaks
in with the now familiar phrase, "From harmony," etc.,
developed as at first. After an antiphonal passage,
"From harmony, to harmony," used as a bridge, a
motif of wide range is worked out for the words "Through
all the compass of the notes it runs"[20], and a descending
scale is treated in imitation for the words, "The Diapason closing full in man." A brief <u>symphony</u> brings the
first chorus to a conclusion.

This opening division of the work occupies thirty-one pages
of the score. It discloses two noteworthy qualities to the listener.
In the first place, the care with which Draghi set the individual
words is apparent on almost every page. He placed every con-

C "Just here begins DR. (MR.) TURNER"

From har - mo-ny, from heav'n-ly har-mo-ny,

MR. ABELL: from heav'nly har - mo - ny;

MR. TURNER: from heav'nly har - - mo-ny;

THE CHORUS AND VIOLINS

etc.

from har-mo - ny, from har-mo-ny;

sonant under its proper note. The word "arise," for instance,
which is sung to a florid figure, is not written in the present-day
manner, thus: "arise . . . ," but precisely as sung, thus: "ari . . .
se."

In the second place, a remarkable variety is here achieved.
Using both viols and voices in many different combinations, and
a contrasted series of themes, Draghi emphasized the import of
the words with great exactitude and expressiveness. Following
his own principles, he paid more attention to meaning than to
poetic form, and a certain disjointedness resulted, for which he
is not altogether responsible. It is true that he achieved a large
measure of unity by the simple procedure of assigning always
the same musical material to the same verbal phrase, and the
opening and closing choruses of this first division do serve to
bind the composition together to some extent. Nevertheless the
effect is more "chaotic" than was desired,[21] and for this Dryden
must share the responsibility.

Dryden certainly did not anticipate the complexity which
Draghi was forced to develop, and did not have clearly in mind
the vital distinction between passages suitable for recitative, for
air, for duet and trio, for semichorus and chorus. Here Draghi's
success, such as it was, was achieved in spite of the unmistakable

E Adagio
   FULL CHORUS

This u - ni - ver - sal, u - ni - ver - sal
frame, this u - ni - ver - sal frame be - gan.

F MR. GOSLING

When Na-ture   underneath a   heap of jar - - -

- - - - - - ring at-oms lay and could not heave her head, and

could not heave her head,   the tunefull voice,   the tunefull
loud

voice was heard, was heard,   was heard,   was heard from high.

443

G One of ye Boys
SOLUS

A - ri - - - - - - - - - - - se, a-

ri - - - - - - - - - - - - se, ye

more than dead, a - rise, a - ri - - - se, ye

more than dead, ye more . . . . than

dead, a - rise, a - rise, ye more . . . . than dead.

defects in this portion of his text. The opening lines, for instance
would puzzle any musician, as they undoubtedly puzzled Draghi.
"From harmony, from heav'nly harmony/This universal frame
began" offers good material for recitative and chorus, but the
verses that immediately follow could not easily be used for furthe
chorus work. Yet they are an integral and seemingly inseparable
part of the stanza; hence the musical interruption, by way of solos
and trio, that must have enlightened Dryden as to the limitations
of his libretto when he heard the performance. Again, the musica
divisions of this stanza could not possibly correspond with or
carry out Dryden's rhyme scheme, which reads well but must hav
been lost to the audience of 1687. "Ye more then dead," sung by
the boy soprano, could hardly have been recognized as the consequent of "raise her head," sung by Gostling to necessarily different music and in a necessarily different manner. Likewise in
the trio, "Then hot and cold," "dry" rhymes with Gostling's "high,
"leap" with his "heap;" "obey" with his "atoms lay." The trio thu
sounds like an interruption to the verse-plan instead of like an ex
position of it. The music, in properly carrying out the ideas,
violates the poetic structure.

 The stanza, "What passion cannot music raise and
quell," is set for counter-tenor accompanied by two violins
and figured bass, and sung by Mr. Abell (Example I). It is
a good example of expressive vocal line, too formal to
be called recitative and too free to be called arioso. The
words are rather simply underlaid: a run to the high D
at "raise," florid passages for "around" and "celestial."
It is both melodic and declamatory.

 On page 35 appears Draghi's great novelty, "The
Trompetts," playing a fanfare in triple time in the key of
C, while the bass viols imitate drum beats (Example J).
The fanfare is bandied back and forth between the two
trumpets and the string quartet, up to the entrance of Mr.
Turner and Mr. Gostling with "The trumpet's loud clangor
excites us to arms." The voices rush vigorously up and
down the scale with the words, "With shrills full of anger
and mortal alarm." The basses become prominent at
"the double, double, double beat" (Example K), the "thundering drum" brings Mr. Gostling down to the low D, and
the violins assist in the effect with rapid repeated notes,
marked "Very Soft." The two voices syncopate the words,

"Hark, ye foes come," the entire chorus enters with a blast on the word "Charge," and "'Tis too late to retreat" is treated in full homophony. A symphony brings this remarkably dramatic movement to a conclusion.

The tonality shifts back to the more subdued C minor on page 46, with the section marked "For the Flutes." Here we find a ground-bass theme, five measures in length, which is played five times in C minor, three times in G minor, and again three times in C minor. Above it the two flutes discourse amiable counterpoint. At the third repetition Mr. Turner enters with his suave air, "The soft complaining flute," etc. (Example L). "Warbling lute" is treated in dotted rhythm, very grateful for the voice, while the instruments indulge in tremolos.

On page 52 "The Violins begin after ye Flutes shall End," with twenty measures of vigorous passage work in G major. Then Messr. Boucher and James Hart sing a

I Close of the Arioso

447

spirited duet to the words, "Sharp violins proclaim their
jealous pangs." The movement is here full of bustle,
and is twice marked "Brisk."

"But oh, what art can teach," etc., a trio for Messrs.
Robart, Church, and Bowman, brings us back through
the key of B flat into C minor (Example M). Here the
accompaniment is sketched out merely in the form of a
figured bass, and is appropriately solemn.

After the usual <u>symphony</u>, Mr. Gostling, accompanied
by all the strings, has the declamatory air, "Orpheus
could lead ye savage Race." The word "unrooted" gets
a descent and an upward swoop, and "sequacious" is
very appropriately repeated to a melodic sequence.
"Raised the wonder higher" naturally ascends, and
"breath" is given an elaborate coloration demanding of
the singer an ample lung-capacity. At "mistaking Earth"
(Example N) the voice sinks to the low G, remaining there

J THE TRUMPETS

K

BRENNECKE

for ten slow beats, and at the final "Heav'n" it rises nearly two full octaves. All this may seem childishly artificial in the telling, but for the listener who can accept it as naïvely as did the Cecilian audiences, it has charm, and musical as well as histrionic and pictorial value.

"The Last Chorus," beginning on page 70, works in the full resources of the band, both vocal and instrumental. "Upon ye words ye Spheres Enters all

451

ye Voices and Viols." The violins rest and reénter with
telling effect. After a symphony, the words "So when
the last and dreadful hour," etc., are assigned as a trio
to Messrs. Robart, Freeman, and Williams, up to "the
trumpet shall be heard on high," whereupon the trumpets
join the violins, and the chorus enters. The tempo is
reduced as (Example O) Mr. Turner declaims, "The
dead shall live;" then Mr. Abell sings, very floridly,
"The Living—" and Mr. Gostling's sepulchral voice
once more reaches the depths with "Dye, dye, dye."
The semichorus, then the instruments alone, then
treble and bass in duet, again a symphony, then Messrs.

M

P All the Voices and Violins till the last

Turner, Abell and Gostling, and finally "All the Voices and Violins Till the Last" extract the utmost expression from the words, "And Musick shall untune the Sky" (Example P).

The last few pages of Draghi's setting contain some passages in which real violence is done the poem. Words are repeated elsewhere, particularly in the choruses, where the procedure may be defended by both precedent and effect, but here we find not only "the trumpet shall be heard, shall be heard," and "the dead shall live, shall live, shall live," but even "and Musick shall untune the sky, untune, untune, and Musick shall, and Musick shall, and Musick shall untune, and Musick shall untune the sky." Here Burney's criticism for once seems to apply:

An absurd custom prevailed in Purcell's time, which he carried to greater excess, probably, than any other

> composer, of repeating a word of one or two syllables
> an unlimited number of times, for the sake of the
> melody, and sometimes before the whole sentence
> has been heard. Such as no, no, no—all, all, all—
> pretty, pretty, pretty, etc., ad infinitum.[22]

More to our purpose, however, is the fact that the same sort of clash between poetic and musical form which we observed in the opening stanza is again apparent. This final stanza did not lend itself readily to purely choral treatment. It abruptly followed choral lines with passages more suitable to solo declamation. Its grammatical scheme, also, while a superb example of sustained poetic thought, is too large and complex to be expounded chorally throughout. After its first four lines of "common" hymn-tune meter, a sudden musical change is demanded, which Draghi supplied with a symphony and solo voices. But thereby some of the poetic unity of the passage is destroyed, and furthermore the composer is sadly embarrassed at the end, by a sheer scarcity of words.

It is true that—with all its colorature, repetition, and formal weakness—this final chorus nevertheless stands as an effort of considerable musical power. Dryden's eloquence, immeasurably superior to the puerilities of his fellow Cecilian poets, was here almost proof against his composer's limited genius and against his own still imperfect realization of the complex nature of his task.

The performance of 1687 thus turned out to be an overwhelming popular success. But it could hardly have been altogether satisfying to so sharp a self-critic as Dryden was. He must have been pleased to observe that his central stanzas were very neatly suited to the varied homophonic treatment that a composer would be inclined to use in the body of his composition. But he also must have observed that his opening and closing passages, excellent as they were as declamatory lyrics, offered unnecessarily awkward problems to the composer. At any rate, he now had the advantage of an invaluable direct experience with the musical as well as the poetic situation, and he must necessarily have become more than ever acutely aware of the peculiar demands of such an occasion. This may be justly regarded as his first Cecilian experiment, in general successful, but by no means flawless; and it provided him with an ample equipment for his culminating effort of ten years later.

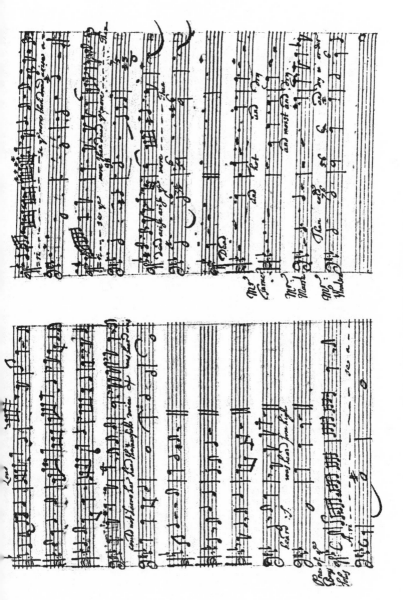

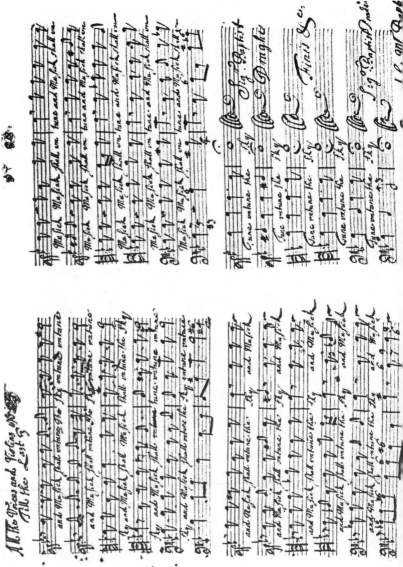

V

For four years after the Dryden-Draghi success there were
no important Cecilian productions. Celebrations were suspended
in 1688 and 1689, probably because of the disturbances attendant
upon the Revolution, but were resumed in 1690, when Thomas
Shadwell wrote the ode. It is a fairly competent poem, echoing
Dryden, of course, but lacking the laureate's mastery of form
and language. The following lines show Dryden's influence:

> You did at first the warring atoms join,
> Made qualities most opposite combine,
> While discords did with pleasing concords join . . . .

> Dirges with sorrow still inspire
> The doleful and lamenting squire . . . .

> Organs and viols sadly groan
> To the voice's dismal tone . . . .

> We touch the soft and tender flute
> The sprinkling and melodious lute . . . .

> How does the thund'ring martial song
> Provoke the military Throng! . . . .

> The clangour of the trumpet's sound
> Fills all the dusty place around, etc.

The music to this effusion, set by Robert King, has been lost.
In the same year the elder Samuel Wesley wrote a Cecilian ode,
which received no music until 1794, when his grandson set it.
Thomas D'Urfey composed the ode for 1691, again a mediocre
performance containing no innovations. Of John Blow's setting,
only two fragments are extant.

The next significant performance took place in 1692, when
the ode was written by Nicholas Brady. It was set by Purcell,
and the result was, musically, the best of all Cecilian compositions up to the time of Handel. A cursory survey of both text
and score[23] will show, first, how far Brady's poem, much admired at the time, depended upon Dryden; second, how far Purcell

457

expanded and elaborated upon Draghi's musical devices of 1687; and finally, how Purcell's striking innovations probably pointed the way to many of the poetic sensations that Dryden was to employ five years later in Alexander's Feast.

Purcell first expanded his orchestra in a remarkable manner. In the overture he uses not only the usual strings and a pair of trumpets, but also kettle drums tuned to D and A, and two oboes. Later he introduces not only two treble flutes but also a bass flute, thus anticipating Wagner's revolutionary device of using combinations of three similar instruments to complete the tone color of each group.[24] Among the soloists for the performance we find again Turner, Woodson, Bowman, and Williams, and Purcell himself.

The overture consists of five contrasted movements, after which a bass recitative takes the words, "Hail, bright Cecilia, hail!" These are repeated by the full chorus, leading to a movement in imitation: "Fill ev'ry heart with love of thee and thy celestial art." Then a duet for alto and tenor: "That thine and music's sacred love," and chorus: "May make the British forest prove as famous as Dodona's vocal Grove." The remainder of the opening stanza,

> Hark! hark! each tree its silence breaks
> The box and fir to talk begin!
> This in the sprightly violin
> That in the flute distinctly speaks! . . .

is set for treble and bass duet with an antiphonal accompaniment for the three flutes and the violins, over a ground-bass in triple time. The second stanza, "'Tis Nature's voice," set for an extremely florid alto solo with figured bass, was "sung with incredible graces" by Purcell.

The third stanza derives unmistakably from Dryden:

> Soul of the world! inspir'd by thee
> The jarring seeds of matter did agree,
> Thou didst the scattered atoms bind,
> Which, by thy laws of true proportion join'd,
> Made up of various parts one perfect harmony.

This is set for a complicated chorus, with tremolos on the chord of the diminished seventh at the words "the jarring seeds of matter," and ending in very simple chords for "one perfect harmony." The remaining two lines of the stanza, "Thou tun'st the world," etc., are given to a treble solo, then to the chorus. The fourth stanza is again reminiscential:

> With that sublime celestial lay
> Dare any earthly sounds compare?
> If any earthly music dare,
>   The noble organ may.
> From heav'n its wondrous notes were giv'n,
> (Cecilia oft conversed with heav'n,)
> Some Angel of the sacred choir
> Did with his breath the pipes inspire,
> And of their notes above the just resemblance gave,
>   Brisk without lightness, without dulness grave.

This is set as a trio for two altos and bass. Passages in colorature are given to the words "celestial," "sounds," and "noble," and the music waxes properly grave at "organ." "Brisk" and "grave" are likewise suggested in melodic figures. The fifth stanza, in praise of the organ, "Wondrous Machine," resulted in one of the most celebrated of Purcell's airs, for bass voice over a ground-bass, accompanied by two oboes. The words "warbling" and "unable" are set to dotted florid passages; the rest of it is purely melodic, and exceedingly pleasurable for both soloists and audience. An alto takes the solo, "The airy violin," and an alto and tenor duet "In vain the am'rous flute," with _ritornelli_ for the flutes. Kettledrums and trumpets establish the mood for "The fife and all the harmony of war," declaimed by the alto voice with the curious repetition, "all, all, all, all, all the harmony." "Let these among themselves contest" is a duet for two basses, and the final stanza, "Hail, bright Cecilia," is given to massive choruses, solo quartet, and full orchestra.

In 1692, Addison wrote his Song for St. Cecilia's Day at Oxford, which was not set to music. In 1693 the ode was written by Theophilus Parsons; it contains only echoes of previous efforts: the invocation to the Saint, the chaos and cosmos idea, the trumpet call, flute rhymed with lute, and so on. Music was provided by Godfrey Finger, and has not been preserved. No odes have been preserved for 1694, 1695, or 1696.

VI

Again the festival languished, and again Dryden was summoned.
He wrote to his sons:[25]

> I am writing a song for St. Cecilia's Feast, who, you
> know, is the patroness of music. This is troublesome,
> and in no way beneficial; but I could not deny the
> stewards of the feast, who came in a body to me to
> desire that kindness.

There is a legend, propagated by Sir Walter Scott, that he composed Alexander's Feast at one sitting, and that Mr. St. John, later Lord Bolingbroke, "found him in unusual agitation of spirits, even to a trembling." There is further evidence that he spent a fortnight in revision, and that he was paid £40 for it. That he appreciated its merits is indicated by his own statement, "A nobler Ode was never produced, nor ever will."[26]

Van Doren[27] has discussed the various sources from which Dryden may have drawn for this poem. And its one line, "Sound the trumpets, beat the drums," is undoubtedly a reminiscence of the title and opening line of Purcell's welcome song of 1687, and affords evidence both of Dryden's familiarity with the music of his day and of his borrowing habits. The originality of this ode's conception is, however, unmistakable. It discards the stale conventions of both the form and the occasion, e.g., the invocation and the parley of instruments, and plunges at once into its central drama. The narrative itself develops the necessary contrasted moods, pompous, amorous, sprightly, tragic, ferocious, and only in the final stanza are Cecilia and the organ and the Angel introduced, to give the "occasional" point to the whole recital. The poem, building on the instrumental resources of Draghi as amplified by Purcell and illustrated in previous settings, demands the use of almost every musical device then current. It marks the climax of Cecilian poetry.

Of special interest, however, are the striking ways in which Alexander's Feast was designed purely as a musician's libretto. It exhibits no such awkward passages for the composer as were found in the opening and close of the 1687 ode. Dryden's experiences had given him a clear recognition of the distinction between recitative or solo declamation, air, and choral effects. Nearly the whole of the ode of 1687 could conceivably have been assigned to both solo and chorus, and Draghi's indecision was often rather apparent. In Alexander's Feast, however, this distinction is clearly shown, in two ways: first, in a contrast in idea and content, for the narrative or solo passages are explicitly set off from the commentary or choral sections; second, in a contrast in phrasing and verbal sound, for the narrative abounds in true dramatic declamation, unsuitable for chorus but grateful to the solo singer.

It is unnecessary to analyse the recitatives to show their essentially declamatory and un-choral character. Verrall[28] notes that with the lines beginning "Behold a ghastly band," the rhythm dies altogether away—an accurate observation, and one which serves to indicate that Dryden here demanded precisely a setting in broken and excited recitative, with agitated interruptions on the part of the orchestra.

The careful division of the stanzas into recitative and aria, with repetition of the aria as chorus, gives explicit direction to the composer and appears in strong contrast to the vagueness of the ode of 1687 in this respect. The choral comment at the conclusion of each stanza is so designed as to be easily adaptable to both air and chorus. These airs and choruses, again, show a clear recognition of the necessity for providing the composer with opportunities for legitimate repetition. Observing that the musician would repeat single words even when such repetition sounds silly, Dryden generously provided both logical and poetic repeats: "Happy, happy, happy pair," and "Fallen, fallen, fallen, fallen, Fallen from his high estate."[29] Likewise he provided those repetitions of phrase so valuable to the composer: "None but the brave, None but the brave, None but the brave deserves the fair," and "A present deity, they shout around: A present deity, the vaulted roofs rebound," "Sweet the pleasure, Sweet is pleasure after pain," "And sigh'd and look'd, sigh'd and look'd, Sigh'd and look'd, and sigh'd again." Notable in these passages is the swift clinching conclusion after the repetition, just the device which is needed by the composer to round off a repetitive or sequential passage.

In vocal writing, any good composer will look to his text for opportunities to employ three musical devices besides that of mere repetition. Dryden must have seen how Draghi used all three under more adverse circumstances, in 1687. The first is vocal polyphony, in which one or two lines may be assigned to voices that enter successively and whose sense may survive being thus scrambled. Dryden supplied many such lines. "With ravish'd ears The monarch hears," for instance, makes sense, no matter how the two lines are reversed or otherwise jumbled; likewise "Assumes the god, Affects to nod." The second device is that of antiphony, by which two lines may be hurled back and forth alternately between two groups of singers without distortion of meaning or poetic effect. Dryden's lines, "Rich the treasure, Sweet the pleasure," and "On the bare earth expos'd he lies. With not a friend to close his eyes" fulfill this requirement perfectly. The third device is that of sequence, by which two or more lines may be assigned to similar musical phrases or motives that follow one another in different registers or tonalities. Alexander's Feast abounds in such: "Flush'd with a purple grace, He shows his honest face," "Gaz'd on the fair Who caus'd his care," "The lovely Thais, by his side Sate like a blooming Eastern bride, In flower of youth and beauty's pride," "He chose a mournful muse, Soft pity to infuse," "Aloft in awful state The godlike hero sate."

In its combination of purely dramatic and poetic with purely musical values, Alexander's Feast thus undoubtedly throws fresh light on Dryden's genius as an artist of the occasion. There was a tradition that he intended to have Purcell compose the setting for the poem.[30] It was almost an inevitable tradition, for it was the curious misfortune of both poetry and music that the greatest composer and the greatest poet of the time never collaborated on an ode. But Purcell had died two years before the feast of 1697. The original setting was actually composed by Jeremiah Clarke, and although it was repeated in concert performance at least twice, the score has not survived. Nor has the second setting, by Clayton, in 1711. In fact, save Philip Hart's inconsequential composition of 1703, no Cecilian music is extant between 1697 and 1736, when Handel set Alexander's Feast. And the odes, which continued to be written annually up to 1703 and sporadically thereafter, are mostly inferior work. Among the efforts of Bishop, Parsons, D'Urfey, and others, only those by Congreve and Pope have any interest. Handel reset Dryden's first ode in 1739, and Thornton's burlesque ode, written in 1749,[31] possibly set by Dr. Arne and later by Burney,[32] with accompaniment of salt-box, jews-harp, marrow-bones, cleavers, and hurdy-gurdy, brought the whole tradition to its natural end.

NOTES

1 William Henry Husk, <u>An Account of the Musical Celebrations</u> <u>on St. Cecilia's Day</u> (London: Bell & Daldy, 1857).— A complete text of the odes is reprinted on pp. 143–236. See also "An Index to the Songs and Musical Allusions in <u>The Gentleman's Journal</u>, 1692–94," <u>The Musical Antiquary</u> (Oxford Univ. Press, 1911), II, 231–234.

2 For the text, critically edited, see <u>The Works of Henry</u> <u>Purcell</u>, Purcell Society edition, X (London: Novello, 1899), p. (1).

3 The score is found in <u>The Works of Henry Purcell</u>, X, 1–25.

4 I.e., a symphony in the older sense of the term, meaning merely an instrumental prelude or interlude. The word is almost synonymous with <u>ritornello</u>.

5 This device, which was later developed into such achievements as Bach's <u>Chaconne</u> for solo violin, his <u>Passacaglia</u> for organ, the <u>Crucifixus</u> of his Mass in B minor, and the last movement of Brahms's Fourth Symphony, was amusingly condemned by Burney in <u>A General History of Music</u> (London, 1789), III, 494: "The composing songs on a ground-base, was an exercise of ingenuity, in which Purcell seems to have much delighted; but though it was much a fashion in his time, as the composing masses on those tunes in the days of Bird and Dr. Bull, in which they all manifested superior abilities, yet the practice was Gothic, and unworthy employment for men possessed of such genius and original resources."

6 Thus the ode occupied but a small portion of the program for 1683. Although Purcell is known to have composed two other Cecilian pieces in this year (<u>Raise the Voice</u>, to words by an unknown poet, and the Latin hymn, <u>Laudate Ceciliam</u>), there is no record of their having been performed on this occasion.

7 It was not until 1690, however, that Purcell wrote any music for the plays of Dryden himself. <u>King Arthur</u>, the most substantial collaboration between Dryden and Purcell, dates from 1691. See Henri Dupré, <u>Purcell</u>, translated by Phillips and Bedford (New York: Knopf, 1928), pp. 201–204.

8 Addison's Song for St. Cecilia's Day at Oxford, 1692, also rhymes day with Cecilia. One might conclude that all Oxford pronounced Cecilia with a stressed fourth syllable, except for the fact that the word is properly treated elsewhere in Fletcher's ode.

9 Mark Van Doren, The Poetry of John Dryden (Cambridge: The Minority Press, 1931), p. 209.

10 A. W. Verrall, Lectures on Dryden (Cambridge: University Press, 1914), pp. 183–185.

11 Van Doren, op. cit., p. 209.

12 W. Nagel, Geschichte der Musik in England, 2. Teil (Strassburg, Trübner, 1897), p. 245.— Sir John Hawkins, A General History of the Science and Practice of Music, new edition (London: Novello, 1875), II, 717–718.

13 In the Catalogue of the Library of the Sacred Harmonic Society (London, 1872), p. 228, under nos. 1904 and 1905. Another copy is listed on p. 227, the sixth item under no. 1897.

14 Including Hawkins, Burney, Grove, and Nagel.

15 Op.cit., II, 752.

16 See Grove's Dictionary, art. Abell.

17 The Cathedral Services, Anthems, Hymns, etc., by Henry Purcell, edited by Vincent Novello (London, n.d.), I, 147–158. In this anthem the bass solo descends to low D.

18 E.g., in the works of the Elizabethan and early Jacobean madrigalists.

19 The key signature is two flats, which would indicate G minor to a modern musician. But in the seventeenth century the signature was still regarded theoretically as an indication of a transposed mode. The minor key being the development of the old Dorian mode, closing on D, one flat would indicate its transposition a fourth higher, to G, and two flats another fourth, to C. Draghi's contemporaries would call his "key" that of "C with the lesser third." The natural sign is not used in the score, a cancelled flat being marked by a sharp.

20 The MS has both "runs" and "run" in place of "ran," which is demanded by the rhyme—an obvious error.

21 Verrall (op.cit.) holds that the idea of chaos is justly represented by the extremely irregular "Pindaric" form of the stanza, and also that the music for such a passage can aid the listener in comprehending its scheme. But there are two fallacies here. Dryden's leading idea is here cosmos and harmony, and not chaos; it presents a true contrast to the thought of the conclusion of the poem. Haydn was justified in writing a beautiful but extremely irregular orchestral prelude to The Creation, to represent chaos, but that was not Dryden's situation here. Again, a musical setting, which is of necessity longer and more elaborate than a mere reading of the words, requires greater, and not less, attention in order that its form may be grasped by the audience.

22 Burney, op.cit., III, 507.

23 Critically edited in The Works of Henry Purcell (London, 1897), vol. VIII.

24 C. H. H. Parry, Oxford History of Music, III (1902), 285.

25 Van Doren, op.cit., p. 211.

26 Husk, op.cit., pp. 41-45.

27 Op.cit., p. 211 ff.

28 Op.cit., p. 201.

29 For this point, the writer is indebted to Prof. Samuel A. Wolff of Columbia University.

30 The tradition was fostered chiefly by Hawkins, who should have known better.

31 The text, entitled Ode on St. Cecilia's Day, adapted to the ancient British Musick, etc., was published by J. & J. Rivington, London, 1749.

32 Boswell, Johnson, Chap. XIII (1763): "Bonnell Thornton had just published a burlesque 'Ode on St. Cecilia's Day.'" Boswell's chronology seems to be fourteen years late. Burney's note on the passage in Boswell reads as follows: "In 1769, I set for Smart and Newberry, Thornton's Burlesque 'Ode on St. Cecilia's Day.' It was performed at Ranelagh in masks, to a very crowded audience as I was told, for I then resided in Norfolk."

DRYDEN'S EPIC MANNER AND VIRGIL

Reuben Arthur Brower

"A heroic poem, truly such, is undoubtedly the greatest work
which the soul of man is capable to perform."[1] While the solem-
nity of this pronouncement is certainly more characteristic of
Rapin than of Dryden, the reverence for epic poetry is quite typical
of the author of An Essay of Heroic Plays. As every reader of
Dryden knows, the influence of Renaissance epic theory is all but
omnipresent in his critical essays and prefaces. It is equally
well known that the epic manner which Dryden often adopted in
his verse owes much in a general way to the idea of the heroic
poem. But fewer readers, I believe, realize the extent to which
Dryden's epic style is directly indebted to his "master," Virgil.

When Dryden tried most consciously to follow the theories
of heroic poetry, almost invariably he heightened his style by
means of echoes and imitations of the "best poet." In such passages we find the heroic convention revived and reënforced by an
uncommon familiarity with Virgil and the Virgilian style. But
the connection between Virgil and the Renaissance idea of the
epic was not made by Dryden; in fact, from early in the sixteenth
century Virgil played only too prominent a part in the voluminous
speculations on the "truly heroic poem."[2] Naturally we must not
hope to draw too fine a line between the influence of Virgil and
that of Homer in shaping these tenuous theories, since with very
few exceptions the critics cite precedents in both poets. Besides,
there are some writers, such as Hobbes and Madame Dacier,
who give Homer, and not Virgil, the first place in their observations. But in spite of references to Homer and Aristotle the
theorists commonly betray an over-fondness for Virgil and "the
pure idea of a Virgilian poem."[3] The Maronolatry[4] of sixteenth-
century Italian critics such as Vida and Scaliger needs no em-

Reprinted by permission of the Modern Language Association from
Publications of the Modern Language Association, Vol. 55 (1940), pp.
119–138, and by permission of the author.

phasizing, while among French critics of both the sixteenth and seventeenth centuries the bias in favor of the Virgilian epic is more than evident.[5] Le Bossu, the most famous of the French writers on the epic, does not praise Virgil at the expense of Homer; but the theories he sets forth find much more support in the Æneid than in the Iliad or the Odyssey. In general, the Renaissance critics and poets alike were in their approach to the epic much nearer to Virgil than Homer. They were able with some reason to cite Virgil's example in justifying some of their most important doctrines, such as the insistence on a conscious moral or patriotic purpose in the epic, the demand that the hero be an exemplar of virtue, and the emphasis on the allegorical interpretation of the action.

If we wish to see quite clearly the influence of the Virgilian tradition in such theorizing, we need only turn to Dryden himself. As will be remembered, Dryden long cherished the notion of writing a poem according to the heroic formula. In his remarks on this project he showed that he was as loyal to Virgil as many of the Continental theorists:

> . . . I could not have wished a nobler occasion to do
> honour . . . to my king, my country, and my friends;
> most of our ancient nobility being concerned in the
> action.[6] . . .

> after Virgil and Spenser, I would have taken occasion
> to represent my living friends and patrons of the
> noblest families, and also shadowed the events of
> future ages, in the succession of our imperial line . . .[7]

The project shows clearly the influence of Virgil in the consciousness of purpose with which the poem is planned and more particularly in the patriotic nature of that purpose. For a seventeenth-century poet, as for Virgil, the heroic fable was not an end in itself, but a vehicle employed for a given object. Dryden further showed his kinship with Virgil in preferring the Augustan age to the era of the Homeric bards: "The times of Virgil please me better, because he had an Augustus for his patron; and, to draw the allegory nearer you [the Earl of Mulgrave], I am sure I shall not want a Maecenas with him."[8] Despite the obvious effort to turn a compliment, Dryden was expressing an instinctive choice:

he was well adapted to an age of patronage, and like Virgil was not averse to suggestions from above.

Dryden never wrote his Virgilian epic, but he was much influenced by the ideal and found other channels which offered him at least a partial fulfillment of it. At the beginning of his career, he found such an outlet in the rhymed heroic plays with which he achieved such great success between 1664 and 1676. Like all of Dryden's works in which he adopted the epic tone, these plays were indebted in a general way to the Renaissance heroic tradition. But they owed their epic quality more directly to a dramatic theory which had been gradually formed through the combined efforts of critics and playwrights. The importance of this application of epic theory to the drama has only recently been recognized by Mr. B. J. Pendlebury:

> Since then the most striking characteristics of the
> heroic play, the epic construction, the unity of tone,
> and the predominance of the hero, cannot be regarded
> as being inherited from Beaumont and Fletcher, it
> is obvious that their origin must be sought in that
> critical theory of heroic poetry which, though it had
> long been connected with dramatic theory in Italy and
> France, and had been adopted to some extent by
> Davenant, Dryden may be said to have been the first
> Englishman to apply consciously and thoroughly in
> the actual composition of plays.[9]

It was Davenant who introduced Dryden to the epic theories of Tasso; it was Davenant, too, who suggested to Dryden the notion of a genre which should combine both epic and drama. In the Preface to Gondibert[10] Davenant had declared that he had constructed his poem on the outlines of a play; while Hobbes, in his Answer, went so far as to declare that "the heroique poem narrative is called an epique poem. The heroic poem dramatique is tragedy."[11] That Dryden's conception of the heroic play was derived largely from Davenant and Hobbes is only too evident from the Essay of Heroic Plays. "For heroic Plays," he wrote, " ... the first light we had of them, on the English theatre, was from the late Sir William D'Avenant."[12] Observing further that "what was wanting to the perfection" of Davenant's Siege of Rhodes " ... was design, and variety of characters," he went on after

Hobbes to add that " . . . an heroic play ought to be an imitation, in little, of an heroic poem."[13] Proceeding on this principle, he criticized Davenant for failing to attain the grandeur of style and spaciousness of design proper to the epic: " . . . in the scanting of his images and design, he complied not enough with the greatness and majesty of an heroic poem."[14]

Such criticisms may imply a theory of drama and dramatic style which strikes us as absurd; but even a bad theory may be very influential, as the heroic plays go to prove. Seeking to give to these dramas "the majesty of an heroic poem," Dryden borrowed heavily from the one epic style with which he was very familiar. The more epic the scene, the more certain he was to adopt a phrase from the Æneid or to imitate some Virgilian expression. As he gradually became convinced that his purpose in these plays was to dramatize heroic poetry, he made an increasing effort to give his style the epic tone. Accordingly we meet with many more reminiscences of Virgil in the two later heroic plays, The Conquest of Granada and Aureng-Zebe than in the two earlier ones, The Indian Emperor and Tyrannic Love. Also, we find that Dryden used his Virgilian echoes for a more definite end in the later than in the earlier plays. In other words, he became more conscious of his epic manner when he undertook The Conquest of Granada, the very play with which he published his theory of epic-drama, An Essay of Heroic Plays.

Most of the Virgilian echoes in The Indian Emperor are of the decorative type so common throughout Dryden's poetry. Two fairly characteristic examples are the reference to the race of Nisus and Euryalus,[15] and the echo of Virgil's sequiturque sequentem.[16] The first occurs in a passage of courtly love; the second, in a song. Two others, "drowned in his sleep"[17] and "when all are buried in their sleep,"[18] are simply reminiscences of a Virgilian metaphor which was a favorite of Dryden's. But in three other passages the imitations play a rôle which is more than purely decorative:

> Behind the covert, where this temple stands
> Thick as the shades, there issue swarming bands
> Of ambushed men . . . .[19]

> As when, upon the sands, the traveller
> Sees the high sea come rolling from afar,[20]

> As callow birds—
> Whose mother's killed in seeking of the prey,
> Cry in their nest, and think her long away;
> And at each leaf that stirs, each blast of wind,
> Gape for the food, which they must never find:
> So cry the people in their misery.[21]

While none of these examples have exact parallels in Virgil, all three suggest his manner; and the third, amusingly enough, Dryden has marked by a hemistich, which at this period he considered eminently Virgilian. All three occur in situations of martial excitement; the approach of Cortez's troops, the pursuit of the defeated Montezuma, and the panic in the besieged city. In each case the simile is "turned on" to give the passage something like epic grandeur. Considering the Virgilian and Homeric tradition, this is good epic practice. For example, in the accounts of the fourth, fifth, and twelfth books of the Iliad, similes appear in much greater numbers than elsewhere. Virgil also makes freer use of figures (often imitated from Homer) in the martial scenes of the ninth and eleventh books of the Æneid.

Dryden, being a dramatist, suffered from a limitation which affected neither of the ancient poets: he could not give such descriptions in his own person. The second of the three examples, an elaborate sea simile, is spoken by Montezuma, who is fleeing from the enemy and who has heretofore shown no knowledge of marine matters. As Dryden later noted, "the image had not been amiss from another man, at another time." But the unconscious reason which led Dryden to employ it—the desire to elevate his style in a passage of great excitement—was not altogether wrong. In fact, the use of a device so inappropriate dramatically shows how much Dryden's style was affected by his regard for epic qualities. The other two similes are more plausibly introduced. The first is put in the lips of a mere messenger, in a speech which describes action off scene. The third is similarly used, in lines which depict the sufferings in the city. In all three passages we have indications of a stylistic device which was to be more purposefully employed in The Conquest of Granada and in Aureng-Zebe.

In the second of Dryden's heroic plays, Tyrannic Love, there is no marked increase in the number of Virgilian echoes; but, interestingly enough, most of those which are found occur in passages of definitely epic character. A legitimate and necessary part of the epic, it will be remembered, was the "machine"—almost any supernatural device used to adorn the tale or to account for what would be incredible if attributed to chance or to a merely human agent.[22] In dramatizing the martyrdom of St. Catherine of Alexandria Dryden found ample justification for venturing into "those enthusiastic parts of poetry." As before, Virgil comes to his aid; and of the three reminiscences occurring in the "machines" of the play, two contain literal translations from the Æneid. The first is found in lines describing the prophetic hocus-pocus of the state magician:

> When first a hollow wind began to blow,
> The sky grew black, and bellied down more low;
> Around the fields did nimble lightning play,
> Which offered us by fits, and snatched the day.[23]

The lines recall a famous description from the Æneid, as is suggested by the tell-tale Latinisms[24] "offered us by fits" and "snatched the day." The second of these echoes occurs also in a scene of supernatural character, in lines picturing the life of evil spirits: "We wander in the fields of air below,"[25] which is partly a literal translation of "vagantur/aëris in campis."[26] The last of this triad is a long and rather beautiful reworking of Virgil's descriptions of Venus, particularly that of the first book of the Æneid.[27] In this passage describing the translation of St. Catherine, we have again a narration of wondrous off-stage action.

Another narrative from the same play announces the death of a hero, Charinus, the Emperor's son. In lines (as Dr. Johnson would say) "of glorious depravity" Charinus' fall is described. He stood,

> . . . like Capaneus defying Jove;
> With his broad sword the boldest beating down.[28]

Bombastic as the narrative is, the passage in which it occurs is of Virgilian inspiration; for surely Dryden had in mind the noble scene from the Æneid when Pallas' body is brought back to Evander.[29] In the play, as the procession draws near, Maximin hears "the hoarse murmurs of a trumpet's sound."[30] The phrase is one of several in which Dryden tried to convey the effect of

Virgil's <u>clangor tubarum</u>. These allusions and imitations from
<u>Tyrannic Love</u>, like those from <u>The Indian Emperor</u>, again sug-
gest that in scenes of epic character, whether of martial or supernatural tone, Dryden tried to heighten his style in an appropriate
manner. And when he did so, echoes from Virgil came.

This suggestion will be greatly reënforced by a study of the
next heroic play, <u>The Conquest of Granada</u>. In the opening scene
of the play the audience learns of Almanzor's feats in a great
bullfight which has just taken place. This scene, as even a brief
glance will show, is nothing more than a long narrative mechanically split up into speeches. Using his vigorous declamatory
vein, Dryden obviously has tried to imitate the Games of the
Æneid, an episode which he especially admired. Within no more
than one hundred lines, he introduced seven or eight reminiscences of Virgil and five "Virgilian" hemistichs. Moreover, the
whole movement of the verse is improved over that of the preceding plays. It is more sonorous and more stately; the rhythmical groups are more varied, a single group extending over five or
six lines, as in Virgil. Near the beginning of the passage the epic
style is suggested by a somewhat awkward Latinism, "the darted
cane."[31] The bulls are described in language which recalls the
<u>Georgics</u>: " . . . with high nostril snuffing up the wind,"[32] echoing

> . . . . bucula caelum
> suspiciens patulis captavit naribus auras.[33]

A longer description shows the blending in memory of various
Virgilian elements:

> One bull, with curled black head, beyond the rest,
> And dew-laps hanging from his brawny chest,
> With nodding front a while did daring stand,
> And with his jetty hoof spurned back the sand;
> Then, leaping forth, he bellowed out aloud:
> The amazed assistants back each other crowd,
> While monarch-like he ranged the listed field;
> Some tossed, some gored, some trampling down he
> killed.[34]

In addition to specific imitations,[35] we should note the Latin use
of the participle ("listed") and the epanaphora which Virgil used

472

so frequently. The lines in which Dryden sketches Almanzor's steed[36] also owe much to Virgil, as is evident to any reader of the Georgics.

But we find Virgilian influence of a more profound character in the speech which closes this narrative:

> Not heads of poppies (when they reap the grain)
> Fall with more ease before the labouring swain,
> Then fell this head:
> It fell so quick, it did even death prevent,
> And made imperfect bellowings as it went.
> Then all the trumpets victory did sound,
> And yet their clangours in our shouts were
>   drown'd.[37]

With this compare:

> purpureus veluti cum flos succisus aratro
> languescit moriens, lassove papavera collo
> demisere caput pluvia cum forte gravantur.[38]

In this passage Dryden is not merely blending two parts of a Virgilian simile into one, or recalling, with no little success, the sonorous trumpets of the Æneid; he is writing in a style which in great part owes its variety of movement and mastery of sound to a thorough appreciation of Virgil's artistry. Hence the easy sweep of the lines with their characteristically Virgilian parentheses; hence the effective use of the caesura after "head" (whatever is the true explanation of the hemistichs); hence too the suggestive use of rime and assonance in "sound . . . shouts . . . drown'd." The whole narrative with which the play opens shows that the full-blown epical manner and the imitation of Virgil were surely connected in Dryden's practice. But since he now realized the absurdity of characters who fought with mouthfuls of classical similes, he tended to restrict this manner to appropriate scenes.

To suppose that Dryden ceased to imitate Virgil in other scenes of the plays is of course unwarranted. On the contrary, there are scattered about in The Conquest of Granada some remarkably close imitations, such as the dream simile,[39] the picture of Venus,[40] and the curse of Turnus.[41] Certainly Virgil was much in Dryden's mind while he was writing the heroic plays, as is suggested by his later defense of a passage from The Conquest of Granada:

> Spite of myself I'll stay, fight, love, despair;
> And I can do all this, because I dare.[42]

"This passage," Professor Noyes notes,[43] "is parodied in The Rehearsal. Dryden, in the second and third quartos, defends it by citing in the margin Virgil's phrase 'possunt quia posse videntur' (Æneid, V. 231)."

Aureng-Zebe, the last of the purely heroic plays, is no less remarkable for the number and significance of its recollections of Virgil. The exposition, like that of The Conquest of Granada, is an epic narrative in dialogue, a description of the war which has broken out among the sons of the Emperor. The opening lines, august and portentous in tone, rise to a climax in a simile drawn from Virgil:[44]

> As at a signal, straight the sons prepare
> For open force, and rush to sudden war:
> Meeting, like winds broke loose upon the main,
> To prove, by arms, whose fate it was to reign.[45]

Within a few lines another simile of much the same type is used to describe the machinations of the ministers, "Whispering, like winds, ere hurricanes arise."[46] Abbas, one of the lords, comes in to tell of the approach of even greater forces: "The vale an iron harvest seems to yield,"[47] a line containing a literal translation of the ferrea telorum seges[48] of Virgil. So once more by means of a narrative in heroic style Dryden sets the tone of the play. A glance over the other echoes from Aureng-Zebe will reveal a number which are especially faithful, such as "argued me of fear,"[49] "birds obscene,"[50] and "conscious virtue."[51] The general character of the night-battle in the city is reminiscent of the fall of Troy, while the last important echo comes again in a narrative speech. Abbas once more enters to report a battle off-stage. His description of the union of the rival forces culminates in lines recalling the famous Laocoön passage:

> In either's flag the golden serpents bear
> Erected crests alike, like volumes rear,
> And mingle friendly hissings in the air.[52]

DRYDEN'S EPIC MANNER AND VIRGIL

It is now fairly clear that Dryden's heroic style was directly indebted to Virgil; as we have seen, in narrative passages describing a martial exploit or an act of divine intervention, Dryden often used Virgilian allusions to suggest the epic tone. Moreover, with the increase in the epic scope of the plays, Dryden tended to restrict this Virgilian style to the exposition, probably feeling that in an opening scene he might adopt a more expansive and leisurely manner than in the heat of the action. In such dramatic narratives when the individuality of the characters was not important, he felt free to indulge in elaborate similes and detailed descriptions closely patterned after Virgil. We have two good instances of this epic style in the opening scenes of The Conquest of Granada and Aureng-Zebe: the first, a spirited description of a bull-fight; the second, a lively picture of the forces led by the king's rebellious sons.

But in their larger features the heroic plays owe relatively little to Virgil. Their epic scope, their unity of tone, and the superhuman stature of their protagonists were due in large part to Renaissance epic theory, to Virgil only indirectly, although it is safe to say that Virgil's influence reënforced the application of the theory at many points now unobservable to us. Occasionally, as in the emphasis on "piety" in the character of Aureng-Zebe, we feel that Dryden was emulating Virgil quite directly. But this play, like the others, was only one of the substitutes for the epic which Dryden always planned, and never wrote. "Some little hope, I have yet remaining," he wrote in the Dedication to Aureng-Zebe, "and those too, considering my abilities, may be vain, that I may make the world some part of amends, for many ill plays, by an heroic poem."[53]

Although Dryden never tried again to transfer epic to the stage, he could not simply give up a dramatic style which he had used for more than a decade. In fact many of Dryden's later plays continued to exhibit definitely heroic qualities. The best plays he ever wrote, All for Love (1677), and Don Sebastian (1689), were essentially dramas of "love and honor"; while plays or operas of less literary value, such as King Arthur[54] and Cleomenes (1692), contained characters and passages in the old heroic vein. For us the point is not so much that the later plays exhibit features characteristic of heroic plays in general; but that still, at times, Dryden used Virgilian allusions to suggest the epic tone. For example, in All for Love, the defeat of the Egyptian navy is announced in words which recall the Æneid:

> O horror, horror!
> Egypt has been; our latest hour is come:
> The queen of nations, from her ancient seat,
> Is sunk for ever in the dark abyss.[55]

The parallel passage is justly famous:

> venit summa dies et ineluctabile tempus
> Dardaniae. fuimus Troes, fuit Ilium et ingens
> gloria Teucrorum.[56]

Again, in The Spanish Friar (1680? 1681?),[57] in two speeches
describing martial uprisings, Dryden used similes based on
Virgil's account of the war of the bees.[58] About four years later,
in the opera Albion and Albanius (1685), Dryden took Virgil as
his guide in describing the intervention of the gods[59] and in picturing the world below.[60] The opera had one scene of martial
character dealing with the disturbances previous to the exile of
the Duke of York ("Albanius" in the opera, later James II). Interestingly enough, Dryden here made a direct allusion to the
passage of the Æneid in which Allecto is summoned to arouse
Queen Amata's wrath:

> Alecto, thou to fair Augusta go,
> And all thy snakes into her bosom throw.[61]

In the next play, Don Sebastian (1689?), Dryden used a bee
simile of the same type as those in The Spanish Friar. Again the
passage is a description of an uprising:

> All crowd in heaps, as, at a night alarm,
> The bees drive out upon each other's backs,
> To emboss their hives in clusters; . . .[62]

Dryden perhaps owed a deeper debt to Virgil in Don Sebastian
than in any of the later plays; for he apparently had Æneas in
mind when he drew the character of the hero: "In the drawing
of his character," he wrote, "I forgot not piety, which anyone
may observe to be one principal ingredient of it, even so far as
to be a habit in him; . . ."[63] And, in fact, Sebastian is depicted
as a second Æneas:

> . . . . he was a man,
> Above man's height, even towering to divinity:
> Brave, pious, generous, great, and liberal;
> Just as the scales of heaven, that weigh the seasons.
> He loved his people; him they idolized.[64]

In the next year after Don Sebastian was played, King Arthur was produced. Whether Dryden felt any irony in using for an opera-masque the grand conception which he was to have carried out in a perfect epic, we cannot know. He certainly tried to inject an heroic quality into the opera, writing a libretto of some dignity and beauty. Echoes from Virgil appear in two of the more exalted passages, the first of which is a description of supernatural manifestations:

> But straight a rumbling sound, like bellowing winds,
> Rose and grew loud; confused with howls of wolves,
> And grunts of bears, and dreadful hiss of snakes;
> Shrieks more than human; globes of hail poured down
> An armed winter, and inverted day.[65]

Evidently Dryden had in mind the passage of the Æneid in which the Sybil's approach is announced by similar wonders:

> sub pedibus mugire solum et iuga coepta moveri
> silvarum, visaeque canes ululare per umbram
> adventante dea . . . .[66]

The second passage indebted to Virgil is a speech in which Arthur offers to end the war by single combat:

> As once Aeneas, my famed ancestor,
> Betwixt the Trojan and Rutilian bands,
> Fought for a crown and bright Lavinia's bed,
> So will I meet thee, ...[67]

But in spite of epic touches, the opera remains a fairy story, a sorry substitute for a "true heroic poem."

In his last tragedy, Cleomenes (1692), Dryden seems to have reverted to his more purely heroic manner, particularly in the characterization of the hero, who is as bold, proud, and stoical

as Almanzor. The play opens with a ranting declamation in which
Cleomenes describes his downfall:

> Unbounded empire hung upon my sword:
> Greece, like a lovely heifer, stood in view,
> To see the rival bulls each other gore,
> But wished the conquest mine.
> I fled; and yet I languish not in exile;
> But here in Egypt whet my blunted horns,
> And meditate new fights, and chew my loss.[68]

This tasteless simile, which recalls the opening scene of The Conquest of Granada, is based on a famous passage from the Georgics:

> pascitur in magna Sila formosa iuvenca:
> illi alternantes multa vi proelia miscent
> vulneribus crebris, lavit ater corpora sanguis,
> versaque in obnixos urgentur cornua vasto
> cum gemitu, reboant silvaeque et longus Olympus.
> nec mos bellantis una stabulare, sed alter
> victus abit longeque ignotis exsulat oris.
> . . . .
> et temptat sese atque irasci in cornua discit
> arboris obnixus trunco, ...[69]

Virgil also had used a simile of the same type in describing
Turnus:

> . . . utque leo, specula cum vidit ab alta
> stare procul campis meditantem in proelia
>   taurum, . . .[70]

Dryden's "meditate new flights" suggests that he had a partial
memory of these particular lines.

Even from such a brief survey of Dryden's later plays, it
becomes evident that on occasion he still used an epic manner
which he sought to heighten by Virgilian allusions. Let us turn
back to the early years of his career and observe the traces of
this style in his non-dramatic poetry. At the very time when
Dryden was writing the heroic plays, he made his one and only
attempt to write a long narrative poem of a partially epic char-

acter—the famous Annus Mirabilis (1667). Everyone will agree with Dryden that however heroic the material may have been, the poem itself is "historical, not epic."[71] Still, the Annus Mirabilis possesses a clinical interest for anyone who wishes to see Dryden's heroic style in the making. "Virgil," he declared in the Preface,

> . . . has been my master in this poem. I have followed him everywhere, I know not with what success, but I am sure with diligence enough; my images are many of them copied from him, and the rest are imitations of him. My expressions also are as near as the idioms of the two languages would admit of in translation.[72]

One of many typical instances will indicate the quality of images so diligently composed:

> Behind, the gen'ral mends his weary pace
> And sullenly to his revenge he sails;
> (p) So glides some trodden serpent on the grass,
> And long behind his wounded volume trails.[73]
> (p) So glides, &c. From Virgil: Quum medii nexus,
> extremaeque agmina caudae Solvuntur; tardosque
> trahit sinus ultimus orbes, &c.

Here as elsewhere, the poem offers depressing evidence of the superficial and imitative qualities of Dryden's epic style. For although he employed various epic devices which are also used by Virgil, such as elaborate similes, declamatory speeches,[74] and supernatural signs,[75] he used them so deliberately, attaching them so externally that the effort appears more heroic than the result.

But it was in satire that Dryden made the most apt use of his epic manner. Here he developed a style which was a compound of the heroic and the satirical, much in the manner of Boileau for whose work he expressed great admiration. In describing Boileau's method in Le Lutrin, Dryden gave a fair account of his own satirical style:

> He writes it [Le Lutrin] in the French heroic verse,
> and calls it an heroic poem; his subject is trivial, but
> his verse is noble. I doubt not but he had Virgil in

> his eye, for we find many admirable imitations of him,
> and some parodies . . . And, as Virgil in his fourth
> Georgic, of the Bees, perpetually raises the lowness of
> his subject, by the loftiness of his words, and ennobles
> it by comparisons drawn from empires, and from
> monarchs . . . we see Boileau pursuing him in the same
> flights, and scarcely yielding to his master. This, I
> think, my Lord, to be the most beautiful and noble kind
> of satire. Here is the majesty of the heroic, finely
> mixed with the venom of the other; and raising the
> delight which otherwise would be flat and vulgar, by
> the sublimity of expression.[76]

In a similar manner, Dryden employed in his satires the vein of
his better heroic plays, heightening his style by common epic
devices and by imitations and parodies of Virgil. As a result,
Dryden's satires have a grandeur which Pope rarely ever attained;
for Dryden came nearer to the epic tone.

Absalom and Achitophel (1681), as many readers have observed, exhibits in general structure a number of features common
to the epic style. The satire opens in a leisurely fashion with a
narrative which explains the situation and prepares the way for the
declamations of Achitophel. In the central part of the poem we
have a kind of epic catalogue transformed into a series of magnificent satirical portraits. And the conclusion comes with a
Jovian warning from the King, whose words are ratified by a sign
from on high:

> He said. Th'Almighty, nodding, gave consent;
> And peals of thunder shook the firmament.
> Henceforth a series of new time began,
> The mighty years in long procession ran:
> Once more the godlike David was restor'd,
> And willing nations knew their lawful lord.[77]

While this description may have been suggested by either Homer
or Virgil,[78] the chances are in favor of a Virgilian origin, especially since Dryden has made a direct allusion to a famous line
in the Fourth Eclogue: magnus ab integro saeclorum nascitur
ordo.[79] There are further signs of Virgilian influence in less
significant passages. For example, when Dryden addressed the

480

muse with the words, "Indulge one labor more, my weary muse," he was following quite literally the first line of the Tenth Eclogue: Extermum hunc, Arethusa, mihi concede laborem.[80] In another passage, for the sake of rhythmical variation he introduced a pseudo-Virgilian hemistich, "And theirs the native right . . ."[81]

But we find in one passage the best illustration of how Dryden used Virgilian allusions to give to his satire the tone of serious epic poetry. Turning in the second section of the poem from his catalogue of the King's enemies, he gives a brief account of the loyal nobles, with Barzillai (the Duke of Ormond) heading the list. Dryden digresses slightly at this point to honor Ormond's son, Thomas, who had recently died:

> His eldest hope, with every grace adorn'd,
> By me (so Heav'n will have it) always mourn'd,
> And always honor'd, snatch'd in manhood's prime
> B'unequal fates, and Providence's crime;
> Yet not before the goal of honor won,
> All parts fulfill'd of subject and of son:
> Swift was the race, but short the time to run.
> O narrow circle, but of pow'r divine,
> Scanted in space, but perfect in thy line!
> By sea, by land, thy matchless worth was known,
> Arms thy delight, and war was all thy own:
> Thy force, infus'd, the fainting Tyrians propp'd;
> And haughty Pharaoh found his fortune stopp'd.
> O ancient honor! O unconquer'd hand,
> Whom foes unpunish'd never could withstand!
> But Israel was unworthy of thy name;
> Short is the date of all immoderate fame.
> It looks as Heav'n our ruin had design'd,
> And durst not trust thy fortune and thy mind.
> Now, free from earth, thy disencumber'd soul
> Mounts up, and leaves behind the clouds and starry
>   pole.[82]

In addition to the phrase "unequal fates" which translates the iniqua fata[83] of the Æneid, we may note three other echoes of Virgil. The first is near the beginning of our passage:

> By me (so Heav'n will have it) always mourn'd,
> And always honor'd, snatch'd in manhood's prime,

a couplet which recalls Æneas' words on the anniversary of his father's death,

> iamque dies, nisi fallor, adest, quem semper acerbum,
> semper honoratum (sic di voluistis) habebo.[84]

In the noble line, "O ancient honor! O unconquer'd hand," we hear Anchises' praise of the young Marcellus and his house,

> heu pietas, heu prisca fides invictaque bello
> dextera! . . . .[85]

And in the last of these reminiscences,

> Now, free from earth, thy disencumber'd soul
> Mounts up, and leaves behind the clouds and starry pole;

Dryden offers a version of lines which he imitated in another poem,[86]

> Candidus insuetum miratur limen Olympi
> sub pedibusque videt nubes et sidera Daphnis.[87]

He presumably drew the general notion for the passage from Virgil's tribute to Marcellus, unconsciously adapting his other allusions to fit this conception. For example, he applied to the young Earl of Ossory the words originally spoken by Æneas on the anniversary of Anchises' death. By preserving Virgil's anaphora and parenthetical phrase, Dryden fashioned a line which recalls remarkably well the movement of the original. The general poetic effect of the allusions in this passage is especially notable, since the most striking qualities of the lines—measured dignity, aristocratic formality, oratorical exaltation, and worshipful tone —are characteristic also of the lines on Anchises and Marcellus to which Dryden made allusion. In particular, we should observe that Æneas' tribute to his father occurs in a speech, the address to his men after landing in Sicily. The tone of his words is not intimate, but appropriate to public utterance; sincere, but formal.

Blessed with the right occasion, Dryden succeeded in giving to his own lines some of the qualities of Virgil's oratorical style. Moreover, by introducing speeches of this type into the context of satire, Dryden produced a rather remarkable effect. For he managed to impart to Absalom and Achitophel as a whole a grandeur quite out of proportion to the characters and events which were being treated. And yet while the tone is obviously mock-epic, it is mock-epic with the minimum sacrifice of epic seriousness. If we want a standard of comparison, we have only to glance at The Rape of the Lock or The Dunciad to see a style in which burlesque has reduced the epic to a much lower level. The impressiveness of Dryden's satire as compared with that of Pope is in no small measure traceable to Dryden's talent for suggesting the tone of serious heroic poetry, a talent which was materially sustained by his exceptional familiarity with the style of the Æneid.

The Medal (1682) is less heroic than Absalom and Achitophel, perhaps because of its brevity. At any rate, Dryden did not make any notable use of Virgil in this poem or in The Second Part of Absalom and Achitophel (1682). Apropos of the later poem, we may note that there is a Virgilian allusion in the very first line of the part generally attributed to Dryden.

It was in Mac Flecknoe (1682?) that Dryden made his finest satirical use of the heroic manner, truly combining the "venom" of the one style with the "majesty" of the other, notably in the famous lines,

> At his right hand our young Ascanius sate,
> Rome's other hope, and pillar of the State.
> His brows thick fogs, instead of glories, grace,
> And lambent dulness play'd around his face. [88]

Only by comparison with the original passages from Virgil can we fully appreciate Dryden's transformation:

> hinc pater Aeneas, Romanae stirpis origo,
> sidereo flagrans clipeo et caelestibus armis
> et iuxta Ascanius, magnae spes altera Romae, [89]
> ecce levis summo de vertice visus Iuli
> fundere lumen apex, tactuque innoxia mollis
> lambere flamma comas et circum tempora pasci. [90]

Externally, Dryden has managed to suggest Virgil's style while producing an entirely different effect. He displayed a similar

power of imaginative synthesis in another passage where he was
again reshaping Virgilian elements to suit his special end:

> The sire then shook the honors of his head,
> And from his brows damps of oblivion shed
> Full on the filial dulness: long he stood,
> Repelling from his breast the raging god:
> At length burst out in this prophetic mood. [91]

Here Dryden combined the Homeric (and Virgilian) picture of
Zeus with Virgil's description of the inspired Sibyl:

> At Phoebi nondum patiens immanis in antro
> bacchatur vates, magnum si pectore possit
> excussisse deum; . . . . [92]

While in these two passages Dryden made his best satirical use
of Virgilian allusion, throughout the poem he maintained the exalted tone proper to epic narrative and in at least one other instance echoed Virgil directly:

> Now Empress Fame had publish'd the renown
> Of Sh——'s coronation thro' the town. [93]

Although the expression "he said," may not necessarily be Virgilian, Dryden certainly used it to give a final heroic touch to his
poem:

> He said: but his last words were scarcely heard;
> For Bruce and Longvil had a trap prepar'd,
> And down they sent the yet declaiming bard. [94]

In the Religio Laici (1682), which Dryden described as an
example of "the legislative style," he found little place for the
epic manner which we are now studying. His aim, as he pointed
out in the preface to the poem, was to imitate the epistolary style
of Horace. But in the preface to his next didactic poem, The Hind
and the Panther (1687), Dryden declared that, in The First Part,
he had " . . . endeavor'd to raise, and give it the majestic turn of
heroic poesy." [95] In the actual writing he did not confine the epic
touches to The First Part of the poem, for the whole of the closing

scene of The Second Part was copied from the seventh book of
the Æneid. Still it is true that the style of the opening section
is more august, even showing traces of the formal diction which
Dryden later used in his Virgil. We note, for example, such
familiar phrases as "vocal blood," "confess'd in sight," and
"vital air." There are also, in The First Part, two further reminiscences of Virgilian lines: "Cov'ring adult'ry with a specious
name."[96] and

> The surly Wolf with secret envy burst,
> Yet could not howl; the Hind had seen
>   him first.[97]

We may note in The Third Part a long Virgilian simile,[98] and a
fable which was strongly influenced by the Georgics.[99]

But while the heroic element is by no means predominant in
the poem, it is a significant fact that Dryden's epic style appears
even in poetry of a didactic character. In the verse published
between The Hind and the Panther (1687) and the Virgil (1697),
Dryden had little opportunity outside the drama to make use of
his heroic style. But the translation of the Æneid at last gave
him a real opportunity to write in a purely epic vein. Dryden
now felt that he might indulge in all the Virgilianisms which he
had long been cultivating. Elsewhere I[100] have described the
qualities of the style which he created, noting particularly its
vague circumlocutions and Latinized vocabulary. I have also
discussed the effect which the translation had upon Dryden's style
in the verse which followed the Virgil, observing that a considerable number of the same circumlocutions and translation phrases
recur in the Fables as a permanent part of Dryden's "poetic diction."

But although the style of the Fables is fairly heroic, the
writing is on the whole more straightforward and simple, a
change which is due in part to Dryden's improved taste and, more
especially, to the example of Chaucer. It is also partly attributable to the nature of the material which Dryden was translating.
For the stories from Chaucer were hardly epic, in spite of Dryden's insistence on the heroic qualities of Palamon and Arcite;
while Ovid's fanciful tales and Boccaccio's melodramatic narratives lent themselves to a style which was less exalted than that
of Virgilian epic. Nevertheless, though moderating the high-heroic

style of the Æneid, Dryden still retained many of his epic expressions, and still sought to elevate the tone by the use of Virgilian allusions. Even in his Chaucerian renderings he found opportunities to introduce reminiscences of a definitely epic character. As Christie has noted, when Dryden described the funeral rites for Arcite, he had ". . . in his mind Virgil's account of the burial-rites after the battle in Æneid XI."[101] A comparison of the three passages[102] shows that Dryden completely transformed Chaucer's lines by applying a balanced antithetical style which owes much to Virgil.

In other poems of this collection we can also point out the frequent use of Virgilian allusions to give the epic tone. For example, in describing the suicide of Sigismonda, Dryden borrowed a detail from Dido's death scene in the fourth book of the Æneid: "This done, she mounts the genial bed."[103] So Dido ordered her sister to place on the pyre exuviasque omnis lectumque iugalem.[104] When she was ready to die, like Sigismonda, she lay down upon her wedding-bed:

> hic, postquam Iliacas vestis notumque cubile
> conspexit, paulum lacrimis et mente morata
> incubuitque toro . . . .[105]

In Theodora and Honoria, when describing a scene of supernatural horror, Dryden again had recourse to Virgil: "Air blacken'd, roll' the thunder, groan'd the ground,"[106] recalling, sub pedibus mugire solum.[107] Once more, in The Flower and the Leaf, as in Palamon and Arcite, a whole passage, the description of the jousting knights,[108] has been remodelled under the influence of a similar passage in the Æneid.[109] In general conception, movement,[110] and in explicit details, Dryden has drawn upon Virgil; and interestingly enough, he has added an allusion taken from a completely different context.[111] But we hardly need to point out further examples from the Fables to prove that Dryden continued to use Virgilian allusions for epic effect.

Indeed, the connection between Virgil and typically heroic motifs was almost mechanically regular throughout Dryden's poetic and dramatic works. When Dryden's immediate theme was a martial exploit, a prince's death, a supernatural manifestation, "games" of warriors, or even a scene of heroic courtesy, when, in other words, his subject was obviously suitable for epic narrative, he almost invariably turned to Virgil for help in expression. In many cases the epic tone of a passage was in great measure conveyed by some Virgilian allusion or by the incorporation of a Virgilian phrase. But it is apparent from the examples we have quoted that the epic touches so introduced were often adventitious in character and superficial in effect. As Dryden knew, he could not make the Annus Mirabilis into a true epic merely by scattering allusions over the surface of the poem. Nor could he by similar methods turn The Conquest of Granada into a dramatized Æneid. But in certain passages and in certain poems of less grandiose pretensions, when the avowed purpose was to convey the impression of epic rather than the reality, Dryden found in the use of Virgilian allusions the surest means of giving to his verse "the majestic turn of heroic poesy."

NOTES

1 Dedication of the Aeneis, Essays of John Dryden, ed. W. P. Ker (Oxford, 1926), II, 154.

2 See J. E. Spingarn, A History of Literary Criticism in the Renaissance (New York, 1908); B. J. Pendlebury, Dryden's Heroic Plays, a Study of the Origins (London, 1923); George Saintsbury, A History of Criticism and Literary Taste in Europe, II, From the Renaissance to the Decline of Eighteenth Century Orthodoxy (Edinburgh and London, 1902); F. Vial, L. Denise, Idées et Doctrines Littéraires du XVIIe Siècle (Paris, 1928).

3 Ker, op. cit., I, xvii.

4 Spingarn, op. cit., p. 108; Saintsbury, op. cit., p. 78.

5 Saintsbury, op. cit., pp. 131, 311–314.

6 The Works of John Dryden, ed. Sir Walter Scott, revised and corrected by George Saintsbury (Edinburgh, 1882–93), V, 196. —Hereafter cited as SS.

7 Ker. op. cit., II, 38.

8 SS., V, 196.

9 Op. cit., p. 8.

10 Sir William D'Avenant, Gondibert, an Heroick Poem (London, 1651), "The author's Preface To his much honour'd friend,

Mr. HOBS [sic]," pp. 1–70; "The Answer of Mr Hobbes to Sr Will. D'Avenant's Preface Before Gondibert," pp. 71–88.

11 Ibid., pp. 72–73.

12 Ker, op. cit., I, 149.

13 Ibid., I, 150.

14 Ibid., I, 151.

15 SS., II, 332; cf. Æn., V, 294–361.

16 SS., II, 380; cf. Æn., XI, 695.

17 SS., II, 359; cf. Æn., II, 265.

18 SS., II, 382.

19 Ibid., II, 334.

20 Ibid., II, 403.

21 Ibid., IV, 376.

22 See Ker, I, 152–153, 189–190.

23 SS., III, 388.

24 Cf. Æn., I, 85–90, especially 88; eripiunt subito nubes caelumque diemque. Scott, loc. cit., notes the Latinism.

25 SS., III, 426.

26 Æn., VI, 886–887.

27 SS., III, 457; cf. Æn., I, 402–417.

28 SS., III, 394; cf. Aegaeon qualis . . .
          . . . Iovis cum fulmina contra Æn., X, 565–567.

29 Æn., XI, 139–181.

30 SS., III, 392.

31 The First Part, SS., IV, 35.

32 Ibid., IV, 36.

33 Georg., I, 375–376.

34 The First Part, SS., IV, 37.

35 Cf. Georg., III, 51–55; 233–234.

36 The First Part, SS., IV, 38; cf. Georg., III, 75–76, 193–195.

37 The First Part, SS., IV, 38–39.

38 Æn., IX, 435–437.

39 The First Part, SS., IV, 61; cf. Æn., XII, 908–913.

40 The Second Part, SS., IV, 151–152; cf. Æn., I, 402–417; II, 589–592.

41 The Second Part, SS., IV, 160; cf. Æn., XII, 941.

42 The Second Part, SS., IV, 154.

43 G. R. Noyes, Selected Dramas of John Dryden (Chicago and New York, 1910), note to p. 92, l. 105, at p. 440.

44 Æn., X, 356–358; cf. Georg., I, 318–320.

45 SS., V, 204.

46 Ibid., V, 205.

47 Ibid., V, 207.

48 Æn., III, 45–46.

49 SS., V, 210.

50 Ibid., V, 215.

51 Ibid., V, 232.

52 Ibid., V, 292.

53 Ibid., V, 196.

54 This opera was nearly finished before the death of Charles II (1685).

55 SS., V, 420.

56 Æn., II, 324–326.

57 In Troilus and Cressida (1678), I find no sure Virgilian allusions.

58 SS., VI, 417, 503.

59 Ibid., VII, 255–256, 279–281.

60 "The Scene is a Poetical Hell." Ibid., VII, 257.

61 Ibid., VII, 259; cf. Æn., VII, 336–350.

62 SS., VII, 404–405.

63 Preface to Don Sebastian, ibid., VII, 311.

64 Ibid., VII, 327.

65 Ibid., VIII, 165.

66 Æn., VI, 256–258. Compare also the storm from the fourth book of the Æneid especially,

> Interea magno misceri murmur caelum
> incipit, insequitur commixta grandine nimbus . . .
> > Æn., IV, 160–161.

67 SS., VIII, 190.

68 Ibid., VIII, 275–276.

69 Georg., III, 219–233.

70 Æn., X, 454–455.

71 Ker, op. cit., I, 11.

72 Ibid., I, 17.

73 Ll. 489–492. All references to Dryden's verse, except in the plays, are to The Poetical Works of John Dryden, ed. G. R. Noyes (Cambridge, Mass., 1909).

74 The addresses of the general, ll. 297–304, 397–404; and Charles II's prayer, ll. 1045–1080.

75 "The cherub with the flaming sword," l. 1082; "the broad extinguisher" sent by God to quench the fire, ll. 1117–1124.

76 A Discourse concerning the Original and Progress of Satire, Ker, op. cit., II, 107–108.

77 Ll. 1026–1131.

78 Cf. Æn., X, 113–115 and Iliad, I, 528–530.

79 Ecl., IV, 5.

80 Ecl., X, 1.

81 L. 87.

82 Ll. 831–851.

83 Æn., II, 257; X, 380.

84 Æn., V, 49–50.

85 Æn., VI, 878–879.

86 On the Death of Amyntas, a Pastoral Elegy, ll. 67–75.

87 Ecl., V, 56–57.

88 Ll. 108–111.

89 Æn., XII, 166–168.

90 Æn., II, 682–684.

91 Ll. 134–138.

92 Æn., VI, 77–79.

93 Ll. 94–95.

94 Ll. 211–213.

95 The Hind and the Panther; To the Reader, Noyes, op. cit., p. 217.

96 L. 354; cf. Æn., IV, 172.

97 Ll. 551–552; cf. Ecl., IX, 53–54.

98 Ll. 1561–1567.

99 Ll. 1721–1932.

100 "Dryden's Poetic Diction and Virgil," Philological Quarterly, XVIII (1939), 211–217.

101 Poetical Works of John Dryden, ed. W. D. Christie (London, 1925), fn. p. 560.

102 The Knight's Tale, ll. 2924–55; Æn., XI, 188–196; Palamon and Arcite, III, 986–997.

103 Sigismonda and Guiscardo, l. 711.

104 Æn., IV, 496.

105 Æn., IV, 648–650.

106 L. 266.

107 Æn., VI, 256.

108 Ll. 285–299.

109 The games of the Trojan boys led by Ascanius, Æn., V, 577–591.

110 ". . . in the passage on the jousting knights Dryden has re-membered the metrical pattern which he used some years before to describe the Trojan boys [i.e. in his Æneis] . . ." Mark Van Doren, The Poetry of John Dryden (New York, 1920), p. 285.

111 Æn., XI, 624–628.

JOHN DRYDEN'S USE OF CLASSICAL RHETORIC

Lillian Feder

In The Senecan Amble (London, 1951), George Williamson, attempting to account for the innovations in prose style in seventeenth-century England, uses the term "anti-Ciceronianism" to describe the movement toward the new simplicity. Yet more than thirty years ago, Morris Croll, in one of his essays on this subject, made it clear that the term "anti-Ciceronianism" is "open to several objections," one of which is that "it may be taken as describing a hostility to Cicero himself, in the opinion of the new leaders, instead of to his sixteenth-century 'apes,' whereas in fact the supreme rhetorical excellence of Cicero was constantly affirmed by them, as it was by the ancient anti-Ciceronians whom they imitated."[1] Certainly Cicero and Quintilian were read and studied in the seventeenth century. Their influence continued to be a strong one during the very period in which the new critical movement was directed against those of their followers who, during the Middle Ages and Renaissance, had debased the study of oratory to a mere concern with the tricks of declamation.

In their attempts to demonstrate the influence of Seneca,[2] of science,[3] or of Puritanism[4] on seventeenth-century prose style, scholars ought not to forget that a tradition as strong as that of classical rhetoric does not die out overnight. Moreover, a writer is never the product of one influence: indeed, sometimes two opposing traditions can be found in the writings of one man who, through his own interpretation of these influences, unites them in his work. Thus, while it cannot be denied that Dryden's critical essays have the simplicity and modernity characteristic of the new style, it can also be shown that their organization and vocabulary sometimes give evidence of the influence of the Roman rhetoricians. Moreover, Dryden's emulation of Cicero and

Reprinted by permission of the Modern Language Association from Publications of the Modern Language Association, Vol. 69 (1954), pp. 1258–1278, and by permission of the author.

Quintilian had a more profound effect on his work than is revealed by an analysis of his prose style, for their influence is reflected in his critical thought and his poetic method. The influence of the Roman rhetoricians on Dryden has been mentioned before,[5] but no one has carefully investigated the subject. This study will attempt to show how Dryden's view of the nature and function of poetry and certain oratorical qualities of his own work may be related to his use of ancient Roman rhetoric.

For Dryden, the rhetorical writings of Cicero and Quintilian were important in two main respects: in their description of the scope and function of oratory and their analysis of the principles governing the art of rhetoric, under which category they considered oratorical training, style, and language. Cicero and Quintilian regarded oratory as the most exalted of the arts and the orator as a figure of great importance to the state. Eloquence, they said, is a divine gift which serves men by exposing vice; it frees the innocent, inspires a nation, leads men to battle, and soothes them by means of reason. What is more, eloquence pleases while it teaches (De Or. I.viii.30–34; Inst. Or. II.xvi.7–10). Behind this attitude lies the important assumption that artistry is a public good, that a man speaking to his fellows must use eloquence to lead them; in other words, that formal speech is true and practical speech and that the spirits of men are reached only by learning and skill.

Since Cicero and Quintilian regarded rhetoric as a great and significant art and not as a mere concern with the tricks of style (De Or. I.v.17; Inst. Or. II.xiii), they demanded that the orator have a careful and thorough education (De Or. II.i.5; Inst. Or. XII. ii.4–iv.2). According to Cicero, the orator must know the entire history of the past; he must employ the cunning of the logician, the ideas of the philosopher, and language close to that of the poet (De Or. I.xxviii.128), for no man can achieve excellence in oratory without a knowledge of human nature and all important arts and sciences (De Or. II.i.5).

Although the rhetorical writings of Cicero and Quintilian do present a program of training which is sometimes very technical and even rigid, they regard the "rules" of their art in no narrow sense. Both men derived their principles from ancient precedent and direct observation, and one of the most interesting aspects of their work is their constant reference to nature as a guide and standard. "Naturam intueamur, hanc sequamur," Quintilian advis

the orator (Inst. Or. VII.iii.71). According to Cicero, art derives
from nature its power to move and please men (De Or. III.li.197).
Standards of judgment are rooted in the "communibus sensibus"
which nature has provided (De Or. III.l.195). Cicero and Quintilian
refer to nature as an objective and reasonable authority. The
rules are nature "methodized." Thus, Cicero says that poetry
arose from natural feelings; later men studied this art and explained it in accordance with theory derived from observation
of a natural phenomenon (Or. liv.183). Quintilian too regards
nature as so ordered and so reasonable an authority that "naturae
ipsi ars inerit" (Inst. Or. IX.iv.120).

As art improves, says Cicero, it more closely imitates
nature. From their observation of the work of past ages, both
Cicero and Quintilian conclude that there is a constant development in the arts. "Nihil est enim et inventum et perfectum"
(Brutus xviii.71; Inst. Or. X.ii.7–10). Moreover, both men realized
that an artist is to some extent the product of his age. Quintilian
mentions the fact that Cato lived in a "rudi saeclo" (Inst. Or. XII.
xi.23). He also says that there were some types of oratory which,
as a result of the "condicione temporum," lacked polish, though
in other respects they showed genius (Inst. Or. X.x.10; Brutus xi.
45). Thus, with both a consideration for what is useful in "veritate
causarum," in the actual practice of men, and with a sense of
historical perspective, Cicero and Quintilian set down the rules
of their art.

In the opinion of the Roman rhetoricians, perhaps the most
important concern of the orator is the rule of propriety: "Semper-
que in omni parte orationis ut vitae quid deceat est considerandum"
(Or. xxi.71). The proper style is determined by the subject, the
character of the speaker and the audience, and the occasion of a
speech (De Or. III.liv.210–211; Inst. Or. VII.ii.1–11; XII.x.70).
An orator employs one style when he speaks before a legislative
audience, another before a judicial body, and a third when he
speaks to the general public at a funeral or other ceremony. It
is interesting that Cicero considers impropriety the worse error
the poet can commit (Or. xxii.74), and he constantly quotes from
the poets examples of various styles he is illustrating for the
student of oratory.

Cicero and Quintilian also emphasize clarity and order. The
orator must use the language of everyday life and that accepted
by general taste, says Cicero (De Or. I.iii.12), but he does not

approve of the language of the street, for diction must be harmonious, graceful, and marked with artistry (De Or. II.xxvii. 120). Quintilian, who praises Cicero's remarks on this subject (Inst. Or. VII.Pr.25), defines correct usage as the agreed manner of speaking of educated men (Inst. Or. I.vi.45). Language, he says, is based upon reason, antiquity, authority, and custom (Inst. Or. I.v.6). Both rhetoricians object strongly to obscurity, ambiguity, solecisms, and archaisms (De Or. III.x.38–40; III.xiii.49—xiv. 52; Inst. Or. VII.ii.12–23). They warn the orator against far-fetched metaphors (De Or. III.iv.163; Inst. Or. VII.vi.17), and are careful to distinguish between bombast and the embellishments of elegance, between empty ranting and fullness or copiousness which heightens the subject matter (De Or. I.xii.51; Inst. Or. XII. x.73). Above all, they feel, one must speak correctly in pure Latin. Even what is said extemporaneously must resemble the written word (De Or. I.xxxiii.152). Though the language of a speech must be simple and like the language used in cultivated conversation, it must be artful and polished. An oration must be a finished product, its form lending significance to the subject matter.

Perhaps the best way to summarize the stylistic principles of the Roman rhetoricians is to translate a brief passage from Quintilian, who says that the orator's work should be "noble but not extravagant, sublime but not bombastic, daring but not rash, severe but not gloomy, grave but not slow, copious but not immoderate, pleasing but not careless, grand but not pompous." He goes on to say, "The principle is the same in all things; the safest way is the mean, for the worst vice is to be found at either extreme."[6] It is important to notice that the "mean" as defined by Quintilian is "sublime," "copious," and "grand." The concept of the mean sets no limits upon the artist's feelings or his ideas. Quintilian, like Cicero and Horace, suggests that the artist achieves the mean only when through arte occulta he molds his deepest feelings and thoughts into restrained and harmonious expression.

The Roman rhetoricians presented an ideal of the man of letters which Dryden accepted and took for his own.[7] To him the writer was a man concerned with public affairs, the religious and political problems of the day or the publica materies of legend. Dryden persuaded men and commented on affairs, never as a private or isolated figure, but as a representative of his

fellows; he translated and imitated, not as an esoteric exercise,
but in order to interpret important material in the light of the
needs of his own day. As critic and poet he assumed in many
respects the role of the ancient orator.

Dryden's critical writings show the influence of rhetorical
theory on the form of his work and give evidence that rhetorical
principles influenced his view of literature. It seems best briefly
to mention certain oratorical qualities in the organization and
vocabulary of Dryden's essays before discussing his critical
thought.

An Essay of Dramatic Poesy (1668) is a dialogue in the
manner of Cicero's De Oratore. Dryden himself tells us, "You
see it is a dialogue sustained by persons of several opinions, all
of them left doubtful, to be determined by the readers in general."[8]
Like the speakers in the De Oratore, each of the persons of the
Essay offers certain aspects of the truth. In the unspoken fusion
of the several points of view lies the whole story. Their very extremes are the boundaries of truth; their differences reveal its
breadth; their arguments and evidence point the way for the
reader's conclusion.

Again Dryden uses rhetorical techniques in A Defence of an
Essay of Dramatic Poesy (1668), where he is answering Sir Robert
Howard's preface to The Great Favorite or the Duke of Lerma.
Dryden says of Howard:

> I must confess he might better have consulted his
> reputation, than by matching himself with so weak an
> adversary. But if his honour be diminished in the
> choice of his antagonist, it is sufficiently recompensed
> in the election of his cause: which by being the weaker,
> in all appearance, as combating the received opinions
> of the best ancient and modern authors, will add to his
> glory, if he overcome, and to the opinion of his gener-
> osity if he be vanquished, since he engages at so great
> odds, and so like a cavalier, undertakes the protection
> of the weaker party. I have only to fear, on my own
> behalf, that so good a cause as mine may not suffer by
> ill management, or weak defence; yet I cannot but in
> honour take the glove when 'tis offered me; though I
> am only a champion by succession, and no more able
> to defend the right of Aristotle and Horace, than an in-
> fant Dimock to maintain the title of a king. (Essays, I, iii)

Dryden here combines the image of the warrior in the chivalric
trial by combat with that of the orator engaged in a verbal battle.
There are interesting parallels in the writings of Cicero and
Quintilian, both of whom frequently use the image of a battle or
a gladiatorial contest when referring to an argument in the law
court or forum. Often in an extended image, combining the
language of oratory with that of physical combat, they picture
the orator debating <u>in aciem forensem</u>.[9] In the same way, Dryden depicts himself as the orator at arms. His cause is a good
one, and, like a good orator, he must find the right arguments
and their proper arrangement. Indeed, this is no mere literary
dispute; it is an argument that will bring <u>honor</u> and <u>glory</u> to the
winner. So significant is the contest that Dryden uses as an image
the hereditary champion of England. Thus, a controversy over
rhyme is given, by the language and the traditional form in which
Dryden conceives it, the significance of a great debate. He continues in the manner of an orator. The question (<u>quaestio</u>) must
first be made clear. Then he sets forth his arguments, answers
his "opponent," foresees future questions and answers them. I
quote merely brief passages to indicate the tone characteristic
of the whole essay: "This argument is so scattered into parts
that it can scarce be united into a syllogism"; and "I plainly deny
his minor proposition"; and "I am almost fearful of illustrating
anything by similitude, lest he should confute it for an argument."
Dryden concludes by informing the <u>world</u> that he will not answer
any further objections to his point of view because of the respect
he has for his opponent (I, 126–133).

There are many examples of a similar form in other critical
essays.[10] Dryden's tone and language suggest that he is consciously modeling himself after the great Roman orators. In defending the "war of opinions," he compares his behavior with
Cicero's (I, 26). When he replies to the arguments of those who
prefer Ovid to Chaucer, Dryden says, "Perhaps I have assumed
somewhat more to myself than they allow me, because I have ad-
ventured to sum up the evidence; but the readers are the jury,
and their privilege remains entire, to decide among the merits
of the cause; or, if they please, to bring it to some other hearing
before some other court" (II, 248). Again Dryden uses the image
of the courtroom in speaking of the qualifications a critic must
have: "He must be a lawyer before he mounts the tribunal; and
the judicature of one court, too, does not qualify a man to preside

in another. He may be an excellent pleader in the Chancery, who is not fit to rule the Common Pleas" (I, 182–183). Almost everywhere in his criticism Dryden argues against an "adversary," and defends his own "cause." He answers objections, offers evidence, and appeals to reason and "the old rule of logic" (I, 69). His very organization, vocabulary, and imagery reflect an interest in and a knowledge of classical rhetorical theory.

Moreover, Dryden's essays also reveal that in forming his conception of the function of the poet and in determining his critical standards, he owed much to the teachings of Cicero and Quintilian. Dryden believed that the poet had an obligation to his nation and a position in the state comparable to that which Cicero and Quintilian assign to the orator. In speaking of his plans for an epic poem, Dryden says, "This, too, I had intended chiefly for the honour of my native country, to which a poet is particularly obliged" (II, 38). He felt that poetry had a moral as well as a public function: "that kind of poetry which excites to virtue the greatest men is of the greatest use to human kind" (Works, IV, 9). Moreover, in defending the satirist in the conventional way as a man who exposes vice, Dryden adds to this idea his own view of the poet's service to the nation. The poet "armed with the power of verse" (Essays, II, 22), exposes a person who has become "a public nuisance" (II, 80). He regards this function as regulated by law, for, if the person attacked "be wrongfully accused, he has his action of slander; and 'tis at the poet's peril if he transgress the law" (II, 260).

Dryden assumed that the poet's subject matter, like that of the ancient orator, must be meaningful in a national or universal sense. Only then did he feel it was fit for public presentation; as he says, "a noble soul is better pleased with a zealous vindicator of Roman liberty than with a temporizing poet, a well-mannered court-slave" (II, 87).

Thus, the poet, according to Dryden, must be equipped to deal with matters of national and public significance. He says: "I am of the opinion that they cannot be good poets who are not accustomed to argue well. False reasonings and colours of speech are the certain marks of one who does not understand the stage; for moral truth is the mistress of the philosopher. Poesy must resemble natural truth, but it must be ethical" (I, 121). True reasoning and the ability to argue well are the means for achieving the highest function of the poet or playwright—the teaching of ethical truth. Dryden believes that the poet, like the ancient orator, employs reason and sound argument for a moral end.

Clearly Dryden regards the poet as a figure who deals with material of public interest and who presents that material in a logical, organized, and often argumentative manner. Literature, in his eyes, is inextricably connected with man's political and social life. When he writes criticism of poetry or drama in the language of the courtroom and the Forum, he does so conscious of the tradition behind such language, for Dryden suggests that the poet has the dignified and responsible position which the ancient orator once had. When Dryden denies Howard's "minor proposition," he denies that "the stage being one place cannot be two." This seems perhaps a question of mere dramatic technique, but to Dryden it is connected ultimately with human reason, imagination, and the nature of liberty. To prove his point that the stage may properly represent two places successively, he says:

> Imagination in a man, or reasonable creature, is
> supposed to participate of Reason, and when that
> governs, as it does in the belief of fiction, Reason
> is not destroyed, but misled or blinded; that can pre-
> scribe to the Reason, during the time of the repre-
> sentation, somewhat like a weak belief of what it sees
> and hears; and Reason suffers itself to be so hood-
> winked, that it may better enjoy the pleasures of the
> fiction; but it is never so wholly a captive, as to be
> drawn headlong into a persuasion of those things which
> are most remote from probability: 'tis in that case a
> free-born subject, not a slave; it will contribute will-
> ingly its assent, as far as it seems convenient, but
> will not be forced to. (I, 127–128)

A literary question is not to be argued on the basis of personal taste or simply aesthetic standards. It is related to the general questions of human capacity and response. The answer to this question represents one aspect of man's solution to the problem of freedom and order, which is the concern of the poet and the playwright.

If the poet is to be concerned with broad and important public issues, he must have an education which will fit him for this responsibility, and Dryden demands that the poet have an education

similar to that which Cicero and Quintilian describe as necessary
for the orator. He seems to be echoing their very words when he
says that both varied knowledge and broad experience are part of
the training of a poet. In the "postscript" to his Remarks on the
Empress of Morocco (1674), he says that "mere poets are as
sottish as mere drunkards are, who live in a continual mist, without seeing or judging anything clearly. A man should be learned
in several sciences, and should have a reasonable, philosophical,
and in some measure, a mathematical head, to be a complete and
excellent poet; and besides this, should have experience in all
sorts and humours and manners of men" (Works, XV, 411). In
The Grounds of Criticism in Tragedy (1679) Dryden goes so far
as to say that "whoever is ignorant" of "natural philosophy, ethics,
and history . . . does not deserve the name of poet" (Essays, I,
214). And, in A Discourse Concerning the Original and Progress
of Satire (1693), he speaks of the ideal poet:

> . . . if any of so happy a genius be now living, or any
> future age can produce a man, who, being conversant
> in the philosophy of Plato, as it is now accommodated
> to Christian use . . . who, to his natural endowments,
> of a large invention, a ripe judgment, and a strong
> memory, has joined the knowledge of the liberal arts
> and sciences, and particularly moral philosophy, the
> mathematics, geography and history, and with all these
> qualifications, is born a poet; knows and can practice
> the variety of numbers, and is master of the language
> in which he writes; — if such a man, I say, be now arisen,
> or shall arise, I am vain enough to think that I have pro-
> posed a model to him, by which he may build a nobler,
> a more beautiful and more perfect poem, than any yet
> extant since the Ancients. (II, 36)

In discussing Dryden's critical ideas, it is necessary to
mention his use of the term "nature," because his conception of
nature is related to his critical values. As is well known, the
term is used loosely and often carelessly during the seventeenth
century. Yet in Dryden's work it seems to have a consistent
meaning, for he uses it, as did the Roman rhetoricians, to denote
an objective guide and standard based on observation and experience as well as on the example of the past. Like Cicero and

Quintilian, Dryden equates nature and good sense. What is natural resides deep in the "communibus sensibus" of all men. Thus, he advises the poet that "the way to please [is] to imitate Nature. . . . For Nature is still the same in all ages" (II, 134). Elsewhere he says that "good sense is the same in all or most ages; and course of time rather improves Nature, than impairs her" (II, 25). The best poets, Dryden says, have followed nature, and, by studying their work, men determined the rules of the art of poetry (II, 134). He seems to be following Cicero and Quintilian when he concludes that the art of rhetoric is also natural law "methodized":

> . . . those things which delight all ages must have been
> an imitation of Nature, which is all I contend. Therefore
> is rhetoric made an art; therefore the names of so many
> tropes and figures were invented; because it was observed
> that they had such and such an effect on the audience.
> Therefore catachreses and hyperboles have found their
> place amongst them; not that they were to be avoided,
> but to be used judiciously, and placed in poetry, as
> heightenings and shadows are in painting, to make the
> figure bolder, and cause it to stand off to the sight.
> (I, 184)

Dryden believed that a development and a refinement could be observed in the arts through the ages. "Nothing is brought to perfection at the first" (II, 259), he says. The word order and diction of this sentence are so similar to Cicero's "Nihil est enim et inventum et perfectum" that one may conclude that, even if Dryden did not translate directly from Cicero, he certainly had the rhetorician's words in mind. Moreover, like Cicero and Quintilian, Dryden approached the literature of the past with a certain historical perspective. He realizes that "the genius of every age is different" (I, 99), and, in discussing the faults of the Elizabethans, he says, "But these absurdities, which those poets committed, may more properly be called the age's fault than theirs; for, besides the want of education and learning (which was their particular unhappiness), they wanted the benefit of converse" (I, 166).

In his criticism Dryden employs the theory and terminology of classical rhetoric both in his broad general statements about the process of creation and in his frequent references to the

principles governing propriety and correctness. In the preface
to Annus Mirabilis (1667), he describes the poetic process as
follows: "the first happiness of the poet's imagination is properly
invention, or finding of the thought; the second is fancy, or the
variation, deriving, or moulding, of that thought, as the judgment
represents it proper to the subject; the third is elocution, or the
art of clothing and adorning that thought, so found and varied, in
apt, significant, and sounding words: the quickness of the imagination is seen in the invention, the fertility in the fancy, and the
accuracy in the expression" (I, 15). Here Dryden adapts the
first three of the traditional divisions of rhetoric[11] to poetic
creation. Moreover, he uses the term "invention" as Cicero and
Quintilian use inventio. Whereas it is true that the word had been
applied to poetry long before Dryden used it, it is significant that
Dryden, unlike medieval and Renaissance authorities,[12] associates
inventio with thought rather than with style. Fancy is here given
the role of dispositio, though elsewhere Dryden calls the same
process "disposition" (Essays, II, 139, 252). The term "elocution"
here and elsewhere in Dryden's work (I, 14, 145, 186; II, 112)
means exactly what it does in the writings of Cicero and Quintilian.

Throughout his life, Dryden was to find similarities in the
"sister arts," and in 1695 he wrote A Parallel of Poetry and Painting as a preface to his translation of Fresnoy's De Arte Graphica.
An interesting passage is the one in which Dryden discusses
"coloring" in both arts, for once again in his analysis of the process of creation he draws upon the rhetorical tradition:

> Our author calls Colouring lena sororis; in plain English
> the bawd of her sister, the design or drawing; she clothes,
> she dresses her up, she paints her, she makes her appear
> more lovely than naturally she is; she procures for the
> design, and makes lovers for her: for the design of itself
> is only so many naked lines. Thus in poetry, the expres-
> sion is that which charms the reader, and beautifies the
> design, which is only the outlines of the fable. It is true,
> the design must of itself be good; if it be vicious, or, in
> one word, unpleasing, the cost of the colouring is thrown
> away upon it: it is an ugly woman in a rich habit set out
> with jewels; — nothing can become her; but granting the
> design to be moderately good, it is like an excellent
> complexion with indifferent features: the white and red

well mingled on the face make what was before but
passable, appear beautiful. (II, 147–148)

Dryden could make this parallel on good classical authority. Not
only are the two arts compared in Horace, but in Cicero and
Quintilian "colores" is used as a critical term as part of elocutio.[13]
Moreover, early in this essay, Dryden quotes a translation of a
passage from the Orator (ii.9) in which Cicero compares oratory
with painting and sculpture (Essays, II, 118). Also, it is interesting that Dryden, in this passage and in the one quoted immediately
preceding it, speaks of the expression as clothing and adorning
the design, for Cicero says that the orator must "vestire atque
ornare oratione" (De Or. I.xxxi.142), thus expressing the same
idea through the same image.

Dryden's remarks on propriety are similar to those of Cicero
and Quintilian on this subject. Like the rhetoricians, Dryden says
that style "should be suited to the occasion, the subject, and the
persons" (Essays, I, 247; II, 256). In the preface to Religio Laici
(1682) he says that when a poem is designed for "instruction . . .
the poet is presumed to be a law-giver." The expression ought
to be "plain, natural, and yet majestic," for these qualities are
proper to the "legislative style." A man is to be "reasoned into
truth" (Works, X, 32). Dryden has learned from the rhetoricians
that different styles are to be used for different purposes, in relation to their effect on the audience. Here he has chosen the
genus tenue, for his purpose is to prove a point.

Frequently in his discussions of language and wit and in certain of his remarks on specific poets, Dryden reveals his dependence on rhetorical theory. He consistently applies rhetorical
terms and principles to poetry. Speaking of the idiom of poetry,
he says, "And certainly, those who, in a logical dispute, keep in
general terms, would hide a fallacy, so those, who do it in any
poetical description, would veil their ignorance" (Essays, I, 13).
He constantly demands of the poet lucidity, order, learning, and
polish, all of the qualities mentioned by the Roman rhetoricians.
Moreover, Dryden is concerned with the "well-placing of words
for sweetness of pronunciation" (I, 165–176, 246; II, 26, 236).
He often recommends "copiousness" (I, 70, 104, 274), perhaps
the best known quality of the Ciceronian style. Though he complains of the "bombast" of Macbeth (I, 167), he repeatedly mentions the virtue of "sounding" and "significant" language (I, 12,

164, 248; II, 15, 29, 234, 266). He desires "language not strained into bombast, but justly elevated" (I, 248), for Dryden accepted the concept of the "mean." He says that "nothing is truly sublime that is not just and proper" (I, 246).

Discussing the faults a good poet must avoid, Dryden admits his dependence on Cicero. After quoting the lines: "And be free / Not heaven itself from thy impiety," he says, "A synchysis or ill-placing of words of which Tully so much complains in oratory."[14] He objects to "false grammar," ambiguity, obscurity, archaisms, and redundance (I, 176, 246, 268; II, 24, 29), and warns the poet against "far-fetched" metaphors (II, 74, 78). In remarking on Cowley's use of hyperbole, Dryden seems to be quoting directly from Cicero when he says that in Cowley's lines, "two words, seemed and methought, have mollified the figure" (I, 184–185). Cicero, in the De Oratore (III.xli.165), mentions this very device, "mollienda est praeposito saepe verbo," and suggests that the poet add to a forceful metaphor the words, "ut ita dicam."

In the Preface to an Evening's Love (1671), Dryden discusses wit. He quotes Quintilian four times within two paragraphs, and says, "I would have more of the urbana, venusta, salsa, faceta, and the rest which Quintilian reckons up as the ornaments of wit." Moreover, he applies to the drama Quintilian's remark on wit in oratory: "Sunt enim longe venustiora omnia in respondendo quam in provocando" (Essays, I, 139). Defining wit in the preface to Annus Mirabilis, Dryden says, "'Tis not the jerk of an epigram, nor the seeming contradiction of a poor antithesis . . . nor the jingle of a poor paronomasia . . . but it is some lively and apt description dressed in such colours of speech, that it sets before your eyes the absent object, as perfectly, and more delightfully than nature" (I, 14–15). Like Cicero and Quintilian, Dryden distinguished between stylistic tricks and the colores which truly represent the subject. Once again, he applies the rhetoricians' standards and their very terms to poetry.

For Dryden, the "distinguishing character of Lucretius (I mean of his soul and genius) is a certain kind of noble pride, and positive assertion of his opinions." He praises Lucretius' confidence in his own arguments, his "perpetual dictatorship," for, though he is sometimes wrong, he "seems to deal bona fide with his reader." Dryden contrasts Lucretius with Hobbes, who he feels "could not but be convinced, or at least doubt of some eternal truths which he has opposed." He admires Lucretius' ability to argue, his capacity to foresee and answer the arguments of his "antagonists," his vehemence, his "scorn and indignation, as if he were assured of the triumph before he entered into the lists." Despite his disagreement with Lucretius' ideas, Dryden is drawn to his "masculine" thoughts, "full of argumentation, and that sufficiently warm" (II, 259).

When he compares Vergil and Homer, Dryden again applies oratorical values to poetry. Explaining the unique gifts of each poet, he says, " 'Tis the same difference which Longinus makes betwixt the effects of eloquence in Demosthenes and Tully; one persuades, the other commands" (II, 254). Moreover, in describing Aeneas trying "to dissuade" Lausus "from pulling on his destiny," Dryden says that Aeneas seems "more like an orator than a soldier" (II, 141).

The foundations of Dryden's critical system are grounded in rhetorical theory. The implications of this fact are important not only for a correct reading of Dryden, but for an understanding of the nature of neo-classicism. Dryden is the first English critic who offered a unified and consistent theory of literary creation.[15] Of course, the rhetoricians were not the only source of Dryden's critical ideas. He studied Horatian theory, and he formulated critical principles from the example of other ancient and modern poets. Also, it is well known that he was influenced by contemporary French thought.[16] However, the basic premises of his criticism are directly connected with his study of ancient rhetoric. He assumes that poetry, drama, and criticism have an important public function and that the writer, like the ancient orator, moves men through his eloquence and persuades them to think or act in a rational way.

Dryden's criticism, although it reveals his personal prejudices and his changing allegiances, is, nevertheless, basically objective; his standards are clearly set down. He objects to Hobbes's criticism of Homer, because he "begins the praise of Homer where he should have ended it." Hobbes had said that the "first beauty of an epic poem consists in diction, that is, in the choice of words and the harmony of numbers." Dryden holds that "the words are the colouring of the work, which in the order of Nature is last to be considered. The design, the disposition, the manners, and the thoughts are all before it." He has trained himself to consider as "natural" the standards he derived from classical theory, which said that elocutio can be considered only after inventio and dispositio. But Dryden's rules never exist merely for their own sake. He goes on to say, "Words indeed, like glaring colours, are the first beauties that arise and strike the sight; but if the draught be false or lame, the figures ill disposed, the manners obscure or inconsistent, or the thoughts unnatural, then the finest colours are but daubing, and the piece is a beautiful monster at best." The rules help one to achieve "an imitation of human life; which is in the very definition of a poem" (II, 252–253). An "imitation of human life" meant to Dryden, as it did to Cicero and Quintilian, an arrangement of reality which gave the impression that human life or "nature" was elegant in form and reasonable in conduct.

Classical rhetoric influenced not only Dryden's critical writings but his poetry as well, and it can be shown that he developed as a poet from the student writing epideictic declamations to the orator inspiring men by reasonable and moving argumentation. A brief survey of Dryden's progress from declamatio to oratio will demonstrate how he adapted certain oratorical techniques to poetry and will indicate how this discipline helped him to find his "true vein" as a poet.

Dryden's elegy Upon the Death of the Lord Hastings (1649) is his first published poem and his earliest example of the poetic declamatio. Ruth Wallerstein has suggested that Dryden was influenced in this poem by "the classical lament," the "theological elegy in the tradition of Donne," and the "praise of character." No doubt these influences were important, but equally important was Dryden's training in writing the declamatio, of which the funeral address and the eulogy were typical examples. Miss Wallerstein suggests that the "classical harmony of the opening and close perhaps [came] to him through the ideal of the classical oration, which he might have known in school studies and in sermons."[17] However, the opening and the close and indeed the whole poem are reminiscent not of the classical oratio but of the declamatio, the oratory of display, which became the decadent and therefore the anti-classical example of the oration. The elegy begins as follows:

> Must noble Hastings immaturely die,
> The honour of his ancient family?
> Beauty and learning thus together meet,
> To bring a winding for a wedding-sheet?
> Must virtue prove death's harbinger? must she,

> With him expiring, feel mortality?
> Is death (sin's wages) grace's now? shall art
> Make us more learned, only to depart?
> If merit be disease, if virtue death;
> To be good, not to be, who'd then bequeath
> Himself to discipline?   (Works, XI, 94)

The passage has all the qualities which Cicero had assigned to the epideictic address.[18] The antitheses are frequent and obvious. They are ornamental rather than organic parts of the arguments. Dryden has not yet learned to use alliteration in antithesis with skill. The similarity of sound in "wedding" and "winding," words whose connotations are so easily and obviously contrasted, only reinforces the facile nature of the antithesis. Because the idea is an obvious one and the symbols are trite, antithesis here does not have the startling effect it is intended to have. "Death" and "grace" create a forced antithesis because the idea expressed in the theoretical question is neither original nor moving. The line, "If merit be disease, if virtue death," is perhaps the most obvious case of the facile antithesis, structural rather than implicit in the thought. Moreover, there are many easy and graceless repetitions of sound and clauses with similar constructions, which Cicero had mentioned as characteristic of the epideictic speech: "Must she" and "shall art"; "who'd then bequeath" and "who'd not esteem." The awkward and obvious combination of the two devices in "To be good, not to be," is unintentionally humorous.

Such stylistic tricks characterize the whole poem; they are too frequent and too obvious, and they indicate that this is a poet's exercise in learning the techniques of the orator. The poem, unlike most classical elegies, though like many of the seventeenth century, is an argument. The question Dryden raises immediately is, "Must Hastings die?" He takes the negative position on this hypothetical quaestio. Next comes the narratio, a further investigation of the question, and Dryden asks, "What does death in this case mean?" Then he defends Hastings' right to life on the basis of his worth, and attacks the imaginary adversary, the small-pox. His tone is both angry and pleading. He says so himself: "Grief makes me rail; sorrow will force its way." Finally, the question is resolved; Hastings, of course, will live.

In this poem, Dryden was struggling with two chief influences: the metaphysical, which he found in Donne and Cowley, and the

JOHN DRYDEN'S USE OF CLASSICAL RHETORIC

Ciceronian, to which his poetic gifts were far better suited. Miss
Wallerstein suggests that in writing this elegy Dryden "may well
have had Donne's Anniversaries in mind," and goes on to say that
Dryden "had not only been subjected to notions of rational thought,
but he had undergone or had sought out for himself severe training in the designing of a poem, on principles very different from
those of Donne's day."[19] Dryden attempts to combine a Donnean
train of thought with the style of a declamation. As a result the
poem is awkward and artificial.

The Heroic Stanzas to the Memory of Oliver Cromwell (1659)
is another occasional poem. It is clear that Dryden has learned
a good deal. He begins dramatically and simply in the tone of the
public oration:

> And now 'tis time; for their officious haste,
>> Who would before have born him to the sky,
> Like eager Romans e'er all rites were past,
>> Did let too soon the sacred eagle fly.   (Works, IX, 8)

Dryden suggests that his poem is a tribute to a great leader without
the false question or the pretended argument. But still he is struggling with the metaphysical influence, which was part of his training. Thus, in the fifth stanza, he plays with the figure of the circle,
a favorite image of the metaphysicals. Also, he is still under the
spell of his own powers to create antitheses and clauses of similar
construction. However, as a whole, in this poem Dryden achieves
a dignity and a simplicity which indicate the direction in which he
is to go.

The poem demonstrates that Dryden learned early to employ
allusions to ancient Rome in order to evoke a literary and historic tradition of dignity and grandeur. Of course, his allusions
and certain of his poetic techniques remind us of the Latin poets
as well as of the rhetoricians. However, it is interesting to notice how well Dryden has fused the Roman association with the
English occasion, employing allusions to Rome to intensify the
emotional effect of his eulogy:

> Fortune, (that easy Mistress to the young,
>> But to her ancient servants coy and hard,)
> Him, at that age, her favourites ranked among,
>> When she her best-loved Pompey did discard.
>>>> (IX, 9)

And again:

> When, past all offerings to Feretrian Jove,
>   He Mars deposed and arms to gowns made yield,
> Successful councils did him soon approve,
>   As fit for close intrigue as open fields. (Works, IX, 11)

Both Roman history and mythology become the background for
Cromwell's victories. Dryden here relates Cromwell's character, his "piety and valour" (the two chief virtues prized by the
Romans) to the great events of the time, and so even his funeral
address, though an epideictic poem, takes on the qualities of the
deliberative oration.

In Astraea Redux (1660) Dryden uses the devices of the orator
with a new sureness and an ease which indicate that they have
become part of his way of thought as well as of his poetic manner.
Thus, he uses antithesis here to describe a violent upset in national affairs and then a restoration of order:

> But you, whose goodness your descent does show
> Your heavenly parentage and earthly too,
> By that same mildness, which your father's crown
> Before did ravish, shall secure your own.   (IX, 38)

In this poem, Dryden interprets the events of his day and leads
his readers to view the facts enlarged and ennobled through a
Roman image. He uses a rhetorical question brilliantly:

> What king, what crown from treason's reach is free,
> If Jove and heaven can violated be?   (IX, 31)

Of Charles he says:

> His wounds he took, like Romans, on his breast,
> Which by his virtue were with laurels drest. (IX, 32)

And he concludes with:

> Oh! Happy age! Oh times like those alone,
> By fate reserved for great Augustus' throne!
> When the joint growth of arms and arts foreshew
> The world a monarch, and that monarch you. (IX, 40)

JOHN DRYDEN'S USE OF CLASSICAL RHETORIC

In the manner of congratulation there is a challenge to the reader to be worthy of the tone in which he is addressed. The final "you" gives the entire poem, which leads up to it, the force of the spoken word rather than the written one.

Thus, by 1660 Dryden had achieved a fusion of the poetic and the rhetorical which is evident in most of his work. In the Epilogue to Amboyna (1673) he takes the role of the orator:

> A poet once the Spartans led to fight,
> And made them conquer in the muse's right;
> So would our poet lead you on this day,
> Showing your tortured fathers in his play. . . .
> As Cato did his Afric fruits display,
> So we before your eyes their Indies lay;
> All loyal English will, like him, conclude,
> Let Caesar live, and Carthage be subdued. (Works, V, 87)

Here Dryden explicitly states that he is the poet revealing a national plight and leading his people to an understanding of it. Dryden is very courageous; he addresses the audience of a Restoration theater, the wits and rakes, Charles and his satellites, as if they were a Roman senate. He again asks them to view a contemporary event in the light of a great tradition.

In other prologues and epilogues,[20] by his manner of addressing his audience, Dryden indicates that he associates the poet's role with that of the orator. Moreover, in a poem complimenting his friend Henry Higden on his translation of the tenth satire of Juvenal, Dryden says, "Satire is our court of chancery" (Works, XI, 55). Thus, he states the position he takes as a poet; often in his major poems, that position is implicit in the very structure of the poetry.

Mark Van Doren says that in Absalom and Achitophel (1681), Dryden has a "speaking voice. . . . Someone seems actually to be reciting" the poem (p. 76). That "someone" is the orator presenting with the eloquence at his command the political positions of both sides in an important public issue. The question is: shall the Duke of York be excluded from the succession by the Whigs, and shall the Duke of Monmouth be put in his place? Shall Shaftesbury and his party succeed? Dryden speaks as a representative of the Tories, and he is aware, as he remarks in his preface, that "he who draws his pen for one party must expect to make enemies of the other." But Dryden always enjoys a good argument, and he says, "The commendation of adversaries is the greatest triumph of a writer" (Works, IX, 210). The poem's appearance was perfectly timed. Absalom and Achitophel appeared while Shaftesbury was in the Tower and just a few days before a bill of indictment was presented against him. The poem's obvious purpose was to influence public opinion.

Dryden's oratorical powers are manifested in the subtle changes of tone in the various orations of which the poem chiefly consists. Achitophel is a crafty speaker, while Absalom "glides unfelt into their secret hearts" (IX, 238); King David speaks majestically, but the most powerful voice is that of the poet himself, who presents the issues simply and clearly and comments on the speeches and actions of the others. Throughout the poem, Dryden speaks with passion and yet with moderation, preparing the reader to judge critically the arguments of the opposition and then giving his reaction to them. Before Achitophel's first speech, Dryden summarizes his arguments and says: "Weak arguments! which yet, he knew full well, / Were strong with people easy to rebel" (IX, 223). Absalom is depicted speaking to his countrymen, eliciting their sympathy by his words and his tears. Then Dryden remarks ironically:

> Youth, beauty, graceful action seldom fail;
> But common interest always will prevail;
> And pity never ceases to be shown
> To him who makes the people's wrongs his own.
> (Works, IX, 239)

As Dryden goes on to consider the behavior of his countrymen, his tone becomes angry, and in his abrupt exclamations one hears the outraged orator. He also employs a favorite Ciceronian device, repeated rhetorical questions. Such questions, by their very phrasing and emphasis, imply agreement between speaker and audience, and are therefore a powerful rhetorical technique:

> O foolish Israel! never warned by ill!
> Still the same bait, and circumvented still!
> Did ever men forsake their present ease,
> In midst of health imagine a disease,
> Take pains contingent mischiefs to foresee,

> Make heirs for monarchs, and for God decree?
> What shall we think? Can people give away,
> Both for themselves and sons, their native sway?
>
> (Works, IX, 240)

Dryden has learned to use repetition and parallel structure brilliantly:

> Shall that false Hebronite escape our curse,
> Judas, that keeps the rebels' pension purse;
> Judas, that pays the treason-writer's fee,
> Judas, that well deserves his namesake's tree.
>
> (IX, 329)

Absalom and Achitophel is full of examples of what Quintilian calls the sententia (Inst. Or. VIII. v. 2). Dryden uses the enthymeme (Inst. Or. VIII. v. 9) constantly: "Scanted in space, and perfect in thy line!" or "How fatal 'tis to be too good a king!" (Works, IX, 241, 242). King David's speech at the close of the first part can be divided into sections on the basis of the epiphonemae he uses. In this poem Dryden uses rhetorical devices to create the tones of reasonable, sorrowful, and excited speech. Thus, his imaginative interpretation of a contemporary political controversy in terms of Biblical society has the liveliness of a great oration and the intensity of feeling and the depth of understanding of a great poem.

In The Hind and the Panther (1687) Dryden reasons in verse on religious issues. The argumentative nature of the poem is obvious, but more important than the fact that it is an argument in verse is a consideration of the artistry that gives meaning to arguments long since unimportant for themselves alone. D. Nichol Smith calls The Hind and the Panther "an official laureate poem, written not only in defence of [Dryden's] new religion, but also in support of the policy of James."[21] And Dryden himself says in the preface: "About a fortnight before I had finished it, his Majesty's Declaration for liberty of conscience came abroad: which if I had so soon expected, I might have spared myself the labour of writing many things which are contained in the third part of it. But I was always in some hope that the church of England might have been persuaded to have taken off the penal laws and the test, which was one design of the poem when I proposed to myself the writing of it" (X, 113). Clearly this is another poem intended to sway public opinion, and once again Dryden, discussing a national problem, gives it significance beyond its own period.

Dr. Johnson calls The Hind and the Panther "an example of poetical ratiocination, in which the argument suffers little from the meter." He objects, in his characteristic way, to the animal fable.[22] However, one can hardly take his objections seriously, for he does not consider the intrinsic connection between the ratiocination which he praises and the fable which he condemns.

In Absalom and Achitophel Dryden argues as a moderate Tory; in The Hind and the Panther, as a moderate Catholic. The Hind is a perfect symbol for him, for here the Hind is his spokes-man, his orator. In the forest of wild beasts, the gentle Hind is alone; she is afraid to approach the "common watering place," and does so timidly only after the lion "bade her fear no more" (X, 136). Yet this gentle creature is able to defeat the Panther at argument. The Hind's delicate appearance, her inferior posi-tion among the animals, and her natural timidity all gain our sympathy. We are moved by the strength and conviction of the arguments which this gracious and delicate creature sets forth. She becomes the artistic symbol for reason itself, "unspotted" because untroubled by human qualification. And because she is not human, she knows the limits of reason and is not tempted to go beyond them. Thus, the Hind is a representation of the noblest quality in man, reason expressed in fruitful and ethical argumenta-tion. In this way, Dryden exceeds the limitations imposed by the contemporary nature of his argument and the particular point of view the Hind takes.

Though they are having a private discussion, the language that the Hind and the Panther use suggests the courtroom and the Forum. Theirs is a formal and logical argument, more like a public debate than a conversation. The Hind, demanding that the Panther "produce plain proofs," compares her behavior with that of a guilty man before a jury:

> As, when the cause goes hard, the guilty man
> Excepts, and thins his jury all he can;
> So, when you stand of other aid bereft,
> You to the twelve apostles would be left.
>
> (Works, X, 169)

JOHN DRYDEN'S USE OF CLASSICAL RHETORIC

At one point in the argument, Dryden describes the Panther's position as follows:

> To this the Panther sharply had replied;
> But, having gained a verdict on her side,
> She wisely gave the loser leave to chide;
> Well satisfied to have the <u>butt and peace</u>,
> And for the plaintiff's cause she cared the less,
> Because she sued <u>in forma pauperis</u>.
> (<u>Works</u>, X, 221–222)

When the Hind declares concisely and majestically

> Few words will serve to finish our dispute;
> Who will not now repeal, would persecute
> (X, 225)

her language and her tone indicate that she is addressing not the Panther alone, but the nation.

It would be possible to quote many other examples giving evidence of the rhetorical tradition in Dryden's work, but "quotations," says Dryden, "are superfluous in an established truth." And it is perhaps fair to say that the truth of this assumption has been established. In emulating the ancient Roman rhetoricians, Dryden did not merely copy them. Instead, through this discipline, he realized himself as a critic and poet. He adapted the standards of Cicero and Quintilian to the needs of his own time and to his own gifts. Writing in the tradition of the classical rhetoricians, Dryden argued simply and artfully on the issues of his day. Both in criticism and poetry, he appealed to man's deepest feelings through powerful and reasonable ideas.

NOTES

1 "Attic Prose in the Seventeenth Century," <u>SP</u>, XVIII (1921), 80.

2 In <u>The Senecan Amble</u>, Williamson quotes Dryden's objections to certain Senecan traits (pp. 225, 331) and admits that there are oratorical qualities in Dryden's style, but he attempts to illustrate Dryden's "progress in conversational prose" (pp. 342–344).

3 Richard F. Jones, "Science and English Prose in the Third
   Quarter of the Seventeenth Century," <u>PMLA</u>, XLV (1930),
   977–1009.

4 Harold Fisch, "The Puritans and the Reform of Prose-Style,"
   <u>ELH</u>, XIX (1952), 229–248.

5 See George Sherburn, "The Restoration and Eighteenth Century," in A. C. Baugh et al., <u>A Literary History of England</u>
   (New York, 1948), pp. 711–722; Mark Van Doren, <u>John Dryden,
   A Study of His Poetry</u> (New York, 1946), p. 47; and T. S. Eliot,
   <u>John Dryden, the Poet, the Dramatist, the Critic</u> (New York,
   1932), p. 17.

6 "Sic erunt magna non nimia, sublimia non abrupta, fortia
   non temeraria, severa non tristia, gravia non tarda, laeta
   non luxuriosa, iucunda non dissoluta, grandia non tumida.
   Similis in ceteris ratio est ac tutissima fere per medium
   via, quia utriusque ultimum vitium est" (<u>Inst. Or.</u> XII.x.80).

7 Dryden's early training at the Westminster School under
   Dr. Richard Busby was significant in shaping his view of
   the man of letters. For evidence of the rhetorical training
   given in English schools of the 17th century, see G. F. Russel
   Barker, <u>Memoir of Richard Busby D.D. (1606–1695)</u> (London,
   1895), pp. 77–82; and Charles Hoole, <u>A New Discovery of
   the Old Art of Teaching School</u>, ed. E. T. Campagnac (London,
   1913), p. 200.

8 W. P. Ker, ed. <u>Essays of John Dryden</u> (Oxford, 1926), I, 124.
   Hereafter cited as <u>Essays</u>.

9 <u>De Or.</u> I.xxxiv.157; II.xvii.71; II.xx.84; II.lxxviii.317; <u>Or.</u> xiii.
   42; lxviii.228; <u>Inst. Or.</u> II.x.8; II.xii.2; X.i.33; XII.vii.3.

10 In his dedication to <u>The Rival Ladies</u> (1664), Dryden tells
   the Earl of Orrery, "Your rhetoric has gained my cause"
   (<u>Essays</u>, I, 9). In <u>A Discourse Concerning the Original and
   Progress of Satire</u> (1693), Dryden says, "In the mean time,
   as a counsellor bred up in the knowledge of the municipal
   and statute laws may honestly inform a just prince how far
   his prerogative extends, so may I be allowed to tell your
   Lordship, who, by an undisputed title, are the king of poets,
   what an extent of power you have, and how lawfully you may

exercise it, over the petulant scribblers of this age" (II, 22–23). Again, in the same essay, he says: "and though all who are my readers will set up to be my judges, I enter my caveat against them, that they ought not so much as to be of my jury; or, if they should be admitted, 'tis but reason that they should first hear what I have to urge in defence of my opinion" (II, 82). See also I, 24, 248; II, 6, 72, 187–188, 223, 225–226, 239, 251, 273; Walter Scott, ed. The Works of John Dryden (London, 1808), III, 351; IX, 209–210, hereafter cited as Works.

11 See De Or. I.xxxi.142–145; Inst. Or. III.iii.

12 For a discussion of the decline of the tradition of ancient rhetoric during the Middle Ages and Renaissance, see C. S. Baldwin, Medieval Rhetoric and Poetic (New York, 1929), and Donald Lemen Clark, Rhetoric and Poetry in the Renaissance (New York, 1922).

13 De Or. III.xxv.96, 98, 100, lii.200; Inst. Or. VI.v.5; VII.i.40; X.i.116, vi.5; XI.i.85.

14 Essays, I, 167. References to Cicero and Quintilian are to be found throughout Dryden's criticism. For further references to Cicero, see Essays, I, 4, 30, 42, 188 (here Dryden does not mention Cicero, but he uses Cicero's phrase oratio soluta as Cicero does [De Or. III.xlviii.184] to mean "prose"), 256; II, 25, 58, 62, 65, 66, 118, 119; Works, II, 149; V, 187, 188; VII, 117–118, 284, 290; XI, 123; and to Quintilian, see Essays, I, 35, 42, 164, 202; II, 53, 58, 62, 64–65; Works, III, 223; VI, 238; VII, 117–118.

15 For another point of view, see Percy Houston, "The Inconsistency of John Dryden," Sewanee Rev., XXII (1914), 469–482. Houston points out certain minor inconsistencies in Dryden's criticism: his attack on Shakespeare in A Defence of the Epilogue and his defense of him in the preface to Aureng-Zebe, or Dryden's emphasis on delight as the chief end of poetry in A Defence of the Essay and his admission, in the preface to Tyrannic Love, that "pleasure is not the only end of poetry," but that "precepts and examples of piety must not be omitted." These inconsistencies are well known, but they do not prove that Dryden's critical standards were

constantly changing. His standards remained consistent in spite of temporary changes in his taste.

16 See A. F. B. Clark, Boileau and the French Classical Critics in England (1660–1830) (Paris, 1925), and Frank L. Huntley, "Dryden's Discovery of Boileau," MP, XLV (1947), 112–117.

17 Studies in Seventeenth-Century Poetic (Univ. of Wisconsin Press, 1950), pp. 128–130.

18 In the Orator (xi.37–38) Cicero speaks slightingly of the epideictic address and says that he will not include it among the various kinds of speeches he will discuss. It is among those speeches "quae absunt a forensi contentione," decorative and elegant addresses which do not deal with problems of public or national interest. Cicero regards the epideictic speech merely as an exercise, a means of learning to be an orator. In such a speech, he says, the ornamentation is obvious and there is no attempt to hide the artistry which creates the intended effects. Antitheses are frequent, and consecutive clauses are made to end in the same way and with similar sounds. These devices are used less frequently and less obviously in actual practice.

19 Wallerstein, pp. 132–133.

20 For example, see the Prologue to the University of Oxford, spoken by Mr. Hart at the acting of "The Silent Woman." Though Dryden begins by addressing his audience as "Athenian judges," he goes on to speak of "Praetorian bands," and says that "Right is in this Senates hands" (Works, X, 379–380). He begins the Epilogue to All For Love with the lines: "Poets, like disputants, when reasons fail / Have one sure refuge left, and that's to rail" (V, 411). In the Prologue to Don Sebastian Dryden humorously compares his audience with a legislative body. The speaker asks the audience to be kind to the author:

> Be not too hard on him with statutes neither;
> Be kind; and do not set your teeth together,
> To stretch the laws, as cobblers do their leather.
> (VII, 304–305)

21 John Dryden (Cambridge, Eng., 1950), p. 63.

22 "John Dryden," Lives of the Poets, ed. Arthur Waugh (London, 1896), II, 239.

DRYDEN'S HEROIC LINE

George Hemphill

Every reader of Dryden's critical essays must recall his concern with the sound as well as the sense of poetry. In the "Original and Progress of Satire," for example, he says that "versification and meter are the greatest pleasures of poetry. . . . When there is anything deficient in numbers, and sound, the reader is uneasy, and dissatisfied; he wants something of his complement; desires somewhat which he finds not." We can be sure, therefore, that Dryden more than some other poets paid close attention to the fabric of his verse. But it is another question whether the regularity or "correctness" which he aimed at, and which he achieved for his translation of Virgil, is generally admired today. If it is admired, it is admired only as one admires an antique. The taste of most modern poets is not for regularity but for liberty bordering on license. In this respect they are like the late Elizabethans and Jacobeans who wrote— to use the phrase which Dryden took from the French—prose mesurée.

This modern bias against regularity colors, if ever so slightly, the best brief account of Dryden's versification I have seen—that of George Young in his English Prosody on Inductive Lines (Cambridge, 1928). In this more detailed examination of the subject I have followed his theory of metrical variation; and his estimate of Dryden as verse-craftsman will serve as my point of departure:

> As an artist in verse of the special kind which was being written in his day, he is first in the first class. The metre which he made his own, the rimed couplet in cinquepace, was, as he himself bears witness, practised with success by at least one precursor, Denham, whose

Reprinted by permission of the Modern Language Association from Publications of the Modern Language Association, Vol. 72 (1957), pp. 863–879, and by permission of the author.

lines on the Thames he praises nobly. His developments by way of prosody were small; and he forbore
to use those of his predecessors. His verse in this
metre is accordingly a throwback to the age of Purism
[i.e., of the early Elizabethans]. His mastery in it is
due to his mastery as a writer of prose; prose of a
time when the language had newly reached its present
level of adaptability to the requirements of modern
thought. To this he added an ear for sound in words
above that of any contemporaries or proximate successors, and a skill in the art of combining smoothness with strength, whereby the asperities of our
monosyllables were converted into ornaments. (p. 244)

This estimate needs little correction but more detail.

I am concerned here with Dryden's purely metrical variations
from the norm of the heroic line, rhymed and unrhymed. This
means that I have nothing to add to the study by Miss Wallerstein
and others of the rhetorical structure of the heroic couplet. And
I am not concerned with Dryden's lyric poems, which should be
studied alongside the music they were written to accompany.[1]
Metrical variations from the norm of the heroic line necessarily
fall into two categories—those affecting the number of syllables
in the line, and those affecting distribution or patterning of
stresses. I have taken no notice of a variation unless at least
one of the following questions about it can be answered affirma-
tively: (1) Have other prosodists mentioned it? (2) Does the poet
himself mention it? (3) Is there a pattern of its occurrence in a
large body of work? The least dubious variations come first in
each list below. First are the variations affecting number of
syllables:

    I. Long or short line for heroic.
    II. Line-ending other than masculine.
    III. Initial truncation.
    IV. Synaloepha.
    V. Colloquial obscuring of syllables in set phrases.
    VI. Dramatic extra syllable.
    VII. Free substitution of feet containing more than two
syllables. And the variations affecting stress-distribution:

VIII. Accent on the first syllable instead of the second (initial trochee established by the accent of a polysyllable).

IX. Accent on an odd-number syllable (mid-line trochee) following a pause.

X. Accent on an odd-numbered syllable (mid-line trochee) without preceding pause.

XI. Trochees, spondees, and pyrrhics established by sentence emphasis.

XII. Deficiency below or excess above five stresses in the heroic line.

All but three of these variations (VI, VII, and XII) meet two or more of the conditions mentioned. In what follows, the variations listed are discussed in turn.

I. The occasional alexandrine is an obvious feature of Dryden's verse. It appears as the third line of a triplet as early as the "Prologue to the University of Oxford" (1673?), and more and more frequently thereafter. In the "Preface to Sylvae" (1685) Dryden seems to be thinking of it as appropriate to lyric: "Since Pindar was the prince of lyric poets, let me have leave to say that, in imitating him, our numbers should, for the most part, be lyrical. For variety, or rather where the majesty of the thought requires it, they may be stretched to the English heroic of five feet, and to the French Alexandrine of six." But in the later and more famous reference to it, in the "Dedication of the Aeneis" (1697), it is defended as appropriate to a heroic poem —to The Faerie Queene and the English Aeneid: "I must acknowledge that Virgil in Latin and Spenser in English, have been my masters. Spenser has also given me the boldness to make use sometimes of his Alexandrine line, which we call, though improperly, the Pindaric, because Mr. Cowley has often employed it in his Odes. It adds a certain majesty to the verse, when 'tis used with judgment, and stops the sense from flowing into another line." The alexandrine, whether necessarily majestic, even when used with judgment (everyone recalls Pope's alexandrine, "That like a wounded snake drags its slow length along"), is with Dryden a deliberate variation. It does not appear in the blank verse of All for Love, where there is no need to stop the sense.

But Dryden very rarely stretches the heroic line to a septenary, and he never refers to it as a legitimate variation. He does mention Chapman's Homer, but only with reference to its triplets, not its continuous septenaries. Here are the six cases of septenary variation which Noyes calls attention to in his edition:

> Thou leap'st o'er all eternal truths in thy Pindaric way
> (The Medal, l. 94)

> The nauseous qualms of ten long months and travel to requite
> (Fourth Pastoral, l. 75)

> But Maurus sweeps whole parishes, and peoples ev'ry grave
> (To John Driden, l. 83)

> And of the Greeks oppress'd in fight to hear the dying sounds
> (Iliad I.666)

> The fanning winds and purling streams continue her repose
> (Cymon and Iphigenia,
> l. 106)

> These lead the lively dance, and those the brimming bowl invite
> (Ibid., l. 568)

There are two more in the Fourth Pastoral (ll. 42 and 73), and two which appeared in the 1685 translations from Virgil:

> With Nisus and Euryalus, the foremost of the band
> (Nisus and Euryalus,
> l. 12)

> Beside him stood Euryalus, his ever faithful friend
> (Ibid., l. 109)

but I think not many more. The last two were reduced by two feet for the Aeneid of 1697, where they appear at V.385 and IX. 228. Noyes and Saintsbury find imitative sound in the first group of lines, but it is certainly not present in the two lines from the episode of Nisus and Euryalus. These lines, and I think some of the others too, are not deliberate variations, but lapses into the Elizabethan fourteener.

Dryden substitutes short as well as long lines for the heroic. But in the "Preface to Tyrannic Love" they require an apology. In that play, he says, he has "from haste not observed equality of numbers." Short lines appear in the 1685 translation of Virgil, but were removed in the 1697 version, even though Virgil himself allowed some to remain in the original. Dryden says he is not "willing to imitate Virgil to a fault"; and that short lines are "the imperfect products of a hasty Muse; like the frogs and serpents in the Nile; part of them kindled into life, and part a lump of unformed unanimated mud." There are a number of short lines in All for Love which may be deliberate; or one might say that in writing blank verse Dryden saw no need to maintain equality of numbers. Rhymed lines of varying length are appropriate to lyric; equality of numbers is a desideratum in the heroic couplet; but line-division itself becomes almost a matter of indifference in blank verse, which is only prose mesurée.

II. Like Puttenham, who wrote that "the cadence which falleth upon the last syllable of a verse is sweetest and most commendable," Dryden shows a marked preference for masculine endings; he reserves feminine endings for special effects. In speaking of the heroic stanzas of Annus Mirabilis he says that "we cannot give ourselves the liberty of . . . using the variety of female rhymes; all of which our fathers practiced, and [which] are still in use among other nations." Dryden consistently limits the use of feminine ending to the less elevated Kinds: lyric, where the conventions of music rather than those of the syllabic stress line hold; and the Prologues and Epilogues, where, as in

> You balk'd him when he was a young beginner,
> And almost spoil'd a very hopeful sinner;
> But, if once more you slight his weak indeavour,
> For aught I know, he may turn tail forever

a comic effect is intended. The variation is also quite frequent in All for Love, where Dryden is following the practice of "the last age" and the "divine Shakespeare." The effect there is of course not comic. Feminine ending in blank verse is a purely rhythmic variation; in disturbing regular meter it gives the effect of slight excess or well-mannered negligence, perhaps, but it may appear in any context of sense. Feminine rhyme in couplets is not nearly so flexible; like a pun, and like masculine rhyme itself to a lesser degree, it invites attention to sense as well as sound.

III. I follow George Young, who in turn got the term from J. B. Mayor, in calling the omission of the first syllable of the line a case of initial truncation. Chaucer's most famous line probably illustrates this variation, and Dryden's well-known censure of Chaucer in the "Preface to the <u>Fables</u>" suggests that he objected to it. Dryden "cannot go so far as [Speght]; for he would have us believe the fault is in our ears, and that there were really ten syllables in a verse when we find but nine." There is good sense in the observation of R. D. Jameson that Dryden's ignorance of Middle English "is not so important here as his demand for syllabic equality in the heroic line";[2] it is not fair to expect Dryden to know as much about Middle English as we do. He was wrong in thinking that there were thousands of cases of initial truncation in Chaucer, but there is no wide agreement even among modern scholars that Chaucer avoided the variation altogether. George Young (pp. 39–43) argues that he tried it and rejected it. But Dryden's objection to heroic lines "which are lame for want of half a foot," though consistent with his practice in the couplet, does not extend to short lines like the following in <u>All for Love</u>:

ˏToo presuming	(II.164)
ˏIf I mix a lie	(II.252)
ˏThat's a trifle	(II.402)
ˏIs this friendly done?	(III.151)
ˏDolabella's Cleopatra	(IV.297)
ˏWere I she	(IV.396)
ˏ'Tis not worth	(V.344)
ˏCoward flesh	(V.482)

There is little doubt that these are deliberate variations. They are remarkable in that they combine shortness with initial truncation (and hence cannot be misread as faulty heroic lines). There are many short lines in the blank verse of the Elizabethan and Jacobean dramatists, and, less frequently, cases of initial truncation, but never this deliberate combining of the two variations. It should be noticed that lines like these disturb alternate stress only when they are preceded by lines with masculine endings, or when, as in II.164, II.402, and IV.297, the short, initially truncated lines themselves have feminine endings and the line immediately following begins normally. All these lines except the first are preceded by lines with feminine endings, with the result that initial truncation does not disturb normal stress-distribution. One is led inevitably to the conclusion that Dryden, even when he was imitating Shakespeare, could not abandon the

metrical pattern of alternate stress. But this is to anticipate discussion of variations VIII–XII.

IV. Prosodists have always had trouble in describing accurately the pronunciation which poets intended when they wrote
expressions like "th' unwieldy," "t' unite," and "for virtu' have
done." "Elision," the term for this phenomenon which Bridges
adopted, led some of his critics, most notably Saintsbury, to believe that he was recommending pronunciations like thŭnwíeldў̆,
tŭnĭ́te, and vírtŭ́ve. Most prosodists since then have recommended
compromise between Bridges' elision and Saintsbury's trisyllabic
substitution. Everyone has noticed, as Jonson's editors Herford
and Simpson put it, that poets of the seventeenth century often
write an apostrophe "between two unelided words to mark a kind
of diphthong having the metrical value of one syllable." Dryden's
term for this phenomenon, "synaloepha," has much to recommend
it. Elision properly refers to the letter which is struck out,
while synaloepha refers to the sounds themselves, which are
smeared together. Dryden's discussion of synaloepha occurs in
the "Dedication of the Examen Poeticum":

> Since I have named the synaloepha, which is the cutting
> off one vowel immediately before another, I will give an
> example of it from Chapman's Homer, which lies before
> me; for the benefit of those who understand not the
> Latin prosodia. 'T is in the first line of the argument
> to the first Iliad:
>
> Apollo's priest to th' Argive fleet doth bring, &c.
>
> There we see he makes it not the Argive, but th' Argive,
> to shun the shock of the two vowels immediately follow-
> ing each other. But in his second argument, in the same
> page, he gives a bad example of the quite contrary kind:
>
> Alpha the pray'r of Chryses sings;
> The army's plague, the strife of kings.
>
> In these words, the army's, the ending with a vowel, and
> army's beginning with another vowel, without cutting off
> the first, which by it had been th' army's, there remains
> a most horrible ill-sounding gap between.

Dryden unfortunately forgets the root meaning of synaloepha here, and gives the definition of elision; and his technical knowledge of phonetics is no better than his knowledge of Middle English. But he undoubtedly had a good ear. By "the shock of the two vowels immediately following each other" in the Argive and the army's he seems to mean a glide from one vowel to another interrupted by a glottal stop. That stop is "a most horrible ill-sounding gap," to be avoided at all costs. But if that is what he meant, he was wrong in saying that the apostrophe cut off a vowel; instead it signals a smooth glide from one vowel to another without intervening glottal stop. And if we take syllable to mean a unit of sound "capable of being pronounced by a single impulse of the voice" (NCD), Bridges rather than Saintsbury is right in thinking of a sound like [ðja] or [ðI'a] as one rather than two syllables. But Saintsbury is right when he calls slurring bad English.

Dryden takes no critical notice of the different metrical situations of th' Argive and the army's. The former occupies the place of two syllables in the meter, the latter three. If the first line were written "Apollo's priest to the Argive fleet doth bring," any reader used to alternate stress and hence not ready to allow an anapaest would be momentarily confused. The other line causes no such trouble. Dryden describes his mature practice in this matter in the "Dedication of the Aeneis":

You may please also to observe, that there is not, to the best of my remembrance, one vowel gaping on another for want of a caesura [an apostrophe] in this whole poem; but, where a vowel ends a word, the next begins either with a consonant, or what is its equivalent; for our W and H aspirate, and our diphthongs [consonantal i and u], are plainly such. The greatest latitude I take is in the letter Y, when it concludes a word and the first syllable of the next begins with a vowel. Neither need I have called this a latitude, which is only an explanation of this general rule, that no vowel can be cut off before another, when we cannot sink the pronunciation of it; as he, she, me, I &c. Virgil thinks it sometimes a beauty to imitate the license of the Greeks, and leave two vowels opening on each other, as in that verse of the Third Pastoral:

Et succus pecori, et lac subducitur agnis.

526

But, <u>nobis non licet esse tam disertis</u>, at least if we study to refine our numbers.

Dryden means, first, that an apostrophe for a suppressed letter marks the place where adjoining vowels in adjoining words make up only one syllable in the meter. In the translation of Virgil, the only letters dropped are the <u>e</u> of the definite article and the <u>o</u> of <u>to</u> when the next word begins with a vowel. I have noticed only one "vowel gaping on another for want of a caesura"—"In rush the Greeks, and all the apartments fill" (<u>Aen</u>. II.675)—and here there is only very slight disturbance of meter. In obvious contrast are the following lines of Milton from <u>Paradise Lost</u>, to which I have added apostrophes:

Thy condescension, and shall be'honoured ever
(VIII.649)

Little inferiour by my'adventure hard
(X.468)

The Glory of that Glory, 'who now become
(722)

Thou didst accept them; wilt thou'enjoy the good
(758)

I had persisted happier, 'had not thy pride
(876)

That cruel Serpent: On me'exercise not
(927)

Against God only, I'against God and thee
(931)

Donne and Jonson use the apostrophe regularly in this metrical situation, sometimes suppressing a letter and sometimes not.[3]

Dryden says further that in the translation of Virgil consonants, including [w], [h], and [j], usually come between adjoining vowels in adjoining words (thereby extending the rule that requires <u>an</u> to be the indefinite article before words beginning with vowels) when the vowels make up not one but two syllables in the meter. This refinement is often ignored, as in

Once more was happy in a Trojan mate
> (<u>Aen</u>. III.385)

O only happy maid of Priam's race
> (415)

O say what dangers I am first to shun
> (471)

but in every such case we cannot, for metrical reasons, "sink
the pronunciation" of either vowel. In the lines from <u>Paradise
Lost</u> listed above we must either sink the pronunciation of a vowel
or admit a trisyllabic foot with, perhaps, "a most horrible ill-
sounding gap" between the vowels. Dryden would undoubtedly
censure Milton's lines, with their colloquial flavor, as indecorous
in a heroic poem. The rule is, not surprisingly, relaxed in <u>All
for Love</u>, where we read

> Then I have washed an Aethiop. Y'are undone;
> Y'are in the toils; y'are taken; y'are destroyed
> (II.225–226)

—permissible in imitation of a tragedy of Shakespeare's, but not
for the translation of Virgil's epic. These <u>y'are</u>'s are, however,
mere colloquial contractions, and noticeably different from Milton's
synaloephas. It may be noticed too that the first and last one (like
the synaloephas in <u>PL</u> VIII.649 and X.931 above) fall in stressed
places in the line. But in Dryden's mature work in the couplet
synaloepha appears regularly in unstressed places only. There is
just one exception in the <u>Aeneid</u>: "While th' other hand sustains
my weighty shield" (II.914). I have noticed that Sidney, like Dryden, and unlike Shakespeare, Donne, Jonson, and Milton, is reluctant to allow synaloepha in stressed places.[4] Sidney and
Dryden may have felt that the glide between vowels was too hard
to achieve when one of them carried accent, or when the diphthong
occupied the stressed place.
    V. Colloquial obscuring of syllables in set phrases is differ-
ent from synaloepha in at least one respect: synaloepha is always
between adjacent vowels, while colloquial obscuring sometimes
takes place between consonants. C. H. Herford and E. P. Simpson[5]
note it in Jonson (as in the line "Active in 's braine, and passive
in his bones"), and it is very common before the Restoration,

where it appears in passages that are satiric, bluff, and hearty
in tone. I agree with Herford and Simpson that Jonson's line does
not contain an English anapaest; we have either an extra semi-
syllable [nəȝ] in a set phrase or, if the n̲ is indistinct (in which
case a better spelling would be i̲' ̲'s̲), an odd kind of synaloepha.
I prefer the first pronunciation. This colloquial obscuring is
frequent in Dryden's boyish Elegy on Hastings (as in "speak'it,"
"in's soul," "i'th'lily," "in's nobler," etc.), and in the Prologues
and Epilogues from the beginning to the end of his career. It
must simply represent pronunciations which, like 'tis and ̲'t̲ ̲will,
have disappeared. The Scott-Saintsbury reading, "But those
damn'd dogs can ne'r be in the right," of line 19 of the Epilogue
to Aureng-zebe does not represent seventeenth-century pronunciation faithfully. Noyes prints "But those damn'd dogs can never
be i'th'right," from the edition of 1692. To level all such variations is to mislead the reader, who should be in a position to
discover the circumstances under which Dryden allowed them
to appear. After the Elegy on Hastings he seems to have allowed
colloquial obscuring in verse written for the stage (the Prologues,
Epilogues, and All for Love), but not for the more elevated satires
and translations. For lack of faithful editions I have not studied
the variation in the heroic plays.

VI. The metrical variation which George Young calls dramatic extra syllable is associated with the name of Shakespeare.
It seems to have been first noticed in William Sidney Walker's
book Shakespeare's Versification (1854), and Young supposes
that it recommended itself to Shakespeare in the following way:
"Composing and realizing his verse by ear rather than eye, he
was early led to a new and fruitful variation, the extra syllable
within the line. . . . Coming to him by analogy with the final extra
syllable, it was not unnatural that an intruding syllable, extraneous
to the norm, should pass muster, if at a pause" (p. 157). The
variation certainly appears in Shakespeare, but it is alien to Dryden. In the Essay of Dramatic Poesy Neander had said that "no
man is tied in modern poesy to observe any farther rule in the
feet of his verse, but that they be dissyllables; whether spondee,
trochee, or iambic, it matters not." Even if it be denied that
Neander is a spokesman for Dryden in his early maturity, it is
still the case that there is a rather close connection between
Neander's rule and the bulk of Dryden's verse. Neander's rule
would allow all the variations listed above except VI and VII (III

only in combination with feminine ending). It can be shown that
Neander tells only part of the truth about Dryden's versification.

If dramatic extra syllables appeared anywhere in Dryden
one would expect them to appear in All for Love, but there are
only two possible cases in that imitation of "the divine Shakespeare":

> See, I have caught it too. Believe me, 'tis not (I. 272)

> And now 'tis near, 'tis lessen'd.
> > Mark the end yet.
> > (II. 239)

The first, however, may be read with feminine ending, and the
second with synaloepha in the ninth place. I would conclude that
dramatic extra syllable is not a deliberate variation in Dryden.
This does not necessarily mean that unlike Shakespeare he composed by eye rather than ear, but only that his ear demanded, in
Jameson's phrase, "syllabic equality in the heroic line." Since
dramatic extra syllable is like feminine ending within the line,
it has the effect of breaking the line in two. Dryden will inter-
polate a short line between two heroic lines, but except in lyric
will never let us forget, even for a moment, the existence of the
heroic line as normal. This is quite in accord with the ethical
and aesthetic principle which permits variety and liberty, but
which disallows chaos and license. George Young, in comparing
the blank verse of Antony and Cleopatra with that of All for Love,
observes that in the latter "there is a tendency always at work
to make the meaning march with the line. It results rather in
[Dryden's] failing after all to 'stop the sense from flowing into
another line,' than in his attaining to that Shakespearean swell
and fall which makes one forget that there is such a thing as a
line" (p. 247). I find it hard to understand why a reader would
want, however, to forget the existence of the line. The sense of
line is only more obvious in Dryden than Shakespeare; it is not
absent in Shakespeare's (or Milton's) most flowing and elevated
verse-paragraphs. To read them otherwise is to read them as
prose heightened by meaning rather than as verse heightened
both by meaning and by the observance of certain metrical conventions. It is a matter of taste whether line-sense is too obvious in Dryden; it is perhaps too obvious for our age, which
likes to have its sense unbridled by convention.

VII. By free substitution of feet other than dissyllabic in
the heroic line I mean such substitution when it is so frequent,
so much a feature of a poet's metrical practice, and so little
to be accounted for under other heads (IV, V, or VI), that it may
be called deliberate. Music of course has something like free
substitution; it is part of classical prosody, and lyric poetry has
followed musical as often as metrical convention, but it has no
continuous history as a variation in syllabic stress verse. Saintsbury thought that excellence in versification depended on the frequent occurrence of trisyllabic feet. Stress-verse has been analyzed as consisting of a great variety of feet, and much modern
verse, if it is not prose mesurée, must be analyzed in the same
way. What Saintsbury did was to put synaloepha ("the abominable
apostrophation of the seventeenth century"), cases of extra semi-
syllables (as in heaven, taken, evil, etc.), colloquial obscuring,
and dramatic extra syllable under the single rubric of trisyllabic
substitution. In doing this he achieved a simplification of terminology, which in itself is desirable, but which in this case had the
effect of confusing several distinct phenomena. The history of
English versification cannot be understood as the checkered career
of the trisyllabic foot. Neander's remark excludes it, and with
some insignificant exceptions it does not appear in Dryden's couplets or blank verse. The only sure cases of trisyllabic substitution in Dryden's heroic verse occur in the deliberate doggerel of
the Prologue to The Mistakes. By an irony of English literary
history the great champion of trisyllabic substitution also edited
Dryden, who limited the use of the variation to the lower Kinds.

VIII. Turning now to the variations affecting stress-distribution, it will be noticed that the first three (VIII–X) are usually
thought of as a single variation—trochaic substitution. Neander's
remark about trochees recommends the use of this term, but there
are more persuasive reasons for avoiding it. For one thing there
is so little agreement as to what it is that where some readers
find a trochee others will find an iamb and still others will find
"level stress." I have avoided this difficulty by taking notice
here and in the next section of indubitable variations only: that
is, of trochees established by the accent of a polysyllable. The
placing of that accent should not be inferred solely from the position of the polysyllable in the line, because to do this is to make
unwarrantable assumptions about a poet's pronunciation and his
habits in allowing variation; linguistic and lexicographical evidence

should supplement metrical evidence. Ideally, all the evidence points to the same conclusion about the accent of a polysyllable. Thus it would be a mistake to assume that the first line of All for Love is other than normal in its stress-distribution. Initial trochees are of course possible in 1677, but we learn from dictionaries that in the seventeenth century portents still had its accent on the second syllable. To assume otherwise is to find in a line like "Vers'd in portents, experienc'd, and inspir'd" (Aen. V.924) a variation almost without parallel in Dryden's elevated style.

The single term trochaic substitution gives, in addition, the false impression that trochees can appear anywhere in the line, but it is well known that VIII is an older and more frequent variation than IX, that X is unusual except in some Jacobean and modern verse. Hence if we wish to understand the differences between the metrical styles of different historical periods we must discuss the three variations separately; only the unhistorical formalist critic will do otherwise.

Of all the variations affecting stress-distribution, the initial trochee is the only one that appears regularly throughout Dryden's verse. It is not noticeably more frequent in his early verse; he does not avoid it either in his maturity or in his most elevated style. About one out of every forty lines begins with a trochee. It is for the most part a purely metrical variation; not, so far as I can detect, an "echo to the sense." The echo may have been sought, however, in this description of the battle-games in the Aeneid:

> Flying they follow, and pursuing shun;
> Broken, they break; and, rallying, they renew
> In other forms the military shew.
>> (V.764–766)

Whatever the effect of the variation on the sense, the organization of sound is very neat, and could not have been accidental. The same cannot be said of the following couplet:

> Evas and Mimas, both of Troy, he slew.
> Mimas his birth from fair Theano drew,
>> (Aen. X.994–995)

where the variations are caused by the accentuations of the proper names. Dryden neither seeks out nor takes pains to avoid this variation.

IX. Both Sidney and Spenser allow an accent to fall on an odd-numbered syllable immediately following a pause; before their time this mid-line trochee was not firmly established, but it became very common early in the seventeenth century. An index of Dryden's use of this variation is its appearance three times in the hundred and thirty-four lines of his two earliest poems:

> Labor a crime? study self-murther deem
> > (Hastings, 1. 12)

> Grief makes me rail: sorrow will force its way
> > (Ibid., 1. 89)

> Thy greedy eyes; looking on this pure gold
> > (To Hoddesdon, 1. 24)

and only four times (exclusive of its appearance because of proper names, as in IX. 780, X. 605, and XI. 131) in the nearly fourteen thousand lines of the Aeneid:

> High o'er the grass, hissing he rolls along
> > (II. 647)

> Confess'd the god's approach. Trembling he springs
> > (VIII. 291)

> Then pois'd the spear, heavy with human weight
> > (XI. 836)

> Deep in the root, whether by fate, or chance
> > (XII. 1118)

The frequency of mid-line trochees after pause in All for Love (see I. 238, 398, 421, 450; II. 291; III. 74, 78, 329, 330, 332, 338; IV. 14, 48, 57, 555; V. 51, 335, 471, 498) and in the boyish poems written before the Heroic Stanzas points to an obvious conclusion: that Dryden associated the variation with "the last age," with that age which had not yet perfected the heroic couplet. He may have felt that variations in stress-distribution anywhere except at the beginning of the line had the effect of breaking the line in two—

> High o'er the grass,
> Hissing he rolls along,
> And brandishes by fits his forky tongue,
>
> Confess'd the god's approach
> Trembling he springs,
> As terror had increas'd his feet with wings,

instead of couplets. The integrity of the couplet must at all costs
be preserved, and the undoubted association of variation in stress-
distribution with line-beginning is a threat (if, as one would think,
a minor threat) to that integrity. Although Neander's theory of
variation would find room for that famous line of Lear's "Never,
never, never, never, never," Dryden himself would not write such
a line, and it would perhaps strike his ear as no line at all.

X. A mid-line trochee without preceding pause is an unusual
variation even among the Jacobeans. It appears, I think, in Paradise Lost (the only question being whether a pause exists when it
is not marked by punctuation), but I have noticed only two likely
cases in Dryden, both, as one might suspect, in All for Love:

> On, sweet eunuch; my dear half-man, proceed
>   (IV.375)
>
> I've thought better; do not deny me twice
>   (V.316)

Since in both of these lines sentence-emphasis demands a trochee
(or something like it) in the first foot, the accent on the third
syllable picks up a rhythm already established. The result is
smoothness rather than roughness; dissyllables accented on the
second syllable replacing eunuch and better would give rhythmi-
cally different but not smoother lines. Dryden can be deliberately
rough in his meters (see his note on Aen. IX.853), but his notion
of roughness does not include the possibility of accenting an odd-
numbered syllable in mid-line without preceding pause or without
other warning (as above) that the rhythm is to be varied.

XI. If Neander's remark about dissyllabic feet were a trust-
worthy guide to Dryden's versification we could reasonably expect
to find not only trochees but also spondees and pyrrhics as occasional variations from the iambic norm. But it is obvious that
accentual spondees and pyrrhics are rarer in English than ac-

centual trochees. English does not lack spondaic words (far-fetched, far-flung, ice cream, steel-blue, well-made, etc.), and in English prose some dissyllabic prepositions have prominence in neither syllable (as in the sentence "He came into money"), but if such words appear in syllabic stress verse they tend to receive alternate stress. The same is true of lines composed wholly of monosyllables:

> Two graves must hide thine and my coarse
> > (Donne's Anniversarie,
> > l. 11)

> Rocks, Caves, Lakes, Fens, Bogs, Dens, and shades of death
> > (PL II.621)

> Thus long my grief has kept me dumb
> > (Threnodia Augustalis,
> > l. 1)

Although in these lines, as in any other, the claims of prose emphasis cannot be ignored, those claims should not jeopardize the claims of conventional stress-distribution; if there are spondees or pyrrhics in the lines they are spondees and pyrrhics established by emphasis.

Trochees established by prose emphasis may be admitted when an article falls in a stressed place in the line. In Dryden's mature practice these occur both initially, as in "Till the loud clamors reach Evander's ear" (Aen. XI.223) and in mid-line with pause preceding, as in "He walks; and the big tears run rolling down his face" (Ibid., 134) or without such marked pause, as in "No more to mother earth or the green stem shall owe" (Ibid., 102). In reading trochees in these lines instead of pyrrhics, I subscribe to the view of George Young (pp. 28 ff.) that most particles can support a stress, but I deny his view that articles can support one.

Most prosodists have argued that alternate accent in English makes spondees and pyrrhics impossible, but two contemporary poets— John Crowe Ransom and Yvor Winters—have made claims in their critical writings that the two feet may appear in sequence in the place of two iambs in syllabic stress verse.[6] Ransom and Winters would have presented a more persuasive case for this variation if they had subjoined a number of examples in which

535

accent as well as sentence emphasis establish it. There are so
many lines of this sort in Dryden (and in Jonson earlier and in
many poets after Dryden) that the variation seems deliberate:

> And all was Britain the wide ocean saw
> > (Annus Mirabilis, XXII. 4)

> They drive, and squander the huge Belgian fleet
> > (Ibid., LXVII. 2)

> Whose waving streamers the glad general knows
> > (Ibid., CV. 2)

> You stand indebted a vast sum to fate
> > (Aureng-zebe, I. 202)

> The vulgar, a scarce animated clod
> > (III. 183)

> The gates are open'd the Portcullis drawn
> > (V. 393)

> Octavius is the minion of blind chance
> > (All for Love, II. 110)

> Not answ'ring the great ends of humankind
> > (Religio Laici, 131)

> Abhorring the supremacy of man
> > (The Hind and the Panther,
> > 195)

> Th'enclosure narrow'd; the sagacious pow'r
> > (Ibid., 577)

> From his apostles the first age receiv'd
> > (Ibid., 879)

> His gracious edict the same franchise yields
> > (Ibid., 2541)

> Behold Torquatus the same track pursue
> > (Aen. VI. 1130)

> Scalp, face, and shoulders the keen steel divides
> > (IX. 1018)

> Where plenteous harvests the fat fields adorn
> > (X. 210)

> Then on their shoulders the sad burden rear
> (XI.96)

> A close caballer; and tongue-valiant lord
> (XI.514)

This list is only representative. In most of the examples an un-
accented final syllable of a polysyllable is followed by an unem-
phatic article in a normally stressed position, which in turn is
followed by an adjective (which if monosyllabic may be emphatic,
and if polysyllabic may carry secondary accent); and a syllable
in stressed position concludes the variation. In these examples
there is a noticeable pyrrhic-spondaic rhythm, but of course none
of the variations is certain, or is established wholly by accent.

XII. Some prosodists would read monosyllabic lines like
those of Donne, Milton, and Dryden quoted above as a succession
of spondees supported by stress and emphasis, and would read
All for Love II.110 with stress only in the second, sixth, and
tenth places ("Octávius is the mínion of blind chánce"). Both
sorts of reading ignore the conventions of stress-distribution;
or to put the matter another way, they concede too much to prose
at the expense of verse. This concession is as much a habit of
the present-day reader as the opposite concession seems to have
been the habit of the Victorian reader who wrenched accents to
fit normal meter.

The foregoing account of Dryden's metrical variations points
to the following conclusions. It is first of all obvious that Dryden himself did what he advised future poets to do, to "study to
refine our numbers." This refining consisted, in part, of refusing to allow certain variations in poems belonging to the more
elevated Kinds. Dryden "forbore to use," as George Young says,
some of the variations of his predecessors; or, more specifically,
his variations affecting stress-distribution are both less frequent
and less obvious than those of "the last age," his variations affecting number of syllables are unmistakable and systematic,
and some variations are outlawed except in the lower Kinds.
Dryden no less than Donne is a man talking to men, but Dryden's
verse finds its counterpart in courtly, public, full-dress manners,
Donne's in the manners of a man speaking in a small group of old
and intimate friends.

Young, furthermore, is right in suggesting that Dryden's
mastery of verse is related to his mastery of prose. The easiest

part of a prosodist's job is to show how the accent of polysyllables
supports normal meter and conventional variations, but to do this
is to fall short of describing Dryden's excellence, or distinguishing it from the achievement of the early Elizabethans. It is Dryden's meaning which converts, as Young says, "the asperities of
our monosyllables . . . into ornaments." Meaning alone sometimes establishes normal meter, as in the final line of this passage from Astræa Redux:

> And welcome now, great monarch, to your own;
> Behold th'approaching cliffs of Albion:
> It is no longer motion cheats your view,
> As you meet it, the land approacheth you.
>   (ll. 250–253)

Meaning also supports the subtlest variations, as in the description of the death of Pandarus:

> the full descending blow
> Cleaves the broad front and beardless cheeks in two.
> Down sinks the giant with a thund'ring sound:
> His pond'rous limbs oppress the trembling ground;
> Blood, brains, and foam gush from the gaping wound:
> Scalp, face, and shoulders the keen steel divides,
> And the shar'd visage hangs on equal sides.
>   (Aen. XI.1012–19)

Meaning, finally, makes the question of norm or variation trivial.
In the following well-known passage, for example, the sound gives
life to the sense, and vice versa.

> My thoughtless youth was wing'd with vain desires
> My manhood, long misled by wand'ring fires,
> Follow'd false lights; and, when their glimpse was gone,
> My pride struck out new sparkles of her own.   75
> Such was I, such by nature still I am;
> Be thine the glory, and be mine the shame.
> Good life be now my task: my doubts are done:
> (What more could fright my faith, than three in one?)
> Can I believe immortal God could lie   80
> Disguis'd in mortal mold and infancy?

538

> That the great Maker of the world could die?
> And after that trust my imperfect sense,
> Which calls in question his omnipotence?
> Can I my reason to my faith compel,   85
> And shall my sight, and touch, and taste rebel?
> Superior faculties are set aside;
> Shall their subservient organs be my guide?
> Then let the moon usurp the rule of day,
> And winking tapers shew the sun his way;   90
> For what my senses can themselves perceive,
> I need no revelation to believe.
>
> (The Hind and the Panther)

There are only a few variations, but neither presence, absence, nor frequency of variations is an index of excellence. Only a very poor reader would miss the passion here, expressed in part in the changes rung on the personal pronouns; those in the first person being, for example, in unstressed places before we get the ringing antithesis of "Be thine the glory, and be mine the shame." Something like a spondee beginning line 80 ("Can I believe") and line 85 ("Can I my reason") would echo the significance of the question. After line 85 the pronouns in the first person go back into unstressed places. This sort of elevation is steady in Paradise Lost; the fact that it is infrequent even in Dryden's most impassioned poem proves only that Dryden and Milton are different sorts of poet. Dryden is always a consummate craftsman of verse and sometimes (if not like Milton always) more than that.

NOTES

1   See C. L. Dav, The Songs of John Dryden (Cambridge, Mass., 1932).

2   "Notes on Dryden's Lost Prosodia," Modern Philology, XX (1923), 247.

3   The specimens from PL I owe to George Young (p. 232), who observed shrewdly that they all come from speeches, but who analyzes them wrongly as cases of dramatic extra syllable. Dryden's finical boast has point when so sensitive a prosodist misreads lines where the apostrophe is missing.

4   I have noticed only two synaloephas in stressed places in Sidney. See Sidney's <u>Works</u>, ed. Albert Feuillerat (Cambridge, Eng., 1912–26), I, 310, l. 7 (MSS. E–M), and II, 71, l. 10.

5   Eds. <u>Ben Jonson</u> (Oxford, 1925–52), II, 429.

6   <u>The New Criticism</u> (Norfolk, Conn., 1941), p. 320, and <u>Primitivism and Decadence</u> (New York, 1937), p. 99.

DRYDEN AND THE ART OF PRAISE

James Kinsley

Much of Dryden's poetry was written to celebrate public
occasions grave and gay, and to laud the merits and acheve-
ments of public persons. Compliment and adulation were not
incidental elements in his work, but an important part of his
function as a professional writer and poet laureate. Poetry, however, was not only his profession, but his art; and in panegyric,
as in every other category of verse he attempted, he worked con-
scientiously at a long-established poetic mode, and gave it something of his own distinctive character and style.

He has been persistently censured for the extravagance of
his panegyrics. "In the meanness and servility of hyperbolical
adulation", says Dr. Johnson, "I know not whether, since the days
in which the Roman emperors were deified, he has ever been
equalled. . . . When once he has undertaken the task of praise
he no longer retains shame in himself, nor supposes it in his
patron."[1] Mr. Van Doren, in the finest general estimate of Dryden's poetry of this century, compares the court society of the
Restoration with that of fourth-century Rome; discovers in it "a
certain pettiness, a certain exclusiveness, a certain blindness,
and a certain pretentious unreality in the official psychology";[2]
and criticises Dryden's panegyrics in this context. It is true
that Dryden was often a time-server, a professional poet singing
the virtues of his benefactors and of those who seemed, by their
position or wealth, to promise some sort of remuneration for
elegant flattery. He praised to live. Yet too much has been made
of this obvious fact. For example, critics have pointed to his
letter to Rochester in 1673, in which he admits writing an extravagant prologue and epilogue for University performances at Oxford:
"And by the event your Lordship will judge how easy 'tis to passe
any thing upon an University; and how grosse flattery the learned

Reprinted from English Studies, Vol. 34 (1953), pp. 57–64, by permission of the author and the publisher.

will endure."[3] Some have argued, rather unconvincingly, that
he was trying to curry favour with the University authorities for
his own advancement;[4] but in any event, he was an artist writing
in an established theatrical mode, and mindful that a dramatist's
essential business, in writing a prologue or an epilogue, is to engage the sympathy, tickle the humour, flatter the vanity, and anticipate the criticism of his audience.

Again, in almost every poem, close reading reveals much of
thought and fancy which lies beyond the limits of mere adulation.
In the panegyrics, as in many of Dryden's prose dedications, a
person or an event serves but as the occasion of his work. There
is reason in the view that, although the initial purpose of a poetic
eulogy may be to praise for gain, the essence of the panegyrical
style is "wit":[5] the poet weaves an intricate and self-sufficient
pattern of "fancy" and "wit" round and through his human or historical subject, and his growing preoccupation with purely artistic
problems carries him, not unwillingly, beyond his apparent theme.
Although Dryden owed much to the example of Waller, who "first
made writing easily an art", and to the darling of his youth, "the
famous Cowley", the chief influence on his early panegyrical style
was Donne, or Donne at second-hand. Waller excelled in a neat,
witty, accomplished middle style; Cowley, in his poems of praise,
oscillates between a talking style and a noisy, hollow rhetoric:
Dryden's essential tones are rich, weighted, and exalted. It was
Donne who drew learning and abstruse wit into the service of
compliment, in the extravagances of the two Anniversaries and
the "elegant epistles in which he delighted and perhaps bewildered
his noble lady friends and patronesses with erudite and transcen-
dental flattery";[6] and on Donne, and the Donne tradition, Dryden
drew heavily for the subtleties of poetic praise.

The "metaphysical" element, however, is not constant in, or
natural to, his panegyrical style. His early poems are laden with
the philosophical and scientific imagery, the extravagant conceits,
and the startling shifts of thought, which mark so much of the
verse of the early and middle seventeenth century; but he always
seems a laborious apprentice in a difficult and uncongenial craft,
drawing his material uneasily from second-hand, and failing to
achieve any synthesis of his developing natural style and the ideas
and imagery which he pretentiously affects.

There is little virtue in the pretence of some, that Dryden
outgrew the fascination of his "false lights". In some measure,

and in his own terms, he realised and demonstrated that the conceited wit of the "metaphysicals" had lost its vital connection with thought and feeling. The ferment of ideas and events, in which the Jacobean poets and dramatists had striven to match mind and imagination with the times, had subsided; and with it went the raison d'être of a bold, intricate, and extravagant poetic style. What had been at its best functional in poetry, and had found its justification in its functional nature, had become decorative and excrescent. Yet Dryden never wholly abandoned the conceit as outmoded or inept. His natural exuberance of mind, his delight in "the irregular and excentrick violence of wit;"[7] the often delusive doctrine of "fancy", the significant example of Ovid's "odoriferous flowers", and the new influence of Longinus on critical thought, combined to hold him in an inconstant allegiance to a tradition which in theory he grew to condemn. But although conceits and witty extravagances adorn his last plays and his last book of poems, and may be found clinging to the smooth classical surface of his mature panegyrics in embarrassed conspicuousness, he began to reject these in some degree quite early in his work, and to develop a more natural style of his own. In the Heroique Stanzas on Cromwell, for example, extravagance and the assured rhetorical exposition of his subject's greatness go hand in hand:

> His Grandeur he derived from Heav'n alone,
>   For he was great, e'er Fortune made him so;
> And Wars, like Mists that rise against the Sun,
>   Made him but greater seem, not greater grow.
>
> He fought, secure of Fortune, as of fame;
>   Till by new Maps, the Island might be shown,
> Of Conquests, which he strew'd where-e'er he came,
>   Thick as the Galaxy with Stars is sown.
>
> Nor dy'd he when his Ebbing Fame went less,
>   But when fresh Laurels courted him to live:
> He seem'd but to prevent some new Success,
>   As if above what Triumphs Earth could give.[8]

In Astraea Redux, the exultation of an England restored to its monarch, and hopeful of an ordered and prosperous reign, is en-

ergetically expressed in terms which swing between ludicrous
exaggeration and the majestic assertion of high ideals. In the
address To my Lord Chancellor, the compression and constant
shift of focus which mark the image-patterns of "metaphysical"
poetry are reduced, steadied, and broadened out: the exaggerated
compliment and fanciful imagery remain; but nothing is forced
or improper to the lofty and serious theme of harmonious government:

> In open Prospect nothing bounds our Eye
> Until the Earth seems join'd unto the Sky:
> So in this Hemisphere our utmost View
> Is only bounded by our King and you.
> Our Sight is limited where you are join'd
> And beyond that no farther Heav'n can find.
> So well your Virtues do with his agree
> That, though your Orbs of different Greatness be,
> Yet both are for each other's use dispos'd,
> His to enclose, and yours to be enclos'd:
> Nor could another in your Room have been,
> Except an Emptiness had come between.
> Well may he then to you his Cares impart
> And share his Burden where he shares his Heart.
> In you his Sleep still wakes; his pleasures find
> Their Share of Business in your labouring Mind.
> So, when the weary Sun his Place resigns,
> He leaves his Light and by Reflection shines.[9]

In the celebration of men and events in Annus Mirabilis, abstruse
and laboured smartness struggles with a simpler, more elevated
and direct utterance in stanza after stanza: Dryden strives to be
at once the poet of a fantastic tradition which is losing its force,
and the earnest disciple of Virgil, "my master in this poem"; and
it is the recurring Virgilian tone which carries the poem to its
modified success. When we turn to Dryden's later panegyrics,
it is confident hyperbole, gracious compliment, and sheer rhetorical power, which persuades and delights:

> When factious Rage to cruel Exile drove
> The Queen of Beauty, and the Court of Love,
> The Muses droop'd with their forsaken Arts,

> And the sad Cupids broke their useless Darts.
> Our fruitful Plains to Wilds and Deserts turn'd,
> Like Eden's Face when banish'd Man it mourn'd:
> Love was no more when Loyalty was gone,
> The great Supporter of his awful Throne.
> Love could no longer after Beauty stay,
> But wander'd northward to the Verge of Day,
> As if the Sun and he had lost their Way.
> But now the illustrious Nymph, return'd again,
> Brings every Grace triumphant in her Train. . .[10]

There is a similar delightful play of fancy, more sustained if less lyrical, round the beauty and virtue of the Duchess of Ormonde, in the address which opens the Fables. In Dryden's praise of the character of his kinsman of Chesterton, "wit" in the sense of "conceit" plays a very small part. "These annals", says Scott, "however simple and vulgar, illuminated by our author's pen, shine like clouds under the influence of a setting sun."[11] Dryden is completely at ease in the evenly sustained elevation of solid virtue, which he manages by weighted generalisation on the right and the good, and by a restrained, judiciously humorous heightening of the subject's character.

His panegyrics are as much opportunities for the exercise of "wit" as they are indirect recognitions of past favours or invitations to patronage. But the type of "wit" they exemplify changes with time. In several places in his critical essays, Dryden repeats the old and conventional definition of "wit" as "sharpness of conceit";[12] but from the beginning of his career, he thought also of "wit" as an essential element, with imagination, in the general creative process.[13] This broader conception is crystallised in his later definition of "wit" as "propriety of thoughts and words". Propriety of thought is "that fancy which arises naturally from the subject, or which the poet adapts to it"; propriety of words is "the clothing of these thoughts with such expressions as are naturally proper to them; and from both of these, if they are judiciously performed, the delight of poetry results."[14] Dryden declares, significantly, that he drew this definition from close consideration of Virgil:

> He is everywhere above conceits of epigrammatic
> wit, and gross hyperboles; he maintains majesty in

the midst of plainness; he shines, but glares not; and
is stately without ambition . . . propriety of thoughts
and words are only to be found in him.[15]

The "wit" which emerges in his mature panegyrical style is,
at its best, a graceful or playful compliment natural to his theme.
The essential function of both imagery and diction in panegyric is
to emphasise and heighten. Although much of the quasi-meta-
physical imagery of Dryden's early poetry is merely decorative
and super-imposed, some of it serves to underline the poet's
praise. But as his voice settled into its adult tones, without fantastic attempts to mimic others, he inclined more and more to
hyperbole and controlled extravagance. His capacity for immense,
assured over-statement, which developed with time and with experiment, proved sufficient for his needs; he had little cause to
drag pretentious novelties from an earlier tradition into a different style which he was engaged in making his own.

With the professional writing-up of the great, and the exercise of "wit" which this provided, there is a third aspect of Dryden's panegyrics worthy of consideration. The key to his method
lies in an observation of Dr. Johnson's (made with derogatory
intent), and in Mr. Van Doren's supplement to it. Dryden appears,
says Johnson,

never to have impoverished his mint of flattery by his
expences, however lavish. He had all forms of excellence, intellectual and moral, combined in his mind,
with endless variation . . . . He never seems to decline
the practice, or lament the necessity; he considers the
great as entitled to encomiastick homage, and brings
praise rather as a tribute than a gift, more delighted
with the fertility of his invention than mortified by the
prostitution of his judgement.[16]

Dryden's official praise, says Mr. Van Doren,

rings with a round Roman grandeur. He writes as if
he lived to praise, not praised to live. His lines speak
contempt for all things small— small passions, small
deeds, small wit. He is warm yet decorous; he is ef-
fectual because of his great confidence and his unremitting eloquence. And his resources are infinite.[17]

These two passages, the one a celebrated Augustan judgment and the other a modern statement of virtues which have long been recognised, together throw light on an aspect of Dryden's panegyrics which criticism has overlooked in its condemnation of his flattery and fantastic extravagance. He could be, when he chose, a perspicacious realist: his comedies, his satires, and occasionally his prose essays, reflect a close observation and a humorous open-eyed assessment of men and affairs. In this, he is but one illustration of the frank, lucid matter-of-factness, in many reduced to a brutal insensitiveness to principle and ideals, which is a mark of his time. But on its other side, Restoration England was resolved to be, if not the nursery, then the forcing-house of the unworldly, exalted, heroic virtues. The difference between the ideal and "the spotted actuality" in the world in which they lived, was always apparent to Dryden and his contemporaries; of this the satire, correspondence, diary literature and comedy of the times provide ample evidence. But the lamentable reality could be countered only by a persistent exemplification of the ideal. Dryden's recognition of the false chivalry, the empty heroics, and the pretence to principle in court and political circles, is epitomised in the sustained mock-heroic of <u>Absalom and Achitophel</u>, in which layers of subtle irony underlie even his praise. On the other hand, there is little suggestion of mere elaborate pretence, little <u>essential</u> artificiality, in the best of his poetic drama. The poetic and the realistic are not the same for Dryden. Poetry can do better than Nature—a venerable thesis, the Renaissance development of the Aristotelian doctrine of an art which is universal, perfect, and higher and more philosophical than history, which Dryden re-states in the <u>Parallel of Poetry and Painting</u>. The artist in paint or words should "form to himself an idea of perfect nature":

> thereby correcting Nature from what she actually is
> in individuals, to what she ought to be, and what she
> was created . . . . Thus in portraits, the painter will not
> take that side of the face which has some notorious
> blemish in it; but either draw it in profile (as Apelles
> did Antigonus, who had lost one of his eyes,) or else
> shadow the more imperfect side. For an ingenious
> flattery is to be allowed to the professors of both arts,
> so long as the likeness is not destroyed.

547

...... Though it must be an idea of perfection, from
which both the epic poet and the history painter draws,
yet all perfections are not suitable to all subjects; but
every one must be designed according to that perfect
beauty which is proper to him.[18]

In poetry lies the antidote to the weaknesses and imperfections
of the real world. The poet's business is not necessarily, or invariably, to depict the actual; he is licensed, by the very nature
and tradition of his art, to raise and make perfect. The influence
of this doctrine is a common-place of criticism; but its implications for the art of panegyric have not been drawn out. Adulation
becomes a justifiable art; and in its art lies its justification. Dryden elevated his imperfect human subjects to the level of ideal ex-
emplars; and his panegyrics are less hymns on individual persons,
than celebrations of the virtues which they exemplify— mixed in
reality with vice and weakness, but raised to perfection by poetry.
Some Restoration portrait-painting provides a significant parallel.
The artist concerns himself, neither with a penetrating personal
interpretation of his subject, nor with mere photographic reproduction, but with the creation of an ideal type-figure elucidating
and perfecting the character and appearance of his sitter.
    The Augustan interest in men and manners, the concern for
civilised virtues, and the predilection for reflection and didactic
comment, encouraged the poet to celebrate public characters and
occasions, personal gain apart, and to raise these themes imagina-
tively to an ideal level without any fundamental insincerity. Thus,
for Dryden, the dead Cromwell is the image of power, disciplined
command, and military prowess; Mary of Modena is the ideal of
beauty and grace in a factious and sordid court; John Driden of
Chesterton is the type of loyal and sagacious squirearchy— "I
have", says Dryden, "not onely drawn the features of my worthy
Kinsman, but have also given my own Opinion, of what an Englishman in Parliament oughto be: & deliver it as a Memorial of my
own Principles to all Posterity."[19] The Duke of Ormonde and
his lady epitomise hereditary dignity, generosity, and courage:
Mrs. Killigrew is the exemplar of the virtues and arts which link
earth and heaven;[20] Bishop Ken, indirectly eulogized in Dryden's
adaptation of Chaucer's portrait of a poor parson, is endowed with
all the ecclesiastical virtues; and the Countess of Abingdon, although never seen by the poet, and praised "for a fat fee,"[21] em-

bodies as Eleonora all the sweetness, charity, and grace of ideal
womanhood.

"The spotted actuality" is absorbed or transcended by the
ideal which the poet's imagination creates against a background
of reality; and in this transcendence, extravagance and hyperbolical compliment play a major, comprehensible part.[22] Dryden's exaggerations have a strict poetic function—they are part
of the "propriety" of panegyric; and the critic's task is not to
deplore their presence and emphasise their contribution to sheer
fantastic flattery, but to assess their value as essential elements
in a boldly artificial type of poetry. In such a test, much of Dryden's early writing fails miserably. His forced flights of fancy
detract from the artistic sincerity of his praise. Where, on the
other hand, he concerns himself less with "sharpness of conceit",
and more with the bold, imaginative over-statement which is a
primary part of his own poetic character, he is remarkably successful. The real is raised to the ideal, and Fancy takes care of
herself.

Dryden continues the Donne tradition in one important respect: Ben Jonson, in his conversations with Drummond, observed
"that Donnes Anniversaries were profane and full of blasphemies:
. . . he told Mr. Donne if it had been written of the Virgin Marie
it had been something; to which he answered that he described the
Idea of a Woman, and not as she was". That Dryden flattered for
his own ends, and indulged his poetic "wit" in the process is obvious; but flattery and wit are not the whole tale, and do not adequately explain either the style or the content of his best panegyrics. His satiric portraits belong to a freer, broader, and more
colourful world than the real world of Restoration politics; strict
verisimilitude is, in them, abandoned in fidelity to the demands
of good art: and what is true of his satiric portraiture is no less
true of his idealised eulogies. Art distorts, heightens, emphasises,
and simplifies reality, for praise and blame alike.

NOTES

1   Lives of the English Poets, ed. G. B. Hill (Oxford, 1905), i.
    399.

2   The Poetry of John Dryden (Cambridge, 1931), p. 116.

3   Letters of John Dryden, ed. C. E. Ward (Durham, N.C., 1942),
    p. 10.

4 See Hugh Macdonald, John Dryden, A Bibliography (Oxford, 1939), pp. 137–8.

5 I develop this from a private suggestion by Professor E. N. Hooker.

6 H. J. C. Grierson, Poems of John Donne (Oxford, 1912), ii. xiv.

7 Johnson, op. cit., i. 460.

8 Stanzas vi, xiv, xxxiii.

9 Lines 31–48.

10 Prologue To the Dutchess, On Her Return from Scotland (1682), lines 1–13.

11 The Works of Dryden (London, 1808), xi. 71–2.

12 Essays of John Dryden, ed. W. P. Ker (Oxford, 1926), i. 138–9, 172.

13 Ibid., i. 15.

14 Ibid., i. 172, 270.

15 Ibid., i. 256.

16 Op. cit., i. 399–400.

17 Op. cit., p. 117.

18 Essays, ii. 125, 127.

19 Letters, ed. C. E. Ward, p. 120.

20 See E. M. W. Tillyard, Five Poems, 1470–1870 (London, 1948), pp. 50 ff.

21 Van Doren, op. cit., p. 132.

22 Cf. Preface to Annus Mirabilis: "the same images serve equally for the Epique Poesie, and for the Historique and Panegyrique, which are branches of it."

DRYDEN AND THE ANALYSIS OF SHAKESPEARE'S TECHNIQUES

Ruth Wallerstein

"All the images of nature were still present to him, and he drew them, not laboriously, but luckily; when he describes anything you more than see it, you feel it too."

I

Recent criticism of Dryden has been of particular interest because it has represented the wide variations of view arising from attempts to re-define the nature of poetry. And it has reflected closely the larger intellectual reorientations of which these attempts are a part. Yet it has been more concerned with the critics' view of Dryden than with a close re-examination of Dryden's own analysis of the techniques of his art. This must be my excuse for attempting another historical study of the problem of Dryden and All for Love and Shakespeare. For I think Dryden's "imitation" of Shakespeare has still something important to yield to our understanding of his view of the imagination and of his methods of work.

Formal and explicit criticism of Shakespeare in the later seventeenth century has been frequently defined and is not here my primary concern. Of the negative criticism involved in the improvements of Shakespeare, there remains nothing to say after Mr. Spencer's and Mr. Nicoll's books.[1] That criticism has the same tendency as the formal criticism in its depreciation of Shakespeare's art in the interests of formal patterns of structure, and of perspicuity, anti-enthusiasm, standardized grammar and diction, and finally in the interests of the accepted social pattern. The positive appreciation of Shakespeare involved in the attempt

Reprinted from Review of English Studies, Vol. 19 (1943), pp. 165–185, by permission of Mrs. Eve W. Fernberger and the publisher.

to imitate him has been less carefully estimated, particularly
in the case of Dryden. Yet that appreciation adds an important
third dimension to the seventeenth-century view of him, and one
from which we gain an important light on Dryden's poetic development in particular. I propose, therefore, to consider in detail
Dryden's "imitation" of Shakespeare in All for Love, and to suggest what light this view of Dryden throws on his conception of
poetry.

II

Dryden came to the imitation of Shakespeare when the whole
intellectual drift of the time had, with enormously increased
speed, focused men's minds on the logical definition of life and
character in types, and when emotion seemed an entity as measurable as water-power. A Suckling, imitating Shakespeare forty odd
years earlier when the Shakespearean and Jacobean drama were
still living artistic traditions, might simply thrust into one play,
The Goblins, elements of the new representation of sentiment and
on the other side direct though fragmentary imitations of Shakespeare's blending of theme and emotion. But when Dryden imitated Antony and Cleopatra, the continuity of the tradition of Shakespearean psychology and techniques of structure and expression
had been broken. Dryden had, indeed, been the chief instrument
in maintaining on the stage the drama of violent action; but this
drama of his had no real connection in form or spirit with the
Shakespearean drama of action. And his most serious formal
endeavour had been the shaping of the drama to the representation of character and ideas in schematic terms.

Nor must the significance of the change in stage conditions
be forgotten. Suckling, to look back again for a moment to The
Goblins, could still, under the physical conditions of his stage,
use a rapid suggestive scene or minor character related to theme
rather than to action, as important elements in his play. But
such elements were barred to Dryden. In the convention of Shakespearean dramaturgy, the scene was essentially abstracted from
the physical stage, which conveyed little to the audience, even
when external setting such as a balcony was made use of; setting
was transferred directly from the minds of the actors to the
spectators. Of this transference, the sunrise in Hamlet, in which

DRYDEN AND SHAKESPEARE'S TECHNIQUES

Horatio's words give voice to the renewed tranquillity of mind
which has come with the return of light to these awestruck and
troubled men, is an example to remind us strikingly that Shakespeare wrote in terms of imaginative and not of factual continuity.
The possibility of using or of understanding that aesthetic form
had been violently disturbed by the radical alteration of the stage
after the Restoration. Those of us who have seen Shakespeare
presented with elaborate changes, scene by scene, in the old
framed stage will know how much the physical form of that stage
with its literal sense impressions of space and time did actually
interfere with the free and mobile suggestions of the lines, and
did make the continuity of atmosphere, action and character in
Shakespeare's plays hard to follow.

Despite these changes in intellectual attitude, in type of
drama, and in stage condition, Dryden was driven back upon
Shakespeare, probably by two things. We must not underestimate
the influence on Dryden of the persistent popularity of Shakespeare. This was a matter of most actual practical moment to
a man dependent for his living on the stage. But when he turned
to Shakespeare, he was driven also by his own sense of a supreme
greatness in Shakespeare which ought to be imitated. On the important issues of the unities, of poetic justice, character type,
and to some extent of decorum and perspicuity, Dryden did not
wish to imitate but to improve Shakespeare. But within the new
form and the new ethical and social patterns he believed that certain supreme aspects of Shakespeare's large and comprehensive
soul could be preserved and imitated. These aspects are to be
found chiefly in the relation of the total situation to the action,
in the passion, the thoughts, and the imagery, and I shall take
them up in that order.

III

But before we consider All for Love, we must glance at another direct imitation of Shakespeare which had come between
Dryden and Suckling, and which by the very ineptitude of its imitation may well have started Dryden on his effort. We shall also
spend a moment on Sedley's play on the Antony and Cleopatra
theme. Otway, a young man of lively feeling and little intellectual
or artistic discipline, but with a keen interest in Racine, had begun

to write for the stage just before All for Love. Otway's Don Carlos is in its central design a study of the destructive force of passion in the King, contrasted with the beauty of self-control in the Queen and Carlos, a self-control motivated by duty and pure love. Doctor R. G. Ham[2] has described the wonderful concision with which Otway made a play out of his prolix source. But as the play stands, it is melodramatic in the endless see-saw of threatened destruction and escape of the latter characters and in the multiplicity of villains who encompass them; it is sentimental melodrama in the repeated titillations of anguished and ever virtuous scenes between Carlos and the Queen. Into its other themes and into its general lack of structure I need not go. What concerns us here is its central passion and the fact that Otway made Othello the model for his scheme of that passion.

It is an imitation of the "invention", however, as art critics call the posture and grouping of figures, not of the passion of Othello. Rui-Gomez-Iago is motivated by ambition and by the desire to revenge himself for Don Carlos's distrust of him. Otway follows in detail the minutiæ of the interchange of speech between Iago and Othello in Iago's temptation; the elements, however, are no longer in coherent relation to each other, to the King's character, or to actual psychological truth. Philip's character is a tabula rasa upon which is written the jealous determination to destroy. The ebb and flow of jealousy and trust are so superficial that the King seems but the dummy for Rui-Gomez-Iago's gleeful taunting. The King has accepted from the first moment and off stage Rui-Gomez's assertion that the Queen and Don Carlos are guilty, and thereafter proclaims his jealousy as if it were a tooth-ache. In the reflux of his natural idealism, trust and love, Othello strives to interpret innocently the evidence which Iago has given him; and Iago pretends to agree, that he may go on without seeming intention into that elaboration of detail by which he inflames his victim's imagination and exults over his own cunning in men's souls. Of this basic motivation Gomez has nothing. He repeats the pretence of being eager to accept their innocence, but without essential psychological purpose and without essential penetration of the King's consciousness. Of course the King's rejection of this view marks no movement in his passion.

A single fragment of dialogue will illustrate Otway's failure to grasp anything in either Iago's character and aim or Othello's experience:

Gomez :	Good heaven forbid that I should ever dare
	To question virtue in a queen so fair.
	Though she her eyes cast on her glorious son
	Men oft see treasures and yet covet none.
King :	Think not to blind me with dark ironies
	The truth disguised in obscure contraries.

But Otway in his own mild language follows the surface invention in great detail. The King, for instance, in a casual encounter with the Queen's lady-in-waiting has a speech which faintly echoes Othello's terrible scene with Æmilia, though it has none of the marks of a disordered and suddenly sensualized imagination which are central in Othello's tragedy.

I have spoken in so much detail of Otway's imitation because it is likely to have set Dryden's imagination off; and it certainly illuminates his way of work.

It may be noted that Otway's expression is rich in figure, especially in simple descriptive metaphor or in simple analogies. The figures are almost all merely decorative, non-dramatic and of a complete sameness, though in one or two, thought and figure move together.

Sedley's Antony and Cleopatra was not an imitation of Shakespeare. Nor is it even substantially an historical play, but a play on current Platonic themes. It may have contributed to Dryden two motives, but nothing of fundamental view or method. The elements which may have been suggestive to Dryden are an opening scene indicating the unrest of the Egyptians, for which the material is in Plutarch, and which receives no further dramatic development by Sedley; and the wooing of Cleopatra by Photinus with Antony's resultant jealousy. By Sedley it is used to illustrate the unworthiness of jealousy.

IV

That Dryden from the first regarded the presentation of passion as Shakespeare's supreme gift we know. The endeavour to imitate that passion was one of the chief aims of All for Love. Incidentally, one may note that Dryden, had he wished it, had the opinion of Bacon and of Hobbes to bear him out that the poets with their fancy had so far done actually more in understanding moral virtue than the philosophers. And it had been passion which Otway, writing just before Dryden and stimulated by Racine, had tried to imitate in Shakespeare. But Otway in his sentimental drama had succeeded in imitating only the posture and grouping of figures of Othello and not the real passion of Othello or the cunning of Iago. Dryden sought to imitate something far deeper than this invention and still more different from anything he had himself previously tried.

Aureng-Zebe, coming just before the imitation of Shakespeare, is replete with the passions, controlled and uncontrolled, which had descended from the heroic play and had been modified by Racine. As compared with the earlier heroic plays, the contrasting passions of Aureng-Zebe had been fundamentally humanized in their conceptions. They are subordinated to a moral view. When Aureng-Zebe argues for the responsible monarch bound by the ideal of public welfare and using his prerogative to that end, he places himself in contrast to the motives of the self-willed and passion-enslaved absolutist, his father; and he sums up more than a century of reflection on monarchy. And this reflection is central to Dryden's conception of the play. This serious ethical motive, deeply rooted in English thought, and growing out of Dryden's real concern for the English state, may have contributed much to the sincerity of tone which separates Aureng-Zebe from its predecessors. But the fundamental structure of the play has matured and not changed. The entire drama proceeds by a series of arguments, arguments upon the conflicting views of the state and of the individual's responsibilities and rights in the political and personal conditions into which the play throws him, and so forth. And the prevailing passion of each character is described in terms of definition and self-analysis clothed in high-flown analogies.

Dryden had in mind a different concept of passion from this logical and schematic one in turning to Shakespeare. Before considering the imitation of the passions proper, however, we may glance at the general effect of All for Love to remind ourselves of the atmosphere in which they are set.

As Mr. Spencer has pointed out, the action of a good bit of All for Love still proceeds, like that of Aureng-Zebe, by a series of confrontations in which rival claims, points of view, or emotions are debated. Yet in All for Love they are but elements of the play, and no longer comprise its whole design. The play opens and closes with scenes which strive not to analyse emotion but to realize it in its direct flow. Upon them much of the atmosphere and meaning of the play depend.

The first scene is an account of portents, which creates an atmosphere of impending disaster. This atmosphere relates itself organically to the action of the play by supplying the motivation of dread in Alexas on which the crisis of the play depends. It is a carefully considered imitation; while it owes something to elements suffused throughout Antony and Cleopatra and in Plutarch, it owes more to the massed effects in Hamlet and in Julius Caesar. And though it achieves nothing like the sense of awful and eternal issues in Hamlet, yet it does affect the imagination with something of that sense of the relation of the individual to the universe which is Shakespearean.

It is by the motivation in Alexas that Dryden sought to give to the external action that unity which is so lacking in Shakespeare's play. If we can forget momentarily the loss of Shakespeare's Cleopatra which is involved in Dryden's conception of this motivation, the study of Alexas's isolation from the normal pleasures of life and his resulting introversion into political fear and into the desire to protect himself at all costs, is one of Dryden's finest things. Place it for a moment beside Otway's superficial plagiarism from Shakespeare's Edmund in his own Don John, and we are sensible at once of the depth of Dryden's study of Shakespeare and of how truly it turned him to a natural view of character.

From the point of view of structural unity the problem is less simple. Shakespeare left the first three acts of Antony and Cleopatra in something of structural and historical chaos. But he used them consistently to draw the characters of Antony and of Cleopatra and to sketch far-reaching social and political issues; and in the last two acts these elements merge in the great tragic conflict between the ultimate force of history and the ultimate social necessity on the one hand, and on the other Antony's and Cleopatra's experience of themselves. Thus Shakespeare cut the Gordian knot of the union of historical play and tragedy. Dryden solved the problem by overlooking it. He created a circumstantial unity which could have had dramatic development only if Alexas had been a principal character; since that development was not present, he created in reality a second plot which is never more than an artificial husk around the essential drama of Antony and

Cleopatra, though it does solve his difficulty in the motivation of Cleopatra. We must allow that Dryden sought to unify Antony and Cleopatra from a point of view which misses Shakespeare's basic theme and therefore the basic organization of his material. And in thus failing to understand the problem he left a central disunity at the heart of his own play. But within his own historical structure he has imitated not without grandeur certain Shakespearean effects. And the instinct which turned him to Hamlet and Julius Cæsar, plays in which the political issue is more overt than in Antony and Cleopatra, was a sound one.

The opening scene is followed by the famous Antony-in-grief scene, which carries forward the preceding scene, first by defining the issues of the play as they centre in Antony, and then by unfolding Antony's character in mid-action. It is composed of: (1) the preliminary discussion of Antony by Ventidius and the gentleman; (2) the brief Egyptian pageant which defines for us what Ventidius has to contend with and prepares for the forward movement of the play; (3) the grief scene proper. In the first two, Dryden must have had in mind to concentrate Shakespeare's opening interpretation of the situation, as it was seen from a Roman point of view, and Enobarbus' account to Mæcenas. We may pass at once to the analysis of the grief scene proper. With this we come to Dryden's treatment of the passions.

The scene has deserved the mirth it has aroused; and no amount of insight into Dryden's aim will ever erase from Antony's tears the incongruous associations aroused by some of the contexts in Shakespeare from which Dryden has borrowed. Yet to understand the play at all we must grant it for the moment an unwilling suspension of disbelief. The fragments from Shakespeare which are gathered together and imitated in the scene are not unconsidered trifles, and the selection of them is significant of Dryden's purpose. They are: the gentleman's description of Antony's appearance and gesture, echoing Desdemona's description of Othello on the eve of his murder of her; the echo of Richard II in Antony's brooding on his own fate; the lines on music which rest upon the Orsino passage at the opening of Twelfth Night (a line in Antony on the power of music may have been the clue in Dryden's memory that brought this passage in); the melancholy Jacques lines; and finally after some detail from the general stigmata of Elizabethan melancholy, the mourning deer passage. In Ventidius' speech, there is the reflection upon Antony, "'Tis

mournful, wondrous mournful", seeming to echo the combined
adjective and adverb and the repetition in a dying fall of Othello's,
"She swore in truth, 'twas strange, 'twas passing strange".

Ventidius had prepared the way for this grief scene by his
interpretation of Antony following the gentleman's description,
and the scene is to be read in the light of this interpretation:

> Just, just his nature.
> Virtue's his path but sometimes 'tis too narrow. . . .
> But, when his danger makes him find his fault,
> Quick to observe, and full of sharp remorse,
> He censures eagerly his own misdeeds,
> Judging himself with malice to himself. . . .

This would suggest a scene of remorse to follow. What we have
in fact is a scene which aims at the delineation of depression.
And one may say that Richard, Jacques, and Orsino do all in fact
represent melancholy, though of course in subtle variation. Following the elements drawn from these characters, the scene dif-
fuses into the general Elizabethan pastoral melancholy theme
and thence via the "sylvan scene" arrives at moss and blasted
oak, the familiar paraphernalia of later seventeenth-century
melancholy, which in Dryden's literary tradition at least still
belonged to the context of religious retreat.[3]

In this sentimentalized presentation of melancholy, we face
at once Dryden's lack of insight into character. To identify
Richard, Orsino, and Jacques, to identify remorse indiscrimi-
nately with melancholy and self-pity is hopeless ignorance of passion. At the same time, it reminds us of the difficulty under
which Dryden laboured in endeavouring to treat these great psychological and ethical issues once more on lines which no longer
had reality in the thought and attitudes of his age. When religion
and the saving of men's souls seemed the all-important issues,
the distinction between remorse and accidie was familiar to the
daily thought of thoughtful men, as we know whether we look at
Red Cross Knight or at a sermon of Perkins' recently re-pub-
lished.[4] It was no longer so in Dryden's day. Granted Dryden's
limitation, the following points deserve our serious note. In attempting this melancholy passion, Dryden was attempting a
serious delineation of an aspect of human nature which broke
completely the bounds of the narrow heroic or Platonistic con-

ceptions then current on the stage. Then the struggle in Antony between virtue and weakness represents a perception by Dryden of the moral interest in Shakespeare and in Racine—and in the Jonson tradition—and of the integral relation of the action of a tragedy to that struggle. The matter of the moral struggle is the old conflict of love and duty. But the real conflict has become that of various passions with reason. And Antony remains throughout a character swayed by emotion and conscious of his own lack of control. Ventidius's interpretation of Antony comes directly from Plutarch, but Dryden may well have observed such a character in the world about him. Rochester comes to mind as an example of a character who swings between enslavement to passion at one moment and at another depression and regret, without ever reaching a norm of self-control.

From this scene we pass to a scene in which Dryden develops another passion, that of friendship, with very close imitation of Shakespeare's Brutus-Cassius scene.

These scenes differ from Otway not only in the bold agglomeration of fragments from many scenes in Shakespeare. They imitate not an invention but passions. They strive, as I have said, to catch passion in direct expression. Yet Dryden is not able to see passion as it is in Shakespeare—the integral product of present experience and habitual individual character. He conceives of it as typical and fixed, and it is this characteristic aspect of it which interests him. Hence it is that he unites passages from so many plays. And for him, passion and judgment have become quite separate entities. He does not in these scenes imitate the main texture of Shakespeare's plays in which the mind is thinking, feeling, acting in one. He can catch only overt sentiment, or passion after it has overmastered reason. And he confuses the two. He chooses first therefore passages from the sentimentalists; and to them in part even Brutus belongs. His other echoes are from passages in which emotion in great characters has become dominant and self-articulate under tragic stress. Such are the "O had she been true" and the "Farewell the tranquil mind" passages from Othello, of which there is perhaps some underlying recollection mingled with elements from Antony and Cleopatra itself in Antony's reflections on the death of Cleopatra.

These passages, like the sentimental passages, he regards as typical of an emotional response to a generic situation and not as arising from a particular tragic stress and in the particu-

lar character which alone would have felt them under that stress.
Cleopatra's cry over the death of Charmian arises from the sudden integration by tragedy of that infinitely various mind which
had been wont to play over sensation and experience in so unchan-
nelled and undisciplined a way. Out of that sensation and experience arise the images which are, or, as Dryden would have put
it, which express, the passion. By Dryden's Antony, the phrases
which imitate Cleopatra are spoken after he is quieted to reflection. As phrases they do reflect the movement of thought in
image; but they have no roots in his character and no play outside themselves. These facts harden their very texture so that
not all their eloquence saves them from sentimentality. Given
to Antony, together with other recollections, they become:

> (Ventidius dies)
> Ant.   Farewell. Ever my leader, ev'n in death!
>   My Queen and you have got the start of me,
>   And I'm the lag of honour. Gone so soon?
>   Is death no more? He used him carelessly,
>   With a familiar kindness ere he knocked,
>   Ran to the door, and took him in his arms,
>   As who should say, Y' are welcome at all hours,
>   A friend need give no warning.

In all these passages Dryden has sought to imitate and understand Shakespeare in the most literal way. He has been blocked
by the total difference of his approach to character and experience. It is paradoxically true that Elizabethan psychology was
functional under a faculty terminology, Dryden's psychology,
really a faculty psychology; for though the faculty terminology
had been simplified and made to sound functional, the conceptions
of process which the earlier terminology sought to describe had
been lost sight of in a rigid conception of reason and passion.
He was also blocked by the very act of imitation. For the whole
history of translation of poetry in the sixteenth and seventeenth
century is a history of the pedantic rigidity which falls upon the
literal translator who explicates the suggestions in the images
of the original poetry.

A different kind of imitation is found in a scene in which
Dryden is representing not a passion, but motivation passing into
action, the scene in Act IV in which Ventidius attempts to wean

561

Antony from Cleopatra by jealousy. Here Dryden is working very
freely, but with clear reference to Shakespeare's psychology and
to his "invention". The blunt irony of Ventidius, different as it is
in character and effect from that of Iago, is real and natural.
And the twisting of Antony's passion out of Ventidius's control is
independent and real, though the anger in him is fustian. The use
of the scene might possibly have been suggested to Dryden by
Otway. But a comparison of Dryden's use with the use of the
same material in Otway, in whom there is verbal echo without
irony and without context of character, brings out strikingly the
deliberateness of Dryden's effort, and, despite all limitations,
his considerable insight.

   There are a number of other elements in the play in which
Dryden imitated the spirit of Shakespeare with considerable freedom and in which he felt the impress of Shakespeare more fully
than where he tried to follow too closely. There are many passages in Shakespeare which Dryden might perhaps have named
either passions, or thoughts, and which embody the mind's reflection on its own movements, on human nature, on man's state
in life. These passages opened up to him a range of his own
observation to which nothing in his earlier attempts in drama
or poetry had awakened him. If such imitations in Dryden are
not always dramatic, they are in eloquence perhaps closer to
Shakespeare than anyone else has ever come.

> Doll.   Men are but children of a larger growth,
> Our appetites as apt to change as theirs,
> And full as craving too, and full as vain;
> And yet the soul shut up in her dark room,
> Viewing so clear abroad, at home sees nothing,
> But, like a mole in earth, busy and blind,
> Works all her folly up and casts it outward
> To the world's open view: thus I discovered,
> And blamed the love of ruin'd Antony;
> Yet wish that I were he, to be so ruined.
>
> Ant.   . . . . Ingrateful woman!
> Who followed me, but as the swallow summer
> Hatching her young ones in my kindly beams,
> Singing her flatteries to my morning wake;
> But, now my winter comes, she spreads her wings,
> And seeks the spring of Caesar.

Alex.   . . . .
              Poor reason! what a wretched aid art thou!
              For still, in spite of thee,
              These two long lovers, soul and body, dread
              Their final separation.

Finally there are many passages in the last two acts which
do not echo but which indefinably reflect Shakespeare's sense of
the human situation, such as Antony's:

              My torch is out; and the world stands before me
              Like a black desert, at th' approach of night:
              I'll lay me down, and stray no farther on.

(How one is tempted not to quote the last line!) Passages of these
sorts create a texture which gives a real sense of the interplay of
human thought and the visible and active world.

To come now to imagery and diction. The nature of Dryden's
treatment of these aspects of his play is implicit in what I have
already said. Yet Dryden certainly thought consciously of his
whole play from the point of view of the diction and the imagery
as well as from that of action, passion, thoughts. It is, therefore, necessary to consider All for Love from that point of view
in order to understand both the full quality of Dryden's play and
his entire view of Shakespeare.

Up to the time of writing All for Love, Dryden had developed
a wonderful facility in writing two kinds of image already present
in the lines on Cromwell: the fustian, inert image which was but
decorative even though in the heroic plays it had become the real
vestment of the sentiments characteristic of those plays; and the
analogy by which he asserts a judgment with stinging speed. To
these in Annus Mirabilis he had added those "Virgilian" tropes
which were later to triumph in his translation of the Æneid.
From such diction the language of All for Love differs widely.
In this play it is the abundance of concrete diction, both direct
and figurative, which strikes us, and the fact that the figures are
largely limited to simile or metaphor. The change was mani-
festly due to Dryden's study of Shakespeare's speech, a study in
many ways parallel to our own contemporary studies of early
seventeenth-century diction. And, indeed, this is no bad place
to remind ourselves that rhetorical as are the terms of Dryden's

critical statement, his view of the relation of language to thought
had in it elements at least as fundamental as our own.

The range of speech in Shakespeare, we must remind ourselves, is very great. In the great tragedies, the diction corresponds both to the characters who speak, and to the plane of the
action in which they speak. Edgar, for instance, is a character in
the middle plane of <u>Lear</u>. By his own nature and by the structure
of the play, he is one of the humane and often choral middle spirits
who carry on the great ethical and social patterns of life from
day to day, and who form that background of normally ordered
social and moral patterns, against which take place in the action
the struggle between order and disorder, self-will and love; and
in the main characters the individual psychological drama. Edgar
speaks in the language of reflection and not in the language of a
Lear at his most intense. Full-rounded and explicit imagery,
sentence structure, level of diction in Edgar, all differ from that
"metaphysical" speech which expresses the labouring and pas-
sion-driven thought of Lear. Still further in the background are
the characters who create the exposition and the atmosphere.
The distinction is one which we have not yet fully understood.
Dryden did not make it. Antony's account of himself to Ventidius,

> But, I have lost my reason, have disgrac'd
> The name of soldier, with inglorious ease.
> In the full vintage of my flowing honours
> Sat still, and saw it pressed by other hands. . . .

is not a character passage but such an interpretive or descriptive passage as might be spoken in the background texture of
<u>Antony and Cleopatra</u> itself, or in, say, the opening description
of Macbeth. It is like them in its deliberately formal type of
expression. Shakespeare, however, uses such a style only in
the plane of background. Even there, as he matures, such speeches
gain their effect by broad descriptions rather than by analyses.
Thus, even in the matter of imagery and diction, we are carried
back to the fundamental profound divergence in approach between
Dryden and Shakespeare, a divergence which Dryden did not understand, which causes him to mingle reflective and dramatic
speech in a way that interrupts psychological continuity.

It is not such reflective speeches but the figures of direct
dramatic representation of which Dryden was most vividly aware

and which he sought chiefly to imitate. A few, chosen because they are representative of the quality of the play where it is most Shakespearean, will illustrate what he achieved.

1. Sera. If he be vanquish'd,
   Or make his peace, Ægypt is doom'd to be
   A Roman province, and our plenteous harvests
   Must then redeem the scarceness of their soil.

2. Alex. [Of Ventidius]
   I saw him in Cilicia first
   When Cleopatra there met Antony:
   A mortal foe he was to us, and Ægypt
   But, let me witness to the worth I hate,
   A braver Roman never drew a sword.
   Firm to his Prince; but as a friend, not slave.
   He ne'r was of his pleasures; but presides
   O'er all his cooler hours and morning counsels.

3. Ant. We have dislodg'd their troops,
   They look on us at distance, and, like curs
   Scap'd from the lion's paw, they bay far off. . . .

4. Ven. [Of Ant.]
   Unbent, unsinew'd, made a woman's toy.

5. Alex. Suppose some shipwrack'd seaman near the shore,
   Dropping and faint, with climbing up the cliff,
   If, from above, some charitable hand
   Pull him to safety, hazarding himself
   To draw the other's weight; would he look back
   And curse him for his pains? The case is yours;
   But one step more, and you have gained the height.

6. Alex. [to Ven.]
   You . . . .
   Lie in his way and stop the paths of death.

7. Ant. . . . . That I settled
   Your father in his throne, was for your sake,
   I left th' acknowledgement for time to ripen.

        Cæsar stepped in, and with a greedy hand
        Pluck'd the green fruit ere the first blush of red
        Yet cleaving to the bough.

8. <u>Ant.</u> O unperforming hand! . . .
                       And death,
        Like a great man, takes state, and makes me wait
        For my admittance.

In all these figures what gives life is the particularized reflection of experience. In the first two the experience is simply and immediately presented to our senses. The power of evocation has only less than the Shakespearean intensity. The third figure is of the same sort, though the description makes use of a simile. The fourth has the same direct perception, but its description is coloured by the passion of Ventidius's judgment. The fifth passage is one of the greatest. Alexas thinks in terms of the image; and the labour of the meeting of the idea and the image is deliberately reflected by Dryden in the incoherence of the syntax and in the personal quality of the rhythm which flows from it. The sixth passage begins in a reflection; but it imitates Shakespeare in restoring the abstraction of death to an actually sensed experience. In Shakespeare that immediate sense of death would be related further to the context of the play and to the minds of the characters; and enlarged by a sense of the meaning of death.

With the seventh, we come to a more deliberate type of figure. A sensuous figure such as we do not find earlier in Dryden, it carries an immediate evocation of the young Cleopatra. The animation and forward movement of the figure itself are not like the forms of speech in Dryden's earlier plays. For this animation, the figure depends upon two things: upon the stages of ripening in the fruit itself, from greenness to the suggested fall; and upon the opening out of the sentence into a participle. And it is to be supposed that Dryden himself was conscious of those technical elements, though doubtless as he wrote this actual image, he was absorbed in the vision of the young Cleopatra. But full of life as it is, it is the image of Dryden and not of Antony. It does not integrate with the first part of Antony's speech nor merge into what follows. It is un-Shakespearean. Yet it sprang from Dryden's study of Shakespeare, and from his perception of the relation of concrete detail, of movement and of syntax, to imaginative truth.

DRYDEN AND SHAKESPEARE'S TECHNIQUES

With the last figure we come to something quite different.
It is, indeed, a verbal imitation of Shakespeare; but with nothing
of Shakespearean texture. As one thinks of the figure which
probably suggested it,

> Oh I could tell,
> Had I but time, as this fell sergeant, Death,
> Is strict in his arrest.

one feels oneself back again among the rhetoric books. Dryden,
as the rhetorics might have taught him, has brought together the
same categories of experience as Shakespeare had brought together in finding a similitude for man's relation to death. But
simile has replaced metaphor and no living images replace fell
and strict. Hamlet's words spring first from the immediate
fact which comes into his consciousness, the sharp prevention
of the completing of his great task. Second, though the stuff
which makes the creative energy of Hamlet's speech eludes our
final definition, behind this immediate experience there certainly
lies Hamlet's and Shakespeare's and our saturation in this play
with the thought of death and our sense of the sudden ironic fulfilment of Hamlet's yearning to confront death. Nor, thirdly,
can we separate our experience of the image from our experience of the play as a whole. For, in the course of the play, the
pressure of time and the urgency of Hamlet's danger have more
and more intensely possessed our minds. Moreover, in Hamlet's
dissolution at the moment of success, all the ironic overtones of
the play are concentrated and resolved. Antony's image has none
of these things. The series of placid reflections and echoes of
which it is a part have no relation to any immediate tension of
feeling in Antony, no relation to anything outside themselves in
Antony or the play, only a deliberately willed and ludicrous logical appropriateness to the external fact that Antony is slow
a-dying.

It is significant that Dryden's most Shakespearean images
are not those spoken by a major character, or at moments of
greatest passion. This may be due in part first to the fact that
Dryden worked more freely in imitating Alexas, Ventidius, Sera-
pion, than in creating Antony, and that his own creative faculty
was therefore in them more free to follow that immediate intuition of Shakespeare, which underlay all his analyses and which

had found voice in "you feel it too". It is true also that Dryden understood Alexas more fully than he could understand Antony. He attempted also to understand him only from a different basis of insight, as a broad general type. The habit of searching for the typical, and of logical abstraction, stood between Dryden and the deeper perception of Shakespeare's characters, even while the wish to imitate Shakespeare's passions prevented Dryden from the free development of Antony's character in his own terms.

This must have been true, I think, even if Dryden had had a larger conception of Antony's character. The point becomes more clear if we turn to Cleopatra's character and to the scenes between Antony and her.

In the conception of Cleopatra and in the action between her and Antony, we are dealing with a different dramatic technique from that used in the scenes which deal with Antony in passion or from those which deal with the Alexas-Serapion element of the design. Though the wish to treat the character of Cleopatra and her relation to Antony naturally and not in terms of heroic concepts owes very much to Shakespeare, and though Cleopatra's closing love and grief follow, in subdued and "perspicuous" terms, much of the movement of Shakespeare's last act, these scenes are developed, not as Shakespearean scenes, but by the method of debate. This remains essentially true, despite the presence of the actual concrete incitements to emotion in them, as in the presence of the children and the fastening of the armour.

If we start with Shakespeare's Cleopatra, it is, of course, impossible that we should make anything of Dryden's. For Shakespeare's Cleopatra offers us not only the variety and fascination of her nature at play with all the forces of empire. She offers us the transformation in a character of supreme spontaneity and energy, of sensationalism, lust, greed and selfishness, into profound emotion, through the instrumentality of suffering and the confrontation with death. Of this transformation Dryden's Cleopatra offers us nothing, nor does she offer that Racinian struggle between passion and reason by which Racine abstracted his dramas out of the formalistic prison of dramatic justice in which the critics were trying to bind the French theatre and into the realm of pure psychological ethics. Dryden conceived her without internal conflict and as a wholly "good" woman. The tragic issue he reduced to the purely formal moral one of her illicit relation to Antony; and even this issue remained actually outside his play, since the play was a study of emotions and not of history. Granting these severe limitations, however, let us look at her as she is.

Dryden did not conceive of her as a passional character, in the sort in which a man was so. All that interested him in her was her capacity for loving in such a way as to make her, in happy circumstances, the final complement of the active and intellectual sides of man's nature. We must remember Dryden's famous comment on the love lyrics of Donne and Cowley. The view was not original with Dryden; he repeated it because it represented the reflection in literary comment of the social attitude of the age. This attitude in general is conveniently defined by Saint-Evremond, speaking of Corneille, though of the range and refinement of Saint-Evremond's conceptions, neither Dryden nor most of his Restoration audience had any grasp.

> Rejeter l'amour de nos tragédies comme indigne des
> héros, c'est ôter ce qui nous fait tenir encore à eux
> par un secret rapport, par je ne sais quelle liaison qui
> demeure encore entre leurs âmes et les nôtres; . . .
> D'ailleurs, comme les femmes sont aussi nécessaires
> pour la représentation que les hommes, il est à propos
> de les faire parler, autant qu'on peut, de ce qui leur
> est le plus naturel et dont elles parlent mieux que
> d'aucune chose. Otez aux unes l'expression des senti-
> ments amoureux et aux autres l'entretien secret où
> les fait entrer la confidence, vous les réduisez ordinaire-
> ment à des conversations fort ennuyeuses. Presque tous
> leurs mouvements, comme leurs discours, doivent être
> les effets de leur passion; leurs joies, leur tristesses,
> leurs craintes, leurs désirs doivent sentir un peu d'amour
> pour nous plaire. . . .
> . . . La douleur des maîtresses, tendre et précieuse,
> nous touche bien plus que l'affliction d'une veuve artificieuse
> ou intéressée, & qui, toute sincère qu'elle est quelquefois,
> nous donne toujours une idée noire des enterrements et
> de leurs cérémonies lugubres.[5]

It is this maîtresse, tendre et précieuse, who forms Dryden's central conception of Cleopatra, and her sufferings are his theme in this aspect of his play. To her he has sought to unite as much of the passion of Shakespeare's Cleopatra as he felt could be absorbed into his idea. It is notable that in the closing scene he has stripped from his imitations of Shakespeare all imperial thoughts either in relation to herself or to Antony and has focused only on the final satisfaction and justification of her tenderness. Sedley, in his Antony and Cleopatra, just before Dryden's play, had handled the relation between Antony and Cleopatra on précieuse or platonician theses. And Antony's jealousy of Photinus—which very conceivably suggested to Dryden the use of the Dolabella incident— is in Sedley met by Cleopatra with a charge of the unworthiness of jealousy. The contrast of this with Dryden's treatment of her suffering tenderness brings out clearly the realism and sincerity in his handling of Cleopatra. Nowhere is his conception more vividly realized than in the close of the fourth act, which is quite independent of Shakespeare.

For this conception of Cleopatra, Dryden's own distinctive style was the proper instrument. Certain motifs of her view of her own life, such as the claim to meet Antony as his wife, derive from Shakespeare though they originate in Plutarch (of their transmogrification into the theme of free love I say nothing); in the earlier part of the play the concrete expression of her sensuousness perhaps owes much to Shakespeare, and in the last act the grave directness of her speech may owe something to the effect on Dryden of Shakespeare's last act. But her moving definition of her own sorrow and fate springs from Dryden's mastery of the analytical drama, and of the poetry of reflection and logical statement.

We meet in All for Love the same critical problem with which we are faced at other high points in Dryden's work. The impressions of the play are essentially fragmentary. Dryden was keenly aware of the logical temper of his own day and of its methods of definition, of its maturity in "judgement". And this awareness was articulate and critical. Yet side by side with this rationalism, we constantly feel the force of Dryden's essentially empirical tradition and temper, and his belief, with the empirical psychologists and with the Renaissance, in imagination and passion. He believed in form and in the conception of Nature as the ideal, at the same time that he believed with the empiricists in the judgment of his audience and in the conception of Nature as the temper of the individual or the mass.[6] He believed in the genre in the traditionalists' sense of the ideal form which had been already found, a belief the depth of which is demonstrated overwhelmingly by his whole method of work, his wish to preserve and imitate the great genres even while he changed them. Yet he had a strong sense of progress and of the growth of any artistic or intellectual achievement through time, as the influences of the age, the place, and the concentration of a given civilization fostered that growth. And this belief, too, he held with that actuality which so often united him to the prevailing currents of his day. In the drama, in particular, he believed, as Ker said, in his own intuition of Shakespeare's greatness.

Dryden's was not, I believe, a profoundly philosophical mind, and his basic grasp of these two worlds, though it rested upon study, was essentially intuitive and creative. He both defined and did not define it. He was not aware of the fundamental philosophical and psychological issues which divided the world of Descartes and the world of Scaliger from the world of empirical thought. The assumptions involved in his conception of judgment in a writer, finding and representing the typical and throwing it into a beautiful expression, had come to him through literary channels and through social attitudes, and he took them too much for granted to examine them and to see in them all that separated them from the spiritual and psychological assumptions of Shakespeare's day and from the psychology of his own. When he turned at last to the serious imitation of the great master, following Otway's superficial imitation and perhaps a little stimulated by Sedley's attempt at a play upon a Shakespearean theme, it must have seemed to him that the methods by which Shakespeare's large soul had operated could be analysed and could be unified with the achievements of judgment in his own day. Dryden would seem to have been much more thoroughly impregnated than his contemporaries with Scaliger's careful distinction between correctness and the qualities of greatness in a style. Hence his wish to unite perspicuity and correctness with Shakespearean fullness.

Shakespeare's greatness lay, as Dryden conceived it, in his mastery of action, the passions, love excepted, and in a general fullness of life and energy of imagination. This last was technically analysable in terms of imagery and diction, or "elocution". For speech depended on the species of things in the mind. He had said in the preface to Annus Mirabilis:

> Wit in the poet . . . is no other than the faculty
> of imagination in the writer, which like a nimble

spaniel beats over and ranges through the field of
memory till it springs the quarry it hunted after.

This was a current conception among psychologists who
stressed the importance of the imagination and the emotions,
men who used the terminology of faculty psychology, but whose
view of the mind was certainly very much more functional than
their language readily shows. Memory is a creative faculty,
"Consors & co-operatrix Rationis", quotes Edward Reynoldes.
The imagination, he goes on to say, is dignified in both office
and latitude. "Its assistance to the understanding is principally
in the matter of invention, readily to supply it with varietie of
objects whereon to work as also to quicken and rayse the minde
with a kind of heate . . . and rapture of the soul, proportional
to extasie in the superior part".[7] This with some modifications
was the basic psychological equivalent of the poetic analysis of
writing as we find it in Scaliger or Ronsard, a brief résumé of
which appears in Reynolde's section on speech. And Dryden
moves from the first section of the definition I have quoted easily
on to the divisions of invention, disposition, and elocution or eloquence. I hope to analyse elsewhere the relation of the poetic
tradition to Neo-platonic psychology and then to the neo-classical
view of Nature, but also to the empirical tradition. Dryden's
definition is of great importance as showing the complex nature
of his view and his defense of the imagination. The writing of
Annus Mirabilis itself seems to me explicable purely in terms
of Dryden's poetic and rhetorical tradition and training, and the
passage from the preface seems a formal rationalization of that.
His saturation in Shakespeare and his analysis of him involved a
profounder view, a real sense of the dependence of Shakespeare's
power upon the multiplicity of life present to him and upon the
direct reflection of this in the passions and in the texture of his
diction. It meant a realization, in a sense which Dryden had not
had before, of how great writing sprang from a rich imagination.

To begin, then, with Shakespeare. He was the
man who of all modern, and perhaps ancient poets,
had the largest and most comprehensive soul. All
the images of Nature were still present to him, and
he drew them, not laboriously, but luckily; when he
describes anything, you more than see it, you feel it

too . . . he needed not the spectacles of books to read
Nature, he looked inwards and found her there.

In the play as a whole, Dryden's attempt could not succeed.
Dryden moved in a spiritually shallow milieu, and was himself
of a vulgar spirit, or subjected to a vulgar spirit, in many areas
of life which had part in the play. The Cleopatra-Octavia scene
is added to the maîtresse tendre. The spiritual Elizabethan conception of the individual and of his relation to the world was ir-
retrievably gone from Dryden; the ethic of Racinian drama lay
equally outside the perception of Restoration society; and no
social conception of the individual so deep as that which Pope
was to give expression to in his Epistle to Dr. Arbuthnot had yet
ripened. The age had no great conception of tragedy and no great
heroes. Moreover, the habit of the heroic plays clung to Dryden's
imagination. And his very wish to unite so much of what by the
instinct of his genius he felt of greatness in the two worlds of
Shakespeare and the age of reason doomed the play to essential
failure and disunity.

And yet the magnitude of his accomplishment is great, whether
we view it for himself or in relation to anything else in the poetry
and the criticism of his day. By the sheer study of Shakespeare's
passions and language, Dryden carried himself into a much larger
world than any in which he had earlier lived. He freed and brought
into play his real observation of human nature; he achieved, though
only in fragments, poetry of an immediacy in its power to relate
thought and experience of the world, such as no after imitator has
come near; he learned, once for all, to unite the rhythms of normal
speech with the formal measures of verse as only he and Shakespeare can.[8] And the play was one of his great assertions of the
significance of the imagination.

Shakespeare's style was the result of generations of direct
and even naïve imitation of human impulse and incident in the
drama, of years of discipline in poetics, united and made organic
by the thought and passion of men such as Marlowe and by his
own vision. Without some such sustaining force, Dryden could
not master that style steadily and in its deeper aspects, nor even
quite hold on to his own insight into it.

We must glance very briefly at the later plays to complete
our picture. Troilus and Cressida is not an imitation but an improvement, an approach which focused Dryden's attention wrongly.

In structure, Shakespeare's Troilus was the play most in need
of unification, as anyone knows most vividly who has seen it on
the stage even with modern Shakespearean staging, and Dryden
did well to try to unify it. But the ethical assumptions and the
view of human nature which underlay Shakespeare's conception
of order, and the ironic and melancholy view from which Shakespeare approached the problem in this play Dryden could little
understand. To the theme of political order, he gives something
of his own political energy without Shakespeare's religious view.
The love theme he handles grossly and mechanically. Both
Troilus' love and Shakespeare's view of it in its world lay beyond
the insight of Dryden. For ampler and more sympathetic passion,
he inserts the friendship motif in Troilus and Hector, and the
Hector-Andromache motif, both with close imitations of Shakespearean invention. The play does not seek to imitate Shakespeare
in the matter of imagery.

Nor do the later plays offer anything consistently Shakespearean. The imagery varies with the type of treatment. Where
they are most characterful and active, Shakespearean directness
and sensuousness and speed of phrasing most prevail, as in
Cleomenes and Don Sebastian. The curious imitation in Don Sebastian of a sensuous image from Spenser confirms our impression
of Dryden's realization of the concreteness of Shakespeare's style,
but it shows how tenuous was his grasp of its actual quality when
he was not immediately saturated with it. Prince Arthur, on the
other hand, illuminates his view of Shakespeare from another
angle. This piece is not a drama of passion but a political allegory of the genre, therefore, of the masque. It required, accordingly, a type of statement in a high vein quite different from that
of the passions. (For this view Ben Jonson's masques might have
been and conceivably were the authority.) In the lyric parts dealing with Emmeline, there is some imitation of Ferdinand and
Miranda. In the allegorical parts, we find without too much surprise Miltonic syntax and formations. Dryden perhaps never
afterwards put into the drama such intense concentration as he
put into All for Love, and his instinct, therefore, never again
worked so deeply. In that play, his failure is a fable for critics.
His success is his own.

DRYDEN AND SHAKESPEARE'S TECHNIQUES

NOTES

1   Hazelton Spencer, Shakespeare Improved, Cambridge, 1927, and Allardyce Nicoll, Dryden as an Adapter of Shakespeare, London, 1922.

2   See R. G. Ham's Otway and Lee, A Study in Baroque Sensibility, New Haven, 1937, pp. 79–80, for a discussion of Otway's critical insight into Racine.

3   See, for instance, Shirley's The Grateful Servant.

4   By S. Thomas, in "The Elizabethan Idea of Melancholy", Modern Language Notes, LVI, 1941, 261–4. But a reading of sermons and treatises of the seventeenth century shows widespread confusion and grossness of interpretation, leading towards Edward Young.

5   Saint-Evremond, "Dissertation sur la tragédie de Racine, intitulée, Alexandre le Grand". Text from Œuvres, Mises en Ordre . . . par René de Planhol, Paris, MDCCCCXXVII, Tome premier.

6   See A. O. Lovejoy, "Nature as Æsthetic Norm", Modern Language Notes, XLII, 1927, 444–50, and H. S. Wilson, "Some Meanings of 'Nature' in Renaissance Literary Theory", Journal of the History of Ideas, II, 1941, 430–46. Dryden's sense of Nature as the temper of the individual or the mass should be connected, I believe, not with older critical conceptions but with the merging of these conceptions in empiricism.

7   Edward Reynoldes, A Treatise of the Passions and Faculties of the Soule of Man, London, 1640, Chapters III and IV. See also Scaliger's own psychology, in the De Subtilitate.

8   To think of Dryden's study of language as merely technical is, as I have already said, to misunderstand the conception of poetry which was the major part of Dryden's assumption about poetry.

ON THE DEATH OF MRS. KILLIGREW: THE PERFECTING OF A GENRE

Ruth Wallerstein

It is often said of Dryden, especially if we are speaking of those poems to which we are least sympathetic, that his frigidity is due to the conception of rhetoric which thought of an art of expression essentially divorced from substance. Or more recently, that to Hobbes's divorce of fancy from judgment may be attributed Dryden's false lights. And the use of the word <u>colors</u> in the famous and ubiquitous comparison is adduced as evidence of his view. But in Dryden's day the use of such a word is no clue to meaning. For the seventeenth century in its criticism still very largely followed the mediaeval pattern of thought in one important respect. It did not start its definitions afresh but accepted the terms of definition handed on by tradition, and altered them by criticism and redefinition from within. Accordingly, in writers of that age, it is particularly important to understand every individual term in the whole context of its use, rather than the reverse. Only so can we grasp both one basic point of view which determines the primary meaning of each term and at the same time that complex of meanings which in the Renaissance adheres around each term and which allows different contexts to attract meanings to different facets as a result of the endeavor to fuse many systems of analysis. But it is not my purpose here to define what the term <u>color</u> or any other term connoted to Dryden. Rather, I wish to ask what we can learn of his method and aims not from his criticism but by a necessary parallel method, by a close consideration of two related poems, his earliest, the elegy on Hastings, and one from his ripest maturity, his ode "To the Memory of Mrs. Killigrew." Taken together, these poems show us Dryden's evolution out of the dying metaphysical age into full neo-classicism without, however, any dimming of his sense of the English tradition. They also show, I think, throughout his

Reprinted from Studies in Philology, Vol. 44 (1947), pp. 519–528, by permission of Mrs. Eve W. Fernberger and the publisher.

art the continuity of an ideal of a poem which we may surmise
to have taken shape in his schooldays under Busby's eye.

The music of his elegy on Hastings is so toneless to our
ears, its imagery falls with such dusty dryness upon our imaginations, what is worse, the bones of its theology and of its social
sentiment rattle so deadly in our thought, that we have been content to dismiss it with the term "metaphysical," using that term
in a more than usually ill-defined sense. Yet it is an astounding
achievement in structure for a boy of eighteen, highly revealing
of Dryden's training. And if we consider it in its context, it is
a valuable harbinger of the ode which succeeded it nearly forty
years later. I propose to sketch the character of this elegy very
briefly, with due apology for the dogmatism such brevity seems
to give my comment, and then against this background to show
how the ode on Mrs. Killigrew evolved.[1]

In his "Elegy upon the Death of the Lord Hastings," Dryden
sought to integrate three types of elegy, pruning them to the compass of his own feeling, all three being part of the living tradition
just before him or contemporary with him. Lacrymae Musarum,
the volume in which the poem appeared, falls in its pagination
into two parts. There were, first, a number of elegies by mature
poets and poetasters, among them Sir John Denham, Robert
Herrick, Andrew Marvell, the latter just coming into print, but
ten years Dryden's senior. Second, several sets of verses by
older hands which had presumably come in late to the printer
and with them a group of laments by Hastings' schoolfellows.
Of these last the others are very brief exercises, of the sort
Busby would commonly have exacted from his students; Dryden's
is a full scope endeavor in the elegy as then practiced by England's leading poets.

Internal evidence makes it probable that the boys had seen
the elegies by maturer hands before they composed their own;
Dryden touches most of the themes sounded in them and hardly
any theme not among them. But besides these immediate models,
he had the larger background of elegies which had formed one of
the most significant and characteristic types of seventeenth-century poetry, such as the numerous poems of the death of Prince
Henry in 1612,[2] and those of the Lycidas volume. Among these
elegies, two forms dominated, pastoral allegory and what we may
call the theological or devotional elegy.

Of the latter Donne had created the form and set the themes.
But while his own elegy on Prince Henry is in the strictest re-

ligious sense a meditation or devotion, cast in the form of a thesis and its resolution, the elegies which followed him were often merely theological reflections, lacking both the metaphysical scope and the prayer form of his "Elegie upon the Death of Prince Henry" and of his "Anniversaries." Yet the form he had created was a powerful and a flexible one. And Denham's elegy on Hastings is the genuine heir of Donne's, though its religious emotion is turned outward upon the state and the martyred king, its verse regularized, and its ordonnance and imagery classicized. Marvell's is classicized in another direction, retaining the contemplative view and the emblem imagery, but arresting itself in a classical appeal to Fate.

Besides the organic forms defined in these two types of poem there still flourished the tradition of poetry-writing which taught the writer how to constitute a poem by aggregation of a selection of motives from a common store of themes suitable to one's subject. This method, which doubtless owed much to the tradition of invention as applied to poetry from the Middle Ages on down, had been clarified or given direction by the study of Quintilian. But it was still inorganic. Scholars have abundantly illustrated the process in relation to the pastoral.[3] Chapman's poem on Prince Henry well illustrates it in the non-pastoral elegy. For the seventeenth century, this method had been restated, and its motives and its devices of style classified by the Jesuit rhetorician Pontanus.[4] Though Scaliger is Pontanus's professed Bible, the work is distinctly what we should call a rhetoric and not a poetic. In tone and teaching it is thoroughly rational. Among the motives which Pontanus most strongly recommends in the funerary elegy is a description or prosopopoeia of the death of the subject, a precept abundantly heeded by the elegists on Hastings, who ring the changes on the smallpox, as eleven years earlier had been done on the watery death of Edward King. In style the Jesuit teaching fosters a witty ingenuity which should be carefully distinguished from the ampler symbolic and metaphysical vein of Donne and the religious poets of the seventeenth century in general except where the two touch in such a poet as Crashaw.

Now, how does Dryden combine the three? Like all the other contributors to the volume, Dryden turns his back upon the pastoral allegorical elegy which had begun in England with Spenser and which Milton had perfected only eleven years before. But though he discarded the allegory and the naturalism of "Lycidas" he kept the rational classical parts of its design. These steps clearly constitute its form: a lament for the particular death; a questioning of the nature of life; an expression of grief, including a lament for the state of the world; a consolation. Within this structure, he combines the theological elegy in the tradition of Donne with inventions taken from rhetoric of the Jesuit kind, they supplying the substance of the classical parts. To Donne belong the discussion of Hastings' character and his significance and the lament for the state of the world; to Pontanus the Death, the most universally used of the inventions and of course frequent in a less rigid form also in the pastoral; the comparison to the great dead; and the social reflection which Dryden draws on both for the lament of the mourners and for the consolation. Of Dryden's school-boy treatment of these grand themes, I shall take time to say only a word on his handling of faith. It is characteristic of the changing age. The tide of seventeenth-century religious emotion which lifts the wave of Donne's prayer

Look to me faith! and look to my faith God!

has fallen. That man's knowledge and virtue are the marks in him of the image of God in which he is created has ceased to be the spur to the most daring contemplative and epistemologic speculation and has become the timid staple of current rational theology. Dryden asserts this truth objectively, as he heard it in sermon and treatise, with a naïvely fresh and honest application of it to his schoolmate. After the theological speculation, we should have expected a consolation in the beatific vision, where instead we find a promise that Hastings will live in the memory of his beloved. But Denham and Marvell have the same classical orientation.

A close study of seventeenth-century poetry shows that particular types of imagery or expression, not mere degrees of elaboration were often held to belong by decorum to particular types of subject matter. The Donnian theme is expressed in accord with this seventeenth-century decorum in an emblematic image. The sickness, by the same decorum, in the type of witty ingenuity which Jesuit elegy and epigram had spread across Europe for such themes.

Perhaps the most notable aspect of the poem, if we look to the future of Dryden's poetry, is its fine ordonnance. Jesuit

rhetoric contains no structural principle. Dryden's opening
question and fine peroration rising in and returning to a single
theme replace Donne's thesis and resolution, classical rhetoric
replacing mediaeval dialectic. They draw his disparate materials
together into a single perspective, the chief light falling on that
aspect of Hastings' death which was probably most significant to
his fellows, his snatching away just as he was leaving his child-
hood and entering into the full responsibilities of his place and
name.

> Must noble Hastings immaturely die,
> The honor of his ancient family,
> Beauty and learning thus together meet,
> To bring a <u>winding</u> for a <u>wedding</u> sheet?
>   . . . his best
> Monument is his spouse's marble breast.

Between this callow poem on Hastings and Dryden's ode "To
the Memory of Mrs. Anne Killigrew" thirty-seven years had
elapsed, but the two are bound together by their relation to a tradition, and by Dryden's unremitting endeavor to realize and re-
define structural forms in terms of the new attitudes he molded
to expression in them. Meanwhile, he had been studying Milton
and Donne, among others, unsparingly. The study of Donne may
be related to Dryden's conversion and to the fact that he was at
this time giving serious attention to religious thought and to
Catholic themes of devotion. Donne offered Dryden the sole great
models in English of solemn verse of compliment in the religious
field; and not only great models, but models Catholic in theme
and spirit. Between the two poems had come also the major part
of Cowley's work, and in particular the establishment by Cowley
of the Pindaric ode as the form for high occasional poetry. The
salient points of an ode upon which Cowley had seized had been
its enthusiastic attack upon great concepts and intellectual events,
the bold play of figures and ideas, and the large and varied metrical structure. He believed in embellishing high poetry; and he
gathers about his central theme a play not only of witty figures
but of scholastic concepts such as Donne had loved to bring to
bear on his experience; but to Cowley they are now obsolete as
thought and exist only as the material of sheer intellectual play,
useful for poetic amplification.[5] Such was the embellishment

suited to his extremely secular, rationalistic, and Epicurean temper; and the undisciplined energy of his meter perhaps does not come amiss to it.

Very different is Dryden's conception of the Pindaric ode as a genre, though he acknowledges Cowley as his authoritative predecessor in the form. Dryden sought to find its most universal forms both of thought and of structure, and he regarded the "embellishment" as a branching out of these. He has left on record his criticism of Cowley's Pindaric measures, namely that Cowley failed to study the organic relation of his varied line lengths to each other.[6] It is clear from his own odes that he did not believe that Cowley had adequately studied the structure of the ode any more than its metre. Such a form he himself seeks to perfect in his ode on Mrs. Killigrew.

In his poem he unites once more the tradition of the Greek and Latin elegy with the tradition of Donne, more particularly the Donne of the "Anniversaries," combining them within the form of a Pindaric ode. The classical lament supplies the main invention, Donne the philosophical meditation on man's fate. He does not, of course, return to the pastoral allegory. Both the descriptions and the personification of nature would have been alien to his taste as to that of his age, and alien to the Pindaric ode. More significantly, that conception of the relation between natural man and man as the creature of grace which enabled Milton to pass so triumphantly from the pagan grief of man and nature to Christian vision is a distinctive attitude of Renaissance Christian humanism, of Platonic humanism, outside the range of Dryden's thought. But the more immediate human grief for human loss which is another treatment of death in central classical poetry had from the time of Jonson taken its appointed place in that sense of order and of the bounds which define order that is the very heart of classicism in Dryden's age. In Dryden's ode, if we compare it with the elegy on Hastings, we find the theme deepened by a closer study of "Lycidas," and, seemingly, of the Sicilian odes themselves. Perhaps also Cartwright offered some suggestions.[7] To this classical theme we are first awakened by echoes of Milton and of the Greeks, echoes as deliberately suggested to our ear as Virgil's of Homer or Milton's of both.

> Whether adopted to some neighboring star,
> Thou rollst above us in thy wandering race, . . .

Cease thy celestial song a little space . . .

But thus Orinda died . . .

If we look at the structure of the ode with "Lycidas" in mind we see clearly these following parts: The statement of the theme of death, here an address to the dead; the praise of the dead; a lament for the times (stanza IV); the admission of the ineluctable claims of fate, closing with a reference to an earlier poetess; the lament of the mourners (stanza VIII); the consolation. But in actual development Dryden's poem has nothing of Milton's sense of the mystery of death and decay; rather Dryden evokes that other classical humanist theme of the Renaissance, only partially submerged by the great impulses of the religious revival and of Platonism, the theme of a great society and of art as the ornament of that society. This difference between Dryden and Milton renders easier and more decorous Dryden's transformation of the pattern of the elegy into the form of the Pindaric ode. On a close consideration of the transformation Dryden's critical and social temper stands forth clearly. The Pindaric was a poem celebrating some great idea. And for this Cowley had used it. In Cowley's Pindarics, however, there is little movement aside from the development of this idea itself, no great lyric structure. Dryden imitated the structural parts of Pindar's odes more closely, adapting the parts of the elegy with amazing neatness to that form. The elegiac praise of the dead transforms itself into what is in the epinicea the praise of the victor. The lament for the times opens out in stanzas V, VI, VII into the celebration of the idea — in this poem a critical definition of the new principles of painting of which Mrs. Killigrew was one of the first practioners.

Thus in general Dryden follows the invention of the classical elegy. The theme of contemplation, however, is drawn from Donne and from the theological elegy.

The poem opens with a vision of Mrs. Killigrew among the blessed, in which there is an echo of Milton, but which is also probably reminiscent of the ascent of the soul of Elizabeth Drury. It closes with a Last Judgment and with a Renaissance and classical coda on fame. Cowley had written a Pindaric on the Judgment, but Dryden is closer to Donne in his development of the theme than is Cowley. And yet despite the resemblance to Donne the

ON THE DEATH OF MRS. KILLIGREW

two scenes might be taken as typical of the difference between
the ages of Donne and of Dryden.

> At the round earth's imagin'd corners, blow
> Your trumpets Angells, and arise, arise
> From death, you numberlesse infinities
> Of soules, and to your scattered bodies goe, . . .
> But let them sleepe, Lord, and mee mourne a space,
> For, if above all these, my sinnes abounde, . . .

> When in mid-air the golden trump shall sound
>   To raise the nations underground;
>   When in the valley of Jehosephat
> The judging God shall close the book of fate,
>   And there the last assizes keep
>   For those who wake and those who sleep;
>   When rattling bones together fly
>   From the four corners of the sky:
> When sinews o'er the skeletons are spread,
> Those clothed with flesh, and life inspires the dead;
> The sacred poets first shall hear the sound . . .

Donne evokes in the first eight lines of his Judgment sonnet the
experience of every single soul surprised by the trumpets blow-
ing at the round earth's imagined corners. In Dryden, the whole
outline of the Judgment scene is blocked in, but the description
is impersonal, general, not carrying us inward to one individual
soul facing itself, but diffusing outward to social comment and
so by an easy step to a defense of poesy.

For Donne and for Milton, in different ways, the world is
symbolic. For Dryden it is, despite his conversion, the essential
imaginative reality. This is the fact which underlies or gives
meaning to Dryden's imagery and to any theory of elocution that
helped to shape it. The ode might well have been a reflective
poem. But the poet has chosen to deal with the general idea of
death, and accordingly to throw his thoughts into the form of the
Pindaric. He must, therefore, develop the poem in the high style
especially suited to the Pindaric ode, a style which will harmonize
all the parts, and which by its imagery will startle and command
our passion suitably to the greatness of the theme. The stanzas
dealing with the thought are sustained by the elaborate statement

of that thought and do not need additional color. It is different
with stanzas I, III, and IX, expressing the lament. Since the
lament is a ritual, these are the stanzas which in Dryden's view,
as we may surmise, needed most amplification to sustain their
passion and to elevate it to the level of the thought of death.
Dryden, therefore, replaces the natural description which he
has discarded by imagery drawn from elementary science and
cosmic lore. These are just such amplifications as he had used
many years before in his formal praise of Cromwell. Only the
palms of Cromwell are become the palms of heaven. The image
of the clustering bees had appeared in Beaumont's elegy on King
James, a fact which reminds us of the deliberately traditional
character of these adornments. Moreover, the play of ideas
shown in amplification constituted the special character of the
Pindaric. The ideas which Dryden brings into play are, unlike
those of Cowley, of genuine interest to him and integrally related
to his theme. He believed, at least at the end of his life, in judicial astrology; and the discussion of the origin of the soul had
still a recognized place in orthodox treatises on the immortality
of the soul. But still they are the outpourings of a discursive
thought, not the substance of a concentrated intuition that draws
thought and feeling inward towards a center.

The music of Dryden's ode, like its invention and its imagery,
is true to neo-classical principles of formal design. Its beauty
is inherent in the pure metrical pattern of the ode itself, objectively conceived, in the varied cadences of the lines within the
stanza. It is conceived and managed with perfect artifice. To
my ear, despite its fine numerousness, it never, like his lines
on Oldham, takes emotion from its theme.

The ode on Mrs. Killigrew is at once illustrative of the
grandeur of Dryden's analysis and reconstitution of the great
formal genres of literature, and of the thin spiritual air he often
had to breathe in his perennial struggle between the fading mediaeval world and the rising world of science and social enlighten-
ment, in the midst of the disillusion of the first Stuart courts.
Sometimes he failed to find a soul to inform what he designed,
leaving it as yet only a bodily essence. But he maintained in
England the tradition of high poetry. And it was by no trivial
ideal of expression but by a profound sense of the forms of great
poems that, even where he could not succeed himself he had left
so much ready to the imaginations of those who followed.

ON THE DEATH OF MRS. KILLIGREW

NOTES

1 I hope shortly to publish a detailed analysis of the elegies against the background of which I am here considering Dryden's poems.

2 For the complete list the reader may refer to Mr. E. C. Wilson's volume, published since I made this study, Prince Henry in English Literature (Ithaca, 1946).

3 See, for instance: Merritt Y. Hughes, "Spenser and the Greek Pastoral Triad," Studies in Philology, XXX (1923), 184–215; T. P. Harrison, Jr., "Spenser and the Earlier Pastoral Elegy," University of Texas Studies in English, XIII (1933), 36–53; Don Cameron Allen, ed., Meres on Poetry (Cambridge, 1938).

4 Jacobi Pontani De Societate Jesu, Poeticarum Institutionum Libri III. I am familiar with Editio Secunda Emendatior (Ingoldstatii, MDXCVIII). Pontanus in the digest of Buechler was certainly widely current, and it is to be presumed that the full book was well known. Dryden certainly used Pontanus's edition of Virgil, which might well have contributed more than has been made account of to his conception of the emotions and of the heroic treatment of character.

5 See Cowley's notes to his Pindarics. Cowley's figures in the odes had of course been defended against the charge of fustian and praised for the beauty of their singular strength by Dryden in his Apology for Heroic Poetry and Poetic License in 1677.

6 Preface to the Sylvae; Essays, ed. Ker, I, 267–268.

7 As is suggested to me by Mr. Gwynne Blackmore Evans, who is shortly to bring out an edition of Cartwright.

ADDITIONAL ARTICLES FOR FURTHER STUDY

Aden, John M. "Dryden and Boileau: The Question of Critical Influence," SP, L (1953), 491–509.

_____. "Dryden and the Imagination: The First Phase," PMLA, LXXIV (1959), 28–40.

Bowers, Fredson. "The 1665 Manuscript of Dryden's Indian Emperour," SP, XLVIII (1951), 738–60.

Brower, Reuben A. "Dryden's Poetic Diction and Virgil," PQ, XVIII (1939), 211–17.

_____. "An Allusion to Europe: Dryden and Tradition," ELH, XIX (1952), 38–48.

Clark, William S. "The Definition of the 'Heroic Play' in the Restoration Period," RES, VIII (1932), 437–44.

Dearing, Vinton A. "Dryden's MacFlecknoe: The Case for Authorial Revision," SB, VII (1955), 85–102.

Evans, G. Blakemore. "The Text of Dryden's MacFlecknoe," Harvard Library Bulletin, VII (1953), 32–54.

Fujimura, Thomas H. "Dryden's Religio Laici: An Anglican Poem," PMLA, LXXVI (1961), 205–17.

Hooker, Helene M. "Dryden's Georgics and English Predecessors," HLQ, IX (1946), 273–310.

Huntley, Frank L. "Dryden's Discovery of Boileau," MP, XLV (1947), 112–17.

Jefferson, D. W. "The Significance of Dryden's Heroic Plays," Proceedings of the Leeds Philosophical and Literary Society, V (1940), 125–39.

Kinsley, James. "Dryden's Bestiary," RES, n. s., IV (1953), 331–36.

Legouis, Pierre. "La Religion dans l'oeuvre de Dryden avant 1682," Revue anglo-américaine, IX (1932), 383–92; 525–36.

Long, Ralph B. "Dryden's Importance as a Spokesman of the Tories," Studies in English, University of Texas, 1941, pp. 79–99.

ADDITIONAL ARTICLES FOR FURTHER STUDY

Lynch, Kathleen M. "Conventions of Platonic Drama in the Heroic Plays of Orrery and Dryden," PMLA, XLIV (1929), 456–71.

McKeithan, D. M. "The Occasion of MacFlecknoe," PMLA, XLVII (1932), 766–71.

MacMillan, Dougald. "The Sources of Dryden's The Indian Emperour," HLQ, XIII (1950), 355–70.

Miltin, William M. "Tempest in a Teapot," ELH, XIV (1947), 207–18.

Miner, Earl. "Dryden and the Issue of Human Progress," PQ, XL (1961), 120–29.

Osborn, James M. "Macdonald's Bibliography of Dryden: An Annotated Check-list of Selected American Libraries," MP, XXXIX (1941), 69–98; 197–212.

Roper, Alan H. "Dryden's Medal and the Divine Analogy," ELH, XXIX (1962), 396–417.

Smith, John Harrington, "Some Sources of Dryden's Toryism, 1682–1684," HLQ, XX (1957), 233–43.

Smith, R. J. "Shadwell's Impact upon John Dryden," RES, XX (1944), 29–44.

Swedenberg, H. T., Jr. "England's Joy: Astraea Redux in its Setting," SP, L (1953), 30–44.

Trowbridge, Hoyt. "Dryden's Essay on the Dramatic Poetry of the Last Age," PQ, XXII (1943), 240–50.

Walcott, Fred G. "John Dryden's Answer to Thomas Rymer's The Tragedies of the Last Age," PQ, XV (1936), 194–214.

Wallerstein, Ruth. "To Madness Near Allied: Shaftesbury and His Place in the Design and Thought of Absalom and Achitophel," HLQ, VI (1943), 445–71.

Ward, Charles E. "The Tempest: A Restoration Opera Problem," ELH, XIII (1946), 119–30.

Wasserman, Earl R. "Dryden's Epistle to Charleton," JEGP, LV (1956), 201–12.

Winterbottom, John. "The Development of the Hero in Dryden's Tragedies," JEGP, LII (1953), 161–73.